BECOMING AMERICA

An Exploration of American Literature from Precolonial to Post-Revolution

Volume I

Edited by Wendy Kurant, Ph.D.

ISBN: 978-1-940771-63-2

Produced by:
University System of Georgia

Published by:
University of North Georgia Press
Dahlonega, Georgia

Author Introductions and Reading and Review Questions contributed by:
Bonnie J. Robinson

Cover Design and Layout Design:
Corey Parson

Cover Image:
"Purple Mountains Majesty" by Kait Thomas of the National Park Service
Arches National Park

For more information, please visit http://ung.edu/university-press
Or email ungpress@ung.edu

If you need this document in another format, please email the University of North Georgia Press at ungpress@ung.edu or call 706-864-1556.

Table of Contents

1 Pre- and Early Colonial Literature

1.1 LEARNING OUTCOMES

After reading this chapter, students will be able to

- Categorize the types of Native American tales and their contribution to their respective tribes' cultures.
- Identify significant tropes and motifs of movement in Native American creation stories.
- Identify the cultural characteristics of Native American creation, trickster, and first contact stories distinct from European cultural characteristics.
- Identify elements of trickster stories.
- Understand how the search for the Westward passage to Asia led to the European discovery of the Americas.
- Understand how the search for commodities led to territorial appropriation of North American land by various European countries.
- Understand the role religion played in European settlement in North America.
- Understand how their intended audience and purpose affected the content and tone of European exploration accounts.

1.2 INTRODUCTION

1.2.1 Native American Accounts

It is well to bear in mind that the selections here should not be understood as representative of Native American culture as a whole. There are thousands of different Native American tribes, all with distinct practices. It would not be possible in the space of a typical anthology to represent just the tribes with whom the colonists had the most contact during the early years of European settlement, or even to say with any precision exactly how many tribes the colonists did interact with since European colonists were often unable to distinguish among different tribes. Additionally, we must realize that these works come to us with omissions and mediations. Many Native American tales are performative as well as oral—the meanings of the words supplemented by expressions, movements, and shared cultural assumptions—and so the words alone do not represent their full significance. That being said, the examples of Native American accounts that follow give us some starting points to consider the different ways in which cultures explain themselves to themselves.

First among a culture's stories are the tales of how the earth was created and how its geographical features and peoples came to be. The Native American creation stories collected here demonstrate two significant tropes within Native American creation stories: the Earth Diver story and the Emergence story. Earth Diver stories often begin with a pregnant female falling from a sky world into a watery world, such as the ones here from the Haudenosaunee (Iroquois) people of the eastern United States and from the Cherokee people from the southern United States. Various animals then work together to create dry land so that the woman may give birth there, starting the process of creating the familiar world and its population. With Emergence stories, here represented by the Zuni creation story, animals and people emerge from within the earth, a distinction from the Earth Diver story that is likely connected to the topography familiar to this tribe from the southwestern United States. Creation stories feature a "culture hero," an extraordinary being who is instrumental in shaping the world in its current form. Other examples in addition to the works here are the Wampanoag culture hero Moshup or Maushop, a giant who shared his meals of whale with the tribe and created the island of Nantucket out of tobacco ash, and Masaw, the Hopi skeleton man and Lord of the Dead who helped the tribe by teaching them agriculture in life and caring for them in death. Some creation tales show similarities to Judeo-Christian theology and suggest parallel development or European influence, quite possible since many of these stories were not put into writing until the nineteenth and twentieth centuries.

Some Native American creation tales show motifs of movement from chaos to duality to order and beings of creation and destruction paired together, themes also found in European accounts of creation. However, these tales feature significant differences to the European way of understanding the world. These tales often show the birth of the land and of the people as either contemporaneous events, as with the Earth Diver stories, or as the former figuratively birthing the latter, as with the Emergence stories. This suggests the context for some tribes' beliefs in the essentialness of land to tribal and personal identity. As Paula Gunn Allen (Laguna Pueblo) asserts in *The Sacred Hoop* (1986), "The land is not really the place (separate from ourselves) where we act out the drama of our isolate destinies . . . It is rather a part of our being, dynamic, significant, real." In addition, Native American creation tales often depict the relationship between man and animals in ways sharply different from European assumptions. In the Haudenosaunee tale and many other Earth Diver tales like it, animals and cultural heroes create the earth and its distinctive features collaboratively.

Like creation stories, Native American trickster stories fulfill an explanatory function about the world; they also explain why social codes exist and why they are needed. The trickster character—often represented as an animal such as a coyote, a raven, or a hare—is a figure of scatological humor, frequently focused on fulfilling and over-fulfilling physical needs to the detriment of those around him. However, above all things the trickster represents fluid boundaries. The trickster can shift between sexes, interacts with both humans and animals, rarely settles down for any period of time, and is crafty and foolish at the same time. Furthermore, the Trickster transgresses what is socially acceptable and often what is physically possible. In one of the best known trickster cycle, that of the Winnebago tribe originating in the Wisconsin region, the trickster Wakdjunkaga has a detachable penis that can act autonomously and sometimes resides in a box. These tales entertain but also function as guides to acceptable social behavior. Through the mishaps the trickster causes and the mishaps s/he suffers, the trickster tends to reinforce social boundaries as much as s/he challenges them and also can function as a culture hero. Much like the culture heroes described previously, the Winnebago trickster Wakdjunkaga also benefits the tribe. In the last tale of the cycle, s/he makes the Mississippi River Valley safe for occupation by killing malevolent spirits and moving a waterfall.

As is apparent in both the creation stories and the Trickster stories, Native American cultures did not differentiate between animal behavior and human behavior to the extent that Europeans did. While the European concept of the Great Chain of Being established animals as inferior to humans and the Bible was understood to grant man dominion over the animals, the Native American stories to follow suggest a sense of equality with the animals and the rest of nature. Animals contributed to the creation of the world upon which humans live, were able to communicate with humans until they chose not to, and followed (or refused to follow) the same social codes as humans, such as meeting in councils to discuss problems as a group and agreeing together on a course of action. Nonetheless, like with the laxative bulb story, there is tension between the helpful and harmful aspects of nature, and these works teach the lesson that nature must be given due respect lest one lose its benefits and suffer its anger.

"In fourteen hundred ninety-two, Columbus sailed the ocean blue": the European perspective on the first contact between Native peoples and European explorers has been taught to Americans from pre-school onward, but the Native American perspective on these events is less familiar. Just like their counterparts, Native American depictions of first contact with European explorers situated them within their accustomed natural, spiritual, and social contexts. The explorers' large ships were interpreted as whales, houses, or islands; their paler complexions were a sign of illness or divinity. The gifts or drinks offered by the strangers are accepted out of politeness and social custom, not naiveté or superstition. As these tales were recorded with hindsight, they often ruefully trace how these explorers and colonists disingenuously relied on the natives' help while appropriating more and more land to themselves and their introduction of alcohol and European commodities into native culture.

1.2.2 European Exploration Accounts

Spain, the first European country to establish a significant foothold in the Americas in the fifteenth century, was not looking for previously unknown lands at all. It was looking for a westward passage to Asia. Earlier in the century, the Ottoman Empire had captured Constantinople and after that point, controlled the territory through which the traditional land-based trade routes to China and India ran, effectively giving the Ottoman Empire a monopoly on trade between Europe and Asia. Spain, like other European nations, looked for a solution by seeking a westward route. Spain at that time did not exist as a unified nation but rather was a collection of kingdoms, sometimes collaborating but more often competing with each other. The move toward nationhood began when King Ferdinand II of Aragon and Queen Isabella I of Castile married in 1469 and unified two of the more powerful Iberian kingdoms. To consolidate their economic and regional power, these monarchs were very interested in securing trade routes for the very lucrative commodities coming from the east. Additional motivation came from a powerful rival within the same peninsula. Portugal had already circumnavigated Africa and looked poised to discover that westward passage. Those influences encouraged King Ferdinand and Queen Isabella to support Christopher Columbus' proposal of finding a western route. Unaware that a landmass intervened between the Atlantic and Pacific Oceans and miscalculating the distance between western Europe and eastern Asia, Columbus thought he had succeeded in his quest when he landed on islands in the Caribbean. He hadn't, but Spain discovered that the New World had desirable commodities too, namely gold and silver mines that funded Spain's empire-building aspirations.

Just as the powerful European nations fought for supremacy within the confines of the European continent, they also grappled over territory in the Americas. Like Spain, other European countries sought new trade routes and, failing that, coveted the new land as a source of commodities such as precious metals, fur, timber, and agricultural products and as an extension of their empires. Spain primarily explored and appropriated areas in South and Central America and in the southeastern and southwestern parts of North America. Holland has the smallest territory for the briefest amount of time in the Americas, controlling the Hudson River Valley from New York City to Albany as well as the western tip of Long Island for little more than fifty years before losing it to the English in 1664 as part of the settlement of the Second Anglo-Dutch War. The French territories concentrated primarily in the Canadian areas of Newfoundland to Quebec as well as around the Great Lakes and a large swath of land in the midsection of the country from the Rocky Mountains to the Mississippi River delta. England, one of the last major European powers to create settlements in North America, ultimately ended up having the largest and most lasting colonial reach, starting with their first permanent settlement in Jamestown in 1608, and expanding along the eastern seaboard where they frequently clashed with Spanish territories to the south and Dutch and French territories to the north and west. A small and densely populated island with a system of primogeniture which increasingly invested land in fewer and fewer hands, England was the European country most in need of agricultural settlements in North America. In addition to supplying food and goods to a mother country, it provided land for younger sons and those without prospects at home as well as a convenient place to send unruly groups within the population.

The relationship between imperialism and the spread of religion in the new world was first cemented during Spanish exploration. In a 1493 papal bull, Pope Alexander VI granted Ferdinand and Isabella and their heirs the right to any lands they "discovered towards the west and south" of a demarcation line that was not already in the possession of a Christian monarch so that "the Catholic faith and the Christian religion [would] be exalted and be everywhere increased and spread." Like the Spanish, French explorers were also accompanied by missionaries to convert North American natives to Catholicism, though they did so with less fervor and less coercion than their co-religionists from Spain. Dutch explorers showed little interest in converting the natives, as Holland had a policy of religious toleration during the time in which it colonized North America. The Church of England had already seceded from the authority of the Catholic Church by the time Jamestown was established, and though the charter from King James emphasized the motive of spreading the Christian faith and church attendance was mandatory in Jamestown's early years, more energy was put into survival and trade than into proselytizing the natives. It was the later colonies founded by Separatists and Puritans that came to the new world with the primary intention of spreading the beliefs of their denominations.

The initial function of the exploration accounts to follow in this section was to report back to the governments and organizations that funded the expeditions. However, the invention of the Gutenberg press with its movable type and increased productivity meant that these accounts could be more easily printed and more widely disseminated. Speaking to a wider audience, these accounts fulfilled other purposes as well. They served as written records of a nation's claim to a territory, as tales of exotic lands and thrilling adventure, and as testimonials to lure more people into investing in and emigrating to these fledgling colonies.

1.3 NATIVE AMERICAN

Image 1.1 | Flag of the Wabanaki Confederacy
Artist | User "GrahamSlam"
Source | Wikimedia Commons
License | CC BY-SA 4.0

The selections of this section come from six tribes whose homelands cover the majority of the United States' eastern seaboard as well as regions in the midwest and southwest. The Micmac or Mi'kmaq tribe belonged to the Wabanaki Confederacy and occupied a region in southeastern Canada's maritime provinces as well as parts of New York and New Jersey. One of the oldest political entities in the new world, the Haudenosaunee Confederacy were called the Iroquois by the French and the Five Nations by the English. The latter refers to the five tribes that made up the confederacy: the Cayuga, Mohawk, Oneida, Onondaga, and Seneca tribes. The name was changed to Six Nations when the Tuscarora tribe joined in the eighteenth century. Their territory covered the majority of New York with some inroads in southern Canada and northern Pennsylvania. Called the Delaware by Europeans, the Lenape tribe's territory included what became New Jersey, eastern Pennsylvania, southeastern New York, northern Delaware, and a bit of southern Connecticut. The Cherokee tribe occupied the southeastern United States as far north as Kentucky and Virginia and as far south as Georgia and Alabama. The Winnebago, or the Ho-chunks, lived in Wisconsin. Finally, the Zuni or the A:shimi were descendants of the ancient Anasazi and Mogollon cultures of the southwestern United States and occupied the area called New Mexico.

Missionaries and ethnologists were some of the first collectors of Native American tales. The missionaries often learned Native American languages and customs as a way to better proselytize the tribes, and some became at least as interested in these studies as in their religious missions. Moravian missionary John Heckewelder recorded the Lenape account of first contact before the American Revolution and published it early in the next century as part of the transactions of the American Philosophical Society, an outgrowth of the Federal era's zeal for knowledge and scientific study. Baptist missionary Silas Rand ministered to the Micmac tribe and recorded the first contact story told to him by Micmac man Josiah Jeremy. A self-taught linguist, Rand also published a Micmac dictionary. Toward the latter half of the nineteenth century, the developing field of ethnology—the analytic study of a culture's customs, religious practices, and social structures—fueled the study of Native American culture. The Cherokee accounts recorded by James Mooney and the Zuni accounts recorded by Ruth Bunzel were first published as part of the annual reports produced by the Bureau of American Ethnology, a federal office in existence from 1879 to 1965 that authorized ethnological studies of tribes throughout America.

Paul Radin—like Bunzel, a student of cultural anthropology pioneer Franz Boas—did his fieldwork for his doctorate among the Winnebago and there recorded the tribe's trickster tales. While many of the accounts come from outsiders embedded for a time within tribes, some accounts were recorded by tribe members themselves. Though previously recounted by others, the Haudenosaunee creation story here is from Tuscarora tribal member David Cusick. A physician and artist, Cusick was one of the first Native American writers to preserve tribal history in his *Sketches of the Ancient History of the Six Nations* (1826). The Haudenosaunee Thanksgiving Address comes from University of Victoria professor Gerald Taiaiake Alfred, a member of the Kahnawake (Mohawk) tribe. Alfred has published several works about Native American culture in the early 21st century.

Image 1.2 | Wampum Belt Commemorating the Iroquis Confederacy
Artist | Unknown
Source | Wikimedia Commons
License | Public Domain

1.3.1 Creation Story (Haudenosaunee (Iroquois))

In the great past, deep water covered all the earth. The air was filled with birds, and great monsters were in possession of the waters, when a beautiful woman was seen by them falling from the sky. Then huge ducks gathered in council and resolved to meet this wonderful creature and break the force of her fall. So they arose, and, with pinion overlapping pinion, unitedly received the dusky burden. Then the monsters of the deep also gathered in council to decide which should hold this celestial being and protect her from the terrors of the water, but none was able except a giant tortoise, who volunteered to endure this lasting weight upon his back. There she was gently placed, while he, constantly increasing in size, soon became a large island. Twin boys were after a time brought forth by the woman—one the spirit of good, who made all good things, and caused the maize, fruit, and tobacco to grow; the other the spirit of evil, who created the weeds and all vermin. Ever the world was increasing in size, although occasional quakings were felt, caused by the efforts of the monster tortoise to stretch out, or by the contraction of his muscles.

After the lapse of ages from the time of his general creation Ta-rhu^{n}-hiă-wăh-ku^{n}, the Sky Holder, resolved upon a special creation of a race which should surpass all others in beauty, strength, and bravery; so from the bosom of the great island, where they had previously subsisted upon moles, Ta-rhu^{n}-hiă-wăh-ku^{n} brought out the six pairs, which were destined to become the greatest of all people.

The Tuscaroras tell us that the first pair were left near a great river, now called the Mohawk. The second family were directed to make their home by the side of a big stone. Their descendants have been termed the Oneidas. Another pair were left on a high hill, and have ever been called the Onondagas. Thus each pair was left with careful instructions in different parts of what is now known as the State of New York, except the Tuscaroras, who were taken up the Roanoke River into North Carolina, where Ta-rhu^{n}-hiă-wăh-ku^{n} also took up his abode, teaching them many useful arts before his departure. This, say they, accounts for the superiority of the Tuscaroras. But each of the six tribes will tell you that his own was the favored one with whom Sky Holder made his terrestrial home, while the Onondagas claim that their possession of the council fire prove them to have been the chosen people.

Later, as the numerous families became scattered over the State, some lived in localities where the bear was the principal game, and were called from that circumstance the clan of the Bear. Others lived where the beavers were trapped, and they were called the Beaver clan. For similar reasons the Snipe, Deer, Wolf, Tortoise, and Eel clans received their appellations.

1.3.2 How the World Was Made (Cherokee)

The earth is a great floating island in a sea of water. At each of the four corners there is a cord hanging down from the sky. The sky is of solid rock. When the world grows old and worn out, the cords will break, and then the earth will sink down into the ocean. Everything will be water again. All the people will be dead. The Indians are much afraid of this.

In the long time ago, when everything was all water, all the animals lived up above in Galun'lati, beyond the stone arch that made the sky. But it was very much crowded. All the animals wanted more room. The animals began to wonder what was below the water and at last Beaver's grandchild, little Water Beetle, offered to go and find out. Water Beetle darted in every direction over the surface of the water, but it could find no place to rest. There was no land at all. Then Water Beetle dived to the bottom of the water and brought up some soft mud. This began to grow and to spread out on every side until it became the island which we call the earth. Afterwards this earth was fastened to the sky with four cords, but no one remembers who did this.

At first the earth was flat and soft and wet. The animals were anxious to get down, and they sent out different birds to see if it was yet dry, but there was no place to alight; so the birds came back to Galun'lati. Then at last it seemed to be time again, so they sent out Buzzard; they told him to go and make ready for them. This was the Great Buzzard, the father of all the buzzards we see now. He flew all over the earth, low down near the ground, and it was still soft. When he reached the Cherokee country, he was very tired; his wings began to flap and strike the ground. Wherever they struck the earth there was a valley; whenever the wings turned upwards again, there was a mountain. When the animals above saw this, they were afraid that the whole world would be mountains, so they called him back, but the Cherokee country remains full of mountains to this day. [This was the original home, in North Carolina.]

When the earth was dry and the animals came down, it was still dark. Therefore they got the sun and set it in a track to go every day across the island from east to west, just overhead. It was too hot this way. Red Crawfish had his shell scorched a bright red, so that his meat was spoiled. Therefore the Cherokees do not eat it.

Then the medicine men raised the sun a handsbreadth in the air, but it was still too hot. They raised it another time; and then another time; at last they had raised it seven handsbreadths so that it was just under the sky arch. Then it was right and they left it so. That is why the medicine men called the high place "the seventh height." Every day the sun goes along under this arch on the under side; it returns at night on the upper side of the arch to its starting place.

There is another world under this earth. It is like this one in every way. The animals, the plants, and the people are the same, but the seasons are different. The streams that come down from the mountains are the trails by which we reach this underworld. The springs at their head are the doorways by which we enter it. But in order to enter the other world, one must fast and then go to the water, and have one of the underground people for a guide. We know that the seasons in the underground world are different, because the water in the spring is always warmer in winter than the air in this world; and in summer the water is cooler.

We do not know who made the first plants and animals. But when they were first made, they were told to watch and keep awake for seven nights. This is the way young men do now when they fast and pray to their medicine. They tried to do this. The first night, nearly all the animals stayed awake. The next night several of them dropped asleep. The third night still more went to sleep. At last, on the seventh night, only the owl, the panther, and one or two more were still awake. Therefore, to these were given the power to see in the dark, to go about as if it were day, and to kill and eat the birds and animals which must sleep during the night.

Even some of the trees went to sleep. Only the cedar, the pine, the spruce, the holly, and the laurel were awake all seven nights. Therefore they are always green. They are also sacred trees. But to the other trees it was said, "Because you did not stay awake, therefore you shall lose your hair every winter."

After the plants and the animals, men began to come to the earth. At first there was only one man and one woman. He hit her with a fish. In seven days a little child came down to the earth. So people came to the earth. They came so rapidly that for a time it seemed as though the earth could not hold them all.

1.3.3 Talk Concerning the First Beginning (Zuni)

Yes, indeed. In this world there was no one at all. Always the sun came up; always he went in. No one in the morning gave him sacred meal; no one gave him prayer sticks; it was very lonely. He said to his two children: "You will go into the fourth womb. Your fathers, your mothers, käeto··-we, tcu-eto·we, mu-eto·we, łhe··-eto-we, all the society priests, society ˆpekwins, society bow priests, you will bring out yonder into the light of your sun father." Thus he said to them. They said, "But how shall we go in?" "That will be all right." Laying their lightning arrow across their rainbow bow, they drew it. Drawing it and shooting down, they entered.

When they entered the fourth womb it was dark inside. They could not distinguish anything. They said, "Which way will it be best to go?" They went toward the west. They met someone face to face. They said, "Whence come you?" "I come from over this way to the west." "What are you doing going around?" "I am going around to look at my crops. Where do you live?" "No, we do not live any place. There above our father the Sun, priest, made us come in. We have come in," they said. "Indeed," the younger brother said. "Come, let us see," he said. They laid down their bow. Putting underneath some dry brush and some dry grass that was lying about, and putting the bow on top, they kindled fire by hand. When they had kindled the fire, light came out from the coals. As it came out, they blew on it and it caught fire. Aglow! It is growing light. "Ouch! What have you there?" he said. He fell down crouching. He had a slimy horn, slimy tail, he was slimy allover, with webbed hands. The elder brother said, "Poor thing! Put out the light." Saying thus, he put out the light. The youth said, "Oh dear, what have you there?" "Why, we have fire," they said. "Well, what (crops) do you have coming up?" "Yes, here are our things coming up." Thus he said. He was going around looking after wild grasses.

He said to them, "Well, now, let us go." They went toward the west, the two leading. There the people were sitting close together. They questioned one another. Thus they said, "Well, now, you two, speak. I think there is something to say. It will not be too long a talk. If you lotus know that we shall always remember it." "That is so, that is so," they said. "Yes, indeed, it is true. There above is our father, Sun. No one ever gives him prayer sticks; no one ever gives him sacred meal; no one ever gives him shells. Because it is thus we have come to you, in order that you may go out standing yonder into the daylight of your sun father. Now you will say which way (you decide)." Thus the two said. "Hayi! Yes, indeed. Because it is thus you have passed us on our roads. Now that you have passed us on our roads here where we stay miserably, far be it from us to speak against it. We can not see one another. Here inside where we just trample on one another, where we just spit on one another, where we just urinate on one another, where we just befoul one another, where we just follow one another about, you have passed us on our roads. None of us can speak against it. But rather, as the priest of the north says, so let it be. Now you two call him." Thus they said to the two, and they came up close toward the north side.

They met the north priest on his road. "You have come," he said. "Yes, we have come. How have you lived these many days?" "Here where I live happily you have passed me on my road. Sit down." When they were seated he questioned them. "Now speak. I think there is something to say. It will not be too long a talk. So now, that you will let me know." "Yes, indeed, it is so. In order that you may go out standing there into the daylight of your sun father we have passed you on your road. However you say, so shall it be." "Yes, indeed, now that you have passed us on our road here where we live thus wretchedly, far be it from me to talk against it. Now that you have come to us here inside where, we just trample on one another, where we just spit on one another, where we just urinate on one another, where we just befoul one another, where we just follow one another about, how should I speak against it?" so he said. Then they arose. They came back. Coming to the village where they were sitting in the middle place, there they questioned one another. "Yes, even now we have met on our roads. Indeed there is something to say; it will not be too long a talk. When you let me know that, I shall always remember it," thus they said to one another. When they had spoken thus, "Yes, indeed. In order that you may go out standing into the daylight of your sun father, we have passed you on your road," thus they said. "Hayi! Yes, indeed. Now that you have passed us on our road here where we cannot see one another, where we just trample on one another, where we just urinate on one another, where we just befoul one another, where we just follow one another around, far be it from me to speak against it. But rather let it be as my younger brother, the priest of the west shall say. When he says, 'Let it be thus,' that way it shall be. So now, you two call him." Thus said the priest of the north and they went and stood close against the west side.

"Well, perhaps by means of the thoughts of someone somewhere it may be that we shall go out standing into the daylight of our sun father." Thus he said. The two thought. "Come, let us go over there to talk with eagle priest." They went. They came to where eagle was staying. "You have come." "Yes." "Sit down." They sat down. "Speak!" "We want you." "Where?" "Near by, to where our fathers, käeto·-we, tcu-eto·we, stay quietly, we summon you." "Haiyi!" So they went. They came to where käeto·-we stayed. "Well, even now when you summoned me, I have passed you on your roads. Surely there is something to say; it will not be too long a talk. So now if you let me know that I shall always remember it," thus he said. "Yes, indeed, it is so. Our fathers, käeto·-we, tcu-eto·we, mu-eto·we, łhe·-eto-we, all the society priests shall go out standing into the daylight of their sun father. You will look for their road." "Very well," he said, "I am going," he said. He went around. Coming back to his starting place he went a little farther out. Coming back to his starting place again he went still farther out. Coming back to his starting place he went way far out. Coming back to his starting place, nothing was visible. He came. To where käeto·-we stayed he came. After he sat down they questioned him. "Now you went yonder looking for the road going out. What did you see in the world?" "Nothing was visible." "Haiyi!" "Very well, I am going now." So he went.

When he had gone the two thought. "Come, let us summon our grandson, cokäpiso," thus they said. They went. They came to where cokäpiso stayed. "Our grandson, how have you lived these days?" "Where I live happily you have passed me on my road. I think perhaps there is something to say; it will not be too long a talk. So now when you let me know that, I shall always remember it," thus he said. "Yes, indeed, it is so. Our fathers, käeto·-we, tcu-eto·we, mu-eto·we, łhe·-eto-we, all the society priests are about to come outstanding into the daylight of their sun father. We summon you that you may be the one to look for their road." "Indeed?" Thus he said. They went. When they got there, they questioned them where they were sitting. "Even now you have summoned me. Surely there is something to say; it will not be too long a talk. So now when you let me know that, I shall always remember it." "Yes, indeed, it is so. When our fathers, our mothers, käeto·-we, tcu-eto·we, mu-eto·we, łhe·-eto-we, the society priests, go forth standing into the daylight of their sun father, you will look for their road." Thus the two said. He went out to the south. He went around. Coming back to the same place, nothing was visible. A second time he went, farther out. Coming back to the same place, nothing was visible. A third time, still farther out he went. Nothing was visible. A fourth time he went, way far, but nothing was visible. When he came to where käeto·-we were staying, the two questioned him. "Now, our grandson, way off yonder you have gone to see the world. What did you see in the world?" Thus the two asked him. "Well, nothing was visible." "Well indeed?" the two said. "Very well, I am going now." Saying this, he went.

When cokäpiso had gone the two thought. "Come, let us go and talk to our grandson chicken hawk." Thus they said. They went. They reached where chicken hawk stayed. "You have come." "Yes." "Sit down." "How have you lived these days?" "Happily. Well now, speak. I think there is something to say; it will not be too long a talk. So now, when you let me know it, I shall always remember that." "Yes, indeed, it is so. When our fathers, käeto·-we, tcu-eto·we, mu-eto·we, łhe·-eto-we, the society priests, go out standing into the sunlight of their sun father, you will look for their road." So they went. When they got there they sat down. There he questioned them. "Yes, even now you summoned me. Perhaps there is something to say; it will not be too long a talk. When you let me know that, I shall always remember it." Thus he said. "Yes, indeed, it is so. When our fathers, käeto·-we, tcu-eto·we, mu-eto·we, łhe·-eto-we, the society priests, go out standing into the daylight of their sun father, you will look for their road." "Is that so?" Saying this, he went out. He went to the south. He went where cokäpiso had been. Coming back to his starting place, nothing was visible. A second time he went, farther out. He came back to his starting place, nothing was visible. He went a third time, along the shore of the encircling ocean. A fourth time farther out he went. He came back to his starting place. Nothing was visible. To where käeto·-we stayed he came. "Nothing is visible." "Haiyi!" Yes, so I am going." "Well, go." So he went.

Then the two thought. "Come on, let us summon our grandson," thus they said. They went. They came to where humming bird was staying. "You have come?"

"Yes, how have you lived these days?" "Where I live happily these days you have passed me on my road. Sit down." When they had sat down: "Well, now, speak. I think there is something to say; it will not be too long a talk. So now if you let me know that, I shall always remember it." "Yes, indeed, it is so. When our fathers, käeto··we, tcu-eto·we, mu-eto·we, łhe··eto-we, the society priests, go out standing into the daylight of their sun father, you shall be the one to look for their road; for that we have summoned you . . . .Is that so?" Saying this, they went. When they got there, he questioned them. "Well, even now you summoned me. Surely there is something to say. It will not be too long a talk. So now when you let me know that I shall always remember it." Thus he said. "Yes, indeed, it is so. When our fathers, käeto··we, tcu-eto·we, mu-eto·we, łhe··eto-we, the society priests, go out into the daylight of their sun father, that you shall be the one to look for their road, for that we have summoned you." Thus the two said. He went out toward the south. He went on. Coming back to his starting place, nothing was visible. Farther out he went. Coming back to the same place, nothing was visible. Then for the third time he went. Coming back to the same place, nothing was visible. For the fourth time he went close along the edge of the sky. Coming back to the same place, nothing was visible. He came. Coming where käeto··we were staying, "Nothing is visible." "Hayi!" "Yes. Well, I am going now." "Very well, go." He went.

The two said, "What had we better do now? That many different kinds of feathered creatures, the ones who go about without ever touching the ground, have failed." Thus the two said. "Come, let us talk with our grandson, locust. Perhaps that one will have a strong spirit because he is like water." Thus they said. They went. Their grandson, locust, they met. "You have come." "Yes, we have come." "Sit down. How have you lived these days?" "Happily." "Well, even now you have passed me, on my road. Surely there is something to say; it will not be too long a talk. So now when you let me know that, that I shall always remember." Thus he said. "Yes, indeed, it is so. In order that our fathers, käeto··we, tcu-eto·we, mu-eto·we, łhe··eto-we, the society priests, may go out standing into the daylight of their sun father, we have come to you." "Is that so?" Saying this, they went. When they arrived they sat down. Where they were sitting, he questioned them. "Well, just now you came to me. Surely there is something to say; it will not be too long a talk. So now if you let me know that, that I shall always remember." "Yes, indeed. In order that our fathers, käeto··we, tcu-eto·we, mu-eto·we, łhe··eto-we, the society priests, may go out standing into the daylight of their sun father, we have summoned you." "Indeed?" Saying this, locust rose right up. He goes up. He went through into another world. And again he goes right up. He went through into another world. And again he goes right up. Again he went through into another world. He goes right up. When he had just gone a little way his strength gave out, he came back to where käeto··we were staying and said, "Three times I went through and the fourth time my strength gave out." "Hayi! Indeed?" Saying this, he went.

When he had gone the two thought. "Come, let us speak with our grandson, Reed Youth. For perhaps that one with his strong point will be all right." Saying this, they went. They came to where Reed Youth stayed. "You have come?" "Yes; how have you lived these days." "Where I stay happily you have passed me on my road. Sit down." Thus he said. They sat down. Then he questioned them. "Yes. Well, even now you have passed me on my road. I think there is something to say; it will not be too long a talk. When you let me know that, that I shall always remember." Thus he said. "Yes, indeed, in order that our fathers, käeto·-we, tcu-eto·we, mu-eto·we, łhe·-eto-we, the society priests, may go out standing into the daylight of their sun father, we have come to you." "Hayi! Is that so?" Having spoken thus, they went. When they arrived they sat down. There he questioned them. "Yes, even now that you have summoned me I have passed you on your roads. Surely there is something to say; it will not be too long a talk. When you let me know that, that I shall always remember.... Yes, indeed, it is so. In order that our fathers, käeto·-we, tcu-eto·we, mu-eto·we, łhe·-eto-we, the society priests, may go forth standing into the daylight of their sun father, we have summoned you." Thus they said. "Hayi! Is that so?" Saying this, he went out. Where Locust had gone out he went out. The first time he passed through, the second time he passed through, the third time he passed through. Having passed through the fourth time and come forth standing into the daylight of his sun father, he went back in. Coming back in he came to where käeto·-we were staying. "You have come?" Thus they said. "Yes," he said. "Far off to see what road there may be you have gone. How may it be there now?" Thus they said. "Yes, indeed, it is so. There it is as you wanted it. As you wished of me, I went forth standing into the daylight of my sun father now." Thus he said. "Halihi! Thank you!" "Now I am going." "Go." Saying this, he went.

After he had gone they were sitting around. Now as they were sitting around, there the two set up a pine tree for a ladder. They stayed there. For four days they stayed there. Four days, they say, but it was four years. There all the different society priests sang their song sequences for one another. The ones sitting in the first row listened carefully. Those sitting next on the second row heard all but a little. Those sitting on the third row heard here and there. Those sitting last on the fourth row heard just a little bit now and then. It was thus because of the rustling of the dry weeds.

When their days there were at an end, gathering together their sacred things they arose. "Now what shall be the name of this place?" "Well, here it shall be sulphur-smell-inside-world; and furthermore, it shall be raw-dust world." Thus they said. "Very well. Perhaps if we call it thus it will be all right." Saying this, they came forth.

After they had come forth, setting down their sacred things in a row at another place, they stayed there quietly. There the two set up a spruce tree as a ladder. When the ladder was up they stayed there for four days. And there again the society priests sang their song sequences for one another. Those sitting on the first row listened carefully. Those sitting there on the second row heard all but a little. Those sitting there on the third row heard here and there. Those sitting last distinguished a single word now and then. It was thus because of the rustling of some plants. When their days there were at an end, gathering together their sacred things there they arose. "Now what shall it be called here?" "Well, here it shall be called soot-inside-world, because we still can not recognize one another." "Yes, perhaps if it is called thus it will be all right." Saying this to one another, they arose.

Passing through to another place, and putting down their sacred things in a row, they stayed there quietly. There the two set up a piñon tree as a ladder. When the piñon tree was put up, there all the society priests and all the priests went through their song sequences for one another. Those sitting in front listened carefully. Those sitting on the second row heard all but a little. Those sitting behind on the third row heard here and there. Those sitting on the fourth row distinguished only a single word now and then. This was because of the rustling of the weeds.

When their days there were at an end, gathering together their sacred things they arose. Having arisen, "Now what shall it be called here?" "Well, here it shall be fog-inside-world, because here just a little bit is visible." "Very well, perhaps if it is called thus it will be all right." Saying this, rising, they came forth.

Passing through to another place, there the two set down their sacred things in a row, and there they sat down. Having sat down, the two set up a cottonwood tree as a ladder. Then all the society priests and all the priests went through their song sequences for one another. Those sitting first heard everything clearly. Those sitting on the second row heard all but a little. Those sitting on the third row heard here and there. Those sitting last on the fourth row distinguished a single word now and then. It was thus because of the rustling of some plants.

When their days there were at an end, after they had been there, when their four days were passed, gathering together their sacred possessions, they arose. When they arose, "Now what shall it be called here?" "Well, here it shall be wing-inner-world, because we see our sun father's wings." Thus they said. They came forth.

Into the daylight of their sun father they came forth standing. Just at early dawn they came forth. After they had come forth there they set down their sacred possessions in a row. The two said, "Now after a little while when your sun father comes forth standing to his sacred place you will see him face to face. Do not close your eyes." Thus he said to them. After a little while the sun came out. When he came out they looked at him. From their eyes the tears rolled down. After they had looked at him, in a little while their eyes became strong. "Alas!" Thus they said. They were covered all over with slime. With slimy tails and slimy horns, with webbed fingers, they saw one another. "Oh dear! is this what we look like?" Thus they said.

Then they could not tell which was which of their sacred possessions. Meanwhile, near by an old man of the Dogwood clan lived alone. Spider said to him, "Put on water. When it gets hot, wash your hair." "Why?" "Our father, our mothers, käeto·-we, tcu-eto·we, mu-eto·we, łhe·-eto-we, all the society priests, into the daylight of their sun father have come forth standing. They can not tell which is which. You will make this plain to them." Thus she said. "Indeed? Impossible.

From afar no one can see them. Where they stay quietly no one can recognize them." Thus he said. "Do not say that. Nevertheless it will be all right. You will not be alone. Now we shall go." Thus she said. When the water was warm he washed his hair.

Meanwhile, while he was washing his hair, the two said, "Come let us go to meet our father, the old man of the Dogwood clan. I think he knows in his thoughts; because among our fathers, käeto·-we, tcu-eto·we, mu-eto·we, łhe·-eto-we, we can not tell which is which." Thus they said. They went. They got there. As they were climbing tip, "Now indeed! They are coming." Thus Spider said to him. She climbed up his body from his toe. She clung behind his ear. The two entered. "You have come," thus he said. "Yes. Our father, how have you lived these days?" "As I live happily you pass me on my road. Sit down." They sat down. "Well, now, speak. I think some word that is not too long, your word will be. Now, if you let me know that, remembering it, I shall live." "Indeed it is so. Our fathers, käeto·-we, tcu-eto·we, mu-eto·we, łhe·-eto-we, all the society priests, into the daylight of their sun father have risen and come out. It is not plain which is which. Therefore we have passed you on your road." "Haiyi, is that so? Impossible! From afar no one can see them. Where they stay quietly no one can recognize them." Thus he said. "Yes, but we have chosen you." Thus the two said. They went. When they came there, "My fathers, my mothers, how have you lived these days?" "Happily, our father, our child. Be seated." Thus they said. He sat down. Then he questioned them. "Yes, now indeed, since you have sent for me, I have passed you on your road. I think some word that is not too long your word will be. Now if you let me know that, remembering it, I shall always live."

Thus he said. "Indeed, it is so. Even though our fathers, our mothers, käeto·-we, tcu-eto·we, mu-eto·we, łhe·-eto-we, have come out standing into the daylight of their sun father, it is not plain which of these is which. Therefore we have sent for you." Thus they said. "Haiyi. Well, let me try." "Impossible. From afar no one can see them. Where they stay quietly no one can tell which is which." "Well, let me try." Thus he said. Where they lay in a row he stood beside them. Spider said to him, "Here, the one that lies here at the end is käeto·-we and these next ones touching it are tcu-eto·we, and this next one is łhe·-eto-we, and these next ones touching it are mu-eto·we." Thus she said. He said, "Now this is käeto·-we, and these all touching it are tcu-eto·we, and this one is łhe·-eto-we, and all these touching it are mu-eto·we." Thus he said. "Halihi! Thank you. How shall be the cycle of the months for them?" Thus he said: "This one Branches-broken-down. This one No-snow-on-the-road. This one Little-sand-storms. This one Great-sand-storms. This the Month-without-a-name. This one Turn-about. This one Branches-broken-down. This one No-snow-on-the-road. This one Little-sand-storms. This one Great-sand-storms. This the Month-without-a-name. This one Turn-about. Thus shall be all the cycle of the months." "Halihi! Thank you. Our father, you shall not be poor. Even though you have no sacred possessions toward which your thoughts bend, whenever Itiwana is revealed to us, because of your thought, the ceremonies of all these shall come around in order. You shall not be a slave." This they said. They gave him the sun. "This shall be your sacred possession." Thus they said. When this had happened thus they lived.

Four days—four days they say, but it was four years—there they stayed. When their days were at an end, the earth rumbled. The two said, "Who was left behind?" "I do not know, but it seems we are all here." Thus they said. Again the earth rumbled. "Well, does it not seem that some one is still left behind?" Thus the two said. They went. Coming to the place where they had come out, there they stood. To the mischief-maker and the Mexicans they said, "Haiyi! Are you still left behind?" "Yes." "Now what are you still good for?" Thus they said. "Well, it is this way. Even though käeto·-we have issued forth into the daylight, the people do not live on the living waters of good corn; on wild grasses only they live. Whenever you come to the middle you will do well to have me. When the people are many and the land is all used up, it will not be well. Because this is so I have come out." Thus he said. "Haiyi! Is that so? So that's what you are. Now what are you good for?" Thus they said. "Indeed, it is so. When you come to the middle, it will be well to have my seeds. Because käeto·-we do not live on the good seeds of the corn, but on wild grasses only. Mine are the seeds of the corn and all the clans of beans." Thus he said. The two took him with them. They came to where käeto·-we were staying. They sat down. Then they questioned him. "Now let us see what you are good for." "Well, this is my seed of the yellow corn." Thus he said. He showed an ear of yellow corn. "Now give me one of your people." Thus he said. They gave him a baby. When they gave him the baby it seems he did something to her. She became sick. After a short time she died. When she had died he said, "Now bury her." They dug a hole and buried her. After four days he said to the two, "Come now. Go and see her." The two went to where they had come out. When they got there the little one was playing in the dirt. When they came, she laughed. She was happy. They saw her and went back. They came to where the people were staying. "Listen! Perhaps it will be all right for you to come. She is still alive. She has not really died." "Well, thus it shall always be." Thus he said.

Gathering together all their sacred possessions, they came hither. To the place called since the first beginning, Moss Spring, they came. There they set down their sacred possessions in a row. There they stayed. Four days they say, but it was four years. There the two washed them. They took from all of them their slimy tails, their slimy horns. "Now, behold! Thus you will be sweet." There they stayed.

When their days were at an end they came hither. Gathering together all their sacred possessions, seeking Itiwana, yonder their roads went. To the place called since the first beginning Massed-cloud Spring, they came. There they set down their sacred possessions in a row. There they stayed quietly. Four days they stayed. Four days they say, but it was four years. There they stayed. There they counted up the days. For käeto·-we, four nights and four days. With fine rain caressing the earth, they passed their days. The days were made for lhe·-eto-we, mu-eto·we. For four days and four nights it snowed. When their days were at an end there they stayed.

When their days were at an end they arose. Gathering together all their sacred possessions, hither their roads went. To the place called since the first beginning Mist Spring their road came. There they sat down quietly. Setting out their sacred possessions in a row, they sat down quietly. There they counted up the days for one another. They watched the world for one another's waters. For käeto··we, four days and four nights, with heavy rain caressing the earth they passed their days. When their days were at an end the days were made for łhe··eto-we and mu-eto·we. Four days and four nights with falling snow the world was filled. When their days were at an end, there they stayed.

When all their days were passed, gathering together all their sacred possessions, hither their road went. To Standing-wood Spring they came. There they sat down quietly. Setting out their sacred possessions in a row, they stayed quietly. There they watched one another's days. For käeto··we, four days and four nights with fine rain caressing the earth, they passed their days. When all their days were at an end, the days were made for lhe-eto:we and mu-eto·we. For four days and four nights, with falling snow, the world was filled. When all their days were at an end, there they stayed.

When all their days were passed, gathering together their sacred possessions, and arising, hither they came. To the place called since the first beginning Upuilima they came. When they came there, setting down their sacred possessions in a row, they stayed quietly. There they strove to outdo one another. There they planted all their seeds. There they watched one another's days for rain. For käeto··we, four days with heavy rain caressing the earth. There their corn matured. It was not palatable, it was bitter. Then the two said, "Now by whose will will our corn become fit to eat?" Thus they said. They summoned raven. He came and pecked at their corn, and it became good to eat. "It is fortunate that you have come." With this then, they lived.

When their days were at an end they arose. Gathering together their sacred possessions, they came hither. To the place called since the first beginning, Cornstalk-place they came. There they set down their sacred possessions in a row. There they stayed four days. Four days they say, but it was four years. There they planted all their seeds. There they watched one another's days for rain. During käeto··we's four days and four nights, heavy rain fell. During lhe-eto:we's and mu-eto·we's four days and four nights, the world was filled with falling snow. Their days were at an end. Their corn matured. When it was mature it was hard. Then the two said, "By whose will will our corn become soft? Well, owl." Thus they said. They summoned owl. Owl came. When he came he pecked at their corn and it became soft.

Then, when they were about to arise, the two said, "Come, let us go talk to the corn priest." Thus they said. They went. They came to where the corn priest stayed. "How have you lived these days?" "As we are living happily you have passed us on our road. Sit down." They sat down. There they questioned one another. "Well, speak. I think some word that is not too long, your word will be. Now, if you let me know that, remembering it, I shall always live." "Indeed, it is so. To-morrow, when we arise, we shall set out to seek Itiwana. Nowhere have we found the middle. Our children, our women, are tired. They are crying. Therefore we have come to you. Tomorrow your two children will look ahead. Perhaps if they find the middle when our fathers, our mothers, käeto·-we, tcu-eto·we, mu-eto·we, lhe-eto:we, all the society priests, come to rest, there our children will rest themselves. Because we have failed to find the middle." "Haiyi! Is that so? With plain words you have passed us on our road. Very well, then, thus it shall be." Thus he said. The two went.

Next morning when they were about to set out they put down a split ear of corn and eggs. They made the corn priest stand up. They said, "Now, my children, some of you will go yonder to the south. You will take these." Thus he said (indicating) the tip of the ear and the macaw egg. And then the ones that were to come this way took the base of the ear and the raven egg. Those that were to go to the south took the tip of the ear and the macaw egg. "Now, my children, yonder to the south you will go. If at any time you come to Itiwana, then some time we shall meet one another." Thus they said. They came hither.

They came to the place that was to be Katcina village. The girl got tired. Her brother said, "Wait, sit down for a while. Let me climb up and look about to see what kind of a place we are going to." Thus he said. His sister sat down. Her brother climbed the hill. When he had climbed up, he stood looking this way. "Eha! Maybe the place where we are going lies in this direction. Maybe it is this kind of a place." Thus he said and came down. Meanwhile his sister had scooped out the sand. She rested against the side of the hill. As she lay sleeping the wind came and raised her apron of grass. It blew up and she lay with her vulva exposed. As he came down he saw her. He desired her. He lay down upon his sister and copulated with her. His sister awoke. "Oh, dear, oh, dear," she was about to say (but she said,) "Watsela, watsela." Her brother said, "Ah!" He sat up. With his foot he drew a line. It became a stream of water. The two went about talking. The brother talked like Koyemci. His sister talked like Komakatsik. The people came.

"Oh alas, alas! Our children have become different beings." Thus they said. The brother speaking: "Now it will be all right for you to cross here." Thus he said. They came and went in. They entered the river. Some of their children turned into water snakes.

Some of them turned into turtles. Some of them turned into frogs. Some of them turned into lizards. They bit their mothers. Their mothers cried out and dropped them. They fell into the river. Only the old people reached the other side. They sat down on the bank. They were half of the people. The two said, "Now wait. Rest here." Thus they said. Some of them sat down to rest. The two said (to the others), "Now you go in. Your children will turn into some kind of dangerous animals and will bite you. But even though you cry out, do not let them go. If, when you come out on the other side, your children do not again become the kind of creatures they are now, then you will throw them into the water." Thus they said to them. They entered the water. Their children became different creatures and bit them. Even though they cried out, they crossed over. Then their children once more became the kind of creatures they had been. "Alas! Perhaps had we done that it would have been all right." Now all had crossed over.

There setting down their sacred possessions in a row, they stayed quietly. They stayed there quietly for four days. Thus they say but they stayed for four years. There each night they lived gaily with loud singing. When all their time was passed, the two said "Come, let us go and talk to Ne-we-kwe." Thus they said. They went to where the Ne-we-kwe were staying. They came there. "How have you passed these days?' "Happily. You have come? Be seated." They sat down. Then they questioned them. "Now speak. I think some word that is not too long your word will be. If you let me know that, remembering it I shall always live." "Indeed it is so. To-morrow we shall arise. Our fathers, our mothers, käeto·-we, tcu-eto·we, mu-eto·we, lhe-eto:we, all the society priests, are going to seek the middle. But nowhere have we come to the middle. Our children and our women are tired. They are crying now. Therefore we have passed you on your road. To-morrow you will look ahead. If perhaps somewhere you come to Itiwana there our children will rest." Thus they said. "Alas! but we are just foolish people. If we make some mistake it will not be right." Thus he said. "Well, that is of no importance. It can't be helped. We have chosen you." Thus they said. "Well indeed?' "Yes. Now we are going." "Go ahead." The two went out.

They came (to where the people were staying). "Come, let us go and speak to our children." Thus they said. They went. They entered the lake. It was full of katcinas. "Now stand still a moment. Our two fathers have come." Thus they said. The katcinas suddenly stopped dancing. When they stopped dancing they said to the two, "Now our two fathers, now indeed you have passed us on our road. I think some word that is not too long your word will be. If you will let us know that we shall always remember it." Thus he said. "Indeed it is so. Tomorrow we shall arise. Therefore we have come to speak to you." "Well indeed? May you go happily. You will tell our parents, 'Do not worry.' We have not perished. In order to remain thus forever we stay here. To Itiwana but one day's travel remains. Therefore we stay nearby. When our world grows old and the waters are exhausted and the seeds are exhausted, none of you will go back to the place of your first beginning. Whenever the waters are exhausted and the seeds are exhausted you will send us prayer sticks. Yonder at the place of our first beginning with them we shall bend over to speak to them. Thus there will not fail to be waters. Therefore we shall stay quietly near by." Thus they said to them. "Well indeed?" "Yes. You will tell my father, my mother, 'Do not worry.' We have not perished." Thus they said. They sent strong words to their parents. "Now we are going. Our children, may you always live happily." "Even thus may you also go." Thus they said to the two. They went out. They arrived. They told them. "Now our children, here your children have stopped. 'They have perished,' you have said. But no. The male children have become youths, and the females have become maidens. They are happy. They live joyously. They have sent you strong words. 'Do not worry,' they said." "Haiyi! Perhaps it is so."

They stayed overnight. Next morning they arose. Gathering together all their sacred possessions, they came hither. They came to Hanlhipingka. Meanwhile the two Ne-we-kwe looked ahead. They came to Rock-in-the-river. There two girls were washing a woolen dress. They killed them. After they had killed them they scalped them. Then someone found them out. When they were found out, because they were raw people, they wrapped themselves in mist. There to where käeto·-we were staying they came. "Alack, alas! We have done wrong!" Thus they said. Then they set the days for the enemy. There they watched one another's days for rain. käeto·-we's four days and four nights passed with the falling of heavy rain. There where a waterfall issued from a cave the foam arose. There the two Ahaiyute appeared. They came to where käeto·-we were staying. Meanwhile, from the fourth inner world, Unasinte, Uhepololo, Kailuhtsawaki, Hattungka, Oloma, Catunka, came out to sit down in the daylight. There they gave them the comatowe Song cycle. Meanwhile, right there, Coyote was going about hunting. He gave them their pottery drum. They sang comatowe.

After this had happened, the two said, "Now, my younger brother, Itiwana is less than one day distant. We shall gather together our children, all the beast priests, and the winged creatures, this night." They went. They came yonder to Comk?äkwe. There they gathered together all the beasts, mountain lion, bear, wolf, wild cat, badger, coyote, fox, squirrel; eagle, buzzard, cokapiso, chicken hawk, baldheaded eagle, raven, owl. All these they gathered together. Now squirrel was among the winged creatures, and owl was among the beasts. "Now my children, you will contest together for your sun father's daylight. Whichever side has the ball, when the sun rises, they shall win their sun father's daylight." Thus the two said. "Indeed?" They went there. They threw up the ball. It fell on the side of the beasts. They hid it. After they had hidden it, the birds came one by one but they could not take it. Each time they paid four straws. They could not take it.

At this time it was early dawn. Meanwhile Squirrel was lying by the fireplace. Thus they came one by one but they could not take it. Eagle said, "Let that one lying there by the fireplace go." They came to him and said, "Are you asleep?" "No. I am not asleep." "Oh dear! Now you go!" Thus they said. "Oh no, I don't want to go," he said. He came back. "The lazy one does not wish to." Thus they said. Someone else went. Again they could not take it. Now it was growing light. "Let that one lying by the fireplace go." Thus they said. Again Buzzard went. "Alas, my boy, you go." "Oh, no, I don't feel like it." Thus he said. Again he went back. "He does not want to," he said. Again some one else went. Again they did not take it. Now it was growing light. Spider said to him, "Next time they come agree to go." Thus she said. Then again they said, "Let that one lying by the fireplace go." Thus they said; and again someone went. When he came there he said, "Alas, my boy, you go." "All right, I shall go." Thus he said and arose. As he arose Spider said to him, "Take that stick." He took up a stick, so short. Taking it, he went. Now the sun was about to rise. They came there. Spider said to him, "Hit those two sitting on the farther side." Thus she said. Bang! He knocked them down. He laid them down. Then, mountain lion, who was standing right there, said, "Hurry up, go after it. See whether you can take it." Thus he said. Spider said to him, "Say to him, 'Oh, no, I don't want to take it.' So she said." "Oh, no, I don't want to take it. Perhaps there is nothing inside. How should I take it? There is nothing in there." "That is right. There is nothing in there. All my children are gathered together. One of them is holding it. If you touch the right one, you will take it." "All right." Now Spider is speaking: "No one who is sitting here has it. That one who goes about dancing, he is holding it." Thus she said. He went. He hit Owl on the hand. The white ball came out. He went. He took up the hollow sticks and took them away with him. Now the birds hid the ball. Spider came down. Over all the sticks she spun her web. She fastened the ball with her web. Now the animals came one by one. Whenever they touched a stick, she pulled (the ball) away. Each time they paid ten straws. The sun rose. After sunrise, he was sitting high in the sky. Then the two came. They said, "Now, all my children, you have won your sun father's daylight, and you, beasts, have lost your sun father's daylight. All day you will sleep. After sunset, at night, you will go about hunting. But you, owl, you have not stayed among the winged creatures. Therefore you have lost your sun father's daylight. You have made a mistake. If by daylight, you go about hunting, the one who has his home above will find you out. He will come down on you. He will scrape off the dirt from his earth mother and put it upon you. Then thinking, 'Let it be here,' you will come to the end of your life. This kind of creature you shall be." Thus they said. They stayed there overnight. The animals all scattered.

The two went. They came to where käeto·-we were staying. Then they arose. Gathering together all their sacred possessions, they arose. Lhe-eto:we said, "Now, my younger brothers, hither to the north I shall take my road. Whenever I think that Itiwana has been revealed to you, then I shall come to you." Thus he said, and went to the north. Now some woman, seeing them, said, "Oh dear! Whither are these going?" Thus she said:

Naiye heni aiye
Naiye heni aiye.
In white stripes of hail they went.

Meanwhile käeto·-we came hither. They came to House Mountain. When they came there they would not let them pass through. They fought together. A giant went back and forth before them. Thus they fought together. Thus evening came. In the evening they came back to Hanlhipingka. Next day they went again. In heavy rain they fought together. In the evening they went back again. Next morning they went again for the third time. Again they fought together. The giant went back and forth in front. Even though she had arrows sticking in her body she did not die. At sunset they went back again. Next morning they went. They came there, and they fought together. Still they would not surrender. The giant went back and forth in front. Although she was wounded with arrows, she would not surrender. Ahaiyute said, "Alas, why is it that these people will not let us pass? Wherever may her heart be, that one that goes back and forth? Where her heart should be we have struck her, yet she does not surrender. It seems we can not overcome her. So finally go up to where your father stays. Without doubt he knows." Thus he said. His younger brother climbed up to where the sun was.

It was nearly noon when he arrived. "You have come?" "Yes, I have come." "Very well, speak. I think some word that is not too long your word will be. So if you let me know that, I shall always remember it." Thus he said. "Indeed, it is so. Our fathers, our mothers, käeto·-we, tcu-eto·we, mu-eto·we, lhe-eto:we, all the society priests, have issued forth into the daylight. Here they go about seeking Itiwana. These people will not let them pass. Where does she have her heart, that one who goes back and forth before them? In vain have we struck her where her heart should be. Even though the arrows stick in her body, she does not surrender." "Haiyi! For nothing are you men! She does not have her heart in her body. In vain have you struck her there. Her heart is in her rattle." Thus he said. "This is for you and this is for your elder brother." Thus he said, and gave him two turquoise rabbit sticks. "Now, when you let these go with my wisdom I shall take back my weapons.' "Haiyi! Is that so? Very well, I am going now." "Go ahead. May you go happily." Thus he said. He came down. His elder brother said to him, "Now, what did he tell you?" "Indeed, it is so. In vain do we shoot at her body. Not there is her heart; but in her rattle is her heart. With these shall we destroy her." Thus he said, and gave his brother one of the rabbit sticks. When he had given his brother the rabbit stick, "Now go ahead, you." Thus he said. The younger brother went about to the right. He threw it and missed. Whiz! The rabbit stick went up to the sun. As the rabbit stick came up the sun took it. "Now go ahead, you try." Thus he said. The elder brother went around to the left. He threw it. As he threw it, zip! His rabbit stick struck his rattle. Tu --- n! They ran away. As they started to run away, their giant died. Then they all ran away. The others ran after them. They came to a village. They went into the houses. "This is my house;" "This is my house;" and "This is mine." Thus they said. They went shooting arrows into the roof. Wherever they first came, they went in. An old woman and a little boy this big and a little girl were inside.

In the center of their room was standing a jar of urine. They stuffed their nostrils with känaite flowers and with cotton wool. Then they thrust their noses into the jar. The people could see them. "Oh, dear! These are ghosts!" Thus they said. Then the two said to them, "Do not harm them, for I think they know something. So even though it is dangerous they are still alive." Thus they said. The two entered. As they came in they questioned them. "And now do you know something? Therefore, even though it is dangerous, you have not perished." "Well, we have a sacred object." "Indeed! Very well, take them. We shall go. Your fathers, your mothers, käeto·-we, tcu-eto·we, mu-eto·we, lhe-eto:we, you will pass on their roads. If your days are the same as theirs you will not be slaves. It does not matter that he is only a little boy. Even so, he will be our father. It does not matter that she is a little girl, she will be our mother." Thus he said. Taking their sacred object they went. They came to where käeto·-we were staying. There they said to them, "Now make your days."

"Oh, no! We shall not be first. When all your days are at an end, then we shall add on our days." Thus they said. Then they worked for käeto·-we. käeto·-we's days were made. Four days and four nights, with fine rain falling, were the days of käeto·-we. When their days were at an end, the two children and their grandmother worked. Their days were made. Four days and four nights, with heavy rain falling, were their days. Then they removed the evil smell. They made flowing canyons. Then they said, "Halihi! Thank you! Just the same is your ceremony. What may your clan be?" "Well, we are of the Yellow Corn clan." Thus they said. "Haiyi! Even though your eton:e is of the Yellow Corn clan, because of your bad smell, you have become black. Therefore you shall be the Black Corn clan." Thus they said to them.

Then they arose. Gathering together all their sacred possessions, they came hither, to the place called, since the first beginning, Halona-Itiwana, their road came. There they saw the Navaho helper, little red bug. "Here! Wait! All this time we have been searching in vain for Itiwana. Nowhere have we seen anything like this." Thus they said. They summoned their grandchild, water bug. He came. "How have you lived these many days?" "Where we have been living happily you have passed us on our road. Be Seated." Thus they said. He sat down. Then he questioned them. "Now, indeed, even now, you have sent for me. I think some word that is not too long your word will be. So now, if you will let me know that, I shall always remember it." "Indeed, it is so. Our fathers, our mothers, käeto·-we, tcu-eto·we, mu-eto·we, lhe-eto:we, all the society priests, having issued forth into the daylight, go about seeking the middle. You will look for the middle for them. This is well. Because of your thoughts, at your heart, our fathers, käeto·-we, tcu-eto·we, mu-eto·we, lhe-eto:we, will sit down quietly. Following after those, toward whom our thoughts bend, we shall pass our days." Thus they said. He sat down facing the east. To the left he stretched out his arm. To the right he stretched out his arm, but it was a little bent. He sat down facing the north. He stretched out his arms on both sides. They were just the same. Both arms touched the horizon. "Come, let us cross over to the north. For on this side my right arm is a little bent." Thus he said. They crossed (the river). They rested. He sat down. To all directions he stretched out his arms. Everywhere it was the same. "Right here is the middle." Thus he said. There his fathers, his mothers, käeto·-we, tcu-eto·we, mu-eto·we, lhe-eto:we, all the society priests, the society pˆekwins, the society bow priests, and all their children came to rest. Thus it happened long ago.

1.3.4 From the Winnebago Trickster Cycle

Trickster's Warpath

https://hotcakencyclopedia.com/ho.TrickstersWarpath.html

Trickster Gets Pregnant

https://hotcakencyclopedia.com/ho.TricksterGetsPregnant.html

Trickster Eats a Laxative Bulb

https://hotcakencyclopedia.com/ho.TricksterEatsLaxative.html

1.3.5 Origin of Disease and Medicine (Cherokee)

In the old days quadrupeds, birds, fishes, and insects could all talk, and they and the human race lived together in peace and friendship. But as time went on the people increased so rapidly that their settlements spread over the whole earth and the poor animals found themselves beginning to be cramped for room. This was bad enough, but to add to their misfortunes man invented bows, knives, blowguns, spears, and hooks, and began to slaughter the larger animals, birds and fishes for the sake of their flesh or their skins, while the smaller creatures, such as the frogs and worms, were crushed and trodden upon without mercy, out of pure carelessness or contempt. In this state of affairs the animals resolved to consult upon measures for their common safety.

The bears were the first to meet in council in their townhouse in Kuwa´hĭ, the "Mulberry Place," and the old White Bear chief presided. After each in turn had made complaint against the way in which man killed their friends, devoured their flesh and used their skins for his own adornment, it was unanimously decided to begin war at once against the human race. Some one asked what weapons man used to accomplish their destruction. "Bows and arrows, of course," cried all the bears in chorus. "And what are they made of?" was the next question. "The bow of wood and the string of our own entrails," replied one of the bears. It was then proposed that they make a bow and some arrows and see if they could not turn man's weapons against himself. So one bear got a nice piece of locust wood and another sacrificed himself for the good of the rest in order to furnish a piece of his entrails for the string. But when everything was ready and the first bear stepped up to make the trial it was found that in letting the arrow fly after drawing back the bow, his long claws caught the string and spoiled the shot. This was annoying, but another suggested that he could overcome the difficulty by cutting his claws, which was accordingly done, and on a second trial it was found that the arrow went straight to the mark. But here the chief, the old White Bear, interposed and said that it was necessary that they should have long claws in order to be able to climb trees. "One of us has already died to furnish the bowstring, and if we now cut off our claws we shall all have to starve together. It is better to trust to the teeth and claws which nature has given us, for it is evident that man's weapons were not intended for us."

No one could suggest any better plan, so the old chief dismissed the council and the bears dispersed to their forest haunts without having concerted any means for preventing the increase of the human race. Had the result of the council been otherwise, we should now be at war with the bears, but as it is the hunter does not even ask the bear's pardon when he kills one.

The deer next held a council under their chief, the Little Deer, and after some deliberation resolved to inflict rheumatism upon every hunter who should kill one of their number, unless he took care to ask their pardon for the offense. They sent notice of their decision to the nearest settlement of Indians and told them at the same time how to make propitiation when necessity forced them to kill one of the deer tribe. Now, whenever the hunter brings down a deer, the Little Deer, who is swift as the wind and can not be wounded, runs quickly up to the spot and bending over the blood stains asks the spirit of the deer if it has heard the prayer of the hunter for pardon. If the reply be "Yes" all is well and the Little Deer goes on his way, but if the reply be in the negative he follows on the trail of the hunter, guided by the drops of blood on the ground, until he arrives at the cabin in the settlement, when the Little Deer enters invisibly and strikes the neglectful hunter with rheumatism, so that he is rendered on the instant a helpless cripple. No hunter who has regard for his health ever fails to ask pardon of the deer for killing it, although some who have not learned the proper formula may attempt to turn aside the Little Deer from his pursuit by building a fire behind them in the trail.

Next came the fishes and reptiles, who had their own grievances against humanity. They held a joint council and determined to make their victims dream of snakes twining about them in slimy folds and blowing their fetid breath in their faces, or to make them dream of eating raw or decaying fish, so that they would lose appetite, sicken, and die. Thus it is that snake and fish dreams are accounted for.

Finally the birds, insects, and smaller animals came together for a like purpose, and the Grubworm presided over the deliberations. It was decided that each in turn should express an opinion and then vote on the question as to whether or not man should be deemed guilty. Seven votes were to be sufficient to condemn him. One after another denounced man's cruelty and injustice toward the other animals and voted in favor of his death. The Frog (walâ´sĭ) spoke first and said: "We must do something to check the increase of the race or people will become so numerous that we shall be crowded from off the earth. See how man has kicked me about because I'm ugly, as he says, until my back is covered with sores;" and here he showed the spots on his skin. Next came the Bird (tsi´skwa; no particular species is indicated), who condemned man because "he burns my feet off," alluding to the way in which the hunter barbecues birds by impaling them on a stick set over the fire, so that their feathers and tender feet are singed and burned. Others followed in the same strain. The Ground Squirrel alone ventured to say a word in behalf of man, who seldom hurt him because he was so small; but this so enraged the others that they fell upon the Ground Squirrel and tore him with their teeth and claws, and the stripes remain on his back to this day.

The assembly then began to devise and name various diseases, one after another, and had not their invention finally failed them not one of the human race would have been able to survive. The Grubworm in his place of honor hailed each new malady with delight, until at last they had reached the end of the list, when some one suggested that it be arranged so that menstruation should sometimes prove fatal to woman. On this he rose up in his place and cried: "Wata´n Thanks! I'm glad some of them will die, for they are getting so thick that they tread on me."

He fairly shook with joy at the thought, so that he fell over backward and could not get on his feet again, but had to wriggle off on his back, as the Grubworm has done ever since.

When the plants, who were friendly to man, heard what had been done by the animals, they determined to defeat their evil designs. Each tree, shrub, and herb, down even to the grasses and mosses, agreed to furnish a remedy for some one of the diseases named, and each said: "I shall appear to help man when he calls upon me in his need." Thus did medicine originate, and the plants, every one of which has its use if we only knew it, furnish the antidote to counteract the evil wrought by the revengeful animals. When the doctor is in doubt what treatment to apply for the relief of a patient, the spirit of the plant suggests to him the proper remedy.

1.3.6 Thanksgiving Address (Haudenosaunee (Iroquois))

https://americanindian.si.edu/environment/pdf/01_02_Thanksgiving_Address.pdf

1.3.7 The Arrival of the Whites (Lenape (Delaware))

https://www.americanheritage.com/content/native-americans-first-view-whites-shore

1.3.8 The Coming of the Whiteman Revealed: Dream of the White Robe and Floating Island (Micmac)

When there were no people in this country but Indians, and before they knew of any others, a young woman had a singular dream. She dreamed that a small island came floating in towards the land, with tall trees on it and living beings, and amongst others a young man dressed in rabbit-skin garments. Next day she interpreted her dream and sought for an interpretation. it was the custom in those days, when any one had a remarkable dream, to consult the wise men and especially the magicians and soothsayers. These pondered over the girl's dream, but they could make nothing of it; but next day an event occurred that explained it all. Getting up in the morning, what should they see but a singular little island, as they took it to be, which had drifted near to land, and had become stationery there. There were trees on it, and branches to the trees, on which a number of bears, as they took them to be, were crawling about. They all seized their bows and arrows and spears and rushed down to the shore, intending to shoot the bears. What was their surprise to find that these supposed bears were men, and that some of them were lowering down into the water a very singular constructed canoe, into which several of them jumped and paddled ashore. Among them was a man dressed in white—a priest with his white stole on, who came towards them making signed of friendliness, raising his hand towards heaven and addressing them in an earnest manner, but in a language which they could not understand. The girl was now questioned respecting her dream. "was it such an island as this that she had seen? was this the man?" She affirmed that they were indeed the same. Some of them, especially the necromancers, were displeased. They did not like it that the coming of the foreigners should have been intimated to this young girl and not to them. Had an enemy of the Indian tribes, with whom they were at war, been about about to make a descent upon them they could have foreseen and foretold it by th epoer of their magic. But of the coming of this teacher of a new religion they could know nothing. The new teacher was gradually received into favor, though the magicians opposed him. The ep[;e received his instructions and submitted to the rite of baptism. The priest learned their tongue, and gave them the prayer-book written in what they call Abòotŭloveëgăsĭk—ornamental mark-writing, a mark standing for a word, and rendering it so difficult to learn that it may be said to be impossible. And this was manifestly done for the purpose of keeping the Indians in ignorance. Had their language been reduced to writing in the ordinary way, the Indians would have learned the use of writing an reading, and would have so advanced knowledge as to have been able to cope with their more enlightened invaders, and it would have been a more difficult matter for the latter to have cheated them out of their lands, etc.

Such was Josiah's story. Whatever were the motives of the priests who gave them their pictorial writing, it is one of the grossest literary blunders that was ever perpetrated. it is bad enough for the Chinese, who language is said to be monosyllabic and unchanged by grammatical inflection. But Micmac is partly syllabic, "endless," in its compounds and grammatical changes, and utterly incapable of being represented by signs.

1.3.9 Reading and Review Questions

1. In the Haudenosaunee (Iroquois), Cherokee, and Zuni Origin Tales, what values of their respective tribes emerge in each tale? How?
2. In the Trickster Cycle, what is the cause of/who causes disruptions? Why? To what effect?
3. What concept of justice, if any, does "Origin of Disease and Medicine" illustrate? How?
4. What do you think is the overall message or purpose of the "Thanksgiving Address?" How does its refrain contribute to this message or purpose? Why?
5. What do "The Arrival of the Whites" and "The Coming of the Whiteman Revealed" suggest the Lenape (Delaware) and the Micmac clearly understood about the meaning of the white man's arrival? What, if anything, about the white man's arrival, is not understood? How do you know?

1.4 CHRISTOPHER COLUMBUS

(1451–1506)

A sailor from his youth, Christopher Columbus sought to discover a mercantile route to Asia via the Atlantic Ocean, a route he calculated as only 3,000 miles across the Atlantic. Winning support in 1492 from Ferdinand and Isabella, monarchs of Spain, Columbus embarked on his historic voyage that failed to discover the route to Asia but instead discovered the New World, where he first landed at what is now the Bahamas. After that voyage with three caravels, Columbus returned to the New World three more times in 1494, 1496, and 1500, founding settlements at Hispaniola and the West Indies and exploring parts of Central and South America.

Image 1.3 | Christopher Columbus
Artist | Sebastiano del Piombo
Source | Wikimedia Commons
License | Public Domain

Columbus compensated for his original mission's failure by taking possession of these new lands and the people he first encountered there—people Columbus significantly noted as wearing gold adornments. Although he hoped to bring peace with him to what he described as paradisiacal landscapes, Columbus's first settlement at Hispaniola, "Villa de la Navidad," proved too grounded in the earthly desires and ambitions of the Old World. The first settlers demanded riches and women from the Native Americans and were in turn massacred. The second settlement, governed by Columbus's brothers, fell into such disorder that Columbus was forced to return to Spain to defend his own activities. Upon his later return to Hispaniola, Columbus had to defend his authority over the settlers and claim authority over the Native Americans, whom he enslaved as laborers and searchers for gold.

In 1500, Columbus returned once more to Spain to defend his reputation and then sought to secure his reputation and fortunes in the New World through further explorations there. This foray into what is now Panama and Jamaica led to disaster, both physical (in a shipwreck) and emotional (in a breakdown). Columbus made his final return to Europe where he died in 1506.

His 1493 *Letter of Discovery* derives from Columbus's manuscripts, was translated into Latin by Aliander de Cosco, and was printed by Stephan Planck. It is addressed to Lord Raphael Sanchez, treasurer to Ferdinand and Isabella, who clearly determines the rhetorical approaches Columbus makes in this letter. It describes the New World in terms amenable to his patrons' desires and ambitions but detrimental to the people he mistakenly named Indians.

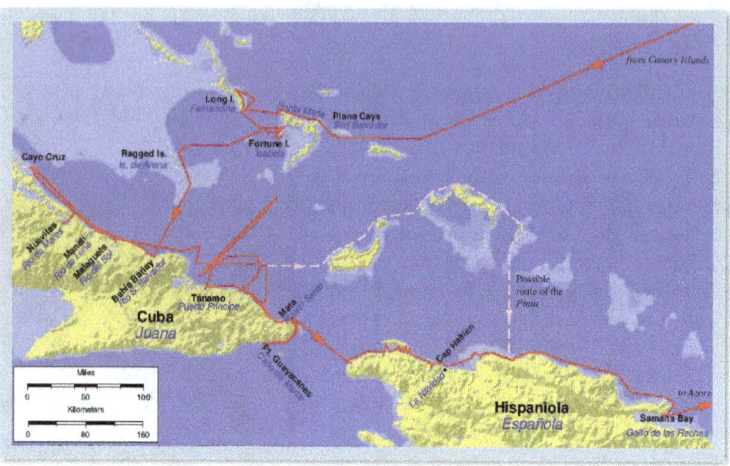

Image 1.4 | Map fo Columbus's First Voyage
Artist | Keith Pickering
Source | Wikimedia Commons
License | CC BY-SA 3.0

1.4.1 Letter of Discovery

(1493)

CHRISTOPHER COLUMBUS TO THE NOBLE LORD RAPHAEL SANCHEZ ANNOUNCING THE DISCOVERY OF AMERICA

As I know that it will afford you pleasure that I have brought my undertaking to a successful result, I have determined to write you this letter to inform you of everything that has been done and discovered in this voyage of mine.

On the thirty-third day after leaving Cadiz I came into the Indian Sea, where I discovered many islands inhabited by numerous people. I took possession of all of them for our most fortunate King by making public proclamation and unfurling his standard, no one making any resistance. To the first of them I have given the name of our blessed Saviour, trusting in whose aid I had reached this and all the rest; but the Indians call it Guanahani. To each of the others also I gave a new name, ordering one to be called Sancta Maria de Concepcion, another Fernandina, another Hysabella, another Johana; and so with all the rest. As soon as we reached the island which I have just said was called Johana, I sailed along its coast some considerable distance towards the West, and found it to be so large, without any apparent end, that I believed it was not an island, but a continent, a province of Cathay. But I saw neither towns nor cities lying on the seaboard, only some villages and country farms, with whose inhabitants I could not get speech, because they fled as soon as they beheld us. I continued on, supposing I should come upon some city, or country-houses. At last, finding that no discoveries rewarded our further progress, and that this course was leading us towards the North, which I was desirous of avoiding, as it was now winter in these regions, and it had always been my intention to proceed Southwards, and the winds also were favorable to such desires, I concluded not to attempt any other adventures; so, turning back, I came again to a certain harbor, which I had remarked. From there I sent two of our men into the country to learn whether there was any king or cities in that land. They journeyed for three days, and found innumerable people and habitations, but small and having no fixed government; on which account they returned. Meanwhile I had learned from some Indians, whom I had seized at this place, that this country was really an island. Consequently I continued along towards the East, as much as 322 miles, always hugging the shore. Where was the very extremity of the island, from there I saw another island to the Eastwards, distant 54 miles from this Johana, which I named Hispana; and proceeded to it, and directed my course for 564 miles East by North as it were, just as I had done at Johana.

The island called Johana, as well as the others in its neighborhood, is exceedingly fertile. It has numerous harbors on all sides, very safe and wide, above comparison with any I have ever seen. Through it flow many very broad and health-giving rivers; and there are in it numerous very lofty mountains. All these islands are very beautiful, and of quite different shapes; easy to be traversed, and full of the greatest variety of trees reaching to the stars. I think these never lose their leaves, as I saw them looking as green and lovely as they are wont to be in the month of May in Spain. Some of them were in leaf, and some in fruit; each flourishing in the condition its nature required. The nightingale was singing and various other little birds, when I was rambling among them in the month of November. There are also in the island called Johana seven or eight kinds of palms, which as readily surpass ours in height and beauty as do all the other trees, herbs and fruits. There are also wonderful pinewoods, fields and extensive meadows; birds of various kinds, and honey; and all the different metals, except iron.

In the island, which I have said before was called Hispana, there are very lofty and beautiful mountains, great farms, groves and fields, most fertile both for cultivation and for pasturage, and well adapted for constructing buildings. The convenience of the harbors in this island, and the excellence of the rivers, in volume and salubrity, surpass human belief, unless one should see them. In it the trees, pasture-lands and fruits differ much from those of Johana. Besides, this Hispana abounds in various kinds of spices, gold and metals. The inhabitants of both sexes of this and of all the other islands I have seen, or of which I have any knowledge, always go as naked as they came into the world, except that some of the women cover their private parts with leaves or branches, or a veil of cotton, which they prepare themselves for this purpose. They are all, as I said before, unprovided with any sort of iron, and they are destitute of arms, which are entirely unknown to them, and for which they are not adapted; not on account of any bodily deformity, for they are well made, but because they are timid and full of terror. They carry, however, canes dried in the sun in place of weapons, upon whose roots they fix a wooden shaft, dried and sharpened to a point. But they never dare to make use of these; for it has often happened, when I have sent two or three of my men to some of their villages to speak with the inhabitants, that a crowd of Indians has sallied forth; but when they saw our men approaching, they speedily took to flight, parents abandoning their children, and children their parents. This happened not because any loss or injury had been inflicted upon any of them. On the contrary I gave whatever I had, cloth and many other things, to whomsoever I approached, or with whom I could get speech, without any return being made to me; but they are by nature fearful and timid. But when they see that they are safe, and all fear is banished, they are very guileless and honest, and very liberal of all they have. No one refuses the asker anything that he possesses; on the contrary they themselves invite us to ask for it. They manifest the greatest affection towards all of us, exchanging valuable things for trifles, content with the very least thing or nothing at all. But I forbade giving them a very trifling thing and of no value, such as bits of plates, dishes, or glass; also nails and straps; although it seemed to them, if they could get such, that they had acquired the most beautiful jewels in the world. For it chanced that a sailor received for a single strap as much weight of gold as three gold solidi; and so others for other things of less price, especially for new blancas, and for some gold coins, for which they gave whatever the seller asked; for instance, an ounce and a half or two ounces of gold, or thirty or forty pounds of cotton, with which they were already familiar. So too for pieces of hoops, jugs, jars and pots they bartered cotton and gold like beasts. This I forbade, because it was plainly unjust; and I gave them many beautiful and pleasing things, which I had brought with me, for no return whatever, in order to win their affection, and that they might become Christians and inclined to love our Kino; and Queen and Princes and all the people of Spain; and that they might be eager to search for and gather and give to us what they abound in and we greatly need.

They do not practice idolatry; on the contrary, they believe that all strength, all power, in short all blessings, are from Heaven, and that I have come down from there with these ships and sailors; and in this spirit was I received everywhere, after they had got over their fear. They are neither lazy nor awkward ; but, on the contrary, are of an excellent and acute understanding. Those who have sailed these seas give excellent accounts of everything; but they have never seen men wearing clothes, or ships like ours.

As soon as I had come into this sea, I took by force some Indians from the first island, in order that they might learn from us, and at the same time tell us what they knew about affairs in these regions. This succeeded admirably; for in a short time we understood them and they us both by gesture and signs and words; and they were of great service to us. They are coming now with me, and have always believed that I have come from Heaven, notwithstanding the long time they have been, and still remain, with us. They were the first who told this wherever we went, one calling to another, with a loud voice, Come, Come, you will see Men from Heaven. Whereupon both women and men, children and adults, young and old, laying aside the fear they had felt a little before, flocked eagerly to see us, a great crowd thronging about our steps, some bringing food, and others drink, with greatest love and incredible good will.

In each island are many boats made of solid wood; though narrow, yet in length and shape similar to our two-bankers, but swifter in motion, and managed by oars only. Some of them are large, some small, and some of medium size; but most are larger than a two-banker rowed by 18 oars. With these they sail to all the islands, which are innumerable; engaging in traffic and commerce with each other. I saw some of these biremes, or boats, which carried 70 or 80 rowers. In all these islands there is no difference in the appearance of the inhabitants, and none in their customs and language, so that all understand one another. This is a circumstance most favorable for what I believe our most serene King especially desires, that is, their conversion to the holy faith of Christ; for which, indeed, so far as I could understand, they are very ready and prone.

I have told already how I sailed in a straight course along the island of Johana from West to East 322 miles. From this voyage and the extent of my journeyings I can say that this Johana is larger than England and Scotland together. For beyond the aforesaid 322 miles, in that portion which looks toward the West, there are two more provinces, which I did not visit. One of them the Indians call Anan, and its inhabitants are born with tails. These provinces extend 180 miles, as I learned from the Indians, whom I am bringing with me, and who are well acquainted with all these islands.

The distance around Hispana is greater than all Spain from Colonia to Fontarabia; as is readily proved, because its fourth side, which I myself traversed in a straight course from West to East, stretches 540 miles. This island is to be coveted, and not to be despised when acquired. As I have already taken possession of all the others, as I have said, for our most invincible King, and the rule over them is entirely committed to the said King, so in this one I have taken special possession of a certain large town, in a most convenient spot, well suited for all profit and commerce, to which I have given the name of the Nativity of our Lord; and there I ordered a fort to be built forthwith, which ought to be finished now. In it I left as many men as seemed necessary, with all kinds of arms, and provisions sufficient for more than a year; also a caravel and men to build others, skilled not only in this trade but in others. I secured for them the good will and remarkable friendship of the King of the island; for these people are very affectionate and kind; so much so that the aforesaid King took a pride in my being called his brother. Although they should change their minds, and wish to harm those who have remained in the fort, they cannot; because they are without arms, go naked and are too timid; so that, in truth, those who hold the aforesaid fort can lay waste the whole of that island, without any danger to themselves, provided they do not violate the rules and instructions I have given them.

In all these islands, as I understand, every man is satisfied with only one wife, except the princes or kings, who are permitted to have 20. The women appear to work more than the men; but I could not well understand whether they have private property, or not; for I saw that what every one had was shared with the others, especially meals, provisions and such things. I found among them no monsters, as very many expected; but men of great deference and kind; nor are they black like the Ethiopians; but they have long, straight hair. They do not dwell where the rays of the Sun have most power, although the Sun's heat is very great there, as this region is twenty-six degrees distant from the equinoctial line. From the summits of the mountains there comes great cold, but the Indians mitigate it by being inured to the weather, and by the help of very hot food, which they consume frequently and in immoderate quantities.

I saw no monsters, neither did I hear accounts of any such except in an island called Charis, the second as one crosses over from Spain to India, which is inhabited by a certain race regarded by their neighbors as very ferocious. They eat human flesh, and make use of several kinds of boats by which they cross over to all the Indian islands, and plunder and carry off whatever they can. But they differ in no respect from the others except in wearing their hair long after the fashion of women. They make use of bows and arrows made of reeds, having pointed shafts fastened to the thicker portion, as we have before described. For this reason they are considered to be ferocious, and the other Indians consequently are terribly afraid of them; but I consider them of no more account than the others. They have intercourse with certain women who dwell alone upon the island of Mateurin, the first as one crosses from Spain to India. These women follow none of the usual occupations of their sex; but they use bows and arrows like those of their husbands, which I have described, and protect themselves with plates of copper, which is found in the greatest abundance among them.

I was informed that there is another island larger than the aforesaid Hispana, whose inhabitants have no hair; and that there is a greater abundance of gold in it than in any of the others. Some of the inhabitants of these islands and of the others I have seen I am bringing over with me to bear testimony to what I have reported. Finally, to sum up in a few words the chief results and advantages of our departure and speedy return, I make this promise to our most invincible Sovereigns, that, if I am supported by some little assistance from them, I will give them as much gold as they have need of, and in addition spices, cotton and mastic, which is found only in Chios, and as much aloes-wood, and as many heathen slaves as their majesties may choose to demand; besides these, rhubarb and other kinds of drugs, which I think the men I left in the fort before alluded to, have already discovered, or will do so; as I have myself delayed nowhere longer than the winds compelled me, except while I was providing for the construction of a fort in the city of Nativity, and for making all things safe.

Although these matters are very wonderful and unheard of, they would have been much more so, if ships to a reasonable amount had been furnished me. But what has been accomplished is great and wonderful, and not at all proportionate to my deserts, but to the sacred Christian faith, and to the piety and religion of our Sovereigns. For what the mind of man could not compass the spirit of God has granted to mortals. For God is wont to listen to his servants who love his precepts, even in impossibilities, as has happened to me in the present instance, who have accomplished what human strength has hitherto never attained. For if any one has written or told any- thing about these islands, all have done so either obscurely or by guesswork, so that it has almost seemed to be fabulous.

Therefore let King and Queen and Princes, and their most fortunate realms, and all other Christian provinces, let us all return thanks to our Lord and Saviour Jesus Christ, who has bestowed so great a victory and reward upon us; let there be processions and solemn sacrifices prepared; let the churches be decked with festal boughs; let Christ rejoice upon Earth as he rejoices in Heaven, as he foresees that so many souls of so many people heretofore lost are to be saved; and let us be glad not only for the exaltation of our faith, but also for the increase of temporal prosperity, in which not only Spain but all Christendom is about to share.

As these things have been accomplished so have they been briefly narrated. Farewell.

CHRISTOPHER COLOM, Admiral of the Ocean Fleet.
Lisbon, March 14th.

1.4.2 Reading and Review Questions

1. Why does Columbus give the islands in the New World new names, even though he knows the names by which they were called by the Native Americans?
2. What are the qualities of the islands' topography to which Columbus brings attention? Why?
3. What characteristics about the Native Americans does Columbus bring attention? Why?
4. What behaviors of the men accompanying Columbus suggest their indifference to the Native Americans' lives and culture? Why?
5. What of Native American culture does Columbus take especial note? Why?

1.5 ALVAR NUNEZ CABEZA DE VACA

(c. 1490–1558)

Alva Nunez Cabeza de Vaca carried a name bestowed upon his maternal grandfather who fought the Moors in Spain and who used a cow's skull to mark a strategic pass through a mountain. Cabeza de Vaca fought in Italy and Spain before leaving with Panfilo de Narvaez (1478–1528) on his 1527 expedition to Florida. Narvaez proved an unwise captain, losing men and all of his six ships to desertion, hurricane, and a failed attempt to discover a port along the Florida shore.

Image 1.5 | Alvar Nunez Cabeza de Vaca
Artist | Unknown
Source | Wikimedia Commons
License | Public Domain

Stranded in Florida along with a fraction of Narvaez's remaining sailors, Cabeza de Vaca was left to fend for himself against threatening Native Americans and an inhospitable land. The men journeyed to what is now Texas. Of the 600 men who undertook the expedition, only four ultimately survived, one of whom was Cabeza de Vaca. For ten years, Cabeza de Vaca faced extraordinary hardships as he traveled along the Texas coast, including being taken as a prisoner by Native Americans (the Karankawa) for over two years. Among the Native Americans, he gained a reputation as a trader and then as a healer, a power he himself attributed to his Christian faith. He ultimately gathered a following of Pimas and Opatas who traveled with him to what is now New Mexico and northern Mexico.

There, he once again encountered fellow Europeans who took Cabeza de Vaca prisoner and enslaved the Native Americans with him. In 1537, Cabeza de Vaca returned to Spain where he vocally protested the predatory behavior of slave hunters like his captor Diego de Alcaraz (c. 1490–1540). He returned again to South America as leader of an expedition but saw his own colony devolve into predatory behaviors. In Rio de Plata, Cabeza de Vaca was removed as leader; he ultimately returned to Spain where he lived the remainder of his life.

The Relation of Alvar Nunez Cabeza de Vaca was begun in 1540 while he was still in Spain. In it, he describes the dangers and suffering he endured from the Narvaez expedition, the Europeans' unjust treatment of Native Americans, and the opportunities for further exploration and colonization in the New World.

Image 1.6 | Map of Cabeza de Vaca's Expedition
Artist | User "Lencer"
Source | Wikimedia Commons

1.5.1 From *The Relation of Alvar Nunez Cabeza de Vaca* (1542)

Chapter XV

WHAT BEFEL US AMONG THE PEOPLE OF MALHADO.

On an Island of which I have spoken, they wished to make us physicians without examination or inquiring for diplomas. They cure by blowing upon the sick, and with that breath and the imposing of hands they cast out infirmity. They ordered that we also should do this, and be of use to them in some way. We laughed at what they did, telling them it was folly, that we knew not how to heal. In consequence, they withheld food from us until we should practice what they required. Seeing our persistence, an Indian told me I knew not what I uttered, in saying that what he knew availed 'nothing; for stones and other matters growing about in the fields, have virtue, and that passing a pebble along the stomach would take away pain and restore health, and certainly then we who were extraordinary men must possess power and efficacy over all other things. At last, finding ourselves in great want we were constrained to obey; but without fear lest we should be blamed for any failure or success.

Their custom is, on finding themselves sick to send for a physician, and after he has applied the cure, they give him not only all they have, but seek among their relatives for more to give. The practitioner scarifies over the seat of pain, and then sucks about the wound. They make cauteries with fire, a remedy among them in high repute, which I have tried on myself and found benefit from it. They afterwards blow on the spot, and having finished, the patient considers that he is relieved.

Our method was to bless the sick, breathing upon them, and recite a Pater-noster and an Ave-Maria, praying with all earnestness to God our Lord that he would give health and influence them to make us some good return. In his clemency he willed that all those for whom we supplicated, should tell the others that they were sound and in health, directly after we made the sign of the blessed cross over them. For this the Indians treated us kindly; they deprived themselves of food that they might give to us, and presented us with skins and some trifles.

So protracted was the hunger we there experienced, that many times I was three days without eating. The natives also endured as much; and it appeared to me a thing impossible that life could be so prolonged, although afterwards I found myself in greater hunger and necessity, which I shall speak of farther on.

The Indians who had Alonzo del Castillo, Andrés Dorantes, and the others that remained alive, were of a different tongue and ancestry from these, and went to the opposite shore of the main to eat oysters, where they staid until the first day of April, when they returned. The distance is two leagues in the widest part. The island is half a league in breadth and five leagues in length.

The inhabitants of all this region go naked. The women alone have any part of their persons covered, and it is with a wool that grows on trees. The damsels dress themselves in deerskin. The people are generous to each other of what they possess. They have no chief. All that are of a lineage keep together. They speak two languages; those of one are called Capoques, those of the other, Han. They have a custom when they meet, or from time to time when they visit, of remaining half an hour before they speak, weeping; and, this over, he that is visited first rises and gives the other all he has, which is received, and after a little while he carries it away, and often goes without saying a word. They have other strange customs; but I have told the principal of them, and the most remarkable, that I may pass on and further relate what befel us.

Chapter XVI

THE CHRISTIANS LEAVE THE ISLAND OF MALHADO.

After Dorantes and Castillo returned to the Island, they brought together the Christians, who were somewhat separated, and found them in all to be fourteen. As I have said, I was opposite on the main, where my Indians had taken me, and where so great sickness had come upon me, that if anything before had given me hopes of life, this were enough to have entirely bereft me of them.

When the Christians heard of my condition, they gave an Indian the cloak of marten skins we had taken from the cacique, as before related, to pass them over to where I was that they might visit me. Twelve of them crossed; for two were so feeble that their comrades could not venture to bring them. The names of those who came were Alonzo del Castillo, Andres Dorantes, Diego Dorantes, Yaldevieso, Estrada, Tostado, Chaves, Gutierrez, Asturiano a clergyman, Diego de Huelva, Estevarico a black, and Benitez; and when they reached the main land, they found another, who was one of our company, named Francisco de Leon. The thirteen together followed along the coast. So soon as they had come over, my Indians informed me of it, and that Hieronymo de Alvaniz and Lope de Oviedo remained on the island. But sickness prevented me from going with my companions or even seeing them.

I was obliged to remain with the people belonging to the island more than a year, and because of the hard work they put upon me and the harsh treatment, I resolved to flee from them and go to those of Charruco, who inhabit the forests and country of the main, the life I led being insupportable. Besides much other labor, I had to get out roots from below the water, and from among the cane where they grew in the ground. From this employment I had my fingers so worn that did a straw but touch them they would bleed. Many of the canes are broken, so they often tore my flesh, and I had to go in the midst of them with only the clothing on I have mentioned.

Accordingly, I put myself to contriving how I might get over to the other Indians, among whom matters turned somewhat more favorably for me. I set to trafficing, and strove to make my employment profitable in the ways I could best contrive, and by that means I got food and good treatment. The Indians would beg me to go from one quarter to another for things of which they have need; for in consequence of incessant hostilities, they cannot traverse the country, nor make many exchanges. With my merchandise and trade I went into the interior as far as I pleased, and traveled along the coast forty or fifty leagues. The principal wares were cones and other pieces of sea-snail, conches used for cutting, and fruit like a bean of the highest value among them, which they use as a medicine and employ in their dances and festivities. Among other matters were sea-beads. Such were what I carried into the interior; and in barter I got and brought back skins; ochre with which they rub and color the face, hard canes of which to make arrows, sinews, cement and flint for the heads, and tassels of the hair of deer that by dyeing they make red. This occupation suited me well; for the travel allowed me liberty to go where I wished, I was not obliged to work, and was not a slave. Wherever I went I received fair treatment, and the Indians gave me to eat out of regard to my commodities. My leading object, while journeying in this business, was to find out the way by which I should go forward, and I became well known. The inhabitants were pleased when they saw me, and I had brought them what they wanted; and those who did not know me sought and desired the acquaintance, for my reputation. The hardships that I underwent in this were long to tell, as well of peril and privation as of storms and cold. Oftentimes they overtook me alone and in the wilderness; but I came forth from them all by the great mercy of God, our Lord. Because of them I avoided pursuing the business in winter, a season in which the natives themselves retire to their huts and ranches, torpid and incapable of exertion.

I was in this country nearly six years, alone among the Indians, and naked like them. The reason why I remained so long, was that I might take with me the Christian, Lope de Oviedo, from the island; Alaniz, his companion, who had been left with him by Alonzo del Castillo, Andrés Dorantes and the rest, died soon after their departure; and to get the survivor out from there, I went over to the island every year, and entreated him that we should go, in the best way we could contrive, in quest of Christians. He put me off every year, saying in the next coming we would start. At last I got him off, crossing him over the bay, and over four rivers in the coast, as he could not swim. In this way we went on with some Indians, until coming to a bay a league in width, and everywhere deep. From the appearance we supposed it to be that which is called Espiritu Sancto. We met some Indians on the other side of it, coming to visit ours, who told us that beyond them were three men like us, and gave their names. We asked for the others, and were told that they were all dead of cold and hunger; that the Indians farther on, of whom they were, for their diversion had killed Diego Dorantes, Valdevieso, and Diego de Huelva, because they left one house for another; and that other Indians, their neighbors with whom Captain Dorantes now was, had in consequence of a dream, killed Esquivel and Mendez. We asked how the living were situated, and they answered that they were very ill used, the boys and some of the Indian men being very idle, out of cruelty gave them many kicks, cuffs and blows with sticks; that such was the life they led.

We desired to be informed of the country ahead, and of the subsistence: they said there was nothing to eat, and that it was thin of people, who suffered of cold, having no skins or other things to cover them. They told us also if we wished to see those three Christians, two days from that time the Indians who had them would come to eat walnuts a league from there on the margin of that river; and that we might know what they told us of the ill usage to be true, they slapped my companion and beat him with a stick, and I was not left without my portion. Many times they threw lumps of mud at us, and every day they put their arrows to our hearts, saying that they were inclined to kill us in the way that they had destroyed our friends. Lope Oviedo, my comrade, in fear said that he wished to go back with the women of those who had crossed the bay with us, the men having remained some distance behind. I contended strongly against his returning, and urged my objections; but in no way could I keep him. So he went back, and I remained alone with those savages. They are called Quevenes, and those with whom he returned, Deaguanes.

Chapter XIX

OUR SEPARATION BY THE INDIANS.

When the six months were over, I had to spend with the Christians to put in execution the plan we had concerted, the Indians went after prickly pears, the place at which they grew being thirty leagues off and when we approached the point of flight, those among whom we were, quarreled about a woman. After striking with fists, heating with sticks and bruising heads in great anger, each took his lodge and went his way, whence it became necessary that the Christians should also separate, and in no way could we come together until another year.

In this time I passed a hard life, caused as much by hunger as ill usage. Three times I was obliged to run from my masters, and each time they went in pursuit and endeavored to slay me; but God our Lord in his mercy chose to protect and preserve me; and when the season of prickly pears returned, we again came together in the same place. After we had arranged our escape, and appointed a time, that very day the Indians separated and all went back. I told my comrades I would wait for them among the prickly pear plants until the moon should be full. This day was the first of September, and the first of the moon; and I said that if in this time they did not come as we had agreed, I would leave and go alone. So we parted, each going with his Indians. I remained with mine until the thirteenth day of the moon, having determined to flee to others when it should be full.

At this time Andrés Dorantes arrived with Estevanico and informed me that they had left Castillo with other Indians near by, called Lanegados; that they had encountered great obstacles and wandered about lost; that the next day the Indian's, among whom we were, would move to where Castillo was, and were going to unite with those who held him and become friends, having been at war until then, and that in this way we should recover Castillo.

We had thirst all the time we ate the pears, which we quenched with their juice. We caught it in a hole made in the earth, and when it was full we drank until satisfied. It is sweet, and the color of must. In this manner they collect it for lack of vessels. There are many kinds of prickly pears, among them some very good, although they all appeared to me to be so, hunger never having given me leisure to choose, nor to reflect upon which were the best.

Nearly all these people drink rain-water, which lies about in spots. Although there are rivers, as the Indians never have fixed habitations, there are no familiar or known places for getting water. Throughout the country are extensive and beautiful plains with good pasturage; and I think it would be a very fruitful region were it worked and inhabited by civilized men. We nowhere saw mountains.

These Indians told us that there was another people next in advance of us, called Camones, living towards the coast, and that they had killed the people who came in the boat of Peñalosa and Tellez, who arrived so feeble that even while being slain they could offer no resistance, and were all destroyed. We were shown their clothes and arms, and were told that the boat lay there stranded. This, the fifth boat, had remained till then unaccounted for. We have already stated how the boat of the Governor had been carried out to sea, and the one of the Comptroller and the Friars had been cast away on the coast, of which Esquevel narrated the fate of the men. We have once told how the two boats in which Castillo, I and Dorantes came, foundered near the Island of Malhado.

Chapter XX

OF OUR ESCAPE.

The second day after we had moved, we commended ourselves to God and set forth with speed, trusting, for all the lateness of the season and that the prickly pears were about ending, with the mast which remained in the woods, we might still be enabled to travel over a large territory. Hurrying on that day in great dread lest the Indians should overtake us, we saw some smokes, and going in the direction of them we arrived there after vespers, and found an Indian. He ran as he discovered us coming, not being willing to wait for us. We sent the negro after him, when he stopped, seeing him alone. The negro told him we were seeking the people who made those fires. He answered that their houses were near by, and he would guide us to them. So we followed him. He ran to make known our approach, and at sunset we saw the houses. Before our arrival, at the distance of two cross-bow shots from them, we found four Indians, who waited for us and received us well. We said in the language of the Mariames, that we were coming to look for them. They were evidently pleased with our company, and took us to their dwellings. Dorantes and the negro were lodged in the house of a physician, Castillo and myself in that of another.

These people speak a different language, and are called Avavares. They are the same that carried bows to those with whom we formerly lived, going to traffic with them, and although they are of a different nation and tongue, they understand the other language. They arrived that day with their lodges, at the place where we found them. The community directly brought us a great many prickly pears, having heard of us before, of our cures, and of the wonders our Lord worked by us, which, although there had been no others, were adequate to open ways for us through a country poor like this, to afford us people where oftentimes there are none, and to lead us through imminent dangers, not permitting us to be killed, sustaining us under great want, and putting into those nations the heart of kindness, as we shall relate hereafter.

Chapter XXI

OUR CURE OF SOME OF THE AFFLICTED.

That same night of our arrival, some Indians came to Castillo and told him that they had great pain in the head, begging him to cure them. After he made over them the sign of the cross, and commended them to God, they instantly said that all the pain had left, and went to their houses bringing us prickly pears, with a piece of venison, a thing to us little known. As the report of Castillo's performances spread, many came to us that night sick, that we should heal them, each bringing a piece of venison, until the quantity became so great we knew not where to dispose of it. We gave many thanks to God, for every day went on increasing his compassion and his gifts. After the sick were attended to, they began to dance and sing, making themselves festive, until sunrise; and because of our arrival, the rejoicing was continued for three days.

When these were ended, we asked the Indians about the country farther on, the people we should find in it, and of the subsistence there. They answered us, that throughout all the region prickly pear plants abounded; but the fruit was now gathered and all the people had gone back to their houses. They said the country was very cold, and there were few skins. Reflecting on this, and that it was already winter, we resolved to pass the season with these Indians.

Five days after our arrival, all the Indians went off, taking us with them to gather more prickly pears, where there were other peoples speaking different tongues. After walking five days in great hunger, since on the way was no manner of fruit, we came to a river and put up our houses. We then went to seek the product of certain trees, which is like peas. As there are no paths in the country, I was detained some time. The others returned, and coming to look for them in the dark, I got lost. Thank God I found a burning tree, and in the warmth of it passed the cold of that night. In the morning, loading myself with sticks, and taking two brands with me, I returned to seek them. In this manner I wandered five days, ever with my fire and load; for if the wood had failed me where none could be found, as many parts are without any, though I might have sought sticks elsewhere, there would have been no fire to kindle them. This was all the protection I had against cold, while walking naked as I was born. Going to the low woods near the rivers, I prepared myself for the night, stopping in them before sunset. I made a hole in the ground and threw in fuel which the trees abundantly afforded, collected in good quantity from those that were fallen and dry. About the whole I made four fires, in the form of a cross, which I watched and made up from time to time. I also gathered some bundles of the coarse straw that there abounds, with which I covered myself in the hole. In this way I was sheltered at night from cold. On one occasion while I slept, the fire fell upon the straw, when it began to blaze so rapidly that notwithstanding the haste I made to get out of it, I carried some marks on my hair of the danger to which I was exposed. All this while I tasted not a mouthful, nor did I find anything I could eat. My feet were bare and bled a good deal. Through the mercy of God, the wind did not blow from the north in all this time, otherwise I should have died.

At the end of the fifth day I arrived on the margin of a river, where I found the Indians, who with the Christians, had considered me dead, supposing that I had been stung by a viper. All were rejoiced to see me, and most so were my companions. They said that up to that time they had struggled with great hunger, which was the cause of their not having sought me. At night, all gave me of their prickly pears, and the next morning we set out for a place where they were in large quantity, with which we satisfied our great craving, the Christians rendering thanks to our Lord that he had ever given us his aid.

1.5.2 Reading and Review Questions

1. In Chapter XV, how does Cabeza de Vaca reconcile his practicing the Indians' healing with his own cultural beliefs?
2. In Chapter XV, what information about the Indians' culture does Cabeza de Vaca convey? How?

3. In Chapter XVI, how do the Indians treat the Spaniards? Why?
4. In Chapter XIX, what does Cabeza de Vaca learn of the people who came in the boat of Peñalosa and Tellez? What is his attitude toward what he learns? How do you know?
5. In Chapter XXI, separated from the Indians and his companions, naked and lost, how does Cabeza de Vaca survive the winter cold? What is his attitude toward his survival? How do you know?

1.6 THOMAS HARRIOT

(1560–1621)

Thomas Harriot began his professional life working for Sir Walter Raleigh (1552–1618) as ship designer, navigational instructor, and accountant. In 1585, he extended his professional activities from England to America, where he served as cartographer and surveyor for Raleigh's second expedition to Virginia which was based at the ill-fated Roanoke, site of the infamous Lost Colony. Named after the English sovereign Queen Elizabeth I, Virginia and Roanoke is now modern day North Carolina. Harriot also served as the expedition's historian, keeping a remarkably-detailed account he later published as *A Briefe and True Report of the New Found Land of Virginia.* In it, he offered a firsthand account written by an Englishman for an English audience. He detailed crops and building materials both as commodities and as means to support colonists. He also offered some details of the culture and lives of the Native Americans he encountered.

Image 1.7 | Thomas Harriot
Artist | Unknown
Source | Wikimedia Commons
License | Public Domain

His last stint with Raleigh was as manager of Raleigh's estates in Waterford, Ireland. Harriot then worked for Henry Percy, the Ninth Earl of Northumberland (1564–1632). From Percy, Harriot received extensive lands and a substantial pension. He devoted the remainder of his life working for himself, so to speak, conducting experiments with the refraction of light and the trajectory of projectiles. His astronomical drawings recorded what later become known as Halley's Comet, and his invention of the perspective trunk led to the invention of the telescope.

Harriot's scientific objectivity, observational powers, and notice of concrete particulars contribute to the valuable record of his *A Briefe and True Report*. This work had an impact not only in England but also the Continent.

Image 1.8 | Thomas Harriot at Syon Park
Artist | Rita Greer
Source | Wikimedia Commons
License | Free Art License

1.6.1 From *A Briefe and True Report of the New Found Land of Virginia*

(1588)

Preface

TO THE RIGHT WORTHIE AND HONORABLE, SIR WALTER RALEGH, KNIGHT, SENESCHAL OF THE DVCHIES OF CORNEWALL AND EXETER, AND L. WARDEN OF THE STANNARIES IN DEUON AND CORNEWALL, T.B. WISHETH TRUE FELICITIE.

SIR, seeing that the parte of the Worlde, which is betwene the FLORIDA and the Cap BRETON nowe nammed VIRGINIA, to the honneur of yours most souueraine Layde and Queene ELIZABETZ, hath ben descouuerd by yours meanes. And great chardges. And that your Collonye hath been theer established to your great honnor and prayse, and noelesser proffit vnto the common welth: Yt ys good raison that euery man euertwe him selfe for to showe the benefit which they haue receue of yt. Theerfore, for my parte I haue been allwayes Desirous for to make yow knowe the good will that I haue to remayne still your most humble særuant. I haue thincke that I cold faynde noe better occasion to declare yt, then takinge the paines to cott in copper (the most diligent ye and well that wear in my possible to doe) the Figures which doe leuelye represent the forme and maner of the Inhabitants of the sane countrye with theirs ceremonies, sollemne feastes, and the manner and situation of their Townes of Villages. Addinge vnto euery figure a brief declaration of the same, to that ende that cuerye man cold the better vnderstand that which is in liuely represented. Moreouer I haue thincke that the aforesaid figures wear of greater commendation, If somme Histoire which traitinge of the commodites and fertillitye of the rapport which Thomas Hariot hath lattely sett foorth, and haue causse them booth togither to be printed for to dedicated vnto you, as a thiuge which by reigtte dooth allreadye apparteyne vnto you. Therfore doe I creaue that you will accept this little Booke, and take yt In goode partte. And desiring that fauor that you will receue me in the nomber of one of your most humble seruantz, besechinge the lord to blese and further you in all yours good doinges and actions, and allso to preserue, and keepe you allwayes in good helthe. And so I comitt you unto the almyhttie, from Franckfort the first of Apprill 1590.

Your most humble seruant,
THEODORVS de BRY.

TO THE ADVENTVRERS, FAVORERS, AND VVELVVILLERS OF THE ENTERPRISE FOR THE INHABITTING AND PLANTING IN VIRGINIA.

SINCE the first vndertaking by Sir Walter Ralegh to deale in the action of discouering of that Countrey which is now called and known by the name of VIRGINIA; many voyages hauing bin thiter made at sundrie times to his great charge; as first in the yeere 1584. and afterwardes in the yeeres 1585. *1586.* and now of late this last yeare of *1587.* There haue bin diuers and variable reportes with some slaunderous and shamefull speeches bruited abroade by many that returned from thence. Especially of that discouery which was made by the Colony transported by Sir Richard Greinuile in the yeare *1585.* being of all the others the most principal and as yet of most effect, the time of their abode in the countrey beeing a whole yeare, when as in the other voyage before they staied but sixe weekes; and the others after were onelie for supply and transportation, nothing more being discouered then had been before. Which reports haue not done a litle wrong to many that otherwise would have also fauoured & aduentured in the action, to the honour and benefite of our nation, besides the particular profite and credite which would redound to them selues the dealers therein; as I hope by the sequele of euents to the shame of those that haue auouched the contrary shalbe manifest: if you the aduenturers, fauourers, and welwillers do but either encrease in number, or in opinion continue, or hauing bin doubtfull renewe your good liking and furtherance to deale therein according to the worthinesse thereof alreadye found and as you shall vnderstand hereafter to be requisite. Touching which woorthines through cause of the diuersitie of relations and reportes, manye of your opinions coulde not bee firme, nor the mindes of some that are well disposed, bee setled in any certaintie.

I haue therefore thought it good beeing one that haue beene in the discouerie and in dealing with the natuall inhabitantes specially imploied; and hauing therefore seene and knowne more then the ordinaire: to imparte so much vnto you of the fruites of our labours, as that you may knowe howe iniuriously the enterprise is slaundered. And that in publike manner at this present chiefelie for two respectes.

First that some of you which are yet ignorant or doubtfull of the state thereof, may see that there is sufficiêt cause why the cheefe enterpriser with the fauour of her Maiestie, notwithstanding suche reportes; hath not onelie since continued the action by sending into the countrey againe, and replanting this last yeere a new Colony; but is also readie, according as the times and meanes will affoorde, to follow and prosecute the same.

Secondly, that you seeing and knowing the continuance of the action by the view hereof you may generally know & learne what the countrey is; & therevpon cõsider how your dealing therein if it proceede, may returne you profit and gaine; bee it either by inhabitting & planting or otherwise in furthering thereof.

And least that the substance of my relation should be doubtful vnto you, as of others by reason of their diuersitie: I will first open the cause in a few wordes wherefore they are so different; referring my selue to your fauourable constructions, and to be adiudged of as by good consideration you shall finde cause.

Of our companie that returned some for their misdemenour and ill dealing in the countrey, haue beene there worthily punished; who by reason of their badde natures, haue maliciously not onelie spoken ill of their Gouernours; but for their sakes slaundered the countrie it selfe. The like also haue those done which were of their confort.

Some beeing ignorant of the state thereof, nothwithstanding since their returne amongest their friendes and acquaintance and also others, especially if they were in companie where they might not be gainesaide; woulde seeme to know so much as no men more; and make no men so great trauailers as themselues. They stood so much as it maie seeme vppon their credite and reputation that hauing been a twelue moneth in the countrey, it woulde haue beene a great disgrace vnto them as they thought, if they coulde not haue saide much wheter it were true or false. Of which some haue spoken of more then euer they saw or otherwise knew to bee there; othersome haue not bin ashamed to make absolute deniall of that which although not by thê, yet by others is most certainely ãd there plêtifully knowne. And othersome make difficulties of those things they haue no skill of.

The cause of their ignorance was, in that they were of that many that were neuer out of the Iland where wee were seated, or not farre, or at the leastwise in few places els, during the time of our aboade in the countrey; or of that many that after golde and siluer was not so soone found, as it was by them looked for, had little or no care of any other thing but to pamper their bellies; or of that many which had little vnderstanding, lesse discretion, and more tongue then was needfull or requisite.

Some also were of a nice bringing vp, only in cities or townes, or such as neuer (as I may say) had seene the world before. Because there were not to bee found any English cities, norsuch faire houses, nor at their owne wish any of their olde accustomed daintie food, nor any soft beds of downe or fethers: the countrey was to them miserable, & their reports thereof according.

Because my purpose was but in briefe to open the cause of the varietie of such speeches; the particularities of them, and of many enuious, malicious, and slaûderous reports and deuises els, by our owne countrey men besides; as trifles that are not worthy of wise men to bee thought vpon, I meane not to trouble you withall: but will passe to the commodities, the substance of that which I haue to make relation of vnto you.

The treatise where of for your more readie view & easier vnderstanding I will diuide into three speciall parts. In the first I will make declaration of such commodities there alreadie found or to be raised, which will not onely serue the ordinary turnes of you which are and shall bee the plãters and inhabitants, but such an ouerplus sufficiently to bee yelded, or by men of skill to bee prouided, as by way of trafficke and exchaunge with our owne nation of England, will enrich your selues the prouiders; those that shal deal with you; the enterprisers in general; and greatly profit our owne countrey men, to supply them with most things which heretofore they haue bene faine to prouide, either of strangers or of our enemies: which commodities for distinction sake, I call *Merchantable.*

In the second, I will set downe all the cõmodities which wee know the countrey by our experience doeth yeld of its selfe for victuall, and sustenance of mans life;

such as is vsually fed vpon by the inhabitants of the countrey, as also by vs during the time we were there.

In the last part I will make mention generally of such other cõmodities besides, as I am able to remember, and as I shall thinke behoofull for those that shall inhabite, and plant there to knowe of; which specially concerne building, as also some other necessary vses: with a briefe description of the nature and maners of the people of the countrey.

Third Part

THE THIRD AND LAST PART, OF SVCH OTHER THINGES AS IS BE HOOFULL FOR THOSE WHICH SHALL PLANT AND INHABIT TO KNOW OF; WITH A DESCRIPTION OF THE NATURE AND MANNERS OF THE PEOPLE OF THE COUNTREY.

Of commodities for building and other necessary uses.

THOSE other things which I am more to make rehearsall of, are such as concerne building, and other mechanicall necessarie vses; as diuers sortes of trees for house & ship timber, and other vses els: Also lime, stone, and brick, least that being not mentioned some might haue bene doubted of, or by some that are malicious reported the contrary.

Okes, there are as faire, straight, tall, and as good timber as any can be, and also great store, and in some places very great.

Walnut trees, as I haue saide before very many, some haue bene seen excellent faire timber of foure & fiue fadome, & aboue fourescore foot streight without bough.

Firre trees fit for masts of ships, some very tall & great. [*Rakíock*]

Rakíock, a kind of trees so called that are sweet wood of which the inhabitans that were neere vnto vs doe commonly make their boats or Canoes of the form of trowes; only with the helpe of fire, harchets of stones, and shels; we haue known some so great being made in that sort of one tree that they haue carried well xx. men at once, besides much baggage: the timber being great, tal, streight, soft, light, & yet tough enough I thinke (besides other vses) to be fit also for masts of ships.

Cedar, a sweet wood good for seelings, Chests, Boxes, Bedsteedes, Lutes, Virginals, and many things els, as I haue also said before. Some of our company which haue wandered in some places where I haue not bene, haue made certaine affirmation of *Cyprus* which for such and other excellent vses, is also a wood of price and no small estimation.

Maple, and also *Wich-hazle*; wherof the inhabitants vse to make their bowes.

Holly a necessary thing for the making of birdlime.

Willowes good for the making of weares and weeles to take fish after the English manner, although the inhabitants vse only reedes, which because they are so strong as also flexible, do serue for that turne very well and sufficiently.

Beech and *Ashe*, good for caske, hoopes: and if neede require, plow worke, as also for many things els.

Elme.

Sassafras trees.

Ascopo a kinde of tree very like vnto Lawrell, the barke is hoat in tast and spicie, it is very like to that tree which Monardus describeth to bee *Cassia Lignea* of the West Indies.

There are many other strange trees whose names I knowe not but in the *Virginian* language, of which I am not nowe able, neither is it so conuenient for the present to trouble you with particular relatiõ: seeing that for timber and other necessary vses I haue named sufficient: And of many of the rest but that they may be applied to good vse, I know no cause to doubt.

Now for Stone, Bricke and Lime, thus it is. Neere vnto the Sea coast where wee dwelt, there are no kind of stones to bee found (except a fewe small pebbles about foure miles off) but such as haue bene brought from farther out of the maine. In some of our voiages wee haue seene diuers hard raggie stones, great pebbles, and a kinde of grey stone like vnto marble, of which the inhabitants make their hatchets to cleeue wood. Vpon inquirie wee heard that a little further vp into the Countrey were all sortes verie many, although of Quarries they are ignorant, neither haue they vse of any store whereupon they should haue occasion to seeke any. For if euerie housholde haue one or two to cracke Nuttes, grinde shelles, whet copper, and sometimes other stones for hatchets, they haue enough: neither vse they any digging, but onely for graues about three foote deepe: and therefore no maruaile that they know neither Quarries, nor lime stones, which both may bee in places neerer than they wot of.

In the meane time vntill there bee discouerie of sufficient store in some place or other cõuenient, the want of you which are and shalbe the planters therein may be as well supplied by Bricke: for the making whereof in diuers places of the countrey there is clay both excellent good, and plentie; and also by lime made of Oister shels, and of others burnt, after the maner as they vse in the Iles of Tenet and Shepy, and also in diuers other places of England: Which kinde of lime is well knowne to bee as good as any other. And of Oister shels there is plentie enough: for besides diuers other particular places where are abundance, there is one shallowe sounde along the coast, where for the space of many miles together in length, and two or three miles in breadth, the grounde is nothing els beeing but halfe a foote or a foote vnder water for the most part.

This much can I say further more of stones, that about 120. miles from our fort neere the water in the side of a hill was founde by a Gentleman of our company, a great veine of hard ragge stones, which I thought good to remember vnto you.

Of the nature and manners of the people.

It resteth I speake a word or two of the naturall inhabitants, their natures and maners, leauing large discourse thereof vntill time more conuenient hereafter:

nowe onely so farre foorth, as that you may know, how that they in respect of troubling our inhabiting and planting, are not to be feared; but that they shall haue cause both to feare and loue vs, that shall inhabite with them.

They are a people clothed with loose mantles made of Deere skins, & aprons of the same rounde about their middles; all els naked; of such as difference of statures only as wee in England; hauing no edge tooles or weapons of yron or steele to offend vs withall, neither know they how to make any: those weapõs that they haue, are onlie bowes made of Witch hazle, & arrowes of reeds; flat edged truncheons also of wood about a yard long, neither haue they any thing to defend themselues but targets made of barcks; and some armours made of stickes wickered together with thread.

Their townes are but small, & neere the sea coast but few, some cõtaining but 10. or 12. houses: some 20. the greatest that we haue seene haue bene but of 30. houses: if they be walled it is only done with barks of trees made fast to stakes, or els with poles onely fixed vpright and close one by another.

Their houses are made of small poles made fast at the tops in rounde forme after the maner as is vsed in many arbories in our gardens of England, in most townes couered with barkes, and in some with artificiall mattes made of long rushes; from the tops of the houses downe to the ground. The length of them is commonly double to the breadth, in some places they are but 12. and 16. yardes long, and in other some wee haue seene of foure and twentie.

In some places of the countrey one onely towne belongeth to the gouernment of a *Wiróans* or chiefe Lorde; in other some two or three, in some sixe, eight, & more; the greatest *Wiróans* that yet we had dealing with had but eighteene townes in his gouernmêt, and able to make not aboue seuen or eight hundred fighting men at the most: The language of euery gouernment is different from any other, and the farther they are distant the greater is the difference.

Their maner of warres amongst themselues is either by sudden surprising one an other most commonly about the dawning of the day, or moone light; or els by ambushes, or some suttle deuises: Set battels are very rare, except if fall out where there are many trees, where eyther part may haue some hope of defence, after the deliuerie of euery arrow, in leaping behind some or other.

If there fall out any warres betweê vs & them; what their fight is likely to bee, we hauing aduantages against them so many maner of waies, as by our discipline, our strange weapons and deuises els; especially by ordinance great and small, it may be easily imagined; by the experience we haue had in some places, the turning vp of their heeles against vs in running away was their best defence.

In respect of vs they are a people poore, and for want of skill and iudgement in the knowledge and vse of our things, doe esteeme our trifles before thinges of greater value: Notwithstanding in their proper manner considering the want of such meanes as we haue, they seeme very ingenious; For although they haue no such tooles, nor any such craftes, sciences and artes as wee; yet in those thinges they doe, they shewe excellencie of wit. And by howe much they vpon due consideration shall finde our manner of knowledges and craftes to exceede theirs in perfection, and speed for doing or execution, by so much the more is it probable that they shoulde desire our friendships & loue, and haue the greater respect for pleasing and obeying vs. Whereby may bee hoped if meanes of good gouernment bee vsed, that they may in short time be brought to ciuilitie, and the imbracing of true religion.

Some religion they haue alreadie, which although it be farre from the truth, yet beyng as it is, there is hope it may bee the easier and sooner reformed.

They beleeue that there are many Gods which they call *Mantóac*, but of different sortes and degrees; one onely chiefe and great God, which hath bene from all eternitie. Who as they affirme when hee purposed to make the worlde, made first other goddes of a principall order to bee as meanes and instruments to bee vsed in the creation and gouernment to follow; and after the Sunne, Moone, and Starres, as pettie goddes and the instruments of the other order more principall. First they say were made waters, out of which by the gods was made all diuersitie of creatures that are visible or inuisible.

For mankind they say a woman was made first, which by the woorking of one of the goddes, conceiued and brought foorth children: And in such sort they say they had their beginning.

But how manie yeeres or ages haue passed since, they say they can make no relation, hauing no letters nor other such meanes as we to keepe recordes of the particularities of times past, but onelie tradition from father to sonne.

They thinke that all the gods are of humane shape, & therfore they represent them by images in the formes of men, which they call *Kewasowok* one alone is called *Kewás*; Them they place in houses appropriate or temples which they call *Mathicómuck*; Where they woorship, praie, sing, and make manie times offerings vnto them. In some *Machicómuck* we haue seene but on *Kewas*, in some two, and in other some three; The common sort thinke them to be also gods.

They beleeue also the immortalitie of the soule, that after this life as soone as the soule is departed from the bodie according to the workes it hath done, it is eyther carried to heauê the habitacle of gods, there to enioy perpetuall blisse and happiness, or els to a great pitte or hole, which they thinke to bee in the furthest partes of their part of the worlde towarde the sunne set, there to burne continually: the place they call *Popogusso*.

For the confirmation of this opinion, they tolde mee two stories of two men that had been lately dead and reuiued againe, the one happened but few yeres before our comming in the countrey of a wicked man which hauing beene dead and buried, the next day the earth of the graue beeing seene to moue, was takê vp againe; Who made declaration where his soule had beene, that is to saie very neere entring into *Popogusso*, had not one of the gods saued him & gaue him leaue to returne againe, and teach his friends what they should doe to auiod that terrible place of tormenr.

The other happened in the same yeere wee were there, but in a towne that was threescore miles from vs, and it was tolde mee for straunge newes that one beeing dead, buried and taken vp againe as the first, shewed that although his bodie had lien dead in the graue, yet his soule was aliue, and had trauailed farre in a long broade waie, on both sides whereof grewe most delicate and pleasaût trees, bearing more rare and excellent fruites then euer hee had seene before or was able to expresse, and at length came to most braue and faire houses, neere which hee met his father, that had beene dead before, who gaue him great charge to goe backe againe and shew his friendes what good they were to doe to enioy the pleasures of that place, which when he had done he should after come againe.

What subtilty soeuer be in the *Wiroances* and Priestes, this opinion worketh so much in manie of the common and simple sort of people that it maketh them haue great respect to their Gouernours, and also great care what they do, to auoid torment after death, and to enjoy blisse; although nothwithstanding there is punishment ordained for malefactours, as stealers, whoremoongers, and other sortes of wicked doers; some punished with death, some with forfeitures, some with beating, according to the greatnes of the factes.

And this is the summe of their religion, which I learned by hauing special familiarity [miliarity] with some of their priestes. Wherein they were not so sure grounded, nor gaue such credite to their traditions and stories but through conuersing with vs they were brought into great doubts of their owne, and no small admiratiõ of ours, with earnest desire in many, to learne more than we had meanes for want of perfect vtterance in their language to expresse.

Most thinges they sawe with vs, as Mathematicall instruments, sea compasses, the vertue of the loadstone in drawing yron, a perspectiue glasse whereby was shewed manie strange sightes, burning glasses, wildefire woorkes, gunnes, bookes, writing and reading, spring clocks that seeme to goe of themselues, and manie other thinges that wee had, were so straunge vnto them, and so farre exceeded their capacities to comprehend the reason and meanes how they should be made and done, that they thought they were rather the works of gods then of men, or at the leastwise they had bin giuen and taught vs of the gods. Which made manie of them to haue such opinions of vs, as that if they knew not the trueth of god and religion already, it was rather to be had from vs, whom God so specially loued then from a people that were so simple, as they found themselues to be in comparison of vs. Whereupon greater credite was giuen vnto that we spake of concerning such matters.

Manie times and in euery towne where I came, according as I was able, I made declaration of the contentes of the Bible; that therein was set foorth the true and onelie GOD, and his mightie woorkes, that therein was contayned the true doctrine of saluation through Christ, which manie particularities of Miracles and chiefe poyntes of religion, as I was able then to vtter, and thought fitte for the time. And although I told them the booke materially & of itself was not of anie such vertue, as I thought they did conceiue, but onely the doctrine therein cõtained; yet would many be glad to touch it, to embrace it, to kisse it, to hold it to their brests and heades, and stroke ouer all their bodie with it; to shew their hungrie desire of that knowledge which was spoken of.

The *Wiroans* with whom we dwelt called *Wingina*, and many of his people would be glad many times to be with vs at our praiers, and many times call vpon vs both in his owne towne, as also in others whither he sometimes accompanied vs, to pray and sing Psalmes; hoping thereby to bee partaker in the same effectes which wee by that meanes also expected.

Twise this *Wiroans* was so greiuously sicke that he was like to die, and as hee laie languishing, doubting of anie helpe by his owne priestes, and thinking he was in such daunger for offending vs and thereby our god, sent for some of vs to praie and bee a meanes to our God that it would please him either that he might liue or after death dwell with him in blisse; so likewise were the requestes of manie others in the like case.

On a time also when their corne began to wither by reason of a drouth which happened extraordinarily, fearing that it had come to passe by reason that in some thing they had displeased vs, many woulde come to vs & desire vs to praie to our God of England, that he would perserue their corne, promising that when it was ripe we also should be partakers of the fruite.

There could at no time happen any strange sicknesse, losses, hurtes, or any other crosse vnto them, but that they would impute to vs the cause or meanes therof for offending or not pleasing vs.

One other rare and strange accident, leauing others, will I mention before I ende, which mooued the whole countrey that either knew or hearde of vs, to haue vs in wonderfull admiration.

There was no towne where we had any subtile deuise practised against vs, we leauing it vnpunished or not reuenged (because wee sought by all meanes possible to win them by gentlenesse) but that within a few dayes after our departure from euerie such towne, the people began to die very fast, and many in short space; in some townes about twentie, in some fourtie, in some sixtie, & in one sixe score, which in trueth was very manie in respect of their numbers. This happened in no place that wee could learne but where wee had bene, where they vsed some practise against vs, and after such time; The disease also so strange, that they neither knew what it was, nor how to cure it; the like by the report of the oldest men in the countrey neuer happened before, time out of minde. A thing specially obserued by vs as also by the naturall inhabitants themselues.

Insomuch that when some of the inhabitantes which were our friends & especially the *Wiroans Wingina* had obserued such effects in foure or fiue towns to follow their wicked practises, they were preswaded that it was the worke of our God through our meanes, and that wee by him might kil and slai whom we would without weapons and not come neere them.

And thereupon when it had happened that they had vnderstanding that any of their enemies had abused vs in our iourneyes, hearing that wee had wrought no reuenge with our weapons, & fearing vpon some cause the matter should so rest: did come and intreate vs that we woulde bee a meanes to our God that they as others that had dealt ill with vs might in like sort die; alleaging howe much it would be for our credite and profite, as also theirs; and hoping furthermore that we would do so much at their requests in respect of the friendship we professe them.

Whose entreaties although wee shewed that they were vngodlie, affirming that our God would not subiect him selfe to anie such praiers and requestes of mê: that in deede all thinges haue beene and were to be done according to his good pleasure as he had ordained: ãd that we to shew ourselues his true seruãts ought rather to make petition for the contrarie, that they with them might liue together with vs, bee made partakers of his truth & serue him in righteousnes; but notwitstanding in such sort, that wee referre that as all other thinges, to bee done according to his diuine will & pleasure, ãd as by his wisedome he had ordained to be best.

Yet because the effect fell out so sodainly and shortly after according to their desires, they thought neuertheless it came to passe by our meanes, and that we in vsing such speeches vnto them did but dissemble in the matter, and therefore came vnto vs to giue vs thankes in their manner that although wee satisfied them not in promise, yet in deedes and effect we had fulfilled their desires.

This maruelous accident in all the countrie wrought so strange opinions of vs, that some people could not tel whether to think vs gods or men, and the rather because that all the space of their sicknesse, there was no man of ours knowne to die, or that was specially sicke: they noted also that we had no women amongst vs, neither that we did care for any of theirs.

Some therefore were of opinion that wee were not borne of women, and therefore not mortall, but that wee were men of an old generation many yeeres past then risen againe to immortalitie.

Some woulde likewise seeme to prophesie that there were more of our generation yet to come, to kill theirs and take their places, as some thought the purpose was by that which was already done.

Those that were immediatly to come after vs they imagined to be in the aire, yet inuisible & without bodies, & that they by our intreaty & for the loue of vs did make the people to die in that sort as they did by shooting inuisible bullets into them.

To confirme this opinion their phisitions to excuse their ignorance in curing the disease, would not be ashemed to say, but earnestly make the simple people beleue, that the strings of blood that they sucked out of the sicke bodies, were the strings wherewithal the inuisible bullets were tied and cast.

Some also thought that we shot them ourselues out of our pieces from the place where we dwelt, and killed the people in any such towne that had offended vs as we listed, how farre distant from vs soeuer it were.

And other some saide that it was the speciall woorke of God for our sakes, as wee our selues haue cause in some sorte to thinke no lesse, whatsoeuer some doe or maie imagine to the contrarie, specially some Astrologers knowing of the Eclipse of the Sunne which wee saw the same yeere before in our voyage thytherward, which vnto them appeared very terrible. And also of a Comet which beganne to appeare but a few daies before the beginning of the said sicknesse. But to exclude them from being the speciall an accident, there are farther reasons then I thinke fit at this present to bee alleadged.

These their opinions I haue set downe the more at large that it may appeare vnto you that there is good hope they may be brought through discreet dealing and gouernement to the imbracing of the trueth, and nsequently to honour, obey, feare and loue vs.

And although some of our companie towardes the ende of the yeare, shewed themselues too fierce, in slaying some of the people, in some towns, vpon causes that on our part, might easily enough haue been borne withall: yet notwithstanding because it was on their part iustly deserued, the alteration of their opinions generally & for the most part concerning vs is the lesse to bee doubted. And whatsoeuer els they may be, by carefulnesse of our selues neede nothing at all to be feared.

The best neuerthelesse in this as in all actions besides is to be endeuoured and hoped, & of the worst that may happen notice to bee taken with consideration, and as much as may be eschewed.

The Conclusion.

NOW I haue as I hope made relation not of so fewe and smal things but that the countrey of men that are indifferent & wel disposed maie be sufficiently liked: If there were no more knowen then I haue mentioned, which doubtlesse and in great reason is nothing to that which remaineth to bee discouered, neither the soile, nor commodities. As we haue reason so to gather by the difference we found in our trauails: for although all which I haue before spoken of, haue bin discouered & experiemented not far from the sea coast where was our abode & most of our trauailing: yet somtimes as we made our iourneies farther into the maine and countrey; we found the soyle to bee fatter; the trees greater and to growe thinner; the grounde more firme and deeper mould; more and larger champions; finer grasse and as good as euer we saw any in England; in some places rockie and farre more high and hillie ground; more plentie of their fruites; more abondance of beastes; the more inhabited with people, and of greater pollicie & larger dominions, with greater townes and houses.

Why may wee not then looke for in good hope from the inner parts of more and greater plentie, as well of other things, as of those which wee haue alreadie discouered? Vnto the Spaniardes happened the like in discouering the maine of the West Indies. The maine also of this countrey of *Virginia*, extending some wayes so many hundreds of leagues, as otherwise then by the relation of the inhabitants wee haue most certaine knowledge of, where yet no Christian Prince hath any possession or dealing, cannot but yeeld many kinds of excellent commodities, which we in our discouerie haue not yet seene.

What hope there is els to be gathered of the nature of the climate, being answerable to the Iland of *Iapan*, the land of *China*, *Persia*, *Jury*, the Ilandes of *Cyprus* and *Candy*, the South parts *Greece*, *Italy*, and *Spaine*, and of many other notable and famous countreis, because I meane not to be tedious, I leaue to your owne consideration.

Whereby also the excellent temperature of the ayre there at all seasons, much warmer then in England, and neuer so violently hot, as sometimes is vnder & between the Tropikes, or neere them; cannot bee vnknowne vnto you without farther relation.

For the holsomnesse thereof I neede to say but thus much: that for all the want of prouision, as first of English victuall; excepting for twentie daies, wee liued only by drinking water and by the victuall of the countrey, of which some sorts were very straunge vnto vs, and might haue bene thought to haue altered our temperatures in such sort as to haue brought vs into some greeuous and dãgerous diseases: secondly the wãt of English meanes, for the taking of beastes, fishe, and foule, which by the helpe only of the inhabitants and their meanes, coulde not bee so suddenly and easily prouided for vs, nor in so great numbers & quantities, nor of that choise as otherwise might haue bene to our better satisfaction and contentment. Some want also wee had of clothes. Furthermore, in all our trauailes which were most speciall and often in the time of winter, our lodging was in the open aire vpon the grounde. And yet I say for all this, there were but foure of our whole company (being one hundred and eight) that died all the yeere and that but at the latter ende thereof and vpon none of the aforesaide causes. For all foure especially three were feeble, weake, and sickly persons before euer they came thither, and those that knewe them much marueyled that they liued so long beeing in that case, or had aduentured to trauaile.

Seing therefore the ayre there is so temperate and holsome, the soyle so fertile and yeelding such commodities as I haue before mentioned, the voyage also thither to and fro beeing sufficiently experimented, to bee perfourmed thrise a yeere with ease and at any season thereof: And the dealing of *Sir Walter Raleigh* so liberall in large giuing and graûting lande there, as is alreadie knowen, with many helpes and furtherances els: (The least that hee hath graunted hath beene fiue hundred acres to a man onely for the aduenture of his person): I hope there reamine no cause whereby the action should be misliked.

If that those which shall thither trauaile to inhabite and plant bee but reasonably prouided for the first yere as those are which were transported the last, and beeing there doe vse but that diligence and care as is requisite, and as they may with eese: There is no doubt but for the time following they may haue victuals that is excellent good and plentie enough; some more Englishe sortes of cattaile also hereafter, as some haue bene before, and are there yet remaining, may and shall bee God willing thiter transported: So likewise our kinde of fruites, rootes, and hearbes may bee there planted and sowed, as some haue bene alreadie, and proue wel: And in short time also they may raise of those sortes of commodities which I haue spoken of as shall both enrich theselues, as also others that shall deale with them.

And this is all the fruites of our labours, that I haue thought necessary to aduertise you of at this present: what els concerneth the nature and manners of the inhabitants of *Virginia*: The number with the particularities of the voyages thither made; and of the actions of such that haue bene by *Sir Walter Raleigh* therein and there imployed, many worthy to bee remembered; as of the first discouerers of the Countrey: of our generall for the time *Sir Richard Greinuile*; and after his departure, of our Gouernour there Master *Rafe Lane*; with diuers other directed and imployed vnder theyr gouernement: Of the Captaynes and Masters of the voyages made since for transporation; of the Gouernour and assistants of those alredie transported, as of many persons, accidêts, and thinges els, I haue ready in a discourse by it selfe in maner of a Chronicle according to the course of times, and when time shall bee thought conuenient shall be also published.

This referring my relation to your fauourable constructions, expecting good successe of the action, from him which is to be acknowledged the authour and gouernour not only of this but of all things els, I take my leaue of you, this moneth of Februarii, 1588.

FINIS.

1.6.2 Reading and Review Questions

1. How does Harriot determine the value of the land's resources in Virginia? Why?
2. What is his attitude towards the British and their place in Virginia? Why?
3. By what standards does Harriot evaluate the lifestyle of the Native Americans he encounters? Their government?
4. Why does Harriot make a point of describing the warfare of the Native Americans he encounters? How do you know?
5. What grounds the Native American's virtues, ethics, and morality, according to Harriot's depiction of them? Why do you think?

1.7 SAMUEL DE CHAMPLAIN

(c. 1570–1635)

Samuel de Champlain was born at Brouage, Saintagone, France. His education focused on seamanship and navigation. In 1599, he undertook the first of several voyages to America, joining a Spanish fleet to the Caribbean. His record of this voyage, including illustrations and first-hand descriptions of the Spanish empire and their rule over American Indians, won him the attention and support of Henry IV, king of France.

Image 1.3 | Samuel de Champlain
Artist | Samuel de Champlain
Source | Wikimedia Commons
License | Public Domain

As Royal Geographer, he joined Francois Pont-Grave's expedition charged with establishing a French colony in America. He sailed up the Saint Lawrence River and proposed a settlement at what is now the lower town of Quebec City. His written reports on America, first with *Des Sauvages* (of the Indians) (1604) followed by his *Les Voyages* (1613) did much to encourage French interest in America.

He defended the small colony through alliances with the Montagnais, the Algonquians, and the Hurons, joining them in a fierce battle against the Mohawk in what is now central New York. He died on Christmas Day in 1635 and was buried at Notre Dame de la Recouvance, a Catholic church he founded in what is now Quebec City. He is still known as the father of New France.

1.7.1 From *The Voyages and Explorations of Sieur de Champlain* (1613)

VOLUME I

BOOK I

Chapter I

Extent of New France and the excellence of its soil. Reasons for establishing Colonies in the New France of the West. Rivers, lakes, ponds, woods, meadows and islands of New France. Its fertility. Its peoples.

The labors that Sieur de Champlain has endured in discovering several countries, lakes, rivers, and islands of New France, during the last twenty-seven years, have not made him lose courage because of the difficulties that have been encountered; but, on the contrary, the dangers and risks that he has met with, instead of lessening, have redoubled his courage. And two very strong reasons in particular have decided him to make new voyages there. The first is that under the reign of King Louis the Just, France should become enriched and increased by a country of which the extent exceeds sixteen hundred leagues in length and nearly five hundred in breadth; the second, that the richness of the soil and the useful things that can be derived from it, whether for commerce or to make life pleasant in that country, are such that one cannot estimate the advantage that the French would gain from it some day, if the French colonies that may be established there should be protected by the favor and authority of His Majesty.

The new discoveries led to the purpose of establishing colonies, which, though at first of little account, have nevertheless in course of time, by means of commerce, become equal to the states of the greatest Icings. One may put in this class several cities that the Spaniards have founded in Peru and other parts of the world within the last hundred and twenty years, which were nothing to begin with. Europe can offer the example of the city of Venice, which was originally a refuge for poor fishermen. Genoa, one of the most superb cities of the world, was built in a region surrounded by mountains, very wild, and so sterile that the inhabitants were obliged to have soil brought from outside to cultivate their garden plots, and their sea is without fish. The city of Marseilles, which formerly was nothing but a great marsh, surrounded by rugged hills and mountains, nevertheless in the course of time made its land fertile, and has become famous and an important seat of commerce. Similarly, many small colonies which had the convenience of ports and harbors have increased in wealth and in reputation.

It must be said also that the country of New France is a new world, and not a kingdom; perfectly beautiful, with very convenient locations, both on the banks of the great river St. Lawrence (the ornament of the country) and on other rivers, lakes, ponds and brooks. It has, too, an infinite number of beautiful islands, and they contain very pleasant and delightful meadows and groves where, during the spring and the summer, may be seen a great number of birds which come there in their time and season. The soil is very fertile for all kinds of grain; the pasturage is abundant; and a network of great rivers and lakes, which are like seas lying across the countries, lend great facility to all the explorations of the interior, whence one could get access to the oceans on the west, the east, the north, and even on the south.

The country is filled with immense tall forests composed of the same kinds of trees that we have in France. The air is salubrious and the water excellent in the latitudes corresponding to ours. The benefit that can be derived from this country, according to what Sieur de Champlain hopes to demonstrate, is sufficient to make the enterprise worth considering, since this country can supply for the service of the King the same advantages that we have in France, as will appear from the following account.

In New France there are a great many savage peoples; some of whom are sedentary, fond of cultivating the soil, and having cities and villages enclosed with palisades; others are roving tribes which live by hunting and fishing, and have no knowledge of God. But there is hope that the clergy who have been sent there and who are beginning to establish themselves and to found seminaries will be able in a few years to make great progress in the conversion of these peoples. This is the first care of His Majesty, who, turning his eyes toward Heaven rather than toward the earth, will support, if it is his good pleasure, such founders as engage to transport clergy to work at this sacred harvest, and propose to establish a Colony as being the only way of making the name of the true God recognized, and of establishing the Christian religion there: such founders, too, as would oblige the French who go there to work, first of all, at tilling the soil, in order to have the necessaries of life on the spot, without being forced to bring them from France. That done, the country will furnish in abundance all that can be wished in life, whether to satisfy needs or pleasures, as will be shown hereafter.

If one cares for hawking, one can find in these places all sorts of birds of prey in as great numbers as one could wish: falcons, gerfalcons, sakers, tassels, sparhawks, goshawks, marlins, muskets, two kinds of eagles, little and big owls, great horned owls of exceptional size, pyes, woodpeckers. And there are other kinds of birds of prey, less common than those named, with grey plumage on the back and white on the belly, as fat and large as a hen, with one foot like the talon of a bird of prey, with which it catches fish; the other like that of a duck. The latter serves for swimming in the water when he dives for fish. This bird is not supposed to be found except in New France.

For hunting with setters, there are three kinds of partridges: some are true pheasants, others are black, and still others white. These last come in winter and have flesh like wood-pigeons, of a very excellent flavor.

As for hunting for other game, river birds abound there; all sorts of ducks, teal, white and grey geese, bustards, little geese, woodcock, snipe, little and big larks, plover, herons, cranes, swans, divers of two or three kinds, coots, ospreys, curlews, thrushes, white and grey sea gulls; and on the coasts and shores of the sea, cormorants, sea parrots, sea pyes, and others in infinite numbers which come there in their season.

In the woods and in the country which is inhabited by the Iroquois, a people of New France, there are many wild turkeys, and at Quebec a quantity of turtle-doves throughout the summer; also blackbirds, linnets, sky larks, and other kinds of birds of varied plumage, which in their season sing very sweetly.

After this kind of hunting may be mentioned another not less pleasant and agreeable, but more difficult. There are in this same country, foxes, common wolves and spotted lynxes, wild cats, porcupines, beavers, muskrats, otters, sables, martens, varieties of badgers, hares, bears, moose, stags, deer, caribous as big as wild asses, kids, flying squirrels, and other kinds of animals which we do not have in France. They can be caught either by lying in wait or with a trap, or, if one suddenly shouts on the islands where they resort most often, one can kill them easily as they throw themselves in the water when they hear the noise; or they can be caught in any other way that the ingenuity of those who take pleasure in it may suggest.

If one is fond of fishing, whether with the line, nets, warrens, weels or other inventions, there are rivers, brooks, lakes and ponds in as great number as one could desire, with an abundance of salmon; very beautiful trout, fine and large, of every kind; sturgeon of three sizes; shad; very good bass, some of which weigh twenty pounds. There are carp of all kinds and some of them are very large; and pike, some of them five feet long; turbot without scales, two or three kinds, big and little; white fish a foot long; gold fish, smelts, tench, perch, tortoises, seal, of which the oil is very good even for frying; white porpoises, and many others that we do not have and that are not found in our rivers and ponds. All these varieties of fish are found in the great river St. Lawrence; besides, cod and whales are caught on the coasts of New France in nearly all seasons. Thus one can judge of the pleasure that the French will have when once they are settled in these places; living a sweet, quiet life, with perfect freedom to hunt, fish, and make homes for themselves according to their desires; with occupation for the mind in building, clearing the ground, working gardens, planting them, grafting, making nurseries, planting all kinds of grains, roots, vegetables, salad greens and other potherbs, over as much land and in as great quantity as they wish. The vines there bear pretty good grapes, even though they are wild. If these are transplanted and cultivated they will yield fruit in abundance. And he who will have thirty acres of cleared land in that country, with the help of a few cattle, and of hunting and fishing, and trading with the savages in conformity to the regulations of the company of New France, will be able to live there with a family of ten as well as those in France who have an income of fifteen or twenty thousand livres.

Chapter II

That Kings and great Princes ought to take more pains to spread the knowledge of the true God and magnify His glory among barbarians than to multiply their states. Voyages of the French to the New World since the year 1504.

THE most illustrious palms and laurels that kings and princes can win in this world are contempt for temporal blessings and the desire to gain the spiritual. They cannot do this more profitably than by converting, through their labor and piety, to the catholic, apostolic and Roman religion, an infinite number of savages, who live without faith, without law, with no knowledge of the true God. For the taking of forts, the winning of battles, and the conquests of countries, are nothing in comparison with the reward of those who prepare for themselves crowns in heaven, unless it be fighting against infidels. In that case, war is not only necessary, but just and holy, since the safety of Christianity, the glory of God and the defence of the faith are at stake. These labors are, in themselves, praiseworthy and very commendable, besides being in conformity to the commandment of God, which says, That the conversion of an infidel is of more value than the conquest of a kingdom. And if all this cannot move us to seek after heavenly blessings at least as passionately as after those of the earth, it is because men's covetousness for this world's blessings is so great that most of them do not care for the conversion of infidels so long as their fortune corresponds to their desires, and everything conforms to their wishes. Moreover, it is this covetousness that has ruined and is wholly ruining the progress and advancement of this enterprise, which is not yet well under way, and is in danger of collapsing, unless His Majesty establishes there conditions as righteous, charitable and just as he is himself; and unless he himself takes pleasure in learning what can be done to increase the glory of God and to benefit his state, repelling the envy of those who should support this enterprise, but who seek its ruin rather than its success.

It is nothing new for the French to make sea voyages for conquest. We know very well that the discovery of new countries and noble enterprises on the sea were begun by our forefathers.

It was the Bretons and Normans who, in the year 1504, were the first Christians to discover the grand bank of the Codfish and the islands of the New World, as is noted in the histories of Niflet and of Antoine Maginus. It is also very certain that in the time of King Francis I, in the year 1523, he sent Verazzano, a Florentine, to discover the lands, coasts and harbors of Florida, as the accounts of his voyages bear testimony; where, after having explored the coast from latitude 33 to latitude 47, just as he was thinking of making a home there, death put an end to his life and his plans. After that, the same King Francis, persuaded by Messire Philip Chabot, Admiral of France, sent Jacques Cartier to discover new lands, and for this purpose he made two voyages in the years 1534 and 1535. In the first he discovered the Island of Newfoundland and the Gulf of Saint Lawrence, with several other islands in this gulf, and he would have gone farther had not the severe season hastened his return. This Jacques Cartier was from the city of St. Malo. He was thoroughly versed and experienced in seamanship; the equal of any one of his times. And St. Malo is under obligation to preserve his memory, for it was his greatest desire to discover new lands. At the request of Charles de Mouy, Sieur de la Mailleres, at that time Vice-Admiral, he undertook the same voyage for the second time; and in order to compass his purpose and to have His Majesty lay the foundation of a colony to increase the honor of God and his royal authority, he gave his commissions with that of the aforesaid Sieur Admiral, who had the direction of this embarkation and contributed all he could to it. When the commissions had been prepared, His Majesty put this same Cartier in charge, and he set sail with two vessels on May 16, 1535. His voyage was so successful that he arrived at the Gulf of Saint Lawrence, entered the river with his ships of 800 tons burden, and even got as far as an island a hundred and twenty leagues up the river, which he called the Isle of Orleans. From there he went some ten leagues farther up the same stream to winter on a small river which is almost dry at low tide. This he named St. Croix, because he arrived there on the day of the Exaltation of the Holy Cross. The place is now called the St. Charles River and at present the Recollect fathers and the Jesuit fathers are stationed there to found a seminary for the instruction of youth. From there Cartier went up the river some sixty leagues, as far as a place which was called Ochelaga in his time and is now called Grand Sault St. Louis. It was inhabited by savages who were sedentary and cultivated the soil. This they no longer do, because of the wars that have made them withdraw into the interior. When Cartier, according to his account, perceived the difficulty of passing up the rapids and that it was impossible, he returned where his vessels were; and the weather and the season were so urgent that he was obliged to winter on the St. Croix River, in the place where the Jesuits live now, on the border of another little river which empties into the St. Croix, called the Jacques Cartier River, as his narratives testify.

Cartier was made so unhappy in this voyage, particularly by the ravages of scurvy, of which the larger part of his men died, that when spring came he returned to France, saddened and disturbed enough at this loss and at the little progress that he thought he had made. He came to the conclusion, as a result of his winter's experience with the scurvy, which he called the disease of the country, that the climate was so different from our own that we could not live in it without great difficulty.

So when he had made his report to the King and to the Sieur Admiral and De Mailleres, who did not go deeply into the matter, the enterprise bore no fruit. But if Cartier could have understood the cause of his sickness, and the beneficial and certain remedy for its prevention, although he and his men did receive some relief from an herb called aneda? just as we did when we were

in the same plight, there is no doubt that the King from that time would not have neglected to forward the plan, as he had already done: for at that time the country was more peopled with sedentary tribes than now. It was this last fact that led His Majesty to have this second voyage made and the undertaking carried on, for he had a holy desire to send colonists there. This was what came of it.

This affair might well have been undertaken by some others than Cartier, who would not have been so soon daunted and would not, on that account, have abandoned an enterprise so well begun. For, to tell the truth, those who are the leaders of explorations are oftentimes those who can put an end to the execution of a praiseworthy project, if people stop to consider their reports. For, if they are believed, it is thought that the enterprise is impossible or so involved in difficulties that it cannot be brought to completion without almost unendurable outlay and trouble. This is the reason why this enterprise did not achieve success. Besides, there are sometimes affairs of so much importance in a state as to cause others to be neglected for awhile; or it may be that those who would gladly have gone on with them, die, and so the years pass with nothing done.

BOOK III

Chapter V

Arrival of the author at Quebec, where he made his place of abode. Habits of the savages of that country.

From the Island of Orleans to Quebec it is one league. When I arrived there on July 3, I looked for a suitable place for our buildings, but I could not find any more convenient or better situated than the point of Quebec, so called by the savages, which is filled with nut trees and vines. I immediately employed some of our workmen in cutting them down, in order to put our buildings there. Some I set to sawing boards, some to digging a cellar and making ditches, and others I sent to Tadoussac with the boat to get our supplies. The first thing that we made was the storehouse in which to put our provisions under cover, which was promptly finished through the diligence of each one and the care that I had of it. Near this place is a pleasant river, where formerly Jacques Cartier passed the winter.

While the ship-carpenters, the woodsawers and other workmen, worked on our lodging I set all the others at clearing the land about the building, in order to make the garden-plots in which to sow grain and seeds, to see how they would all turn out, for the soil appeared very good.

Meanwhile a great many savages were in cabins near us, fishing for eels, which begin to come about September 15 and go away on October 15. At this time all the savages live on this manna and dry enough of it to last through the winter to the month of February, when the snow is about two and a half feet deep, or three at the most. And when the eels and other things that they collect have been prepared they go to hunt the beaver, which they do until the beginning of January. They were not very successful in the beaver hunt, for the water was too high and the rivers had overflowed, as they told us. When their eels give out they have recourse to hunting the elk and other wild beasts, which they can find, while waiting for the spring. At that time I was able to supply them with several things. I made a special study of their customs.

All these people are so much in want that sometimes they are driven to live on certain kinds of shellfish and to eat their dogs and the skins with which they protect themselves against the cold. If some one should show them how to live and teach them how to till the soil, and other things, they would learn very easily, for there are a good many of them who have good judgment and reply intelligently to what is asked of them. There is an evil tendency among them to be revengeful, and to be great liars, and one cannot rely upon them, except with caution and when one is armed. They make promises enough, but keep few of them, most of them being without law, as far as I could see, and, besides, full of false beliefs. I asked them what ceremonies they employed in praying to their god; they told me that they made use of none, except that each prayed in his heart as he wished. This is why they have no law, and do not know what it is to worship God and pray to Him, but live like brute beasts; but I think that they would soon be converted to Christianity if some people would settle among them and cultivate their soil, which is what most of them wish. They have among them some savages whom they call Pilotois, who, they believe, talk with the devil face to face, who tells them what they must do, whether in case of war or in regard to other matters; and if he should command them to carry out a certain enterprise they would obey his command at once. They believe, also, that all the dreams that they have are true; and, in fact, there are a great many of them who say that they have seen and dreamed things which have come to pass or will take place. But, to tell the truth about the matter, these are diabolical visions, which deceive them and lead them astray. This is all that I have been able to learn about their brutish belief.

All these people are well-built, without deformity, and are active. The women are equally well-formed, plump, and of a tawny complexion, because of certain pigments which they put on which make them look olive-colored. They are dressed in skins; a part of the body is covered, the rest is naked; but in winter they make up for it, for they are dressed in good furs, like elk, otter, beaver, bear, seal, deer and roe, which they have in great quantity. In winter, when there is a great deal of snow, they make a sort of racquets, which are three or four times as large as those in France, which they attach to their feet, and in this way they can go in the snow without sinking in; without them they could not hunt or go in many places. They have an odd sort of marriage, namely: when a girl is fourteen or fifteen years old, and she has several suitors, she may associate with all of them that she likes. Then at the end of five or six years she makes her own choice from them of a husband, and they live together to the end of their lives. But if, after living some time together, there are no children, then the man may unmarry himself and take another wife, saying that his own is good for nothing. Thus the girls are freer thar the women.

After marriage they are chaste, and the husbands are, for the most part, jealous. They give presents to the fathers or relatives of the girls whom they have married. These are the ceremonies and ways that they employ in their marriages.

As for their burials, when a man or a woman dies, they dig a big grave, where they put all the possessions that they had, such as kettles, furs, axes, bows, arrows, robes and other things; then they put the body in the grave and cover it with earth, and put a great many large pieces of wood on top, and one piece erect This they paint red on the upper part They believe in the immortality of the soul, and say that they will be happy in other lands with their relatives and friends who are dead. In the case of captains and others in positions of authority, they come, after the death, three times a year for a celebration and dance, and sing on the grave.

They are very timid and constantly fear their enemies, and scarcely sleep at all wherever they are, although I reassured them every day as much as I could and advised them to do as we do, namely: let some watch while others sleep, and let each one have his arms ready, like him who was on guard; and that they should not take dreams for the truth, on which to rely. But these teachings were of little use, and they said that we understood better than they how to protect ourselves against these things, and that in time, if we should come to live in their country, they would learn.

Chapter VII

Journey from Quebec to the Island of St. Eloi, and the meeting that I had with some Algonquin and Ochtaiguin savages.

With this purpose I departed on the eighteenth of the month. The river begins to widen here, sometimes to a league and even a league and a half in some places. The country becomes more and more beautiful. The banks of the river are partly hills and partly level land without rocks, except a very few. As for the river, it is dangerous in many places, because of sandbars and rocks, and is not good to sail in without the lead in hand. The river is very abundantly supplied with several sorts of fish, not only such as we have on this side of the sea, but others that we have not. The country is all covered with large, high forests of the same kinds of trees that we have about our settlement. There are also many vines and nut trees on the bank of the river and a great many little brooks and rivers which are navigable only with canoes. We passed near Point St. Croix. This point is sandy. It projects a little into the river, and is exposed to the northwest wind, which beats upon it. There are some meadows, but they are submerged every time the tide is high. The tide falls nearly two and a half fathoms. This passage is very dangerous to go through, on account of the quantity of rocks that lie across the river, although there is a good channel which is very crooked, where the river runs like a mill-race, and one must take plenty of time for the passage. This place has deceived a great many people, who thought that they could not go through it except at high tide for lack of a channel, but we have found the contrary. As for going down, one can do it at low tide; but to go up would be very difficult, unless there should be a high wind, because of the great current; and so it is necessary to wait until the tide is one-third flood to pass, when the current in the channel is 6, 8, 10, 12 and 15 fathoms deep.

Continuing our course we came to a river which is very pleasant. It is nine leagues from St. Croix and twenty-four from Quebec. We named it St. Mary's River. The whole length of this river from St. Croix is very beautiful.

Continuing our route I met two or three hundred savages, who were in cabins near a little island called St. Eloi, a league and a half from St. Mary. We investigated and found that they were some tribes of savages called Ochateguins and Algonquins, who were going to Quebec, to assist us in exploration of the countries of the Iroquois, against whom they carry on mortal combat, sparing nothing that belongs to them.

After having recognized them I went ashore to see them and asked who their chief was. They told me that they had two of them one named Iroquet and the other Ochasteguin, whom they pointed out to me and I went to their cabin, where they received me well, according to their custom. I began to explain to them the purpose of my journey, with which they were very much pleased; and, after talking of several things, I withdrew. Some time afterward they came to my shallop, where they made me accept some skins, showing a good many signs of pleasure, and then they returned to land.

The next day the two chiefs came to find me. Then they remained some time without saying a word, meditating and smoking constantly. After having thought it all over, they began to harangue in a loud voice all their companions who were on the river bank, their arms in their hands, listening very attentively to what their chiefs said to them, namely: that nearly ten moons ago, as they reckoned, Iroquet's son had seen me, and that I had given him a kind reception, and that we desired to assist them against their enemies, with whom they had been at war for a long time, because of a great deal of cruelty that the enemy had shown toward their tribe, on the pretext of friendship; and that, having always desired vengeance since that time, they had asked all the savages on the bank of the river to come to us, to form an alliance with us, and that they never had seen Christians, which had also induced them to come to see us, and that I might do as I wished with them and their companions; that they had no children with them, but men who knew how to fight and were full of courage, and who were familiar with the country and the rivers in the country of the Iroquois; and that now they begged me to return to our settlement, that they might see our houses; that after three days we should return all together to the war, and that for a sign of great friendship and joy I should have muskets and arquebuses fired, and that they would be very much pleased; which I did. They gave great cries of astonishment, and especially those who never had heard nor seen them before.

After I had heard them I replied to them that to please them I should be very glad to go back to our settlement, to give them more pleasure, and that they might infer that I had no other intention than to engage in war, since I carried with me nothing but arms, and not merchandise for barter, as they had been led to understand; that my desire was only to accomplish that which I had promised them; and that if I had known of any one who had made evil reports to them, I should regard such as enemies more than they themselves did. They told me that they did not believe any of it, and that they had heard nothing said; but the contrary was true, for there were some savages who told ours. I contented myself in waiting for an opportunity to be able to show them in reality something different from what they could have expected of me.

Chapter IX

Departure from the rapids of the Iroquois River. Description of a large lake. Of tke encounter with the enemy that we had at this lake, and of the manner in which they attacked the Iroquois.

I left these rapids of the Iroquois River on July 2. All the savages began to carry their canoes, arms and baggage by land about half a league, in order to get by the swiftness and force of the rapids. This was quickly accomplished.

Then they put them all in the water, and two men in each boat, with their baggage; and they made one of the men from each canoe go by land about a league and a half, the length of the rapid, which is not so violent as at its mouth, except in certain places where rocks obstruct the river, which is not more than 300 or 400 paces wide. After we had passed the rapid, which was not without difficulty, all the savages who had gone by land by a pretty good path and level country, although there were a great many trees, re-embarked in their canoes. My men went by land, too, and I by water, in a canoe. They had a review of all their men and found that they had twenty-four canoes, with sixty men in them. When they had had their review, we continued on our way as far as an island three leagues long, covered with the most beautiful pines that I had ever seen. They hunted, and caught some wild animals there. Going on farther, about three leagues from there, we encamped, to rest that night.

Immediately they all began, some to cut wood, others to strip off the bark of trees to cover their cabins, to provide shelter for themselves; others began to fell big trees for a barricade on the bank of the river about their cabins. They know so well how to do this that in less than two hours five hundred of their enemy would have had a good deal of trouble to attack them without losing a great many of their number. They do not barricade the side toward the river, where their canoes are drawn up, so as to be able to embark, if occasion requires.

When they were lodged they sent three canoes with nine good men, as is their custom in all their encampments, to reconnoitre for two or three leagues, to see if they can discover anything. Later these come back. They sleep all night, relying upon the exploration of these scouts, which is a very bad custom among them; for sometimes they are surprised while asleep by their enemies, who knock them in the head before they have a chance to get up to defend themselves.

Being aware of that, I explained to them the mistake that they were making, and told them that they ought to watch, as they had seen us do every night, and have men on the lookout, to listen and see if they saw anything; and that they should not live like beasts. They told me that they could not keep watch, and that they worked enough by day in hunting; and, above all, when they go to war, they divide their bands into three parts, viz., one part to hunt, distributed in various places; one to constitute the main body, who are always under arms; and the other part as scouts, to explore along the rivers, to see if there is any mark or sign to indicate that their enemies have passed, or their friends. This they recognize by certain marks that the chiefs of different tribes exchange. These are not always alike, and they inform themselves from time to time when they are changed. In this way they recognize whether those who have passed are friends or enemies. The hunters never hunt in advance of the main body, or of the scouts, in order not to cause alarm or disorder, but in the rear, and in the direction where they do not expect their enemies; and they continue thus until they are two or three days journey from their enemies, when they go at night by stealth, all in a body, except the scouts. And by day they retire within the thickest part of the woods, where they rest, without wandering off, or making any noise, or lighting any fire, even when necessary for food, during this time, in order not to be noticed if, by chance, their enemies should pass. They do not make any fire, except for smoking; and they eat Indian meal cooked, which they soak in water, like porridge. They preserve this meal for times of need, and when they are near their enemies, or when they are retreating after an attack, they do not care to hunt, but retreat at once.

In all their encampments they have their Pilotois, or Ostemoy, a kind of persons who act as soothsayers, in whom these people believe. The soothsayer builds a cabin surrounded by sticks of wood, and covers it with his robe. When it is done he ensconces himself inside in such a way that he cannot be seen at all; then he takes hold of one of the posts of his cabin and shakes it, muttering some words between his teeth, by which he says he invokes the devil, who appears to him in the form of a stone and tells him whether they will find their enemies and kill many of them. This Pilotois lies flat on the ground, motionless, only making believe to speak to the devil; then suddenly he rises to his feet, talking and writhing in such a way that, although he is naked, he is all in a perspiration. All the people are about the cabin, seated on their buttocks like monkeys. They told me often that the shaking of the cabin that I saw was caused by the devil and not by the man who was inside, although I observed the contrary; for it was (as I have already said) the Pilotois who seized one of the props of the cabin and made it move so. They also told me that I should see fire come out of the top, which I did not see at all. These rogues also disguise their voices and make them sound big and clear and speak in a language that is unfamiliar to the other savages; and when they make it sound broken the savages believe that it is the devil who speaks, and that he is saying what is to happen in their war, and what they must do. Nevertheless, all these rascals who play soothsayer do not speak two true words out of a hundred and impose upon these poor folk, like plenty of others in the world, in order to get their living from the people. I often admonished them that all that they did was sheer folly, and that they ought not to put faith in it.

Now, after they have learned from their soothsayers what is to happen to them, they take as many sticks, a foot long, as they themselves number, and represent their chiefs by others a little longer. Then they go into the woods and clear a place five or six feet square, where the chief, as field sergeant, arranges all the sticks in the order that seems good to him; then he calls all his companions, who all come armed, and shows them the rank and order that they are to keep when they fight with their enemies. All the savages watch this attentively, noticing the figure which their chief has made with these sticks, and afterward they retire and begin to arrange themselves as they have seen these sticks, and then mingle with one another, and return directly to their order; continuing this two or three times, and doing it at all their encampments, without needing a sergeant to make them keep in their ranks, which they know well how to keep, without getting into confusion. This is the rule that they abide by in their warfare.

We left the next day, continuing our course in the river as far as the entrance to the lake. In this there are many pretty islands, which are low, covered with very beautiful woods and meadows, where there is a quantity of game, and animals for hunting, such as stags, fallow-deer, fawns, roebucks, bears and other animals which come from the mainland to these islands. We caught a great many of them. There are also many beavers, not only in this river, but in many other little ones which empty into it. These places, although they are pleasant, are not inhabited by any savages, on account of their wars. They withdraw as far as possible from the river into the interior, in order not to be suddenly surprised. The next day we entered the lake, which is of great extent, perhaps 50 or 60 leagues long. There I saw four beautiful islands 10, 12 and 15 leagues long, which formerly had been inhabited by savages, like the River of the Iroquois; but they had been abandoned since they had been at war with one another. There are also several rivers which flow into the lake that are bordered by many fine trees, of the same sorts that we have in France, with a quantity of vines more beautiful than any I had seen in any other place; many chestnut trees, and I have not seen any at all before, except on the shores of the lake, where there is a great abundance of fish of a good many varieties. Among other kinds there is one called by the savages Chaousarou, which is of various lengths; but the longest, as these people told me, is eight or ten feet. I saw some of them five feet long, as big as a man's thigh, with a head as large as two fists, a snout two and a half feet long, and a double row of very sharp and dangerous teeth. Its body is, in all respects, like that of the pike, but it is armed with scales so strong that a dagger could not pierce them, and it is silver grey in color. And the end of its snout is like that of a pig. This fish fights all the others in the lakes and rivers, and is wonderfully cunning, to judge from what the people have assured me, which is, that when it wishes to catch certain birds, it goes into the rushes or weeds which border the lake in several places, and puts its snout out of the water without moving at all, so that when the birds come to light on its snout, thinking that it is the trunk of a tree, the fish is so skillful in closing its snout, which had been half open, that it draws the birds under the water by the feet. The savages gave me a head of one of them. They set great store by them, saying that when they have a headache they Weed themselves with the teeth of this fish where the pain is, and it passes off at once.

Continuing our course in this lake on the west side I saw, as I was observing the country, some very high mountains on the east side, with snow on the top of them. I inquired of the savages if these places were inhabited. They told me that they were by the Iroquois and that in these places there were beautiful valleys and open stretches fertile in grain, such as I had eaten in this country, with a great many other fruits; and that the lake went near some mountains, which were perhaps, as it seemed to me, about fifteen leagues from us. I saw on the south others not less high than the first, but they had no snow at all. The savages told me that it was there that we were to go to find their enemies, and that these mountains were thickly peopled. They also said it was necessary to pass a rapid, which I saw afterward, and from there to enter another lake, three or four leagues long; and that when we had reached the end of that it would be necessary to follow a trail for four leagues, and to pass over a river which empties on the coast of the Almouchiquois, near the coast of Norumbegue; and that it was only two days journey by their canoes, as I have [also] learned since from some prisoners that we took, who described to me very much in detail all that they had found out themselves about the matter through some Algonquin interpreters who knew the Iroquois language.

Now, as we began to approach within two or three days' journey of the home of their enemies, we did not advance more, except at night, and by day we rested. Nevertheless, they did not omit, at any time, the practice of their customary superstitions, to find out how much of their undertakings would succeed, and they often came to me to ask if I had dreamed, and if I had seen their enemies. I answered them "no," and told them to be of good courage and to keep up hope. When night came we pursued our journey until daylight, when we withdrew into the thickest part of the woods and passed the rest of the day there. About ten or eleven o'clock, after having taken a little walk around our encampment, I went to rest; and I dreamed that I saw the Iroquois, our enemies, in the lake, near a mountain, drowning within our sight; and when I wished to help them our savage allies told me that we must let them all die, and that they were worthless. When I woke up they did not fail to ask me, as is their custom, if I had dreamed anything. I told them the substance of what I had dreamed. This gave them so much faith that they no longer doubted that good was to befall them.

When evening came we embarked in our canoes to continue on our way; and, as we were going along very quietly, and without making any noise, on the twenty-ninth of the month, we met the Iroquois at ten o'clock at night at the end of a cape that projects into the lake on the west side, and they were coming to war. We both began to make loud cries, each getting his arms ready. We withdrew toward the water and the Iroquois went ashore and arranged their canoes in line, and began to cut down trees with poor axes, which they get in war sometimes, and also with others of stone; and they barricaded themselves very well.

Our men also passed the whole night with their canoes drawn up close together, fastened to poles, so that they might not get scattered, and might fight all together, if there were need of it; we were on the water within arrow range of the side where their barricades were.

When they were armed and in array, they sent two canoes set apart from the others to learn from their enemies if they wanted to fight. They replied that they desired nothing else; but that, at the moment, there was not much light and that they must wait for the daylight to recognize each other, and that as soon as the sun rose they would open the battle. This was accepted by our men; and while we waited, the whole night was passed in dances and songs, as much on one side as on the other, with endless insults, and other talk, such as the little courage they had, their feebleness and inability to make resistance against their arms, and that when day came they should feel it to their ruin. Our men also were not lacking in retort, telling them that they should see such power of arms as never before; and much other talk, as is customary in the siege of a city. After plenty of singing, dancing, and parleying with one another, daylight came. My companions and I remained concealed for fear that the enemy should see us, preparing our arms the best that we could, separated, however, each in one of the canoes of the Montagnais savages. After arming ourselves with light armor, each of us took an arquebuse and went ashore. I saw the enemy come out of their barricade, nearly 200 men, strong and robust to look at, coming slowly toward us with a dignity and assurance that pleased me very much. At their head there were three chiefs. Our men also went forth in the same order, and they told me that those who wore three large plumes were the chiefs; and that there were only three of them; and that they were recognizable by these plumes, which were a great deal larger than those of their companions; and that I should do all I could to kill them. I promised them to do all in my power, and said that I was very sorry that they could not understand me well, so that I might give order and system to their attack of the enemy, in which case we should undoubtedly destroy them all; but that this could not be remedied; that I was very glad to encourage them and to show them the good-will that I felt, when we should engage in battle.

As soon as we were ashore they began to run about 200 paces toward their enemy, who were standing firmly and had not yet noticed my companions, who went into the woods with some savages. Our men began to call me with loud cries; and, to give me a passageway, they divided into two parts a;ul put me at their head, where I marched about twenty paces in front of them until I was thirty paces from the enemy. They at once saw me and halted, looking at me, and I at them. When I saw them making a move to shoot at us, I rested my arquebuse against my cheek and aimed directly at one of the three chiefs. With the same shot two of them fell to the ground, and one of their companions, who was wounded and afterward died. I put four balls into my arquebuse. When our men saw this shot so favorable for them, they began to make cries so loud that one could not have heard it thunder. Meanwhile the arrows did not fail to fly from both sides. The Iroquois were much astonished that two men had been so quickly killed, although they were provided with armor woven from cotton thread and from wood, proof against their arrows. This alarmed them greatly. As I was loading again, one of my companions fired a shot from the woods, which astonished them again to such a degree that, seeing their chiefs dead, they lost courage, took to flight and abandoned the field and their fort, fleeing into the depths of the woods. Pursuing them thither I killed some more of them. Our savages also killed several of them and took ten or twelve of them prisoners. The rest escaped with the wounded. There were fifteen or sixteen of our men wounded by arrow shots, who were soon healed.

After we had gained the victory they amused themselves by taking a great quantity of Indian corn and meal from their enemies, and also their arms, which they had left in order to run better. And having made good cheer, danced and sung, we returned three hours afterward with the prisoners.

This place, where this charge was made, is in latitude 43 degrees and some minutes, and I named the lake Lake Champlain.

Chapter X

Return from the battle, and what happened on the way.

After going eight leagues, toward evening they took one of the prisoners and harangued him about the cruelties that he and his people had inflicted on them, without having any consideration for them; and said that similarly he ought to make up his mind to receive as much. They commanded him to sing, if he had any courage; which he did, but it was a song very sad to hear.

Meanwhile our men lighted a fire, and when it was blazing well, each one took a brand and burned this poor wretch little by little, to make him suffer greater torment. Sometimes they stopped and threw water on his back. Then they tore out his nails and put the fire on the ends of his fingers and on his privy member. Afterward they flayed the top of his head and dripped on top of it a kind of gum all hot; then they pierced his arms near the wrists, and with sticks pulled the sinews, and tore them out by force; and when they saw that they could not get them, they cut them. This poor wretch uttered strange cries, and I pitied him when I saw him treated in this way; and yet he showed such endurance that one would have said that, at times, he did not feel any pain.

They strongly urged me to take some fire and do as they were doing, but I explained to them that we did not use such cruelties at all, and that we killed them at once, and that if they wished me to fire a musket shot at him I would do it gladly. They said "no," and that he would not feel any pain. I went away from them, distressed to see so much cruelty as they were practising upon this body. When they saw that I was not pleased at it, they called me and told me to fire a musket shot at him; which I did without his seeing it at all. After he was dead they were not satisfied, for they opened his belly and threw his entrails into the lake; then they cut off his head, his arms, and his legs, which they scattered in different directions, and kept the scalp, which they had skinned off, as they had done with all the others that they had killed in the battle.

They committed also another wickedness, which was to take the heart, which they cut into several pieces and gave to a brother of his and others of his companions, who were prisoners, to eat. They put it into their mouths, but would not swallow it. Some Algonquin savages, who were guarding them, made some of them spit it out and threw it into the water. This is how these people treat those whom they capture in war; and it would be better for them to die in fighting, or to kill themselves on the spur of the moment, as there are many who do, rather than fall into the hands of their enemies. After this execution we resumed our march to return with the rest of the prisoners, who always went along singing, without any hope of being better treated than the other. When we arrived at the rapids of the River of the Iroquois, the Algonquins returned to their country, and also the

Ochateguins with some of the prisoners. They were well pleased with what had taken place in the war, and that I had gone with them readily. So we separated with great protestations of friendship, and they asked me if I did not wish to go into their country to aid them always as a brother. I promised that I would do so, and I returned with the Montagnais.

After informing myself, through the prisoners, about their country, and about how large it might be, we packed up the baggage to return; which we did with such speed that every day we made 25 or 30 leagues in their canoes, which is the ordinary rate. When we were at the mouth of the River Iroquois, there were some of the savages who dreamed that their enemies were pursuing them. This dream at once led them to move the camp, although the night was very bad on account of winds and rain; and they went to pass the night among some high reeds, which are in Lake St. Peter, until the next day. Two days afterward we reached our settlement, where I had them given bread, peas and beads, which they asked me for to ornament the heads of their enemies, in order to make merry on their arrival. The next day I went with them in their canoes to Tadoussac, to see their ceremonies. As they approached the shore each one took a stick with the heads of their enemies hung on the ends, with these beads on them, singing one and all. When they were near the shore the women undressed entirely naked and threw themselves into the water, going in front of the canoes, to take the heads to hang afterward to their necks, like a precious chain. Some days afterward they made me a present of one of these heads and of two sets of their enemies' weapons, to preserve, in order to show them to the King; which I promised to do, to give them pleasure.

1.7.2 Reading and Review Questions

1. According to what criteria does Champlain value/evaluate New France? How do his criteria compare with those of John Smith?
2. Why, and to what effect, does Champlain allude to Old World/European examples of successful colonization of places that at first seemed to promise little success ie Venice, Genoa, Marseilles?
3. What cultural adaptations, if any, does Champlain foresee for Frenchmen who cultivate/colonize New France?
4. Why do you think Champlain extolls converting Canadian Indians to Christianity as the true virtue of kings?
5. What attitude does Champlain take to the Canadian Indians' culture(s)? Why? How do you know? How does his attitude compare with that of de Vaca or Smith? Why and to what effect does Champlain detail the torturing of a Mohawk Iroquois prisoner of war by the Montagnais (with whom Champlain fought)?

1.8 JOHN SMITH

(1580–1657)

Born into a farming family in Lincolnshire, John Smith early on sought a more adventurous life. At the age of sixteen, he joined in the (Protestant) Dutch War of Independence from the (Catholic) Philip II of Spain. He next saw action in the Mediterranean and in the Austrian war against the Turks. His service in this war earned him the rank of Captain. Wounded in battle and captured by the Turks, Smith escaped slavery by assassinating his owner and fleeing to Eastern Europe. He eventually returned to England in 1604.

Image 1.10 | Captain John Smith
Artist | Unknown
Source | Wikimedia Commons
License | Public Domain

Smith's military experience led to his being appointed to the ruling council of the Virginia Company, a company of investors who supported colonizing efforts in North America. Himself somewhat unruly and bad-tempered, Smith was placed under arrest on the voyage over and was even threatened with execution. Once having reached their destination, Smith took his place on the governing council and became governor of the colony in 1607. Although active in maintaining the settlement, especially in the face of sickness and starvation, Smith made extensive explorations of Virginia.

Image 1.11 | Pocahontas
Artist | Unknown
Source | Wikimedia Commons
License | Public Domain

During one of these exploratory treks, Smith was captured by the Chesapeake Bay Indians, then ruled by Powhatan (1545–1618) whose daughter Pocahontas (d. 1617) saved Smith from execution. He was almost executed by the Jamestown colonists for the death of two of his soldiers but escaped punishment upon the arrival of a much-needed supply ship. After suffering injury from an accidental explosion of gunpowder, Smith returned to England. There he wrote of his experiences and explorations of Virginia and New England in terms that captivated the imagination of future settlers. His own imagination may have colored many of the events he detailed, including his famous encounter with Pocahontas, an encounter that many modern-day historians doubt ever occurred.

The Generall Historie of Virginia, New-England, and the Summer Isles (1624) compiled previously-published accounts with Smith's own writing. In it, he offered lavish details of the land's bountiful resources, countered biased views of Native Americans as simple savages and nomads by describing the Powhatan confederacy, and advocated strong leaders and leadership for maintaining colonies.

1.8.1 From *The Generall Historie of Virginia, New-England, and the Summer Isles*

(1624)

Third Book

Chapter 2

Being thus left to our fortunes, it fortuned that within ten dayes scarce ten amongst vs could either goe, or well stand, such extreame weaknes and sicknes oppressed vs. And thereat none need marvaile, if they consider the cause and reason, which was this; whilest the ships stayed, our allowance was somewhat bettered, by a daily proportion of Bisket, which the sailers would pilfer to sell, giue, or exchange with vs, for money, Saxefras, furres, or loue. But when they departed, there remained neither taverne, beere-house, nor place of reliefe, but the common Kettell. Had we beene as free from all sinnes as gluttony, and drunkennesse, we might haue beene canonized for Saints; But our President would never haue beene admitted, for ingrossing to his private, Oatmeale, Sacke, Oyle, *Aquavitæ*, Beefe, Egges, or what not, but the Kettell; that indeed he allowed equally to be distributed, and that was halfe a pint of wheat, and as much barley boyled with water for a man a day, and this having fryed some 26. weekes in the ships hold, contained as many wormes as graines; so that we might truely call it rather so much bran then corne, our drinke was water, our lodgings Castles in the ayre: with this lodging and dyet, our extreame toile in bearing and planting Pallisadoes, so strained and bruised vs, and our continuall labour in the extremitie of the heat had so weakned vs, as were cause sufficient to haue made vs as miserable in our natiue Countrey, or any other place in the world. From May, to September, those that escaped, liued vpon Sturgeon, and Sea-crabs, fiftie in this time we buried, the rest seeing the Presidents proiects to escape these miseries in our Pinnace by flight (who all this time had neither felt want nor sicknes) so moved our dead spirits, as we deposed him; and established *Ratcliffe* in his place, (Gosnoll being dead) *Kendall* deposed, *Smith* newly recovered, *Martin* and *Ratcliffe* was by his care preserved and relieued, and the most of the souldiers recovered, with the skilfull diligence of Mr *Thomas Wotton* our Chirurgian generall. But now was all our provision spent, the Sturgeon gone, all helps abandoned, each houre expecting the fury of the Salvages; when

God the patron of all good indevours, in that desperate extremitie so changed the hearts of the Salvages, that they brought such plenty of their fruits, and provision, as no man wanted.

And now where some affirmed it was ill done of the Councell to send forth men so badly provided, this incontradictable reason will shew them plainely they are too ill advised to nourish such ill conceits; first, the fault of our going was our owne, what could be thought fitting or necessary we had, but what we should find, or want, or where we should be, we were all ignorant, and supposing to make our passage in two moneths, with victuall to liue, and the advantage of the spring to worke; we were at Sea fiue moneths, where we both spent our victuall and lost the opportunitie of the time, and season to plant, by the vnskilfull presumption of our ignorant transporters, that vnderstood not at all, what they vndertooke.

Such actions haue ever since the worlds beginning beene subiect to such accidents, and every thing of worth is found full of difficulties, but nothing so difficult as to establish a Common-wealth so farre remote from men and meanes, and where mens mindes are so vntoward as neither doe well themselues, nor suffer others. But to proceed.

The new President and *Martin*, being little beloved, of weake iudgement in dangers, and lesse industrie in peace, committed the managing of all things abroad to Captaine *Smith*: who by his owne example, good words, and faire promises, set some to mow, others to binde thatch, some to build houses, others to thatch them, himselfe alwayes bearing the greatest taske for his owne share, so that in short time, he provided most of them lodgings, neglecting any for himselfe. This done, seeing the Salvages superfluitie beginne to decrease (with some of his workemen) shipped himselfe in the Shallop to search the Country for trade. The want of the language, knowledge to mannage his boat without sailes, the want of a sufficient power, (knowing the multitude of the Salvages) apparell for his men, and other necessaries, were infinite impediments, yet no discouragement. Being but six or seauen in company he went downe the river to *Kecoughtan*, where at first they scorned him, as a famished man, and would in derision offer him a handfull of Corne, a peece of bread, for their swords and muskets, and such like proportions also for their apparell. But seeing by trade and courtesie there was nothing to be had, he made bold to try such conclusions as necessitie inforced, though contrary to his Commission: Let fly his muskets, ran his boat on shore, whereat they all fled into the woods. So marching towards their houses, they might see great heapes of corne: much adoe he had to restraine his hungry souldiers from present taking of it, expecting as it hapned that the Salvages would assault them, as not long after they did with a most hydeous noyse. Sixtie or seaventie of them, some blacke, some red, some white, some party-coloured, came in a square order, singing and dauncing out of the woods, with their Okee (which was an Idoll made of skinnes, stuffed with mosse, all painted and hung with chaines and copper) borne before them: and in this manner being well armed, with Clubs, Targets, Bowes and Arrowes, they charged the English, that so kindly receiued them with their muskets loaden with

Pistoll shot, that downe fell their God, and divers lay sprauling on the ground; the rest fled againe to the woods, and ere long sent one of their *Quiyoughkasoucks* to offer peace, and redeeme their *Okee*. *Smith*told them, if onely six of them would come vnarmed and loade his boat, he would not only be their friend, but restore them their *Okee*, and giue them Beads, Copper, and Hatchets besides: which on both sides was to their contents performed: and then they brought him Venison, Turkies, wild foule, bread, and what they had, singing and dauncing in signe of friendship till they departed. In his returne he discovered the Towne and Country of *Warraskoyack*.

Thus God vnboundlesse by his power,
Made them thus kind, would vs deuour.

Smith perceiving (notwithstanding their late miserie) not any regarded but from hand to mouth (the company being well recovered) caused the Pinnace to be provided with things fitting to get provision for the yeare following; but in the interim he made 3. or 4. iournies and discovered the people of Chickahamania: yet what he carefully provided the rest carelesly spent Wingfield and *Kendall* liuing in disgrace, seeing all things at randome in the absence of *Smith*, the companies dislike of their Presidents weaknes, and their small loue to *Martins* never mending sicknes, strengthened themselues with the sailers, and other confederates to regaine their former credit and authority, or at least such meanes abord the Pinnace, (being fitted to saile as *Smith* had appointed for trade) to alter her course and to goe for *England*. *Smith* vnexpectedly returning had the plot discovered to him, much trouble he had to prevent it, till with store of sakre and musket shot he forced them stay or sinke in the riuer, which action cost the life of captaine *Kendall*. These brawles are so disgustfull, as some will say they were better forgotten, yet all men of good iudgement will conclude, it were better their basenes should be manifest to the world, then the busines beare the scorne and shame of their excused disorders. The President and captaine *Archer* not long after intended also to haue abandoned the country, which proiect also was curbed, and suppressed by *Smith*. The *Spaniard* never more greedily desired gold then he victuall, nor his souldiers more to abandon the Country, then he to keepe it. But finding plentie of Corne in the riuer of *Chickahamania* where hundreds of Salvages in diuers places stood with baskets expecting his comming. And now the winter approaching, the rivers became so covered with swans, geese, duckes, and cranes, that we daily feasted with good bread, Virginia pease, pumpions, and putchamins, fish, fowle, and diverse sorts of wild beasts as fat as we could eate them: so that none of our Tuftaffaty humorists desired to goe for *England*. But our *Comœdies* never endured long without a *Tragedie;* some idle exceptions being muttered against Captaine *Smith*, for not discovering the head of *Chickahamania* river, and taxed by the Councell, to be too slow in so worthy an attempt. The next voyage hee proceeded so farre that with much labour by cutting of trees in sunder he made his passage, but when his Barge could passe no farther, he left her in a broad bay out of danger of shot, commanding none should goe a shore till his returne: himselfe with two English and two Salvages went vp higher in a Canowe, but hee was not long absent, but his men went a shore, whose want of government, gaue both occasion and opportunity to the Salvages to surprise one *George Cassen*, whom they slew, and much failed not to haue cut of the boat and all the rest. *Smith* little dreaming of that accident, being got to the marshes at the rivers head, twentie myles in the desert, had his two men slaine (as is supposed) sleeping by the Canowe, whilst himselfe by fowling sought them victuall, who finding he was beset with 200. Salvages, two of them hee slew, still defending himselfe with the ayd of a Salvage his guid, whom he bound to his arme with his garters, and vsed him as a buckler, yet he was shot in his thigh a little, and had many arrowes that stucke in his cloathes but no great hurt, till at last they tooke him prisoner. When this newes came to *Iames* towne, much was their sorrow for his losse, fewe expecting what ensued. Sixe or seuen weekes those Barbarians kept him prisoner, many strange triumphes and coniurations they made of him, yet hee so demeaned himselfe amongst them, as he not onely diverted them from surprising the Fort, but procured his owne libertie, and got himselfe and his company such estimation amongst them, that those Salvages admired him more then their owne *Quiyouckosucks*. The manner how they vsed and deliuered him, is as followeth.

The Salvages hauing drawne from *George Cassen* whether Captaine *Smith* was gone, prosecuting that oportunity they followed him with. 300. bowmen, conducted by the King of Pamavnkee, who in diuisions searching the turnings of the riuer, found *Robinson*and *Emry* by the fire side, those they shot full of arrowes and slew. Then finding the Captaine, as is said, that vsed the Salvage that was his guide as his sheld (three of them being slaine and diuers other so gauld) all the rest would not come neere him. Thinking thus to haue returned to his boat, regarding them, as he marched, more then his way, slipped vp to the middle in an oasie creeke & his Salvage with him, yet durst they not come to him till being neere dead with cold, he threw away his armes. Then according to their composition they drew him forth and led him to the fire, where his men were slaine. Diligently they chafed his benummed limbs. He demanding for their Captaine, they shewed him Opechankanough, King of *Pamavnkee*, to whom he gaue a round Ivory double compass Dyall. Much they marvailed at the playing of the Fly and Needle, which they could see so plainely, and yet not touch it, because of the glasse that covered them. But when he demonstrated by that Globe-like Iewell, the roundnesse of the earth, and skies, the spheare of the Sunne, Moone, and Starres, and how the Sunne did chase the night round about the world continually; the greatnesse of the Land and Sea, the diversitie of Nations, varietie of complexions, and how we were to them *Antipodes*, and many other such like matters, they all stood as amazed with admiration. Notwithstanding, within an houre after they tyed him to a tree, and as many as could stand about him prepared to shoot him, but the King holding vp the Compass in his hand, they all laid downe their Bowes and Arrowes, and in a triumphant manner led him to *Orapaks*, where he was after their manner kindly feasted, and well vsed.

Their order in conducting him was thus; Drawing themselues all in fyle, the King in the middest had all their Peeces and Swords borne before him. Captaine *Smith* was led after him by three great Salvages, holding him fast by each arme: and on each side six went in fyle with their Arrowes nocked. But arriving at the Towne (which was but onely thirtie or fortie hunting houses made of Mats, which they remoue as they please, as we our tents) all the women and children staring to behold him, the souldiers first all in fyle performed the forme of a *Bissom* so well as could be; and on each flanke, officers as Serieants to see them keepe their order. A good time they continued this exercise, and then cast themselues in a ring, dauncing in such severall Postures, and singing and yelling out such hellish notes and screeches; being strangely painted, every one his quiver of Arrowes, and at his backe a club; on his arme a Fox or an Otters skinne, or some such matter for his vambrace; their heads and shoulders painted red, with Oyle and *Pocones* mingled together, which Scarlet-like colour made an exceeding handsome shew; his Bow in his hand, and the skinne of a Bird with her wings abroad dryed, tyed on his head, a peece of copper, a white shell, a long feather, with a small rattle growing at the tayles of their snaks tyed to it, or some such like toy. All this while *Smith* and the King stood in the middest guarded, as before is said, and after three dances they all departed. *Smith* they conducted to a long house, where thirtie or fortie tall fellowes did guard him, and ere long more bread and venison was brought him then would haue served twentie men, I thinke his stomacke at that time was not very good; what he left they put in baskets and tyed over his head. About midnight they set the meate againe before him, all this time not one of them would eate a bit with him, till the next morning they brought him as much more, and then did they eate all the old, & reserved the new as they had done the other, which made him thinke they would fat him to eat him. Yet in this desperate estate to defend him from the cold, one *Maocassater* brought him his gowne, in requitall of some beads and toyes *Smith* had given him at his first arrivall in *Virginia*.

Two dayes after a man would haue slaine him (but that the guard prevented it) for the death of his sonne, to whom they conducted him to recover the poore man then breathing his last. *Smith* told them that at *Iames* towne he had a water would doe it, if they would let him fetch it, but they would not permit that; but made all the preparations they could to assault *Iames* towne, crauing his advice, and for recompence he should haue life, libertie, land, and women. In part of a Table booke he writ his minde to them at the Fort, what was intended, how they should follow that direction to affright the messengers, and without fayle send him such things as he writ for. And an Inventory with them. The difficultie and danger, he told the Salvages, of the Mines, great gunnes, and other Engins exceedingly affrighted them, yet according to his request they went to *Iames* towne, in as bitter weather as could be of frost and snow, and within three dayes returned with an answer.

But when they came to *Iame* towne, seeing men sally out as he had told them they would, they fled; yet in the night they came againe to the same place where he had told them they should receiue an answer, and such things as he had promised them, which they found accordingly, and with which they returned with no small expedition, to the wonder of them all that heard it, that he could either divine, or the paper could speake: then they led him to the *Youthtanunds*, the Mattapanients, the *Payankatanks*, the *Nantaughtacunds*, and *Onawmanients* vpon the rivers of *Rapahanock*, and *Patawomek*, over all those rivers, and backe againe by divers other severall Nations, to the Kings habitation at *Pamavnkee*, where they entertained him with most strange and fearefull Coniurations;

As if neare led to hell,
Amongst the Devils to dwell.

Not long after, early in a morning a great fire was made in a long house, and a mat spread on the one side, as on the other, on the one they caused him to sit, and all the guard went out of the house, and presently came skipping in a great grim fellow, all painted over with coale, mingled with oyle; and many Snakes and Wesels skins stuffed with mosse, and all their tayles tyed together, so as they met on the crowne of his head in a tassell; and round about the tassell was as a Coronet of feathers, the skins hanging round about his head, backe, and shoulders, and in a manner covered his face; with a hellish voyce and a rattle in his hand. With most strange gestures and passions he began his invocation, and environed the fire with a circle of meale; which done, three more such like devils came rushing in with the like antique tricks, painted halfe blacke, halfe red: but all their eyes were painted white, and some red stroakes like Mutchato's, along their cheekes: round about him those fiends daunced a pretty while, and then came in three more as vgly as the rest; with red eyes, and white stroakes over their blacke faces, at last they all sat downe right against him; three of them on the one hand of the chiefe Priest, and three on the other. Then all with their rattles began a song, which ended, the chiefe Priest layd downe fiue wheat cornes: then strayning his armes and hands with such violence that he sweat, and his veynes swelled, he began a short Oration: at the conclusion they all gaue a short groane; and then layd down three graines more. After that, began their song againe, and then another Oration, ever laying downe so many cornes as before, till they had twice incirculed the fire; that done, they tooke a bunch of little stickes prepared for that purpose, continuing still their devotion, and at the end of every song and Oration, they layd downe a sticke betwixt the divisions of Corne. Till night, neither he nor they did either eate or drinke, and then they feasted merrily, with the best provisions they could make. Three dayes they vsed this Ceremony; the meaning whereof they told him, was to know if he intended them well or no. The circle of meale signified their Country, the circles of corne the bounds of the Sea, and the stickes his Country. They imagined the world to be flat and round, like a trencher, and they in the middest. After this they brought him a bagge of gunpowder, which they carefully preferved till the next spring, to plant as they did their corne; because they would be acquainted with the nature of that seede. *Opitchapam* the Kings brother invited him to his house, where, with as many platters of bread, foule, and wild beasts, as did environ him, he bid him wellcome; but not any of them would eate a bit with him, but put vp all the remainder in Baskets. At his returne to *Opechancanoughs*, all the Kings women, and their children, flocked about him for their parts, as a due by Custome, to be merry with such fragments.

But his waking mind in hydeous dreames did oft see wondrous shapes,
Of bodies strange, and huge in growth, and of stupendious makes.

At last they brought him to Meronocomoco, where was Powhatan their Emperor. Here more then two hundred of those grim Courtiers stood wondering at him, as he had beene a monster; till *Powhatan* and his trayne had put themselues in their greatest braveries. Before a fire vpon a seat like a bedsted, he sat covered with a great robe, made of *Rarowcun* skinnes, and all the tayles hanging by. On either hand did sit a young wench of 16 to 18 yeares, and along on each side the house, two rowes of men, and behind them as many women, with all their heads and shoulders painted red; many of their heads bedecked with the white downe of Birds; but every one with something: and a great chayne of white beads about their necks. At his entrance before the King, all the people gaue a great shout. The Queene of *Appamatuck* was appointed to bring him water to wash his hands, and another brought him a bunch of feathers, in stead of a Towell to dry them: having feasted him after their best barbarous manner they could, a long consultation was held, but the conclusion was, two great stones were brought before *Powhatan*: then as many as could layd hands on him, dragged him to them, and thereon laid his head, and being ready with their clubs, to beate out his braines, *Pocahontas* the Kings dearest daughter, when no intreaty could prevaile, got his head in her armes, and laid her owne vpon his to saue him from death: whereat the Emperour was contented he should liue to make him hatchets, and her bells, beads, and copper; for they thought him as well of all occupations as themselues. For the King himselfe will make his owne robes, shooes, bowes, arrowes, pots; plant, hunt, or doe any thing so well as the rest.

They say he bore a pleasant shew
But sure his heart was sad.
For who can pleasant be, and rest
That liues in feare and dread
And having life suspected, doth
It still suspected lead.

Two dayes after, *Powhatan* having disguised himselfe in the most fearefullest manner he could, caused Capt *Smith* to be brought forth to a great house in the woods, and there vpon a mat by the fire to be left alone. Not long after from behinde a mat that divided the house, was made the most dolefullest noyse he ever heard; then *Powhatan* more like a devill then a man with some two hundred more as blacke as himselfe, came vnto him and told him now they were friends, and presently he should goe to *Iames* towne, to send him two great gunnes, and a gryndstone, for which he would giue him the Country of *Capahowosick*, and for ever esteeme him as his sonne *Nantaquoud*. So to *Iames* towne with 12 guides *Powhatan* sent him. That night they quarterd in the woods, he still expecting (as he had done all this long time of his imprisonment) every houre to be put to one death or other: for all their feasting. But almightie God (by his divine providence) had mollified the hearts of those sterne *Barbarians* with compassion. The next morning betimes they came to the Fort, where *Smith* having vsed the Salvages with what kindnesse he could, he shewed *Rawhunt, Powhatans* trusty servant two demi-Culverings & a millstone to carry *Powhatan*: they found them somewhat too heavie; but when they did see him discharge them, being loaded with stones, among the boughs of a great tree loaded with Isickles, the yce and branches came so tumbling downe, that the poore Salvages ran away halfe dead with feare. But at last we regained some conference with them, and gaue them such toyes; and sent to *Powhatan*, his women, and children such presents, as gaue them in generall full content. Now in *Iames* Towne they were all in combustion, the strongest preparing once more to run away with the Pinnace; which with the hazzard of his life, with Sakrefalcon and musket shot, *Smith* forced now the third time to stay or sinke. Some no better then they should be, had plotted with the President, the next day to haue put him to death by the Leviticall law, for the liues of *Robinson* and *Emry*, pretending the fault was his that had led them to their ends: but he quickly tooke such order with such Lawyers, that he layd them by the heeles till he sent some of them prisoners for *England*. Now ever once in foure or fiue dayes, *Pocahontas* with her attendants, brought him so much provision, that saved many of their liues, that els for all this had starved with hunger.

Thus from numbe death our good God sent reliefe,
The sweete asswager of all other griefe.

His relation of the plenty he had seene, especially at *Werawocomoco*, and of the state and bountie of *Powhatan*, (which till that time was vnknowne) so revived their dead spirits (especially the loue of *Pocahontas*) as all mens feare was abandoned. Thus you may see what difficulties still crossed any good indevour: and the good successe of the businesse being thus oft brought to the very period of destruction; yet you see by what strange means God hath still delivered it. As for the insufficiency of them admitted in Commission, that error could not be prevented by the Electors; there being no other choise, and all strangers to each others education, qualities, or disposition. And if any deeme it a shame to our Nation to haue any mention made of those inormities, let them pervse the Histories of the

Spanyards Discoveries and Plantations, where they may see how many mutinies, disorders, and dissentions haue accompanied them, and crossed their attempts: which being knowne to be particular mens offences; doth take away the generall scorne and contempt, which malice, presumption, covetousnesse, or ignorance might produce; to the scandall and reproach of those, whose actions and valiant resolutions deserue a more worthy respect.

Now whether it had beene better for Captaine *Smith,* to haue concluded with any of those severall proiects, to haue abandoned the Countrey, with some ten or twelue of them, who were called the better sort, and haue left Mr *Hunt* our Preacher, Master *Anthony Gosnoll,* a most honest, worthy, and industrious Gentleman, Master *Thomas Wotton,* and some 27 others of his Countrymen to the fury of the Salvages, famine, and all manner of mischiefes, and inconveniences, (for they were but fortie in all to keepe possession of this large Country;) or starue himselfe with them for company, for want of lodging: or but adventuring abroad to make them provision, or by his opposition to preserue the action, and saue all their liues; I leaue to the censure of all honest men to consider. But

We men imagine in our Iolitie
That 'tis all one, or good or bad to be.
But then anone wee alter this againe
If happily wee feele the sence of paine;
For then we're turn'd into a mourning vaine.

1.8.2 Reading and Review Questions

1. How does Smith's account of his experiences in the New World compare with the descriptions and assumptions of Columbus, Cabeza de Vaca, or Harriot?
2. What grounds Smith's assessment of events that he recounts, events like the men's starving at the settlement? Does he ground his assessment in cause and effect? In Providence? Why, either way, do you think?
3. Compare the way the Native Americans treat Smith after capturing him with the way his own men treat him before he leaves to follow the Council's bidding. What, if anything, causes the differences, do you think?
4. How does Smith use scientific knowledge against the Native Americans or for his own defense? Why?
5. What introduction, if any, does Smith give to Pocahontas? Why? What purpose lies behind Smith's probably inventing his rescue by Pocahontas? What role, if any, does it play in legitimizing a cultural as well as military conquest?

1.9 ADRIAEN VAN DER DONCK

(1618–1655)

Image 1.12 | Presumed Portrait of Adriaen van der Donck
Artist | Unknown
Source | Wikimedia Commons
License | Public Domain

Adriaen van der Donck was born in Breda, Netherlands. His maternal grandfather, Adrian van Bergen took part in the Eighty Years' War against Spain and helped capture the city of Breda in 1590. Starting in 1638, van der Donck attended the University of Leiden, where he studied law, earning a degree in both civil and canon law.

Van der Donck's interest in the New World led him to obtain a post as *schout*, a sheriff and prosecutor, from Kiliaen van Rensselaer, who owned territory near what is now Albany. He later worked for the Dutch West India Company. As a reward for negotiating peace with American Indian tribes, the Dutch West India Company gifted van der Donck land north of what is now the island of Manhattan. There, he became known as the Gentleman, or *Jonker* in Dutch, from which the modern day Yonkers derives.

He worked as administrator to Peter Stuyvesant and was appointed to the Council of Nine, New Amsterdam's governing body. His petitioning for democratic reform in the colony won him the ire of Peter Stuyvesant, who briefly jailed van der Donck. Van der Donck returned to the Netherlands, where he continued to petition the Dutch government for democratic reform. He also wrote *A Description of New Netherland, the Country*. He returned to America in 1653 and lived on his estate until his death in 1655.

1.9.1 From *A Description of New Netherland, the Country*

Where, and by whom, New-Netherlands was first discovered.

This country was first found and discovered in the year of our Lord 1609; when, at the cost of the incorporated East India Company, a ship named the Half-Moon was fitted out to discover a westerly passage to the kingdom of China. This ship was commanded by Hendrick Hudson, as captain and supercargo, who was an Englishman by birth, and had resided many years in Holland, during which he had been in the employment of the East India Company. This ship sailed from the Canary Islands, steering a course north by west; and, after sailing twenty days with good speed, land was discovered, which, by their calculation, lay 320 degrees by west. On approaching the land, and observing the coast and shore convenient, they landed, and examined the country as well as they could at the time, and as opportunity offered; from which they were well satisfied that no Christian people had ever been there before, and that they were the first who by Providence had been guided to the discovery of the country.

The Netherlanders the First Possessors of New-Netherland.

Although the possession and title which the Netherlanders have to New-Netherlands are amply treated of in their length and breadth, in the *Representation of the Commonalty*, and little more can be said in relation to them unless access be had to the Registers of the Honorable West India Company, we will nevertheless, touch upon them briefly, *en passant*. When this country was first discovered by the Netherlanders in the year 1609, and it was told them by the natives that they were the first Christian explorers in that region, they took possession of it in the name and on behalf of their High Mightinesses, the Lords of the States-General of the United Netherlands, first in the South Bay at Cape *Hinloopen*, which they so called at that time, and which still retains that name; and so all along the coast and up the rivers, giving names to the different places as far as the great North River, a great distance up which they sailed, and which some of the English will still call Hudson's River, but which was then named *Mauritius* River after Prince Maurice, who at that time was governor in Netherland; from whence they sailed further along till they went beyond Cape Cod, of which they also took possession, and which they named New Holland. And our Netherlanders have sailed there and traded at the same places thus taken into possession from time to time since then, until the charter was granted to the West Indian Company, when they passed under its jurisdiction. And although before we had there in our favor the circumstances of fifty families and cattle, yet since the year 1622 several forts have been built, farms and plantations taken up, much of the land bought of the natives, and then tokens of possession shown as is to be seen at length in the *Representation of the Commonalty of New-Netherland*, to which we refer the curious reader. It is therefore unusual, unhandsome, and unreasonable for any other nation to assert title or jurisdiction over these places or over those situated between such as were first discovered by the Netherlanders.

Of Agricultural Production

The pursuit of agriculture is not heavy and expensive there, as it is in the Netherlands. First, because the fencing and enclosing of the land does not cost much; for, instead of the Netherlands dykes and ditches, they set up post and rail, or palisado fences, and when new clearings are made, they commonly have fencing timber enough on the land to remove, which costs nothing but the labour, which is reasonably cheap to those who have their own hands, and without domestic labour very little can be effected. The land whereon there are few standing trees, and which has been grubbed and ploughed twice, we hold to be prepared for a crop of winter grain. For summer grain one ploughing is sufficient. If it is intended to sow the same field again with winter grain, then the stubble is ploughed in, and the land is sowed with wheat or rye, which in ordinary seasons will yield a fine crop.

I can affirm that during my residence of nine years in the country I have never seen land manured, and it is seldom done. The land is kept in order by tillage, which is often done to keep down weeds and brush, but for which it would have rest. Some persons (which I also hold to be good management), when their land becomes foul and weedy, break it up and sow the same with peas, because a crop of peas softens the land and makes it clean; but most of the land is too rich for peas, which when sown on the same grow so rank that the crop falls and rots on the land. Some of the land must be reduced by cropping it with wheat and barley, before it is proper to sow the same with peas. We have frequently seen the straw of wheat and barley grow so luxuriant that the crops yielded very little grain.

I deem it worthy of notice that with proper attention, in ordinary seasons, two ripe crops of peas can be raised on the same land in one season, in the New-Netherlands. It has frequently been done in the following manner, viz. The first crop was sown in the last of March or first of April, which will ripen about the first of July; the crop is then removed, and the land ploughed, and sowed again with peas of the first crop. The second crop will ripen in September, or about the first of October, when the weather is still fine and warm. The same can also be done with buckwheat, which has frequently been proved; but the first crop is usually much injured by finches and other birds, and, as wheat and rye are plenty, therefore there is very little buckwheat sown. The maize (Indian corn) is carefully attended to, and is sufficient to the wants of the country.

The Turkey wheat, or maize, as the grain is named, many persons suppose to be the same kind of grain which Jesse sent parched by his son David to his other sons of the army of Israel. This is a hardy grain, and is fit for the sustenance of man and animals. It is easily cultivated and will grow in almost every kind of land . . . . After a corn crop is gathered, the land may be sowed with winter grain in the fall without previous ploughing. When this is intended, the corn is gathered, the stalks are pulled up and burnt, the hills levelled, and the land sown and harrowed smooth and level. Good crops are raised in this manner. I have seen rye sown as before described, which grew so tall that a man of common size would bind the ears together above his head, which yielded seven and eight *schepels*, Amsterdam measure, per *vin* of 108 sheaves, of which two *vins* made a wagon load.

The Rev. Johannis Megapolensis, Junior, minister of the colony of Rensselaerwyck, in certain letters which he has written to his friends, which were printed (as he has told me) without his consent, but may be fully credited,—he being a man of truth and of great learning, who writes in a vigorous style,—states, with other matters, that a certain farmer had cropped one field with wheat eleven years in succession, which to many persons will seem extraordinary, and may not be credited. Still it is true, and the residents of the place testify to the same, and they add that this same land was ploughed but twelve times in the eleven seasons,—twice in the first year, and once in every succeeding year, when the stubble was ploughed in, the wheat sown and harrowed under. I owned land adjoining the land referred to, and have seen the eleventh crop, which was tolerably good. The man who did this is named Brandt Pelen; he was born in the district of Utrecht, and at the time was a magistrate (schepen) of the colony of Rensselaerwyck. We acknowledge that this relation appears to be marvellous, but in the country it is not so, for there are many thousand *morgens* of as good land there as the land of which we have spoken.

During the period when I resided in the New-Netherlands, a certain honorable gentleman, named John Everts Bout (who was recommended to the colonists by their High Mightinesses, &c.), laid a wager that he could raise a crop of barley on a field containing seven *morgens* of land, which would grow so tall in every part of the field that the ears could easily be tied together above his head. I went to see the field of barley, and found that the straw, land by land, was from six to seven feet high, and very little of it any shorter. It has also been stated to me as a fact that barley has frequently been raised, although not common, which yielded eleven *schepel*, Amsterdam measure, per *vin* of 108 sheaves. Therefore, all persons who are acquainted with the New-Netherlands judge the country to be as well adapted for the cultivation of grain as any part of the world which is known to the Netherlanders, or is in their possession.

With the other productions of the land we must include tobacco, which is also cultivated in the country, and is, as well as the maize, well adapted to prepare the land for other agricultural purposes, which also, with proper attention, grows fine, and yields more profit. Not only myself, but hundreds of others, have raised tobacco the leaves of which were three-fourths of a yard long. The tobacco raised here is of different kind, but principally of the Virginia kind, from which it differs little in flavour, although the Virginia is the best. Still it does not differ so much in quality as in price. Next to the Virginia it will be the best; many persons esteem it better, and give it a preference. It is even probable that when the people extend the cultivation of the article, and more tobacco is planted, that it will gain more reputation and esteem. Many persons are of opinion that the defect in flavour arises from the newness of the land, and hasty cultivation, which will gradually be removed.

Barley grows well in the country, but it is not much needed. Cummin seed, canary seed, and the like, have been tried, and Commander Minuit testifies that those articles succeed well, but are not sought after. Flax and hemp will grow fine, but as the women do not spin much, and the Indians have hemp in abundance in the woods from which they make strong ropes and nets, for these reasons very little flax is raised; but the persons who do sow the seed find that the land is of the proper quality for such articles.

Of their bodily form and appearance, and why we named them (*Wilden*) Wild Men.

Having briefly remarked on the situation and· advantages of the country, we deem it worth our attention to treat concerning the nature of the original native inhabitants of the land; that after the Christians have multiplied and the natives have disappeared and melted away, a memorial of them may be preserved.

Their appearance and bodily form, as well of the men as of the women, are well proportioned, and equal in height to the Netherlanders, varying little from the common size. Their limbs are properly formed, and they are sprightly and active. They can run very fast for a long time, and they can carry heavy packs. To all bodily exertions they are very competent, as far as their dispositions extend; but to heavy slavish labour the men have a particular aversion, and they manage their affairs accordingly, so that they need not labour much. Misshapen or ill-formed persons are very rare amongst them. During the whole time of my residence in the country, I have not seen more than one who was born deformed. Cripples, hunch-backed, or other bodily infirmities, are so rare, that we may say that there are none amongst them; and when we see or hear of one who is crippled or lame, we on inquiry find the same to have originated by accident or in war. They are all properly formed and well proportioned persons. None are gross or uncommonly heavy. Although nature has not given them abundant wisdom, still they exercise their talents with discretion. No lunatics or fools are found amongst them, nor any mad or raving persons of either sex. The men and women commonly have broad shoulders and slender waists. Their hair, before old age, is jet black, sleek and uncurled, and nearly as coarse as a horse's tail. Hair of any other colour they dislike and despise. On the skin, the breast, under the arms, and on other parts of the body, they have little or no hair, and if any appear on their chins they pluck it out by the roots, and it seldom sprouts again. Their old men sometimes have a little stubble on their chins. The men and women all have fine brown eyes, and snow white teeth. Purblind, cross-eyed persons are rare objects, and I have never heard of a native who was born blind, and they seldom lose their sight by accident. One I have seen who had lost his eye-sight by the small pox; and when they become old, their sight does not fail so early in life as ours. The colour of their skin is not so white as ours; still we see some of them who have a fine skin, and they are mostly born with good complexions; otherwise they have a yellowish colour like the Tartars, or heathen who are seen in Holland, or like the Outlanders who keep in the fields and go uncovered as they do. Their yellowness is no fault of nature, but it is caused by the heat of the scorching sun, which is hotter and more powerful in that country than in Holland, which from generation to generation has been shining on that people, and exhibits its effects stronger. Although this yellowness of the skin appears more or less on all this race, still we find very comely men and women amongst them. It is true that they appear singular and strange to our nation, because their complexion, speech and dress are so different, but this, on acquaintance, is disregarded. Their women are well favoured and fascinating. Several of our Netherlanders were connected with them before our women came over, and remain firm in their attachments. Their faces and countenances are as various as they are in Holland, seldom very handsome, and rarely very ugly, and if they were instructed as our women are, there then would be little or no difference in their qualifications.

The original natives of the country, (for now there are native born Christians also,) although they are composed of different tribes, and speak different tongues, all pass by the appellation of (Wilden) wild men; and this name was given them, as far as we can learn, at the first discovery of the country, which for various reasons seems very appropriate. First, on account of their religion, of which they have very little, and that is very strange; and secondly, on account of their marriages, wherein they differ from civilized societies; thirdly, on account of their laws, which are so singular as to deserve the name of wild regulations. And the Christians hold different names necessary to distinguish different nations, such as Turks, Mamelukes, and Barbarians; and as the name of Heathen is very little used in foreign lands, therefore they would not distinguish the native Americans by either of these names;. and as they trade in foreign countries with dark and fair coloured people, and with those who resemble ourselves, in distinction from negroes, and as the American tribes are bordering on an olive colour, the name of *wild men* suits them best. Thus without deliberation, and as it were by chance at the first word, (as we suppose,) they were called Wild Men. And as unlearned persons never reflect much but speak their first thoughts in this manner, it has probably happened that this people received their national name, because they seemed to be wild and strangers to the Christian religion.

Of the Nature and Diversions of the Indians

The Indians are naturally (with few exceptions) of taciturn, steady and pensive dispositions and tempers, and of few words, which are well considered, uttered slowly, and long remembered; they say no more than is necessary to the subject in hand. When they want to buy or to sell any article, they say no more than is necessary to the bargain. On the other occasions, they talk of no subjects except hunting, fishing, and war. Their young men frequently entertain each other on their gallantry with young female connections. They despise lying, and still they are not very precise in the performance of their engagements. Swearing and scolding are not heard among them, unless it be among those who have learned those habits from us. They do not possess great wisdom or extensive knowledge, but reasonable understanding, resulting from practical experience, which they certainly possess without any desire for further instruction; they are naturally civil and well disposed, and quick enough to distinguish between good and evil, but after they have associated amongst us, they become cunning and deceitful, They are slovenly, careless, and dirty of their persons, and are troubled with the evils which attend filthiness. They are very revengeful and obstinate even unto death, and when in trouble they disregard and despise all pain and torture that can be done to them, and will sing with proud contempt until death terminates their sufferings. They are all stingy and inclined to beggary, and cannot be trusted too far because they also are thievish; denying them the least trifle does not offend them. They are all free by nature and will not bear any domineering or lording over them; they will not bear any insult, unless they have done wrong, and they will bear chastisement without resentment. Delicious food or drink they disregard; they fear no accidents, and can endure heat, cold, hunger, and thirst, in a wonderful manner, and they can all swim like ducks from their childhood. When abroad, they spend their time in hunting, fishing or war; at home they smoke tobacco, and play a game with pieces of reeds, resembling our card playing. The old men knit nets, and make wooden bowls and ladles. Labour among the young men is uncommon, and nearly all the necessary labour is done by the females.

Of their Religion, and whether they can be brought over to the Christian Faith.

The natives are all heathen and without any religious devotions. Idols are neither known nor worshipped among them. When they take an oath they swear by the sun, which, they say, sees all things. They think much of the moon, and believe it has great influence over vegetation. Although they know all the planets from the other stars, by appropriate names, still they pay no idolatrous worship to the same, yet by the planets and other signs they are somewhat weatherwise. The offering up of prayers, or the making of any distinction between days, or any matter of the kind, is unknown among them. They neither know or say any thing of God; but they possess great fear of the devil, who they believe causes diseases, and does them much injury. When they go on a hunting or fishing excursion they usually cast a part of what is first taken into the fire, without using any ceremony on the occasion, then saying "stay thou devil, eat thou that." They love to hear usspeak of God and of our religion; and are very attentive and still during divine service and prayers, and apparently are inclined to devotion; but in truth they know nothing about it, and live without any religion, or without any inward or outward godly fear, nor do they know of any superstition or idolatry; they only follow the instilled laws of nature, therefore some suppose they can easily be brought to the knowledge and fear of God. Among some nations the word Sunday is known by the name of Kintowen. The oldest among them say that in former times the knowledge and fear of God had been known among them, and they remark, that since they can neither read nor write, in process of time the Sunday will be forgotten, all knowledge of the same lost. Their old men, when we reason earnestly with them on the matter, seem to feel pensive or sorrowful, but manifest no other emotions or agitations—when we reprove them for bad conduct and reason with them on its impropriety, and say that there is a God in heaven above whom they offend, their common answer is—'We do not know that God, we have never seen him, we know not who he is—if you know him and fear him, as you say you do, how does it then happen that so many thieves, drunkards, and evil-doers are found among you. Certainly that God will punish you severely, because he has warned you to beware of those deeds, which he has never done to us. We know nothing about it, and therefore we do not deserve such punishment.' Very seldom do they adopt our religion, nor have there been any political measures taken for their conversion. When their children are young some of them are frequently taken into our families for assistants, who are, according to opportunity, instructed in our religion, but as soon as they are grown up, and turn lovers and associate again with the Indians, they forget their religious impressions and adopt the Indian customs. The Jesuits have taken great pains and trouble in Canada to convert the Indians to the Roman Church, and outwardly many profess that religion; but inasmuch as they are not well instructed in its fundamental principles, they fall off lightly and make sport of the subject and its doctrine.

In the year 1639, when a certain merchant, who is still living with us, went into that country to trade with an Indian chief who spoke good French, after he had drank two or three glasses of wine, they began to converse on the subject of religion. The chief said that he had been instructed so far that he often said mass among the Indians, and that on a certain occasion the place where the altar stood caught fire by accident, and our people made preparations to put out the fire, which he forbade them to do, saying that God, who stands there, is almighty, and he will put out the fire himself; and we waited with great attention, but the fire continued till all was burned up, with your almighty God himself and with all the fine things about him. Since that time I have never held to that religion, but regard the sun and moon much more, as being better than all your Gods are; for they warm the earth and cause the fruits to grow, when your lovely Gods cannot preserve themselves from the fire. In the whole country I know no more than one Indian who is firm in his religious profession, nor can any change be expected among them, as long as matters are permitted to remain as heretofore. If they are to be brought over to the Christian faith, then the public hand must be extended to them and continued; we must establish good schools at convenient places among them, for the instruction of their children; let them learn to write our catechism, and let them be thoroughly instructed in the fundamental principles of our religion, so that in process of time they may be enabled to instruct each other and become attached thereto. It certainly would be attended with some trouble and expense to the government, still, without such means and measures, it will be difficult to do any good, among them. Our negligence on those matters is very reprehensible, for the Indians themselves say that they are very desirous to have their children instructed in our language and religion.

Of their hope after this present life.

It is a wonderful truth which affords strong evidence against unbelievers and free-thinking spirits, that this barbarous wild race of people of whom we have treated, should know that there is a distinction between the body and the soul, and believe, as they actually do, that the one is perishable and the other immortal. The soul, they say, is that spirit which directs all the actions of the body, and is the producing cause of all good and evil conduct, which, when the body dies, separates from it and removes to a place towards the south, where the climate is so fine that no covering against the cold will be necessary, and where the heat will never be troublesome. To this place the souls of all those who have been good and valuable in this life will go, where they will be satisfied and have an abundance of good things, without any trouble or labour for the same, forever; and they who have been bad in this life, after death will go to another place, where their condition will be directly contrary to the first; where they will never enjoy peace and contentment, as the good will do. But I have never been able rightly to discover whether they believe the soul will be hereafter united to the body. I have, however, spoken with Christians who remark, that they have heard them state such to be their belief. But they do not affirm to this fact. When they hear voices or noises in the woods at night, which frequently happens, and which, we believe, usually proceed from wild animals, but which they declare, with fear and astonishment, are made by the wicked, the souls of whom are thus doomed to wander at night in the woods and solitary palaces for punishment in unhappy situations. The Indians, because they fear those subjects, do not travel by night unless it be necessary, and then go in parties or companies; when they go alone they always carry a fire-brand with them, with which they believe they can keep off those evil spirits and prevent them from doing them any injury, which, they say, are always disposed to frighten them and do them wrong. They acknowledge also that the soul proceeds from God, and that the same is his gift. This we sometimes learn from their old men of understanding, when an opportunity presents itself in conversation and we probably would discover more of them in relation to this matter, if we did perfectly understand their languages. Among their common or young people we do not hear those spoken of. In this we still see the providence of God, who, by the common light of nature, has given to this people the knowledge that there is, after this life, a reward for the just, and a punishment for the unjust, which all mankind may expect.

1.9.2 Reading and Review Questions

1. How, why, and to what effect does van der Donck assert the right of the Dutch to possess New Netherland? What assumptions about law and jurisdiction does he make, and why?
2. What details of Dutch culture can be inferred by van der Donck's description of the land, crops, and people in New Netherland? How does van der Donck's description in this way differ from that of other New World accounts?
3. Van der Donck records details of American Indian lives and culture to prevent regret over their inevitable disappearance. According to van der Donck, who will feel this regret? Why?
4. Why did the Dutch "name" American Indians the "wilden?" How does van der Donck justify this name as appropriate, even as he acknowledges that different tribes and groups exist, each with their own distinct name?
5. Van der Donck recounts an American Indian noting how the Christian God allows himself to be burnt (when a Christian altar and relics catch fire and burn). Van der Donck declares that the American Indian mocked the Christian God. Why does van der Donck recount this event and this so-called mockery? What do you think is van der Donck's point?

2 Seventeenth Century English Colonial Literature

2.1 LEARNING OUTCOMES

After reading this chapter, students will be able to

- Understand both the shared and distinctive motives leading to different European groups' traveling to and settling in the new world.
- Understand how their respective founding charters shaped the ideologies of the different European settlements in the new world.
- Understand the adverse effects on the relationship of the English and the Native American tribes of the ongoing European expansion of English colonies in North America.
- Understand the significance of the Pequod War and the so-called King Philip's War.
- Identify the introduction, growth, and effects of African slavery in the colonies.
- Understand the significance of Puritanism to seventeenth century literature and culture in the new world.
- Identify the aesthetic features of the Puritan plain style in literature.

2.2 INTRODUCTION

The Puritans tend to be overrepresented in the histories and literature of the seventeenth century English colonies in North America; however, they were hardly the only group from England to travel to the new world. Some groups came for similar reasons as the Puritans–to practice their religion freely–though many came for secular reasons. The Jamestown colony in Virginia, a territory which originally included not only the current state of Virginia but also the northern parts of North Carolina up to the Long Island Sound in New York, was founded as a commercial venture. In addition, people with commercial interests in the new world traveled alongside William Bradford's pilgrims on the *Mayflower*, and considerable tension existed between settlements with secular interests and those of the Puritans, as we see in William Bradford's account of Thomas Morton (c. 1579–1647) and the residents of Merrymount.

More colonies soon joined those in Massachusetts and Virginia. In 1632, Lord Baltimore (1605–1675) was given a charter for land north of the Potomac River. A Catholic, Baltimore established the colony of Maryland as a place of religious tolerance. A charter for the Carolinas, a territory which extended well beyond the modern borders of those states, was granted in 1663 and settlers established one of the first colonies under this charter near Charleston, South Carolina. In 1681, Pennsylvania was granted by King Charles II to William Penn (1644–1718) in repayment of a debt owed to Penn's father. The colony became a refuge for members of the Society of Friends or Quakers, as Penn was a recent convert to the denomination. Georgia was the last of the original colonies. Founded in 1732, the colony was intended primarily as a bulwark between the English colonies to the north and the Spanish colonies to the south.

Certainly, this ongoing expansion of English colonies caused continual tension with the Native American tribes already occupying the territory. The Powhatan Confederacy, a union of tribes occupying the tidewater Virginia region, alternately collaborated with and fought against the Jamestown colony from its founding until 1645, when the English forced the confederacy to surrender and cede land. In New England, the Pequod War (1636–1638) was one of the first significant fights between the colonies in Massachusetts and the local tribes, pitting the Pequod tribe against the Massachusetts Bay, Plymouth, and Saybrook colonies and their allies, the Narragansett tribe. The natives of New England continued attempting to hold back English encroachments, making their last major effort when the Wampanoag, Narragansett, and other allied tribes, led by Metacom (1638–1675)—called King Philip by the English—attacked frontier towns. The so-called King Philip's War lasted from 1675 to 1676, when Metacom was captured and executed.

The use of African slaves in the colonies also grew during this century. African slavery had first been introduced to North America by the Spanish, especially after the Catholic Church started cracking down on enslaving Native Americans. Slaves were first brought to the English colony of Jamestown in 1619, to Connecticut in 1629, and to Massachusetts in 1637. The widespread adoption of slavery languished initially as it proved to be too expensive of an option for the struggling colonists. Indentured servants were a more economical option, but as wages rose in England toward the end of the century and dried up the supply of indentured servants, the use of enslaved Africans grew in the colonies. Though slavery was most prevalent in the southern colonies because of their greater focus on agriculture, the New England colonies were the first to codify slavery (in Massachusetts in 1641) and the first to forbid it (in Rhode Island in 1652). Even before America was a nation officially, America had a slavery problem. As Samuel Sewall's anti-slavery tract shows, the arguments for and against slavery made during this century are some of the same ones that will be made again and again in the following two centuries.

While the Puritans were only one of many groups settling the English colonies, they were the one with the most cultural power. For that reason, it is necessarily to understand who they were and how they saw the world to understand many of the readings of this section. The Puritans were groups who felt that the Church of England, otherwise known as the Anglican Church, retained too much of the doctrine and culture of the Catholic Church after the Protestant reformation. Their name derived from their desire to purify the church of these Catholic vestiges. There were also non-separatist and separatist groups within the Puritans as a whole. The non-separatists, like John Winthrop's company, believed that the Puritans should remain within the Anglican Church and correct it from within the system; the separatists, represented by William Bradford's Plymouth company, felt the Church of England was a lost cause from which the Puritans should separate themselves. The restoration of King James I to the throne and the subsequent persecutions of dissenters made the distinction moot. The only way to safely practice views that differed from the orthodoxy was to put considerable distance between oneself and English authorities, which both Winthrop's and Bradford's groups did.

The Puritans came to the new world with the goal of building a community constructed around religious principles that could stand as a model—a "city upon a hill," as Winthrop put it—for a Christian community. The Puritans subscribed to Calvinist theology, and Calvinism's assumptions about humanity and its relationship to God influence their works. First, Calvinism held that mankind was born depraved as a result of Adam's original sin. The presence of sin within the human soul meant that all of man's impulses, desires, and beliefs were tainted. As John Calvin put it in his *Institutes of the Christian Religion* (1536):

> Let it stand, therefore, as an indubitable truth, which no engines can shake, that the mind of man is so entirely alienated from the righteousness of God that he cannot conceive, desire, or design any thing but what is wicked, distorted, foul, impure, and iniquitous; that his heart is so thoroughly envenomed by sin that it can breathe out nothing but corruption and rottenness; that if some men occasionally make a show of goodness, their mind is ever interwoven with hypocrisy and deceit, their soul inwardly bound with the fetters of wickedness.

Congenitally incapable of righteousness, humanity was incapable of achieving salvation on their own. Only God's intervention could save people from the damnation they deserved.

According to Calvinism, some of the faithful will be saved because of unconditional election. Election, or God's decision to replace a person's original depraved spirit with a clean one capable of understanding and following God's will, could not be earned through good behavior; it was unconditional in that it had nothing to do with choices the person made or would make. It was also limited to a relatively small number of people rather than all of humanity. A logical outgrowth of these points of theology was the concept of predestination, which Calvin described in *Institutes* as "the eternal decree of God, by which He hath determined in Himself what He would have to become of every individual of mankind . . . . eternal life is foreordained for some, and eternal damnation for others." Whatever one's predestined fate was, one could do nothing to change it. Nonetheless, the Puritans held that one should always behave piously regardless of one's destined outcome and emphasized the weaning of affections from the things of this world. Puritans were instructed to develop an attitude of indifference toward material things—to "wean" themselves of their natural attraction to the worldly—as well as to personal relationships, including one's own family. This was not to encourage hard-heartedness but rather to make spiritual things the main priority of one's life because the things of this world will not last; only the life of the spirit was permanent for the Puritans.

Given their beliefs in the total fallibility of mankind, Puritans looked outside of themselves for guidance in following God's will. The first source of guidance was the Bible, which the Puritans took to be the most direct expression of God's will. The Puritans, like other scholars of the Bible before them, believed in a typological relationship between the Old Testament and the New Testament. Stories of the Old Testament were types or, as Hebrews 10:1 puts it, "a shadow of good things to come," that foreshadowed the antitypes or "the very image of the good things" in the New Testament. For example, Jonah's release from the whale in the Old Testament would be considered a type to the antitype of Jesus' resurrection in the New Testament. However, the Puritans did not confine typological interpretation to the Bible alone. Typology assumes that all of human history and experience is part of a larger pattern of meanings that communicate God's will, so any event—as big as smallpox decimating the native populations in greater numbers than the colonial populations or as small as a snake failing to ingest a mouse as recorded in John Winthrop's journal—could be considered part of that pattern and signs of God's approbation or disapprobation.

Despite vigorous policing of their theological borders against antinomians (who argued that salvation through faith meant that one needn't follow the laws of a church); Quakers who disagreed with the beliefs of total depravity and salvation for only a limited number; and others who criticized Puritan practices, the Puritans' power eventually faded along with the membership of the denomination by the end of the seventeenth century. Initially, the bar for membership in the church was quite high. Believing that only the elect, or those who are destined to be saved, should be members of the church and thereby be able to choose leaders for both the church and the state, prospective members were required to testify of their conversion experience and be interrogated by the other members of the church. It was a rigorous experience that more and more people decided to forego, and eventually, church members in the colonies were outnumbered by non-church members. To increase their ranks and hold on to political power, Puritan churches adopted the Half-Way Covenant in 1662. Under this covenant, the children of church members could become members without testifying to their conversion.

Despite this measure, the political power of the Puritan churches continued to decline, though their cultural power continues to influence American culture.

Finally, in the spirit of purification and a return to a simpler practice, many of the works in this section demonstrate the Puritan aesthetic of plain style. In contrast to the more ornate style of writers like William Shakespeare, the Puritans and some other Protestant denominations felt that the best style was that which lacked embellishment or ornamentation and strove for simplicity and accessibility to the average person. Plain-style writing typically eschewed classical allusions, preferring to use figurative language originating either in the Bible or in everyday experience; was didactic (intended to teach a lesson) rather than entertaining; and featured limited variation in syntactical structures—though those structures might seem complex to a modern reader. This aesthetic can also be seen in the narrow color range of Puritan clothing and the distinct lack of gilding, statuary, and altars in Puritan churches.

2.3 WILLIAM BRADFORD

(1590–1657)

William Bradford was born in Austerfield, Yorkshire and reared as a farmer. In 1606, inspired by the preaching of non-conformist minister Richard Clyfton (d. 1616), Bradford joined the Separatist group tied to William Brewster (1568–1644) in Scrooby, Nottinghamshire. As Separatists from the Church of England headed by the English monarch, this group (and similar others) engaged in treason against the English crown. To escape the consequent-enforced secrecy and persecution, the group left England for the Netherlands. In 1609, Bradford joined them there, became a weaver, and started his own business upon inheriting money from his family.

Image 2.1 | William Bradford
Artist | Unknown
Source | Wikimedia Commons
License | Public Domain

To escape further persecution, the group petitioned for and won a land grant in North America. Bradford was one of the pilgrims who sailed from Southampton, England in 1620 on the *Mayflower* to settle in the land granted. Their land grant was originally meant to be in Virginia but, due to difficulty navigating in storms, they landed at Plymouth, Massachusetts. William Bradford helped define for themselves and future generations their Puritan settlement and endeavor at Plymouth Plantation. After the death of their elected governor John Carver (1576–1621), Bradford was elected governor. He was re-elected thirty times, serving as governor for almost all but the last five years of his life. He signed the Mayflower Compact that ordered their earthly rule (even as a means to prepare for heavenly rule); held to the Compact's democratic principles in his governorship; worked to repay the debt to the British investors who funded their project in America; and did much to organize and lead the pilgrims' lives.

Self-educated particularly in languages—including Hebrew—and an avid reader, Bradford applied his knowledge and skills to recording the history *Of Plymouth Plantation*. He started this chronicle largely in response to the growth of Non-Separatist settlers in the colony, settlers whom he saw as competing with the Separatists. His history records such important events as the pilgrims' landing at Plymouth, the *Mayflower Compact*, the first Thanksgiving, and the Puritan ethic in action as it was put to trial and served as testimony of God's designs. These designs included the pilgrims' persecutions, voyage to and landing at Plymouth, suffering starvation and sickness there, as well as experiencing increasing tensions between themselves and the Native Americans. In the Puritan plain style, Bradford offers simple yet monumental truths of their lives.

Image 2.2 | Landing of the pilgrims at Plymouth 11th Dec. 1620
Artist | N. Currier
Source | Wikimedia Commons
License | Public Domain

2.3.1 *Of Plymouth Plantation*

(1620–1647)

BOOK I

Chapter I

It is well knowne unto ye godly and judicious, how ever since ye first breaking out of ye lighte of ye gospell in our Honourable Nation of England, (which was ye first of nations whom ye Lord adorned ther with, affter yt grosse darknes of popery which had covered & overspred ye Christian worled,) what warrs & opposissions ever since, Satan hath raised, maintained, and continued against the Saincts, from time to time, in one sorte or other. Some times by bloody death and cruell torments; other whiles imprisonments, banishments, & other hard usages; as being loath his kingdom should goe downe, the trueth prevaile, and yechurches of God reverte to their anciente puritie, and recover their primative order, libertie, & bewtie. But when he could not prevaile by these means, against the maine trueths of ye gospell, but that they began to take rootting in many places, being watered with ye blooud of ye martires, and blessed from heaven with a gracious encrease; He then begane to take him to his anciente strategemes, used of old against the first Christians. That when by ye bloody & barbarous persecutions of ye Heathen Emperours, he could not stoppe & subuerte the course of ye gospell, but that it speedily overspred with a wounderfull celeritie the then best known parts of ye world, He then begane to sow errours, heresies, and wounderfull dissentions amongst yeprofessours them selves, (working upon their pride & ambition, with other corrupte passions incidente to all mortall men, yea to ye saints them selves in some measure,) by which wofull effects followed; as not only bitter contentions, & hartburnings, schismes, with other horrible confusions, but Satan tooke occasion & advantage therby to foyst in a number of vile ceremoneys, with many unproffitable cannons & decrees, which have since been as snares to many poore & peaceable souls even to this day. So as in ye anciente times, the persecutions by ye heathen & their Emperours, was not greater then of the Christians one against other; the Arians & other their complices against ye orthodoxe & true Christians. As witneseth Socrates in his 2. booke. His words are these; *The violence truly* (saith he) *was no less than that of ould practised towards ye Christians when they were compelled & drawne to sacrifice to idoles; for many indured sundrie kinds of tormente, often rackings, & dismembering of their joynts; confiscating of ther goods; some bereaved of their native soyle; others departed this life under ye hands of ye tormentor; and some died in banishmēte, & never saw ther cuntrie againe, &c.*

The like methode Satan hath seemed to hold in these later times, since ye trueth begane to springe & spread after ye great defection made by Antichrist, yt man of siñe.

For to let pass ye infinite examples in sundrie nations and severall places of ye world, and instance in our owne, when as yt old serpente could not prevaile by those firie flames & other his cruell tragedies, which he by his instruments put in ure every wher in ye days of queene Mary & before, he then begane an other kind of warre, & went more closly to worke; not only to oppuggen, but even to ruinate & destroy ye kingdom of Christ, by more secrete & subtile means, by kindling ye flames of contention and sowing yeseeds of discorde & bitter enmitie amongst ye proffessors & seeming reformed them selves. For when he could not prevaile by ye former means against the principall doctrins of faith, he bente his force against the holy discipline & outward regimente of the kingdom of Christ, by which those holy doctrines should be conserved, & true pietie maintained amongest the saints & people of God.

Mr. Foxe recordeth how yt besids those worthy martires & confessors which were burned in queene Marys days & otherwise tormented, *many (both studients & others) fled out of ye land, to ye number of 800. And became severall congregations. At Wesell, Frankford, Bassill, Emden, Markpurge, Strausborugh, & Geneva, &c.* Amongst whom (but especialy those at Frankford) begane yt bitter warr of contention & persecutiō aboute ye ceremonies, & servise-booke, and other popish and antichristian stuffe, the plague of England to this day, which are like ye highplases in Israell, wch the prophets cried out against, & were their ruine; which ye better parte sought, according to ye puritie of ye gospell, to roote out and utterly to abandon. And the other parte (under veiled pretences) for their ouwn ends & advancments, sought as stifly to continue, maintaine, & defend. As appeareth by ye discourse therof published in printe, Ano: 1575; a booke ytdeserves better to be knowne and considred.

The one side laboured to have ye right worship of God & discipline of Christ established in ye church, according to ye simplicitie of ye gospell, without the mixture of mens inventions, and to have & to be ruled by ye laws of Gods word, dispensed in those offices, & by those officers of Pastors, Teachers, & Elders, &c. according to ye Scripturs. The other partie, though under many colours & pretences, endevored to have yeepiscopall dignitie (affter ye popish mañer) with their large power & jurisdiction still retained; with all those courts, cannons, & ceremonies, togeather with all such livings, revenues, & subordinate officers, with other such means as formerly upheld their antichristian greatnes, and enabled them with lordly & tyranous power to persecute ye poore servants of God. This contention was so great, as neither ye honour of God, the commone persecution, nor ye mediation of Mr. Calvin & other worthies of ye Lord in those places, could prevaile with those thus episcopally minded, but they proceeded by all means to disturbe ye peace of this poor persecuted church, even so farr as to charge (very unjustly, & ungodlily, yet prelatelike) some of their cheefe opposers, with rebellion & hightreason against ye Emperour, & other such crimes.

And this contētion dyed not with queene Mary, nor was left beyonde ye seas, but at her death these people returning into England under gracious queene Elizabeth, many of them being preferred to bishopricks & other promotions, according to their aimes and desires, that inveterate hatered against ye holy discipline of Christ in his church hath continued to this day. In somuch that for fear it should preveile, all plotts & devices have been used to keepe it out, incensing ye queene & state against it as dangerous for ye comon wealth; and that it was most needfull yt ye fundamentall poynts of Religion should be preached in those ignorante & superstitious times; and to wiñe ye weake & ignorante, they might retaine diverse harmles ceremoneis; and though it were to be wished yt diverse things were reformed, yet this was not a season for it. And many the like, to stop ye mouthes of ye more godly, to bring them over to yeeld to one ceremoney after another, and one corruption after another; by these wyles begyleing some & corrupting others till at length they begane to persecute all ye zealous professors in ye land (though they knew little what this discipline mente) both by word & deed, if they would not submitte to their ceremonies, & become slaves to them & their popish trash, which have no ground in ye word of God, but are relikes of yt man of sine. And the more ye light of ye gospell grew, ye more yey urged their subscriptions to these corruptions. So as (notwithstanding all their former pretences & fair colures) they whose eyes God had not justly blinded might easily see wherto these things tended. And to cast contempte the more upon ye sincere servants of God, they opprobriously & most injuriously gave unto, & imposed upon them, that name of Puritans, which [it] is said the Novatians out of prid did assume & take unto themselves. And lamentable it is to see ye effects which have followed. Religion hath been disgraced, the godly greeved, afflicted, persecuted, and many exiled, sundrie have lost their lives in prisones & otherways. On the other hand, sin hath been countenanced, ignorance, profannes, & atheisme increased, & the papists encouraged to hope againe for a day.

This made that holy man Mr. Perkins crie out in his exhortation to repentance, upon Zeph. 2. *Religion* (saith he) *hath been amongst us this 35. years; but the more it is published, the more it is contemned & reproached of many, &c. Thus not prophanes nor wickednes, but Religion it selfe is a byword, a moking-stock, & a matter of reproach; so that in England at this day the man or woman yt begines to profes Religion, & to serve God, must resolve with him selfe to sustaine mocks & injueries even as though he lived amongst ye enimies of Religion.* And this comone experience hath confirmed & made too apparente.

A late observation, as it were by the way, worthy to be Noted.

Full litle did I thinke, yt the downfall of ye Bishops, with their courts, cannons, & ceremonies, &c. had been so neare, when I first begane these scribled writings (which was aboute ye year 1630, and so peeced up at times of leasure afterward), or that I should have lived to have seene or heard of ye same; but it is ye Lords doing, and ought to be marvelous in our eyes! Every plante which mine heavenly father hath not planted (saith our Saviour) shall be rooted up. Mat: 15. 13. I have snared the, and thou art taken, O Babell (Bishops), and thou wast not aware; thou art found, and also caught, because thou hast striven against the Lord. Jer. 50. 24. But will they needs strive against ye truth, against yeservants of God; what, & against the Lord him selfe? Doe they provoke the Lord to anger? Are they stronger than he? 1. Cor: 10. 22. No, no, they have mete with their match. Behold, I come unto ye, O proud man, saith the Lord God of hosts; for thy day is come, even the time that I will visite the. Jer: 50. 31. May not the people of God now say (and these pore people among ye rest), The Lord hath brought forth our righteousnes; come, let us declare in Sion the work of the Lord our God. Jer: 51. 10. Let all flesh be still before the Lord; for he is raised up out of his holy place. Zach: 2. 13.

In this case, these poore people may say (among ye thousands of Israll), *When the Lord brougt againe the captivite of Zion, we were like them that dreame. Psa: 126. 1. The Lord hath done greate things for us, wherof we rejoyce. v. 3. They that sow in teares, shall reap in joye. They wente weeping, and carried precious seede, but they shall returne with joye, and bring their sheaves, v. 5, 6.*

Doe you not now see ye fruits of your labours, O all yee servants of ye Lord that have suffered for his truth, and have been faithfull witneses of ye same, and yee litle handfull amongst ye rest, ye least amongest ye thousands of Israll? You have not only had a seede time, but many of you have seene yejoyefull harvest; should you not then rejoyse, yea, and againe rejoyce, and say Hallelu-iah, salvation, and glorie, and honour, and power, be to ye Lord our God; for true and righteous are his judgments. Rev. 19. 1, 2.

But thou wilte aske what is ye mater? What is done? Why, art thou a stranger in Israll, that thou shouldest not know what is done? Are not those Jebusites overcome that have vexed the people of Israll so long, even holding Jerusalem till Davids days, and been as thorns in their sids, so many ages; and now begane to scorne that any David should meadle with them; they begane to fortifie their tower, as that of the old Babelonians; but those proud Anakimes are throwne downe, and their glory laid in yedust. The tiranous bishops are ejected, their courts dissolved, their cannons forceless, their servise casheired, their ceremonies uselese and despised; their plots for popery prevented, and all their superstitions discarded & returned to Roome from whence they came, and ye monuments of idolatrie rooted out of ye land. And the proud and profane suporters, and cruell defenders of these (as bloody papists & wicked athists, and their malignante consorts) marvelously over throwne. And are not these greate things? Who can deney it?

But who hath done it? Who, even he that siteth on ye white horse, who is caled faithfull, & true, and judgeth and fighteth righteously, Rev: 19. 11. whose garments are dipte in blood, and his name was caled the word of God, v. 13. for he shall rule them with a rode of iron; for it is he that treadeth the winepress of the feircenes and wrath of God almighty. And he hath upon his garmente, and upon his thigh, a name writen, The King of Kings, and Lord of Lords, v. 15, 16.

Hallelu-iah.

Anno Dom: 1646.

But that I may come more near my intendmente; when as by the travell & diligence of some godly & zealous preachers, & Gods blessing on their labours, as in other places of ye land, so in ye North parts, many became inlightened by the word of God, and had their ignorance & sins discovered unto them, and begane by his grace to reforme their lives, and make conscience of their wayes, the worke of God was no sooner manifest in them, but presently they were both scoffed and scorned by ye prophane multitude, and yeministers urged with ye yoak of subscription, or els must be silenced; and ye poore people were so vexed with apparators, & pursuants, & ye comissarie courts, as truly their affliction was not smale; which, notwithstanding, they bore sundrie years with much patience, till they were occasioned (by ye continuance & encrease of these troubls, and other means which the Lord raised up in those days) to see further into things by the light of ye word of God. How not only these base and beggerly ceremonies were unlawfull, but also that ye lordly & tiranous power of ye prelats ought not to be submitted unto; which thus, contrary to the freedome of the gospell, would load & burden mens consciences, and by their compulsive power make a prophane mixture of persons & things in the worship of God. And that their offices & calings, courts & cannons, &c. were unlawfull and antichristian; being such as have no warrante in ye word of God; but the same yt were used in poperie, & still retained. Of which a famous author thus writeth in his Dutch comtaries. At the coming of king James into England; *The new king* (saith he) *found their established ye reformed religion, according to ye reformed religion of king Edward ye 6. Retaining, or keeping still ye spirituall state of ye Bishops, &c. after ye ould maner, much varying & differing from ye reformed churches in Scotland, France, & ye Neatherlands, Embden, Geneva, &c. whose reformation is cut, or shapen much nerer ye first Christian churches, as it was used in ye Apostles times.*

So many therfore of these proffessors as saw ye evill of these things, in thes parts, and whose harts yeLord had touched wth heavenly zeale for his trueth, they shooke of this yoake of antichristian bondage, and as ye Lords free people, joyned them selves (by a covenant of the Lord) into a church estate, in ye felowship of ye gospell, to walke in all his wayes, made known, or to be made known unto them, according to their best endeavours, whatsoever it should cost them, the Lord assisting them. And that it cost them something this ensewing historie will declare.

These people became 2. distincte bodys or churches, & in regarde of distance of place did congregate severally; for they were of sundrie townes & vilages, some in Notingamshire, some of Lincollinshire, and some of Yorkshire, wher they border nearest togeather. In one of these churches (besids others of note) was Mr. John Smith, a man of able gifts, & a good preacher, who afterwards was chosen their pastor. But these afterwards falling into some errours in ye Low Countries, ther (for ye most part) buried them selves, & their names.

But in this other church (wch must be ye subjecte of our discourse) besids other worthy men, was Mr. Richard Clifton, a grave and reverēd preacher, who by his paines and dilligens had done much good, and under God had ben a means of ye conversion of many. And also that famous and worthy man Mr. John Robinson, who afterwards was their pastor for many years, till ye Lord tooke him away by death. Also Mr. William Brewster a reverent man, who afterwards was chosen an elder of ye church and lived with them till old age.

But after these things they could not long continue in any peaceable condition, but were hunted & persecuted on every side, so as their former afflictions were but as flea-bitings in comparison of these which now came upon them. For some were taken & clapt up in prison, others had their houses besett & watcht night and day, & hardly escaped their hands; and ye most were faine to flie & leave their howses & habitations, and the means of their livelehood. Yet these & many other sharper things which affterward befell them, were no other then they looked for, and therfore were ye better prepared to bear them by ye assistance of Gods grace & spirite. Yet seeing them selves thus molested, and that ther was no hope of their continuance ther, by a joynte consente they resolved to goe into ye Low-Countries, wher they heard was freedome of Religion for all men; as also how sundrie from London, & other parts of ye land, had been exiled and persecuted for ye same cause, & were gone thither, and lived at Amsterdam, & in other places of ye land. So affter they had continued togeither aboute a year, and kept their meetings every Saboth in one place or other, exercising the worship of God amongst them selves, notwithstanding all ye dilligence & malice of their adverssaries, they seeing they could no longer continue in yt condition, they resolved to get over into Hollād as they could; which was in ye year 1607. & 1608.; of which more at large in ye next chap.

Chapter IV

Showing ye reasons & causes of their remoovall.

After they had lived in this citie about some 11. or 12. years, (which is ye more observable being ye whole time of yt famose truce between that state & ye Spaniards,) and sundrie of them were taken away by death, & many others begane to be well striken in years, the grave mistris Experience haveing taught them many things, those prudent governours with sundrie of yesagest members begane both deeply to apprehend their present dangers, & wisely to foresee yefuture, & thinke of timly remedy. In ye agitation of their thoughts, and much discours of things hear aboute, at length they began to incline to this conclusion, of remoovall to some other place. Not out of any newfanglednes, or other such like giddie humor, by which men are oftentimes transported to their great hurt & danger, but for sundrie weightie & solid reasons; some of yecheefe of which I will hear breefly touch. And first, they saw & found by experience the hardnes of ye place & countrie to be such, as few in comparison would come to them, and fewer that would bide it out, and continew with them. For many yt came to them, and many more yt desired to be with them, could not endure yt great labor and hard fare, with other inconveniences which they underwent & were contented with. But though they loved their persons, approved their cause, and honoured their sufferings, yet they left them as it weer weeping, as Orpah did her mother in law Naomie, or as those Romans did Cato in Utica, who desired to be excused & borne with, though they could not all be Catoes. For many, though they desired to injoye yeordinances of God in their puritie, and ye libertie of the gospell with them, yet, alass, they admitted of bondage, with danger of conscience, rather then to indure these hardships; yea, some preferred & chose ye prisons in England, rather then this libertie in Holland, with these afflictions. But it was thought that if a better and easier place of living could be had, it would draw many, & take away these discouragments. Yea, their pastor would often say, that many of those wo both wrate & preached now against them, if they were in a place wher they might have libertie and live comfortably, they would then practise as they did.

2ly. They saw that though ye people generally bore all these difficulties very cherfully, & with a resolute courage, being in ye best & strength of their years, yet old age began to steale on many of them, (and their great & continuall labours, with other crosses and sorrows, hastened it before ye time,) so as it was not only probably thought, but apparently seen, that within a few years more they would be in danger to scatter, by necessities pressing them, or sinke under their burdens, or both. And therfore according to ye devine proverb, yt a wise man seeth ye plague when it cometh, & hideth him selfe, Pro. 22. 3., so they like skillfull & beaten souldiers were fearfull either to be intrapped or surrounded by their enimies, so as they should neither be able to fight nor flie; and therfor thought it better to dislodge betimes to some place of better advantage & less danger, if any such could be found. Thirdly; as necessitie was a taskmaster over them, so they were forced to be such, not only to their servants, but in a sorte, to their dearest chilldren; the which as it did not a litle wound ye tender harts of many a loving father & mother, so it produced likwise sundrie sad & sorowful effects. For many of their children, that were of best dispositions and gracious inclinations, haveing lernde to bear ye yoake in their youth, and willing to bear parte of their parents burden, were, often times, so oppressed with their hevie labours, that though their minds were free and willing, yet their bodies bowed under ye weight of ye same, and became decreped in their early youth; the vigor of nature being consumed in ye very budd as it were. But that which was more lamentable, and of all sorowes most heavie to be borne, was that many of their children, by these occasions, and ye great licentiousnes of youth in yt countrie, and ye manifold temptations of the place, were drawne away by evill examples into extravagante & dangerous courses, getting ye raines off their neks, & departing from their parents. Some became souldiers, others tooke upon them farr viages by sea, and other some worse courses, tending to dissolutnes & the danger of their soules, to ye great greefe of their parents and dishonour of God. So that they saw their posteritie would be in danger to degenerate & be corrupted.

Lastly, (and which was not least,) a great hope & inward zeall they had of laying some good foundation, or at least to make some way therunto, for ye propagating & advancing ye gospell of ye kingdom of Christ in those remote parts of ye world; yea, though they should be but even as stepping-stones unto others for ye performing of so great a work.

These, & some other like reasons, moved them to undertake this resolution of their removall; the which they afterward prosecuted with so great difficulties, as by the sequell will appeare.

The place they had thoughts on was some of those vast & unpeopled countries of America, which are frutfull & fitt for habitation, being devoyd of all civill inhabitants, wher ther are only salvage & brutish men, which range up and downe, litle otherwise then ye wild beasts of the same. This proposition being made publike and coming to ye scaning of all, it raised many variable opinions amongst men, and caused many fears & doubts amongst them selves. Some, from their reasons & hops conceived, laboured to stirr up & incourage the rest to undertake & prosecute ye same; others, againe, out of their fears, objected against it, & sought to diverte from it, aledging many things, and those neither unreasonable nor unprobable; as that it was a great designe, and subjecte to many unconceivable perills & dangers; as, besids the casulties of ye seas (which none can be freed from) the length of ye vioage was such, as ye weake bodys of women and other persons worne out with age & traville (as many of them were) could never be able to endure. And yet if they should, the miseries of ye land which they should be exposed unto, would be to hard to be borne; and lickly, some or all of them togeither, to consume & utterly to ruinate them. For ther they should be liable to famine, and nakednes, & ye wante, in a maner, of all things. The chang of aire, diate, & drinking of water, would infecte their bodies with sore sicknes, and greevous diseases. And also those which should escape or overcome these difficulties, should yett be in continuall danger of ye salvage people, who are cruell, barbarous, & most trecherous, being most furious in their rage, and merciles wher they overcome; not being contente only to kill, & take away life, but delight to tormente men in ye most bloodie mañer that may be; fleaing some alive with ye shells of fishes, cutting of ye members & joynts of others by peesmeale, and broiling on ye coles, eate ye collops of their flesh in their sight whilst they live; with other cruelties horrible to be related. And surely it could not be thought but ye very hearing of these things could not but move ye very bowels of men to grate within them, and make ye weake to quake & tremble. It was furder objected, that it would require greater sum̃es of money to furnish such a voiage, and to fitt them with necessaries, then their consumed estats would amounte too; and yett they must as well looke to be seconded with supplies, as presently to be trãsported. Also many presidents of ill success, & lamentable misseries befalne others in the like designes, were easie to be found, and not forgotten to be aledged; besids their owne experience, in their former troubles & hardships in their removall into Holand, and how hard a thing it was for them to live in that strange place, though it was a neighbour countrie, & a civill and rich comone wealth.

It was answered, that all great & honourable actions are accompanied with great difficulties, and must be both enterprised and overcome with answerable courages. It was granted ye dangers were great, but not desperate; the difficulties were many, but not invincible. For though their were many of them likly, yet they were not cartaine; it might be sundrie of ye things feared might never befale; others by providente care & ye use of good means, might in a great measure be prevented; and all of them, through ye help of God, by fortitude and patience, might either be borne, or overcome. True it was, that such atempts were not to be made and undertaken without good ground & reason; not rashly or lightly as many have done for curiositie or hope of gaine, &c. But their condition was not ordinarie; their ends were good & honourable; their calling lawfull, & urgente; and therfore they might expecte ye blessing of God in their proceding. Yea, though they should loose their lives in this action, yet might they have comforte in the same, and their endeavors would be honourable. They lived hear but as men in exile, & in a poore condition; and as great miseries might possibly befale them in this place, for ye 12. years of truce were now out, & ther was nothing but beating of drumes, and preparing for warr, the events wherof are allway uncertaine. Ye Spaniard might prove as cruell as the salvages of America, and ye famine and pestelence as sore hear as ther, & their libertie less to looke out for remedie. After many other perticuler things answered & aledged on both sids, it was fully concluded by ye major parte, to put this designe in execution, and to prosecute it by the best means they could.

Chapter IX

Of their vioage, & how they passed ye sea, and of their safe arrivall at Cape Codd.

Septr: 6. These troubls being blowne over, and now all being compacte togeather in one shipe, they put to sea againe with a prosperus winde, which continued diverce days togeather, which was some incouragmente unto them; yet according to ye usuall maner many were afflicted with sea-sicknes. And I may not omite hear a spetiall worke of Gods providence. Ther was a proud & very profane yonge man, one of ye sea-men, of a lustie, able body, which made him the more hauty; he would allway be contemning ye poore people in their sicknes, & cursing them dayly with greēous execrations, and did not let to tell them, that he hoped to help to cast halfe of them over board before they came to their jurneys end, and to make mery with what they had; and if he were by any gently reproved, he would curse and swear most bitterly. But it plased God before they came halfe seas over, to smite this yong man with a greeveous disease, of which he dyed in a desperate maner, and so was him selfe ye first yt was throwne overbord. Thus his curses light on his owne head; and it was an astonishmente to all his fellows, for they noted it to be ye just hand of God upon him.

After they had injoyed faire winds and weather for a season, they were incountred many times with crosse winds, and mette with many feirce stormes, with which ye shipe was shroudly shaken, and her upper works made very leakie; and one of the maine beames in ye midd ships was bowed & craked, which put them in some fear that ye shipe could not be able to performe ye vioage. So some of ye cheefe of ye company, perceiveing ye mariners to feare ye suffisiencie of ye shipe, as appeared by their mutterings, they entred into serious consulltation with ye mr. & other officers of ye ship, to consider in time of ye danger; and rather to returne then to cast them selves into a desperate & inevitable perill. And truly ther was great distraction & differance of opinion amongst ye mariners them selves; faine would they doe what could be done for their wages sake, (being now halfe the seas over,) and on ye other hand they were loath to hazard their lives too desperatly. But in examening of all opinions, the mr. & others affirmed they knew ye ship to be stronge & firme under water; and for the buckling of ye maine beame, ther was a great iron scrue ye passengers brought out of Holland, which would raise ye beame into his place; ye which being done, the carpenter & mr. affirmed that with a post put under it, set firme in ye lower deck, & otherways bounde, he would make it sufficiente. And as for ye decks & uper workes they would calke them as well as they could, and though with ye workeing of ye ship they would not longe keepe stanch, yet ther would otherwise be no great danger, if they did not overpress her with sails. So they comited them selves to ye will of God, & resolved to proseede. In sundrie of these stormes the winds were so feirce, & ye seas so high, as they could not beare a knote of saile, but were forced to hull, for diverce days togither. And in one of them, as they thus lay at hull, in a mighty storme, a lustie yonge man (called John Howland) coming upon some occasion above ye grattings, was, with a seele of the shipe throwne into [ye] sea; but it pleased God yt he caught hould of ye top-saile halliards, which hunge over board, & rane out at length; yet he held his hould (though he was sundrie fadomes under water) till he was hald up by ye same rope to ye brime of ye water, and then with a boat hooke & other means got into ye shipe againe, & his life saved; and though he was something ill with it, yet he lived many years after, and became a profitable member both in church & comone wealthe. In all this viage ther died but one of ye passengers, which was William Butten, a youth, servant to Samuell Fuller, when they drew near ye coast. But to omite other things, (that I may be breefe,) after longe beating at sea they fell with that land which is called Cape Cod; the which being made & certainly knowne to be it, they were not a litle joyfull. After some deliberation had amongst them selves & with ye mr. of ye ship, they tacked aboute and resolved to stande for ye southward (ye wind & weather being faire) to finde some place aboute Hudsons river for their habitation. But after they had sailed yt course aboute halfe ye day, they fell amongst deangerous shoulds and roring breakers, and they were so farr intangled ther with as they conceived them selves in great danger; & ye wind shrinking upon them withall, they resolved to bear up againe for the Cape, and thought them selves hapy to gett out of those dangers before night overtooke them, as by Gods providence they did. And ye next day they gott into ye Cape-harbor wher they ridd in saftie. A word or too by ye way of this cape; it was thus first named by Capten Gosnole & his company, Anno: 1602, and after by Capten Smith was caled Cape James; but it retains ye former name amongst seamen. Also yt pointe which first shewed those dangerous shoulds unto them, they called Pointe Care, & Tuckers Terrour; but ye

French & Dutch to this day call it Malabarr, by reason of those perilous shoulds, and ye losses they have suffered their.

Being thus arived in a good harbor and brought safe to land, they fell upon their knees & blessed ye God of heaven, who had brought them over ye vast & furious ocean, and delivered them from all ye periles & miseries therof, againe to set their feete on ye firme and stable earth, their proper elemente. And no marvell if they were thus joyefull, seeing wise Seneca was so affected with sailing a few miles on ye coast of his owne Italy; as he affirmed, that he had rather remaine twentie years on his way by land, then pass by sea to any place in a short time; so tedious & dreadfull was ye same unto him.

But hear I cannot but stay and make a pause, and stand half amased at this poore peoples presente condition; and so I thinke will the reader too, when he well considers ye same. Being thus passed ye vast ocean, and a sea of troubles before in their preparation (as may be remembred by yt which wente before), they had now no freinds to wellcome them, nor inns to entertaine or refresh their weatherbeaten bodys, no houses or much less townes to repaire too, to seeke for succoure. It is recorded in scripture as a mercie to ye apostle & his shipwraked company, yt the barbarians shewed them no smale kindnes in refreshing them, but these savage barbarians, when they mette with them (as after will appeare) were readier to fill their sids full of arrows then otherwise. And for ye season it was winter, and they that know ye winters of yt cuntrie know them to be sharp & violent, & subjecte to cruell & feirce stormes, deangerous to travill to known places, much more to serch an unknown coast. Besids, what could they see but a hidious & desolate wildernes, full of wild beasts & willd men? and what multituds ther might be of them they knew not. Nether could they, as it were, goe up to ye tope of Pisgah, to vew from this willdernes a more goodly cuntrie to feed their hops; for which way soever they turnd their eys (save upward to ye heavens) they could have litle solace or content in respecte of any outward objects. For sum̃er being done, all things stand upon them with a wetherbeaten face; and ye whole countrie, full of woods & thickets, represented a wild & savage heiw. If they looked behind them, ther was ye mighty ocean which they had passed, and was now as a maine barr & goulfe to seperate them from all ye civill parts of ye world. If it be said they had a ship to sucour them, it is trew; but what heard they daly from ye mr. & company? but yt with speede they should looke out a place with their shallop, wher they would be at some near distance; for ye season was shuch as he would not stirr from thence till a safe harbor was discovered by them wher they would be, and he might goe without danger; and that victells consumed apace, but he must & would keepe sufficient for them selves & their returne. Yea, it was muttered by some, that if they gott not a place in time, they would turne them & their goods ashore & leave them. Let it also be considred what weake hopes of supply & succoure they left behinde them, yt might bear up their minds in this sade condition and trialls they were under; and they could not but be very smale. It is true, indeed, ye affections & love of their brethren at Leyden was cordiall & entire towards them, but they had litle power to help them, or them selves; and how ye case stode betweene them & ye marchants at their coming away, hath allready been declared. What could now sustaine them but the spirite of God & his grace? May not & ought not the children of these fathers rightly say: *Our faithers were Englishmen which came over this great ocean, and were ready to perish in this willdernes; but they cried unto ye Lord, and he heard their voyce, and looked on their adversitie, &c. Let them therfore praise ye Lord, because he is good, & his mercies endure for ever. Yea, let them which have been redeemed of ye Lord, shew how he hath delivered them from ye hand of ye oppressour. When they wandered in ye deserte willdernes out of ye way, and found no citie to dwell in, both hungrie, & thirstie, their sowle was overwhelmed in them. Let them confess before ye Lord his loving kindnes, and his wonderfull works before ye sons of men.*

Chapter X

Showing how they sought out a place of habitation, and what befell them theraboute.

Being thus arrived at Cap-Cod ye 11. of November, and necessitie calling them to looke out a place for habitation, (as well as the maisters & mariners importunitie,) they having brought a large shalop with them out of England, stowed in quarters in ye ship, they now gott her out & sett their carpenters to worke to trime her up; but being much brused & shatered in ye shipe wth foule weather, they saw she would be longe in mending. Wherupon a few of them tendered them selves to goe by land and discovere those nearest places, whilst ye shallop was in mending; and ye rather because as they wente into yt harbor ther seemed to be an opening some 2. or 3 leagues of, which ye maister judged to be a river. It was conceived ther might be some danger in ye attempte, yet seeing them resolute, they were permited to goe, being 16. of them well armed, under ye conduct of Captain Standish, having shuch instructions given them as was thought meete. They sett forth ye 15. of Novebr: and when they had marched aboute the space of a mile by ye sea side, they espied 5. or 6. persons with a dogg coming towards them, who were salvages; but they fled from them, & rañe up into ye woods, and ye English followed them, partly to see if they could speake with them, and partly to discover if ther might not be more of them lying in ambush. But ye Indeans seeing them selves thus followed, they againe forsooke the woods, & rane away on ye sands as hard as they could, so as they could not come near them, but followed them by ye tracte of their feet sundrie miles, and saw that they had come the same way. So, night coming on, they made their randevous & set out their sentinels, and rested in quiete yt night, and the next morning followed their tracte till they had headed a great creake, & so left the sands, & turned an other way into ye woods. But they still followed them by geuss, hopeing to find their dwellings; but they soone lost both them & them selves, falling into shuch thickets as were ready to tear their cloaths & armore in peeces, but were most distresed for wante of drinke. But at length they found water & refreshed them selves, being ye first New-England water they drunke of, and was now in thir great thirste as pleasante unto them as wine or bear had been in for-times. Afterwards they directed their course to come to ye other shore, for they knew it was a necke of land they were to crosse over, and so at length gott to ye sea-side, and marched to this supposed river, & by ye way found a pond of clear fresh water, and shortly after a good quantitie of clear ground wher ye Indeans had formerly set corne, and some of their graves. And proceeding furder they saw new-stuble wher corne had been set ye same year, also they found wher latly a house had been, wher some planks and a great ketle was remaining, and heaps of sand newly padled with their hands, which they, digging up, found in them diverce faire Indean baskets filled with corne, and some in eares, faire and good, of diverce collours, which seemed to them a very goodly sight, (haveing never seen any shuch before). This was near ye place of that supposed river they came to seeck; unto which they wente and found it to open it selfe into 2. armes with a high cliffe of sand in ye enterance, but more like to be crikes of salte water then any fresh, for ought they saw; and that ther was good harborige for their shalope; leaving it further to be discovered by their shalop when she was ready. So their time limeted them being expired, they returned to ye ship, least they should be in fear of their saftie; and tooke with them parte of ye corne, and buried up ye rest, and so like ye men from Eshcoll carried with them of ye fruits of ye land, & showed their breethren; of which, & their returne, they were marvelusly glad, and their harts incouraged.

After this, ye shalop being got ready, they set out againe for ye better discovery of this place, & ye mr. of ye ship desired to goe him selfe, so ther went some 30. men, but found it to be no harbor for ships but only for boats; ther was allso found 2. of their houses covered with matts, & sundrie of their implements in them, but ye people were rune away & could not be seen; also ther was found more of their corne, & of their beans of various collours. The corne & beans they brought away, purposing to give them full satisfaction when they should meete with any of them (as about some 6. months afterward they did, to their good contente). And here is to be noted a spetiall providence of God, and a great mercie to this poore people, that hear they gott seed to plant them corne ye next year, or els they might have starved, for they had none, nor any liklyhood to get any till ye season had beene past (as ye sequell did manyfest). Neither is it lickly they had had this, if ye first viage had not been made, for the ground was now all covered with snow, & hard frozen. But the Lord is never wanting unto his in their greatest needs; let his holy name have all ye praise.

The month of November being spente in these affairs, & much foule weather falling in, the 6. of Desemr: they sente out their shallop againe with 10. of their principall men, & some sea men, upon further discovery, intending to circulate that deepe bay of Cap-codd. The weather was very could, & it frose so hard as ye sprea of ye sea lighting on their coats, they were as if they had been glased; yet that night betimes they gott downe into ye botome of ye bay, and as they drue nere ye shore they saw some 10. or 12. Indeans very busie aboute some thing. They landed aboute a league or 2. from them, and had much a doe to put a shore any wher, it lay so full of flats. Being landed, it grew late, and they made them selves a barricade with loggs & bowes as well as they could in ye time, & set out their sentenill & betooke them to rest, and saw ye smoake of ye fire ye savages made yt night. When morning was come they devided their company, some to coaste along ye shore in ye boate, and the rest marched throw ye woods to see ye land, if any fit place might be for their dwelling. They came allso to ye place wher they saw the Indans ye night before, & found they had been cuting up a great fish like a grampus, being some 2. inches thike of fate like a hogg, some peeces wher of they had left by ye way; and ye shallop found 2. more of these fishes dead on ye sands, a thing usuall after storms in yt place, by reason of ye great flats of sand that lye of. So they ranged up and doune all yt day, but found no people, nor any place they liked. When ye sune grue low, they hasted out of ye woods to meete with their shallop, to whom they made signes to come to them into a creeke hardby, the which they did at highwater; of which they were very glad, for they had not seen each other all yt day, since ye morning. So they made them a barricado (as usually they did every night) with loggs, staks, & thike pine bowes, ye height of a man, leaving it open to leeward, partly to shelter them from ye could & wind (making their fire in ye midle, & lying round aboute it), and partly to defend them from any sudden assaults of ye savags, if they should surround them. So being very weary, they betooke them to rest. But aboute midnight, they heard a hideous & great crie, and their sentinell caled, "Arme, arme"; so they bestired them & stood to their armes, & shote of a cupple of moskets, and then the noys seased. They concluded it was a companie of wolves, or such like willd beasts; for one of ye sea men tould them he had often heard shuch a noyse in New-found land. So they rested till about 5. of ye clock in the morning; for ye tide, & ther purposs to goe from thence, made them be stiring betimes. So after praier they prepared for breakfast, and it being day dawning, it was thought best to be carring things downe to ye boate. But some said it was not best to carrie ye armes downe, others said they would be the readier, for they had laped them up in their coats from ye dew. But some 3. or 4. would not cary theirs till they wente them selves, yet as it fell out, ye water being not high enough, they layed them downe on ye banke side, & came up to breakfast. But presently, all on ye sudain, they heard a great & strange crie, which they knew to be the same voyces they heard in ye night, though they varied their notes, & one of their company being abroad came runing in, & cried, "Men, Indeans, Indeans"; and wthall, their arowes came flying amongst them. Their men rane with all speed to recover their armes, as by ye good providence of God they did. In ye mean time, of those that were ther ready, tow muskets were discharged at them, & 2. more stood ready in ye enterance of ther randevoue, but were comanded not to shoote till they could take full aime at them; & ye other 2. charged againe with all speed, for ther were only 4. had armes ther, & defended ye baricado which was first assalted. The crie of ye Indeans was dreadfull, espetially when they saw ther men rune out of ye randevoue towourds ye shallop, to recover their armes, the Indeans wheeling aboute upon them. But some ruñing out with coats of malle on, & cutlasses in their hands, they soone got their armes, & let flye amongs them, and quickly stopped their violence. Yet ther was a lustie man, and no less valiante, stood behind a tree within halfe a musket shot, and let his arrows flie at them. He was seen shoot 3. arrowes, which were all avoyded. He stood 3. shot of a musket, till one taking full aime at him, and made ye barke or splinters of ye tree fly about his ears, after which he gave an extraordinary shrike, and away they wente all of them. They left some to keep ye shalop, and followed them aboute a quarter of a mille, and shouted once or twise, and shot of 2. or 3. peces, & so returned. This they did, that they might conceive that they were not affrade of them or any way discouraged. Thus it pleased God to vanquish their enimies, and give them deliverance; and by his spetiall providence so to dispose that not any one of them were either hurte, or hitt, though their arrows came close by them, & on every side them, and sundry of their coats, which hunge up in ye barricado, were shot throw & throw. Aterwards they gave God sollamne thanks & praise for their deliverance, & gathered up a bundle of their arrows, & sente them into England afterward by ye mr. of ye ship, and called that place ye first encounter. From hence they departed, & costed all along, but discerned no place likly for harbor; & therfore hasted to a place that their pillote, (one Mr. Coppin who had bine in ye cuntrie before) did assure them was a good harbor, which he had been in, and they might fetch it before night; of which they were glad, for it begane to be foule weather. After some houres sailing, it begane to snow & raine, & about ye midle of ye afternoone, ye wind increased, & ye sea became very rough, and they broake their rudder, & it was as much as 2. men could doe to steere her with a cupple of oares. But their pillott bad them be of good cheere, for he saw ye harbor; but ye storme increasing, & night drawing on, they bore what saile they could to gett in, while they could see. But herwith they broake their mast in 3. peeces, & their saill fell over bord, in a very grown sea, so as they had like to have been cast away; yet by Gods mercie they recovered them selves, & having ye floud with them, struck into ye harbore. But when it came too, ye pillott was deceived in ye place, and said, ye Lord be mercifull unto them, for his eys never saw yt place before; & he & the mr. mate would have rune her ashore, in a cove full of breakers, before ye winde. But a lusty seaman which steered, bad those which rowed, if they were men, about with her, or ells they were all cast away; the which they did with speed. So he bid them be of good cheere & row lustly, for ther was a faire sound before them, & he doubted not but they should find one place or other wher they might ride in saftie. And though it was *very darke*, and rained sore, yet in ye end they gott under ye lee of a smalle iland, and remained ther all yt night in saftie. But they knew not this to be an iland till morning, but were devided in their minds; some would keepe ye boate for fear they might be amongst ye Indians; others were so weake and could, they could not endure, but got a shore, & with much adoe got fire, (all things being so wett,) and ye rest were glad to come to them; for after midnight ye wind shifted to the north-west, & it frose hard. But though this had been a day & night of much trouble & danger unto them, yet God gave them a morning of comforte & refreshing (as usually he doth to his children), for ye next day was a faire sunshinīg day, and they found them sellvs to be on an iland secure from ye Indeans, wher they might drie their stufe, fixe their peeces, & rest them selves, and gave God thanks for his mercies, in their manifould deliverances. And this being the last day of ye weeke, they prepared ther to keepe ye Sabath. On Munday they sounded ye harbor, and founde it fitt for shipping; and marched into ye land, & found diverse cornfeilds, & litle runing brooks, a place (as they supposed) fitt for situation; at least it was ye best they could find, and ye season, & their presente necessitie, made them glad to accepte of it. So they returned to their shipp againe with this news to ye rest of their people, which did much comforte their harts.

On ye 15. *of Desemr*: they wayed anchor to goe to ye place they had discovered, & came within 2. leagues of it, but were faine to bear up againe; but ye 16. day ye winde came faire, and they arrived safe in this harbor. And after wards tooke better view of ye place, and resolved wher to pitch their dwelling; and ye 25. day begane to erecte ye first house for comone use to receive them and their goods.

BOOK II

Chapter X

In these hard & difficulte beginings they found some discontents & murmurings arise amongst some, and mutinous speeches & carriags in other; but they were soone quelled & overcome by ye wisdome, patience, and just & equall carrage of things by ye Govr and better part, wch clave faithfully togeather in ye maine. But that which was most sadd & lamentable was, that in 2. or 3. moneths time halfe of their company dyed, espetialy in Jan: & February, being ye depth of winter, and wanting houses & other comforts; being infected with ye scurvie & other diseases, which this long vioage & their inacomodate condition had brought upon them; so as ther dyed some times 2. or 3. of a day, in ye foresaid time; that of 100. & odd persons, scarce 50. remained. And of these in ye time of most distres, ther was but 6. or 7. sound persons, who, to their great comendations be it spoken, spared no pains, night nor day, but with abundance of toyle and hazard of their owne health, fetched them woode, made them fires, drest them meat, made their beads, washed their lothsome cloaths, cloathed & uncloathed them; in a word, did all ye homly & necessarie offices for them wch dainty & quesie stomacks cannot endure to hear named; and all this willingly & cherfully, without any grudging in ye least, shewing herein their true love unto their freinds & bretheren. A rare example & worthy to be remembred. Tow of these 7. were Mr. William Brewster, ther reverend Elder, & Myles Standish, ther Captein & military comander, unto whom my selfe, & many others, were much beholden in our low & sicke condition. And yet the Lord so upheld these persons, as in this generall calamity they were not at all infected either with sicknes, or lamnes. And what I have said of these, I may say of many others who dyed in this generall vissitation, & others yet living, that whilst they had health, yea, or any strength continuing, they were not wanting to any that had need of them. And I doute not but their recompence is with ye Lord.

But I may not hear pass by an other remarkable passage not to be forgotten. As this calamitie fell among ye passengers that were to be left here to plant, and were hasted a shore and made to drinke water, that ye sea-men might have ye more bear, and one in his sicknes desiring but a small cann of beere, it was answered, that if he were their owne father he should have none; the disease begane to fall amongst them also, so as allmost halfe of their company dyed before they went away, and many of their officers and lustyest men, as ye boatson, gunner, 3. quarter-maisters, the cooke, & others. At wch ye mr. was something strucken and sent to ye sick a shore and tould ye Govr he should send for beer for them that had need of it, though he drunke water homward bound. But now amongst his company ther was farr another kind of carriage in this miserie then amongst ye passengers; for they that before had been boone companions in drinking & joyllity in ye time of their health & wellfare, begane now to deserte one another in this calamitie, saing they would not hasard ther lives for them, they should be infected by coming to help them in their cabins, and so, after they came to dye by it, would doe litle or nothing for them, but if they dyed let them dye. But shuch of ye passengers as were yet abord shewed them what mercy they could, wch made some of their harts relente, as ye boatson (& some others), who was a prowd yonge man, and would often curse & scofe at ye passengers; but when he grew weak, they had compassion on him and helped him; then he confessed he did not deserve it at their hands, he had abused them in word & deed. O! saith he, you, I now see, shew your love like Christians indeed one to another, but we let one another lye & dye like doggs. Another lay cursing his wife, saing if it had not ben for her he had never come this unlucky viage, and anone cursing his felows, saing he had done this & that, for some of them, he had spente so much, & so much, amongst them, and they were now weary of him, and did not help him, having need. Another gave his companion all he had, if he died, to help him in his weaknes; he went and got a litle spise & made him a mess of meat once or twise, and because he dyed not so soone as he expected, he went amongst his fellows, & swore ye rogue would cousen him, he would see him choaked before he made him any more meate; and yet ye pore fellow dyed before morning.

All this while ye Indians came skulking about them, and would sometimes show them selves aloofe of, but when any aproached near them, they would rune away. And once they stoale away their tools wher they had been at worke, & were gone to diner. But about ye 16. *of March* a certaine Indian came bouldly amongst them, and spoke to them in broken English, which they could well understand, but marvelled at it. At length they understood by discourse with him, that he was not of these parts, but belonged to ye eastrene parts, wher some English-ships came to fhish, with whom he was aquainted, & could name sundrie of them by their names, amongst whom he had gott his language. He became proftable to them in aquainting them with many things concerning ye state of ye cuntry in ye east-parts wher he lived, which was afterwards profitable unto them; as also of ye people hear, of their names, number, & strength; of their situation & distance from this place, and who was cheefe amongst them. His name was *Samaset*; he tould them also of another Indian whos name was *Squanto*, a native of this place, who had been in England & could speake better English then him selfe. Being, after some time of entertainmente & gifts, dismist, a while after he came againe, & 5. more with him, & they brought againe all ye tooles that were stolen away before, and made way for ye coming of their great Sachem, called *Massasoyt*; who, about *4. or 5. days after*, came with the cheefe of his freinds & other attendance, with the aforesaid *Squanto*. With whom, after frendly entertainment, & some gifts given him, they made a peace with him (which hath now continued this 24. years) in these terms.

1. That neither he nor any of his, should injurie or doe hurte to any of their peopl.
2. That if any of his did any hurte to any of theirs, he should send ye offender, that they might punish him.
3. That if any thing were taken away from any of theirs, he should cause it to be restored; and they should doe ye like to his.
4. If any did unjustly warr against him, they would aide him; if any did warr against them, he should aide them.
5. He should send to his neighbours confederats, to certifie them of this, that they might not wrong them, but might be likewise comprised in ye conditions of peace.
6. That when ther men came to them, they should leave their bows & arrows behind them.

After these things he returned to his place caled *Sowams*, some 40. mile from this place, but *Squanto* continued with them, and was their interpreter, and was a spetiall instrument sent of God for their good beyond their expectation. He directed them how to set their corne, wher to take fish, and to procure other comodities, and was also their pilott to bring them to unknowne places for their profitt, and never left them till he dyed. He was a *native of this place*, & scarce any left alive besids him selfe. He was caried away with diverce others by one *Hunt*, a mr. of a ship, who thought to sell them for slaves in Spaine; but he got away for England, and was entertained by a marchante in London, & imployed to New-foundland & other parts, & lastly brought hither into these parts by one Mr. *Dermer*, a gentleman imployed by Sr. Ferdinando Gorges & others, for discovery, & other designes in these parts. Of whom I shall say some thing, because it is mentioned in a booke set forth Ano: 1622. by the Presidente & Counsell for New-England, that he made ye peace betweene ye salvages of these parts & ye English; of which this plantation, as it is intimated, had ye benefite. But what a peace it was, may apeare by what befell him & his men.

This Mr. Dermer was hear the same year that these people came, as apears by a relation written by him, & given me by a friend, bearing date June 30. Ano: 1620. And they came in Novembr: following, so ther was but 4. months differance. In which relation to his honored freind, he hath these passages of this very place.

> I will first begine (saith he) wth that place from whence *Squanto*, or *Tisquantem*, was taken away; wch in Cap: *Smiths mape* is called *Plimoth*: and I would that Plimoth had ye like comodities. I would that the first plantation might hear be seated, if ther come to the number of 50. persons, or upward. Otherwise at Charlton, because ther ye savages are lese to be feared. The *Pocanawkits*, which live to ye *west* of *Plimoth*, bear an inveterate malice to ye English, and are of more streingth then all ye savags from thence to Penobscote. Their desire of revenge was occasioned by an English man, who having many of them on bord, made a great slaughter with their murderers & smale shot, when as (they say) they offered no injurie on their parts. Whether they were English or no, it may be douted; yet they beleeve they were, for ye Frenche have so possest them; for which cause *Squanto* cañot deney but they would have kiled me when I was at *Namasket*, had he not entreated hard for me. The soyle of ye borders of this great bay, may be compared to most of ye plantations which I have seene in Virginia. The land is of diverce sorts; for *Patuxite* is a hardy but strong soyle, *Nawsel & Saughtughtett* are for ye most part a blakish & deep mould, much like that wher groweth ye best Tobaco in Virginia. In ye botume of yt great bay is store of Codd & basse, or mulett, &c.

But above all he comends *Pacanawkite* for ye richest soyle, and much open ground fitt for English graine, &c.

> *Massachussets* is about 9. leagues from *Plimoth*, & situate in ye mids betweene both, is full of ilands & peninsules very fertill for ye most parte.

With sundrie shuch relations which I forbear to transcribe, being now better knowne then they were to him.

He was taken prisoner by ye Indeans at *Manamoiak* (a place not farr from hence, now well knowne). He gave them what they demanded for his liberty, but when they had gott what they desired, they kept him still & indevored to kill his men; but he was freed by seasing on some of them, and kept them bound till they gave him a cannows load of corne. Of which, see Purch: lib. 9. fol. 1778. But this was Ano: 1619.

After ye writing of ye former relation he came to ye Ile of *Capawack* (which lyes south of this place in ye way to Virginia), and ye foresaid *Squanto* wth him, wher he going a shore amongst ye Indans to trad, as he used to doe, was betrayed & assaulted by them, & *all his men slaine, but one that kept the boat*; but him selfe gott abord very sore wounded, & they had cut of his head upon ye cudy of his boat, had not ye man reskued him with a sword. And so they got away, & made shift to gett into Virginia, wher he dyed; whether of his wounds or ye diseases of ye cuntrie, or both togeather, is uncertaine. By all which it may appeare how farr these people were from peace, and with what danger this plantation was begune, save as ye powerfull hand of the Lord did protect them. These things were partly the reason why they kept aloofe & were so long before they came to the English. An other reason (as after them selvs made know̃) was how aboute 3. *years before*, a French-ship was cast away at *Cap-Codd*, but ye men gott ashore, & saved their lives, and much of their victails, & other goods; but after ye Indeans heard of it, they geathered togeather from these parts, and never left watching & dogging them till they got advantage, and *kild them all but 3. or 4.* which they kept, & sent from one Sachem to another, to make sporte with, and used them worse then slaves; (of which ye foresaid Mr. Dermer redeemed 2. of them;) and they conceived this ship was now come to revenge it.

Also, (as after was made knowne,) before they came to ye English to make freindship, they gott all the *Powachs* of ye cuntrie, for 3. days togeather, in a horid and divellish maner to curse & execrate them with their cunjurations, which asembly & service they held in a darke & dismale swampe.

But to returne. The spring now approaching, it pleased God the mortalitie begane to cease amongst them, and ye sick and lame recovered apace, which put as it were new life into them; though they had borne their sadd affliction with much patience & contentednes, as I thinke any people could doe. But it was ye Lord which upheld them, and had beforehand prepared them; many having long borne ye yoake, yea from their youth. Many other smaler maters I omite, sundrie of them having been allready published in a Jurnall made by one of the company; and some other passages of jurneys and relations allredy published, to which I referr those that are willing to know them more perticulerly. And being now come to ye 25. of March I shall begine ye year 1621.

Chapter XIX

This year the Dutch sent againe unto them from their plantation, both kind leterss, and also diverse comodities, as suger, linen cloth, Holand finer & courser stufes, &c. They came up with their barke to Manamete, to their house ther, in which came their Secretarie Rasier; who was accompanied with a noyse of trumpeters, and some other attendants; and desired that they would send a boat for him, for he could not travill so farr over land. So they sent a boat to Manonscussett, and brought him to ye plantation, with ye cheefe of his company. And after some few days entertainmente, he returned to his barke, and some of them wente with him, and bought sundry of his goods; after which begining thus made, they sente often times to ye same place, and had entercourse togeather for diverce years; and amongst other comodities, they vended much tobaco for linen cloath, stuffs, &c., which was a good benefite to ye people, till the Virginians found out their plantation. But that which turned most to their profite, in time, was an entrance into the trade of Wampampeake; for they now bought aboute 50li. worth of it of them; and they tould them how vendable it was at their forte Orania; and did perswade them they would find it so at Kenebeck; and so it came to pass in time, though at first it stuck, & it was 2. years before they could put of this small quantity, till ye inland people knew of it; and afterwards they could scarce ever gett enough for them, for many years togeather. And so this, with their other provissions, cutt of they trade quite from ye fisher-men, and in great part from other of ye stragling planters. And strange it was to see the great allteration it made in a few years amonge ye Indeans them selves; for all the Indeans of these parts, & ye Massachussets, had none or very litle of it, but ye sachems & some spetiall persons that wore a litle of it for ornamente. Only it was made & kepte amonge ye Nariganssets, & Pequents, which grew rich & potent by it, and these people were poore & begerly, and had no use of it. Neither did the English of this plantation, or any other in ye land, till now that they had knowledg of it from ye Dutch, so much as know what it was, much less yt it was a com̃oditie of that worth & valew. But after it grue thus to be a comoditie in these parts, these Indeans fell into it allso, and to learne how to make it; for ye Narigansets doe geather ye shells of which yey make it from their shors. And it hath now continued a current comoditie aboute this 20. years, and it may prove a drugg in time. In ye mean time it maks ye Indeans of these parts rich & power full and also prowd therby; and fills them with peeces, powder, and shote, which no laws can restraine, by reasone of ye bassnes of sundry unworthy persons, both English, Dutch, & French, which may turne to ye ruine of many. Hithertoo ye Indeans of these parts had no peeces nor other armes but their bowes & arrowes, nor of many years after; nether durst they scarce handle a gune, so much were they affraid of them; and ye very sight of one (though out of kilter) was a terrour unto them. But those Indeans to ye east parts, which had com̃erce with ye French, got peces of them, and they in the end made a commone trade of it; and in time our English fisher-men, led with ye like covetoussnes, followed their example, for their owne gaine; but upon complainte against them, it pleased the kings majestie to prohibite ye same by a stricte proclaimation, commanding that no sorte of armes, or munition, should by any of his subjects be traded with them.

Aboute some 3. or 4. years before this time, ther came over one Captaine Wolastone, (a man of pretie parts,) and with him 3. or 4. more of some eminencie, who brought with them a great many servants, with provissions & other implments for to begine a plantation; and pitched them selves in a place within the Massachusets, which they called, after their Captains name, Mount-Wollaston. Amongst whom was one Mr. Morton, who, it should seeme, had some small adventure (of his owne or other mens) amongst them; but had litle respecte amongst them, and was sleghted by ye meanest servants. Haveing continued ther some time, and not finding things to answer their expectations, nor profite to arise as they looked for, Captaine Wollaston takes a great part of ye sarvants, and transports them to Virginia, wher he puts them of at good rates, selling their time to other men; and writs back to one Mr. Rassdall, one of his cheefe partners, and accounted their marchant, to bring another parte of them to Verginia likewise, intending to put them of ther as he had done ye rest. And he, wth ye consente of ye said Rasdall, appoynted one Fitcher to be his Livetenante, and governe ye remaines of ye plantation, till he or Rasdall returned to take further order theraboute. But this Morton abovesaid, haveing more craft then honestie, (who had been a kind of petie-fogger, of Furnefells Inne,) in ye others absence, watches an oppertunitie, (commons being but hard amongst them,) and gott some strong drinck & other junkats, & made them a feast; and after they were merie, he begane to tell them, he would give them good counsell. You see (saith he) that many of your fellows are carried to Virginia; and if you stay till this Rasdall returne, you will also be carried away and sould for slaves with ye rest. Therfore I would advise you to thruste out this Levetenant Fitcher; and I, having a parte in the plantation, will receive you as my partners and consociats; so may you be free from service, and we will converse, trad, plante, & live togeather as equalls, & supporte & protecte one another, or to like effecte. This counsell was easily received; so they tooke oppertunitie, and thrust Levetenante Fitcher out a dores, and would suffer him to come no more amongst them, but forct him to seeke bread to eate, and other releefe from his neigbours, till he could gett passages for England. After this they fell to great licenciousnes, and led a dissolute life, powering out them selves into all profanenes. And Morton became lord of misrule, and maintained (as it were) a schoole of Athisme. And after they had gott some good into their hands, and gott much by trading with ye Indeans, they spent it as vainly, in quaffing & drinking both wine & strong waters in great exsess, and, as some reported, 10li. worth in a morning. They allso set up a May-pole, drinking and dancing aboute it many days togeather, inviting the Indean women, for their consorts, dancing and frisking togither, (like so many fairies, or furies rather,) and worse practises. As if they had anew revived & celebrated the feasts of ye Roman Goddes Flora, or ye beasly practieses of ye madd Bacchinalians. Morton likwise (to shew his poetrie) composed sundry rimes & verses, some tending to lasciviousnes, and others to ye detraction & scandall of some persons, which he affixed to this idle or idoll May-polle. They chainged allso the name of their place, and in stead of calling it Mounte Wollaston, they call it Merie-mounte, as if this joylity would have lasted ever. But this continued not long, for after Morton was sent for England, (as follows to be declared,) shortly after came over that worthy gentlman, Mr. John Indecott, who brought over a patent under ye broad seall, for ye govermente of ye Massachusets, who visiting those parts caused yt May-polle to be cutt downe, and rebuked them for their profannes, and admonished them to looke ther should be better walking; so they now, or others, changed ye name of their place againe, and called it Mounte-Dagon.

Now to maintaine this riotous prodigallitie and profuse excess, Morton, thinking him selfe lawless, and hearing what gaine ye French & fisher-men made by trading of peeces, powder, & shotte to ye Indeans, he, as ye head of this consortship, begane ye practise of ye same in these parts; and first he taught them how to use them, to charge, & discharg, and what proportion of powder to give ye peece, according to ye sise or bignes of ye same; and what shotte to use for foule, and what for deare. And having thus instructed them, he imployed some of them to hunte & fowle for him, so as they became farr more active in that imploymente then any of ye English, by reason of ther swiftnes of foote, & nimblnes of body, being also quick-sighted, and by continuall exercise well knowing ye hants of all sorts of game. So as when they saw ye execution that a peece would doe, and ye benefite that might come by ye same, they became madd, as it were, after them, and would not stick to give any prise they could attaine too for them; accounting their bowes & arrowes but bables in comparison of them.

And here I may take occasion to bewaile ye mischefe that this wicked man began in these parts, and which since base covetousnes prevailing in men that should know better, has now at length gott ye upper hand, and made this thing comone, notwithstanding any laws to ye contrary; so as ye Indeans are full of peeces all over, both fouling peeces, muskets, pistols, &c. They have also their moulds to make shotte, of all sorts, as muskett bulletts, pistoll bullets, swane & gose shote, & of smaler sorts; yea, some have seen them have their scruplats to make scrupins them selves, when they wante them, with sundery other implements, wherwith they are ordinarily better fited & furnished then ye English them selves. Yea, it is well knowne that they will have powder & shot, when the English want it, nor cannot gett it; and yt in a time of warr or danger, as experience hath manifested, that when lead hath been scarce, and men for their owne defence would gladly have given a groat a l which is dear enoughe, yet hath it bene bought up & sent to other places, and sould to shuch as trade it with ye Indeans, at 12. pence ye li.; and it is like they give 3. or 4.s ye pound, for they will have it at any rate. And these things have been done in ye same times, when some of their neigbours & freinds are daly killed by ye Indeans, or are in deanger therof, and live but at ye Indeans mercie. Yea, some (as they have aquainted them with all other things) have tould them how gunpowder is made, and all ye materialls in it, and that they are to be had in their owne land; and I am confidente, could they attaine to make saltpeter, they would teach them to make powder. O the horiblnes of this vilanie! how many both Dutch & English have been latly slaine by those Indeans, thus furnished; and no remedie provided, nay, ye evill more increased, and ye blood of their brethren sould for gaine, as is to be feared; and in what danger all these colonies are in is too well known. Oh! that princes & parlements would take some timly order to prevente this mischeefe, and at length to suppress it, by some exemplerie punishmente upon some of these gaine thirstie murderers, (for they deserve no better title,) before their collonies in these parts be over throwne by these barbarous savages, thus armed with their owne weapons, by these evill instruments, and traytors to their neigbors and cuntrie. But I have forgott my selfe, and have been to longe in this digression; but now to returne. This Morton having thus taught them ye use of peeces, he sould them all he could spare; and he and his consorts detirmined to send for many out of England, and had by some of ye ships sente for above a score. The which being knowne, and his neigbours meeting ye Indeans in ye woods armed with guns in this sorte, it was a terrour unto them, who lived straglingly, and were of no strenght in any place. And other places (though more remote) saw this mischeefe would quietly spread over all, if not prevented. Besides, they saw they should keep no servants, for Morton would entertaine any, how vile soever, and all ye scume of ye countrie, or any discontents, would flock to him from all places, if this nest was not broken; and they should stand in more fear of their lives & goods (in short time) from this wicked & deboste crue, then from ye salvages them selves.

So sundrie of ye cheefe of ye stragling plantations, meeting togither, agreed by mutuall consente to sollissite those of Plimoth (who were then of more strength then them all) to joyne with them, to prevente ye further grouth of this mischeefe, and suppress Morton & his consortes before yey grewe to further head and strength. Those that joyned in this acction (and after contributed to the charge of sending him for England) were from Pascataway, Namkeake, Winisimett, Weesagascusett, Natasco, and other places wher any English were seated. Those of Plimoth being thus sought too by their messengers & letters, and waying both their reasons, and the com̃one danger, were willing to afford them their help; though them selves had least cause of fear or hurte. So, to be short, they first resolved joyntly to write to him, and in a freindly & neigborly way to admonish him to forbear these courses, & sent a messenger with their letters to bring his answer. But he was so highe as he scorned all advise, and asked who had to doe with him; he had and would trade peeces with ye Indeans in dispite of all, with many other scurillous termes full of disdaine. They sente to him a second time, and bad him be better advised, and more temperate in his termes, for ye countrie could not beare ye injure he did; it was against their comone saftie, and against ye king's proclamation. He answerd in high terms as before, and that ye kings proclamation was no law; demanding what penaltie was upon it. It was answered, more then he could bear, his majesties displeasure. But insolently he persisted, and said ye king was dead and his displeasure with him, & many ye like things; and threatened withall that if any came to molest him, let them looke to them selves, for he would prepare for them. Upon which they saw ther was no way but to take him by force; and having so farr proceeded, now to give over would make him farr more hautie & insolente. So they mutually resolved to proceed, and obtained of ye Govr of Plimoth to send Captaine Standish, & some other aide with him, to take Morton by force. The which accordingly was done; but they found him to stand stifly in his defence, having made fast his dors, armed his consorts, set diverse dishes of powder & bullets ready on ye table; and if they had not been over armed with drinke, more hurt might have been done. They som̃aned him to yeeld, but he kept his house, and they could gett nothing but scofes & scorns from him; but at length, fearing they would doe some violence to ye house, he and some of his crue came out, but not to yeeld, but to shoote; but they were so steeld with drinke as their peeces were to heavie for them; him selfe with a carbine (over charged & allmost halfe fild with powder & shote, as was after found) had thought to have shot Captaine Standish; but he stept to him, & put by his peece, & tooke him. Neither was ther any hurte done to any of either side, save yt one was so drunke yt he rane his owne nose upon ye pointe of a sword yt one held before him as he entred ye house; but he lost but a litle of his hott blood. Morton they brought away to Plimoth, wher he was kepte, till a ship went from ye Ile of Shols for England, with which he was sente to ye Counsell of New-England; and letters writen to give them information of his course & cariage; and also one was sent at their comone charge to informe their Hors more perticulerly, & to prosecute against him. But he foold of ye messenger, after he was gone from hence, and though he wente for England, yet nothing was done to him, not so much as rebukte, for ought was heard; but returned ye nexte year. Some of ye worst of ye company were disperst, and some of ye more modest kepte ye house till he should be heard from. But I have been too long aboute so un-worthy a person, and bad a cause.

This year Mr. Allerton brought over a yonge man for a minister to ye people hear, wheather upon his owne head, or at ye motion of some freinds ther, I well know not, but it was without ye churches sending; for they had bene so bitten by Mr. Lyford, as they desired to know ye person well whom they should invite amongst them. His name was Mr. Rogers; but they perceived, upon some triall, that he was crased in his braine; so they were faine to be at further charge to send him back againe ye nexte year, and loose all ye charge that was expended in his hither bringing, which was not smalle by Mr. Allerton's accounte, in provissions, aparell, bedding, &c. After his returne he grue quite distracted, and Mr. Allerton was much blamed yt he would bring such a man over, they having charge enough otherwise.

Chapter XXIII

Also ye people of ye plantation begane to grow in their owtward estats, by reason of ye flowing of many people into ye cuntrie, espetially into ye Bay of ye Massachusets; by which means corne & catle rose to a great prise, by wch many were much inriched, and comodities grue plentifull; and yet in other regards this benefite turned to their hurte, and this accession of strength to their weaknes. For now as their stocks increased, and ye increse vendible, ther was no longer any holding them togeather, but now they must of necessitie goe to their great lots; they could not other wise keep their katle; and having oxen growne, they must have land for plowing & tillage. And no man now thought he could live, except he had catle and a great deale of ground to keep them; all striving to increase their stocks. By which means they were scatered all over ye bay, quickly, and ye towne, in which they lived compactly till now, was left very thine, and in a short time allmost desolate. And if this had been all, it had been less, thoug to much; but ye church must also be devided, and those yt had lived so long togeather in Christian & comfortable fellowship must now part and suffer many divissions. First, those that lived on their lots on ye other side of the bay (called Duxberie) they could not long bring their wives & children to ye publick worship & church meetings here, but with such burthen, as, growing to some competente number, they sued to be dismissed and become a body of them selves; and so they were dismiste (about this time), though very unwillingly. But to touch this sadd matter, and handle things together that fell out afterward. To prevent any further scatering from this place, and weakning of ye same, it was thought best to give out some good farms to spetiall persons, yt would promise to live at Plimoth, and lickly to be helpfull to ye church or comonewelth, and so tye ye lands to Plimoth as farmes for the same; and ther they might keepe their catle & tillage by some servants, and retaine their dwellings here. And so some spetiall lands were granted at a place generall, called Greens Harbor, wher no allotments had been in ye former divission, a plase very weell meadowed, and fitt to keep & rear catle, good store. But alass! this remedy proved worse then ye disease; for wthin a few years those that had thus gott footing ther rente them selves away, partly by force, and partly wearing ye rest with importunitie and pleas of necessitie, so as they must either suffer them to goe, or live in continuall opposition and contention. And others still, as yey conceived them selves straitened, or to want accom̃odation, break away under one pretence or other, thinking their owne conceived necessitie, and the example of others, a warrente sufficente for them. And this, I fear, will be ye ruine of New-England, at least of ye churches of God ther, & will provock ye Lords displeasure against them.

Chapter XXVII

In ye year 1634, the Pequents (a stoute and warlike people), who had made warrs with sundry of their neigbours, and puft up with many victories, grue now at varience with ye Narigansets, a great people bordering upon them. These Narigansets held correspondance and termes of freindship with ye English of ye Massachusetts. Now ye Pequents, being conscious of ye guilte of Captain-Stones death, whom they knew to be an-English man, as also those yt were with him, and being fallen out with ye Dutch, least they should have over many enemies at once, sought to make freindship with ye English of ye Massachusetts; and for yt end sent both messengers & gifts unto them, as appears by some letters sent from ye Govr hither.

> Dear & worthy Sr: &c. To let you know somwhat of our affairs, you may understand that ye Pequents have sent some of theirs to us, to desire our freindship, and offered much wampam & beaver, &c. The first messengers were dismissed without answer; with ye next we had diverce dayes conferance, and taking ye advice of some of our ministers, and seeking the Lord in it, we concluded a peace & freindship with them, upon these conditions: that they should deliver up to us those men who were guilty of Stones death, &c. And if we desired to plant in Conightecute, they should give up their right to us, and so we would send to trade with them as our freinds (which was ye cheefe thing

we aimed at, being now in warr with ye Dutch and ye rest of their neigbours). To this they readily agreed; and that we should meadiate a peace betweene them and the Narigansetts; for which end they were contente we should give the Narigansets parte of yt presente, they would bestow on us (for they stood so much on their honour, as they would not be seen to give any thing of them selves). As for Captein Stone, they tould us ther were but 2. left of those who had any hand in his death; and that they killed him in a just quarell, for (say they) he surprised 2. of our men, and bound them, to make them by force to shew him ye way up ye river; and he with 2. other coming on shore, 9. Indeans watched him, and when they were a sleepe in ye night, they kiled them, to deliver their owne men; and some of them going afterwards to ye pinass, it was suddainly blowne up. We are now preparing to send a pinass unto them, &c.

In an other of his, dated ye 12. of ye first month, he hath this.

Our pinass is latly returned from ye Pequents; they put of but litle comoditie, and found them a very false people, so as they mean to have no more to doe with them. I have diverce other things to write unto you, &c.

Yours ever assured,
Jo: Winthrop.
Boston, 12. of ye 1. month, 1634.

After these things, and, as I take, this year, John Oldom, (of whom much is spoken before,) being now an inhabitant of ye Massachusetts, went wth a small vessell, & slenderly mand, a trading into these south parts, and upon a quarell betweene him & ye Indeans was cutt of by them (as hath been before noted) at an iland called by ye Indeans Munisses, but since by ye English Block Iland. This, with ye former about the death of Stone, and the baffoyling of ye Pequents with ye English of ye Massachusetts, moved them to set out some to take revenge, and require satisfaction for these wrongs; but it was done so superfitially, and without their acquainting of those of Conightecute & other neighbours with ye same, as they did litle good. But their neigbours had more hurt done, for some of ye murderers of Oldome fled to ye Pequents, and though the English went to ye Pequents, and had some parley with them, yet they did but delude them, & ye English returned without doing any thing to purpose, being frustrate of their oppertunitie by ye others deceite. After ye English were returned, the Pequents tooke their time and oppertunitie to cut of some of ye English as they passed in boats, and went on fouling, and assaulted them ye next spring at their habytations, as will appear in its place. I doe but touch these things, because I make no question they wall be more fully & distinctly handled by them selves, who had more exacte knowledg of them, and whom they did more properly concerne.

Chapter XXVIII

Anno Dom: 1637.

In ye fore parte of this year, the Pequents fell openly upon ye English at Conightecute, in ye lower parts of ye river, and slew sundry of them, (as they were at work in ye feilds,) both men & women, to ye great terrour of ye rest; and wente away in great prid & triumph, with many high threats. They allso assalted a fort at ye rivers mouth, though strong and well defended; and though they did not their prevaile, yet it struk them with much fear & astonishmente to see their bould attempts in the face of danger; which made them in all places to stand upon their gard, and to prepare for resistance, and ernestly to solissite their freinds and confederats in ye Bay of Massachusets to send them speedy aide, for they looked for more forcible assaults. Mr. Vane, being then Govr, write from their Generall Courte to them hear, to joyne with them in this warr; to which they were cordially willing, but tooke opportunitie to write to them aboute some former things, as well as presente, considerable hereaboute. The which will best appear in ye Govr answer which he returned to ye same, which I shall here inserte.

> Sr: The Lord having so disposed, as that your letters to our late Govr is fallen to my lott to make answer unto, I could have wished I might have been at more freedome of time & thoughts also, that I might have done it more to your & my owne satisfaction. But what shall be wanting now may be supplyed hereafter. For ye matters which from your selfe & counsell were propounded & objected to us, we thought not fitte to make them so publicke as ye cognizance of our Generall Courte. But as they have been considered by those of our counsell, this answer we thinke fitt to returne unto you. (1.) Wereas you signifie your willingnes to joyne with us in this warr against ye Pequents, though you cannot ingage your selves without ye consente of your Generall Courte, we acknowledg your good affection towards us, (which we never had cause to doubt of,) and are willing to attend your full resolution, when it may most seasonably be ripened. (2ly.) Wheras you make this warr to be our peopls, and not to conceirne your selves, otherwise then by consequence, we do in parte consente to you therin; yet we suppose, that, in case of perill, you will not stand upon such terms, as we hope we should not doe towards you; and withall we conceive that you looke at ye Pequents, and all other Indeans, as a comone enimie, who, though he may take occasion of ye begining of his rage, from some one parte of ye English, yet if he prevaile, will surly pursue his advantage, to ye rooting out of ye whole nation. Therfore when we desired your help, we did it not without respecte to your owne saftie, as ours. (3ly.) Wheras you desire we should be ingaged to aide you, upon all like occasions; we are perswaded you doe not doubte of it; yet as we now deale with you as a free people, and at libertie, so as we cannot draw you into this warr with us, otherwise then as reason may guid & provock you; so we desire we may be at ye like freedome, when any occasion may call for help

from us. And wheras it is objected to us, that we refused to aide you against ye French; we conceive ye case was not alicke; yet we cannot wholy excuse our failing in that matter. (4ly.) Weras you objecte that we began ye warr without your privitie, & managed it contrary to your advise; the truth is, that our first intentions being only against Block Iland, and ye interprice seeming of small difficultie, we did not so much as consider of taking advice, or looking out for aide abroad. And when we had resolved upon ye Pequents, we sent presently, or not long after, to you aboute it; but ye answer received, it was not seasonable for us to chaing our counsells, excepte we had seen and waighed your grounds, which might have out wayed our owne.

(5ly.) For our peoples trading at Kenebeck, we assure you (to our knowledge) it hath not been by any allowance from us; and what we have provided in this and like cases, at our last Courte, Mr. E. W. can certifie you.

And (6ly); wheras you objecte to us yt we should hold trade & correspondancie with ye French, your enemise; we answer, you are misinformed, for, besids some letters which hath passed betweene our late Govr and them, to which we were privie, we have neither sente nor incouraged ours to trade with them; only one vessell or tow, for ye better conveãce of our letters, had licens from our Govr to sayle thither.

Diverce other things have been privatly objected to us, by our worthy freind, wherunto he received some answer; but most of them concerning ye apprehention of perticuler discurteseis, or injueries from some perticuler persons amongst us. It concernes us not to give any other answer to them then this; that, if ye offenders shall be brought forth in a right way, we shall be ready to doe justice as ye case shall require. In the meane time, we desire you to rest assured, that such things are without our privity, and not a litle greeveous to us.

Now for ye joyning with us in this warr, which indeed concerns us no other wise then it may your selves, viz.: the releeving of our freinds & Christian breethren, who are now first in ye danger; though you may thinke us able to make it good without you, (as, if ye Lord please to be with us, we may,) yet 3. things we offer to your consideration, which (we conceive) may have some waight with you. (First) yt if we should sinck under this burden, your opportunitie of seasonable help would be lost in 3. respects. 1. You cannot recover us, or secure your selves ther, with 3. times ye charge & hazard which now ye may. 2ly. The sorrowes which we should lye under (if through your neglect) would much abate of ye acceptablenes of your help afterwards. 3ly. Those of yours who are now full of courage and forwardnes, would be much damped, and so less able to undergoe so great a burden. The (2.) thing is this, that it concernes us much to hasten this warr to an end before ye end of this somer, otherwise ye newes of it will discourage both your & our freinds from coming to us next year; with what further hazard & losse it may expose us unto, your selves may judge.

The (3.) thing is this, that if ye Lord shall please to blesse our endeaours, so as we end ye warr, or put it in a hopefull way without you, it may breed such ill thoughts in our people towards yours, as will be hard to entertaine such opinione of your good will towards us, as were fitt to be nurished among such neigbours & brethren as we are. And what ill consequences may follow, on both sids, wise men may fear, & would rather prevente then hope to redress. So with my harty salutations to you selfe, and all your counsell, and other our good freinds with you, I rest

Yours most assured in ye Lord,
Jo: Winthrop.
Boston, ye 20. of ye 3. month, 1637.

In ye mean time, the Pequents, espetially in ye winter before, sought to make peace with ye Narigansets, and used very pernicious arguments to move them therunto: as that ye English were stranegers and begane to overspred their countrie, and would deprive them therof in time, if they were suffered to grow & increse; and if ye Narigansets did assist ye English to subdue them, they did but make way for their owne overthrow, for if they were rooted out, the English would soone take occasion to subjugate them; and if they would harken to them, they should not neede to fear ye strength of ye English; for they would not come to open battle with them, but fire their houses, kill their katle, and lye in ambush for them as they went abroad upon their occasions; and all this they might easily doe without any or litle danger to them selves. The which course being held, they well saw the English could not long subsiste, but they would either be starved with hunger, or be forced to forsake the countrie; with many ye like things; insomuch that ye Narigansets were once wavering, and were halfe minded to have made peace with them, and joy̅ed against ye English. But againe when they considered, how much wrong they had received from the Pequents, and what an oppertunitie they now had by ye help of ye English to right them selves, revenge was so sweete unto them, as it prevailed above all ye rest; so as they resolved to joyne with ye English against them, & did. The Court here agreed forwith to send 50. men at their owne charg; and wth as much speed as posiblie they could, gott them armed, and had made them ready under sufficiente leaders, and provided a barke to carrie them provisions & tend upon them for all occasions; but when they were ready to march (with a supply from ye Bay) they had word to stay, for ye enimy was as good as vanquished, and their would be no neede.

I shall not take upon me exactly to describe their proceedings in these things, because I expecte it will be fully done by them selves, who best know the carrage & circumstances of things; I shall therfore but touch them in generall. From Connightecute (who were most sencible of ye hurt sustained, & ye present danger), they sett out a partie of men, and an other partie mett them from ye Bay, at ye Narigansets, who were to joyne with them. Ye Narigansets were ernest to be gone before ye English were well rested and refreshte, espetially some of them which came last. It should seeme their desire was to come upon ye enemie sudenly, & undiscovered. Ther was a barke of this place, newly put in ther, which was come from Conightecutte, who did incourage them to lay hold of ye Indeans forwardnes, and to shew as great forwardnes as they, for it would incorage them, and expedition might prove to their great advantage. So they went on, and so ordered their march, as the Indeans brought them to a forte of ye enimies (in which most of their cheefe men were) before day. They approached ye same with great silence, and surrounded it both with English & Indeans, that they might not breake out; and so assualted them with great courage, shooting amongst them, and entered ye forte with all speed; and those yt first entered found sharp resistance from the enimie, who both shott at & grapled with them; others rane into their howses, & brought out fire, and sett them on fire, which soone tooke in their matts, &, standing close togeather, with ye wind, all was quickly on a flame, and therby more were burnte to death then was otherwise slain; it burnte their bowstrings, and made them unservisable. Those yt scaped ye fire were slaine with ye sword; some hewed to peeces, others rune throw with their rapiers, so as they were quickly dispatchte, and very few escaped. It was conceived they thus destroyed about 400. at this time. It was a fearfull sight to see them thus frying in ye fyer, and ye streams of blood quenching ye same, and horrible was ye stinck & sente ther of; but ye victory seemed a sweete sacrifice, and they gave the prays therof to God, who had wrought so wonderfuly for them, thus to inclose their enimise in their hands, and give them so speedy a victory over so proud & insulting an enimie. The Narigansett Indeans, all this while, stood round aboute, but aloofe from all danger, and left ye whole execution to ye English, exept it were ye stoping of any yt broke away, insulting over their enimies in this their ruine & miserie, when they saw them dancing in ye flames, calling them by a word in their owne language, signifing, O brave Pequents! which they used familierly among them selves in their own prayes, in songs of triumph after their victories. After this servis was thus happily accomplished, they marcht to the water side, wher they mett with some of their vesells, by which they had refreishing with victualls & other necessaries. But in their march ye rest of ye Pequents drew into a body, and acoasted them, thinking to have some advantage against them by reason of a neck of land; but when they saw the English prepare for them, they kept a loofe, so as they neither did hurt, nor could receive any. After their refreishing & repair to geather for further counsell & directions, they resolved to pursue their victory, and follow ye warr against ye rest, but ye Narigansett Indeans most of them forsooke them, and such of them as they had with them for guids, or otherwise, they found them very could and backward in ye bussines, ether out of envie, or yt they saw ye English would make more profite of ye victorie then they were willing they should, or els deprive them of such advantage as them selves desired by having them become tributaries unto them, or ye like.

For ye rest of this bussines, I shall only relate ye same as it is in a leter which came from Mr. Winthrop to ye Govr hear, as followeth.

Worthy Sr: I received your loving letter, and am much provocked to express my affections towards you, but straitnes of time forbids me; for my desire is to acquainte you with ye Lords greate mercies towards us, in our prevailing against his & our enimies; that you may rejoyce and praise his name with us. About 80. of our men, haveing costed along towards ye Dutch plantation, (some times by water, but most by land,) mett hear & ther with some Pequents, whom they slew or tooke prisoners. 2. sachems they tooke, & beheaded; and not hearing of Sassacous, (the cheefe sachem,) they gave a prisoner his life, to goe and find him out. He wente and brought them word where he was, but Sassacouse, suspecting him to be a spie, after he was gone, fled away with some 20. more to ye Mowakes, so our men missed of him. Yet, deviding them selves, and ranging up & downe, as ye providence of God guided them (for ye Indeans were all gone, save 3. or 4. and they knew not whither to guid them, or els would not), upon ye 13. of this month, they light upon a great company of them, viz. 80. strong men, & 200. women & children, in a small Indean towne, fast by a hideous swamp, which they all slipped into before our men could gett to them. Our captains were not then come togeither, but ther was Mr. Ludlow and Captaine Masson, with some 10. of their men, & Captaine Patrick with some 20. or more of his, who, shooting at ye Indeans, Captaine Trask with 50. more came soone in at ye noyse. Then they gave order to surround ye swampe, it being aboute a mile aboute; but Levetenante Davenporte & some 12. more, not hearing that com̃and, fell into ye swampe among ye Indeans. The swampe was so thicke with shrub-woode, & so boggie with all, that some of them stuck fast, and received many shott. Levetenant Davenport was dangerously wounded aboute his armehole, and another shott in ye head, so as, fainting, they were in great danger to have been taken by ye Indeans. But Sargante Rigges, & Jeffery, and 2. or 3. more, rescued them, and slew diverse of ye Indeans with their swords. After they were drawne out, the Indeans desired parley, & were offered (by Thomas Stanton, our interpretour) that, if they would come out, and yeeld them selves, they should have their lives, all that had not their hands in ye English blood. Wherupon ye sachem of ye place came forth, and an old man or 2. & their wives and children, and after that some other women & children, and so they spake 2. howers, till it was night. Then Thomas Stanton was sente into them againe, to call them forth; but they said they would selle their lives their, and so shott at him so thicke as, if he had not cried out, and been presently rescued, they had slaine him. Then our men cutt of a place of ye swampe with their swords, and cooped the Indeans into so narrow a compass, as they could easier kill them throw ye thickets. So they continued all ye night, standing aboute 12. foote one from an other, and ye Indeans, coming close up to our men, shot their arrows so thicke, as they pierced their hatte brimes, & their sleeves, & stockins, & other parts of their cloaths, yet so miraculously did the Lord preserve them as not one of them was wounded, save those 3. who rashly went into ye swampe. When it was nere day, it grue very darke, so as those of them which were left dropt away betweene our men, though they stood but 12. or 14. foote assunder; but were presenly discovered, & some killed in ye pursute. Upon searching of ye swampe, ye next morning, they found 9. slaine, & some they pulled up, whom ye Indeans had buried in ye mire, so as they doe thinke that, of all this company, not 20. did escape, for they after found some who dyed in their flight of their wounds received. The prisoners were devided, some to those of ye river, and the rest to us. Of these we send ye male children to Bermuda, by Mr. William Peirce, & ye women & maid children are disposed aboute in the townes. Ther have been now slaine & taken, in all, aboute 700. The rest are dispersed, and the Indeans in all quarters so terrified as all their friends are affraid to receive them. 2. of ye sachems of Long Iland came to Mr. Stoughton and tendered them selves to be tributaries under our protection. And 2. of ye Neepnett sachems have been with me to seeke our frendship. Amonge the prisoners we have ye wife & children of Mononotto, a womon of a very modest countenance and behaviour. It was by her mediation that the 2. English maids were spared from death, and were kindly used by her; so that I have taken charge of her. One of her first requests was, that the English would not abuse her body, and that her children might not be taken from her. Those which were wounded were fetched of soone by John Galopp, who came with his shalop in a happie houre, to bring them victuals, and to carrie their wounded men to ye pinass, wher our cheefe surgeon was, wth Mr. Willson, being aboute 8. leagues off. Our people are all in health, (ye Lord be praised,) and allthough they had marched in their armes all ye day, and had been in fight all ye night, yet they professed they found them selves so fresh as they could willingly have gone to such another bussines.

This is ye substance of that which I received, though I am forced to omite many considerable circomstances. So, being in much straitnes of time, (the ships being to departe within this 4. days, and in them the Lord Lee and Mr. Vane,) I hear breake of, and with harty saluts to, &c., I rest

Yours assured,
Jo: Winthrop.
The 28. of ye 5. month, 1637.

The captains reporte we have slaine 13. sachems; but Sassacouse & Monotto are yet living.

That I may make an end of this matter: this Sassacouse (ye Pequents cheefe sachem) being fled to ye Mowhakes, they cutt of his head, with some other of ye cheefe of them, whether to satisfie ye English, or rather ye Nariganset, (who, as I have since heard, hired them to doe it,) or for their owne advantage, I well know not; but thus this warr tooke end. The rest of ye Pequents were wholy driven from their place, and some of them submitted them selves to ye Narigansets, & lived under them; others of them betooke them selves to ye Monhiggs, under Uncass, their sachem, wth the approbation of ye English of Conightecutt, under whose protection Uncass lived, and he and his men had been faithful to them in this warr, & done them very good service. But this did so vexe the Narrigansetts, that they had not ye whole sweay over them, as they have never ceased plotting and contriving how to bring them under, and because they cannot attaine their ends, because of ye English who have protected them, they have sought to raise a generall conspiracie against ye English, as will appear in an other place.

Chapter XXXIV

Anno Dom: 1644.

Mr. Edward Winslow was chosen Govr this year.

Many having left this place (as is before noted) by reason of the straightnes & barrennes of ye same, and their finding of better accommodations elsewher, more sutable to their ends & minds; and sundrie others still upon every occasion desiring their dismissions, the church begane seriously to thinke whether it were not better joyntly to remove to some other place, then to be thus weakened, and as it were insensibly dissolved. Many meetings and much consultation was held hearaboute, and diverse were mens minds and opinions. Some were still for staying togeather in this place, aledging men might hear live, if they would be contente with their condition; and yt it was not for wante or necessitie so much yt they removed, as for ye enriching of them selves. Others were resolute upon removall, and so signified yt hear yey could not stay; but if ye church did not remove, they must; insomuch as many were swayed, rather then ther should be a dissolution, to condescend to a removall, if a fitt place could be found, that might more conveniently and comfortablie receive ye whole, with such accession of others as might come to them, for their better strength & subsistence; and some such like cautions and limitations. So as, with ye afforesaide provissos, ye greater parte consented to a removall to a place called Nawsett, which had been superficially veiwed and ye good will of ye purchassers (to whom it belonged) obtained, with some addition thertoo from ye Courte. But now they begane to see their errour, that they had given away already the best & most com̃odious places to others, and now wanted them selves; for this place was about 50. myles from hence, and at an outside of ye countrie, remote from all society; also, that it would prove so straite, as it would not be competente to receive ye whole body, much less be capable of any addition or increase; so as (at least in a shorte time) they should be worse ther then they are now hear. The which, with sundery other like considerations and inconveniences, made them chaing their resolutions; but such as were before resolved upon removall tooke advantage of this agreemente, & wente on notwithstanding, neither could ye rest hinder them, they haveing made some begiñing. And thus was this poore church left, like an anciente mother, growne olde, and forsaken of her children, (though not in their affections,) yett in regarde of their bodily presence and personall helpfullness. Her anciente members being most of them worne away by death; and these of later time being like children translated into other families, and she like a widow left only to trust in God. Thus she that had made many rich became her selfe poore.

2.3.2 Reading and Review Questions

1. How does Bradford connect the Pilgrims' experience typologically with the Old Testament? Why does he do so?
2. Why and how does Bradford place the Puritan faith within the larger Christian struggle against Satan and related history of martyrs and pilgrims such as the Marian exiles?
3. How does Bradford measure God's approval of the Puritan efforts? Why? Are his views consistent? Why or why not?
4. What governing (versus religious) principles shape the Mayflower Compact? Why?
5. What is Bradford's attitude towards Native Americans? What shapes his attitude? How do you know?

2.4 JOHN WINTHROP

(1588–1649)

John Winthrop was born into a prosperous family in Groton, England, and followed the path of many such prosperous gentlemen by studying at Cambridge University. Though he practiced law at the Inner Temple, he soon shifted paths when he became a Puritan, devoted to purifying the Anglican Church from within and eschewing lingering Catholic practices and rituals. When Charles I ascended the throne, Puritans such as Winthrop faced being ruled by a monarch with clear and expressed sympathies for Catholicism. To avoid losing his earthly possessions to the throne, Winthrop joined a group of Puritans who obtained permission from the king to leave England for America. They gained a charter from the Council for New England and formed themselves as "The Company of Massachusetts Bay in New England," free to found a religious colony beyond the king's rule. Their colony would in time become New England's chief colony.

Image 2.3 | John Winthrop
Artist | Charles Osgood
Source | Wikimedia Commons
License | Public Domain

In 1629, Winthrop was chosen governor, a position he would hold for twenty years. The initial group of colonists left England on April 8, 1630, sailing on the

Image 2.4 | Massachusetts Bay Colony Seal
Artist | Unknown
Source | Wikimedia Commons
License | Public Domain

Arbella. Either before embarkation or early in the voyage itself, Winthrop gave his sermon *A Model of Christian Charity* which envisaged a harmonious Puritan community that would serve as guide and model for future emigrants. Preparing the colonists to face adversity and temptation, the sermon also prepared for their future society's being built on and guided by Christian principles. As governor of the colony, Winthrop himself modeled these principles through his steadfast morality and selfless concern for others.

A Model of Christian Charity speaks plainly and clearly of an earthly life in the wilderness guiding towards God's heavenly city, the new Jerusalem.

2.4.1 *A Model of Christian Charity*

(1630)

WRITTEN ON BOARD THE ARBELLA, ON THE ATLANTIC OCEAN.

By the Hon. John Winthrop Esqr. In his passage (with a great company of Religious people, of which Christian tribes he was the Brave Leader and famous Governor;) from the Island of Great Brittaine to New-England in the North America. Anno 1630.

A Modell hereof.

God Almighty in his most holy and wise providence, hath soe disposed of the condition of mankind, as in all times some must be rich, some poore, some high and eminent in power and dignitie; others mean and in submission.

The Reason hereof.

1 *Reas.* First to hold conformity with the rest of his world, being delighted to show forth the glory of his wisdom in the variety and difference of the creatures, and the glory of his power in ordering all these differences for the preservation and good of the whole; and the glory of his greatness, that as it is the glory of princes to have many officers, soe this great king will haue many stewards, counting himself more honoured in dispensing his gifts to man by man, than if he did it by his owne immediate hands.

2 *Reas.* Secondly that he might haue the more occasion to manifest the work of his Spirit: first upon the wicked in moderating and restraining them: soe that the riche and mighty should not eate upp the poore nor the poore and dispised rise upp against and shake off theire yoake. 2ly In the regenerate, in exerciseing his graces in them, as in the grate ones, theire love, mercy, gentleness, temperance &c., in the poore and inferior sorte, theire faithe, patience, obedience &c.

3 *Reas.* Thirdly, that every man might have need of others, and from hence they might be all knitt more nearly together in the Bonds of brotherly affection. From hence it appears plainly that noe man is made more honourable than another or more wealthy &c., out of any particular and singular respect to himselfe, but for the glory of his creator and the common good of the creature, man. Therefore God still reserves the propperty of these gifts to himself as Ezek. 16. 17. he there calls wealthe, his gold and his silver, and Prov. 3. 9. he claims theire service as his due, *honor the Lord with thy riches* &c.—All men being thus (by divine providence) ranked into two sorts, riche and poore; under the first are comprehended all such as are able to live comfortably by their own meanes duely improved; and all others are poore according to the former distribution. There are two rules whereby we are to walk one towards another: Justice and Mercy. These are always distinguished in their act and in their object, yet may they both concurre in the same subject in eache respect; as sometimes there may be an occasion of showing mercy to a rich man in some sudden danger or distresse, and alsoe doeing of meere justice to a poor man in regard of some perticular contract &c. There is likewise a double Lawe by which wee are regulated in our conversation towardes another; in both the former respects, the lawe of nature and the lawe of grace, or the morrall lawe or the lawe of the gospell, to omitt the rule of justice as not propperly belonging to this purpose otherwise than it may fall into consideration in some perticular cases. By the first of these lawes man as he was enabled soe withall is commanded to love his neighbour as himself. Upon this ground stands all the precepts of the morrall lawe, which concernes our dealings with men. To apply this to the works of mercy; this lawe requires two things. First that every man afford his help to another in every want or distresse. Secondly, that hee performe this out of the same affection which makes him carefull of his owne goods, according to that of our Savior, (Math.) Whatsoever ye would that men should do to you. This was practised by Abraham and Lot in entertaining the angells and the old man of Gibea. The lawe of Grace or of the Gospell hath some difference from the former; as in these respects, First the lawe of nature was given to man in the estate of innocency; this of the Gospell in the estate of regeneracy. 2ly, the former propounds one man to another, as the same flesh and image of God; this as a brother in Christ allsoe, and in the communion of the same Spirit, and soe teacheth to put a difference between christians and others. Doe good to all, especially to the household of faith; upon this ground the Israelites were to putt a difference betweene the brethren of such as were strangers though not of the Canaanites.

3ly. The Lawe of nature would give no rules for dealing with enemies, for all are to be considered as friends in the state of innocency, but the Gospell commands loue to an enemy. Proofe. *If thine Enemy hunger, feed him; Love your Enemies, doe good to them that hate you.* Math. 5. 44.

This lawe of the Gospell propounds likewise a difference of seasons and occasions. There is a time when a christian must sell all and give to the poor, as they did in the Apostles times. There is a time allsoe when christians (though they give not all yet) must give beyond their abillity, as they of Macedonia, Cor. 2, 6. Likewise community of perills calls for extraordinary liberality, and soe doth community in some speciall service for the churche. Lastly, when there is no other means whereby our christian brother may be relieved in his distress, we must help him beyond our ability rather than tempt God in putting him upon help by miraculous or extraordinary meanes.

This duty of mercy is exercised in the kinds, Giueving, lending and forgiving.—

Quest. What rule shall a man observe in giueving in respect of the measure?

Ans. If the time and occasion be ordinary he is to giue out of his abundance. *Let him lay aside as God hath blessed him.* If the time and occasion be extraordinary, he must be ruled by them; taking this withall, that then a man cannot likely doe too much, especially if he may leave himselfe and his family under probable means of comfortable subsistence.

Object. A man must lay upp for posterity, the fathers lay upp for posterity and children, and *he is worse than an infidell that pronideth not for his owne.*

Ans. For the first, it is plaine that it being spoken by way of comparison, it must be meant of the ordinary and usuall course of fathers, and cannot extend to times and occasions extraordinary. For the other place the Apostle speaks against such as walked inordinately, and it is without question, that he is worse than an infidell who through his owne sloathe and voluptuousness shall neglect to provide for his family.—

Object. The wise man's Eies are in his head, saith Solomon, *and foreseeth the plague*; therefore he must forecast and lay upp against evill times when hee or his may stand in need of all he can gather.

Ans. This very Argument Solomon useth to persuade to liberallity, Eccle.: *Cast thy bread upon the waters, and for thou knowest not what evill may come upon the land.* Luke 26. *Make you friends of the riches of iniquity*; you will ask how this shall be? very well. For first he that giues to the poore, lends to the lord and he will repay him even in this life an hundredfold to him or his.—*The righteous is ever mercifull and lendeth and his seed enjoyeth the blessing*; and besides wee know what advantage it will be to us in the day of account when many such witnesses shall stand forth for us to witnesse the improvement of our tallent. And I would know of those whoe pleade soe much for laying up for time to come, whether they holde that to be Gospell, Math. 16. 19. *Lay not upp for yourselves Treasures upon Earth* &c. If they acknowledge it, what extent will they allowe it? if only to those primitive times, let them consider the reason whereopon our Saviour groundes it.

The first is that they are subject to the moathe, the rust, the theife. Secondly, They will steale away the hearte; *where the treasure is there will ye heart be allsoe.* The reasons are of like force at all times. Therefore the exhortation must be generall and perpetuall, withallwayes in respect of the love and affection to riches and in regard of the things themselves when any speciall seruice for the churche or perticular Distresse of our brother doe call for the use of them; otherwise it is not only lawfull but necessary to lay upp as Joseph did to haue ready uppon such occasions, as the Lord (whose stewards wee are of them) shall call for them from us; Christ giues us an Instance of the first, when hee sent his disciples for the Ass, and bidds them answer the owner thus, the Lord hath need of him: soe when the Tabernacle was to be built, he sends to his people to call for their silver and gold, &c; and yeildes noe other reason but that it was for his worke. When Elisha comes to the widow of Sareptah and findes her preparing to make ready her pittance for herselfe and family, he bids her first provide for him, he challengeth first God's parte which she must first give before shee must serve her owne family. All these teache us that the Lord lookes that when hee is pleased to call for his right in any thing wee haue, our owne interest wee haue, must stand aside till his turne be served. For the other, wee need looke noe further then to that of John 1. *he whoe hath this world's goodes and seeth his brother to neede and shutts upp his compassion from him, how dwelleth the loue of God in him,* which comes punctually to this conclusion; if thy brother be in want and thou canst help him, thou needst not make doubt, what thou shouldst doe; if thou louest God thou must help him.

Quest. What rule must wee observe in lending?

Ans. Thou must observe whether thy brother hath present or probable or possible means of repaying thee, if there be none of those, thou must give him according to his necessity, rather then lend him as he requires; if he hath present means of repaying thee, thou art to look at him not as an act of mercy, but by way of Commerce, wherein thou arte to walk by the rule of justice; but if his means of repaying thee be only probable or possible, then is hee an object of thy mercy, thou must lend him, though there be danger of losing it, Deut. 15. 7. *If any of thy brethren be poore* &c., *thou shalt lend him sufficient.* That men might not shift off this duty by the apparent hazzard, he tells them that though the yeare of Jubile were at hand (when he must remitt it, if hee were not able to repay it before) yet he must lend him and that chearefully. *It may not greive thee to giue him* (saith hee) and because some might object, why soe I should soone impoverishe myself and my family, he adds with all thy worke &c; for our Saviour, Math. 5. 42. *From him that would borrow of thee turne not away.*

Quest. What rule must we observe in forgiuing?

Ans. Whether thou didst lend by way of commerce or in mercy, if he hath nothing to pay thee, must forgive, (except in cause where thou hast a surety or a lawfull pleadge) Deut. 15. 2. Every seaventh yeare the Creditor was to quitt that which he lent to his brother if he were poore as appears ver. 8. *Save when there shall be no poore with thee.* In all these and like cases, Christ was a generall rule,

Math. 7. 22. *Whatsoever ye would that men should doe to you, doe yee the same to them allsoe.*

Quest. What rule must wee observe and walke by in cause of community of perill?

Ans. The same as before, but with more enlargement towards others and lesse respect towards ourselves and our owne right. Hence it was that in the primitive Churche they sold all, had all things in common, neither did any man say that which he possessed was his owne. Likewise in theire returne out of the captivity, because the worke was greate for the restoring of the church and the danger of enemies was common to all, Nehemiah directs the Jews to liberallity and readiness in remitting theire debts to theire brethren, and disposing liberally to such as wanted, and stand not upon their owne dues which they might have demanded of them. Thus did some of our Forefathers in times of persecution in England, and soe did many of the faithful of other churches, whereof wee keepe an honorable remembrance of them; and it is to be observed that both in Scriptures and latter stories of the churches that such as have beene most bountifull to the poore saintes, especially in those extraordinary times and occasions, God hath left them highly commended to posterity, as Zacheus, Cornelius, Dorcas, Bishop Hooper, the Cuttler of Brussells and divers others. Observe againe that the Scripture gives noe caussion to restraine any from being over liberall this way; but all men to the liberall and cherefull practise hereof by the sweeter promises; as to instance one for many, Isaiah 58. 6. *Is not this the fast I have chosen to loose the bonds of wickedness, to take off the heavy burdens, to lett the oppressed go free and to breake every yoake, to deale thy bread to the hungry and to bring the poore that wander into thy house, when thou seest the naked to cover them; and then shall thy light brake forth as the morning and thy healthe shall growe speedily, thy righteousness shall goe before God, and the glory of the Lord shall embrace thee; then thou shall call and the Lord shall answer thee* &c., Ch. 2. 10. *If thou power out thy soule to the hungry, then shall thy light spring out in darkness, and the Lord shall guide thee continually, and satisfie thy soule in draught, and make falt thy bones, thou shalt be like a watered garden, and they shalt be of thee that shall build the old wast places* &c. On the contrary most heavy cursses are layed upon such as are straightened towards the Lord and his people, Judg. 5. *Cursse the Meroshe because he came not to help the Lord. Hee whoe shutteth his eares from hearing the cry of the poore, he shall cry and shall not be heard*; Math. 25. *Goe ye curssed into everlasting fire* &c. I *was hungry and ye fedd mee not*, Cor. 2. 9. 16. He that soweth sparingly shall reape sparingly. Haveing already sett forth the practice of mercy according to the rule of God's lawe, it will be useful to lay open the groundes of it allsoe, being the other parte of the Commandment and that is the affection from which this exercise of mercy must arise, the Apostle tells us that this *love is the fullfilling of the lawe*, not that it is enough to loue our brother and soe noe further; but in regard of the excellency of his partes giueing any motion to the other as the soule to the body and the power it hath to sett all the faculties on worke in the outward exercise of this duty; as when wee bid one make the clocke strike, he doth not lay hand on the hammer, which is the immediate instrument of the sound, but setts on worke the first mouer or maine wheele; knoweing that will certainely produce the sound which he intends. Soe the way to drawe men to the workes of mercy, is not by force of Argument from the goodness or necessity of the worke; for though this cause may enforce, a rationall minde to some present act of mercy, as is frequent in experience, yet it cannot worke such a habit in a soule, as shall make it prompt upon all occasions to produce the same effect, but by frameing these affections of loue in the hearte which will as naturally bring forthe the other, as any cause doth produce the effect.

The deffinition which the Scripture giues us of loue is this. *Love is the bond of perfection*, first it is a bond or ligament. 2ly it makes the worke perfect. There is noe body but consists of partes and that which knitts these partes together, giues the body its perfection, because it makes eache parte soe contiguous to others as thereby they doe mutually participate with each other, both in strengthe and infirmity, in pleasure and paine. To instance in the most perfect of all bodies; Christ and his Church make one body; the severall partes of this body considered a parte before they were united, were as disproportionate and as much disordering as soe many contrary quallities or elements, but when Christ comes, and by his spirit and loue knitts all these partes to himselfe and each to other, it is become the most perfect and best proportioned body in the world, Eph. 4. 16. *Christ, by whome all the body being knitt together by every joint for the furniture thereof, according to the effectuall power which is in the measure of every perfection of partes, a glorious body without spott or wrinkle*; the ligaments hereof being Christ, or his love, for Christ is love, 1 John 4. 8. Soe this definition is right. *Love is the bond of perfection.*

From hence we may frame these conclusions. 1. First of all, true Christians are of one body in Christ, 1 Cor. 12. 12. 13. 17. *Ye are the body of Christ and members of their parte.* All the partes of this body being thus vnited are made soe contiguous in a speciall relation as they must needes partake of each other's strength and infirmity; joy and sorrowe, weale and woe. 1 Cor. 12. 26. *If one member suffers, all suffer with it, if one be in honor, all rejoyce with it.* 2ly. The ligaments of this body which knitt together are loue. 3ly. Noe body can be perfect which wants its propar ligament. 5ly. This sensibleness and sympathy of each other's conditions will necessarily infuse into each parte a native desire and endeavour, to strengthen, defend, preserve and comfort the other. To insist a little on this conclusion being the product of all the former, the truthe hereof will appeare both by precept and patterne. 1 John 3. 10. *Yee ought to lay doune your lives for the brethren.* Gal. 6. 2. *beare ye one another's burthen's and soe fulfill the lawe of Christ.* For patterns wee haue that first of our Saviour whoe out of his good will in obedience to his father, becomeing a parte of this body and being knitt with it in the bond of loue, found such a natiue sensibleness of our infirmities and sorrowes as he willingly yielded himselfe to deathe to ease the infirmities of the rest of his body, and soe healed theire sorrowes. From the like sympathy of partes did the Apostles and many thousands of the Saintes lay doune theire lives for Christ. Againe the like wee may see in the members of this body among themselves. 1 Rom. 9. Paule could have been contented to have been separated from Christ, that the Jewes might not be cutt off from the body. It is very observable what hee professeth of his affectionate partaking with every member; *whoe is weake* (saith hee) *and I am not weake? whoe is offended and I burne not*; and againe, 2 Cor. 7. 13. *therefore wee are comforted because yee were comforted.* Of Epaphroditus he speaketh, Phil. 2. 30. *that he regarded not his owne life to do him service.* Soe Phebe and others are called *the servants of the churche.* Now it is apparent that they served not for wages, or by constrainte, but out of loue. The like we shall finde in the histories of the churche, in all ages; the sweete sympathie of affections which was in the members of this body one towards another; theire chearfullness in serueing and suffering together; how liberall they were without repineing, harbourers without grudgeing, and helpfull without reproaching; and all from hence, because they had feruent loue amongst them; which onely makes the practise of mercy constant and easie.

The next consideration is how this loue comes to be wrought. Adam in his first estate was a perfect modell of mankinde in all their generations, and in him this loue was perfected in regard of the habit. But Adam, rent himselfe from his Creator, rent all his posterity allsoe one from another; whence it comes that every man is borne with this principle in him to loue and seeke himselfe onely, and thus a man continueth till Christ comes and takes possession of the soule and infuseth another principle, loue to God and our brother, and this latter haueing continuall supply from Christ, as the head and roote by which he is vnited, gets the predomining in the soule, soe by little and little expells the former. 1 John 4. 7. *loue cometh of God and every one that loueth is borne of God,* soe that this loue is the fruite of the new birthe, and none can have it but the new creature. Now when this quallity is thus formed in the soules of men, it workes like the Spirit upon the drie bones. Ezek. 39. *bone came to bone.* It gathers together the scattered bones, or perfect old man Adam, and knitts them into one body againe in Christ, whereby a man is become againe a living soule.

The third consideration is concerning the exercise of this loue, which is twofold, inward or outward. The outward hath beene handled in the former preface of this discourse. From unfolding the other wee must take in our way that maxime of philosophy. *Simile simili gaudet,* or like will to like; for as of things which are turned with disaffection to eache other, the ground of it is from a dissimilitude or ariseing from the contrary or different nature of the things themselves; for the ground of loue is an apprehension of some resemblance in the things loued to that which affects it. This is the cause why the Lord loues the creature, soe farre as it hathe any of his Image in it; he loues his elect because they are like himselfe, he beholds them in his beloued sonne. So a mother loues her childe, because shee throughly conceives a resemblance of herselfe in it. Thus it is betweene the members of Christ; eache discernes, by the worke of the Spirit, his oune Image and resemblance in another, and therefore cannot but loue him as he loues himself. Now when the soule, which is of a sociable nature, findes anything like to itselfe, it is like Adam when Eve was brought to him. She must be one with himselfe. *This is flesh of my flesh* (saith he) *and bone of my bone.* Soe the soule conceives a greate delighte in it; therefore shee desires nearness and familiarity with it. Shee hath a greate propensity to doe it good and receiues such content in it, as fearing the miscarriage of her beloved, shee bestowes it in the inmost closett of her heart. Shee will not endure that it shall want any good which shee can giue it. If by occasion shee be withdrawne from the company of it, shee is still looking towardes the place where shee left her beloved. If shee heard it groane, shee is with it presently. If shee finde it sadd and disconsolate, shee sighes and moanes with it. Shee hath noe such joy as to see her beloved merry and thriving. If shee see it wronged, shee cannot hear it without passion. Shee setts noe boundes to her affections, nor hath any thought of reward. Shee findes recompense enough in the exercise of her loue towardes it. Wee may see this acted to life in Jonathan and David. Jonathan a valiant man endued with the spirit of love, soe soone as he discovered the same spirit in David had presently his hearte knitt to him by this ligament of loue; soe that it is said he loued him as his owne soule, he takes soe great pleasure in him, that hee stripps himselfe to adorne his beloved. His father's kingdome was not soe precious to him as his beloved David, David shall haue it with all his hearte. Himself desires noe more but that hee may be neare to him to rejoyce in his good. Hee chooseth to converse with him in the wildernesse even to the hazzard of his oune life, rather than with the greate Courtiers in his father's Pallace. When hee sees danger towards him, hee spares neither rare paines nor perill to direct it. When injury was offered his beloued David, hee would not beare it, though from his oune father. And when they must parte for a season onely, they thought theire heartes would have broake for sorrowe, had not theire affections found vent by abundance of teares. Other instances might be brought to showe the nature of this affection; as of Ruthe and Naomi, and many others; but this truthe is cleared enough. If any shall object that it is not possible that loue shall be bred or upheld without hope of requitall, it is graunted; but that is not our cause; for this loue is alluayes vnder reward. It never giues, but it alluayes receives with advantage; First in regard that among the members of the same body, loue and affection are reciprocall in a most equall and sweete kinde of commerce.

2nly. In regard of the pleasure and content that the exercise of loue carries with it, as wee may see in the naturall body. The mouth is at all the paines to receive and mince the foode which serves for the nourishment of all the other partes of the body; yet it hath noe cause to complaine; for first the other partes send backe, by severall passages, a due proportion of the same nourishment, in a better forme for the strengthening and comforting the mouthe. 2ly the laboure of the mouthe is accompanied with such pleasure and content as farre exceedes the paines it takes. Soe is it in all the labour of love among Christians. The partie louing, reapes loue again, as was showed before, which the soule covetts more then all the wealthe in the world. 3ly. Nothing yeildes more pleasure and content to the soule then when it findes that which it may loue fervently; for to love and live beloved is the soule's paradise both here and in heaven. In the State of wedlock there be many comforts to learne out of the troubles of that Condition; but let such as have tryed the most, say if there be any sweetness in that Condition comparable to the exercise of mutuall loue.

From the former Considerations arise these Conclusions.—1. First, This loue among Christians is a reall thing, not imaginarie. 2ly. This loue is as absolutely necessary to the being of the body of Christ, as the sinews and other ligaments of a naturall body are to the being of that body. 3ly. This loue is a divine, spirituall, nature; free, active, strong, couragious, permanent; undervaluing all things beneathe its propper object and of all the graces, this makes us nearer to resemble the virtues of our heavenly father. 4thly It rests in the loue and wellfare of its beloued. For the full certain knowledge of those truthes concerning the nature, use, and excellency of this grace, that which the holy ghost hath left recorded, 1 Cor. 13, may give full satisfaction, which is needful for every true member of this louely body of the Lord Jesus, to worke upon theire heartes by prayer, meditation continuall exercise at least of the speciall [influence] of this grace, till Christ be formed in them and they in him, all in eache other, knitt together by this bond of loue.

It rests now to make some application of this discourse, by the present designe, which gaue the occasion of writing of it. Herein are 4 things to he propounded; *first* the persons, 2ly the worke, 3ly the end, 4thly the meanes. 1. For *the persons.* Wee are a company professing ourselves fellow members of Christ, in which respect onely though wee were absent from each other many miles, and had our imployments as farre distant, yet wee ought to account ourselves knitt together by this bond of loue, and, live in the exercise of it, if wee would have comforte of our being in Christ. This was notorious in the practise of the Christians in former times; as is testified of the Waldenses, from the mouth of one of the adversaries Æneas Sylvius "mutuo ament pere antequam norunt," they use to loue any of theire owne religion even before they were acquainted with them. 2nly for the *worke* wee have in hand. It is by a mutuall consent, through a speciall overvaluing providence and a more than an ordinary approbation of the Churches of Christ, to seeke out a place of cohabitation and Consorteshipp under a due forme of Government both ciuill and ecclesiasticall. In such cases as this, the care of the publique must oversway all private respects, by which, not only conscience, but meare civill pollicy, dothe binde us. For it is a true rule that particular Estates cannot subsist in the ruin of the publique. 3ly The *end* is to improve our lives to doe more service to the Lord; the comforte and encrease of the body of Christe, whereof we are members; that ourselves and posterity may be the better preserved from the common corruptions of this evill world, to serve the Lord and worke out our Salvation under the power and purity of his holy ordinances. 4thly for the *meanes* whereby this must be effected. They are twofold, a conformity with the worke and end wee aime at. These wee see are extraordinary, therefore wee must not content ourselves with usuall ordinary meanes. Whatsoever wee did, or ought to have, done, when wee liued in England, the same must wee doe, and more allsoe, where wee goe. That which the most in theire churches mainetaine as truthe in profession onely, wee must bring into familiar and constant practise; as in this duty of loue, wee must loue brotherly without dissimulation, wee must loue one another with a pure hearte fervently. Wee must beare one anothers burthens. We must not looke onely on our owne things, but allsoe on the things of our brethren. Neither must wee thinke that the Lord will beare with such faileings at our hands as he dothe from those among whome wee have lived; and that for these 3 Reasons; 1. In regard of the more neare bond of mariage between him and us, wherein hee hath taken us to be his, after a most strickt and peculiar manner, which will make them the more jealous of our loue and obedience. Soe he tells the people of Israell, *you onely have I knowne of all the families of the Earthe, therefore will I punishe you for your Transgressions.* 2ly, because *the Lord will be sanctified in them that come neare him.* We know that there were many that corrupted the service of the Lord; some setting upp altars before his owne; others offering both strange fire and strange sacrifices allsoe; yet there came noe fire from heaven, or other sudden judgement upon them, as did upon Nadab and Abihu, whoe yet wee may think did not sinne presumptuously. 3ly When God gives a speciall commission he lookes to have it strictly observed in every article, When he gave Saule a commission to destroy Amaleck, Hee indented with him upon certain articles, and because hee failed in one of the least, and that upon a faire pretense, it lost him the kingdom, which should have beene his reward, if hee had observed his commission. Thus stands the cause betweene God and us. We are entered into Covenant with Him for this worke. Wee haue taken out a commission. The Lord hath given us leave to drawe our own articles. Wee haue professed to enterprise these and those accounts, upon these and those ends. Wee have hereupon besought Him of favour and blessing. Now if the Lord shall please to heare us, and bring us in peace to the place we desire, then hath hee ratified this covenant and sealed our Commission, and will expect a strict performance of the articles contained in it; but if wee shall neglect the observation of these articles which are the ends wee have propounded, and, dissembling with our God, shall fall to embrace this present world and prosecute our carnall intentions, seeking greate things for ourselves and our posterity, the Lord will surely breake out in wrathe against us; be revenged of such a [sinful] people and make us knowe the price of the breache of such a covenant.

Now the onely way to avoyde this shipwracke, and to provide for our posterity, is to followe the counsell of Micah, *to doe justly, to love mercy, to walk humbly with our God.* For this end, wee must be knitt together, in this worke, as one man. Wee must entertaine each other in brotherly affection. Wee must be willing to abridge ourselves of our superfluities, for the supply of other's necessities. Wee must uphold a familiar commerce together in all meekeness, gentlenes, patience and liberality. Wee must delight in eache other; make other's conditions our oune;

rejoice together, mourne together, labour and suffer together, allwayes haueving before our eyes our commission and community in the worke, as members of the same body. Soe shall wee *keepe the unitie of the spirit in the bond of peace*. The Lord will be our God, and delight to dwell among us, as his oune people, and will command a blessing upon us in all our wayes. Soe that wee shall see much more of his wisdome, power, goodness and truthe, than formerly wee haue been acquainted with. Wee shall finde that the God of Israell is among us, when ten of us shall be able to resist a thousand of our enemies; when hee shall make us a prayse and glory that men shall say of succeeding plantations, "the Lord make it likely that of *New England*." For wee must consider that wee shall be as a citty upon a hill. The eies of all people are uppon us. Soe that if wee shall deale falsely with our God in this worke wee haue undertaken, and soe cause him to withdrawe his present help from us, wee shall be made a story and a by-word through the world. Wee shall open the mouthes of enemies to speake evill of the wayes of God, and all professors for God's sake. Wee shall shame the faces of many of God's worthy servants, and cause theire prayers to be turned into curses upon us till wee be consumed out of the good land whither wee are a goeing.

I shall shutt upp this discourse with that exhortation of Moses, that faithfull servant of the Lord, in his last farewell to Israell, Deut. 30. *Beloued there is now sett before us life and good, Death and evill, in that wee are commanded this day to loue the Lord our God, and to loue one another, to walke in his wayes and to keepe his Commandements and his Ordinance and his lawes*, and the articles of our Covenant with him, that *wee may liue and be multiplied, and that the Lord our God may blesse us in the land whither wee goe to possesse it. But if our heartes shall turne away, soe that wee will not obey, but shall be seduced, and worshipp and serue other Gods*, our pleasure and proffitts, *and serue them*; it is propounded unto us this day, *wee shall surely perishe out of the good land whither wee passe over this vast sea to possesse it*;

> Therefore lett us choose life
> that wee, and our seede
> may liue, by obeyeing His
> voyce and cleaveing to Him,
> for Hee is our life and
> our prosperity.

2.4.2 Reading and Review Questions

1. In what ways, if any, is *A Model of Christian Charity* a theodicy, that is, a vindication of divine goodness in the face of existing evil, justifying the ways of God to man? Why? How do you know?
2. What temptations, if any, does Winthrop believe the Puritans will face in America? Why does he view them as temptations rather than opportunities?

3. According to Winthrop, what causes social distinctions, or inequalities? What does he think counters or answers them? Why?
4. Why is self-love not a form of love, according to Winthrop? Why does he think self-love should be avoided, and what are the benefits he sees for doing so?
5. Why does Winthrop believe that the Massachusetts Bay Colony should be seen as a city on a hill? What is he cautioning against through this allusion? What is he promising?

2.5 ROGER WILLIAMS

(c. 1603–1683)

Born in London, Roger Williams hailed from a merchant family. His work as a stenographer for Sir Edward Coke (1552–1634) led to Williams' attending a grammar school in London and then enrolling as a scholarship student at Cambridge University in 1623. He earned his BA with honors and, in order to graduate, signed an oath to the Anglican Church, which was headed by the English monarch. He began a course of study for an MA in theology; however, growing estranged from what he saw as the corrupt practices of the Anglican Church, he withdrew without obtaining the degree and converted to Puritanism.

The religious controversies in England were tied to the crown, and the civil war between the Royalists and the Parliamentarians was already fomenting. To escape threatened persecutions against the Puritans, Roger Williams and his wife Mary Barnard (m. 1629–d. 1676) left for religious freedom in America.

He soon deemed the refuge he sought as unobtainable at the Massachusetts Bay Colony and other such established religious colonies. He objected to their intolerance of religious dissent, appropriation of Native American land, and uniting government with the church. His objections and criticisms led the General Court of Massachusetts Bay to eject Rogers from the colony in 1636. He again sought refuge, this time at Narragansett Bay, where he purchased land from the Native Americans and founded Providence in what is now Rhode Island, a city he envisaged as a religious sanctuary for true Dissenters and Separatists.

Williams viewed existing churches and institutions—as well as Christians themselves—as imperfect and unable to achieve true purity until the return of Christ, or the millennium. From this perspective, he believed that the church had no dominion over individual conscience and should therefore not enforce religious conformity in its civil rule or organization.

He returned to England in 1644 to obtain a patent for Rhode Island, returning again in 1651 to have it renewed upon its expiration or annulment. Williams thereby ensured a place open to liberty of conscience and relative tolerance of religious and racial differences. In 1654, he was elected as the colony's president, a position he held for three succeeding terms.

He wrote several important polemical tracts, attacking the theology at Massachusetts Bay Colony and advocating for the separation of church and state. His *Christenings Make Not Christians* calls out those in the New World who claim to be practicing Christians, who cling more to form than real practice of charity for all humans on earth, including Native Americans.

Image 2.5 | The Return of Roger Williams
Artist | C. R. Grant
Source | Wikimedia Commons
License | Public Domain

2.5.1 *Christenings Make Not Christians*

(1645)

A Briefe Discourse concerning that name HEATHEN Commonly given to the Indians. As also concerning that great point of their conversion.

Shall first be humbly bold to inquire into the name Heathen, which the English give them, & the Dutch approve and practise in their name Heydenen, signifying Heathen or Nations. How oft have I heard both the English and Dutch (not onely the civill, but the most ded bauched and profane) fay, These *Heathen* Dogges, better kill a thousand of them then that we *Christians* should be indangered or troubled with them; Better they were all cut off, & then we shall be no more troubled with them: They have spilt our *Christian* bloud, the best way to make riddance of them, cut them all off, and fo make way for Christians.

I shall therefore humbly intreat my country-men of all forts to consider, that although men have used to apply this word *Heathen* to the Indians that go naked, and have not heard of that One-God, yet this word *Heathen* is most improperly sinfully, and unchristianly so used in this fence. The word *Heathen* signifieth no more then *Nations* or *Gentiles*; so do our Translations from the Hebrew and the Greeke in the old and New Testament promiscuoufly render these words *Gentiles, Nations, Heathens.*

Why Nations? Because the Jewes being the onely People and Nation of God, esteemed (and that rightly) all other People, not only those that went naked, but the famous BABYLONIANS, CALDEANS, MEDES, and PERSIANS, GREEKES and ROMANES, their stately Cities and Citizens, inferiour themselves, and not partakers of their glorious privileges, but Ethnicke, Gentiles, Heathen, or the Nations of the world.

Now then we must enquire who are the People of God, his *holy nation*, snce the comming of the Lord Jesus, and the rejection of his first typicall holy Nation the Jewes.

It is confest by all, that the CHRISTIANS the followers of Jesus, are now the onely People of God, his *holy nation*, &c. 1. *Pet.* 2. 9.

Who are then the *nations*, *heathen*, or *gentiles*, in opposition to this People of Goa? I answer, All People, *civilized* as well as *uncivilized*, even the most famous States, Cities, and the Kingdomes of the World: For all must come within that distinction. 1. Cor. 5. *within* or *without*.

Within the *People of God*, his Church at CORNITH: *Without* the City of CORINTH worshipping *Idols*, and so consequently all other People, HEATHENS, or NATIONS, opposed, to the People of God, the true *Jewes*: And therefore now the naturall *Jewes* themselves, not being of this People, are *Heathens Nations* or *Gentiles*. Yea, this will by many hands be yeelded, but what say you to the *Christian world*? What say you to *Christendome*? I answer, what do you thinke *Peter* or *John*, or *Paul*, or any of the first Messengers of the Lord Jesus; Yea if the Lord Jesus himselfe were here, (as he will be shortly) and were to make answer, what would they, what would he fay to a CHRISTIAN WORLD? To CHRISTENDOME? And otherwise then what He would speak, that is indeed what he hath spoken, and will shortly speake, must no man speak that names himselfe a Christian.

Herdious in his Map of his CHRISTIAN WORLD takes in all *Asia*, *Europe*, a vaste part of *Africa*, and a great part also of *America*, so far as the *Popes Christnings* have reached to.

This is the CHRISSION WORLD, or Christendome, in which respect men stand upon their tearmes of *high opposition* between the CHRISTIAN and the TVRKE, (the Chriftian shore, and the Turkish shore) betweene the CHRISTIANS of this Christian WORLD and the JEVV, and the CHRISTIAN and the HEATHEN, that is the naked *American*.

But since *Without* is turned to be *Within*, the WORLD turned CHRISTIAN, and athe*ittle* flocke of JESVS CHRIST hath so marvelllously increased in such wonderfull converfions, let me be bold to aske what is Christ? What are the Christians? The Hebrew and the Greeke will tell us that Christ was and is the *Anointed* of God, whom the Prophets and Kings and preists of Israel in their *anointings* did prefigure and type out; whence his followers are called christians, that is *Anointed* also: So that indeed to be a *christian* implyes two things, first, to be afollower of that anointed one in all his Offices; secondly, to pertake of his anointings, for the Anointing of the Lord Jesus (like to the anointings of AARON, to which none might make the like on pain of death) descend to the skirt of his garments.

To come nearer to this Christion world, (where the world becomes christian holy, anointed, Gods People, &c.) what faith John? What faith the Angel? Yea, What faith Jesus Christ and his Father (from whom the Revelation came *Revel* 1. 1.) What fay they uuto the Beast and his Worshippers *Revel.* 13.

If that beast be not the *Turke*, northe *Roman Emperour* (as the grosest interpret- but either the generall councels, or the catholike church of *Rome*, or the Popes or Papacy (as the most refined interpret) why then all the *world, Revel.* 13. wonders after the *Beast*, worships the *Beast*, followeth the *Beast*, and boasts of the *Beast*, that there is none like him, and all People, Tongues, and Nations, come under the power of this *Beast*, & no man shall buy nor fell, nor live, who hath not the marke of the *Beast* in his *Fore-head*, or in his hand, or the number of his name.

If this *world* or *earth* then be not intended of the whole terrestriall Globe, *Europe, Asia, Africa* and *America*, (which fence and experience denyes) but of the *Roman earth*, or world, and the People, Languages, and Nations, of the *Roman Monarchy*, transferred from the Roman Emperour to the *Roman Popes*, and the Popish *Kingdomes*, branches of that ROMAN-ROOT, (as all *history* and consent of time make evident.)

Then we know by this time what the Lord Jesus would say of the Christian world and of the *Christian*: Indeed what he saith *Revel.* 14. If any man worship the *Beast* or his *picture*, he shall drinke &c. even the dread fullest cup that the whole Booke of God ever held forth to snners. Grant this, say some of Popish Countries, that notwithstanding they make up Christendome, or Christian world, yet submitting to that *Beast*, they are the earth or world and must drinke of that most dreadfull cup: But now for those nations that have withdrawn their necks from that *beastly yoke*, & protesting against him, are not Papists, but Protestants, shall we, may we thinke of them, that they, or any of them may also be called (in true Scripture fence) *Heathens*, that is Nations or Gentiles, in opposition to the People of God, which is the onely holy Nation.

I answer, that all Nations now called Protestants were at first part of that whole Earth, or main (ANTICHRISTIAN) Continent, that wondered after, worshipped the *Beast*, &c. This must then with holy feare and trembling (because it concernes the KINGDOME of God, and salvation) be attended to, Whether such a departure from the *Beast*, and coming out from ANTICHRISTIAN abominations, from his markes in a false converson, and a false constitution, or framing of NATIONAL CHVRCHES in false MINISTERIES, and ministrations of BAPTISME, *Supper of the Lord, Admonitions, Excommunications* as amounts to a true perfect Iland, cut off from that Earth which wonderd after and worshipped the *Beast*: or-whether, not being so cut off, they remaine not *Peninsulâ* or necks of land, contiguous and joyned still unto his *Christtendome*? If now the bodies of Protestant Nations remaine in an unrePentant, unregenerate, naturall estate, and so consequently farre from hearing the admonitions of the Lord Jesus, Math 18. I lay they must sadly consder and know (least their profession of the name of Jesus prove at last but an aggravation of condemnation) that Christ Jesus hath faid, they are but as *Heathens and Publcanes*, vers. 17. How might I therefore humbly beseech my counry men to consider what deepe cause they have to fearch their conversons from that *Beast* and his *Pisture*?' And whether having no more of Christ then the name (besde the invented wayes of worship, derived from, or drawn after *Romes pattern*) their hearts and conversations will not evince them unconverted and *unchristian Christians*, and not yet knowing what it is to come by true Regeneration within, to the true spirituall Jew from without amongst the Nations, that is *Heathens or Gentiles*.

How deeply and eternally this concerns each foule to search into! yea, and much more deeply such as professe to be Guides, Leaders, and Builders of the HOUSE OF GOD.

First, as they look to *Formes* and *Frame* of Buildings, or Churches.

Secondly, as they attend to *Meanes* and *Instruments*, &c.

Thirdly, as they would lay sure Foundations; and lasting Groundfells.

Fourthly, as they account the cost and charge such buildings will amount unto.

Fifthly, so they may not forget the true spirituall matter and mateaials of which a true House, Citty, Kingdome, or Nation of of God, now in the new Testament are to be composed or gathered.

Now Secondly, for the hopes of CONVERSION, and turning the People of *America* unto God: There is no respect of Persons with him, for we are all the worke of his hands; from the rising of the Sunne to the going downe thereof, his name shall be great among the nations from the Eats: & and from the West, &c. If we respect theirsfins, they are far short of *European* sinners: They neither abuse such corporall mercies for they have them not; nor sin they against the Gospell light, (which shines not amongst them) as the men of *Europe* do: And yet if they were greater sinners then they are, or greater sinners then the *Europeans*, they are not the further from the great *Ocean* of mercy in that respect.

Laftly, they are intelligent, many very ingenuous, plaine-hearted, inquisitive and (as I said before) prepared with many convictions, &c.

Now secondly, for the Catholicks conversion, although I believe I may safely hope that God hath his in Rome, in Spaine, yet if Antichrist be their false head (as most true it is) the body, faith, baptisme, hope (opposte to the true, Ephef. 4.) are all false also; yea consequently their preachings, conversons, salvations (leaving fecret things to God) must all be of the same false nature likewise.

If the reports (yea some of their owne *Historians*) be true, what monstrous and molt inhumane conversons have they made; baptizing thousands, yea ten thousands of the poore Natives, sometimes by wiles and subtle devices, sometimes by force compelling them to submit to that which they understood not, neither before nor after such their monstrous Christning of them. Thirdly, for our *New-endland* parts; I can speake uprightly and confidently, I know it to have been easie for my selfe, long ere this, to have brought many thousands of these Natives, yea the whole country, to a far greater Antichristian conversion then ever was yet heard of in *America*. I have reported something in the Chapter of their Religion, how readily I could have brought the whole Country to have observed one day in seven; I adde to have received a *Baptisme* (or washing) though it were in Rivers (as the first *Christians* and the Lord Jesus himselfe did) to have come to a *stated Church meeting*, maintained priests and formes of prayer, and a whole forme of *Antichristian* worship in life and death. Let none wonder at this, for *plausible perswations* in the mouths of those whom naturall men esteem and love: for the power of prevailing forces and armies hath done this in all the Nations (as men speake) of *Christendome*. Yea what lamentable experience have we of the *Turnings* and *Turnings* of the *body* of this Land in point of Religion in few yeares?

When *England* was all *Popish* under Henry the the seventh, how ease is conversion wrought to halfe Papist halfe-Protestant under *Henry* the eighth?

From halfe-Proteftanifme halfe-Popery under *Henry* the eight, to absolute Protestanisme under Edward the sxth: from absoluer Protestation under *Edward* the sixt to absalute popery under Quegne *Mary*, and from absolute Popery under Queene *Mary*, (just like the Weather-cocke, with the breatq of every Prince) to absolute Protestanisme under Queene *Elizabeth* &c.

For all this, yet some may aske, why hath there been such a price in my hand not improved? why have I not brought them to such a conversion as I speake of? I answer, woe be to me, if I call light darknesse, or darknesse light; sweet bitter, or bitter sweet; woe be to me if I call that conversion unto God, which is indeed subversion of the soules of Millions in *Christendome*, from one false worship to another, and the prophanation of the holy name of God, his holy Son and blessed Ordinances. *America* (as Europe and all nations) lyes dead in sin and trespasses: It is not a fuite of crimson Satten will make a dead man live, take off and change his crimson into white he is dead still, off with that, and shift him into cloth of gold, end from that to cloth of diamonds, he is but a dead man still: For it is not a forme, nor the change of one forme into another, a finer, and a finer, and yet more fine, that makes a man a convert I meane such a convert as is acceptable to God in Jesus Christ, according to the visible Rule of his last will and Testament. I speake not of Hypocrites, (which may but glister, and be no solid gold as *Simon Magus, Judas* &c.) But of a true externall converson; I say then, woe be to me if intending to catch men (as the Lord Jesus said to *Peter*) I should pretend converson) and the bringing of men as mistical fish, into a *Church-estate*, that is a converted estate, and so build them up with *Ordinances* as a converted Christian People, and yet afterward still pretend to catch them by an after converson. I question not but that it hath pleased God in his infinit pitty and patience, to fuffer this among us, yea and to convert thousands, whom all men, yea and the persons (in their personall estates converted) have esteemed themselves good converts before.

But I question whether this hath been so frequent in these late yeares, when the times of ignorance (which God pleaseth to pase by) are over, and now a greater light concerning the Church, Ministery, and conversion, is arisen. I question whether if such rare talents, which God hath betrusted many of his precious Worthies with, were laid out (as they shall be in the Lord's molt holy season) according to the first pattern; I say, I question whether or no, where there hath been one (in his personall estate converted) there have not been, and I hope in the Lords time shall be, thousands truly converted from *Antichristian Idols* (both in *person* and *worship*) to serve the living and true God.

And lastly, it is out of question to me, that I may not pretend a *false conversion*, and *false state of worship*, to the true Lord Jesus.

If any noble *Berean* shall make inquiry what is that true conversion I intend; I answer first negatively.

First, it is not a converson of a People from one false worship to another, as *Nebuchadnezzer* compeld all Nations under his Monarchy.

Secondly, it is not to a mixture of the manner or worship of the true God, the God of Israel, with false gods & their worships, as the People were converted by the King of *Assyria*, 2, *Kin*. 17. in which worship for many Generations did these *Samaritans* continue, having a forme of many wholsome truths amongst them, concerning God and the Messiah, Ioh. 4.

Thirdly, it is not from the true to a false, as IEREBOAM turned the ten Tribes to their mine and disperson unto this day, 1. Kin. 12.

Fourthly, it must not be a conversion to some externall submisson to Gods Ordinances upon earthly respects, as JACOBS sons converted the *Sichemites*, Gen. 34.

Fiftly it mustnot be, (it is not poslible it should be in truth) a converson of People to the worship of the Lord Jesus, by force of Armes and swords of steele: So indeed did *Nebuchadnezzer* deale with all the world, *Dan*. 3. to doth his *Antitype* and *successorr* the *Beast* deal with all the earth, *Rev*. 13. &c.

But so did never the Lord Jesus bring any unto his most pure worship, for he abhorres (as all men, yea the very *Indians* doe) an unwilling Spouse, and to enter into a forced bed: The will in worship, if true, is like a free Vote, *nec cogit, nec cogitur*: JESVS CHRIST compells by the mighty perswasons of his Messengers to come in, but otherwise with earthly weapons he never did compell nor can be compelled. The not discerning of this truth hath let out the bloud of thousands in civill combustions in all ages; and made the whore drunke, & the Earth drunk with the bloud of the Saints, and witnesses of Jesus.

And it is yet like to be the destruction & and dissolution of (that which is called) the Christian world, unlesse the God of peace and pity looke downe upon it, and satisfy the soules of men, that he hath not so required. I should be far yet from unsecuring the peace of a City, of. a Land, (which I confesse ought to be maintained by civill weapons, & which I have so much cause to be earnest with God for;) Nor would I leave a gap open to any mutinous hand or tongue, nor wish a weapon left in the hand of any known to be mutinous and peace-breakers.

I know (lastly) the consciences of many are otherwise perswaded, both from Israels state of old, and other Allegations; yet I shall be humbly bold to lay, I am able to present such considerations to the eyes of all who love the Prince of truth and Peace, that shall discover the weaknesse of all such allegations, aud answer all objections, that have been, or can be made in this point. So much negatively. Secondly, affirmatively: I answer in generall, A true Conversion (whether of *Americans* or *Europeans*) must be such as those Conversions were of the first pattern, either of the Jewes or the Heathens; That Rule is the golden *Mece wand* in the hand of the Angell or Messenger, *rev*. 11. 1. besde which all other are leaden and crooked.

In particular: First, it must be by the free proclaiming or preaching of Repentance & forgivenesse of sins. *Luk*. 24. by such Messengers as can prove their lawfull fending and Commission from the Lord Jesus, to make Disciples out of all nations: and so to baptize or wash them into the *name* or *profession* of the holy Trinity, *Mat*, 28. 19 Rom. 10. 14. 15.

Secondly, such a conversion (so farre as mans Judgement can reach which is fallible, (as was the judgement of the first Messengers, as in *Simon Magus*, &c.) as is a turning of the whole man from the power of *Sathan* unto God, *act*. 26. Such a change, as if an old man became a new Babe *Ioh*. 3. yea, as amounts to Gods new creation in the soule, *Ephes*, 2. 10.Thirdly, Visibly it is a turning from Idols not only of *conversation* but of *worhsip* (whether *Pagan*, Turkish, Jewish, or Antichristian) to the Living and true God in the waies of his holy worship, appointed by his Son, 1 *Thes*. 1. 9.

I know Objections use to be made against this, but the *golden Rule*, if well attended to, will discover all crooked *swervings* and *aberrations*.

If any now say unto me, Why then if this be *Conversion*, and you have such a *Key* of *Language*, and such a dore of *opportunity*, in the knowledge of the Country and the inhabitants, why proceed you not to produce in *America* some patternes of such conversions as you speake of?

I answer, first, it must be a great deale of practise, and mighty paines and hardship undergone by my selfe, or any that would proceed to such a further degree of the Language, as to be able in propriety of speech to open matters of salvation to them. In matters of Earth men will helpe to spell out each other, but in matters of Heaven (to which the soule is naturally so averse) how far are the Eares of man hedged up from listening to all improper Language?

Secondly, my dsfires and endeavours are constant (by the helpe of God) to attaine a propriety of Language.

Thirdly, I confesse to the honour of my worthy Countrymen in the *Bay of Massachuset*, and elsewhere, that I received not longsfince expressions of their holy desires and prossers of assistance in the worke, by the hand of my worthy friend Colonell *Humphreys*, during his abode there.

Yet fourthly, I answer, if a man were as affectionate and zealous as *David* to build an house for God, and as wife and holy to advise and incourage, as *Nathan*, attempt this worke without a *Word*, a *Warrant* and *Comimission*, for *matter*, and *manner*, from GOD himselfe, they must afterwards heare a voice (though accepting good desires, yet reproving want of Commission) *Did I ever speak a word saith the Lord?* &c. 2. *Sam*. 7. 7.

The truth is, having not been without (through the mercy of God) abundant and constant thoughts about a true Commission for such an Embassie and Ministery. I must ingenuousy confesse the restlesse unsatisfiednesse of my soule in divers *main particulars*:

As first, whether (snce the Law must go forth from *Zion*, and the word of the Lord from Jerusalem) I say whether Gods great businesse between Christ Jesus the holy Son of God and Antichrist the man of sin and Sonne of perdition, must not be first over, and *Zion* and *Jerusalem* be re-built and re-established, before the Law and word of life be sent forth to the rest of the Nations of the World, who have not heard of Christ: The Prophets are deep concerning this.

Secondly snce there can be no preaching (according to the last Will and Testament of Christ Jesus) without a true sending *Rom*. 14. 15 Where the power and authority of *sending* and *giving* that *Commission on Math*. 28 &c. I say the question is where that power now lyes?

It is here unseasonable to number up all that lay claime to this *Power*, with their grounds for their pretences, either those of the *Romish* fort, or those of the *Reforming* or *Re-building* fort, and the mighty controverses which are this day in all parts about it: in due place (haply) I may present such sad *Queries* to consideration, that may occasion some to cry with DANIEL (concer-JERVSALEMS desolation *Dan*. 9.) *Under the whole Heaven hath not been done, as hath* been done to JERVSALEM: and with JEREMY in the fame respect, Lam. 2. 12. *Have you no respect all you that passe by, behold and see there were ever sorrow like to my sorrow, wherewith the Lord hath afflicted me in the day of his fierce wrath.*

That may make us ashamed for all that wee have done, *Ezek*. 43 and loath our selves, for that (in whorish worships) wee have broken him with our whorish hearts *Ezek*. 9. To fall dead at the feet of JESVS, *Rev*. 1. as JOHN did, and to weepe much as hee *Rev*. 5. that so the LAMB may please to open unto us that WONDERFVLL BOOK and the seven SEALED MYSTERIES thereof.

Your unworthy Country-man
ROGER WILLIAMS.

2.5.2 Reading and Review Questions

1. How does Williams distinguish Native Americans from "heathens?" Why, do you think?
2. What criticisms does Williams make against many Christians who have converted Native Americans? Why?

3. What hypocrisies, if any, does Williams perceive among the Puritans in America? Why?
4. How does Williams's view of the Puritans' purpose and place in America differ from Bradford's or Winthrop's? Why?
5. What views does Williams express that foreshadow America's post-Revolutionary separation of church and state?

2.6 CECIL CALVERT, LORD BALTIMORE

(1605–1675)

From his father George Calvert, Cecil Calvert inherited the title of Lord Baltimore and the charter from King Charles I to establish a colony at the Province of Maryland, comprising ten to twelve million acres of land in what is now the state of Maryland. Calvert governed the colony from England, sending his *Instructions to the Colonists by Lord Baltimore* to his brother Leonard, who served as the colony's first governor. Calvert's instructions served as the foundation for Maryland's laws.

Throughout his proprietorship, Cecil Calvert fostered religious tolerance in the colony of Maryland. After Leonard's death, Calvert commissioned a Protestant, William Stone, to serve as governor. He gave Stone a new law to be voted on by the Maryland Assembly, a law that came to be known as the Act of Toleration. This new law allowed colonists freedom of worship in any Christian faith, provided they maintained loyalty to Cecil Calvert and Maryland's government.

2.6.1 From *A Relation of the Lord Baltemore's Plantation in Maryland*

Chapter I

His most Excellent Majestie having by his Letters Patent, under the Great Seale of *England*, granted a certaine Countrey in *America* (now called *Maryland*, in honour of our gratious Queene) unto the Lord *Baltemore*, with divers Priviledges, and encouragements to all those that should adventure with his Lordship in the Planting of that Countrey: the benefit and honour of such an action was readily apprehended by divers Gentlemen, of good birth and qualitie, who thereupon resolved to adventure their Persons, and a good part of their fortunes with his Lordship, in the pursuite of so noble and (in all likelihood) so advantagious an enterprize. His Lordship was at first resolved to goe in person; but the more important reasons perswading his stay at home, hee appointed his brother, Mr. *Leonard Caluert* to goe Governour in his stead, with whom he joyned in Commission, Mr. *Jerome Hawley*, and Mr. *Thomas Cornwallis* (two worthy and able Gentlemen.) These with the other Gentlemen adventurers, and their servants to the number of neere 200. people, imbarked theselves for the voyage, in the good ship called the *Arke*, of 300. tunne & upward, which was attended by his Lordships Pinnace, called the *Dove*, of about 50. tunne. And so on Friday, the 22. of *November*, 1633. a small gale of winde coming gently from the *Northwest*, they weighed from the *Cowes* in the *Isle of Wight*, about ten in the morning; And having stayed by the way Twenty dayes at the *Barbada's*, and Fourteene dayes at Saint *Christophers* (upon some necessary occasions) they arrived at *Point Comfort* in *Virginia*, on the foure & twentyeth of *February* following. They had Letters from his Majesty, in favor of them, to the Governour of *Virginia*, in obedience whereunto, he used them with much courtesie and humanitie. At this time, one Captaine *Cleyborne* (one of the Councel of Virginia) comming from the parts whether they intended to goe, told them that all the Natives were in preparation of defence by reason of a rumor some had raised amongst them, that 6. shippes were to come with many people, who would drive all the inhabitants out of the Countrey.

On the 3. of *March*, they left *Point-Comfort*, & 2. dayes after, they came to *Patowmeck* river, which is about 24. leagues distant, there they began to give names to places, and called the *Southerne* point of that River, Saint *Gregories*; and the *Northerne* point, Saint *Michaels*.

They sayled up the River, till they came to *Heron* Island, which is about 14. leagues, and there came to an Anchor under an Island neere unto it, which they called S. *Clements*. Where they set up a Crosse, and tooke possession of this Countrey for our Saviour, and for our Soveraigne Lord the King of England.

Heere the Governor thought fit for the ship to stay, untill hee had discovered more of the Countrey: and so hee tooke two Pinnaces, and went up the River some 4. leagues, and landed on the *South* side, where he found the Indians fled for feare, from thence hee sayled some 9. leagues higher to *Patowmeck* Towne where the *Werowance* being a child, Archibau his unckle (who governed him and his Countrey for him) gave all the company good wellcome, and one of the company having entered into a little discourse with him, touching the errours of their religion, hee seemed well pleased therewith; and at his going away, desired him to returne thither againe, saying he should live with him, his men should hunt for him, and hee would divide all with him.

From hence the Governor went to *Paschatoway*, about 20. leagues higher, where he found many *Indians* assembled, and heere he met with one Captaine *Henry Fleete* an *English-man*, who had lived many yeeres among the *Indians*, and by that meanes spake the Countrey language very well, and was much esteemed of by the natives. Him our Governour sent a shore to invite the *Werowance* to a parley, who thereupon came with him aboard privatly, where he was courteously entertained, and after some parley being demanded by the Governour, whether hee would be content that he and his people should set downe in his Countrey, in case he should find a place convenient for him, his answere was, *"that he would not bid him goe, neither would hee bid him stay, but that he might use his owne discretion."*

While this *Werowance* was aboard, many of his people came to the water side, fearing that he might be surprised, whereupon the *Werowance* commanded two *Indians* that came with him, to goe on shore, to quit them of this feare, but they answered, they feared they would kill them; The *Werowance* therefore shewed himselfe upon the decke, and told them hee was in safety, wherewith they were satisfied.

Whilest the Governour was abroad, the neighbouring *Indians*, where the ship lay, began to cast off feare, and to come to their Court of guard, which they kept night and day upon Saint *Clements* Ile, partly to defend their barge, which was brought in pieces out of *England*, and there made up; and partly to defend their men which were imployed in felling of trees, and cleaving pales for a Palizado, and at last they ventured to come aboard the ship.

The Governour finding it not fit, for many reasons, to seate himselfe as yet so high in the River, resolved to returne backe againe, and to take a more exact view of the lower part, and so leaving the Ship & Pinnaces there, he tooke his Barge (as most fit to search the Creekes, and small rivers) and was conducted by Captaine *Fleete* (who knew well the Countrey) to a River on the North-side of *Patomeck* river, within 4. or 5. leagues from the mouth thereof, which they called Saint *Georges* River. They went up this river about 4. Leagues, and anchored at the Towne of *Yoacomaco*: from whence the *Indians* of that part of the Countrey, are called *Yoacomacoes*:

At their comming to this place, the Governour went on shoare, and treated friendly with the *Werowance* there, and acquainted him with the intent of his comming thither, to which hee made little answere (as it is their manner, to any new or suddaine question) but entertained him, and his company that night in his house, and gave him his owne bed to lie on (which is a matt layd on boords) and the next day, went to shew him the country, and that day being spent in viewing the places about that towne, and the fresh waters, which there are very plentifull and excellent good (but the maine rivers are salt) the Governor determined to make the first Colony there, and so gave order for the Ship and Pinnaces to come thither.

This place he found to be a very commodious situation for a Towne, in regard the land is good, the ayre wholsome and pleasant, the River affords a safe harbour for ships of any burthen, and a very bould shoare; fresh water, and wood there is in great plenty, and the place so naturally fortified, as with little difficultie, it will be defended from any enemie.

To make his entry peaceable and safe, hee thought fit to present the *Werowance* and the *Wisoes* of the Towne with some *English* Cloth, (such as is used in trade with the *Indians*) Axes, Howes, and Knives, which they accepted very kindly, and freely gave consent that hee and his company should dwell in one part of their Towne, and reserved the other for themselves; and those *Indians* that dwelt in that part of the Towne, which was allotted for the *English*, freely left them their houses, and some corne that they had begun to plant: It was also agreed between them, that at the end of harvest they should leave the whole towne; which they did accordingly: And they made mutuall promises to each other, to live friendly and peaceably together, and if any injury should happen to be done on any part, that satisfaction should be made for the same, and thus upon the 27. day of *March*,

Anno Domini, 1634. the Governour tooke possession of the place, and named the Towne Saint *Maries.*

There was an occasion that much facilitated their treaty with these *Indians*, which was this: The *Sasquehanocks* (a warlike people that inhabite betweene *Chesopeack* bay, and *Delaware* bay) did usually make warres, and incursions upon the neighbouring *Indians*, partly for superiority, partly for to get their Women, and what other purchase they could meet with, which these *Indians* of *Yocomaco* fearing, had the yeere before our arivall there, made a resolution, for their safety, to remove themselves higher into the Countrey where it was more populous, and many of them were gone thither before the *English* arrived.

Three dayes after their comming to *Yoacomaco* the Arke with the two Pinaces arived there. The Indians much wondred to see such ships, and at the thundering of the Ordnance when they came to an Anchor.

The next day they began to prepare for their houses, and first of all a Court of Guard, and a Store-house; in the meane time they lay abord the ship: They had not beene there many dayes before *Sir John Haruie* the governor of *Virginea* came thither to visit them: Also some Indian *Werowances*, and many other Indians from severall parts came to see them, amongst others the *Werowance* of *Patuxent* came to visit the Governour, and being brought into the great Cabin of the ship, was placed betweene the Governour of *Virginea*, and the Governour of *Mary-land*; and a Patuxent Indian that came with him, comming into the Cabin, and finding the *Werowance* thus sitting betweene the two Governours, started backe, fearing the *Werowance* was surprised, and was ready to have leapt overboard, and could not be perswaded to come into the Cabin, untill the *Werowance* came himselfe unto him; for he remembered how the said *Werowance* had formerly beene taken prisoner by the *English* of *Virginia.*

After they had finished the store-house, and unladed the ship, the Governour thought fit to bring the Colours on shore, which were attended by all the Gentlemen, and the rest of the servants in armes; who received the Colours with a volley of shot, which was answered by the Ordnance from the ships; At this Ceremony were present, the *Werowances* of *Patuxent*, and *Yoacomaco*, with many other Indians; and the *Werowance* of *Patuxent* hereupon tooke occasion to advise the Indians of *Yoacomaco* to be carefull to keepe the league that they had made with the *English.* He stayed with them divers dayes, and used many Indian Complements, and at his departure hee said to the Governour. "I love the English so well, that if they should goe about to kill me, if I had but so much breath as to speake; I would command the people, not to revenge my death; for I know they would not doe such a thing, except it were through mine owne default."

They brought thither with them some store of Indian Corne, from the *Barbado's*, which at their first arivall they began to use (thinking fit to reserve their English provision of Meale and Oatemeale) and the Indian women seeing their servants to bee unacquainted with the manner of dressing it, would make bread thereof for them, and teach them how to doe the like: They found also the countrey well stored with Corne (which they bought with truck, such as there is desired, the Natives having no knowledge of the use of money) whereof they sold them such plenty, as that they sent 1,000. bushells of it to *New-England*, to provide them some salt-fish, and other commodities which they wanted.

During the time that the *Indians* stai'd by the English at *Yoacomaco*, they went dayly to hunt with them for Deere and Turkies, whereof some they gave them for Presents, and the meaner sort would sell them to them, for knives, beades and the like: Also of Fish, the natives brought them great store, and in all things dealt very friendly with them; their women and children came very frequently amongst them, which was a certaine signe of their confidence of them, it being found by experience, that they never attempt any ill, where the women are, or may be in danger.

Their comming thus to feate upon an Indian Towne, where they found ground cleered to their hands, gave them opportunity (although they came late in the yeere) to plant some Corne, and to make them gardens, which they sowed with English seeds of all sorts, and they prospered exceeding well. They also made what haste they could to finish their houses; but before they could accomplish all these things, one Captaine *Cleyborne* (who had a desire to appropriate the trade of those parts unto himselfe) began to cast out words amongst the Indians, saying, That those of *Yoacomaco* were *Spaniards* and his enemies; and by this meanes endeavoured to alienate the mindes of the Natives from them, so that they did not receive them so friendly as formerly they had done. This caused them to lay aside all other workes, and to finish their Fort, which they did within the space of one moneth; where they mounted some Ordnance, and furnished it with some murtherers, and such other meanes of defence as they thought fit for their safeties: which being done, they proceeded with their Houses and finished them, with convenient accommodations belonging thereto: And although they had thus put themselves in safety, yet they ceased not to procure to put these jealousies out of the Natives minds, by treating and using them in the most courteous manner they could, and at last prevailed therein, and setled a very firme peace and friendship with them. They procured from *Virginia*, Hogges, Poultrey, and some Cowes, and some male cattell, which hath given them a foundation for breed and increase; and whoso desires it, may furnish himselfe with store of Cattell from thence, but the hogges and Poultrey are already increased in *Maryland*, to a great stocke, sufficient to serve the Colonie very plentifully. They have also set up a Water-mill

for the grinding of Corne, adjoyning to the Towne.

Thus within the space of fixe moneths, was laid the foundation of the Colonie in *Maryland*; and whosoever intends now to goe thither, shall finde the way so troden, that hee may proceed with much more ease and confidence then these first adventurers could, who were ignorant both of Place, People, and all things else, and could expect to find nothing but what nature produced: besides, they could not in reason but thinke, the Natives would oppose them; whereas now the Countrey is is discovered, and friendship with the natives is assured, houses built, and many other accommodations, as Cattell, Hogges, Poultry, Fruits and the like brought thither from *England*, *Virginea*, and other places, which are usefull, both for profit and Pleasure: and without boasting it may be said, that this Colony hath arived to more in fixe moneths, then *Virginia* did in as many yeeres. If any man say, they are beholding to *Virginea* for so speedy a supply of many of those things which they of *Virginia* were forced to fetch from *England* and other remote places, they will confesse it, and acknowledge themselves glad that Virginea is so neere a neighbour, and that it is so well stored of all necessaries for to make those parts happy, and the people to live as plentifully as in any other part of the world, only they wish that they would be content their neighbours might live in peace by them, and then no doubt they should find a great comfort each in other.

Chapter III

The Commodities which this Countrey affords naturally.

This Countrey affords naturally, many excellent things for Physicke and Surgery, the perfect use of which, the *English* cannot yet learne from the Natives: They have a roote which is an excellent preservative against Poylon, called by the *English*, the *Snake roote*. Other herbes and rootes they have, wherewith they cure all manner of woundes; also *Saxafras*, Gummes, and *Balfum*. An *Indian* seeing one of the English, much troubled with the tooth-ake, fetched of the roote of a tree, and gave the party some of it to hold in his mouth, and it eased the paine presently. They have other rootes fit for dyes, wherewith they make colours to paint themselves.

The Timber of these parts is very good, and in aboundance, it is usefull for building of houses, and shippes; the white Oake is good for Pipe-staves, the red Oake for wainescot. There is also Walnut, Cedar, Pine, & Cipresse, Chesnut, Elme, Ashe, and Popler, all which are for Building, and Husbandry. Also there are divers sorts of Fruit-trees, as Mulberries, Persimons, with severall other kind of Plummes, and Vines, in great aboundance. The Mast and the Chesnuts, and what rootes they find in the woods, doe feede the Swine very fat, and will breede great store, both for their owne provision, or for merchandise, and such as is not inferior to the Bacon of *Westphalia*.

Of Strawberries, there is plenty, which are ripe in *Aprill*: Mulberries in *May*; and Raspices in *June*; Maracocks which is somewhat like a Limon, are ripe in *August*.

In the Spring, there are severall sorts of herbes, as Corn-fallet, Violets, Sorrell, Purflaine, all which are very good and wholsome, and by the English, used for sallets, and in broth.

In the upper parts of the Countrey, there are Bufeloes, Elkes, Lions, Beares, Wolues, and Deare there are in great store, in all places that are not too much frequented, as also Beavers, Foxes, Otters, and many other sorts of Beasts.

Of Birds, there is the Eagle, Goshawke, Falcon, Lanner, Sparrow-hawke, and Merlin, also wild Turkeys in great aboundance, whereof many weigh 50. pounds, and upwards; and of Partridge plenty: There are likewise sundry sorts of Birds which sing, whereof some are red, some blew, others blacke and yellow, some like our Black-birds, others like Thrushes, but not of the same kind, with many more, for which wee know no names.

In Winter there is great plenty of Swannes, Cranes, Geese, Herons, Ducke, Teale, Widgeon, Brants, and Pidgeons, with other sorts, whereof there are none in *England*.

The Sea, the Bayes of *Chesopeack*, and *Delaware*, and generally all the Rivers, doe abound with Fish of severall sorts; for many of them we have no *English* names: There are Whales, Sturgeons very large and good, and in great aboundance; Grampuses, Porpuses, Mullets, Trouts, Soules, Place, Mackerell, Perch, Crabs, Oysters, Cockles, and Mussles; But above all these, the fish that have no English names, are the best except the Sturgeons: There is also a fish like the Thornebacke in *England*, which hath a taile a yard long, wherein are sharpe prickles, with which if it strike a man, it will put him to much paine and torment, but it is very good meate: also the Todefish, which will swell till it be ready to burst, if it be taken out of the water.

The Mineralls have not yet beene much searched after, yet there is discovered Iron Oare; and Earth fitt to make Allum, *Terra lemnia*, and a red soile like Bolearmonicke, with sundry other sorts of Mineralls, which wee have not yet beene able to make any tryall of.

The soile generally is very rich, like that which is about *Cheesweeke* neere *London*, where it is worth 20. shillings an Acre yeerely to Tillage in the Common-fields, and in very many places, you shall have two foote of blacke rich mould, wherein you shall scarce find a stone, it is like a sifted Garden-mould, and is so rich that if it be not first planted with *Indian* corne, *Tobacco*, Hempe, or some such thing that may take off the ranknesse thereof, it will not be fit for any *English* graine; and under that, there is found good loame, where-of wee have made as good bricke as any in *England*; there is great store of Marish ground also, that with good husbandry, will make as rich Medow, as any in the world: There is store of Marie, both blue, and white, and in many places, excellent clay for pots, and tyles; and to conclude, there is nothing that can be reasonably expected in a place lying in the latitude which this doth, but you shall either find it here to grow naturally: or Industry, and good husbandry will produce it.

Chapter IIII

The commodities that may be procured in Maryland by industry.

Hee that well considers the situation of this Countrey, and findes it placed betweene *Virginia* and *New-England*, cannot but, by his owne reason, conclude that it must needs participate of the naturall commodities of both places, and be capable of those which industry brings into either, the distances being so small betweene them: you (hall find in the Southerne parts of *Maryland*, all that *Virginia* hath naturally; and in the Northerne parts, what *New-England* produceth: and he that reades Captaine *John Smith* shall see at large discoursed what is in *Virginia*, and in Master *William Wood*, who this yeere hath written a treatise of *New-England*, he may know what is there to be expected.

Yet to say something of it in particular.

In the first place I name Corne, as the thing most necessary to sustaine man; That which the Natives use in the Countrey, makes very good bread, and also a meate which they call *Omene*, it's like our *Furmety*, and is very savory and wholesome; it will Mault and make good Beere; Also the Natives have a sort of *Pulse*, which we call *Pease* and *Beanes*, that are very good. This Corne yeelds a great increase, so doth the *Pease* and *Beanes*: One man may in a season, well plant so much as will yeeld a hundred bustiells of this Corne, 20 bushells of Beanes and Pease, and yet attend a crop of *Tobacco*: which according to the goodnesse of the ground may be more or lesse, but is ordinarily accompted betweene 800 and 100 pound weight.

They have made tryall of English *Pease*, and they grow very well, also *Musk-mellons, Water-melons, Cow-cumbers*, with all sorts of garden Roots and Herbes, as *Carrots, Parsenips, Turnips, Cabbages, Radish* with many more; and in *Virginia* they have sowed English *Wheate* and *Barley*, and it yeelds twise as much increase as in *England*; and although there be not many that doe apply themselves to plant Gardens and Orchards, yet those that doe it, find much profit and pleasure thereby: They have Peares, Apples, and severall forts of Plummes, Peaches in abundance, and as good as those of *Italy*; so are the Mellons and Pumpions: Apricocks, Figgs and Pomegranates prosper exceedingly; they have lately planted Orange and Limon trees which thrive very wel: and in fine, there is scarce any fruit that growes in England, France, Spaine or Italy, but hath been tryed there, and prospers well. You may there also have hemp and Flax, Pitch and Tarre, with little labour; it's apt for Rapefeed, and Annis-seed, Woad, Madder, Saffron, &c. There may be had, Silke-wormes, the Countrey being stored with Mulberries: and the superfluity of wood will produce Potashes.

And for *Wine*, there is no doubt but it will be made there in plenty, for the ground doth naturally bring foorth Vines, in such aboundance, that they are as frequent there, as Brambles are here. Iron may be made there with little charge; Brave ships may be built, without requiring any materials from other parts: Clabboard, Wainscott, Pipe-staves and Masts for mips the woods will afford plentifully. In fine, *Butter* and *Cheese, Porke* and *Bacon*, to transport to other countrys will be no small commodity, which by industry may be quickly had there in great plenty, &c. And if there were no other staple commodities to be hoped for, but Silke and Linnen (the materialls of which, apparantly will grow there) it were sufficient to enrich the inhabitants.

Chapter V

Of the Naturall disposition of the Indians which Inhabite the parts of Maryland where the English are seated: And their manner of living.

Hee that hath a Curiosity to know all that hath beene observed of the Customes and manners of the *Indians*, may find large discourses thereof in Captaine *Smiths* Booke of *Virginia*, and Mr. *Woods* of *New-England*: but he that is desirous to goe to *Maryland*, shall here find enough to informe him of what is necessary for him to know touching them. By Captaine *Smith's*, and many other Relations you may be informed, that the People are War-licke, and have done much harme to the *English*; and thereby are made very terrible. Others say that they are a base and cowardly People, and to be contemned: and it is thought by some who would be esteemed States-men, that the only point of pollicie that the *English* can use, is, to destroy the *Indians*, or to drive them out of the Countrey, without which, it is not to be hoped that they can be secure. The truth is, if they be injured, they may well be feared, they being People that have able bodies, and generally, taller, and bigger limbed then the *English*, and want not courage; but the oddes wee have of them in our weapons, keepes them in awe, otherwise they would not flie from the *English*, as they have done in the time of Warres with those of Virginia, and out of that respect, a small number of our men being armed, will adventure upon a great troope of theirs, and for no other reason, for they are resolute and subtile enough: But from hence to conclude, that there can be no safety to live with them, is a very great errour. Experience hath taught us, that by kind and faire usage, the Natives are not onely become peaceable, but also friendly, and have upon all occasions performed as many friendly Offices to the *English* in *Maryland*, and *New-England*, as any neighbour or friend uses to doe in the most Civill parts of Christendome: Therefore any wise man will hold it a far more just and reasonable way to treat the People of the Countrey well, thereby to induce them to civility, and to teach them the use of husbandry, and Mechanick trades, whereof they are capable, which may in time be very usefull to the *English*; and the Planters to keepe themselves strong, and united in Townes, at least for a competent number, and then noe man can reasonably doubt, either surprise, or any other ill dealing from them.

But to proceede, hee that sees them, may know how men lived whilest the world was under the Law of Nature; and, as by nature, so amongst them, all men are free, but yet subject to command for the publike defence. Their Government is Monarchicall, he that governes in chiefe, is called the *Werowance*, and is assisted by some that consult with him of the common affaires, who are called *Wisoes*: They have no Lawes, but the Law of Nature and discretion, by which all things are ruled, onely Custome hath introduced a law for the Succession of the Government, which is this; when a *Werowance* dieth, his eldest sonne succeeds, and after him the second, and so the rest, each for their Hues, and when all the sonnes are dead, then the sons of the *Werowances* eldest daughter shall succeede, and so if he have more daughters; for they hold, that the issue of the daughters hath more of his blood in them than the issue of his sonnes. The *Wisoes* are chosen at the pleasure of the *Werowance*, yet commonly they are chosen of the same family, if they be of yeeres capable: The yong men generally beare a very great respect to the elder.

They have also *Cockorooses* that are their Captains in time of war, to whom they are very obedient: But the *Werowance* himselfe plants Corne, makes his owne Bow and Arrowes, his Canoo, his Mantle, Shooes, and what ever else belongs unto him, as any other common Indian; and commonly the Commanders are the best and most ingenious and active in all those things which are in esteeme amongst them. The woman serve their husbands, make their bread, dresse their meate, such as they kill in hunting, or get by fishing; and if they have more wives than one, as some of them have (but that is not generall) then the best beloved wife performes all the offices of the house, and they take great content therein. The women also (beside the houshold businesse) use to make Matts, which serve to cover their houses, and for beds; also they make baskets, some of Rushes, others of Silke-grasse, which are very handsom.

The Children live with their Parents; the Boyes untill they come to the full growth of men; (for they reckon not by yeeres, as we doe) then they are put into the number of Bow-men, and are called Blacke-boyes (and so continue until they take them wives) When they are to be made Black-boyes, the ancient men that governe the yonger, tell them, That if they will be valiant and obedient to the *Werowance*, *Wisos*, and *Cockorooses*, then their god will love them, all men will esteeme of them, and they shall kill Deere, and Turkies, catch Fish, and all things shall goe well with them; but if otherwise, then shall all goe contrary: which perswasion mooves in them an incredible obedience to their commands; If they bid them take fire in their hands or mouthes, they will doe it, or any other desperate thing, although with the apparant danger of their lives.

The woman remaine with their Parents until they have huasonds, and if the Parents bee dead, then with some other of their friends. If the husband die, he leaves all that he hath to his wife, except his bow and arrowes, and some Beades (which they usually bury with them) and she is to keepe the children untill the sons come to be men, and then they live where they please, for all mens houses are free unto them; and the daughters untill they have husbands. The manner of their marriages is thus; he that would have a wife, treates with the father, or if he be dead, with the friend that take care of her whom he desires to have to wife, and agrees with him for a quantity of Beades, or some such other thing which is accepted amongst them; which he is to give for her, and must be payed at the day of their marriage; and then the day being appointed, all the friends of both parts meet at the mans house that is to have the wife, and each one brings a present of meate, and the woman that is to be married also brings her present: when the company is all come, the man he sits at the upper end of the house, and the womans friends leade her up, and place her by him, then all the company sit down upon mats, on the ground (as their manner is) and the woman riseth and serves dinner, First to her husband, then to all the company the rest of the day they spend in singing and dancing (which is not unpleasant) at night the company leaves the, and comonly they live very peaceably and lovingly together; Yet it falls out sometimes, that a man puts away one wife and takes another: then she and her children returne to her friends again. They are generally very obedient to their husbands, and you shal seldome heare a woman speake in the presence of her husband, except he aske her some question.

This people live to a great age, which appeares, in that although they marry not so yong as we doe in *England*, yet you may see many of them great-grandfathers to children of good bignesse; and continue at that age, very able and strong men: The Men and Women have all blacke haire, which is much bigger and harsher then ours, it is rare to see any of them to waxe gray, although they be very old, but never bauld: It is seldome seene that any of the men have beards, but they weare long locks, which reach to their shoulders, and some of them to their wasts: they are of a comely stature, well favoured, and excellently well limbed, and seldome any deformed. In their warres, and hunting, they use Bowes and Arrowes (but the Arrowes are not poysoned, as in other places.) The Arrow-heads are made of a Flint-stone, the top of a Deares horn, or some Fish-bone, which they fasten with a sort of glew, which they make. They also use in warres, a short club of a cubite long, which they call a *Tomahawk*.

They live for the most part in Townes, like Countrey Villages in *England*; Their houses are made like our Arboures, covered some with matts, others with barke of trees, which defend them from the injury of the weather: The fiers are in the midst of the house, and a hole in the top for the smoake to goe out at. In length, some of them are 30. others 40. some a 100. foote; and in breadth about 12. foote. They have some things amongst them which may well become Christians to imitate, as their temperance in eating and drinking, their Justice each to other, for it is never heard of, that those of a Nation will rob or steale one from another; and the *English* doe often trust them with truck, to deale for them as factors, and they have performed it very justly: Also they have sent letters by them to Virginia, and into other parts of of the Countrey, unto their servants that have beene trading abroad, and they have delivered them, and brought backe answere thereof unto those that sent thfcm; Also their conuersation each with other, is peaceable, and free from all scurrulous words, which may give offence; They are very hospitable to their owne people, and to strangers ; they are also of a grave comportment: Some of the Adventurers at a time, was at one of their feasts, when Two hundred of them did meet together; they eate of but one dish at a meale, and every man, although there be never so many, is serued in a dish by himselfe; their dishes are made of wood, but handsomely wrought; The dinner lasted two houres; and after dinner, they sung and danced about two houres more, in all which time, not one word or action past amongst them that could give the least disturbance to the company; In the most grave assembly, no man can expect to find so much time past with more silence and gravitie: Some *Indians* comming on a time to *James Towne* in *Virginia*, it happened, that there then fate the Councell to heare causes, and the *Indians* feeing such an assembly, asked what it meant? Answere was made, there was held a *Match-comaco* (which the Indians call their place of Councell) the Indian replyed, that they all talke at once, but wee doe not so in our *Match-comaco*.

Their attire is decent and modest; about their wasts, they weare a covering of Deares skinnes, which reacheth to their knees, and upon their shoulders a large mantle of skinnes, which comes downe to the middle of the legge, and some to the heele; in winter they weare it furred, in summer without; When men hunt they put off their Mantles, so doe the women when they worke, if the weather be hot: The women affect to weare chaines and bracelets of beades, some of the better sort of them, weare ropes of Pearle about their necks, and some hanging in their eares, which are of a large sort, but spoyled with burning the Oysters in the fire, and the rude boaring of them. And they and the young men use to paint their faces with severall colours, but since the *English* came thither, those about them have quite left it; and in many things (hew a great inclination to conforme themselues to the English manner of living. The *Werowance* of *Paschatoway* desired the Governor to send him a man that could build him a house like the English, and in sundry respects, commended our manner of living, as much better then their owne: The *Werowance* of *Patuxent*, goes frequently in *English* Attire, so doth he of *Portoback*, and many others that have bought Clothes of the *English*: These *Werowances* have made request, that some of their children may be brought up amongst the *English*, and every way, shew great demonstrations of friendship, and good affection unto them.

These People acknowledge a God, who is the giver of al the good things, wherewith their life is maintained; and to him they sacrifice of the first fruits of their Corne, and of that which they get by hunting and fishing: The sacrifice is performed by an Ancient man, who makes a speech unto their God (not without something of Barbarisme) which being ended, hee burnes part of the sacrifice, and then eates of the rest, then the People that are present, eate also, and untill the Ceremony be performed, they will not touch one bit thereof: They hold the Immortalitie of the soule, and that there is a place of Joy, and another of torment after death, and that those which kill, steale, or lye, shall goe to the place of torment, but those which doe no harme, to the good place; where they shall have all sorts of pleasure.

It happened the last yeere, that some of the *Sasquehanocks* and the *Wicomesses* (who are enemies) met at the Hand of *Monoponson*, where Captaine *Cleyborne* liveth, they all came to trade, and one of the *Sasquehanocks* did an Injury to a *Wicomesse*, whereat some of *Cleybornes* people that saw it, did laugh. The *Wicomesses* seeing themselves thus injured and despised (as they thought) went away, and lay in ambush for the returne of the *Sasquehanocks*, and killed five of them, onely two escaped; and then they returned againe, and killed three of *Cleybornes* People, and some of his Cattle; about two moneths after this was done, the *Wicomesses* sent a messenger unto his Lordships Governor, to excuse the fact, and to offer satisfaction for the harme that was done to the *English*: The *Wicomesse* that came with the message, brought in his company an *Indian*, of the Towne of *Patuxent*, which is the next neighbouring Towne unto the *English* at Saint *Maries*, with whom they have good correspondence, and hee spake to the Governour in this manner.

> I am a Native of *Patuxent*, as this man (whom you know) can tell you, true it is, I married a wife amongst the *Wicomesses*, where I have lived ever since, and they have sent me to tell you, that they are sorry for the harme, which was lately done by some of their people, to the *English* at *Monaponson*; and hope you will not make the rash act of a few young men (which was done in heate) a quarrell to their Nation, who desire to live in peace and love with you, and are ready to make satisfaction for the Injury, desiring to know what will give you content, and that they will returne such things as were then taken from thence; But withall, they desire you not to thinke that they doe this for feare, for they have warres with the *Sasquehanocks*, who have by a surprise, lately killed many of their men, but they would not sue to them for peace, intending to revenge the injuries, as they could find opportunitie, yet their desire was to have peace with the English.

The Governour returned answere to the *Wicomesse* ;since you acknowledge the Injury, and are sorry for it, and onely desire to know what I expect for satisfaction; I tell you I expect that those men, who have done this out-rage, should be delivered unto me, to do with them as I shall thinke fit, and likewise that you restore all such things as you then tooke from the *English*; and withall, charged him with a second Injury attempted upon some of his owne People, since that time, by the *Wicomesses*.

The *Wicomesse* after a little pause, replyed; It is the manner amongst us *Indians*, that if any such like accident happen, wee doe redeeme the life of a man that is so slaine, with a 100. armes length of *Roanoke* (which is a sort of Beades that they make, and use for money) and since that you are heere strangers, and come into our Countrey, you should rather conforme your selves to the Customes of our Countrey, then impose yours upon us; But as for the second matter, I know nothing of it, nor can give any answere thereunto.

The Governour then told him; It seemes you come not sufficiently instructed in the businesse which wee have with the *Wicomesses*, therefore tell them what I have said; and that I expect a speedy answere; and so dismist him.

It fell in the way of my discourse, to speake of the *Indian* money of those parts, It is of two sorts, *Wompompeag* and *Roanoake*; both of them are made of a fish-shell, that they gather by the Sea side, *Wompompeag* is of the greater sort, and *Roanoake* of the lesser, and the *Wompompeag* is three times the value of *Roanoake*; and these serve as Gold and Silver doe heere; they barter also one commoditie for another, and are very glad of trafficke and commerce, so farre as to supply their necessities: They shew no great desire of heaping wealth, yet some they will have to be buryed with them; If they were Christians, and would live so free from covetousnesse, and many other vices, which abound in Christendome, they would be a brave people.

I therefore conclude, that since God Almighty hath made this Countrey so large and fruitfull, and that the people be such as you have heard them described;

It is much more Prudence, and Charity, to Civilize, and make them Christians, then to kill, robbe, and hunt them from place to place, as you would doe a wolfe. By reducing of them, God shall be served, his Majesties Empire enlarged by the addition of many thousand Subjects, as well as of large Territories, our Nation honoured, and the Planters themselves enriched by the trafficke and commerce which may be had with them; and in many other things, they may be usefull, but presudiciall they cannot be, if it be not through their owne faults, by negligence of fortifying themselves, and not consering military discipline.

2.6.2 Reading and Review Questions

1. What, if any, significance do you see in the voyagers on the *Dove* and the *Arke* hearing as soon as they arrived at the Patowmeck river that (a) hostile American Indians were gathering against them, and (b) they raised a cross on the island of S. Clements, taking possession of "this Countrey for our Saviour, and for our Soveraigne Lord the King of England?"
2. How does the experience of these colonizers compare with those at Jamestown or Plymouth Plantation? Why? How does the purpose of these colonizers differ from earlier groups?
3. Why does Calvert make such a point about the approval and support these colonizers gained from the start from the Native Americans? What evidence does he give?
4. What values, in terms of material wealth and prosperity, are apparent in Calvert's account of the commodities procurable through industry? How do these values compare to those of other colonizers?
5. How much attention does Calvert give to gender issues among the American Indians? Why? What is his attitude towards American Indian women? How do you know? How does his description of gender issues differ from those of other accounts, like van der Donck's or Champlain's?

2.7 ANNE BRADSTREET

(1612–1672)

Like many women of her era, Anne Bradstreet's life quite literally depended upon those of her male relatives. In Bradstreet's case, these relatives were her father, Thomas Dudley (1576–1653), and her husband Simon Bradstreet (1603–1697). Her father encouraged Bradstreet's literary bent; her husband caused her emigration from England to America. Both guided her Puritan faith. She met Simon Bradstreet through his and her father's working for the estate of the Earl of Lincoln (1600–1667), a Puritan. Simon Bradstreet helped form the Massachusetts Bay Company. With him, Anne Bradstreet sailed on the *Arbella* to become a member of that colony.

Despite this dependence, Bradstreet showed independence of mind and spirit quite remarkable for a woman of her era. She felt that the Bible was not fulfilling the religious enlightenment and transcendence she sought. In America, she eventually saw firsthand, so to speak, the hand of the God to whom she would devote herself. Even as she fulfilled a woman's "appointed" domestic role and duties as wife and mother, Bradstreet realized her individual voice and vision through the poetry she wrote from her childhood on. Her poetic ambitions appear through the complex poetic forms in which she wrote, including rhymed discourses and "Quaternions," or four-part poems focusing on four topics of fours: the four elements, the four humors, the four ages of man, and the four seasons. Her ambitions show also in the poets whose work she emulated or learned from, poets including Sir Philip Sidney (1554–1586), Edmund Spenser (1552–1599), and John Donne (1572–1631).

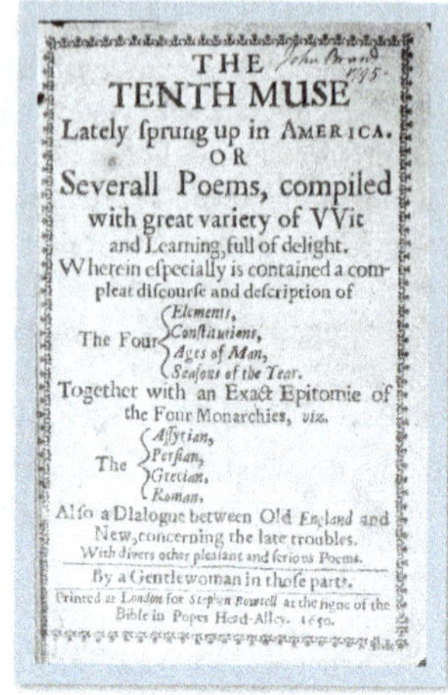
THE
TENTH MUSE
Lately ſprung up in AMERICA.
OR
Severall Poems, compiled
with great variety of VVit
and Learning, full of delight.
Wherein eſpecially is contained a compleat diſcourſe and deſcription of
The Four *Elements, Conſtitutions, Ages of Man, Seaſons of the Year.*
Together with an Exact Epitomie of the Four Monarchies, *viz.*
The *Aſſyrian, Perſian, Grecian, Roman.*
Alſo a Dialogue between Old *England* and New, concerning the late troubles.
With divers other pleaſant and ſerious Poems.
By a Gentlewoman in thoſe parts.
Printed at *London* for *Stephen Bowtell* at the ſigne of the Bible in Popes Head-Alley. 1650.

Image 2.6 | "The Tenth Muse"
Author | Anne Bradstreet
Source | Wikimedia Commons
License | Public Domain

Her ambition may not have been to publish her work. It was due to another male relative, her brother-in-law John Woodbridge (1613–1696), that her manuscript of poems was published. He brought the manuscript with him to London where it was published in 1651 as *The Tenth Muse Lately Spring Up in America, By a Gentlewoman of Those Parts.* The first book of poetry published by an American, it gained strong notice in England and Europe.

Image 2.7 | Etching of a House from *The Works of Anne Bradstreet in Prose and Verse*
Artist | Unknown
Source | Wikimedia Commons
License | Public Domain

These poems use allusion and erudition to characterize Bradstreet's unique, "womanly" voice. Poems later added to this book, some after her death, augment this voice through their simplicity and their attention to the concrete details of daily life. With personal lyricism, these poems give voice to Bradstreet's meditations on God and God's trials—such as her own illness, the burning of her house, and the deaths of grandchildren—as well as God's gifts, such as marital love.

2.7.1 "The Prologue"

I

To sing of Wars, of Captains, and of Kings,
Of Cities founded, Common-wealths begun,
For my mean pen are too superior things:
Or how they all, or each their dates have run
Let Poets and Historians set these forth,
My obscure Lines shall not so dim their worth.

II

But when my wondring eyes and envious heart
Great Bartas sugar'd lines, do but read o're
Fool I do grudge the Muses did not part
'Twixt him and me that overfluent store,
A Bartas can, do what a Bartas will
But simple I according to my skill.

III

From school-boyes tongue no rhet'rick we expect
Nor yet a sweet Consort from broken strings,
Nor perfect beauty, where's a main defect:
My foolish, broken blemish'd Muse so sings
And this to mend, alas, no Art is able,
'Cause nature, made it so irreparable.

IV

Nor can I, like that fluent sweet-tongu'd Greek,
Who lisp'd at first, in future times speak plain
By Art he gladly found what he did seek
A full requital of his, striving pain
Art can do much, but this maxime's most sure
A weak or wounded brain admits no cure.

V

I am obnoxious to each carping tongue
Who says my hand a needle better fits.
A Poets pen all scorn I should thus wrong.
For such despite they cast on Female wits:
If what I do prove well, it won't advance,
They'l say it's stoln, or else it was by chance.

VI

But sure the Antique Greeks were far more mild,
Else of our Sexe why feigned they those Nine
And poesy made, Calliope's own child;
So 'mongst the rest they placed the Arts Divine:
But this weak knot, they will full soon untie,
The Greeks did nought, but play the fools & lye.

VII

Let Greeks be Greeks, and women what they are.
Men have precedency, and still excell.
It is but vain unjustly to wage warre,
Men can do best, and women know it well
Preheminence in all and each is yours;
Yet grant some small acknowledgement of ours.

VIII

And oh ye high flown quills that soar the Skies,
And ever with your prey still catch your praise,
If e're you daigne these lowly lines your eyes
Give Thyme or Parsley wreath; I ask no bayes,
This mean and unrefined ore of mine
Will make you glistring gold, but more to shine:

2.7.2 "The Author to Her Book"

Thou ill-form'd offspring of my feeble brain,
Who after birth did'st by my side remain,
Till snatcht from thence by friends, less wise then true
Who thee abroad, expos'd to publick view,
Made thee in raggs, halting to th' press to trudg,
Where errors were not lessened (all may judg)
At thy return my blushing was not small,
My rambling brat (in print) should mother call,
I cast thee by as one unfit for light,
Thy Visage was so irksome in my sight;
Yet being mine own, at length affection would
Thy blemishes amend, if so I could:
I wash'd thy face, but more defects I saw,
And rubbing off a spot, still made a flaw.
I stretcht thy joynts to make thee even feet,
Yet still thou run'st more hobling then is meet;

In better dress to trim thee was my mind,
But nought save home-spun Cloth, i' th' house I find
In this array, 'mongst Vulgars mayst thou roam
In Criticks hands, beware thou dost not come;
And take thy way where yet thou art not known,
If for thy Father askt, say, thou hadst none:
And for thy Mother she alas is poor,
Which caus'd her thus to send thee out of door.

2.7.3 "To My Dear and Loving Husband"

If ever two were one, then surely we.
If ever man were lov'd by wife, then thee,
If ever wife was happy in a man,
Compare with me ye women if you can.
I prize thy love more then whole Mines of gold,
Or all the riches that the East doth hold,
My love is such that Rivers cannot quench,
Nor ought but love from thee, give recompence.
Thy love is such I can no way repay,
The heavens reward thee manifold I pray.
Then while we live, in love lets so persever,
That when we live no more, we may live ever.

2.7.4 "Contemplations"

I

Sometime now past in the Autumnal Tide,
When Phœbus wanted but one hour to bed,
The trees all richly clad, yet void of pride,
Were gilded o're by his rich golden head.
Their leaves & fruits seem'd painted, but was true
Of green, of red, of yellow, mixed hew,
Rapt were my sences at this delectable view.

II

I wist not what to wish, yet sure thought I,
If so much excellence abide below,
How excellent is he that dwells on high?
Whose power and beauty by his works we know.
Sure he is goodness, wisdome, glory, light,
That hath this under world so richly dight:
More Heaven then Earth was here, no winter & no night.

III

Then on a stately Oak I cast mine Eye,
Whose ruffling top the Clouds seem'd to aspire.
How long since thou wast in thine Infancy?
Thy strength, and stature, more thy years admire,
Hath hundred winters past since thou wast born,
Or thousand since thou brakest thy shell of horn,
If so, all these as nought, Eternity doth scorn.

IV

Then higher on the glistering Sun I gaz'd,
Whose beams was shaded by the leavie Tree.
The more I look'd, the more I grew amaz'd
And softly said, what glory's like to thee?
Soul of this world, this Universes Eye,
No wonder, some made thee a Deity:
Had I not better known, (alas) the same had I.

V

Thou as a Bridegroom from thy Chamber rushes
And as a strong man, joyes to run a race,
The morn doth usher thee, with smiles & blushes.
The Earth reflects her glances in thy face.
Birds, insects, Animals with Vegative,
Thy heart from death and dulness doth revive;
And in the darksome womb of fruitful nature dive.

VI

Thy swift Annual, and diurnal Course,
Thy daily streight, and yearly oblique path,
Thy pleasing fervor, and thy scorching force,
All mortals here the feeling knowledg hath
Thy presence makes it day, thy absence night,
Quaternal Seasons caused by thy might:
Hail Creature, full of sweetness, beauty & delight.

VII

Art thou so full of glory, that no Eye
Hath strength, thy shining Rayes once to behold?
And is thy splendid Throne erect so high?
As to approach it, can no earthly mould.

How full of glory then must thy Creator be?
Who gave this bright light luster unto thee:
Admir'd, ador'd for ever, be that Majesty.

VIII

Silent alone, where none or saw, or heard,
In pathless paths I lead my wandring feet,
My humble Eyes to lofty Skyes I rear'd
To sing some Song, my mazed Muse thought meet.
My great Creator I would magnifie,
That nature had, thus decked liberally:
But Ah, and Ah, again, my imbecility!

IX

I heard the merry grasshopper then sing,
The black clad Cricket, bear a second part,
They kept one tune, and played on the same string,
Seeming to glory in their little Art.
Shall Creatures abject, thus their voices raise?
And in their kind resound their makers praise:
Whilst I as mute, can warble forth no higher layes.

X

When present times look back to Ages past,
And men in being fancy those are dead,
It makes things gone perpetually to last
And calls back moneths and years that long since fled
It makes a man more aged in conceit,
Then was Methuselah or's grand-sire great:
While of their persons & their acts his mind doth treat.

XI

Sometimes in Eden fair, he seems to be,
Sees glorious Adam there made Lord of all,
Fancies the Apple, dangle on the Tree,
That turn'd his Sovereign to a naked thral.
Who like a miscreant's driven from that place,
To get his bread with pain, and sweat of face:
A penalty impos'd on his backsliding Race.

XII

Here sits our Grandame in retired place,
And in her lap, her bloody Cain new born,
The weeping Imp oft looks her in the face,
Bewails his unknown hap, and fate forlorn;
His Mother sighs, to think of Paradise,
And how she lost her bliss, to be more wise,
Believing him that was, and is, Father of lyes.

XIII

Here *Cain* and *Abel* come to sacrifice,
Fruits of the Earth; and Fatlings each do bring,
On *Abels* gift the fire descends from Skies,
But no such sign on false *Cain's* offering;
With sullen hateful looks he goes his wayes,
Hath thousand thoughts to end his brothers dayes,
Upon whose blood his future good he hopes to raise.

XIV

There Abel keeps his sheep, no ill he thinks,
His brother comes, then acts his fratricide,
The Virgin Earth of blood her first draught drinks
But since that time she often hath been cloy'd;
The wretch with gastly face and dreadful mind,
Thinks each he sees will serve him in his kind,
Though none on Earth but kindred near then could he find.

XV

Who fancyes not his looks now at the Barr,
His face like death, his heart with horror fraught,
Nor Male-factor ever felt like warr,
When deep dispair, with wish of life hath fought,
Branded with guilt, and crusht with treble woes,
A Vagabond to Land of Nod he goes,
A City builds, that walls might him secure from foes.

XVI

Who thinks not oft upon the Father's ages.
Their long descent how nephews sons they saw,
The starry observations of those Sages,
And how their precepts to their sons were law,

How Adam sighed to see his Progeny,
Cloath'd all in his black, sinfull Livery,
Who neither guilt, not yet the punishment could fly.

XVII

Our Life compare we with their length of dayes
Who to the tenth of theirs doth now arrive?
And though thus short, we shorten many wayes,
Living so little while we are alive;
In eating, drinking, sleeping, vain delight
So unawares comes on perpetual night,
And puts all pleasures vain unto eternal flight.

XVIII

When I behold the heavens as in their prime
And then the earth (though old) still clad in green,
The stones and trees, insensible of time,
Nor age nor wrinkle on their front are seen;
If winter come and greeness then do fade,
A Spring returns, and they more youthfull made,
But Man grows old, lies down, remains where once he's laid.

XIX

By birth more noble then those creatures all,
Yet seems by nature and by custome curs'd,
No sooner born, but grief and care makes fall
That state obliterate he had at first:
Nor youth, nor strength, nor wisdom spring again,
Nor habitations long their names retain,
But in oblivion to the final day remain.

XX

Shall I then praise the heavens the trees, the earth
Because their beauty and their strength last longer
Shall I wish there, or never to had birth,
Because they're bigger, & their bodyes stronger?
Nay, they shall darken, perish, fade and dye,
And when unmade, so ever shall they lye.
But man was made for endless immortality.

XXI

Under the cooling shadow of a stately Elm
Close sate I by a goodly Rivers side,
Where gliding streams the Rocks did overwhelm;
A lonely place, with pleasures dignifi'd.
I once that lov'd the shady woods so well,
Now thought the rivers did the trees excel,
And if the sun would ever shine, there would I dwell.

XXII

While on the stealing stream I fixt mine eye
Which to the long'd for Ocean held its course,
I markt, nor crooks, nor rubs that there did lye
Could hinder ought, but still augment its force.
O happy Flood, quoth I, that holds thy race
Till thou arrive at thy beloved place,
Nor is it rocks or shoals that can obstruct thy pace.

XXIII

Nor is't enough, that thou alone may'st slide,
But hundred brooks in thy cleer waves do meet,
So hand in hand along with thee they glide
To Thetis house, where all imbrace and greet:
Thou Emblem true, of what I count the best,
O could I lead my Rivolets to rest,
So may we press to that vast mansion, ever blest.

XXIV

Ye Fish which in this liquid Region 'bide
That for each season, have your habitation,
Now salt, now fresh where you think best to glide
To unknown coasts to give a visitation,
In Lakes and ponds, you leave your numerous fry,
So nature taught and yet you know not why,
You watry folk that know not your felicity.

XXV

Look how the wantons frisk to tast the air,
Then to the colder bottome streight they dive,
Eftsoon to Neptun's glassie Hall repair
To see what trade they great ones there do drive,

Who forrage o're the spacious sea-green field
And take the trembling prey before it yield,
Whose armour is their scales, their spreading fins their shield.

XXVI

While musing thus with contemplation fed,
And thousand fancies buzzing in my brain,
The sweet-tongu'd Philomel percht o're my head,
And chanted forth a most melodious strain
Which rapt me so with wonder and delight,
I judg's my hearing better then my sight,
And wisht me wings with her a while to take my flight.

XXVII

O merry Bird (said I) that fears no snares,
That neither toyls nor hoards up in thy barn,
Feels no sad thoughts, nor cruciating cares
To gain more good, or shun what might thee harm
Thy cloaths ne're wear, thy meat is everywhere,
Thy bed a bough, thy drink the water cleer,
Reminds not what is past, nor whats to come dost fear.

XXVIII

The dawning morn with songs thou dost prevent,
Sets hundred notes unto thy feathered crew,
So each one tunes his pretty instrument,
And warbling out the old, begin anew,
And thus they pass their youth in summer season,
Then follow thee into a better Region,
Where winter's never felt by that sweet airy legion.

XXIX

Man at the best a creature frail and vain,
In knowledg ignorant, in strength but weak,
Subject to sorrows, losses, sickness, pain,
Each storm his state, his mind, his body break.
From some of these he never finds cessation,
But day or night, within, without, vexation,
Troubles from foes, from friends, from dearest, near'st Relation.

XXX

And yet this sinfull creature, frail and vain,
This lump of wretchedness, of sin and sorrow,
This weather-beaten vessel wrackt with pain,
Joyes not in hope of an eternal morrow.
Nor all his losses, crosses, and vexation,
In weight, in frequency and long duration
Can make him deeply groan for that divine Translation.

XXXI

The Mariner that on smooth waves doth glide,
Sings merrily, and steers his Barque with ease,
As if he had command of wind and tide,
And now becomes great Master of the seas;
But suddenly a storm spoiles all the sport.
And makes him long for a more quiet port.
Which 'gainst all adverse winds may serve for fort.

XXXII

So he that faileth in this world of pleasure,
Feeding on sweets, that never bit of th' sowre,
That's full of friends, of honour and of treasure,
Fond fool, he takes this earth ev'n for heav'ns bower.
But sad affliction comes & makes him see
Here's neither honour, wealth, nor safety.
Only above is found all with security.

XXXIII

O Time the fatal wrack of mortal things,
That draws oblivions curtains over kings,
Their sumptuous monuments, men know them not;
Their names without a Record are forgot.
Their parts, their ports, their pomp's all laid in th' dust
Nor wit nor gold, nor buildings scape times rust,
But he whose name is grav'd in the white stone
Shall last and shine when all of these are gone.

2.7.5 "Here Follows Some Verses upon the Burning of Our House"

In silent night when rest I took,
For sorrow neer I did not look,

I waken'd was with thundring nois
And Piteous shreiks of dreadfull voice.
That fearfull sound of fire and fire,
Let no man know is my Desire.

I, starting up, the light did spye,
And to my God my heart did cry
To strengthen me in my Distresse
And not to leave me succourlesse.
Then coming out beheld a space,
The flame consume my dwelling place.

And, when I could no longer look,
I blest his Name that gave and took,
That layd my goods now in the dust:
Yea so it was, and so 'twas just.
It was his own: it was not mine;
far be it that I should repine.

He might of All justly bereft,
But yet sufficient for us left.
When by the Ruines oft I pasft,
My sorrowing eyes aside did cast,
And here and there the places spye
Where oft I fate, and long did lye.

Here stood that Trunk, and there that chest;
There lay that store I counted best:
My pleasant things in ashes lye,
And them behold no more shall I.
Under thy roof no guest shall sitt,
Nor at thy Table eat a bitt.

No pleasant tale shall 'ere be told,
Nor things recounted done of old.
No Candle 'ere shall shine in Thee,
Nor bridegroom's voice ere heard shall bee.
In silence ever shalt thou lye;
Adeiu, Adeiu; All's vanity.

Then streight I 'gin my heart to chide,
And did thy wealth on earth abide?
Didst fix thy hope on mouldring dust,

The arm of flesh didst make thy trust?
Raise up thy thoughts above the skye
That dunghill mists away may flie.

Thou haft an house on high erect,
Fram'd by that mighty Architect,
With glory richly furnished,
Stands permanent tho: this bee fled.
'Its purchased, and paid for too
By him who hath enough to doe.

A Prise so vast as is unknown,
Yet, by his Gift, is made thine own.
Ther's wealth enough, I need no more;
Farewell my Pelf, farewell my Store.
The world no longer let me Love,
My hope and Treasure lyes Above.

2.7.6 "In Memory of My Dear Grandchild Elizabeth Bradstreet"

I

Farewel dear babe, my hearts too much content,
Farewel sweet babe, the pleasure of mine eye,
Farewel fair flower that for a space was lent,
Then ta'en away unto Eternity.
Blest babe why should I once bewail thy fate,
Or sigh the dayes so soon were terminate;
Sith thou art setled in an Everlasting state.

II

By nature Trees do rot when they are grown,
And Plumbs and Apples throughly ripe do fall,
And Corn and grass are in their season mown,
And time brings down what is both strong and tall.
But plants new set to be eradicate,
And buds new blown to have so short a date,
Is by his hand alone that guides nature and fate.

2.7.7 "In Memory of My Dear Grandchild Anne Bradstreet"

With troubled heart & trembling hand I write,
The Heavens have chang'd to sorrow my delight.
How oft with disappointment have I met,

When I on fading things my hopes have set?
Experience might 'fore this have made me wise,
To value things according to their price:
Was ever stable joy yet found below?
Or perfect bliss without mixture of woe.
I knew she was but as a withering flour,
That's here to day perhaps gone in an hour;
Like as a bubble, or the brittle glass,
Or like a shadow turning as it was.
More fool then I to look on that was lent,
As if mine own, when thus impermanent.
Farewel dear child, thou ne re shall come to me,
But yet a while and I shall go to thee.
Mean time my throbbing heart's chear'd up with this
Thou with thy Saviour art in endless bliss.

2.7.8 "On My Dear Grandchild Simon Bradstreet"

No sooner come, but gone, and fal'n asleep,
Acquaintance short, yet parting caus'd us weep.
Three flours, two scarcely blown, the last i'th' bud,
Cropt by th' Almighties hand; yet is he good,
With dreadful awe before him let's be mute,
Such was his will, but why, let's not dispute,
With humble hearts and mouths put in the dust,
Let's say he's merciful as well as just.
He will return, and make up all our losses,
And smile again, after our bitter crosses.
Go pretty babe go rest with Sisters twain
Among the blest in endless joyes remain.

2.7.9 Reading and Review Questions

1. In "The Prologue," what are her "inherent defects" to which Bradstreet brings attention? Why does she do so? Does the poem as a whole bear out these "defects" as actual defects? To what degree, if any, do these defects reflect Bradstreet's sense of her gender and her religion?
2. Why do you think Bradstreet essentially records her knowledge of literature and the classics in "The Prologue?"
3. In "The Author to Her Book," what conventional maternal behaviors does Bradstreet apply to her book? Why? Why does she make an especial note of her "offspring" not having a father?

4. In "To My Dear and Loving Husband," what conventions and tropes often used in the sonnet form does Bradstreet use? What, if anything, is unconventional in her using them? Why?
5. How does Bradstreet console herself for such losses and suffering as the deaths of her grandchildren and the burning of her house? How, if at all, does her religious faith support her as a woman?

2.8 MICHAEL WIGGLESWORTH

(1631–1705)

Michael Wigglesworth's parents, Edward and Esther Wigglesworth, brought him with them when they emigrated to the American colonies in 1683. Wigglesworth was educated in America, first at home under the tutelage of Ezekiel Cheever (1514–1708), then at Harvard. In 1652, he earned his MA from Harvard and remained there as lecturer.

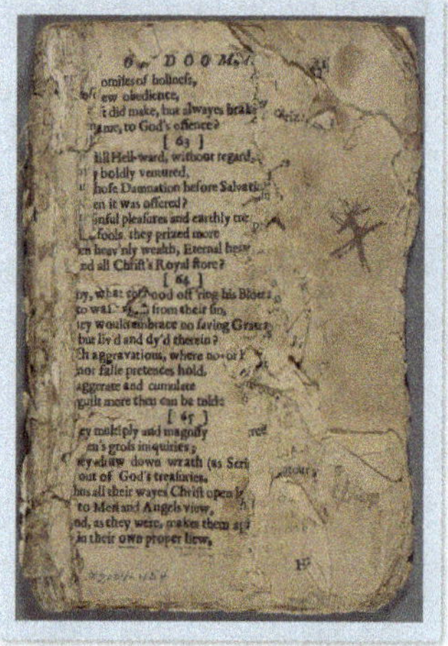

Image 2.4 | First Edition of *The Day of Doom*
Author | Michael Wigglesworth
Source | Wikimedia Commons
License | Public Domain

After his graduation, Wigglesworth also began preaching; he ultimately became an ordained minister at Malden, Massachusetts in 1656. Chronic illness curtailed his ministry activities, ministry that he nevertheless maintained through his writing. His *The Day of Doom: Or, A Description of the Great and Last Judgment, with a Short Discourse about Eternity* (1662) is a didactic religious poem, exhorting his parishioners to adhere to true Puritan doctrines and ideals. Its publication coincided with the controversy over church membership, later resolved in what became known as the Half-Way Covenant, allowing church membership without conversion testimony. The Covenant intended to bring colonists to the fervid faith held by first-generation settlers. This historical context may help explain the purpose of Wigglesworth's work.

Its effectiveness as a didactic piece appears in its extraordinary popularity (selling over 1,800 copies) and its being used to teach children Puritan theology. Its 224 eight-line stanzas—all with striking details and often terrifying images—arrest the attention of wandering minds and souls threatening to fall into sins of omission and commission, souls that may repent too late before the inevitable judgment day. Its stanzaic lines alternate between eight and six syllables; with internal rhymes in the eight-syllable lines, and end rhymes in alternating pairs of the six-syllable lines. Through its artistry and style combined with substance, through its sweetness and light, *The Day of Doom* fulfills poetry's highest purpose (according to Sir Phillip Sidney) in encouraging right living.

2.8.1 *The Day of Doom* Or, *A Description of the Great and Last Judgment*

(1662)

I
Still was the night, serene and bright,
when all men sleeping lay;
Calm was the season, & car [. . .] l reason
thought so 'twould last [. . .] or ay.
Soul take thine ease, let sorrow cease,
much good thou hast in store;
This was their song their cups among
the evening before.

II
Wallowing in all kind of sin,
vile wretches lay secure,
The best of men had scarcely then
their Lamps kept in good ure.
Virgins unwise, who through disguise
amongst the best were number'd,
Had clos'd their eyes; yea, and the Wise
through sloth and frailty slumber'd.

III
Like as of old, when men grew bold
Gods threatnings to contemn,
(Who stopt their ear, and would not hear
when mercy warned them?
But took their course, without remorse,
till God began to pour
Destruction the world upon,
in a tempestuous show [. . .]

IV
They put away the evil day
and drown'd their cares and fears,
Till drown'd were they, and swept away
by vengeance unawares:

So at the last, whilest men sleep fast
in their security,
Surpriz'd they are in such a snare
as cometh suddenly.

V

For at midnight broke forth a light,
which turn'd the night to day:
And speedily an hideous cry
did all the world dismay.
Sinners awake, their hearts do ake,
trembling their loyns surprizeth;
Am [. . .] z'd with fear, by what they hear,
each one of them ariseth.

VI

They rush from beds with giddy heads,
and to their windows run,
Viewing this Light, which shines more bright
than doth the noon-day Sun.
Straightway appears (they see't with [. . .] ears)
the Son of God most dread,
Who with his train comes on amain
to judge both Quick and Dead.

VII

Before his face the Heavens give place,
and Skies are rent asunder,
With mighty voice and hideous noise,
more terrible then Thunder.
His brightness damps Heav'ns glorious l [. . .] mps,
and makes them hide their heads:
As if afraid, and quite dismaid,
they quit their won [. . .] ed steads.

VIII

Ye sons of men that durst contemn
the threatnings of Gods word,
How cheer you now? your hearts (I trow)
are thrill'd as with a sword.
Now Atheist blind, whose bru [. . .] ish min [. . .]
a God could never see,

Dost thou perceive, dost now believe
that Christ thy Judge shall be [. . .]

IX
Stout courages (whose hardiness
could death and hell out-face)
Are you as bold now you behold
your Judge draw near apace?
They cry, No, no: alas and wo [. . .]
our courage all is gone:
Our hardiness, ([. . .]ool-hardiness)
hath us undone, undone.

X
No heart so b [. . .]ld but now grows cold,
and almost dead with fear:
No eye so dry but now can cry,
and pour out many a tear.
Earths Po [. . .] entates and pow'rful States,
Captains and men of Might
Are qui [. . .] e abasht, their courage dasht.
At this most dreadful sight.

XI
Mean men lament, great men do r [. . .] nt
their robes and tear their hair:
They do not spare their flesh to tear
through horrible despair.
All kindreds wail, their hearts do fail:
horrour the world doth fill
Wi [. . .] weeping eyes, and loud out-cries,
yet knows not how to kill.

XII
Some hide themselves in Caves and Delves,
and pl [. . .] ces under ground:
Some rashly leap into the deep,
to, scape by being drown'd:
Some to the Rocks, (O sensless blocks)
and woody Mountains run,
T [. . .] a [. . .] there they might this fearful [. . .] ight
and dreaded Presence shun.

XIII

In v [. . .] in do they to Mountains say,
Fall on us, and us hide
From Judges i [. . .] e, more hot then fire,
For who may it abide?
No hiding place can from his face
sinners at all conceal,
Whose flaming eye hid things doth spy,
and darkest things reveal.

XIV

The Judge draws nigh, exalted high
upon a lofty Throne,
Amids the throng of Angels strong,
LIKE Israel's [. . .] oly One.
The excellence of whose Presence,
and awful Majesty,
Am [. . .] zeth Nature, and every Crea [. . .] ure
doth more then terrifie.

XV

The Mountains smo [. . .] k, the Hills are shook,
the Earth is rent and torn,
As if she should be clean dissolv'd,
or from her Cen [. . .] re born.
The Sea doth roar, forsakes the sho [. . .] e,
and shrinks away for fear:
The wild beasts flee into the Sea
so soon as he draws nea [. . .].

XVI

Whose glory bright, whose wond [. . .] ous might,
whose Power Imperial,
So far surpass what ever was
in Realms Terrestrial;
That tongues of men (nor Angels pen)
cannot the same express:
And the [. . .] efore I must pass it by,
lest speaking should transgress.

XVII

Before his throne a Trump is blown,
proclaiming th' day of Doom:

Forthwith he c [. . .] ies, Ye dead arise,
and unto Judgement come.
No sooner said, but 'tis obey'd;
Sepulch [. . .] es open'd are;
Dead bodies all [. . .] ise at his call,
and's mig [. . .] y power declare.

XVIII
Both s [. . .] a and land at his command,
their dead at once surrender:
The fire and air constrained are
also [. . .] heir de [. . .] d to [. . .] ender.
The mighty wo [. . .] d of [. . .] his great Lord
links body and soul toge [. . .] her,
Both of the just and the unjust,
to part no more for ever.

XIX
The same translates from mortal states
[. . .] o imm [. . .] tality,
All that survive, and be alive,
i'th' twinkling of an eye.
That so they may abide for ay
to endless weal or woe;
Both the Renate and Reprobate
are made to dye no moe.

XX
His winged Hosts fly through all Coasts,
together gathering
Both good and bad, both quick and dead,
and all to Judgement bring.
Out of their holes these creeping Moles,
that hid themselves for fear,
By force they take, and quickly make
before the Judge appear.

XXI
Thus every one before the Throne
of Christ the Judge is brought,
Both righteous and impious,
that good or ill had wrought.
A sepa [. . .] ation, and diff'ring station

by Christ appointed is
To sinners sad (‘ [. . .] wixt good and bad,)
‘ [. . .] wixt Heirs of woe, and bliss.

XXII
At Christ’s right hand the sheep do st [. . .] nd,
his Holy Martyrs who
For his dear Name, suffering shame,
calamity, and woe,
Like Champions stood, and with their blood
their Testimony sealed;
Whose innocence, without off [. . .] nce
to Christ their Judge appealed.

XXIII
Next unto whom there find a room,
all Christs [. . .] fflicted one [. . .],
Who being chastis’d, neither despis’d,
nor sank amidsts their g [. . .] oans:
Who by the Rod were turn’d to God,
and loved him the more,
N [. . .] murmuring nor quarrelling [. . .]
when they were chast’ned sore.

XXIV
Moreover such as loved much,
that had not such a trial,
As might constrain to so great pain,
and such deep sel [. . .]-denial;
Yet ready were the Cross to bear,
when Christ them call’d thereto,
And did rejoyce to hear his voice,
they’r counted Sheep also.

XXV
Christ’s flock of Lambs there also stands,
whose Faith was weak, yet true;
All sound Believers (Gospel-receivers)
whose grace was small, but grew.
And them among an infant throng
of Babes, for whom Christ dy’d;
Whom [. . .] or his own, by ways unknown.
to men, he sanctify’d.

XXVI
All stand before their Saviour
in long white Robes [. . .] clad,
Their countenance [. . .] ull of pleasance,
appearing wondrous glad.
O glorious sight I behold how bright
dust heaps are made to shine,
Conformed so their Lord unto,
whose glory is divine.

XXVII
At Christs left hand the Goats do stand,
all whining Hypocrites,
Who for self-ends did seem Christ's friends,
but fost'red guileful sprites:
Who Sheep resembled, but they dissembled
(their heart was not sincere)
Who once did throng Christ's Lambs among;
but now must not come near.

XXVIII
Apostata's, and Run-away's,
such as have Christ forsaken,
(Of whom the the Devil, with seven more evil,
hath fresh possession taken:
Sinners in grain, reserv'd to pain
and torments most severe)
Because 'gainst light they sinn'd with spight,
are also placed there.

XXIX
There also stand a num'rous band,
that no profession made
Of Godliness, nor to redress
their wayes at all assay'd:
Who better knew, but (sin [. . .] ul Crew [. . .])
Gospel and Law despised;
Who all Christ's knocks withstood like blocks,
and would not be advised.

XXX
Moreover there with them appear
a number numberless

Of great and small, vile wretches all,
that did Gods Law transgress:
Idolaters, false Worshippers,
Prophaners of Gods Name,
Who not at all thereon did call,
or took in vain the same.

XXXI
Blasphemers lewd, and Swearers shrewd,
Scoffers at Purity,
That hated God, contemn'd his Rod,
and lov'd security.
Sabbath-polluters, Saints Persecuters,
Presumptuous men, and Proud,
Who never lov'd those that reprov'd;
all stand amongst this crowd.

XXXII
Adulterers and Whoremongers
were there, with all unchast.
There Covetou [. . .] , and Ravenous,
that Riches got too fast:
Who us'd vile ways themselves to raise
t' Estates and worldly wealth,
Oppression by, or Knavery,
by Force, or Fraud, or Stealth.

XXXIII
Moreover, there together were
Children fl [. . .] gitious,
And Parents who did them undo
by nature vicious.
False-witness-bearers, and self-forswearers,
Murd'rers and men of blood,
Witches, Inchanters, and Alehouse-haunters,
beyond account there stood.

XXXIV
Their place there find all Heathen blind,
that Natures light abused,
Although they had no tidings glad
of Gospel-grace re [. . .] used.
There stand all Nations and Generations

of Adam's Progeny,
Whom Christ redeem'd not, who Christ esteem'd not
throught infidelity.

XXXV

Who no Peace-maker, no Undertaker
to shrowd them from God's ire
Ever obtained; they must be pained
with everlasting fire.
These num'rous bands, wringing their hands,
and weeping, all stand there,
Filled with anguish, whose hearts do languish
through self-tormenting fear.

XXX

Fast by them stand at Christ's left hand
the Lion fierce and fell,
The Dragon bold, that Serpent old
that hurried Souls to Hell.
There also stand, under command,
Legions of Sprights unclean.
And hellish Fiends that are no friends
to God, nor unto men.

XXXVII

With dismal chains and strong reins,
like prisoners of Hell,
They'r held in place before Christ's face,
till he their Doom shall tell.
These void of tears, but fill'd with fears,
and dreadful expectation
Of endless pains, and scalding flames,
stand waiting for Damnation.

XXXVIII

All silence kept, both Goats and Sheep,
before the Judges Throne:
With mild aspect to his Elect
then spake the Holy One:
My Sheep draw near, your sentence hear,
which is to you no dread,
Who clearly now discern, and know
your sins are pardoned.

XXXIX
'Twas meet that ye should judged be,
that so the world may 'spy
No cause of grudge, when as I judge
and deal impartially,
Know therefore all both great and small,
the ground and reason why
These men do stand at my right hand,
and look so chearfully.

XL
These men be those my Father chose
before the world's foundation,
And to me gave that I should save
from death and condemnation.
For whose dear sake I flesh did take,
was of a woman born,
And did inure my self t'endure
unjust reproach and scorn.

XLI
For them it was that I did pass
through sorrows many a one:
That I drank up that bitter Cup,
which made me sigh and groan.
The Cross his pain I did sustain;
yea more, my Fathers ire
I under-went, my bloud I spent
to save them from Hell fire.

XLII
Thus I esteem'd, thus I redeem'd
all these from every Nation,
that they might be (as now you see)
a chosen Generation.
What if ere-while they were as vile
and bad as any be,
[. . .] nd yet from all their guilt and thrall
at once I set them free?

XLIII
My grace to one is wrong to none:
none can Election claim.

Amongst all those their souls that lose,
none can Rejection blame.
He that may chuse, or else refuse,
all men to save or spill,
May this man chuse, and that refuse,
redeeming whom he will.

XLIV
But as for those whom I have chose
Salvations heirs to be,
I u [. . .] derwent their punishment,
and therefore set them free.
I bore their grief, and their relief
by suffering procur'd,
That they of bliss and happiness
[. . .] ight firmly be assur'd.

XLV
And this my g [. . .] ace they did embrace,
believing on my name;
Which Faith was true, the fruits do shew
proceeding from the same.
Their Penitence, their Patience,
their Love, their Self-den [. . .] al;
In suffering losses and bearing crosses,
when put upon the trial:

XLVI
Their sin forsaking, their cheerful taking
my yoke; their chari [. . .] ee
Unto the Saints in all their wants,
and in them unto me.
These things do clear, and make appear
their Faith to be unfeigned:
And that a part in my desert
and purchase they have gained.

XLVII
Their debts are paid, their peace is made,
their sins remitted are;
Therefore at once I do pronounce
and openly declare,
That Heaven is theirs, that they be Heir [. . .]

of Life and of Salvation;
Nor ever shall they come at all
to death or to damnation.

XLVIII
Come, blessed ones, and sit on Thrones,
judging the world with me:
Come, and possess your happiness,
and bought [. . .] elicitee.
Henceforth no fears, no care, no tears,
no sin shal you annoy,
Nor any thing that grief doth bring;
eternal rest enjoy.

XLIX
You bore the Cross, you suffered loss
of all [. . .] or my Names sake:
Receive the Crown that's now your own;
come, and a kingdom take.
Thus spake the Judge: the wicked grudge,
and grind their teeth in vain;
They see with groans these plac'd on throne [. . .]
which addeth to their pain:

L
That those whom they did wrong and slay,
must now their judgement see!
Such whom they sleighted and once de [. . .] spighte [. . .]
must of their Judges be!
Thus 'tis decreed, such is their meed
and guerdon glorious:
With Christ they sit, judging it fit
to plague the impious.

LI
The wicked are brought to the Bar
like guilty malefactors,
That oftentimes of bloody crimes
and treasons have been actors.
Of wicked men none are so mean
as there to be neglected:
Nor none so high in dignity,
as there to be respected.

LII
The glorious Judge will priviledge
nor Emperour nor King:
But every one that hath misdone
doth into judgement bring;
And every one that hath misdone,
the Judge impartially
Condemneth to eternal wo,
and endless misery.

LIII
Thus one and all, thus great and small,
the rich as well as poor,
And those of place, as the most base,
do stand their Judge before:
They are arraign'd, and there detain'd
before Christ's judgement seat
With trembling fear their Doom to hear,
and feel his angers heat.

LIV
There Christ demands at all their hands
a strict and straight account
Of all things done under the Sun;
who [. . .] e numbers far surmount
Man's wit and thought: yet all are brought
unto this solemn trial;
And each offence with evidence,
so that there's no denial.

LV
There's no excuses for their abuse [. . .]
since their own consciences
More proof give in of each man's sin;
then thousand witnesses.
Though formerly this faculty
had grosly been abused,
(Men could it stifle, or with it trifle,
whenas it them accused.)

LVI
Now it comes in, and every si [. . .]
unto mans charge doth lay:

It judgeth them, and doth condemn,
though all the world say nay.
It so stingeth and tortureth,
it worketh such di [. . .] tress,
That each mans self against himself
is forced to confess.

LVII
It's vain, moreover, for men to cover
the least iniquity;
The Judge hath seen and privy been
to all their villany.
He unto light and open sight
the works of darkness b [. . .] ings:
He doth unfold both new and old,
both known and hidden things.

LVIII
All filthy facts and secret acts,
however closely done
And long conceal'd, are there reveal'd.
before the mid-day Sun.
Deeds of the night shunning the light,
which darkest corners sought,
To fearful blame and endless shame,
are there most justly brought.

LIX
And as all facts and grosser acts,
so every word and thought,
Erroneous notion and lust [. . .] ul motion,
are into judg [. . .] ment brought.
No sin so small and trivial,
but hi [. . .] her it must come:
[. . .] or so long past, but now at last
it must receive a doom.

LX
[. . .] t this sad season Christ asks a reason
(with just austerity)
Of Grace refus'd, of Light abus'd
so oft, so wilfully:
O [. . .] Talents lent, by them-mispent,

and on their lusts bestown;
Which if improv'd as it behoov'd,
Heaven might have been their own.

LXI
Of time neglected, of meanes rejected,
of God's long-suffering,
And patience, to penitence
that sought hard hearts to bring.
Why cords of love did nothing move
to shame or to remorse?
Why warnings grave, and councels have
nought chang'd their sinful course?

LXII
Why chastenings and evil [. . .] hings,
why judgments so severe
Prevailed not with them a jo [. . .],
nor wrought an awful fear?
Why promises of holiness,
and new obedience,
[. . .] hey oft did make, but always break
the [. . .] ame to Gods offence?

LXIII
Why, still Hell-ward, without regard,
the boldly ventured,
And chose Damnation before Salvation
when it was offered?
Why sinful pleasures and earthly treasures,
like fools they prized more
Then heavenly wealth, eternal health,
and all Christs Royal store?

LXIV
Why, when he stood off'ring his Bloud
to wash them from their sin,
They would embrace no saving Grace,
but liv'd and di'd therein?
Such aggravations, where no evasions
nor false pretences hold,
Exagerate and cumulate
guilt more then can be told:

LXV

They multiply and magnifie
mens gross iniquities;
They draw down wrath (as Scripture saith)
out of God's treasuries [. . .]
Thu [. . .] all their ways Christ open lays
to Men and Angels view,
And, as they were, makes them appear
in their own proper hue.

LXVI

Thus he doth find of all ma [. . .] kind
that stand at his left hand
No mothers son but hath misdone,
and broken God's command.
All have transgrest, even the best,
and merited God's wrath
[. . .] nto their own perdition,
and everlasting scath.

LXVII

Earth's dwellers all both great and small,
have wrought iniquity,
And suffer must (for it is just)
eternal misery.
Amongst the many there come not any
before the Judge's face,
That able are themselves to clear,
of all this curled race.

LXVIII

Nevertheless they all express,
Christ granting liberty,
What for their way they have to say,
how they have liv'd, and why.
They all draw near, and seek to clear
themselves by making plea's.
There hypocrites, false-hearted wights,
do make such pleas as these.

LXIX

Lord, in thy Name, and by the same
we Devils dispossest:

We rais'd the dead, and ministred
succour to the distrest.
Our painful preaching and pow'rful teaching,
by thine own wond'rous might,
Did throughly win from God to sin
many a wretched wight.

LXX

All this (quoth he) may granted be [. . .]
and your case little better'd,
Who still remain under a chain,
and many irons fetter'd.
You that the dead have quickened,
and rescu'd from the grave,
Your selves were dead, yet never ned
a Christ your Souls to save.

LXXI

You that could preach, and others teach
wh [. . .] t way to life doth lead;
Why were you slack to find that track,
and in that way to tread?
How could you bear to see or hear
of others freed at last
From Satans Paws, whilst in his jaws
your selves were held more fa [. . .] t?

LXXII

Who though you kne [. . .] Repentance true
and faith in my great Name,
The only mean to quit you clean
from punishment and blame,
Yet took no pain true faith to gain,
(such as might not deceive)
Nor would repent wi [. . .] h true intent
[. . .] our evil deeds to leave.

LXXIII

[. . .] is Masters will how to fulfil
[. . .] he servant that well knew,
[. . .] et left undone his duty known,
more plagues to him are due.
[. . .] ou against Light perverted Right;

[. . .] herefore it shall be now
[. . .] or *Sidon* and for *Sodom*'s Land
[. . .] ore easie then for you.

LXXIV
[. . .] ut we have in thy presence bin,
say some, and eaten there.
[. . .] id we not eat thy flesh for meat,
and feed on heavenly cheer?
Whereon who feed shall never need,
as thou thy self dost say,
[. . .] or shall they die eternally,
but live with thee for ay.

LXXV
We may alledge, thou gav'st a pledge
of thy dea [. . .] love to us
[. . .] Wine and B [. . .] e [. . .] d, [. . .] hich figured
[. . .] hy grace bestowed thus.
Of streng [. . .] hning seals, of s [. . .] eetest meals
have we so oft partaken?
[. . .] nd shall we be cast off by thee,
and utterly forsaken?

LXXVI
[. . .] whom the Lord thu [. . .] in a word
[. . .] eturns a short reply:
I never k [. . .] ew any of you
that wrought iniquity.
You say y' have bin, my Presence in;
bu [. . .] , f [. . .] iends, how came you there
Wi [. . .] h Raiment vile, that did defile
and quite disgrace my cheer?

LXXVII
Durst you draw near without due fear
unto my holy Table?
Du [. . .] st you prophane and render vain
so far as you were able,
Those Mysteries? which whoso prize
and carefully improve,
Shall saved be undoubtedly,
and nothing shall them move.

LXXVIII

How du [. . .] st you venture, bold guests, to enter
in such a [. . .] ordid hi [. . .] e,
Amongst my guests, unto those feasts
that were not made for you?
How durst you eat for spir'tual meat
your bane, and drink damnation,
Whilst by your guile you rendred vile
so rare and great salvation?

LXXIX

Your fancies fed on heav'nly bread;
your hearts fed on some lust:
You lov'd the Creature more then th'Creator
your soules clave to the dust.
And think you by hypocrisie
and cloaked wickedness,
To enter in, laden with sin,
to lasting happiness.

LXXX

This your excuse shews your abuse
of things ordain'd for good;
And do declare you guilty are
of my dear Flesh and Bloud.
Wherefore those Seals and precious Meals
you put so much upon
As things divine, they seal and sign
you to perdition.

LXXXI

Then forth issue another Crew,
(those being silenced)
Who drawing nigh to the most High
adventure thus to plead:
We sinners were, say they, 'tis clear,
deserving Condemnation:
But did not we rely on thee,
O Christ, for whole Salvation?

LXXXII

We did believe, and of receive
thy gracious Promises:

We took great care to get a share
in endless happiness:
We pray'd and wept, we Fast-days kept,
lewd ways we did eschew:
We joyful were thy Word to h [. . .] ar,
we fo [. . .] m'd our lives anew.

LXXXIII

We thought our sin had pardon'd bi [. . .],
that our estate was good,
Our debts all paid, [. . .] ur peace well made,
our Souls wash [. . .] wi [. . .] h [. . .] hy B [. . .] oud.
Lord, why dost thou rej [. . .] ct us now,
who have not thee rejected,
Nor utterly true sanctity
and holy li [. . .] e neglected?

LXXXIV

The Judge ince [. . .] sed at their pretenced
self-vaunting piety,
With such a look as trembling strook
into them, made reply;
O impudent, impeni [. . .] ent,
and guile [. . .] ul generation!
Think you that I cannot descry
your hearts abomination?

LXXXV

You not receiv'd, nor yet believ [. . .] d
my promises of grace;
Nor were you wise enough to prize
my reconciled face:
But did presume, that to assume
which was not yours to take,
And challenged the childrens bread,
yet would not sin forsake.

LXXXVI

B [. . .] ing too bold you laid fast hold
where int' [. . .] est you had none,
Your selves deceiving by your believing;
all which you might have known.
You [. . .] an away (but ran astray)

with Gospel promises,
And perished, being still dead
in sins and trespasse [. . .].

LXXXVII

How oft did I hypocrisie
and hearts deceits unmask
Before your sight, giving you ligh [. . .]
to know a Christians task?
But you held fast unto the last
your own conceits so vain:
No warning could prevail, you would
your own deceits re [. . .] ain.

LXXXVIII

As for your care to get a share
in bliss, the fear of Hell,
And of a part in endless smart,
did thereunto compel.
Your holiness and ways redress,
such as it was, did spring
From no true love to things above,
but from some other thing.

LXXXIX

You pray'd and wept, you Fast-days kept,
but did you this to me?
No, but for [. . .] n you sought to win
the greater liberte [. . .].
For all your vaunts, you had vile haunt's;
for which your consciences
Did you alarm, whose voice to charm
you us'd these practises.

XC

Your penitence, your diligence
to read, to pray, to hear,
Were but to drown the clam'rous sound
of conscience in your ea [. . .]
If light you lov'd, vain-glory mov'd
your selves therewith to store,
Th [. . .] t seeming wise, men might you prize,
and honour you the more.

XCI
Thus from your selves unto your selves
your duties all do tend:
And as self-love the wheels do move,
so in self-love they end.
Thus Ch [. . .] ist detects their vain projects,
and close impiety,
And plainly shews that all their shows
were but hypocrisie.

XCII
Then were brought nigh a company
of [. . .] ivil honest men,
That lov'd true dealing, and hated stealing,
[. . .] e wrong'd their brethren:
Who pleaded thus, Thou knowest us
that we were blamele [. . .] s livers;
No whore-mongers, no murderers,
no quarrellers nor strivers.

XCIII
Idolaters, Adulterers,
Church-robbers we were none;
Nor false dealers, nor couzeners,
but paid each man his own.
Our way was fair, our dealing square,
we were no wastful spenders,
No lewd toss-pots, no drunken sots,
no scandalous offenders.

XCIV
We hated vice, and set great price
by vertuous conversation:
And by the same we got a name,
and no small commendation.
God's Laws express that righteousness
is that which he doth prize;
And to obey, as he doth say,
is more then sacrifice.

XCV
Thus to obey, hath been our way;
let our good deeds, we pray,

Find some regard, and good rewa [. . .] d
with thee, O Lord, this day.
And whereas we transgressors be;
of Adam's Race were n [. . .] ne,
(No not the best) but have confes [. . .]
themselves to h [. . .] ve mis [. . .] one.

XCVI

Then answered, un [. . .] o their dread,
the Judge, True piety
God doth desire, and eke requi [. . .] e
no less then honesty.
Justice demands at all your hands
perfect Obedience:
If but in part you have come sh [. . .],
that is a just offence.

XCVII

On earth below where men did owe
a thousand pounds and more,
Could twenty pence it recompence?
could that have clear'd the score?
Think you to buy felicity
with part of what's due debt?
O [. . .] for desert of one small part
the whole should off be set?

XCVIII

And yet that part (whose great desert
you think to reach so far
For your excuse) doth you accuse,
and will your boasting mar.
However fair, however square
your way, and work h [. . .] th bin
Before mens eyes, yet God espies
iniquity therein.

XCIX

God looks upon th' [. . .] ff [. . .] ction
and temper of the heart;
Not only on the action,
and the external part.
Whatever end vain men pretend,

God knows the v [. . .] ri [. . .] y [. . .]
And by the end which they intend
their words and deeds doth try.

C

Without true faith, the Scripture saith,
God cannot take delight
In any deed, that doth proceed
from any si [. . .] ful wight.
And withou [. . .] love all actions prove
but barren empty things:
Dead works they be, and vanity,
the which vexation brings.

CI

Nor from true faith, which quencheth wrath
hath your obedience flown:
Nor from true love, which wont to move
believers, hath it grown.
Your argument shews your intent
in all that you have done:
You thought to [. . .] cale heavens lofty wall,
by ladders o [. . .] your own.

CII

Your blinded spirit, hoping to merit
by your own righteousness,
Needed no Saviour, but your b [. . .] haviour
and blameless ca [. . .] riages [. . .]
You trusted to what you could do,
and in no need you stood:
Your haughty pride laid me aside,
and trampled on my Bloud.

CIII

All men have gone astray, and done
that which God's Law [. . .] condemn:
But my Purchase and offered Grace
all men did not contemn.
The Ninevites and Sodomites
had no such sin as this:
Yet as if all your sins were small,
you say, All did amiss.

CIV
Again, you thought, and mainly sought
a name with men t' acquire:
Pride bare the B [. . .] ll that made you swell,
and your own selves admire.
M [. . .] an frui [. . .] it is, and vile, I wis,
that sp [. . .] ings from such a root:
Vertue divine and genuine
wants not from pride to shoor.

CV
Such deeds as you are worse then poo [. . .],
they are but sins guilt over
With silver dross, whose glistering gloss
[. . .] an them no longer cover.
The best of them would you condemn,
and [. . .] uine you alone,
Al [. . .] hough you were from faults so clear,
that other you had none.

CVI
Your gold is dross, you [. . .] silver brass,
your righteousness is sin:
And think you by such honesty
Eternall life to win?
You much mistake, if for it's sake
you dream of acceptation;
Whereas the same deserveth shame,
and meriteth damnation.

CVII
A wond'rous Crowd then 'gan aloud
thus for themselves to say;
We did intend, Lord to mend,
and to reform our way:
Ou [. . .] true intent was to repent,
and make our peace with thee;
But sudden death stopping our breath,
left us no libertee.

CVIII
Short was our time; for in his prime
our youthful flow'r was cropt:

We dy'd in youth, before full growth;
so was our purpose stopt.
Let our good will to turne from ill,
and sin to have forsaken,
Accepted be O Lord, by thee,
and in good part be taken.

CIX
To whom the Judg; Where you alledge
the shortness of the space
That from your bi [. . .] th you liv'd on earth,
to compass S [. . .] ving Grace:
It was free-grace, that any space
wa [. . .] given you at all
To turn from evil, defie the Devil,
and upon God to call.

CX
One day, one week, wherein to seek
Gods face with all your hearts,
A favour was that far did pass
the best of your deserts.
You had a season; what was your Reason
such preciou [. . .] hours to waste?
What could you find, what could you mind
that was of greater haste?

CXI
Could you find time for vain pastime?
for loose licentious mirth?
For fruitless toys, and fading joyes
that perish in the birth?
Had you good leisure for Carnal pleasure
in days of health and youth?
And yet no space to seek Gods face,
and turn to him in truth?

CXII
In younger years, beyond your fears,
what if you were surprised?
You put away the evil day,
and of long life devised.
You oft were told, and might behold,

that Death no age would spare.
Why then did you your time foreslow,
and slight your Souls welfare?

CXIII
H [. . .] d your intent been to Repent,
and had you it desir'd,
There would have been endeavours seen
before your time expir'd.
God makes no [. . .] reasure nor hath he pleasure
in idle purpo [. . .] es:
Such fair pretences are foul offences,
and cloaks for wickedness.

CXIV
Then were brought in and charg'd with sin
another Compa [. . .] y,
Who by Petition obtain'd permission
to make apology:
They argued; We were mis-led,
as is well known to thee,
By their Example, that had more ample
abilities than we.

CXV
Such as profest we did detest
and hate each wicked way:
Whose seeming grace whil'st we did trace,
our Souls were led astray.
When men of Parts, Learning and Arts,
professing Piety,
Did thus and thus, it seem'd to us
we might take liberty.

CXVI
The Judge Replies; I gave you eyes,
a [. . .] d light to see your way:
Which had you lov'd and well improv'd
you had not gone astray.
My Word was pure, the Rule was sure;
why did you it forsake,
Or thereon trample, and men's Example
your Directory make?

CXVII
This you well know, that God is true,
and that most men are liars,
In word professing holiness,
in deed thereof deniers [. . .]
O simple [. . .] ools! that having Rules
your lives to Regulate,
Would them refuse, and rather chuse
vile men to imitate.

CXVIII
But Lord, say they, we we [. . .] astray,
and did more wickedly,
By means of those whom thou hast chose
Salvations Heirs to be.
To whom the Judge; What you alledge
doth nothing help the case,
But makes appear how vile you were,
and rend'reth you more ba [. . .] e.

CXIX
You understood that what was good
was to be [. . .] ollowed,
And that you ought that which was nought
to have relinquished.
Contrariwise, it was your guise,
only to imitate
Good mens defects, and their neglects
that were Regenerate.

CXX
But to express their holiness,
or imitate their Grace,
Yet little ca [. . .] 'd, not once prepar'd
your hearts to seek my face.
They did Repent, and truly Rent
their hearts for all known sin:
You did Offend, but not Amend,
to follow them therein.

CXXI
We had thy Word, (said some) O Lord,
but wiser men then wee

Could never yet interpret it,
but always disagree.
How could we fools be led by Rules
so far beyond our ken,
Which to explain, did so much pain
and puzzle wisest men?

CXXII
Was all my Word obscure and hard?
the Judge then answered:
It did contain much Truth so plain,
you might have run and read.
But what was hard you never car'd
to know, nor studied:
And things that were most plain and clear,
you never practised.

CXXIII
The Mystery of Pie [. . .] y
God unto Babes reveals;
When to the wise he it denies,
and from the world co [. . .] ceals.
If [. . .] o fulfill Gods holy will
had seemed good to you,
You would have sought light as you ought,
and done the good y [. . .] u knew.

CXXIV
Then came in view ano [. . .] her Crew,
and 'gan to make their plea's;
Amongst the rest, some of the best
had such poor [. . .] hifts as these:
Thou know'st right well, who all canst tell,
we liv'd amongst thy foes,
Who the Renate did sorely hate,
and goodness much oppose.

CXXV
We Holiness durst not profess,
fearing to be forlorn
Of all our friends, and for amends
to be the wicked's scorn.
We knew thei [. . .] anger would much endanger

our lives and our estates:
Therefore for fear we durst appear
no better than our mates.

CXXVI
To whom the Lord returns this word;
O wonderful deceits!
To cast off aw of Gods strict Law,
and fear mens wrath and th [. . .] eats!
To fear Hell-fire and Gods fierce ire
less then the rage of men!
As if Gods wrath could do less scath
than wrath of bretheren!

CXXVII
To use such strife to temp'ral life
to rescue and secure!
And be so b [. . .] ind as not to mind
that life that will endure!
This was you [. . .] case, who carnal peace
more then [. . .] ue joyes did savour:
Who fed on dus [. . .] , clave to your lust,
and spurned at my [. . .] avour.

CXXVIII
To please your kin, mens loves to win,
to flow in wo [. . .] ldly wealth,
To save your skin, these things have bin
more than Eternal health.
You had your choice, wherein rejoyce,
it was your portion,
For which you chose your Souls t' expose
unto Perdition.

CXXIX.
Who did not hate friends, life, and state,
with all things else for me,
And all forsake, and's Cross up take,
shall never happy be.
Well worthy they do die for ay,
who death then life had rather:
Death is their due that so value
the friendship of my Father.

CXXX
Others argue, and not a few,
is not God gracious?
His Equity and Clemency
are they not marvellous?
Thus we believ'd; are we deceiv'd?
cannot his Mercy great,
(As hath been told to us of old)
asswage his anger's heat?

CXXXI
How can it be that God should see
his Creatures endless pain?
O [. . .] hear their groans or ruefull moanes,
and still his wrath retain?
Can it agree with equitee?
can Mercy have the heart,
To Recompence few years offence
with Everlasting smart?

CXXXII
Can God delight in such a sight
as sinners Misery?
Or what great good can this our bloud
bring unto the most High?
Oh thou that dost thy Glory most
in pard'ning sin display!
Lord! might it please thee to release,
and pardon us this day?

CXXXIII
Unto thy Name more glorious fame
would not such Mercy bring?
Would it not raise thine endless praise,
more than our suffering?
With that they cease, holding their peace,
but cease not still to weep;
Griefe ministers a flood to tears,
in which their words do steep:

CXXXIV
But all too late; Grief's out of date
when Life is at an end.

The glorious King thus answering,
all to his voice attend:
God gracious is, quoth he, like his
no Mercy can be found;
His Equity and Clemency
to sinners do abound.

CXXXV

As may appear by those that here
are plac'd at my right hand;
Whose stripes I bore and clear'd the score
that they might quitted stand.
For surely none but God alone,
whose Grace transcends man's thought,
For such as those that were his foes
like wonders would have wrought.

CXXXVI

And none but he such lenitee
and patience would have shown
To you so long, who did him wrong,
and pull'd his judgements down.
How long a space (O stiff-neck't Race!)
did patience you afford?
How oft did love you gently move
to turn unto the Lord?

CXXXVII

With cords of Love God often strove
your stubborn hearts to tame:
Nevertheless, your wickedness
did still resist the same.
If now at last Mercy be past
from you for evermore,
And Justice come in Mercies room,
yet grudge you no [. . .] therefore.

CXXXVIII

If into wrath God tu [. . .] ed hath
his Long-long [. . .] uffe [. . .] ing,
And now for Love you Vengeance prove,
it is an equal thing.
Your waxing worse, hath stopt the course

of wonted Clemency:
Mercy refus'd, and Grace misus'd,
call for severity.

CXXXIX
It's now high time that every Crime
be brought to punishment:
VVrath long contain'd, and oft refrain'd,
at last must have a vent.
Justice [. . .] evere cannot fo [. . .] bear
to plague sin any longer;
But must inflict with hand mo [. . .] t strict
mischief upon the wronger.

CXL
In vain do they for Mercy pray,
the season being past,
Who had no care to get a share
therein, while time did last.
The men whose ear refus'd to hear
the voice of Wisdom's cry,
Earn'd this reward, that none regard
him in his misery.

CXLI
It doth agree with Equitee,
and with God's holy Law,
That those should dy eternally,
that death upon them draw.
The Soul that sin's damnation win's;
for so the Law ordains:
Which Law is just [. . .] and therefore must
such suffer endless pains.

CXLII
Etern [. . .] l smart is the desert
ev'n of the least offence;
Then wonder not if I allot
to you this Recompence:
But wonder more that, since so sore
and lasting plagues are due
To every sin, you liv'd therein,
who well the danger knew.

CXLIII
God hath no joy to crush or 'stroy,
and ruine wretched wights:
But to display the glorious ray
of Justice he delights.
To manifest he doth detest
and throughly hate all sin,
By plaguing it, as is most fit,
this shall him glory win.

CXLIV
Then at the Bar arraigned are
an impudenter sort,
Who to evade the guilt that's laid
upon them, thus retort;
How could we cease thus to transgress?
how could we Hell avoid,
Whom God's Decree shut out from thee,
and sign'd to be destroy'd?

CXLV
Whom God ordains to endless pains
by Laws unalterable,
Repentance true, Obedience new,
to save such are unable:
Sorrow for sin no good can win
to such as are rejected;
Ne can they give, not yet believe
that never were elected.

CXLVI
Of man's faln Race who can true Grace
or Holiness obtain?
Who can convert or change his heart,
if God with-hold the same?
Had we apply'd our selves, and tri'd
as much as who did most
Gods love to gain, our busie pain
and labour had been lost.

CXLVII
Christ readily makes this reply;
I damn you not because
You are rejected, or not elected;

but you have broke my Laws.
It is but vain your wits to strain
the E [. . .] d and Me [. . .] ns to sever:
Men fondly seek to dart or break
what God hath link'd together.

CXLVIII
Whom God will save, such he will have
the means of life to use:
Whom he'l pass by, shall chuse to di [. . .],
and ways of life refuse.
He that fore-sees and fore-decrees,
in wisdom order'd has,
That man's free-will electing ill
shall bring his Will to pass.

CXLIX
High God's Decree, as it is free,
so doth it none compel
Against their will to good or ill;
i [. . .] forceth none to Hell.
They have their wish whose Souls perish
with torments in Hell-fire:
Who rather chose their souls to lose,
then leave a loose desire.

CL
God did ordain sinners to pain;
and I to hell send none,
But such as swe [. . .] v'd, and have deserv'd
destruction as their own.
His pleasure is, that none fr [. . .] ss
and endless happiness
Be barr'd, but such as wrong [. . .] much
by wilful wickedness.

CLI
You (sinful crew!) no other knew
but you might be elect:
Why did you then your selves condemn?
why did you me reject?
Where was your strife to gain that life
which lasteth evermore?

You never knock't, yet say God lock't
against you heavens door.

CLII
'Twas no vain task to knock, to ask,
whilst life continued.
Who ever sought Heav'n as he ought,
and seeking perished?
The lowly-meek who truly seek
for Christ and for salvation,
There's no Decree whereby such be
ordain'd to condemnation.

CLIII
You argue then; But abject men,
whom God resolves to spill,
Cannot repent, nor their hearts rent;
ne can they change their will.
Not for his Can is any man
adjudged unto hell:
But for his Will [. . .] to do what's ill,
and nilling to do well.

CLIV
I often stood tend'ring my Bloud
to wash away your guilt:
And eke my Sprite to frame you right,
lest your souls should be spilt.
But you, vile race, rejected Grace
when Grace was freely proffer'd:
No changed heart, no heav'nly part
would you, when it was offer'd.

CLV
Who wilfully the remedy
of Grace and Life contemned,
Cause have the same themselves to blame,
if now they be co [. . .] demned.
You have your selves, you and none else,
your selves have done to die:
You chose the way to your decay,
and perish'd wilfully.

CLVI
These words apale and daunt them all;
dismai'd, and all amort,
Like stocks they stand at Christs left hand,
and dare no more retort.
Then were brought near, with trembling fear
a number numberless
Of blind Heathen and b [. . .] utish men,
that did Gods Law transgress.

CLVII
Whose wicked ways, Christ open lays,
and makes their sins appear,
They making plea's the case to ease,
if not themselves to clear.
Thy written word (say they) good Lord
we never did enjoy:
We not refus'd nor it abus'd,
Oh do not us destroy.

CLVIII
You ne'r abus'd nor yet refus'd
my written Word, you plead;
That's t [. . .] ue, (quoth he) therefore shall ye
the less be punished.
You shall not smart for any part
of other mens offence,
But for your own transgression
receive due recompence.

CLIX
But we were blind, say [. . .] hey, in mind;
too dim was natures light,
Our only guide (as hath been try [. . .] d)
to bring us to the sight
Of our estate degenerate,
and cu [. . .] st by Adam's fall;
How we were born and lay forlorn
in bondage and in th [. . .] all.

CLX
We did not know a Christ till now,
nor bow fal [. . .] man he saved:

Else should we not, right well we wo [. . .] ,
have so our selves behaved.
We should have mourn'd, we should have turn'd
from sin at thy reproof,
And been more wise through thine advice
for our own Souls behoof.

CLXI
But natures light shin'd not so bright
to teach us the right way:
We might have lov'd it, & well improv'd it,
and yet have gone astray.
The Judge most high makes this reply;
you ignorance pretend,
Dimness of sight, and want of light
your course Heav'n-ward to bend:

CLXII
How came your mind to be so blind?
I once you knowledge gave,
Clearness of sight, and judgement right;
who did the same deprave?
If to your cost you have it lost,
and quite defac'd the same;
Your own desert hath caus'd your smart,
you ought not me to blame.

CLXIII
Your selves into a pit of wo
your own transgressions led:
If I to none my grace had shown,
who had been injured?
If to a few, and not to you,
I shew'd a way of life,
My Grace so free, you clearly see,
gives you no ground of strife.

CLXIV
'Tis [. . .] ain to tell, you wot full well,
if you in time had known
Your Misery and Remedy,
your actions had it shown.
You, sinful crew, have not been true

unto the light of Nature;
No [. . .] done the good you understood,
nor owned your Creator.

CLXV
He that the Light, because 'tis Light,
hath used to despize,
Would not the Light, shining more bright,
be likely for to prize.
If you had lov'd and well improv'd
your knowledge and dim sight,
Herein your pain had not been vain,
your plagues had been more light.

CLXVI
Then to the Bar all they drew near
who dy'd in infancy,
And never had or good or bad
effected pers'nally;
But from the womb unto the tomb
were straightway carried,
(Or at the least, ere they transgrest)
who thus began to plead.

CLXVII
If for our own transgression,
or disobedience,
We here did stand at thy left hand,
j [. . .] st were the recompence:
But Adam's guilt our souls hath spilt,
his fault is charg'd upon us;
And that alone hath overthrown,
and utterly undone us.

CLXVIII
Not we, but he, a [. . .] e of the Tree,
whose fruit was interdicted:
Yet on us all of his sad fall
the punishment's inflicted.
How could we sin who had not bin?
or how is his sin our
Without consent, which to prevent
we never had a pow'r?

CLXIX
O great Creator, why was our nature
depraved and forlorn?
Why so defil'd, and made so vild
Whilst we were yet unborn?
If it be just, and needs we must
transgressors reckon'd be,
Thy mercy, Lord, to us afford,
which sinners hath set free.

CLXX
Behold, we see Adam [. . .] et free,
and sav'd from his tre [. . .] pass,
Whose sinful fall hath split us all,
and brought us to this pass.
Canst thou deny us once to try,
or grace to us to tender,
When he finds grace before thy face,
that was the chief offender?

CLXXI
Then answered the Judge most dread;
God doth such doom forbid,
T [. . .] at men should die eternally
for what they never did.
But what you call old Adam's Fall,
and only his Trespass,
You call amiss to call it his:
both his and yours it was.

CLXXII
He was design'd of all mankind
to be a publick Head,
A common Root whence all should shoot,
and stood in all their stead:
He stood and fell, did ill or well,
not for himself alone,
But for you all, who now his Fall
and trespass would disown.

CLXXIII
If he had stood, then all his brood
had been established

In Gods true love, never to move,
nor once awry to tread:
Then all his Race my Fathers Grace
should have enjoy'd for ever,
And wicked Sprights by subtil sleights
could them have harmed never.

CLXXIV
Would you have griev'd to have receiv'd
through Adam so much good,
As had been your for evermore,
if he at first had stood?
Would you have said, We ne'r obey'd
nor did thy Laws regard;
It ill befits with benefits
us, Lord, so to reward?

CLXXV
Since then to share in his welfare
you could have been content,
You may with reason share in his treason,
and in the punishment.
Hence you were born in state forlorn,
with natures so dep [. . .] aved:
Death was your due, because that you
had thus your selves behaved.

CLXXVI
You think if we had been as he,
whom God did so betrust,
all for a paltry lust.
Had you been made in Adam's stead,
you would like things have wrought;
And so into the self-same wo
your selves and yours have brought.

CLXXVII
I may deny you once to try,
or Grace to you to tender,
Though he finds grace be [. . .] ore my face
who was the chief offender:
Else should my Grace cease to be Grace,
for it should not be free,

If to release whom I shall please
I have not libertee.

CLXXVIII
I [. . .] upon one what's due to none
I frankly shall bestow,
And on the rest shall not think best
compassions skirt to throw,
Whom injure I? will you envy,
and grudge at others weal?
Or me accuse, who do refuse
your selves to help and heal?

CLXXIX
Am I alone of what's my own
no Master or [. . .] o Lord?
Or if I am, how can you claim
w [. . .] at I to some afford?
Will you demand G [. . .] ace at my hand,
and challenge what is mine?
Will you teach me whom to set free,
and thus my Grace confine?

CLXXX
You sinners are, and such a share
as sinners may expect,
Such you shall have, for I do save
none but mine own Elect.
Yet to compare your sin with their
who liv'd a longer time,
I do confess yours is much less,
though ev'ry sin's a crime:

CLXXXI
A crime it is: therefore in bliss
you may not hope to dwell:
But unto you I shall allow
the easiest room in hell.
The glorious King thus answering,
they cease and plead no longer:
Their consciences must needs confess
his Reasons are the stronger.

CLXXXII
Thus all mens plea's the Judge with ease
doth answer and confute,
Until that all both great and small,
are silenced and mute.
Vain hopes are cropt, all mouths are stopt,
sinners have nought to say,
But that 'tis just, and equal most
they should be damn'd for ay.

CLXXXIII
Now what remains, but that to pains
and everlasting smart
Christ should condemn the sons of men,
which is their just desert?
Oh ru [. . .] ul plights of sinful wights!
Oh wretches all forlorn!
That happy been they ne'r had seen
the Sun, or not been born.

CLXXXIV
Yea, now it would be good they could [. . .]
themselves annihilate,
And cease to be, themselves to free
from such a fearful state.
Oh happy Dogs, and Swine, and Frogs!
yea, Serpents generation!
Who do not fear this doom to hear,
and sentence of D [. . .] mnation!

CLXXXV
This is their state so de [. . .] perate:
their sins are fully known;
Their vani [. . .] ies and villanies
Before the world are shown.
As they are gross and impious,
so are their numbers more
Then motes i' th' air, or then their hair,
or sands upon the shore.

CLXXXVI
Divine Justice offended is,
a [. . .] d Satisfaction claime [. . .] h:

Gods wrathful ire kindled like fire
against them fiercely flameth.
Their Judge severe doth quite cashire
and all their Pleas off take,
That never a man, or dare, or can
a further Answer make.

CLXXXVII

Their mouthes are shut, each man i [. . .] put
to silence and to shame:
Nor have they ought within their thought
Christs Justice for to blame;
The Judge is just, and plague them must,
nor will he mercy shew
(For Mercy's day is past away)
to any of this Crew.

CLXXXVIII

The Judge is strong; doers of wrong
cannot his Power withstand:
None can by flight run out of sight,
nor scape out of his hand.
Sad is their sta [. . .] e; for Advocate
to plead their Cause there's none:
None to prevent their punishment,
or misery to bemo [. . .] e.

CLXXXIX

O dismal day! whither shall they
for help or succour flee?
To God above, with hopes to move
their greatest Enemee?
His wrath is g [. . .] eat, whose burning heat
to flood of Tears can [. . .] lake:
His word stands fast, that they be cast
into the burning Lake.

CXC

To Chr [. . .] st their Judge? he doth adjudge
them to the Pit of Sorrow:
Nor will he hear or cry, or tear,
nor respite them on morrow.
To Heav'n? Alas they cannot pass,

it is against them shut:
To enter there (O heavy chear!)
they out of hopes are put.

CXCI

U [. . .] to their Treasures, or to their Pleasures?
all these have been forsaken:
Had they full Coffers to make large offers,
their Gold would not be taken.
Unto the place where whilome was
their birth and education?
Lo! Christ begins for their great sins
to fire the Earths foundation:

CXCII

And by and by the flaming Sky
shall drop like moulten Lead
About their ears, t' increase their fears
and aggravate their dread.
To Angels good that ever stood
in their integrity,
Should they betake themselves, and make
their suit incessantly?

CXCIII

They neither skill, nor do they will
to work them any ease:
They will not mourn to see them burn,
nor beg for their release.
To wicked men, their brethren
in sin and wickedness,
Should they make mone? their case is one;
they're in the same distress.

CXCIV

Ah, cold comfort, and mean support
from such like Comforters!
Ah, little joy of Company,
and fellow-sufferers!
Such shall increase their hearts disease,
and add unto their wo,
Because that they brought to decay
themselves and many moe.

CXCV
Unto the Saints with sad complaints.
should they themselves apply?
They're not dejected nor ought affected
with all their misery.
Friends stand aloof, and make no proof
what Prayers or Tears can do:
Your godly friends are now more friends
to Christ then unto you.

CXCVI
Where tender love mens hearts did move
unto a sympathy,
And bearing part of others smart
in their anxiety;
Now such compassion is out of fashion,
and wholly laid aside:
No friend so near, but Saints to hear
their judgement can abide.

CXCVII
One natural Brother beholds another
in this astonied fit,
Yet sorrows not thereat a jot,
nor pities him a whit.
The godly wife conceives no grief,
nor can she shed a tear
For the sad state of her dear Mate,
when she his doom doth hear.

CXCVIII
He that was erst a Husband pierc't
with sense of Wives distress,
Whose tender heart did bear a part
of all her grievances,
Shall mourn no more as heretofore
because of her ill plight;
Although he see her now to be
a damn'd forsaken wight.

CXCIX
The tender Mother will own no other
of all her numerous brood,

But such as stand at Christs right hand
acquitted through his Blood.
The pious Father had now much rather
his graceless Son should lye
In Hell with Devils, for all his evils
burning eternally:

CC
Then God most High should injury
by sparing him sustain;
And doth rejoyce to hear Christs voice
adjudging him to pain.
Who having all (both great and small)
convinc't and silenced,
Did then proceed their Doom to read,
and thus it uttered;

CCI
Ye [. . .] inful wights, and cursed sprights,
that work Iniquity,
Depart together from me for ever
to endless Misery.
Your portion take in that sad Lake
where Fire and Brimstone flameth:
Suffer the smart, which your desert
as its du [. . .] wages claimeth.

CCII
Oh pierceing words more sharp then Swords!
what, to depart from Thee,
Whose face before for evermore
the best of Pleasures be!
What! to depart (unto our smart)
from thee Eternally!
To be for ay banish't away
with Devils company!

CCIII
What! to be sent to Punishment,
and flames of Burning Fire!
To be surrounded, and eke confounded
with God's Revengeful Ire!
What! to abide, not for a tide,

these Torments, but for Ever!
To be released, or to be eased,
not after years, but Never!

CCIV

Oh, fearful Doom! now there's no room
for hope, or help at all:
Sentence is past which ay shall last,
Christ will not it recall.
There might you hear them rent and tear
the Air with their out-c [. . .] ies:
The hideous noise of their sad voice
ascendeth to the skies.

CCV

They wring their hands, their caitiff-hands,
and gnash their teeth for terrour:
They cry, they rore for anguish sore,
and gnaw their tongues for horrour.
But get away without delay;
Christ pities not your cry:
Depart to Hell [. . .] there may you yell
and roar Eternally.

CCVI

That word Depart, maugre their heart;
drives every wicked one,
With mighty pow'r, the self-same hour
far from the Judges throne.
Away they're cast by the strong blast
of his Death-threatning mouth:
They [. . .] lee full fast, as if in hast;
although they be full loath.

CCVII

As chaff that's dry, and dust doth fly
before the Northern wind:
Right so are they chased away,
and can no Refuge find.
They hasten to the Pit of wo,
guarded by Angels stout:
Who to fulfil Christ's holy will
attend this wicked Rout.

CCVIII
Whom having brought, as they are taught
unto the brink of Hell
(That dismal place far from Christ's face,
where Death and Darkness dwell:
Where God's fierce ire kindleth the fire,
and Vengeance feeds the flame
With piles of wood, and brimstone flood,
that none can quench the same.)

CCIX
With Iron bands they bind their hands
and cursed feet together,
And cast them all, both great and small,
into that Lake for ever.
Where day and night, without respite,
they wail, and cry, and howl
For tor' [. . .] ring pain, which they sustain
in Body and in Soul.

CCX
For day and night, in their despight,
their torments smoak ascendeth:
Their pain and grief have no relief,
their anguish never endeth.
There must they lye, and never dye;
though dying every day:
There must they dying ever lye;
and not consume away.

CCXI
Dye fain they would, if dye they cou [. . .]
but death will not be had [. . .]
Gods dire [. . .] ul wrath their bodies hath
for ev'r Immortal made.
They live to lie in misery.
and bear eternal wo:
And live they must whil'st God is just,
that he may plague them so.

CCXII
But who can tell the plagues of Hell,
and torments exquisite?

Who can relate their dismal state,
and terrours infinite?
Who fare the best, and feel the least,
yet feel that Punishment
Whereby to nought they should be brought,
if God did not prevent.

CCXIII

The least degree of misery
there felt's incomparable,
The lightest pain they there sustain
more then intollerable.
But Gods great pow'r from hour to hour
upholds them in the fire,
That they shall not consume a jot,
nor by its force expire.

CCXIV

But ah, the wo they u [. . .] dergo
(they more then all beside)
Who had the light, and knew the right,
yet would not it abide!
The sev' [. . .] -fold smart, which to their part
and portion doth fall,
Who Christ his Grace would not embrace,
nor hearken to his call!

CCXV

The Amorites and Sodomites,
although their plagues be sore,
Yet find some ease, compar'd to these,
who feel a great deal more.
Almighty God, whose Iron Rod
to smite them never [. . .] ins,
Doth most declare his Justice rare
in plaguing these mens [. . .] ins.

CCXVI

The pain of loss their souls doth toss
[. . .] nd wond'rously distress,
To think what they have cast away
by wilful wickedness.
We might have been redeem'd from si [. . .],

think they, and liv'd above,
Being possest of heav'nly rest,
and joying in Gods love.

CCXVII

But wo, wo, wo our souls unto!
we would not happy be;
And therefore bear Gods vengeance here
to all Eternitee.
Experience and woful sence
must be our painful teachers,
Who [. . .] ' ould believe, nor credit give
unto our faithful Preachers.

CCXVIII

Thus shall they lie, and wail, and cry,
tormented, and tormenting
Their galled hearts with poyson'd darts;
but now too late repenting.
There let them dwell i' th' flames of hell,
there leave we them to burn,
And back agen unto the men
whom Christ acquits return.

CCXIX

The Saints behold with courage bold,
and tha [. . .] kful wonderment,
To see all those that were their foes
thus sent to punishment:
Then do they sing unto their King
a song of endless praise [. . .]

They praise his Name, and do proclaim,
that just are all his ways.

CCXX

Thus with great joy and melody
to Heav'n they all ascend,
Him there to praise with sweetest layes,
And Hymns that never end.
Where with long Rest they shall be blest,
and nought shall them annoy:

Where they shall see as seen they be,
and whom they love, enjoy.

CCXXI
O glorious Place! where face to face
Jehovah may be seen,
By such as were sinners whilere,
and no dark vail between.
Where the Sun-shine, and Light divine,
of Gods bright Countenance
Doth rest upon them every one
with sweetest influence.

CCXXII
O blessed state of the Renate!
O Wond'rous Happiness
To which they'r brought, beyond what thought
can reach, or words express!
Grief's water-course, and Sorrow's sourse
are turn'd to joyful streams.
Their old distress and heaviness
a [. . .] e vanished like dreams.

CCXXIII
For God above in arms of love
doth dearly them embrace,
And fills their sprights with such delights
and pleasures in his grace;
As shall not fail, nor yet grow stale
through frequency of use:
Nor do they fear Gods Favour there
to forfeit by abuse.

CCXXIV
For there the Saints are perfect Saints,
and holy ones indeed,
From [. . .] ll the sin, that dwelt within
their mortal bodies, freed:
Made Kings and Priests to God, through Christs
dear loves transcendency,
There to remain, and there to reign
with him Eternally.

2.8.2 Reading and Review Questions

1. Who are the sinners whom Wigglesworth identifies in *The Day of Doom*? How do you know?
2. How does Wigglesworth characterize God's approaching judgment of the sinner? Why?
3. What knowledge of the Puritan faith and the Elect does this poem offer? How? To what effect? How, if at all, does he make his "message" palatable to his readers?
4. Against what possible failures in Puritan's faith does Wigglesworth caution? Why?
5. Who does Wigglesworth believe can hope for God's mercy? Why?

2.9 MARY ROWLANDSON

(c. 1637–1711)

Mary Rowlandson (née White) was born in Somersetshire, England around 1637. Two years later, her family joined the Puritan migration to America and settled in the Massachusetts Bay Colony. They then lived in Salem, Massachusetts, before moving to Lancaster, a frontier settlement comprising of fifty families and six garrisons. In 1656, she married Joseph Rowlandson (1631–1678) who became an ordained minister. They had four children, one of whom died in infancy.

Image 2.9 | Illustration of Mary Rowlandson from *A Narrative of the Captivity, Sufferings and Removes of Mrs. Mary Rowlandson*
Artist | Coverly/Rowlandson
Source | Wikimedia Commons
License | Public Domain

In 1676, Lancaster was attacked in the ongoing conflict now known as King Philip's War (1675–1678). Metacomet (1638–1676), called King Philip by the Puritans, was chief of the Wampanoags. His father, Massasoit (1580–1661), signed a treaty with the Pilgrims at Plymouth in 1621. By 1675, white settlers were pushing Native Americans from their land to such a degree that Algonquian tribes formed a coalition and raided white settlements. Among these was Lancaster, where Rowlandson's garrison was attacked and burned. She, along with twenty-three other survivors, was taken prisoner by the Native Americans.

Her captivity lasted eleven weeks and five days, during which time the Algonquians walked up to Chesterfield, New Hampshire and back to Princeton, Massachusetts. There, Rowlandson was ransomed for twenty pounds in goods. In 1677, her family—including the surviving children taken captive along with Rowlandson—moved to Wethersfield, Connecticut where Joseph Rowlandson had acquired a position as minister. He died in 1678; one year later, Rowlandson married Captain Samuel Talcott. She remained in Connecticut, where she died in 1711.

Soon after her release from captivity and before her first husband died, Rowlandson began to write of her experiences with the Native Americans. Published in 1682, her memoir became immensely popular as a captivity narrative, a popular genre in the seventeenth century. These captivity narratives record stories of individuals who are captured by people considered as uncivilized enemies, opposed to a Puritan way of life. Much of their popularity stemmed from their testimony of the Puritan God's providence. Rowlandson's narrative adheres to Puritan covenantal obligations, alludes to pertinent Biblical exemplum, and finds God's chastising and loving hand in her suffering and ultimate redemption. Her suffering includes fear, hunger, and witnessing the deaths of other captives. She describes the Native Americans as savage and hellish scourges of God. She acclaims the wonder of God's power when these same Native Americans offer her food, help her find shelter, and provide her with a Bible. Her rhetorical strategies and the ambivalences and ambiguities in her account—particularly in regards to cultural assimilation, cross-cultural contact, and gender issues of social construction of identity, voice, and authority—contribute to its continuing popularity to this day.

Image 2.10 | King Phillip or Metacom
Artist | S. G. Drake
Source | Wikimedia Commons
License | Public Domain

2.9.1 From *The Captivity and Restoration of Mary Rowlandson* (1682)

Preface

The sovereignty and goodness of God, together with the faithfulness of his promises displayed, being a narrative of the captivity and restoration of Mrs. Mary Rowlandson, commended by her, to all that desires to know the Lord's doings to, and dealings with her. Especially to her dear children and relations. The second Addition [sic] Corrected and amended. Written by her own hand for her private use, and now made public at the earnest desire of some friends, and for the benefit of the afflicted. Deut. 32.39. See now that I, even I am he, and there is no god with me, I kill and I make alive, I wound and I heal, neither is there any can deliver out of my hand.

On the tenth of February 1675, came the Indians with great numbers upon Lancaster: their first coming was about sunrising; hearing the noise of some guns, we looked out; several houses were burning, and the smoke ascending to heaven. There were five persons taken in one house; the father, and the mother and a sucking child, they knocked on the head; the other two they took and carried away alive. There were two others, who being out of their garrison upon some occasion were set upon; one was knocked on the head, the other escaped; another there was who running along was shot and wounded, and fell down; he begged of them his life, promising them money (as they told me) but they would not hearken to him but knocked him in head, and stripped him naked, and split open his bowels. Another, seeing many of the Indians about his barn, ventured and went out, but was quickly shot down. There were three others belonging to the same garrison who were killed; the Indians getting up upon the roof of the barn, had advantage to shoot down upon them over their fortification. Thus these murderous wretches went on, burning, and destroying before them.

At length they came and beset our own house, and quickly it was the dolefulest day that ever mine eyes saw. The house stood upon the edge of a hill; some of the Indians got behind the hill, others into the barn, and others behind anything that could shelter them; from all which places they shot against the house, so that the bullets seemed to fly like hail; and quickly they wounded one man among us, then another, and then a third. About two hours (according to my observation, in that amazing time) they had been about the house before they prevailed to fire it (which they did with flax and hemp, which they brought out of the barn, and there being no defense about the house, only two flankers at two opposite corners and one of them not finished); they fired it once and one ventured out and quenched it, but they quickly fired it again, and that took. Now is the dreadful hour come, that I have often heard of (in time of war, as it was the case of others), but now mine eyes see it. Some in our house were fighting for their lives, others wallowing in their blood, the house on fire over our heads, and the bloody heathen ready to knock us on the head, if we stirred out. Now might we hear mothers and children crying out for themselves, and one another, "Lord, what shall we do?" Then I took my children (and one of my sisters', hers) to go forth and leave the house: but as soon as we came to the door and appeared, the Indians shot so thick that the bullets rattled against the house, as if one had taken an handful of stones and threw them, so that we were fain to give back. We had six stout dogs belonging to our garrison, but none of them would stir, though another time, if any Indian had come to the door, they were ready to fly upon him and tear him down. The Lord hereby would make us the more acknowledge His hand, and to see that our help is always in Him. But out we must go, the fire increasing, and coming along behind us, roaring, and the Indians gaping before us with their guns, spears, and hatchets to devour us. No sooner were we out of the house, but my brother-in-law (being before wounded, in defending the house, in or near the throat) fell down dead, whereat the Indians scornfully shouted, and hallowed, and were presently upon him, stripping off his clothes, the bullets flying thick, one went through my side, and the same (as would seem) through the bowels and hand of my dear child in my arms. One of my elder sisters' children, named William, had then his leg broken, which the Indians perceiving, they knocked him on [his] head. Thus were we butchered by those merciless heathen, standing amazed, with the blood running down to our heels. My eldest sister being yet in the house, and seeing those woeful sights, the infidels hauling mothers one way, and children another, and some wallowing in their blood: and her elder son telling her that her son William was dead, and myself was wounded, she said, "And Lord, let me die with them," which was no sooner said, but she was struck with a bullet, and fell down dead over the threshold. I hope she is reaping the fruit of her good labors, being faithful to the service of God in her place. In her younger years she lay under much trouble upon spiritual accounts, till it pleased God to make that precious scripture take hold of her heart, "And he said unto me, my Grace is sufficient for thee" (2 Corinthians 12.9). More than twenty years after, I have heard her tell how sweet and comfortable that place was to her. But to return: the Indians laid hold of us, pulling me one way, and the children another, and said, "Come go along with us"; I told them they would kill me: they answered, if I were willing to go along with them, they would not hurt me.

Oh the doleful sight that now was to behold at this house! "Come, behold the works of the Lord, what desolations he has made in the earth." Of thirty-seven persons who were in this one house, none escaped either present death, or a bitter captivity, save only one, who might say as he, "And I only am escaped alone to tell the News" (Job 1.15). There were twelve killed, some shot, some stabbed with their spears, some knocked down with their hatchets. When we are in prosperity, Oh the little that we think of such dreadful sights, and to see our dear friends, and relations lie bleeding out their heart-blood upon the ground. There was one who was chopped into the head with a hatchet, and stripped naked, and yet was crawling up and down. It is a solemn sight to see so many Christians lying in their blood, some here, and some there, like a company of sheep torn by wolves, all of them stripped naked by a company of hell-hounds, roaring, singing, ranting, and insulting, as if they would have torn our very hearts out; yet the Lord by His almighty power preserved a number of us from death, for there were twenty-four of us taken alive and carried captive.

I had often before this said that if the Indians should come, I should choose rather to be killed by them than taken alive, but when it came to the trial my mind changed; their glittering weapons so daunted my spirit, that I chose rather to go along with those (as I may say) ravenous beasts, than that moment to end my days; and that I may the better declare what happened to me during that grievous captivity, I shall particularly speak of the several removes we had up and down the wilderness.

The First Remove

Now away we must go with those barbarous creatures, with our bodies wounded and bleeding, and our hearts no less than our bodies. About a mile we went that night, up upon a hill within sight of the town, where they intended to lodge. There was hard by a vacant house (deserted by the English before, for fear of the Indians). I asked them whether I might not lodge in the house that night, to which they answered, "What, will you love English men still?" This was the dolefulest night that ever my eyes saw. Oh the roaring, and singing and dancing, and yelling of those black creatures in the night, which made the place a lively resemblance of hell. And as miserable was the waste that was there made of horses, cattle, sheep, swine, calves, lambs, roasting pigs, and fowl (which they had plundered in the town), some roasting, some lying and burning, and some boiling to feed our merciless enemies; who were joyful enough, though we were disconsolate. To add to the dolefulness of the former day, and the dismalness of the present night, my thoughts ran upon my losses and sad bereaved condition. All was gone, my husband gone (at least separated from me, he being in the Bay; and to add to my grief, the Indians told me they would kill him as he came homeward), my children gone, my relations and friends gone, our house and home and all our comforts—within door and without—all was gone (except my life), and I knew not but the next moment that might go too. There remained nothing to me but one poor wounded babe, and it seemed at present worse than death that it was in such a pitiful condition, bespeaking compassion, and I had no refreshing for it, nor suitable things to revive it. Little do many think what is the savageness and brutishness of this barbarous enemy, Ay, even those that seem to profess more than others among them, when the English have fallen into their hands.

Those seven that were killed at Lancaster the summer before upon a Sabbath day, and the one that was afterward killed upon a weekday, were slain and mangled in a barbarous manner, by one-eyed John, and Marlborough's Praying Indians, which Capt. Mosely brought to Boston, as the Indians told me.

The Second Remove

But now, the next morning, I must turn my back upon the town, and travel with them into the vast and desolate wilderness, I knew not whither. It is not my tongue, or pen, can express the sorrows of my heart, and bitterness of my spirit that I had at this departure: but God was with me in a wonderful manner, carrying me along, and bearing up my spirit, that it did not quite fail. One of the Indians carried my poor wounded babe upon a horse; it went moaning all along, "I shall die, I shall die." I went on foot after it, with sorrow that cannot be expressed. At length I took it off the horse, and carried it in my arms till my strength failed, and I fell down with it. Then they set me upon a horse with my wounded child in my lap, and there being no furniture upon the horse's back, as we were going down a steep hill we both fell over the horse's head, at which they, like inhumane creatures, laughed, and rejoiced to see it, though I thought we should there have ended our days, as overcome with so many difficulties. But the Lord renewed my strength still, and carried me along, that I might see more of His power; yea, so much that I could never have thought of, had I not experienced it.

After this it quickly began to snow, and when night came on, they stopped, and now down I must sit in the snow, by a little fire, and a few boughs behind me, with my sick child in my lap; and calling much for water, being now (through the wound) fallen into a violent fever. My own wound also growing so stiff that I could scarce sit down or rise up; yet so it must be, that I must sit all this cold winter night upon the cold snowy ground, with my sick child in my arms, looking that every hour would be the last of its life; and having no Christian friend near me, either to comfort or help me. Oh, I may see the wonderful power of God, that my Spirit did not utterly sink under my affliction: still the Lord upheld me with His gracious and merciful spirit, and we were both alive to see the light of the next morning.

The Third Remove

The morning being come, they prepared to go on their way. One of the Indians got up upon a horse, and they set me up behind him, with my poor sick babe in my lap. A very wearisome and tedious day I had of it; what with my own wound, and my child's being so exceeding sick, and in a lamentable condition with her wound. It may be easily judged what a poor feeble condition we were in, there being not the least crumb of refreshing that came within either of our mouths from Wednesday night to Saturday night, except only a little cold water. This day in the afternoon, about an hour by sun, we came to the place where they intended, viz. an Indian town, called Wenimesset, northward of Quabaug. When we were come, Oh the number of pagans (now merciless enemies) that there came about me, that I may say as David, "I had fainted, unless I had believed, etc" (Psalm 27.13). The next day was the Sabbath. I then remembered how careless I had been of God's holy time; how many Sabbaths I had lost and misspent, and how evilly I had walked in God's sight; which lay so close unto my spirit, that it was easy for me to see how righteous it was with God to cut off the thread of my life and cast me out of His presence forever. Yet the Lord still showed mercy to me, and upheld me; and as He wounded me with one hand, so he healed me with the other. This day there came to me one Robert Pepper (a man belonging to Roxbury) who was taken in Captain Beers's fight, and had been now a considerable time with the Indians; and up with them almost as far as Albany, to see King Philip, as he told me, and was now very lately come into these parts. Hearing, I say, that I was in this Indian town, he obtained leave to come and see me. He told me he himself was wounded in the leg at Captain Beer's fight; and was not able some time to go, but as they carried him, and as he took oaken leaves and laid to his wound, and through the blessing of God he was able to travel again. Then I took oaken leaves and laid to my side, and with the blessing of God it cured me also; yet before the cure was wrought, I may say, as it is in Psalm 38.5-6 "My wounds stink and are corrupt, I am troubled,

I am bowed down greatly, I go mourning all the day long." I sat much alone with a poor wounded child in my lap, which moaned night and day, having nothing to revive the body, or cheer the spirits of her, but instead of that, sometimes one Indian would come and tell me one hour that "your master will knock your child in the head," and then a second, and then a third, "your master will quickly knock your child in the head."

This was the comfort I had from them, miserable comforters are ye all, as he said. Thus nine days I sat upon my knees, with my babe in my lap, till my flesh was raw again; my child being even ready to depart this sorrowful world, they bade me carry it out to another wigwam (I suppose because they would not be troubled with such spectacles) whither I went with a very heavy heart, and down I sat with the picture of death in my lap. About two hours in the night, my sweet babe like a lamb departed this life on Feb. 18, 1675. It being about six years, and five months old. It was nine days from the first wounding, in this miserable condition, without any refreshing of one nature or other, except a little cold water. I cannot but take notice how at another time I could not bear to be in the room where any dead person was, but now the case is changed; I must and could lie down by my dead babe, side by side all the night after. I have thought since of the wonderful goodness of God to me in preserving me in the use of my reason and senses in that distressed time, that I did not use wicked and violent means to end my own miserable life. In the morning, when they understood that my child was dead they sent for me home to my master's wigwam (by my master in this writing, must be understood Quinnapin, who was a Sagamore, and married King Philip's wife's sister; not that he first took me, but I was sold to him by another Narragansett Indian, who took me when first I came out of the garrison). I went to take up my dead child in my arms to carry it with me, but they bid me let it alone; there was no resisting, but go I must and leave it. When I had been at my master's wigwam, I took the first opportunity I could get to go look after my dead child. When I came I asked them what they had done with it; then they told me it was upon the hill. Then they went and showed me where it was, where I saw the ground was newly digged, and there they told me they had buried it. There I left that child in the wilderness, and must commit it, and myself also in this wilderness condition, to Him who is above all. God having taken away this dear child, I went to see my daughter Mary, who was at this same Indian town, at a wigwam not very far off, though we had little liberty or opportunity to see one another. She was about ten years old, and taken from the door at first by a Praying Ind. and afterward sold for a gun. When I came in sight, she would fall aweeping; at which they were provoked, and would not let me come near her, but bade me be gone; which was a heart-cutting word to me. I had one child dead, another in the wilderness, I knew not where, the third they would not let me come near to: "Me (as he said) have ye bereaved of my Children, Joseph is not, and Simeon is not, and ye will take Benjamin also, all these things are against me." I could not sit still in this condition, but kept walking from one place to another. And as I was going along, my heart was even overwhelmed with the thoughts of my condition, and that I should have children, and a nation which I knew not, ruled over them. Whereupon I earnestly entreated the Lord, that He would consider my low estate, and show me a token for good, and if it were His blessed will, some sign and hope of some relief. And indeed quickly the Lord answered, in some measure, my poor prayers; for as I was going up and down mourning and lamenting my condition, my son came to me, and asked me how I did. I had not seen him before, since the destruction of the town, and I knew not where he was, till I was informed by himself, that he was amongst a smaller parcel of Indians, whose place was about six miles off. With tears in his eyes, he asked me whether his sister Sarah was dead; and told me he had seen his sister Mary; and prayed me, that I would not be troubled in reference to himself. The occasion of his coming to see me at this time, was this: there was, as I said, about six miles from us, a small plantation of Indians, where it seems he had been during his captivity; and at this time, there were some forces of the Ind. gathered out of our company, and some also from them (among whom was my son's master) to go to assault and burn Medfield. In this time of the absence of his master, his dame brought him to see me. I took this to be some gracious answer to my earnest and unfeigned desire. The next day, viz. to this, the Indians returned from Medfield, all the company, for those that belonged to the other small company, came through the town that now we were at. But before they came to us, Oh! the outrageous roaring and hooping that there was. They began their din about a mile before they came to us. By their noise and hooping they signified how many they had destroyed (which was at that time twenty-three). Those that were with us at home were gathered together as soon as they heard the hooping, and every time that the other went over their number, these at home gave a shout, that the very earth rung again. And thus they continued till those that had been upon the expedition were come up to the Sagamore's wigwam; and then, Oh, the hideous insulting and triumphing that there was over some Englishmen's scalps that they had taken (as their manner is) and brought with them. I cannot but take notice of the wonderful mercy of God to me in those afflictions, in sending me a Bible. One of the Indians that came from Medfield fight, had brought some plunder, came to me, and asked me, if I would have a Bible, he had got one in his basket. I was glad of it, and asked him, whether he thought the Indians would let me read? He answered, yes. So I took the Bible, and in that melancholy time, it came into my mind to read first the 28th chapter of Deuteronomy, which I did, and when I had read it, my dark heart wrought on this manner: that there was no mercy for me, that the blessings were gone, and the curses come in their room, and that I had lost my opportunity. But the Lord helped me still to go on reading till I came to Chap. 30, the seven first verses, where I found, there was mercy promised again, if we would return to Him by repentance; and though we were scattered from one end of the earth to the other, yet the Lord would gather us together, and turn all those curses upon our enemies. I do not desire to live to forget this Scripture, and what comfort it was to me.

Now the Ind. began to talk of removing from this place, some one way, and some another. There were now besides myself nine English captives in this place (all of them children, except one woman). I got an opportunity to go and take my leave of them. They being to go one way, and I another, I asked them whether they were earnest with God for deliverance. They told me they did as they were able, and it was some comfort to me, that the Lord stirred up children to look to Him. The woman, viz. goodwife Joslin, told me she should never see me again, and that she could find in her heart to run away. I wished her not to run away by any means, for we were near thirty miles from any English town, and she very big with child, and had but one week to reckon, and another child in her arms, two years old, and bad rivers there were to go over, and we were feeble, with our poor and coarse entertainment. I had my Bible with me, I pulled it out, and asked her whether she would read. We opened the Bible and lighted on Psalm 27, in which Psalm we especially took notice of that, ver. ult., "Wait on the Lord, Be of good courage, and he shall strengthen thine Heart, wait I say on the Lord."

The Fourth Remove

And now I must part with that little company I had. Here I parted from my daughter Mary (whom I never saw again till I saw her in Dorchester, returned from captivity), and from four little cousins and neighbors, some of which I never saw afterward: the Lord only knows the end of them. Amongst them also was that poor woman before mentioned, who came to a sad end, as some of the company told me in my travel: she having much grief upon her spirit about her miserable condition, being so near her time, she would be often asking the Indians to let her go home; they not being willing to that, and yet vexed with her importunity, gathered a great company together about her and stripped her naked, and set her in the midst of them, and when they had sung and danced about her (in their hellish manner) as long as they pleased they knocked her on head, and the child in her arms with her. When they had done that they made a fire and put them both into it, and told the other children that were with them that if they attempted to go home, they would serve them in like manner. The children said she did not shed one tear, but prayed all the while. But to return to my own journey, we traveled about half a day or little more, and came to a desolate place in the wilderness, where there were no wigwams or inhabitants before; we came about the middle of the afternoon to this place, cold and wet, and snowy, and hungry, and weary, and no refreshing for man but the cold ground to sit on, and our poor Indian cheer.

Heart-aching thoughts here I had about my poor children, who were scattered up and down among the wild beasts of the forest. My head was light and dizzy (either through hunger or hard lodging, or trouble or all together), my knees feeble, my body raw by sitting double night and day, that I cannot express to man the affliction that lay upon my spirit, but the Lord helped me at that time to express it to Himself. I opened my Bible to read, and the Lord brought that precious Scripture to me. "Thus saith the Lord, refrain thy voice from weeping, and thine eyes from tears, for thy work shall be rewarded, and they shall come again from the land of the enemy" (Jeremiah 31.16). This was a sweet cordial to me when I was ready to faint; many and many a time have I sat down and wept sweetly over this Scripture. At this place we continued about four days.

The Fifth Remove

The occasion (as I thought) of their moving at this time was the English army, it being near and following them. For they went as if they had gone for their lives, for some considerable way, and then they made a stop, and chose some of their stoutest men, and sent them back to hold the English army in play whilst the rest escaped. And then, like Jehu, they marched on furiously, with their old and with their young: some carried their old decrepit mothers, some carried one, and some another. Four of them carried a great Indian upon a bier; but going through a thick wood with him, they were hindered, and could make no haste, whereupon they took him upon their backs, and carried him, one at a time, till they came to Banquaug river. Upon a Friday, a little after noon, we came to this river. When all the company was come up, and were gathered together, I thought to count the number of them, but they were so many, and being somewhat in motion, it was beyond my skill. In this travel, because of my wound, I was somewhat favored in my load; I carried only my knitting work and two quarts of parched meal. Being very faint I asked my mistress to give me one spoonful of the meal, but she would not give me a taste. They quickly fell to cutting dry trees, to make rafts to carry them over the river: and soon my turn came to go over. By the advantage of some brush which they had laid upon the raft to sit upon, I did not wet my foot (which many of themselves at the other end were mid-leg deep) which cannot but be acknowledged as a favor of God to my weakened body, it being a very cold time. I was not before acquainted with such kind of doings or dangers. "When thou passeth through the waters I will be with thee, and through the rivers they shall not overflow thee" (Isaiah 43.2). A certain number of us got over the river that night, but it was the night after the Sabbath before all the company was got over. On the Saturday they boiled an old horse's leg which they had got, and so we drank of the broth, as soon as they thought it was ready, and when it was almost all gone, they filled it up again.

The first week of my being among them I hardly ate any thing; the second week I found my stomach grow very faint for want of something; and yet it was very hard to get down their filthy trash; but the third week, though I could think how formerly my stomach would turn against this or that, and I could starve and die before I could eat such things, yet they were sweet and savory to my taste. I was at this time knitting a pair of white cotton stockings for my mistress; and had not yet wrought upon a Sabbath day. When the Sabbath came they bade me go to work. I told them it was the Sabbath day, and desired them to let me rest, and told them I would do as much more tomorrow; to which they answered me they would break my face. And here I cannot but take notice of the strange providence of God in preserving the heathen. They were many hundreds, old and young, some sick, and some lame;

many had papooses at their backs. The greatest number at this time with us were squaws, and they traveled with all they had, bag and baggage, and yet they got over this river aforesaid; and on Monday they set their wigwams on fire, and away they went. On that very day came the English army after them to this river, and saw the smoke of their wigwams, and yet this river put a stop to them. God did not give them courage or activity to go over after us. We were not ready for so great a mercy as victory and deliverance. If we had been God would have found out a way for the English to have passed this river, as well as for the Indians with their squaws and children, and all their luggage. "Oh that my people had hearkened to me, and Israel had walked in my ways, I should soon have subdued their enemies, and turned my hand against their adversaries" (Psalm 81.13-14).

The Eighth Remove

On the morrow morning we must go over the river, i.e. Connecticut, to meet with King Philip. Two canoes full they had carried over; the next turn I myself was to go. But as my foot was upon the canoe to step in there was a sudden outcry among them, and I must step back, and instead of going over the river, I must go four or five miles up the river farther northward. Some of the Indians ran one way, and some another. The cause of this rout was, as I thought, their espying some English scouts, who were thereabout. In this travel up the river about noon the company made a stop, and sat down; some to eat, and others to rest them. As I sat amongst them, musing of things past, my son Joseph unexpectedly came to me. We asked of each other's welfare, bemoaning our doleful condition, and the change that had come upon us. We had husband and father, and children, and sisters, and friends, and relations, and house, and home, and many comforts of this life: but now we may say, as Job, "Naked came I out of my mother's womb, and naked shall I return: the Lord gave, the Lord hath taken away, blessed be the name of the Lord." I asked him whether he would read. He told me he earnestly desired it, I gave him my Bible, and he lighted upon that comfortable Scripture "I shall not die but live, and declare the works of the Lord: the Lord hath chastened me sore yet he hath not given me over to death" (Psalm 118.17-18). "Look here, mother," says he, "did you read this?" And here I may take occasion to mention one principal ground of my setting forth these lines: even as the psalmist says, to declare the works of the Lord, and His wonderful power in carrying us along, preserving us in the wilderness, while under the enemy's hand, and returning of us in safety again. And His goodness in bringing to my hand so many comfortable and suitable scriptures in my distress. But to return, we traveled on till night; and in the morning, we must go over the river to Philip's crew. When I was in the canoe I could not but be amazed at the numerous crew of pagans that were on the bank on the other side. When I came ashore, they gathered all about me, I sitting alone in the midst. I observed they asked one another questions, and laughed, and rejoiced over their gains and victories. Then my heart began to fail: and I fell aweeping, which was the first time to my remembrance, that I wept before them. Although

I had met with so much affliction, and my heart was many times ready to break, yet could I not shed one tear in their sight; but rather had been all this while in a maze, and like one astonished. But now I may say as Psalm 137.1, "By the Rivers of Babylon, there we sate down: yea, we wept when we remembered Zion." There one of them asked me why I wept. I could hardly tell what to say: Yet I answered, they would kill me. "No," said he, "none will hurt you." Then came one of them and gave me two spoonfuls of meal to comfort me, and another gave me half a pint of peas; which was more worth than many bushels at another time. Then I went to see King Philip. He bade me come in and sit down, and asked me whether I would smoke it (a usual compliment nowadays amongst saints and sinners) but this no way suited me. For though I had formerly used tobacco, yet I had left it ever since I was first taken. It seems to be a bait the devil lays to make men lose their precious time. I remember with shame how formerly, when I had taken two or three pipes, I was presently ready for another, such a bewitching thing it is. But I thank God, He has now given me power over it; surely there are many who may be better employed than to lie sucking a stinking tobacco-pipe.

Now the Indians gather their forces to go against Northampton. Over night one went about yelling and hooting to give notice of the design. Whereupon they fell to boiling of ground nuts, and parching of corn (as many as had it) for their provision; and in the morning away they went. During my abode in this place, Philip spake to me to make a shirt for his boy, which I did, for which he gave me a shilling. I offered the money to my master, but he bade me keep it; and with it I bought a piece of horse flesh. Afterwards he asked me to make a cap for his boy, for which he invited me to dinner. I went, and he gave me a pancake, about as big as two fingers. It was made of parched wheat, beaten, and fried in bear's grease, but I thought I never tasted pleasanter meat in my life. There was a squaw who spake to me to make a shirt for her sannup, for which she gave me a piece of bear. Another asked me to knit a pair of stockings, for which she gave me a quart of peas. I boiled my peas and bear together, and invited my master and mistress to dinner; but the proud gossip, because I served them both in one dish, would eat nothing, except one bit that he gave her upon the point of his knife. Hearing that my son was come to this place, I went to see him, and found him lying flat upon the ground. I asked him how he could sleep so? He answered me that he was not asleep, but at prayer; and lay so, that they might not observe what he was doing. I pray God he may remember these things now he is returned in safety. At this place (the sun now getting higher) what with the beams and heat of the sun, and the smoke of the wigwams, I thought I should have been blind. I could scarce discern one wigwam from another. There was here one Mary Thurston of Medfield, who seeing how it was with me, lent me a hat to wear; but as soon as I was gone, the squaw (who owned that Mary Thurston) came running after me, and got it away again. Here was the squaw that gave me one spoonful of meal. I put it in my pocket to keep it safe. Yet notwithstanding, somebody stole it, but put five Indian corns in the room of it; which corns were the greatest provisions I had in my travel for one day.

The Indians returning from Northampton, brought with them some horses, and sheep, and other things which they had taken; I desired them that they would carry me to Albany upon one of those horses, and sell me for powder: for so they had sometimes discoursed. I was utterly hopeless of getting home on foot, the way that I came. I could hardly bear to think of the many weary steps I had taken, to come to this place.

The Thirteenth Remove

Instead of going toward the Bay, which was that I desired, I must go with them five or six miles down the river into a mighty thicket of brush; where we abode almost a fortnight. Here one asked me to make a shirt for her papoose, for which she gave me a mess of broth, which was thickened with meal made of the bark of a tree, and to make it the better, she had put into it about a handful of peas, and a few roasted ground nuts. I had not seen my son a pretty while, and here was an Indian of whom I made inquiry after him, and asked him when he saw him. He answered me that such a time his master roasted him, and that himself did eat a piece of him, as big as his two fingers, and that he was very good meat. But the Lord upheld my Spirit, under this discouragement; and I considered their horrible addictedness to lying, and that there is not one of them that makes the least conscience of speaking of truth. In this place, on a cold night, as I lay by the fire, I removed a stick that kept the heat from me. A squaw moved it down again, at which I looked up, and she threw a handful of ashes in mine eyes. I thought I should have been quite blinded, and have never seen more, but lying down, the water run out of my eyes, and carried the dirt with it, that by the morning I recovered my sight again. Yet upon this, and the like occasions, I hope it is not too much to say with Job, "Have pity upon me, O ye my Friends, for the Hand of the Lord has touched me." And here I cannot but remember how many times sitting in their wigwams, and musing on things past, I should suddenly leap up and run out, as if I had been at home, forgetting where I was, and what my condition was; but when I was without, and saw nothing but wilderness, and woods, and a company of barbarous heathens, my mind quickly returned to me, which made me think of that, spoken concerning Sampson, who said, "I will go out and shake myself as at other times, but he wist not that the Lord was departed from him." About this time I began to think that all my hopes of restoration would come to nothing. I thought of the English army, and hoped for their coming, and being taken by them, but that failed. I hoped to be carried to Albany, as the Indians had discoursed before, but that failed also. I thought of being sold to my husband, as my master spake, but instead of that, my master himself was gone, and I left behind, so that my spirit was now quite ready to sink. I asked them to let me go out and pick up some sticks, that I might get alone, and pour out my heart unto the Lord. Then also I took my Bible to read, but I found no comfort here neither, which many times I was wont to find. So easy a thing it is with God to dry up the streams of Scripture comfort from us. Yet I can say, that in all my sorrows and afflictions, God did not leave me to have my impatience work towards Himself, as if His ways were unrighteous. But I knew that He laid upon me less than I deserved. Afterward, before this doleful time ended with me, I was turning the leaves of my Bible, and the Lord brought to me some Scriptures, which did a little revive me, as that [in] Isaiah 55.8: "For my thoughts are not your thoughts, neither are your ways my ways, saith the Lord." And also that [in] Psalm 37.5: "Commit thy way unto the Lord; trust also in him; and he shall bring it to pass." About this time they came yelping from Hadley, where they had killed three Englishmen, and brought one captive with them, viz. Thomas Read. They all gathered about the poor man, asking him many questions. I desired also to go and see him; and when I came, he was crying bitterly, supposing they would quickly kill him. Whereupon I asked one of them, whether they intended to kill him; he answered me, they would not. He being a little cheered with that, I asked him about the welfare of my husband. He told me he saw him such a time in the Bay, and he was well, but very melancholy. By which I certainly understood (though I suspected it before) that whatsoever the Indians told me respecting him was vanity and lies. Some of them told me he was dead, and they had killed him; some said he was married again, and that the Governor wished him to marry; and told him he should have his choice, and that all persuaded I was dead. So like were these barbarous creatures to him who was a liar from the beginning.

As I was sitting once in the wigwam here, Philip's maid came in with the child in her arms, and asked me to give her a piece of my apron, to make a flap for it. I told her I would not. Then my mistress bade me give it, but still I said no. The maid told me if I would not give her a piece, she would tear a piece off it. I told her I would tear her coat then. With that my mistress rises up, and take up a stick big enough to have killed me, and struck at me with it. But I stepped out, and she struck the stick into the mat of the wigwam. But while she was pulling of it out I ran to the maid and gave her all my apron, and so that storm went over.

Hearing that my son was come to this place, I went to see him, and told him his father was well, but melancholy. He told me he was as much grieved for his father as for himself. I wondered at his speech, for I thought I had enough upon my spirit in reference to myself, to make me mindless of my husband and everyone else; they being safe among their friends. He told me also, that awhile before, his master (together with other Indians) were going to the French for powder; but by the way the Mohawks met with them, and killed four of their company, which made the rest turn back again, for it might have been worse with him, had he been sold to the French, than it proved to be in his remaining with the Indians.

I went to see an English youth in this place, one John Gilbert of Springfield. I found him lying without doors, upon the ground. I asked him how he did? He told me he was very sick of a flux, with eating so much blood. They had turned him out of the wigwam, and with him an Indian papoose, almost dead (whose parents had been killed), in a bitter cold day, without fire or clothes. The young man himself had nothing on but his shirt and waistcoat. This sight was enough to melt a heart of flint. There they lay quivering in the cold, the youth round like a dog, the papoose stretched out with his eyes and nose and mouth full of dirt, and yet alive, and groaning. I advised John to go and get to some fire. He told me he could not stand, but I persuaded him still, lest he should lie there and die. And with much ado I got him to a fire, and went myself home. As soon as I was got home his master's daughter came after me, to know what I had done with the Englishman. I told her I had got him to a fire in such a place. Now had I need to pray Paul's Prayer "That we may be delivered from unreasonable and wicked men" (2 Thessalonians 3.2). For her satisfaction I went along with her, and brought her to him; but before I got home again it was noised about that I was running away and getting the English youth, along with me; that as soon as I came in they began to rant and domineer, asking me where I had been, and what I had been doing? and saying they would knock him on the head. I told them I had been seeing the English youth, and that I would not run away. They told me I lied, and taking up a hatchet, they came to me, and said they would knock me down if I stirred out again, and so confined me to the wigwam. Now may I say with David, "I am in a great strait" (2 Samuel 24.14). If I keep in, I must die with hunger, and if I go out, I must be knocked in head. This distressed condition held that day, and half the next. And then the Lord remembered me, whose mercies are great. Then came an Indian to me with a pair of stockings that were too big for him, and he would have me ravel them out, and knit them fit for him. I showed myself willing, and bid him ask my mistress if I might go along with him a little way; she said yes, I might, but I was not a little refreshed with that news, that I had my liberty again. Then I went along with him, and he gave me some roasted ground nuts, which did again revive my feeble stomach.

Being got out of her sight, I had time and liberty again to look into my Bible; which was my guide by day, and my pillow by night. Now that comfortable Scripture presented itself to me, "For a small moment have I forsaken thee, but with great mercies will I gather thee" (Isaiah 54.7). Thus the Lord carried me along from one time to another, and made good to me this precious promise, and many others. Then my son came to see me, and I asked his master to let him stay awhile with me, that I might comb his head, and look over him, for he was almost overcome with lice. He told me, when I had done, that he was very hungry, but I had nothing to relieve him, but bid him go into the wigwams as he went along, and see if he could get any thing among them. Which he did, and it seems tarried a little too long; for his master was angry with him, and beat him, and then sold him. Then he came running to tell me he had a new master, and that he had given him some ground nuts already. Then I went along with him to his new master who told me he loved him, and he should not want. So his master carried him away, and I never saw him afterward, till I saw him at Piscataqua in Portsmouth.

That night they bade me go out of the wigwam again. My mistress's papoose was sick, and it died that night, and there was one benefit in it—that there was more room. I went to a wigwam, and they bade me come in, and gave me a skin to lie upon, and a mess of venison and ground nuts, which was a choice dish among them. On the morrow they buried the papoose, and afterward, both morning and evening, there came a company to mourn and howl with her; though I confess I could not much condole with them. Many sorrowful days I had in this place, often getting alone. "Like a crane, or a swallow, so did I chatter; I did mourn as a dove, mine eyes ail with looking upward. Oh, Lord, I am oppressed; undertake for me" (Isaiah 38.14). I could tell the Lord, as Hezekiah, "Remember now O Lord, I beseech thee, how I have walked before thee in truth." Now had I time to examine all my ways: my conscience did not accuse me of unrighteousness toward one or other; yet I saw how in my walk with God, I had been a careless creature. As David said, "Against thee, thee only have I sinned": and I might say with the poor publican, "God be merciful unto me a sinner." On the Sabbath days, I could look upon the sun and think how people were going to the house of God, to have their souls refreshed; and then home, and their bodies also; but I was destitute of both; and might say as the poor prodigal, "He would fain have filled his belly with the husks that the swine did eat, and no man gave unto him" (Luke 15.16). For I must say with him, "Father, I have sinned against Heaven and in thy sight." I remembered how on the night before and after the Sabbath, when my family was about me, and relations and neighbors with us, we could pray and sing, and then refresh our bodies with the good creatures of God; and then have a comfortable bed to lie down on; but instead of all this, I had only a little swill for the body and then, like a swine, must lie down on the ground. I cannot express to man the sorrow that lay upon my spirit; the Lord knows it. Yet that comfortable Scripture would often come to mind, "For a small moment have I forsaken thee, but with great mercies will I gather thee."

The Eighteenth Remove

We took up our packs and along we went, but a wearisome day I had of it. As we went along I saw an Englishman stripped naked, and lying dead upon the ground, but knew not who it was. Then we came to another Indian town, where we stayed all night. In this town there were four English children, captives; and one of them my own sister's. I went to see how she did, and she was well, considering her captive condition. I would have tarried that night with her, but they that owned her would not suffer it. Then I went into another wigwam, where they were boiling corn and beans, which was a lovely sight to see, but I could not get a taste thereof. Then I went to another wigwam, where there were two of the English children; the squaw was boiling horses feet; then she cut me off a little piece, and gave one of the English children a piece also. Being very hungry I had quickly eat up mine, but the child could not bite it, it was so tough and sinewy, but lay sucking, gnawing, chewing and slabbering of it in the mouth and hand. Then I took it of the child, and eat it myself, and savory it was to my taste. Then I may say as Job 6.7, "The things that my soul refused to touch are as my sorrowful meat." Thus the Lord made that pleasant refreshing, which another time would have been an abomination. Then I went home to my mistress's wigwam; and they told me I disgraced my master with begging, and if I did so any more, they would knock me in the head. I told them, they had as good knock me in head as starve me to death.

The Nineteenth Remove

They said, when we went out, that we must travel to Wachusett this day. But a bitter weary day I had of it, traveling now three days together, without resting any day between. At last, after many weary steps, I saw Wachusett hills, but many miles off. Then we came to a great swamp, through which we traveled, up to the knees in mud and water, which was heavy going to one tired before. Being almost spent, I thought I should have sunk down at last, and never got out; but I may say, as in Psalm 94.18, "When my foot slipped, thy mercy, O Lord, held me up." Going along, having indeed my life, but little spirit, Philip, who was in the company, came up and took me by the hand, and said, two weeks more and you shall be mistress again. I asked him, if he spake true? He answered, "Yes, and quickly you shall come to your master again; who had been gone from us three weeks." After many weary steps we came to Wachusett, where he was: and glad I was to see him. He asked me, when I washed me? I told him not this month. Then he fetched me some water himself, and bid me wash, and gave me the glass to see how I looked; and bid his squaw give me something to eat. So she gave me a mess of beans and meat, and a little ground nut cake. I was wonderfully revived with this favor showed me: "He made them also to be pitied of all those that carried them captives" (Psalm 106.46).

My master had three squaws, living sometimes with one, and sometimes with another one, this old squaw, at whose wigwam I was, and with whom my master had been those three weeks. Another was Wattimore [Weetamoo] with whom I had lived and served all this while. A severe and proud dame she was, bestowing every day in dressing herself neat as much time as any of the gentry of the land: powdering her hair, and painting her face, going with necklaces, with jewels in her ears, and bracelets upon her hands. When she had dressed herself, her work was to make girdles of wampum and beads. The third squaw was a younger one, by whom he had two papooses. By the time I was refreshed by the old squaw, with whom my master was, Weetamoo's maid came to call me home, at which I fell aweeping. Then the old squaw told me, to encourage me, that if I wanted victuals, I should come to her, and that I should lie there in her wigwam. Then I went with the maid, and quickly came again and lodged there. The squaw laid a mat under me, and a good rug over me; the first time I had any such kindness showed me. I understood that Weetamoo thought that if she should let me go and serve with the old squaw, she would be in danger to lose not only my service, but the redemption pay also. And I was not a little glad to hear this; being by it raised in my hopes, that in God's due time there would be an end of this sorrowful hour. Then came an Indian, and asked me to knit him three pair of stockings, for which I had a hat, and a silk handkerchief. Then another asked me to make her a shift, for which she gave me an apron.

Then came Tom and Peter, with the second letter from the council, about the captives. Though they were Indians, I got them by the hand, and burst out into tears. My heart was so full that I could not speak to them; but recovering myself, I asked them how my husband did, and all my friends and acquaintance? They said, "They are all very well but melancholy." They brought me two biscuits, and a pound of tobacco. The tobacco I quickly gave away. When it was all gone, one asked me to give him a pipe of tobacco. I told him it was all gone. Then began he to rant and threaten. I told him when my husband came I would give him some. Hang him rogue (says he) I will knock out his brains, if he comes here. And then again, in the same breath they would say that if there should come an hundred without guns, they would do them no hurt. So unstable and like madmen they were. So that fearing the worst, I durst not send to my husband, though there were some thoughts of his coming to redeem and fetch me, not knowing what might follow. For there was little more trust to them than to the master they served. When the letter was come, the Sagamores met to consult about the captives, and called me to them to inquire how much my husband would give to redeem me. When I came I sat down among them, as I was wont to do, as their manner is. Then they bade me stand up, and said they were the General Court. They bid me speak what I thought he would give. Now knowing that all we had was destroyed by the Indians, I was in a great strait. I thought if I should speak of but a little it would be slighted, and hinder the matter; if of a great sum, I knew not where it would be procured. Yet at a venture I said "Twenty pounds," yet desired them to take less. But they would not hear of that, but sent that message to Boston, that for twenty pounds I should be redeemed. It was a Praying Indian that wrote their letter for them. There was another Praying Indian, who told me, that he had a brother, that would not eat horse; his conscience was so tender and scrupulous (though as large as hell, for the destruction of poor Christians). Then he said, he read that Scripture to him, "There was a famine in Samaria, and behold they besieged it, until an ass's head was sold for four-score pieces of silver, and the fourth part of a cab of dove's dung for five pieces of silver" (2 Kings 6.25). He expounded this place to his brother, and showed him that it was lawful to eat that in a famine which is not at another time. And now, says he, he will eat horse with any Indian of them all. There was another Praying Indian, who when he had done all the mischief that he could, betrayed his own father into the English hands, thereby to purchase his own life. Another Praying Indian was at Sudbury fight, though, as he deserved, he was afterward hanged for it. There was another Praying Indian, so wicked and cruel, as to wear a string about his neck, strung with Christians' fingers. Another Praying Indian, when they went to Sudbury fight, went with them, and his squaw also with him, with her papoose at her back. Before they went to that fight they got a company together to pow-wow. The manner was as followeth: there was one that kneeled upon a deerskin, with the company round him in a ring who kneeled, and striking upon the ground with their hands, and with sticks, and muttering or humming with their mouths. Besides him who kneeled in the ring, there also stood one with a gun in his hand. Then he on the deerskin made a speech, and all manifested assent to it; and so they did many times together. Then they bade him with the gun go out of the ring, which he did. But when he was out, they called him in again; but he seemed to make a stand; then they called the more earnestly, till he returned again. Then they all sang. Then they gave him two guns, in either hand one. And so he on the deerskin began again; and at the end of every sentence in his speaking, they all assented, humming or muttering with their mouths, and striking upon the ground with their hands. Then they bade him with the two guns go out of the ring again; which he did, a little way. Then they called him in again, but he made a stand. So they called him with greater earnestness; but he stood reeling and wavering as if he knew not whither he should stand or fall, or which way to go. Then they called him with exceeding great vehemency, all of them, one and another. After a little while he turned in, staggering as he went, with his arms stretched out, in either hand a gun. As soon as he came in they all sang and rejoiced exceedingly a while. And then he upon the deerskin, made another speech unto which they all assented in a rejoicing manner. And so they ended their business, and forthwith went to Sudbury fight. To my thinking they went without any scruple, but that they should prosper, and gain the victory. And they went out not so rejoicing, but they came home with as great a victory. For they said they had killed two captains and almost an hundred men. One Englishman they brought along with them: and he said, it was too true, for they had made sad work at Sudbury, as indeed it proved. Yet they came home without that rejoicing and triumphing over their victory which they were wont to show at other times; but rather like dogs (as they say) which have lost their ears. Yet I could not perceive that it was for their own loss of men. They said they had not lost above five or six; and I missed none, except in one wigwam. When they went, they acted as if the devil had told them that they should gain the victory; and now they acted as if the devil had told them they should have a fall. Whither it were so or no, I cannot tell, but so it proved, for quickly they began to fall, and so held on that summer, till they came to utter ruin. They came home on a Sabbath day, and the Powaw that kneeled upon the deer-skin came home (I may say, without abuse) as black as the devil. When my master came home, he came to me and bid me make a shirt for his papoose, of a holland-laced pillowbere. About that time there came an Indian to me and bid me come to his wigwam at night, and he would give me some pork and ground nuts. Which I did, and as I was eating, another Indian said to me, he seems to be your good friend, but he killed two Englishmen at Sudbury, and there lie their clothes behind you: I looked behind me, and there I saw bloody clothes, with bullet-holes in them. Yet the Lord suffered not this wretch to do me any hurt. Yea, instead of that, he many times refreshed me; five or six times did he and his squaw refresh my feeble carcass. If I went to their wigwam at any time, they would always give me something, and yet they were strangers that I never saw before. Another squaw gave me a piece of fresh pork, and a little salt with it, and lent me her pan to fry it in; and I cannot but remember what a sweet, pleasant and delightful relish that bit had to me, to this day. So little do we prize common mercies when we have them to the full.

The Twentieth Remove

It was their usual manner to remove, when they had done any mischief, lest they should be found out; and so they did at this time. We went about three or four miles, and there they built a great wigwam, big enough to hold an hundred Indians, which they did in preparation to a great day of dancing. They would say now amongst themselves, that the governor would be so angry for his loss at Sudbury, that he would send no more about the captives, which made me grieve and tremble. My sister being not far from the place where we now were, and hearing that I was here, desired her master to let her come and see me, and he was willing to it, and would go with her; but she being ready before him, told him she would go before, and was come within a mile or two of the place. Then he overtook her, and began to rant as if he had been mad, and made her go back again in the rain; so that I never saw her till I saw her in Charlestown. But the Lord requited many of their ill doings, for this Indian her master, was hanged afterward at Boston. The Indians now began to come from all quarters, against their merry dancing day. Among some of them came one goodwife Kettle. I told her my heart was so heavy that it was ready to break. "So is mine too," said she, but yet said, "I hope we shall hear some good news shortly." I could hear how earnestly my sister desired to see me, and I as earnestly desired to see her; and yet neither of us could get an opportunity. My daughter was also now about a mile off, and I had not seen her in nine or ten weeks, as I had not seen my sister since our first taking. I earnestly desired them to let me go and see them: yea, I entreated, begged, and persuaded them, but to let me see my daughter; and yet so hard-hearted were they, that they would not suffer it. They made use of their tyrannical power whilst they had it; but through the Lord's wonderful mercy, their time was now but short.

On a Sabbath day, the sun being about an hour high in the afternoon, came Mr. John Hoar (the council permitting him, and his own foreward spirit inclining him), together with the two forementioned Indians, Tom and Peter, with their third letter from the council. When they came near, I was abroad. Though I saw them not, they presently called me in, and bade me sit down and not stir. Then they catched up their guns, and away they ran, as if an enemy had been at hand, and the guns went off apace. I manifested some great trouble, and they asked me what was the matter? I told them I thought they had killed the Englishman (for they had in the meantime informed me that an Englishman was come). They said, no. They shot over his horse and under and before his horse, and they pushed him this way and that way, at their pleasure, showing what they could do. Then they let them come to their wigwams. I begged of them to let me see the Englishman, but they would not. But there was I fain to sit their pleasure. When they had talked their fill with him, they suffered me to go to him. We asked each other of our welfare, and how my husband did, and all my friends? He told me they were all well, and would be glad to see me. Amongst other things which my husband sent me, there came a pound of tobacco, which I sold for nine shillings in money; for many of the Indians for want of tobacco, smoked hemlock, and ground ivy. It was a great mistake in any, who thought I sent for tobacco; for through the favor of God, that desire was overcome. I now asked them whether I should go home with Mr. Hoar? They answered no, one and another of them, and it being night, we lay down with that answer. In the morning Mr. Hoar invited the Sagamores to dinner; but when we went to get it ready we found that they had stolen the greatest part of the provision Mr. Hoar had brought, out of his bags, in the night. And we may see the wonderful power of God, in that one passage, in that when there was such a great number of the Indians together, and so greedy of a little good food, and no English there but Mr. Hoar and myself, that there they did not knock us in the head, and take what we had, there being not only some provision, but also trading-cloth, a part of the twenty pounds agreed upon. But instead of doing us any mischief, they seemed to be ashamed of the fact, and said, it were some matchit Indian that did it. Oh, that we could believe that there is nothing too hard for God! God showed His power over the heathen in this, as He did over the hungry lions when Daniel was cast into the den. Mr. Hoar called them betime to dinner, but they ate very little, they being so busy in dressing themselves, and getting ready for their dance, which was carried on by eight of them, four men and four squaws. My master and mistress being two. He was dressed in his holland shirt, with great laces sewed at the tail of it; he had his silver buttons, his white stockings, his garters were hung round with shillings, and he had girdles of wampum upon his head and shoulders. She had a kersey coat, and covered with girdles of wampum from the loins upward. Her arms from her elbows to her hands were covered with bracelets; there were handfuls of necklaces about her neck, and several sorts of jewels in her ears. She had fine red stockings, and white shoes, her hair powdered and face painted red, that was always before black. And all the dancers were after the same manner. There were two others singing and knocking on a kettle for their music. They kept hopping up and down one after another, with a kettle of water in the midst, standing warm upon some embers, to drink of when they were dry. They held on till it was almost night, throwing out wampum to the standers by. At night I asked them again, if I should go home? They all as one said no, except my husband would come for me. When we were lain down, my master went out of the wigwam, and by and by sent in an Indian called James the Printer, who told Mr. Hoar, that my master would let me go home tomorrow, if he would let him have one pint of liquors. Then Mr. Hoar called his own Indians, Tom and Peter, and bid them go and see whether he would promise it before them three; and if he would, he should have it; which he did, and he had it. Then Philip smelling the business called me to him, and asked me what I would give him, to tell me some good news, and speak a good word for me. I told him I could not tell what to give him. I would [give him] anything I had, and asked him what he would have? He said two coats and twenty shillings in money, and half a bushel of seed corn, and some tobacco. I thanked him for his love; but I knew the good news as well as the crafty fox. My master after he had had his drink, quickly came ranting into the wigwam again, and called for Mr. Hoar, drinking to him, and saying, he was a good man, and then again he would say, "hang him rogue." Being almost drunk, he would drink to him, and yet presently say he should be hanged. Then he called for me. I trembled to hear him, yet I was fain to go to him, and he drank to me, showing no incivility. He was the first Indian I saw drunk all the while that I was amongst them. At last his squaw ran out, and he after her, round the wigwam, with his money jingling at his knees. But she escaped him. But having an old squaw he ran to her; and so through the Lord's mercy, we were no more troubled that night. Yet I had not a comfortable night's rest; for I think I can say, I did not sleep for three nights together. The night before the letter came from the council, I could not rest, I was so full of fears and troubles, God many times leaving us most in the dark, when deliverance is nearest. Yea, at this time I could not rest night nor day. The next night I was overjoyed, Mr. Hoar being come, and that with such good tidings. The third night I was even swallowed up with the thoughts of things, viz. that ever I should go home again; and that I must go, leaving my children behind me in the wilderness; so that sleep was now almost departed from mine eyes.

On Tuesday morning they called their general court (as they call it) to consult and determine, whether I should go home or no. And they all as one man did seemingly consent to it, that I should go home; except Philip, who would not come among them.

But before I go any further, I would take leave to mention a few remarkable passages of providence, which I took special notice of in my afflicted time.

1. Of the fair opportunity lost in the long march, a little after the fort fight, when our English army was so numerous, and in pursuit of the enemy, and so near as to take several and destroy them, and the enemy in such distress for food that our men might track them by their rooting in the earth for ground nuts, whilst they were flying for their lives. I say, that then our army should want provision, and be forced to leave their pursuit and return homeward; and the very next week the enemy came upon our town, like bears bereft of their whelps, or so many ravenous wolves, rending us and our lambs to death. But what shall I say? God seemed to leave his People to themselves, and order all things for His own holy ends. Shall there be evil in the City and the Lord hath not done it? They are not grieved for the affliction of Joseph, therefore shall they go captive, with the first that go captive. It is the Lord's doing, and it should be marvelous in our eyes.
2. I cannot but remember how the Indians derided the slowness, and dullness of the English army, in its setting out. For after the desolations at Lancaster and Medfield, as I went along with them, they asked me when I thought the English army would come after them? I told them I could not tell. "It may be they will come in May," said they. Thus did they scoff at us, as if the English would be a quarter of a year getting ready.

3. Which also I have hinted before, when the English army with new supplies were sent forth to pursue after the enemy, and they understanding it, fled before them till they came to Banquang river, where they forthwith went over safely; that that river should be impassable to the English. I can but admire to see the wonderful providence of God in preserving the heathen for further affliction to our poor country. They could go in great numbers over, but the English must stop. God had an over-ruling hand in all those things.
4. It was thought, if their corn were cut down, they would starve and die with hunger, and all their corn that could be found, was destroyed, and they driven from that little they had in store, into the woods in the midst of winter; and yet how to admiration did the Lord preserve them for His holy ends, and the destruction of many still amongst the English! strangely did the Lord provide for them; that I did not see (all the time I was among them) one man, woman, or child, die with hunger.

Though many times they would eat that, that a hog or a dog would hardly touch; yet by that God strengthened them to be a scourge to His people.

The chief and commonest food was ground nuts. They eat also nuts and acorns, artichokes, lilly roots, ground beans, and several other weeds and roots, that I know not.

They would pick up old bones, and cut them to pieces at the joints, and if they were full of worms and maggots, they would scald them over the fire to make the vermine come out, and then boil them, and drink up the liquor, and then beat the great ends of them in a mortar, and so eat them. They would eat horse's guts, and ears, and all sorts of wild birds which they could catch; also bear, venison, beaver, tortoise, frogs, squirrels, dogs, skunks, rattlesnakes; yea, the very bark of trees; besides all sorts of creatures, and provision which they plundered from the English. I can but stand in admiration to see the wonderful power of God in providing for such a vast number of our enemies in the wilderness, where there was nothing to be seen, but from hand to mouth. Many times in a morning, the generality of them would eat up all they had, and yet have some further supply against they wanted. It is said, "Oh, that my People had hearkened to me, and Israel had walked in my ways, I should soon have subdued their Enemies, and turned my hand against their Adversaries" (Psalm 81.13-14). But now our perverse and evil carriages in the sight of the Lord, have so offended Him, that instead of turning His hand against them, the Lord feeds and nourishes them up to be a scourge to the whole land.

5. Another thing that I would observe is the strange providence of God, in turning things about when the Indians was at the highest, and the English at the lowest. I was with the enemy eleven weeks and five days, and not one week passed without the fury of the enemy, and some desolation by fire and sword upon one place or other. They mourned

> (with their black faces) for their own losses, yet triumphed and rejoiced in their inhumane, and many times devilish cruelty to the English. They would boast much of their victories; saying that in two hours time they had destroyed such a captain and his company at such a place; and boast how many towns they had destroyed, and then scoff, and say they had done them a good turn to send them to Heaven so soon. Again, they would say this summer that they would knock all the rogues in the head, or drive them into the sea, or make them fly the country; thinking surely, Agag-like, "The bitterness of Death is past." Now the heathen begins to think all is their own, and the poor Christians' hopes to fail (as to man) and now their eyes are more to God, and their hearts sigh heavenward; and to say in good earnest, "Help Lord, or we perish." When the Lord had brought His people to this, that they saw no help in anything but Himself; then He takes the quarrel into His own hand; and though they had made a pit, in their own imaginations, as deep as hell for the Christians that summer, yet the Lord hurled themselves into it. And the Lord had not so many ways before to preserve them, but now He hath as many to destroy them.

But to return again to my going home, where we may see a remarkable change of providence. At first they were all against it, except my husband would come for me, but afterwards they assented to it, and seemed much to rejoice in it; some asked me to send them some bread, others some tobacco, others shaking me by the hand, offering me a hood and scarfe to ride in; not one moving hand or tongue against it. Thus hath the Lord answered my poor desire, and the many earnest requests of others put up unto God for me. In my travels an Indian came to me and told me, if I were willing, he and his squaw would run away, and go home along with me. I told him no: I was not willing to run away, but desired to wait God's time, that I might go home quietly, and without fear. And now God hath granted me my desire. O the wonderful power of God that I have seen, and the experience that I have had. I have been in the midst of those roaring lions, and savage bears, that feared neither God, nor man, nor the devil, by night and day, alone and in company, sleeping all sorts together, and yet not one of them ever offered me the least abuse of unchastity to me, in word or action. Though some are ready to say I speak it for my own credit; but I speak it in the presence of God, and to His Glory. God's power is as great now, and as sufficient to save, as when He preserved Daniel in the lion's den; or the three children in the fiery furnace. I may well say as his Psalm 107.12 "Oh give thanks unto the Lord for he is good, for his mercy endureth for ever." Let the redeemed of the Lord say so, whom He hath redeemed from the hand of the enemy, especially that I should come away in the midst of so many hundreds of enemies quietly and peaceably, and not a dog moving his tongue. So I took my leave of them, and in coming along my heart melted into tears, more than all the while I was with them, and I was almost swallowed up with the thoughts that ever I should go home again. About the sun going down, Mr. Hoar, and myself, and the two Indians came to Lancaster, and a solemn sight it was to me. There had I lived many comfortable years amongst my relations and neighbors, and now not one Christian to be seen, nor one house left standing. We went on to a farmhouse that was yet standing, where we lay all night, and a comfortable lodging we had, though nothing but straw to lie on. The Lord preserved us in safety that night, and raised us up again in the morning, and carried us along, that before noon, we came to Concord. Now was I full of joy, and yet not without sorrow; joy to see such a lovely sight, so many Christians together, and some of them my neighbors. There I met with my brother, and my brother-in-law, who asked me, if I knew where his wife was? Poor heart! he had helped to bury her, and knew it not. She being shot down by the house was partly burnt, so that those who were at Boston at the desolation of the town, and came back afterward, and buried the dead, did not know her. Yet I was not without sorrow, to think how many were looking and longing, and my own children amongst the rest, to enjoy that deliverance that I had now received, and I did not know whether ever I should see them again. Being recruited with food and raiment we went to Boston that day, where I met with my dear husband, but the thoughts of our dear children, one being dead, and the other we could not tell where, abated our comfort each to other. I was not before so much hemmed in with the merciless and cruel heathen, but now as much with pitiful, tender-hearted and compassionate Christians. In that poor, and distressed, and beggarly condition I was received in; I was kindly entertained in several houses. So much love I received from several (some of whom I knew, and others I knew not) that I am not capable to declare it. But the Lord knows them all by name. The Lord reward them sevenfold into their bosoms of His spirituals, for their temporals. The twenty pounds, the price of my redemption, was raised by some Boston gentlemen, and Mrs. Usher, whose bounty and religious charity, I would not forget to make mention of. Then Mr. Thomas Shepard of Charlestown received us into his house, where we continued eleven weeks; and a father and mother they were to us. And many more tender-hearted friends we met with in that place. We were now in the midst of love, yet not without much and frequent heaviness of heart for our poor children, and other relations, who were still in affliction. The week following, after my coming in, the governor and council sent forth to the Indians again; and that not without success; for they brought in my sister, and goodwife Kettle. Their not knowing where our children were was a sore trial to us still, and yet we were not without secret hopes that we should see them again. That which was dead lay heavier upon my spirit, than those which were alive and amongst the heathen: thinking how it suffered with its wounds, and I was no way able to relieve it; and how it was buried by the heathen in the wilderness from among all Christians. We were hurried up and down in our thoughts, sometime we should hear a report that they were gone this way, and sometimes that; and that they were come in, in this place or that. We kept inquiring and listening to hear concerning them, but no certain news as yet. About this time the council had ordered a day of public thanksgiving. Though I thought I had still cause of mourning, and being unsettled in our minds, we thought we would ride toward the eastward, to see if we could hear anything concerning our children. And as we were riding along (God is the wise disposer of all things) between Ipswich and Rowley we met with Mr. William Hubbard, who told us that our son Joseph was come in to Major Waldron's, and another with him, which was my sister's son. I asked him how he knew it? He said the major himself told him so. So along we went till we came to Newbury; and their minister being absent, they desired my husband to preach the thanksgiving for them; but he was not willing to stay there that night, but would go over to Salisbury, to hear further, and come again in the morning, which he did, and preached there that day. At night, when he had done, one came and told him that his daughter was come in at Providence. Here was mercy on both hands. Now hath God fulfilled that precious Scripture which was such a comfort to me in my distressed condition. When my heart was ready to sink into the earth (my children being gone, I could not tell whither) and my knees trembling under me, and I was walking through the valley of the shadow of death; then the Lord brought, and now has fulfilled that reviving word unto me: "Thus saith the Lord, Refrain thy voice from weeping, and thine eyes from tears, for thy Work shall be rewarded, saith the Lord, and they shall come again from the Land of the Enemy." Now we were between them, the one on the east, and the other on the west. Our son being nearest, we went to him first, to Portsmouth, where we met with him, and with the Major also, who told us he had done what he could, but could not redeem him under seven pounds, which the good people thereabouts were pleased to pay. The Lord reward the major, and all the rest, though unknown to me, for their labor of Love. My sister's son was redeemed for four pounds, which the council gave order for the payment of. Having now received one of our children, we hastened toward the other. Going back through Newbury my husband preached there on the Sabbath day; for which they rewarded him many fold.

On Monday we came to Charlestown, where we heard that the governor of Rhode Island had sent over for our daughter, to take care of her, being now within his jurisdiction; which should not pass without our acknowledgments. But she being nearer Rehoboth than Rhode Island, Mr. Newman went over, and took care of her and brought her to his own house. And the goodness of God was admirable to us in our low estate, in that He raised up passionate friends on every side to us, when we had nothing to recompense any for their love. The Indians were now gone that way, that it was apprehended dangerous to go to her. But the carts which carried provision to the English army, being guarded, brought her with them to Dorchester, where we received her safe. Blessed be the Lord for it, for great is His power, and He can do whatsoever seemeth Him good. Her coming in was after this manner: she was traveling one day with the Indians, with her basket at her back; the company of Indians were got before her, and gone out of sight, all except one squaw; she followed the squaw till night, and then both of them lay down, having nothing over them but the heavens and under them but the earth. Thus she traveled three days together, not knowing whither she was going; having nothing to eat or drink but water, and green hirtle-berries. At last they came into Providence, where she was kindly entertained by several of that town. The Indians often said that I should never have her under twenty pounds. But now the Lord hath brought her in upon free-cost, and given her to me the second time. The Lord make us a blessing indeed, each to others. Now have I seen that Scripture also fulfilled, "If any of thine be driven out to the outmost parts of heaven, from thence will the Lord thy God gather thee, and from thence will he fetch thee. And the Lord thy God will put all these curses upon thine enemies, and on them which hate thee, which persecuted thee" (Deuteronomy 30.4-7). Thus hath the Lord brought me and mine out of that horrible pit, and hath set us in the midst of tender-hearted and compassionate Christians. It is the desire of my soul that we may walk worthy of the mercies received, and which we are receiving.

Our family being now gathered together (those of us that were living), the South Church in Boston hired an house for us. Then we removed from Mr. Shepard's, those cordial friends, and went to Boston, where we continued about three-quarters of a year. Still the Lord went along with us, and provided graciously for us. I thought it somewhat strange to set up house-keeping with bare walls; but as Solomon says, "Money answers all things" and that we had through the benevolence of Christian friends, some in this town, and some in that, and others; and some from England; that in a little time we might look, and see the house furnished with love. The Lord hath been exceeding good to us in our low estate, in that when we had neither house nor home, nor other necessaries, the Lord so moved the hearts of these and those towards us, that we wanted neither food, nor raiment for ourselves or ours: "There is a Friend which sticketh closer than a Brother" (Proverbs 18.24). And how many such friends have we found, and now living amongst? And truly such a friend have we found him to be unto us, in whose house we lived, viz. Mr. James Whitcomb, a friend unto us near hand, and afar off.

I can remember the time when I used to sleep quietly without workings in my thoughts, whole nights together, but now it is other ways with me. When all are fast about me, and no eye open, but His who ever waketh, my thoughts are upon things past, upon the awful dispensation of the Lord towards us, upon His wonderful power and might, in carrying of us through so many difficulties, in returning us in safety, and suffering none to hurt us. I remember in the night season, how the other day I was in the midst of thousands of enemies, and nothing but death before me. It is then hard work to persuade myself, that ever I should be satisfied with bread again. But now we are fed with the finest of the wheat, and, as I may say, with honey out of the rock. Instead of the husk, we have the fatted calf. The thoughts of these things in the particulars of them, and of the love and goodness of God towards us, make it true of me, what David said of himself, "I watered my Couch with my tears" (Psalm 6.6). Oh! the wonderful power of God that mine eyes have seen, affording matter enough for my thoughts to run in, that when others are sleeping mine eyes are weeping.

I have seen the extreme vanity of this world: One hour I have been in health, and wealthy, wanting nothing. But the next hour in sickness and wounds, and death, having nothing but sorrow and affliction.

Before I knew what affliction meant, I was ready sometimes to wish for it. When I lived in prosperity, having the comforts of the world about me, my relations by me, my heart cheerful, and taking little care for anything, and yet seeing many, whom I preferred before myself, under many trials and afflictions, in sickness, weakness, poverty, losses, crosses, and cares of the world, I should be sometimes jealous least I should have my portion in this life, and that Scripture would come to my mind, "For whom the Lord loveth he chasteneth, and scourgeth every Son whom he receiveth" (Hebrews 12.6). But now I see the Lord had His time to scourge and chasten me. The portion of some is to have their afflictions by drops, now one drop and then another; but the dregs of the cup, the wine of astonishment, like a sweeping rain that leaveth no food, did the Lord prepare to be my portion. Affliction I wanted, and affliction I had, full measure (I thought), pressed down and running over. Yet I see, when God calls a person to anything, and through never so many difficulties, yet He is fully able to carry them through and make them see, and say they have been gainers thereby. And I hope I can say in some measure, as David did, "It is good for me that I have been afflicted." The Lord hath showed me the vanity of these outward things. That they are the vanity of vanities, and vexation of spirit, that they are but a shadow, a blast, a bubble, and things of no continuance. That we must rely on God Himself, and our whole dependance must be upon Him. If trouble from smaller matters begin to arise in me, I have something at hand to check myself with, and say, why am I troubled? It was but the other day that if I had had the world, I would have given it for my freedom, or to have been a servant to a Christian. I have learned to look beyond present and smaller troubles, and to be quieted under them. As Moses said, "Stand still and see the salvation of the Lord" (Exodus 14.13).

2.9.2 Reading and Review Questions

1. How does Rowlandson's view of Providence—including God's providence in preserving Native Americans—relate to that of Bradford's, Winthrop's, and Bradstreet's? Why?
2. How does Rowlandson's theodicy compare with Winthrop's? Why?
3. What interpretation does Rowlandson give to Native American's social behavior and practices? Consider her view of their use of tobacco—which she had herself used before her captivity.
4. How and why does Rowlandson distinguish her Christian virtues and behavior from the behavior of the Native Americans towards her, and from the Christianity of what she calls Praying-Indians? Why?
5. How, if at all, does Rowlandson's captivity become a sort of felix culpa (or fortunate fall) bringing her closer to an understanding and appreciation of God's mercies?

2.10 EDWARD TAYLOR

(c. 1642–1729)

Little is known of Edward Taylor's early life in England. His poetry displays a Leicestershire dialect; he was probably born in Sketchly, Leicestershire County, where his father was a yeoman farmer. He may have been educated in England. He seems to have read and been influenced by seventeenth-century English literature, including John Milton's (1608–1674) epic poetry and the Metaphysical poetry of John Donne and George Herbert (1593–1633). Epics are long, heroic poems tied to a nation's history. Metaphysical poetry is a type of highly intellectual, complex poetry using unexpected metaphors, incongruous imagery, and such linguistic feats as puns and paradoxes.

To escape the religious controversies and persecutions of the early 1660s and to avoid signing an oath of loyalty to the Church of England, Taylor emigrated to America in 1668. He studied at Harvard for three years and eschewed the teaching profession (that he practiced for a few years) for that of the ministry. In 1671, he was called to serve as minister at Westfield, Massachusetts, where he lived for the remainder of his life. He maintained friendships with such prominent Puritans as Increase Mather (1639–1723) and Samuel Sewall (1652–1730); married twice; fathered fourteen children; upheld Puritan theocracy; and wrote poetry.

None of his poetry was published during Taylor's lifetime. His poems were discovered by Thomas H. Johnson in the 1930s at the Yale Library. They had been deposited there by Ezra Stiles (1727–1795), Taylor's grandson and a President of Yale. Taylor seems to have written his poems as private devotions and communions with God. They express his rejection of worldly matters and dependence on God in his own struggle against Satan and evil. In his *Preparatory Meditations*, for example, Taylor prepares to celebrate the Lord's Supper and so ponders the mystery of the incarnation, of God as flesh, and the transubstantiation of God's blood and flesh into the wine and bread of the communion. Their variety of genres–including elegies, lyrics, and meditations–attests to his education in the classics and modern languages. Their original use of the metaphysical conceits (metaphors that yoke together two apparently highly dissimilar things), paradoxes, and puns attest to the Puritan God that was Taylor's absolute that drew together all incongruities. The poems' domestic details of everyday life reveal not only his Puritan faith but also seventeenth-century life in America.

2.10.1 "Prologue" to *Preparatory Meditations*

Lord, Can a Crumb of Earth the Earth outweigh:
    Outmatch all mountains, nay the Chrystall Sky?
Imbosom in't designs that shall Display
    And trace into the Boundless Deity?
    Yea, hand a Pen whose moysture doth guild ore
    Eternall Glory with a glorious glore.

If it its Pen had of an Angels Quill,
And sharpend on a Pretious Stone ground tite,
And dipt in Liquid Gold, and mov'de by skill
In Christall leaves should golden Letters write,
It would but blot and blur: yea, jag and jar,
Unless thou mak'st the Pen and Scribener.

I am this Crumb of Dust which is design'd
To make my Pen unto thy Praise alone,
And my dull Phancy I would gladly grinde
Unto an Edge on Zions Pretious Stone:
And Write in Liquid Gold upon thy Name
My Letters till thy glory forth doth flame.

Let not th' attempts breake down my Dust I pray,
Nor laugh thou them to scorn, but pardon give.
Inspire this Crumb of Dust till it display
Thy Glory through 't: and then thy dust shall live.
Its failings then thou'lt overlook I trust,
They being Slips slipt from thy Crumb of Dust.

Thy Crumb of Dust breaths two words from its breast;
That thou wilt guide its pen to write aright
To Prove thou art, and that thou art the best,
And shew thy Properties to shine most bright.
And then thy Works will shine as flowers on Stems,
Or as in Jewellary Shops, do jems.

2.10.2 "Preface" to *God's Determination*

Infinity, when all things it beheld,
In Nothing, and of Nothing all did build,
Upon what Base was fixt the Lath, wherein
He turn'd this Globe, and riggalld it so trim?
Who blew the Bellows of his Furnace Vast?
Or held the Mould wherein the world was Cast?
Who laid its Corner Stone? Or whose Command?
Where stand the Pillars upon which it stands?
Who Lac'de and Fillitted the earth so fine,
With Rivers like green Ribbons Smaragdine?
Who made the Sea's its Selvedge, and it locks
Like a Quilt Ball within a Silver Box?
Who Spread its Canopy? Or Curtains Spun?
Who in this Bowling Alley bowld the Sun?

Who made it always when it rises set:
To go at once both down, and up to get?
Who th' Curtain rods made for this Tapistry?
Who hung the twinckling Lanthorns in the Sky?
Who? who did this? or who is he? Why, know
It's Onely Might Almighty this did doe.
His hand hath made this noble worke which Stands
His Glorious Handywork not made by hands.
Who spake all things from nothing; and with ease
Can speake all things to nothing, if he please.
Whose Little finger at his pleasure Can
Out mete ten thousand worlds with halfe a Span:
Whose Might Almighty can by half a looks
Root up the rocks and rock the hills by th' roots.
Can take this mighty World up in his hande,
And shake it like a Squitchen or a Wand.
Whose single Frown will make the Heavens shake
Like as an aspen leafe the Winde makes quake.
Oh! what a might is this! Whose single frown
Doth shake the world as it would shake it down?
Which All from Nothing fet, from Nothing, All:
Hath All on Nothing set, lets Nothing fall.
Gave All to nothing Man indeed, whereby
Through nothing man all might him Glorify.
In Nothing is imbosst the brightest Gem
More pretious than all pretiousness in them.
But Nothing man did throw down all by sin:
And darkened that lightsom Gem in him,
    That now his Brightest Diamond is grown
    Darker by far than any Coalpit Stone.

2.10.3 "Meditation 8" (First Series)

John VI: 5i: I am the living bread.

I ken[n]ing through Astronomy Divine
    The Worlds bright Battlement, wherein I spy
A Golden Path my Pensill cannot line
    From that bright Throne unto my Threshold ly.
    And while my puzzled thoughts about it pore,
    I find the Bread of Life in't at my doore.

When that this Bird of Paradise put in
    This Wicker Cage (my Corps) to tweedle praise

Had peckt the Fruite forbid: and so did fling
    Away its Food, and lost its golden dayes,
    It fell into Celestiall Famine sore,
    And never could attain a morsell more.

Alas! alas! Poore Bird, what wilt thou doe?
    This Creatures field no food for Souls e're gave:
And if thou knock at Angells dores, they show
    An Empty Barrell: they no soul bread have.
    Alas! Poore Bird, the Worlds White Loafe is done,
    And cannot yield thee here the smallest Crumb.

In this sad state, Gods Tender Bowells run
    Out streams of Grace: And he to end all strife,
The Purest Wheate in Heaven, his deare-dear Son
    Grinds, and kneads up into this Bread of Life:
    Which Bread of Life from Heaven down came and stands
    Disht in thy Table up by Angells Hands.

Did God mould up this Bread in Heaven, and bake,
    Which from his Table came, and to thine goeth?
Doth he bespeake thee thus: This Soule Bread take;
    Come, Eate thy fill of this, thy Gods White Loafe?
    Its Food too fine for Angells; yet come, take
    And Eate thy fill! Its Heavens Sugar Cake.

What Grace is this knead in this Loafe? This thing
    Souls are but petty things it to admire.
Yee Angells, help: This fill would to the brim
    Heav'ns whelm'd-down Chrystall meele Bowle, yea and higher.
    This Bread of Life dropt in thy mouth doth Cry:
    Eate, Eate me, Soul, and thou shalt never dy.

2.10.4 "Medication 32" (First Series)

https://allpoetry.com/Preparatory-Meditations---First-Series:-32

2.10.5 "A Fig for Thee, O Death"

https://www.poetrynook.com/poem/fig-thee-oh-death

2.10.6 "Upon Wedlock, and Death of Children"

A Curious Knot God made in Paradise,
    And drew it out inamled neatly Fresh.

It was the True-Love Knot, more sweet than spice,
And set with all the flowres of Graces dress.
Its Weddens Knot, that ne're can be unti'de:
No Alexanders Sword can it divide.

The slips here planted, gay and glorious grow:
Unless an Hellish breath do sindge their Plumes.
Here Primrose, Cowslips, Roses, Lilies blow,
With Violets and Pinkes that voide perfumes:
Whose beautious leaves are lac'd with Hony Dew,
And Chanting birds Chirp out Sweet Musick true.

When in this Knot I planted was, my Stock
Soon knotted, and a manly flower out brake.
And after it my branch again did knot:
Brought out another Flowre: its sweet breath'd mate.
One knot gave tother and tothers place;
Thence Checkling Smiles fought in each others face.

But oh! a glorious hand from glory came,
Guarded with Angells, soon did Crop this flowre,
Which almost tore the root up of the same,
At that unlookt for, Dolesome, darksome houre.
In Pray're to Christ perfum'de it did ascend,
And Angells bright did it to heaven tend.

But pausing on't this Sweet perfum'd my thought,
Christ would in Glory have a Flowre, Choice, Prime.
And having Choice, chose this my branch forth brought.
Lord, take! I thanke thee, thou takst ought of mine;
It is my pledg in glory; part of mee
Is now in it, Lord, glorifi'de with thee.

But praying o're my branch, my branch did sprout,
And bore another manly flower, and gay,
And after that another, sweet brake out,
The which the former hand soon got away.
But oh I the torture, Vomit, screechings, groans:
And six weeks fever would pierce hearts like stones.

Griefe o're doth flow: and nature fault would finde
Were not thy Will my Spell, Charm, Joy, and Gem:
That as I said, I say, take, Lord, they're thine:

I piecemeale pass to Glory bright in them.
I joy, may I sweet Flowers for Glory breed,
Whether thou getst them green, or lets them seed.

2.10.7 Reading and Review Questions

1. In "Prologue," when referring to himself as a poet, why does Taylor describe himself as a crumb of dust? How does this self-representation compare to those of Bradstreet's and Wigglesworth's?
2. In "Preface to God's Determination," why and to what effect does Taylor present God's creation in terms of craftsmanship and domesticity?
3. What metaphors, or metaphysical conceits, does Taylor use in "Meditation 32" and "Meditation 8"? How does Taylor make their dissimilar elements similar? To what end?
4. In "A Fig for Thee, O Death," why does Taylor refer to his body as a strumpet? In what other ways does he refer to his body? What do these metaphors, or metaphysical conceits, have in common?
5. In "Upon Wedlock, and Death of Children," how does Taylor console himself for the loss of his child Elizabeth? How does his consolation compare with those of Bradstreet's for her losses?

2.11 SAMUEL SEWALL

(1652–1730)

Samuel Sewall was born in England to a wealthy family that had property in Massachusetts. Upon the Restoration of the Monarchy with Charles II's accession to the throne, the Sewall family emigrated to New England. There, Sewall continued his education and graduated from Harvard in 1674 with an MA. Soon thereafter, he married Hannah Hull (d. 1717), daughter of the wealthy John Hull (1624–1683), Master of the Mint of Massachusetts Bay Colony. Sewall remained in Boston, where he took his place as one of its wealthiest citizens. Despite his wealth, Sewall devoted much of his life to public service, a life he recorded in his now famous *Diary*.

Image 2.11 | Samuel Sewell
Artist | John Smybert
Source | Wikimedia Commons
License | Public Domain

Sewall managed Boston's printing press and served as deputy of the General Court in 1683 and as member of the Council from 1684 to 1686. He helped negotiate a restoration of the Massachusetts Charter, causing him to stay in England almost a full year. A new Charter was granted in 1692; it named Sewall as member of the Council, a position he held for thirty-three years. Also in 1692, he was appointed justice of the Superior Court; he eventually rose to be chief justice of Massachusetts (1718–1728).

Sir William Phips (1651–1695), the new governor of Massachusetts, placed Sewall as one of the three judges at the Salem witch trials (1692–1693) that condemned twelve people to death, eleven by hanging and one by pressing. Four years later, Sewall became the only one of these three judges to recant his judgment.

In 1700, he published what is thought to be the first American antislavery tract: *The Selling of Joseph: A Memorial.* Its title derives from the Biblical account of Joseph being sold into slavery in Egypt by his own brothers. The title speaks to Sewall's view that God's covenant with Adam and Eve gave all their "heirs" liberty. He countered arguments claiming blacks' descent from Noah's cursed son Ham—condemned to be slave to his brothers—and pointed to the Bible's prohibition against kidnapping, an act by which most blacks were enslaved. Sewall maintained his views against slavery in the *Boston News-Letter* (June 12, 1706) and expanded upon them in his *Diary*. This *Diary,* which he kept from 1673 to 1729, was not published until 1787.

Image 2.12 | Slaves working in 17th-century Virginia
Artist | Unknown
Source | Wikimedia Commons
License | Public Domain

2.11.1 "The Selling of Joseph: A Memorial" (1700)

Forasmuch *as* Liberty *is in real value next unto* Life: *None ought to part with* it themselves, or deprive others of it, but upon most mature Consideration.

The Numerousness of Slaves at this day in the Province, and the Uneasiness of them under their Slavery, hath put many upon thinking whether the Foundation of it be firmly and well laid; so as to sustain the Vast Weight that is built upon it. It is most certain that all Men, as they are the Sons of *Adam*, are Coheirs; and have equal Right unto Liberty, and all other outward Comforts of Life. GOD *hath given the Earth* [with all its Commodities] *unto the Sons of Adam, Psal* 115. 16. *And hath made of One Blood, all Nations of Men, for to dwell on all the face of the Earth; and hath determined the Times before appointed, and the bounds of their habitation: That they should seek the Lord. Forasmuch then as we are the Offspring of GOD* &c. Act 17.26, 27, 29. Now although the Title given by the last ADAM, doth infinitely better Mens Estates, respecting GOD and themselves; and grants them a most beneficial and inviolable Lease under the Broad Seal of Heaven, who were before only Tenants at Will: Yet through the Indulgence of GOD to our First Parents after the Fall, the outward Estate of all and every of the Children, remains the same, as to one another. So that Originally, and Naturally, there is no such thing as Slavery. *Joseph* was rightfully no more a Slave to his Brethren, then they were to him: and they had no more Authority to *Sell* him, than they had to *Slay* him. And if *they* had nothing to do to Sell him; the *Ishmaelites* bargaining with them, and paying down Twenty pieces of Silver, could not make a Title. Neither could *Potiphar* have any better Interest in him than the *Ishmaelites* had. Gen. 37. 20, 27, 28. For he that shall in this case plead *Alteration of Property*, seems to have forfeited a great part of his own claim to Humanity. There is no proportion between Twenty Pieces of Silver, and LIBERTY. The Commodity it self is the Claimer. If *Arabian* Gold be imported in any quantities, most are afraid to meddle with it, though they might have it at easy rates; lest if it should have been wrongfully taken from the Owners, it should kindle a fire to the Consumption of their whole Estate. 'Tis pity there should be more Caution used in buying a Horse, or a little lifeless dust; than there is in purchasing Men and Women: Whenas they are the Offspring of GOD, and their Liberty is,

----------------*Auro pretiosior Omni.*

And seeing GOD hath said, *He that Stealeth a Man and Selleth him, or if he be found in his hand, he shall surely be put to Death.* Exod. 12.16. This Law being of Everlasting Equity, wherein Man Stealing is ranked amongst the most atrocious of Capital Crimes: What louder Cry can there be made of the Celebrated Warning,

Caveat Emptor!

And all thing considered, it would conduce more to the Welfare of the Province, to have White Servants for a Term of Years, than to have Slaves for Life. Few can endure to hear of a Negro's being made free; and indeed they can seldom use their freedom well; yet their continual aspiring after their forbidden Liberty, renders them Unwilling Servants. And there is such a disparity in their Conditions, Color & Hair, that they can never embody with us, and grow up into orderly Families, to the Peopling of the Land: but still remain in our Body Politick as a kind of extravasat Blood. As many Negro men as there are among us, so many empty places there are in our Train Bands, and the places taken up of Men that might make Husbands for our Daughters. And the Sons and Daughters of *New England* would become more like *Jacob*, and *Rachel*, if this Slavery were thrust quite out of doors. Moreover it is too well known what Temptations Masters are under, to connive at the Fornification of their Slaves; lest they should be obliged to find them Wives, or pay their Fines. It seems to be practically pleaded that they might be Lawless; 'tis thought much of, that the Law should have Satisfaction for their Thefts, and other Immoralities; by which means, *Holiness to the Lord*, is more rarely engraven upon this sort of Servitude. It is likewise most lamentable to think, how in taking Negros out of *Africa*, and Selling of them here, That which GOD ha's joyned together men do boldly rend asunder; Men from their Country, Husbands from their Wives, Parents from their Children. How horrible is the Uncleanness, Mortality, if not Murder, that the Ships are guilty of that bring great Crouds of these miserable Men, and Women. Methinks, when we are bemoaning the barbarous Usage of our Friends and Kinsfolk in *Africa*: it might not be unseasonable to inquire whether we are not culpable in forcing the Africans to become Slaves amongst our selves. And it may be a question whether all the Benefit received by *Negro* Slaves, will balance the Accompt of Cash laid out upon them; and for the Redemption of our own enslaved Friends out of *Africa*. Besides all the Persons and Estates that have perished there.

Obj. 1. *These Blackamores are of the Posterity of Cham, and therefore are under the Curse of Slavery*. Gen. 9.25, 26, 27.

Answ. Of all Offices, one would not begg this; viz. Uncall'd for, to be an Executioner of the Vindictive Wrath of God; the extent and duration of which is to us uncertain. If this ever was a Commission; How do we know but that it is long since out of date? Many have found it to their Cost, that a Prophetical Denunciation of Judgment against a Person or People, would not warrant them to inflict that evil. If it would, *Hazael* might justify himself in all he did against his Master, and the *Israelites*, from 2 *Kings* 8. 10, 12.

But it is possible that by cursory reading, this Text may have been mistaken. For Canaan is the Person Cursed three times over, without the mentioning of Cham. Good Expositors suppose the Curse entailed on him, and that this Prophesie was accomplished in the Extirpation of the *Canaanites*, and in the Servitude of the *Gibeonites*, *Vide Pareum*. Whereas the Blackmores are not descended of *Canaan*, but of *Cush*. Psal. 68. 31. *Princes shall come out of Egypt* [Mizraim] *Ethopia* [Cush] *shall soon* stretch out her hands unto God. *Under which Names, all* Africa *may be comprehended; and the Promised Conversion ought to be prayed for*. Jer. *13, 23*. Can the Ethiopian change his skin? *This shews that Black Men are the Posterity of*

Cush: *Who* time out of mind have been distinguished by their Colour. And for want of the true, *Ovid* assigns a fabulous cause of it.

Sanguine tum credunt in corpora summa vocato
Æthiopum populos nigrum traxisse colorem.
Metamorph. lib.2.

Obj. 2. *The Nigers are brought out of a Pagan Country, into places where the Gospel is Preached.*

Answ. Evil must not be done, that good may come of it. The extraordinary and comprehensive Benefit accruing to the Church of God, and to *Joseph* personally, did not rectify his brethrens Sale of him.

Obj. 3. *The Africans have Wars with one another: our Ships bring lawful Captives taken in those Wars.*

Answ. For ought is known, their Wars are much such as were between *Jacob's* Sons and their Brother *Joseph*. If they be between Town and Town; Provincial, or National: Every War is upon one side Unjust. An Unlawful War can't make lawful Captives. And by Receiving, we are in danger to promote, and partake in their Barbarous Cruelties. I am sure, if some Gentlemen should go down to the *Brewsters* to take the Air, and Fish: And a stronger party from *Hull* should Surprise them, and Sell them for Slaves to a Ship outward bound: they would think themselves unjustly dealt with; both by Sellers and Buyers. And yet 'tis to be feared, we have no other kind of Title to our *Nigers. Therefore all things whatsoever ye would that men should do to you, do ye even so to them: for this is the Law and the Prophets.* Matt. 7. 12.

Obj. 4. *Abraham had servants bought with his Money, and born in his House.*

Answ. Until the Circumstances of *Abraham's* purchase be recorded, no Argument can be drawn from it. In the mean time, Charity obliges us to conclude, that He knew it was lawful and good.

It is Observable that the *Israelites* were strictly forbidden the buying, or selling one another for Slaves. *Levit.* 25. 39, 46. *Jer.* 34. 8——22. And GOD gaged His Blessing in lieu of any loss they might conceipt they suffered thereby. *Deut.* 15. 18. And since the partition Wall is broken down, inordinate Self love should likewise be demolished. GOD expects that Christians should be of a more Ingenuous and benign frame of spirit. Christians should carry it to all the World, as the *Israelites* were to carry it one towards another. And for men obstinately to persist in holding their Neighbours and Brethren under the Rigor of perpetual Bondage, seems to be no proper way of gaining Assurance that God ha's given them Spiritual Freedom. Our Blessed Saviour ha's altered the Measures of the Ancient Love-Song, and set it to a most Excellent New Tune, which all ought to be ambitious of Learning. *Matt.* 5. 43, 44. *John* 13. 34. These *Ethiopians*, as black as they are; seeing they are the Sons and Daughters of the First *Adam*, the Brethren and Sister of the Last ADAM, and the Offspring of GOD; They ought to be treated with a Respect agreeable.

Servitus perfecta voluntaria, inter Christianum & Christiainum, ex parte servi patientis saepe est licita, quia est necessaria: sed ex parte domini agentis, & procurando & exercendo, vix potest esse licita: quia non convenit regulae illi generali:

Quaecunque volueritis ut faciant vobis homines, ita & vos facite eis. Matt. 7.12.

Perfecta servitus poenae, non potest jure locum habere, nisi ex delicto gravi quod ultimum supplicum aliquo modo meretur: quia Libertas ex naturali aestimatione proxime accedit ad vitam ipsam, & eidem a multis proeferri solet.

Ames. Cas. Consc. Lib. 5. Cap. 23. Thes. 2, 3.

2.11.2 Reading and Review Questions

1. What intrinsic rights does Sewall attribute to Joseph? Why? How?
2. How does Sewall characterize slave-holders? What Biblical allusions does he make to shape this characterization?
3. What concrete distinctions does Sewall make between blacks and whites? Why? How do these distinctions support his condemnation of slavery?
4. How, and to what effect, does Sewall refute the argument that, because slave-holders bring blacks to the "light" of Christianity, slavery benefits blacks?
5. How convincing is Sewall's argument against slave-holders' using Abrahams purchase of servants as justification for their enslaving blacks? Why?

2.12 GABRIEL THOMAS

(1661–1714)

Gabriel Thomas was born at Poentmoil, Wales. A friend of William Penn and a member of the Society of Friends, Thomas sailed for Pennsylvania on the *John and Sarah*, arriving near the time of that colony's inception. He lived in Pennsylvania for fifteen years before returning to England. There, Thomas published his description in England, an account that sought to encourage settlements along the Delaware River. Eight or so years after the publication of his book, Thomas returned to America. He settled in Prime Hook Neck, in modern-day Delaware, where he died in 1714.

2.12.1 From *An Historical and Geographical Account of the Province and Country of Pensilvania; and of West-New-Jersey in America*

Pensilvania lies between the Latitude of Forty and Forty fire Degrees; *West-Jersey* on the East, *Virginia* the West, Mary-*Land* South, and *Canada* on the North. In Length three hundred, and in Breadth one hundred and eighty Miles.

The Natives, or first Inhabitants of this Country in their Original, are suppos'd by most People to have been of the Ten Scattered Tribes, for they resemble the *Jews* very much in the *Make* of their *Persons*, and *Tineture* of their *Complexions*: They observe New *Moons*, they offer their first Fruits to a *Maneto*, or suppos'd Deity, whereof they have two, one, as they fansie, above (good,) another below (bad,) and have a kind of *Feast* of *Tabernales*, laying their *Altars* upon *Twelve Stones*, observe a fort of *Mourning* twelve Months, *Customs of Women*, and many other *Rites* to be toucht (here) rather than dwelt upon, because they shall be handled more at large at the latter end of this Treatise.

They are very Charitable to one another, the Lame and the Blind (amongst them) living as well as the best; they are also very kind and obliging to the *Christians*.

The next that came there, were the *Dutch*, (who call'd the Country *New Neitherland*) between Fifty and Sixty Years ago, and were the First *Planters* in those Parts; but they made little or no Improvement, (applying themselves wholly to Trafique in Skins and Furs, which the *Indians* or *Natives* furnish'd them with, and which they Barter'd for Rum, Strong Liquors, and Sugar, with others, thereby gaining great Profit) till near the time or the Wars between *England* and *Them*, about Thirty or Forty Years ago.

Soon after them came the *Swedes* and *Fins*, who apply'd themselves to Husbandry, and were the first *Christian* People that made any considerable Improvement there.

There were some Disputes between these two Nations some Years, the *Dutch* looking upon the *Swedes* as Intruders upon their Purchase and Possession, which was absolutely terminated in the Surrender made by *John Rizeing* the Swedes Governour, to *Peter Styreant*, Governour for the *Dutch*, in 1655. In the *Holland* War about the Year 1665. Sir *Robert Carr* took the Country from the *Dutch* for the *English*, and left his Cousin, Captain *Carr*, Governor of that place; but in a short time after, the *Dutch* re-took the Country from the *English*, and kept it in their Possession till the Peace was concluded between the *English* and them, when the *Dutch* Surrendered that *Country* with *East* and *West-Jersey*, *New-York*, (with the whole Countries belonging to that Government) to the *English* again. But it remain'd with very little Impovement till the Year 1681. in which *William Penn* Esq; had the Country given him by King *Charles* the *Second*, in lieu of Money that was due to (and signal Service done by) his Father, Sir *William Penn* and from him bore the Name of *Pensilvania*.

Since that time, the Industrious (nay Indefatigable) Inhabitants have built a *Noble* and *Beautiful* City, and called it *Philadelphia*, which contains above two thousand Houses, all Inhabited; and most of them Stately, and of Brick, generally three Stories high, after the Mode in *London*, and as many several Families in each. There are very many *Lanes* and *Alley*, as first, *Huttons-Lane*, *Morris-Lane*, *Jones's-Lane*, wherein are very good Buildings. *Shorters-Alley*, *Towers-Lane*, *Wallers-Alley*, *Turners-Lane*, *Sikes-Alley* and *Flowers-Alley*. All these *Alleys* and *Lanes* extend from the *Front Street* to the *Second Street*. There is another Alley in the *Second Street,* called *Carters-Alley.* There are also besides these *Alleys* and *Lanes,* several fine *Squares* and *Courts* Within this Magnificent City, (for so I may justly call it,) As for the particular Names of the several Streets contained therein, the Principal areas follows, *viz, Walnut-Street, Vine-Street, Mulberry-Street, Chesnut-Street, Sassafras-Street,* taking their Names from the abundance of those Trees that formerly grew there; *High-Street, Broad-Street, Delaware-Street, Front-Street,* with several of less Note, too tedious to insert here.

It hath in it Three *Fairs* every Year, and Two *Markets* every Week, They kill above Twenty *Fat Bullocks* every Week, in the hottest time in Summer, for their present spending in that City, besides many *Sheep* , *Calves,* and *Hogs.*

This City is Situated between *Schoolkill-River* and the great River Delaware, which derives its Name from Captain *Delaware,* who came there pretty early: Ships of Two or Three Hundred Tuns may come up to this City, by either of these two Rivers. Moreover, in this Province are Four Great *Market-Towns,* viz, *Chester,* the German Town, *New-Caslle,* and *Lewis-Town,* which are mightily Enlarged in this latter Improvement. Between these Towns, the Water-Men constantly Ply their *Wherries;* like-wife all those Towns have *Fairs* kept in them, besides there are several Country Villages, *viz. Dublin, Harford, Merioneth,* and *Radnor* in *Cambry,* all which *Towns, Villages* and *Rivers,* took their Names from the several *Countries* whence the present Inhabitants came.

The *Air* here is very delicate, pleasant, and wholesom; the *Heavens* serene, rarely overcast, bearing mighty resemblance to the better part of *France;* after Rain they have commonly a very clear Sky, the Climate is something Colder in the depth of Winter, and Hotter in the height of Summer; (the cause of which is it. being a Main Land or Continent; the Days also are two Hours longer in the shortest Day in Winter, and shorter by two Hours in the longest Day of Summer) than here in *England,* which makes the Fruit so good, and the Earth so fertil.

The Corn-Harvest is ended before the middle of *July,* and most Years they have commonly between Twenty and Thirty Bushels of Wheat for every one they Sow. Their Ground is harrowed with Wooden Tyned Harrows, twice over in a, place is sufficient; twice mending of their Plow-Irons in a Years time will serve. Their Horses commonly go without being shod; two Men may clear between Twenty and Thirty Acres of Land in one Year, fit for the Plough, in which Oxen are chiefly us'd, though Horses are not wanting, and of them Good and well shap'd. A Cart or a Wain may go through the middle of the Woods, between the Trees without getting any damage, and of such Land in a convenient place, the Purchase will cost between *Ten* and *Fifteen Pounds* for a Hundred Acres. Here is much Meadow Ground. Poor People both Men and Women, will get near three times more Wages for their Labour in this Country, than they can earn either in *England* or *Wales.*

What is Inhabited of this Country, is divided into Six *Counties,* though there is not the Twentieth Part of it yet Peopled by the *Christians.* It hath in it several Navigable Rivers for Shipping to come in, besides the Capital *Celaware,* wherein a Ship of Two Hundred Tuns may Sail Two Hundred Miles up. There are also several other small Rivers, in number hardly Credible; these, as the Brooks, have for the most part gravelly and hard Bottoms; and it is suppos'd that there are many other further up in the Country, which are nor yet discover'd; the Names of the aforesaid Rivers, are, *Hoorkill-River*, alias *Lewis River*, which runs up to *Lewis Town*, the chiefest in *Suffex County*; *Cedar-River*, *Muskmellon-River*, all taking their Names from the great plenty of these things growing thereabouts; *Mother-kill* alias *Dover-River*, St. *Jones* alias *Cranbrook-River*, where one *John Curtice* lives, who hath Three Hundred Head of Neat Beasts, besides great Numbers of *Hogs*, *Horses* and *Sheep*; *Great Duck-River*, *Little Duck-River*, *Black-Bird-River*, these also took their Original Names from the great Numbers of those Fowls which are found there in vast quantities: *Apequinemy-River*, where their Goods come to be Carted over to *Mary-Land*, St. *George's-River*, *Christen-River*, *Brandy-Wine-River*, *Upland* alias *Chester-River*, which runs by *Chester-Town*, being the Shire or Country-Town; *Schoolkill-River*, *Frankford-River*, near which, *Arthur Cook* hath a most Stately Brick-House; and *Nishamany-River*, where Judge *Growden* hath a very Noble and Fine House, very pleasantly Situated, and likewise a Famous Orchard adjoining to it, wherein are contain'd above a Thousand Apple Trees of various forts; likewise there is the famous *Derby-River*, which comes down from the *Cumbry* by *Derby-Town*, wherein are several *Mills*, viz. *Fulling-Mills*, *Corn-Mills*, &c.

There is curious *Building-Stone* and *Paving-Stone*, also *Tile-Stone*, with which latter, Governor *Penn* covered his *Great* and *Stately Pile*, which he call'd *Pennsbury-House*, the Name it still retains. There is likewise *Iron-Stone* or *Oar*, (lately found) which far exceeds that in *England*, being Richer and Less Drossy, some Preparations have been made to carry on an Iron-Work: There is also a very good *Lime-Stone* in great plenty, and cheap, of great use in Buildings, and also in Manuring Land, (if there were occasion) but Nature has made that of it self sufficiently Fruitful; besides here are *Load-Stone*, *Issing-Glass*, and (that Wonder of Stones) the *Salamander-Stone*, found near *Brandy-Wine-River*, having *Cotton* in Veins within it, which will not consume in the Firel though held there a long time.

As to *Minerals*, or *Metals*, there is very good *Copper*, far exceeding ours in *England*, being much Finer, and of a more glorious Colour. Not two Mile from the *Metropolis*, are also *Purging Mineral-Waters*, that pass both by Siege and *Vrine*, all out as good as *Epsom*; and I have reason to believe, there are good *Coals* also, for I observ'd, the Runs of Water have the fame Colour as that which proceeds from the *Coal-Mines* in *Wales*.

Here is curious Diversion in Hunting, Fishing, and Fowling, especially upon that Great and Famou River *Suskahanah*, which runs down quite through the heart of the Country to *Mary-Land*, where it makes the Head of *Chesepeck-Bay*, in which place there are an Infinite Number of Sea and Land Fowl, of most forts. *viz. Swans*, *Ducks*, *Brands*, *Snipe*, *Curlew*; as also *Eagles*, *Turkies* (of Forty or Fifty Pound Weight) *Pheasants*, *Partridges*, *Pidgeons*, *Heath-Birds*, *Black-Birds*; and that Strange and Remarkable Fowl, call'd (in these Parts) the *Mocking-Bird*, that Imitates all sorts of Birds in their various Notes. And for Fish, there are prodigious quantities of most sorts, *viz. Shadds Cats Heads, Sheeps-Heads, Herrings, Smelts, Roach, Eels, Perch*. As also the large fort of Fish, as *Whales* (of which a great deal of Oyl is made) *Salmon, Trout, Sturgeon, Rock, Oysters*, (some six Inches long) *Crabs, Cockles* (some as big as Stewing *Oysters* of which are made a Choice Soupe or Broth) *Canok* and *Mussels*, with many other sorts of Fish, which would be too tedious to insert.

There are several sorts of wild *Beasts* of great Profit, and good Food; *viz. Panthers, Woolves, Fither, Deer, Beaver, Otter, Hares, Musk-Rats, Minks, Wild Cats, Foxes, Rackoons, Rabits*, and that strange Creature, the *Possam*, the having a false belly to swallow her Yonng ones, by which means she preserveth them from danger, when any thing comes to disturb them. There are also *Bears* some *Wolves*, are pretty well destroy'd by the *Indians*, for the sake of the Reward given them by the *Christian* for that Service. Here is also that Remarkable Creature the *Flying-Squirrel*, having a kind of Skinny Wings, almost like those of the *Batt*, though it hath the like Hair and Colour of the Common *Squirrel*, but is much less in Bodily Substance; I have (my self) seen it fly from one Tree to another in the Woods, but how long it can maintain its Flight is not yet exactly known.

There are in the Woods abundance of *Red Deer* (vulgarly called *Stags*) for I have bought of the *Indians* a whole *Buck*, (both skin and Carcass) for two Gills of Gunpowder. Excellent Food, most delicious, far exceeding that in *Europe*, in the Opinion of most that are Nice and Curious People. There are vast Numbers of other Wild Creatures, as *Elks, Bufalos*, &c. all which as well Beast. Fowl, and Fish, are free and common to any Person who can shoot or take them, without any left, hinderance or Opposition whatsoever.

There are among other various sorts of *Frogs*, the *Bull-Frog*, which makes a roaring noise, hardly to be distinguished from that well known of the Beast, from whom it takes its Name: There is another sort of *Frog* that crawls up to the tops of Trees, there seeming to imitate the Notes of several *Birds*, with many other strange and various Creatures, which would take up too much room here to mention.

Next, I shall proceed to instance in the several sorts of Wild Fruits, as excellent *Grapes, Red, Black, White, Muscadel*, and *Fox*, which upon frequent Experience have produc'd Choice Wine, being daily Cultivated by skillful *Vinerons*; they will in a short space of time, have very good Liquor of their own, and some to supply their Neighbors, to their great advantage; as these Wines are more pure, so much more wholesom; the Brewing Trade of Sophisticating and Adulterating of Wines, as in *England, Holland* (especially) and in some other places not being known there yet, nor in all probability will it in many Years, through a natural Probity so fixed a implanted in the Inhabitants, and (I hope) like to continue. *Wallnuts, Chesnuts, Filberts, Hockery-Nuts, Hartleberries, Mulberries*, (white and black) *Rasberries, Strawberries, Cramberries, Pumbs* of several sorts, and many other Wild Fruits, in great plenty, which are common and free for any to gather to particularize the

Names of them all, would take up too much time; tire, not gratifie the Reader, and be inconsistent with the intended Brevity of this little Volume.

The common Planting *Fruit-Trees,* are *Apples,* which from a Kernel (without Inoculating) will shoot up to be a large Tree, and produce very delicious, large, and pleasant Fruit, of which much excellent *Cyder* is made, in taste resembling that in *England* press'd from *Pippins* and *Pearmains,* sold commonly for between Ten and Fifteen Shillings *per* Barrell. *ears, Peaches,* &c. of which they distil a Liquor much like the taste of *Rumm,* or *Brandy,* which they Yearly make in great quantities: There are *Quinces, Cherries, Goosberries, Currants, Squashes, Pumpkins, Water-Mellons, Muskmellons,* and other *Fruits* in great Numbers, which seldom fail of yielding great plenty. There are also many curious and excellent *Physical Wild Herbs, Roots,* and *Drugs* of great Verture, and very fanative, as the *Sassafras,* and *Sarsaparilla,* so much us'd in Diet-Drinks for the Cure of the Veneral Disease, which makes the *Indians* by a right application of them, as able *Doctors* and *Surgeons* as any in *Europe,* performing celebrated Cures, therewith, and by the use of some particular *Plants* only, find Remedy in all *Swellings, Burnings, Cute,* &c. There grows also in great plenty the *Black Snake-Root, Poke-Roots,* call in *England Jallop,* with several other beneficial *Herbs, Plants* and *Roots,* which *Physicians* have approved of, far exceeding in Nature and Vertue, those of other Countries.

The Names of the Connties are as followeth; First, *Philadelphia County*; Second, *Bucks County*; Third, *Chester County*; Fourth, *New-Castle County*; Fifth, *Kent County*; Sixth, *Suffex County.* The chiefest and most commodious places for raising Tebacco, as also Breeding and Improving all sorts of Cattle, are the Counties of *Kent* and *New-Castle*; the other chiefly depend upon Raising and Improving *English Grain,* of which they have a prodigious Encrease, which I have particularly instanced in the beginning of this Book, both as to their Quality and Quantity: All those Counties also very much abound in all sorts of *Cattle,* both small and great, for the Use and Service of Man.

Their sorts of *Grain* are, *Wheat, Rye, Pease, Oates, Barley, Buck-Wheat, Rice, Indian-Corn, Indian-Pease,* and *Beans,* with great quantities of *Hemp* and *Flax*; as also several sorts of eating Roots, as *Turnips, Potatoes, Carrats, Persnips,* &c. all which are produc'd Yearly in greater quantities than in *England,* those *Roots* being much larger, and altogether as sweet, if not more delicious; *Cucumbers, Coshaws, Artichokes,* with many others; most sorts of Saladings, besides what grows naturally Wild in the Country, and tat in great plenty also, as *Mustard,* Rye, Sage, *Mint, Tanzy, Wormwood, Penny-Royal* and *Purslain,* and most of the Herbs and Roots found in the Gardens in *England.* There are several Husband Men, who sow Yearly between Seventy and Eighty Acres of *Wheat* each, besides *Barley, Oates, Rye, Pease, Beans,* and other Grain.

They ave commonly *Tw Harvest* in the Year; First of *English Wheat,* and next of *Buck,* (or *French*) Wheat. They have great Stocks both of *Hogs* and *Horses,* kept in the Woods, out of which, I saw a *Hog* kill'd, of about a Year old, which weigh'd

Two Hundred weight; whose Flesh is much sweeter, and even more luscious tan that in *England*, because they feed and fatten on the rich (though wild) Fruits, besides those fatned at home by *Peaches, Cherries* and *Apples*. Their *Hoses* are very hot with riding or otherwise, they are turn'd out into the Woods at the same Instant, and yet receive no hard; some Farmers have Forty, some Sixty, and from that Number to Two or Three Hundred Head f *Cattle*: Their Oxen usually weigh Two Hundred Pounds a Quarter. They are commonly fatter of Flesh, and yield more Tallow (by feeding only on Grass) than the Cattle in *England*. And for *Sheep*, they have considerable Numbers which are generally free from those infectious Diseases which are incident to those Creatures in *England*, as the *Rot, Scab*, or *Maggots*; They commonly bring forth two *Lambs* at once, some *twise in one Year*, and the Wooll is very fine, and thick, and also very white.

Bees thrive and multipl exceedingly in those Parts, and *Sweeds* often get great store of them in the Woods, where they are free for any Body. Honey (and choice too) is sold in the Capital City for Five Pence *per* Pound. Wax is also plentiful, cheap, and a considerable Commerce. Tame Fowls, as *Chickens, Hens, Geese, Ducks, Turkeys*, &c. are large, and very plentiful all over this Countrey.

And now for their Lots and Lands in City and Countrey, in their great Advancement since they were first laid out, which was within the compass of about Twelve Years, that which might have been bought for Fifteen or Eighteen Shillings, is not solde for Fourscore Pounds in ready Silver; and some other Lots, that might have been then Purchased for Three Pounds, within the space of Two Years, were sold for a Hundred Pounds a piece, and likewise some Land that lies near the City, that Sixteen Years ago might have been Purchas'd for Six or Eight Pounds the Hundred Acres, cannot now be bough under One Hundred and Fifty, or Two Hundred Pounds.

Now the true Reason why this Fruitful Countrey and Florishing City advance so considerably in the Purchase of Lands both in the one and the other, is their great and extended Traffique and Commerce both by Sea and Land, *viz.* to *New-York, New-England, Virginia, Mary-Land, Carolina, Jamaica, Barbadoes, Nevis, Monserat, Antego*, St. *Cristophers, Barmudoes, New-Found-Land, Maderas, Saltetudeous*, and *Old-England*; besides several other places. Their Merchandize chiefly consists in *Horses, Pipe-Staves, Pork* and *Beef* Salted and Barrelled up, *Bread*, and *Flower*, all sorts of Grain, *Peases, Beans, Skins, Furs, Taobacco*, or *Pot-Ashes, Wax*, &c. which are Barter'd for *Rumm, Sugar, Molasses, Silver, Negroes, Salt, Wine, Linen, Household-Goods*, &c.

However there still remain Lots of Land both in the aforesaid City and Country, that any may Purchase almost as cheap as they could at the first Laying out of Parcelling of either City or Country; which is, (in the Judgment of most People) the likeliest to turn to account to those that lay their Money out upon it, and in a shorter time than the aforementioned Lots and Lands that are already improved, and for several Reasons. In the first place, the Countrey is now well inhabited by the Christians, who have great Stocks of all sorts of Cattle that increase extraordinarily, and upon tat account they are oblig'd to go farther up into the Countreym because there is the chiefest and best place for their Stocks, and for them that go back into the Countrey, they get the richest Land, for the best lies thereabouts.

Secondly, Farther into the Countrey is the Principal Place to Trade with the *Indians* for all sorts of *Pelt*, as *Skins* and *Furs*, and also *Fat Venison*, of whom People may Purchase cheaper by three Parts in four than they can at the City of *Philadelphia*.

Thirdly, Backwards in the Countrey lies the *Mines* where is *Copper* and *Iron*, besides other *Metals*, and *Minerals*, of which there is some Improvement made already in order to bring them, to greater Perfection; and that will be a means to erect more Inland Market-Towns, which exceedingly promote Traffick.

Fourthly, and lastly, Because the Countrey and the first, laying out, was void of Inhabitants (except the Heathens, or very few Chrstians not worth naming)) and not many People caring to abandon a quiet and easier (at least tolderable) Life in their Native Countrey (usually the most agreeable to all Mankind) to seek out a new hazardous, and careful one in a Foreign Wilderness or Desart Countrey, wholly destitute of Chrstian Inhabitants, and even to arrive at which, they must pass over a vast Ocean, expos'd to some Dangers, and not a few Inconveniencies: but now all those Cares, Fears and Hazards are vanished, for the Countrey is pretty well Peopled, and very much Improv'd, and will be more every Day, now the Dove is return'd with the Olive-branch of Peace in her Mouth.

I must needs say, even the present Encouragements are very great and inviting, for Poor People (both Men and Women) of all kinds, can here get three times the Wages for their Labour they can in *England* or *Wales*.

I shall instance in a few which may serve; any, and will hold in all the rest. The first was a *Black-Smith* (my next Neighbour) who himself and one Negro Man he had, got Fifty Shillings in one Day, by working up a Hundred Pound Weight of Iron, which at Six Pence *per* Pound (and that is the common Price in that Countrey) amounts to that Summ.

And for *Carpenters*, both *House* and *Ships*, *Brick-layers*, *Masons*, either of these Trades-Men, will get between Five and Six Shillings every Day, constantly. As to *Journey-Men Shooe-Makers*, they have Two Shillings *per* Pair both for Men and Womens Shooes: And *Journey-Men Taylors* have Twelve Shillings *per* Week and their Diet. *Sawyers* get between Six and Seven Shillings the Hundred for Cutting of Pine-Boards. And for *Weavers*, they have Ten or Twelve. Pence the Yard for Weaving of that which is little more than half a Yard in breadth. *Wooll-Combers*, have for combing Twelve Pence *per* Pound. *Potters* have Sixteen Pence for an Earthen Pot which may be bought in *England* for Four Pence. *Tanners*, may buy their Hides green for Three Half Pence *per* Pound, and sell their Leather for Twelve Pence *per* Pound. And *Curriers* have Three Shillings and Four Pence *per* Hide for Dressing it; they buy their Oyl at Twenty Pence *per* Gallon. *Brick-Makers* have Twenty Shillings *per* Thousand for their Bricks at the Kiln. *Felt-Makers* will have for their Hats Seven Shillings a piece, such as may be bought in *England* for Two Shillings a piece; yet they buy their *Wooll* commonly for Twelves or Fifteen Pence *per* Pound. And as to the *Glaziers*, they will have Five Pence a Quarry for their Glass. The Rule for the *Coopers* I have almost forgot; but this I can affirm of some who went from *Bristol*, (as their Neighbours report) that could hardly get their Livelihoods there, are now reckon'd in *Pensilvania*, by a modest Computation to be worth some Hundred, (if not Thousands) of Pounds. The *Bakers* make as White Bread as any in *London*, and as for their Rule, it is the same in all Parts of the World that I have been in. The *Butchers* for killing a Beast, have Five Shillings and their Diet; and they may buy a good fat large Cow for Three Pounds, or thereabouts. The *Brewers* sell such Beer as is equal in Strength to that in London, half Ale and half Stout for Fifteen Shillings *per* Barrel; and their Beer hath a better Name, that is, is in more esteem than *English beer* in *Barbadoes*, and is sold for a higher Price there. And for *Silver-Smiths*, they have between Half a Crown and Three Shillings an Ounce for working their Silver, and for Gold equivalent. *Plasterers* have commonly Eighteen Pence *per* Yard for *Plastering*. *Laft-Makers* have Two Shillings a dozen for their Lafts. and *Heel-Makers* have Two Shillings a dozen for their Heels. *Wheel* and *Mill-Wrights, Joyners, Brasierz, Pewterers, Dyers, Fullers, Comb-Makers, Wyer-Drawers, Cage-Makers, Card-Makers, Painters, Cutlers, Rope-Makers, Carversm Block-Makers, Turners, Button-Makers, Hair* and *Wood Sieve-Makers, Bodies-Makers, Gun-Smithers, Lock-Smiths, Nailers, File-Cuters, Skinners, Furriers, Glovers, Patten-Makers, Watch-Makers, Clock-Makers, Sadlers, Coller-Makers, Barbers, Printers, Book-Binders*, and all other *trades-Men*, their Gaines and Wages, are about the same proportion as the forementioned Trades in their Advancements, as to what they have in *England*.

Of *Lawyers* and *Physicians* I shall say nothing, because this Countrey is very Peaceable and Healty; long may it so continue and never have occasion for the Tongue of the one, nore the Pen of the Other, both equally destructive to Mens Estates and Lives; besides forsooth, they, Hang-Man like, have a License to Murder and make Mischief. *Labouring-Men* have commonly here, between 14 and 15 Pounds a Year, and their Meat, Drink, Washing and Lodging; and by the Day their Wages is generally between Eighteen Pence and Half a Crown, and Diet also; But in Harvest they have usually between Three and Four Shilling each Day, and Diet. they *Maid Servant Wages* is commonly betwixt Six and Ten Pounds *per Annum*, with very good Accommodation. And for the *Women* who get their Livelihood by their own Industry, their Labour is very dear, for I can buy in London a Cheese-Cake for Two Pence, bigger than theirs at that price when at the same time their Milk is as cheap as we can buy it in *London*, and their Flour cheaper by one half.

Corn and Flesh, and what else serves man for Drink, Food and Rayment, is much cheaper here than in *Endgland*, or elsewhere; but the chief reason why Wages of Servants of all sorts if much higher here than there, arises from the great Fertility and Produce of the Place; besides, if these large Stipends were refused them, they would quickly set up for themselves, for they can have Provision very cheap, and Land for a very small matter, or next to nothing in comparison of the

Purchase of Lands in *England*; and the farmers there can better addord to give that great Wages than the Farmers in *England* can, for several Reasons very obvious.

As First, their Land costs them (as I said but just now) little or nothing in comparison, of which the Farmers commonly will get twice the increase of Corn for every Bushel they sow, that the Farmers in *England* can from the richest Land they have.

In the Second place, they have constantly good price for their Corn, by reason of the great and quick vent into *Barbadoes* and other Islands; through which means Silver is become more plentiful than here in *England*, considering the Number of People, and that causes a quick Trade for both Corn and Cattle; and that is the reason that corn differs now from the Price formerly, else it would be at half the Price it was at then; for a Brother of mine (to my own particular knowledge) sold within the compass of one Week, about One Hundred and Twenty fat Beasts, most of them good handsom large Oxen.

Thirdly, They pay no *Tithes*, and their *Taxes* are inconsiderable; the Place is free for all persuasions, in a Sober and Civil way; for the Church of *England* and the *Quakers* bear equal Share in the Government. They live Friendly and Well together; there is no Persecution for Religion, nor ever like to be; 'tis this that knocks all Commerce on the Head, together with high Imposts, strict Laws, and cramping Orders. Before I end this Paragraph, I shall add another Reason why Womens Wages are so exorbitant; they are not yet very numerous, which makes them stand upon high Terms for their several Services, in *Sempstering, Washing, Spinning, Knitting, Serving*, and in all the other parts of their Employments; for they have for Spinning either Worsted or Linen, Two Shillings a Pound, and commonly for Knitting a very Course pair of Yarn Stockings, they have half a Crown a Pair; moreover they are usually Marry'd before they are Twenty Years of Age, and when once in the Nose, are for the most part a little uneasier, and make their Husbands so too, till they procure them a Maid Servant to bear theburden of the Work, as also in some measure to wait on them too.

it is now time to return to the City of *Brotherly-Love* (for so much of the *Greek* Word or Name *Philadelphia* imports) which though at present so obscure, that neither the *Map-Makers*, nor *Geographers* have taken the least notice of her, tho she far exceeds her Namesake of *Lydia*, (having above Two Thousand Noble Houses for her Five Hundred Ordinary) or *Celisia*, or *Cœlesyria*; yet in a very short space of time the will, in all probability, make a fine Figure in the World, and be a most Celebrated *Emporeum*. Here is lately built a Noble *Town-House* or *Guild-Hall*, also a Handsom *Market-House*, and a convenient *Prison*. The Number of Christians both Old and Young Inhabiting in that Countrey, are by a Modest Computation, adjudged to amount to above Twenty Thousand.

The Laws of this Countrey, are the same with those in *England*; our Constitution being on the same Foot: Many Disputes and Differences are determined and composed by Arbitration; and all Causes are decided with great Care and Expedition, being concluded (generally) at furthest at the Second Court, unless they happen to be very Nice and Difficult Cases; under Forty Shillings any one Justice of the Peace has Power to Try the Cause. Thieves of all sorts, are oblig'd to restore four fold after they have been Whipt and Imprison'd,a ccording to the Nature of their Crime; and if they be not of Ability to restore four fold, they must be in Servitude till 'tis satisfied. They have Curious Wharfs as also several large and fine Timber-Yards, both at *Philadelphia*, and *New-Castle*, especially at the *Metropolis*, before *Robert Turner*'s Great and Famous House, where are built Ships of considerable Burthen; they Cart their Goods from that Wharf into the Cirt of *Philadelphia*, under an Arch, over which part of the Street is built, which is called *Chesnut-Street-Warf*, besides other *Wharfs*, as *High-Street Warf*, *Mulberry Street Wharf*, and *Vine-Street Wharf*, and all those are Common Wharfs; and likewise there are very pleasant Stairs, as *Trus* and *Carpenter-Stairs*, besides several others. There are above Thirty Carts belonging to that City, Four or Five Horses to each. There is likewise a very convenient Wharf called *Carpenter's Wharf*, which hath a fine necessary *Craine* belonging to it, with suitable *Grainaries*, and *Store-Houses*. A Ship of Two Hundred Tun may load and unload by the side of it, and there are other Wharfs (with *Magazines* and *Ware-Houses*) which front the City all along the River, as also a Curious and Commodious *Dock* with a *Draw-Bridge* to it, for the convenient Reception of Vessels; where have been built some Ships of Two or Three Hundred Tuns each: They have very Stately Oaks to build Ships with, some of which are between Fifty and Sixty Foot long, and clear from Knots, being very straight and well Grain'd. In this famous City of *Philadelphia* there are several *Rope-Makers*, who have large and curious *Rope-Walks* especially one *Joseph Wilcox*. Also Three or Four Spacious *Malt-Houses*, as many large *Brew-Houses*, and many handsom *Bake-Houses* for Publick Use.

In the said City are several good *Schools of Learning* for Youth, in order to the Attainment of *Arts* and *Sciences*, as also *Reading*, *Writing*, &c. Here is to be had on any Day in the Week, *Tarts*, *Pies*, *Cakes*, &c. We have also several *Cooks-Shops*, both *Roasting* and *Boyling*, as in the City of *London*; *Bread*, *Beer*, *Beef*, and *Pork*, are sold at any time much cheaper than in *England* (which arises from their Plenty) our Wheat is very white and clear from Tares, making as good and white Bread as any in *Europe*. Happy Blessings, for which we owe the highest Gratitude to our Plentiful Provider, the great Creator of Heaven and Earth. The *Water-Mills* far exceed those in England, both for quickness and grinding good Meal, their being great choice of good Timber, and earlier Corn than in the aforesaid Place, they are made by one *Peter Deal*, a Famous and Ingenious Workman, especially for inventing such like Machines.

All sorts of very good *Paper* are made in the *German-Town*; as also very fine *German linen*, such as no person of Quality need be asham'd to wear; and in several places they make very good *Druggets*, *Crapes*, *Camblets*, and *Serges*, besides other *Woollen Cloaths*, the Manufacture of all which daily improves: And in most parts of the Countrey there are many Curious and Spacious Building, which several of the *Gentry* have erected for their Country-Houses. As for the Fruit-Trees they

Plant, they arrive at such Perfection, that they bear in a little more than half the time that they commonly do in *England.*

The *Christian Children* born here are generally *well-favoured,* and *Beautiful* to behold; I never knew any come into the World with the least blemish on any part of its Body, being in the general, observ'd to be *better Natur'd, Milder,* and more *tender Hearted* than those born in *England.*

There are very fine and delightful *Gardens* and *Orchards,* in most part of this Countrey; but *Edward Shippey* (who lives near the Capital City) has an Orchard and Gardens adjoining to his Great Hous that equalizes (if not exceeds) any I have ever seen, having a very famous and pleasant Summer-House erected in the middle of his extraordinary fine and large Garden abounding with *Tulips, Pinks, Carnations, Roses,* (of several sorts) *Lilies,* not to mention those that grow wild in the Fields.

Reader, what I have here written is not a *Fiction, Flam, Whim,* or any sinister *Design,* either to impose upon the Ignorant, or Credulous, or to curry Favour with the Rich and Mighty, but in meer Pity and pure Compassion to the Numbers of Poor Labouring Men, Women, and Children in *England,* half starv'd, visible in their meagre looks, that are continually wandering up and down looking for Employment without finding any, who here need not lie idle a moment, nor want due Encouragement or Reward for their Work, much less Vagabond or Drone it about. Here there are no Beggars to be seen (it is a Shame and Disgrace to the State that there are so many in *England*) nor indeed have any here that least Occasion or Temptation to take up that Scandalous Lazy Life.

Jealousie among Men is here very rare; and barrenness among Women hardly to be heard of, nor are old Maids to be met with; for all commonly Marry before they are Twenty Years of Age, and seldom any young Married Women but hath a Child in her Belly, or one upon her Lap.

What I have delivere'd concerning this *Province,* is indisputably true, I was an Eye-Witness to it all, for I went in the first Ship that was bound from *England* for that Countery, since it received the Name of *Pensilvania,* which was in the Year 1681. The Ship's Name was the *John and Sarah* of *London, Henry Smith* Commander. I have declin'd giving any Account of several things which I have only heard others speak of, because I did not see them my self, for I never held that way infallible, to make Reports from Hear-say. I saw the first Cellar when it was digging for the use of our Governour *Will. Penn.*

I shall now haste to a Conclusion, and only hint a little concerning the *Natives* or *Aborigines,* their *Persons, Language, Manners, Religion* and *Government*; Of *Person* they are ordinarily Tall, Straight, well-turn'd, and true Propotion'd; their Treat strong and clever, generally walking with a lofty Chin. Of Complexion *Black,* but by design, *Gypsie-like,* greasing themselves with Bears-Fat Clarified, and using no defense against the Injuries of *the* Sun and *Weather,* their Skins fail not to be Swarthy. Their *Eyes* are small and black. *Thick lips and flat Noses* so frequent with *Negroes* and *East Indians*, are rare with them. They have Comely Faces and Tolerable Complexions, some of their Noses having a rise like the *Roman*.

Their *Language* is Lofty and Elegant, but not Copious; *One* Word serveth in the stead of *Three*, imperfect and ungrammatical, which defects are supply'd by the Understanding of the Hearers. *Sweet*, of *Noble Sound* and *Accent*. Take here a Specimen.

Hodi hita nee huska a peechi nee, machi
Pensilvania *huska dogwachi, keshow a peechi*
Nowa, huska hayly, Chetena koon peo.

Thus in *English*.

Farewel Friend, I will very quickly go to
Pensilvania, very cold Mon will come presently,
And very great hard frosts will come quickly.

I might Treat largely of their *Customs* and *Manners*, but that will not agree with my proposed Brevity.

As soon as their Children are born, they wash them in cold *Water*, especially in *cold Weather*. To harden and embolden them, they plunge them in the River, they find their Feet early, usually at Nine Months they can go. The Boys Fish till Fifteen, then hunt, and having given proof of their Manhood, by a large return of Skins, they may Marry (else 'tis ashame to think of a Wife) which is usually at the Age of Seventeen or Eighteen; the Girls stay with their Mothers, and help to hoe the Ground, Plant Corn, bear Burdens, and Marry about Thirteen or Fourteen.

Their Houses are *Matts*, or *Barks* of *Trees* set on Poles, Barn-like, not higher than a Man, so not exposed to Winds. They lie upon *Reeds* or *Grass*. In *Travel* they lodge in the *Woods* about a great Fire, with the Mantle of Duffils they wear wrapt about them, and a few Boughs stuck round them.

They live chiefly on *Maze*, or *Indian Corn* softed in the Ashes, sometimes beaten and boyl'd with Water, called *Homine*. They have Cakes, not unpleasant; also Beans and Pease, which Nourish much, but the Woods and Rivers afford them their Provision; they ear Morning and Evening; their Seats and Tables are the Ground; they are reserv'd, apt to resent and retain long: Their Women are Chaste (at least after Marriage) and when with Child, will not admit of their Husband Embraces any more till Deliver'd. Exceeding Liberal and Generous; Kind and Affable; uneasie in Sicknesse, to remedy which, they drink a Decoction of Roots in Spring-Water, forbearing Flesh, which is they happen to eat, it must be the Female; they commonly bury their Kettles and part of their goods with their Friends when they die, suspecting (poor souls) they shall make use of them again at the Resurrection. They Mourn a whole Year, but it is no other than blacking their Faces.

Their Government is Monarchical, and Successive, and ever od the Mothers (the surest) side, to prevent a Spurious Issue. The Distaff (as in *France*) is excluded the Regal Inheritance. Their Princes are Powerful, yet do nothing without the Concurrence of their Senate, or Councils, consisting chiefly of Old, but mixt with Young Men; slow and deliberate, (*Spaniard*-like) in resolving, naturally wise, and hardly to be out-witted. Their Punishments are Pecuniary. Murder may be aton'd for by Feasts and Presents, in Proportion to the Quality of the Offence, Person, or Sex injur'd: for if a Woman be kill'd, the Mulct is double, because she brings forth Children. They seldom quarel when Sober, and if Boozy, (which of late they are more apt to be, having learn'd to drink, a little too much Rum of the Christians, to their shame) they readily pardon it, alledging the Liquor is Criminal not the Man.

The way of Worship the *Sweeds* use in this COuntrey, is the *Lutheran*; the *English* have four sorts of Assemblies or Religious Meetings here: as first, The Church of *England*, who built a very fine Church in the City of *Philadelphia* in the Year 1695. Secondly, the *Anabaptists*: Thirdly, the *Presbyterians*, and two sorts of *Quakers* (of all the most numerous by much) one Part held with *George Keith*; but whether both Parties will joyn together again in one I cannot tell, for that Gentleman hath alter'd his Judgement since he came to *England*, concerning his Church-Orders in *Pensilvania*, by telling and shewing them Precepts that were lawful in the time of the Law, but forbidden under the Gospel to pay Tithes, or Ministers to Preach for Hire, &c. As also to sprinkle Infants; and he tells the *Presbyterian Minister*, That he must go to the Pope of *Rome* for his Call, for he had no Scripture for it, and that Water-Baptism and the Outward Supper are not of the nature of the Everlasting Gospel; nor essential parts of it, see his *Truth Advanced* page 173. He gives likewise a strict Charge concerning plain Language and plain Habit, and that they should not be concern'd in the compelling part of the Worldly Government, and that they should let their *Negroes* at Liberty after some reasonable time of Service; likewise, they they should not take the Advantage of the Law against one another, as to procure them any Corporeal Punishment: These Orders he tells his Followers, would make Distinction between them and *Jews* and moral heathens, this was in the Year 1693. in *Pensilvania*: But now the Year 1697. since he came to *England*, his Judgement is chang'd, for he tells his Disciples, that Water-Baptism is come in the room of Circumcision; and by so doing, they would distinguish themselves from either *Jews*, *Pagans*, or Moral *Heathens*: He keeps his Meeting once a Week at *Turners-Hall* in *Fill-Pot-Lane*, *London*, on *Sundays* in the Afternoon; he begins between Two and Three of the Clock and commonly ends between Four and Five.

Friendly Reader, by this thou mayst see how wavering and mutable Men of great Outward Learning are, if the Truth of this be by an Body question'd, let them look in the *Creed*, and the Paper against *Christians being concern'd in Worldly Government*, and the *Paper concerning Negroes*, that was given forth by the Appointment of the Meeting held by *George Keith* at *Philip James*'s House in the City of *Philadelphia*, in *Pensilvania*; and his *Letter also in* Mary-Land *against the Presbysterian Catechism*, Printed at *Boston* in *New-England* in 1695. with the *Answer* to it bound up together in one Book and in *Truth Advanced*, page 173. And for what relates to hime since in *England*, let them look into the *Quaker Arguments Refuted, Concerning Water-Baptism and the Lord's Supper*, page 70. And now Reader, I shall take my leave of thee, recommending thee with my own self to the Directions of the Spirit of God in our Conscience, and that will agree with all the Holy Scriptures in its right place; and when we find our selves so, we have no need to take any Thought or Care what any Body shall say of us.

2.12.2 Reading and Review Questions

1. Compare Gabriel Thomas's conjectures regarding the roots of American Indians with those of Adriaen van der Donck's. From what value base is Thomas functioning? How do you know?
2. Why does Thomas dismiss the claims to possession of previous colonizers, including the Dutch and the Swedes, due to their having made no improvements to the land? What does he mean by improvements? How do you know? What does William Penn's followers' being industrious suggest about their characters and rights?
3. What's the effect of Thomas's grouping "negroes" among such bartered goods as rum, sugar, molasses, silver, salt, wine, linen, and household goods? What is suggested by this reference to negroes? Why?
4. According to Thomas, why do women receive unusually high wages in Pennsylvania? What's his attitude to their "exorbitant" wages? How do you know?

2.13 JOHN NORRIS

(unknown)

Very little is known about John Norris that is not derived from his 1712 pamphlet, *Profitable Advice for Rich and Poor*. This pamphlet encouraged poor Englishmen to establish small farms in the colonial South where they could gain independent subsistence. He particularly encouraged tradesmen who could not make their living in England to reap "profit and delight" in what is now South Carolina. His pamphlet addressed possible causes for reluctance to settle in South Carolina, including the fear that "English people, and others" would be enslaved when they entered the colonies.

2.13.1 From *Profitable Advice for Rich and Poor*

(1712)

http://nationalhumanitiescenter.org/pds/becomingamer/growth/text1/carolinarandolphnorris.pdf

2.13.2 Reading and Review Questions

1. What's the purpose and effect of the first question in this dialogue being about the settlers and their religion? Why?
2. What justification, if any, does the planter James Freeman give to the presence of slaves in this colony? How does he distinguish between "Blackmoors" and "Red Dun, or Tan'd Skin'd" slaves? Why? What rights or protections, if any, do slaves have?
3. Why does Question make a point of asking about the possibility of "English people, and others" being made slaves upon their arrival in America? How does Freeman reassure Question? What attitudes towards "Blackmoors" and "Red Dun, or Tan'd Skin'd" slaves does Freeman reveal in his reassurance? What rights or protections, if any, do such indentured servants have?
4. What advantages might laborers from England gain from apprenticing or indenturing themselves in order to emigrate to America?
5. What relationship between the colony and England does Freeman describe? What is his attitude towards this relationship? How do you know?

3 Revolutionary and Early National Period Literature

3.1 LEARNING OUTCOMES

After reading this chapter, students will be able to

- Identify historical characteristics of the Revolutionary or Early National period in America.
- Place the French and Indian War within its larger social, cultural, and historical context, in both North America and Europe.
- Understand the diverse and numerous circumstances contributing to the Revolutionary War, starting with the Battles of Lexington and Concord (1775).
- Understand the purpose and effect of the Second Continental Congress and its Articles of Confederation.
- Understand the purposes and effects of the Constitutional Convention (1787).
- Identify the political viewpoints of the Federalists and the Anti-federalists and their respective contributions to the development of the United States federal government.
- Understand the influence of the Enlightenment on eighteenth century American culture, particularly with the shift from Puritan theology to science, philosophy, and the empirical method.
- Understand the relationship of eighteenth century American literature with the goal of human perfectibility.
- Understand the inconsistent application of Enlightenment values of individual will, equality, and freedom among African slaves, Native Americans, and women.
- Understand how the Enlightenment encouraged alternative religions and philosophies, such as Deism and Unitarianism, as well as a resurgence of Calvinism in the Great Awakening and evangelizing.

3.2 INTRODUCTION

The American eighteenth century—often called the Revolutionary or Early National period because it coincided with the establishment of the soon-to-be United States—was one punctuated by warfare and nation building. The country's first major experience with warfare in the century came with the French and Indian War. Part of the broader Seven Years War, this North American phase began in 1754 with territorial disputes over the upper Ohio River Valley by traders and settlers of New France and traders and setters of the Virginia and Pennsylvania colonies. The dispute escalated when both territories established forts in the area and escalated again when they called their respective mother countries into the argument. The fight between the colonies was another extension of the historic enmity between France and England and was also mirrored by enmities between different Native American tribes who allied themselves to the side which best served their interests and desire to defeat rival tribes. The North American phase of the war concluded in 1760. The larger conflict was not settled until 1763, and France was compelled to cede Canada and lands east of the Mississippi to England.

American colonies' participation in the French and Indian War affected the American Revolution in two ways: American militias gained valuable military experience that was put to use in the later conflict, and American dissatisfaction with England erupted once they started getting the bills from the war. The British government and public felt that it was only right that the American colonists help pay the costs of conducting the French and Indian War since it was on their behalf. The American colonists disagreed since they had no representation in the government that decided what to tax and how much. American resentment of and resistance to England peaked with the so-called Intolerable Acts of 1774, which added the insult of usurped governance to the injury of taxation. Among other things, the Intolerable Acts closed the port of Boston until the tea destroyed in the Boston Tea Party was repaid. It also put the Massachusetts government under direct British control and required American colonists to quarter the British soldiers there to enforce that control. In response, all the colonies with the exception of Georgia convened the First Continental Congress and sent a Declaration of Rights and Grievances to England in late 1774. England's reply was to send troops to put down colonial resistance, and the Battles of Lexington and Concord in April of 1775 initiated the American Revolutionary War.

Soon after those battles, the colonists set about establishing a government. The Second Continental Congress met to draft the Articles of Confederation. Codifying a loose connection among sovereign states with a limited central government, the Articles also established the new name of the country and a bicameral federal legislature, one side with representation proportionate to population and the other with equal representation. Completed in 1777 and finally ratified in 1781, the Articles proved to be problematic after peace with England was officially declared with the Treaty of Paris in 1783. While the new Congress had the power to pass laws, it lacked the power to enforce them, and it became clear within four years of nationhood that a new plan was needed.

When the delegates to the Constitutional Convention met in 1787, they all agreed to the rule of secrecy—no details of the new Constitution would be leaked until the draft was complete and offered to the states for ratification. It was only when the draft was released in 1789 that the national debate about its principles began in earnest. Two major positions quickly coalesced. The Federalists, who included George Washington and Benjamin Franklin, supported the Constitution as written, favoring a strong central government composed of executive and judicial branches added to the legislative branch and relatively weaker state governments. Anti-Federalists like Patrick Henry were leery of the consolidation of power by a federal government headed by a President, arguing that the Constitution replicated a system like the one from which they had just separated. They wanted strong state governments because they thought states would be more likely to protect individual freedoms. Anti-federalists ultimately influenced the new form of the federal government by the addition of the Bill of Rights, designed to protect individual rights from the power of the federal government. The Constitution and the Bill of Rights containing ten amendments were finally ratified by the last state in 1790.

The Enlightenment was the major cultural influence on eighteenth century America, and through it, the early colonial worldview dominated by Puritan theology shifted into a world view influenced by science and philosophy. There was an explosion of improved scientific technologies during the seventeenth century, and as a result, scientists were able to collect more precise data and challenge previously held ideas about how the world functioned. To illustrate the effect that scientific discoveries and theories had on the time period, consider Isaac Newton's law of universal gravitation. If one had previously been told, as the seventeenth century Puritans had, that the workings of nature were actuated by God's inscrutable will and were beyond humanity's ability to understand, the discovery of a formula that could predict one of those workings of nature with accuracy every time (so long as the mass of the objects and the distance between them were known) would cause a seismic change in one's perceptions. The existence of laws like Newton's asserted that the universe was ordered on rational principles that man could understand using reason. As a result, the use of reason gained greater respect echoed in the era's other name, the Age of Reason, and human ability was held in much higher regard.

In the eighteenth century, science and philosophy were not considered distinct fields of knowledge, and so it is not surprising that some philosophers too prioritized reason in examining the nature of humanity. English philosopher John Locke and his articulation of Empiricism show not only the supremacy of what is now called the scientific method but also a view of human nature that differed considerably from that of the Puritans. In his *Essay Concerning Human Understanding* (1689), Locke asserts that "all ideas come from sensation or reflection." In other words, all human knowledge is founded in sensory information—what we see, hear, smell, taste, or feel—and inferences that can be logically drawn from that information. It then follows that the nature of an infant at birth, assumed to have had no sensory experiences until that moment, must be like a *tabula rasa* or blank slate, untainted by original sin. While the Puritans believed that humanity is born bad, Locke asserted that humanity was born blank. The sensory experiences that followed and the inferences drawn from them as a result of a good or faulty education would dictate the kind of person one would become.

Though Empiricism held that human nature could be swayed either way, this period was nothing if not optimistic. Some Enlightenment and Federal era thinkers emphasized the goal of human perfectibility. Despite the concept's name, they did not actually think humans could become perfect; however, they did believe that individuals and humanity in total could continually improve, if reason was applied to determine the best ways to be and the best ways to learn those ways. This period ushered in the establishment of many a library, athenaeum, and study group like Franklin's Junto Club—all institutions available to the person wishing for self-improvement because people now believed that it was possible to become better through one's own efforts. For these reasons, American literature of the eighteenth century is frequently intended to instruct, whether it be Benjamin Franklin's "bold and arduous project of arriving at moral perfection" or the frequent cautions about the dangers of vanity and frivolity for women in Hannah Webster Foster's *The Coquette.*

Though reason had a new place of prominence in the eighteenth century, its inadequacies were also explored. Franklin lays out an eminently rational system of inculcating virtue, then goes on to admit that he never could learn some of those virtuous qualities. In an echo of his younger self rationalizing the break with his vegetarian principles when the smell of cooked fish becomes too tempting, Franklin slyly acknowledges that, sometimes, a "speckled" or only partially virtuous self is best. Foster too creates a tension between the textbook virtuous women who advise her heroine to abandon her flirtatious ways and settle for the life of a dutiful minister's wife and that same heroine's clear and persuasive understanding that this proposed life would be both unsuitable for her personality and deadly boring.

This new respect for human ability and potentiality lead the period to reimagine the relationship between the individual and the community. For Puritans, individualism was the cause of much evil, and so in John Robinson's letter read to William Bradford's group when they embarked for the New World, each traveler is instructed to "repress in himself and the whole body in each person, as so many rebels against the common good, all private respects of men's selves, not sorting with the general conveniency." For writers of the Enlightenment, the individual and the community were not antagonists but collaborators finding a balance that benefitted both. Remarking on individual freedom, Locke in his *Second Treatise on Civil Government* (1689) asserts

> But though this be a state of liberty, yet it is not a state of license . . .The state of nature has a law of Nature to govern it, which obliges every one, and reason,

> which is that law, teaches all mankind who will but consult it, that being all equal and independent, no one ought to harm another in his life, health, liberty, or possessions.

In other words, the individual is free to do what he wants as long as it does not curtain the freedom of another; individual freedom must balance with group freedom. Locke's statement also references two other influential concepts of the period—natural law and the golden mean—which were borrowed from classical Greek and Roman philosophy. The natural law concept argues that, to be just, laws should be founded in the observable operations of nature. Particularly in ethical arguments, this period also advocated for the desirability of finding the "golden mean" in any action and charting a middle course between two extremes of excess and paucity.

One might have supposed that the primacy of reason and an emphasis on the equality of all human beings would have vanquished prejudice against those who were not white males, but this period also illustrates that rationality is not invulnerable to bias. For some Americans such as Benjamin Franklin, it seemed obvious that one cannot both declare that all men are created equal and also support slavery. However, American slaveholders like Thomas Jefferson managed to rationalize the cognitive dissonance, arguing the paternalist position that Africans were not as fully developed as European descendants and needed to be controlled by the latter until they had moved further along on the continuum of civilization. Similar arguments were made about Native Americans, and the evidence of their advanced civilization was ignored or explained away. For example, it was a widely held belief that Native American burial mounds had been constructed by some earlier civilization that the Native Americans had overrun. Women, too, were excluded from the protections of the Constitution and the Bill of Rights and were erased by the practice of coverture, which asserted that women's legal rights were "covered" by those of her father or husband; women did not have a separate legal existence from their male relatives. Some white women were offered a limited ticket to participate in Enlightenment ideals through the concept of Republican Motherhood. This concept argued that women needed to be educated, to have some level of financial security, and to have knowledge of the political system so that they could raise sons who would be good American citizens. While Republican Motherhood increased access to education for a small group of women, their rights were still subsumed by the priorities of white men.

Though science and philosophy had increased influence on eighteenth century American culture, religion had not vanished from the scene. However, the hegemony of Calvinist theology was challenged by non-denominational groups as well as by a segment within the one of its major denomination. Some American intellectuals who identified with Enlightenment principles embraced deism, often called "natural religion" in reference to natural law. More a philosophy than an organized religion, deism had little in the way of dogma and no institutional structure. This belief system followed the principles of Empiricism by asserting that religious belief should derive from reason rather than tradition. Deists believed in God, rationally deducing the existence of a Creator from the orderliness of nature observed through their senses. As Thomas Paine, perhaps the most famous deist in America, asserts in "The Existence of God" (1797), "The Universe is the bible of a true Theophilanthropist. It is there that he reads of God. It is there that the proofs of his existence are to be sought and to be found." However, deists did not see God as behind every tiny working of nature. Unlike the Puritans, who might describe any natural event as occurring because God was pleased or displeased with them, deists believed that nature operated itself along the orderly principles created by God and revealed by science. Finally, deists, like the period in general, were humanist, following a philosophy which prioritized human concerns and needs in its ethical beliefs. Whereas a Puritan would judge an action based on whether it was in accordance with or contrary to God's will, a humanist deist would judge it according to its effect on people.

Unitarianism was a more moderate religious belief of the time period, attempting to strike the preferred middle position between Calvinist beliefs and Enlightenment beliefs. Unitarianism grew out of the Congregationalist denomination—one of the major denominations of the Puritans who settled in the English colonies. Unlike deists, Unitarians valued the Bible as a sacred text; however, influenced by Empiricism, Unitarians argued that the Bible and religious traditions must be subjected to reason and accepted or rejected on that basis. One such tradition Unitarians felt did not pass rational muster was the belief in a three-person God, and their name is taken from this position. Also in accordance with Empirical beliefs, Unitarians rejected the Calvinist views of corrupt human nature and the inevitability of damnation for the majority and believed, in a religious version of human perfectibility, that all souls were capable of working toward salvation.

Colonial membership in Calvinist Protestant denominations experienced a resurgence in the eighteenth century especially from the 1730s to the 1750s when the Great Awakening, a movement of revitalized piety originating in Europe, arrived in America. While continuing to hold many tenets in contradiction to Enlightenment emphases, the Calvinism of the Great Awakening showed signs of the influence of that intellectual movement. Their views still held that man was born corrupt and unworthy of the salvation that God granted to some. However, the movement pushed back against the prioritization of rationality with the idea that one could prepare oneself to be open to God's grace by a public and emotional testimony about one's religious experience. For some of the foremost ministers of this movement, it was not enough to understand Biblical teachings intellectually; to truly understand God's will and prepare oneself for the gift of grace, should one be saved, one needed to feel those teachings emotionally. The movement also directed its adherents to evangelize (publicly testify about one's religious experience) to help others arrive at that deeper understanding and in that way, shows some influence of humanism.

3.3 JONATHAN EDWARDS

(1703–1758)

Jonathan Edwards was born in East Windsor, Connecticut to Reverend Timothy Edwards and Esther Stoddard Edwards, daughter of the Reverend Solomon Stoddard (1643–1729), an important religious figure in western Massachusetts. Nurtured by Calvinistic authorities in the Puritan Faith, Edwards nevertheless relied on his own understanding and observation of the world around him. Before reaching his teens, he refuted materialism in an essay and wrote a study of the flying spider. Upon entering Yale at the age of thirteen, he came to terms (on his own terms) with Puritan doctrine, particularly the idea of the elect and of God's complete sovereignty. As strict Calvinists, the Puritans held that God to be all-powerful and completely sovereign and all humans to be naturally depraved. God elected only a few for salvation.

Image 3.1 | Jonathan Edwards
Artist | Unknown
Source | Wikimedia Commons
License | Public Domain

Edwards' fervent acceptance of Puritan doctrine was heightened by his study of John Locke's (1632–1704) *Essay Concerning Human Understanding* (1689). This philosophical treatise encouraged empiricism, experience, and sensation. It tied abstract ideas to concrete particulars. To paraphrase the later Romantic poet John Keats (1795–1821), Edwards came to feel his abstract faith in his pulses. He recorded his conversion in his *Personal Narrative* (1765). After graduating from Yale, Edwards was ordained as minister at Northampton, Massachusetts, assisting his grandfather Solomon Stoddard before succeeding him upon his death. In 1727, Edwards married Sarah Pierrepont; together, they raised ten children.

As minister, Edwards sought to bring his congregation to an understanding of the Puritan faith that involved a physical (as well as metaphysical) experience of faith. His preaching was so successful that it contributed to the wave of revivalism now known as the first Great Awakening that swept through the colonies in the 1730s and 1740s. Listeners to Edwards' sermons were gripped by a full-bodied conviction of God's mercy for the elect, a conviction characterized by strong emotions and sentiment.

The Great Awakening led to schisms within churches with some members opposing revivals as sources of hysteria and disorder, particularly as they empowered uneducated itinerant ministers, inspired individual authority in many women, and converted a number of blacks to Christianity. The early sovereignty of

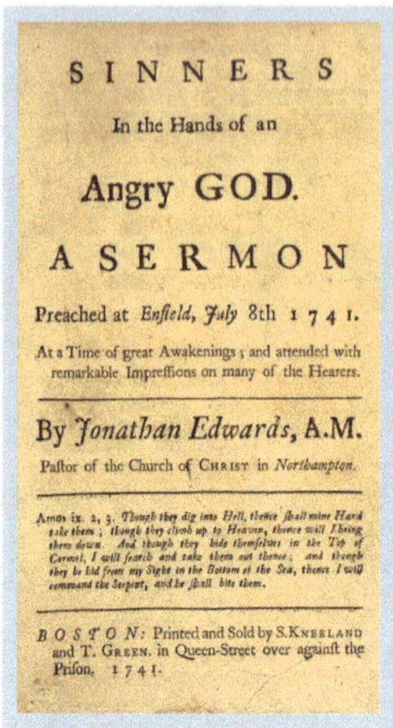

SINNERS

In the Hands of an

Angry GOD.

A SERMON

Preached at *Enfield*, *July* 8th 1741.

At a Time of great Awakenings; and attended with remarkable Impreſſions on many of the Hearers.

By *Jonathan Edwards*, A.M.

Paſtor of the Church of CHRIST in *Northampton*.

Amos ix. 2, 3. *Though they dig into Hell, thence ſhall mine Hand take them; though they climb up to Heaven, thence will I bring them down. And though they hide themſelves in the Top of Carmel, I will ſearch and take them out thence; and though they be hid from my Sight in the Bottom of the Sea, thence I will command the Serpent, and he ſhall bite them.*

BOSTON: Printed and Sold by S. KNEELAND and T. GREEN, in Queen-Street over againſt the Priſon. 1741.

Image 3.2 | *Sinners in the Hands of an Angry God*
Author | Jonathan Edwards
Source | Wikimedia Commons
License | Public Domain

Puritan faith in America thus gave way to more liberal and differing denominations and even deism. Edwards himself tried to tamp down these shifts with such works as *A Faithful Narrative of the Surprising Work of God* (1737), a work seeking to balance emotionalism and mindfulness, and his *A Treatise Concerning Religious Affections* (1746), a work that distinguished genuine from false religious experiences.

In 1741, Edwards gave the sermon *Sinners in the Hands of an Angry God*, a sermon emphasizing human depravity and God's unfathomable mercy. It uses natural and observable details and terrifying images to give a compelling depiction of that yawning hell burning beneath all, particularly the unwary and unready. Its depiction of punishment almost, but ultimately does not, overwhelm the sermon's purpose: the promise of God's mercy.

Edwards exhorted a return to traditional Puritan orthodoxy, claiming authority to denounce "backsliders" in his congregation and refuse communion to those sanctioned by the Half-Way Covenant, that is, the members of his church who did not publicly declare themselves as saved. In 1750, his congregation rejected Edwards by vote and dismissed him from the church.

He then served as missionary to the Housatonnuck Indians in Stockbridge. In 1758, he became president of the College of New Jersey, now known as Princeton. He died from smallpox after receiving an inoculation against this infectious disease.

3.3.1 "Personal Narrative"

(1765)

http://edwards.yale.edu/archive?path=aHR0cDovL2Vkd2FyZHMueWFsZS5lZHUvY2dpLWJpbi9uZXdwaGlsby9nZXRvYmplY3QucGw/Yy4xNTo3NDo1LndqZW8

3.3.2 Reading and Review Questions

1. How does Edwards convey his sense of himself as being unique, as uniquely religious, both before and after his "awakening?"

2. What stylistic elements does Edwards use? How aware of his audience is Edwards? What means, if any, does Edwards use to engage his audience? How do you know?
3. How does Edwards' narrative serve as a model to his audience? How, if at all, does it confer his potential authority over its audience? Why? How do you know?
4. What religious conflicts, fears, or uncertainties does this narrative address? How universal do you think these were among Edwards' audience? How does he resolve these conflicts, fears, and uncertainties? How convincing (to you as a reader and to Edwards' contemporaries) are his resolutions?
5. How appealing does Edwards make his faith and understanding of the Christian God? Why?

3.4 BENJAMIN FRANKLIN

(1706–1790)

Born in Boston, Benjamin Franklin was the youngest son of the youngest son five generations back. His father, Josiah Franklin, left Northamptonshire, England for America in reaction against the Church of England. Though he tried to have his son educated formally by enrolling him in the Boston Grammar School, Josiah was forced by financial circumstances to bring Benjamin into his tallow chandler and soap boiling business. Franklin hated the business, particularly the smell, so he was eventually apprenticed to his brother James, who had learned the printing trade in England and started a newspaper, *The New England Courant.*

Image 3.3 | Benjamin Franklin
Artist | Joseph Duplessis
Source | Wikimedia Commons
License | Public Domain

Franklin took to printing and the printed word, reading voraciously not only the business's publications but also the books loaned to him by its patrons and friends. Through reading and using texts as models, Franklin acquired great facility in writing. An editorial he wrote under the pseudonym of "Silence Dogood" was published by his brother, who had no idea of the piece's true authorship. James was imprisoned after quarreling with

Massachusetts authorities, leaving Franklin to run the business during his absence. Franklin was only sixteen.

James also quarreled with Benjamin, who sought freedom from James's temper and tyranny by running away, determined to make his own way in the world. In 1723, he arrived in Philadelphia and walked up the Market Street wharf munching on one of three large puffy rolls and carrying small change in his pocket. He found work as a printer there until, upon what proved to be the groundless encouragement of William Keith (1669–1749), a governor of the province, Franklin traveled to England to purchase printing equipment and start a new printing business of his own. He worked for others at printing houses for two years before returning home. While in England, he also read widely, and saw first-hand the growing importance of the periodical, the long periodical essay, and the persona of an author who served as intermediary between a large audience of readers and the news and events of the day.

He put this knowledge to good purpose once he returned to Philadelphia, first co-owning then owning outright a new printing business that published *The Pennsylvania Gazette*; books from the Continent; and, from 1733 to 1758, an almanac using the persona of Poor Richard, or Richard Saunders. *Poor Richard's Almanac* became immensely popular, eventually selling 10,000 copies per year. With wit, puns, and word play, Franklin offered distinctly American aphorisms, maxims, and proverbs on reason versus faith, household management, thrift, the work ethic, and good manners.

In 1730, he married Deborah Read who bore two children and helped raise Franklin's illegitimate son William. It was for William that Franklin wrote the first part of *The Autobiography of Benjamin Franklin*. The quintessential self-made man, his business success allowed Franklin to retire at the age of forty-two and focus his energies on the common good and public affairs. He had already contributed a great deal to both, including inventing an eponymous stove and founding the first circulating library; the American Philosophical Society; and the Pennsylvania Hospital. He also promoted the establishment of the University of Pennsylvania, an institution of higher learning grounded in secular education.

He applied the tenets of this education in first-hand observation and study of the natural world, from earthquakes to electricity. His *Experiments and Observations on Electricity* (1751–1753) won him the respect of scientists around the world. Like other humanist-deist thinkers of his day, Franklin used reason to overcome institutional tyrannies over mind and body. Between the years 1757 and 1775, he actively sought to overcome England's tyranny over the colonies in two separate diplomatic missions to England, representing Pennsylvania, Georgia, Massachusetts, and New Jersey and also protesting the Stamp Act.

The rising sense of injustice against England led to the First and then the Second Continental Congresses, at the latter of which Franklin represented Pennsylvania and served with Thomas Jefferson on the committee that drafted the 1776 Declaration of Independence, a declaration that represented all thirteen colonies. Central to the beginning of the American Revolution, Franklin was also central to its end in 1783 through the Treaty of Paris that he, John Jay, and John Adams shaped and signed. And he helped shape the future of the United States of America by serving on the Constitutional Convention that wrote the Constitution and the Bill of Rights.

Throughout all these great actions and events, Franklin wrote didactic works leavened by an extraordinary blend of worldliness and earnestness and enlivened by wit, humor, and sometimes deceptive irony.

Image 3.4 | Congress Voting Independence
Artists | Robert Edge Pine and Edward Savage
Source | Wikimedia Commons
License | Public Domain

3.4.1 "The Way to Wealth"

(1758)

COURTEOUS READER,

I have heard that nothing gives an author so great pleasure, as to find his works respectfully quoted by others. Judge, then, how much I must have been gratified by an incident I am going to relate to you. I stopped my horse, lately, where a great number of people were collected at an auction of merchants' goods. The hour of the sale not being come, they were conversing on the badness of the times; and one of the company called to a plain, clean, old man, with white locks, 'Pray, Father Abraham, what think you of the times? Will not those heavy taxes quite ruin the country! How shall we be ever able to pay them? What would you advise us to?'——Father Abraham stood up, and replied, 'If you would have my advice, I will give it you in short; "for a word to the wise is enough," as Poor Richard says.' They joined in desiring him to speak his mind, and, gathering round him, he proceeded as follows:

'Friends,' says he, 'the taxes are indeed very heavy; and, if those laid on by the government were the only ones we had to pay, we might more easily discharge them; but we have many others, and much more grievous to some of us. We are taxed twice as much by our idleness, three times as much by our pride, and four times as much by our folly; and from these taxes the commissioners cannot ease or deliver us by allowing an abatement. However, let us hearken to good advice, and something may be done for us; "God helps them that help themselves," as Poor Richard says.

I. 'It would be thought a hard government that should tax its people one-tenth part of their time to be employed in its service: but idleness taxes many of us much more; sloth, by bringing on diseases, absolutely shortens life.

"Sloth, like rust, consumes faster than labour wears, while the used key is always bright," as Poor Richard says.—"But, dost thou love life? then do not squander time, for that is the stuff life is made of," as Poor Richard says.—How much more than is necessary do we spend in sleep! forgetting that, "the sleeping fox catches no poultry, and that there will be sleeping enough in the grave," as Poor Richard says.

"If time be of all things the most precious, wasting time must be" as Poor Richard says, "the greatest prodigality;" since, as he elsewhere tells us, "Lost time is never found again; and what we call time enough, always proves little enough." Let us then up and be doing, and doing to the purpose: so by diligence shall we do more with less perplexity. "Sloth makes all things difficult, but industry all easy; and he that riseth late, must trot all day, and shall scarce overtake his business at night; while laziness travels so slowly, that poverty soon overtakes him. Drive thy business, let not that drive thee; and early to bed, and early to rise, makes a man healthy, wealthy, and wise," as Poor Richard says.

'So what signifies wishing and hoping for better times? We may make these times better, if we bestir ourselves. "Industry need not wish, and he that lives upon hope will die fasting. There are no gains without pains; then help hands, for I have no lands;" or if I have, they are smartly taxed. "He that hath a trade, hath an estate; and he that hath a calling, hath an office of profit and honour," as Poor Richard says; but then the trade must be worked at, and the calling well followed, or neither the estate nor the office will enable us to pay our taxes.—If we are industrious, we shall never starve; for "at the working man's house hunger looks in, but dares not enter." Nor will the bailiff or the constable enter, for "industry pays debts, while despair increaseth them." What, though you have found no treasure, nor has any rich relation left you a legacy. "Diligence is the mother of good luck, and God gives all things to industry. Then plow deep, while sluggards sleep, and you shall have corn to sell and to keep." Work while it is called to-day, for you know not how much you may be hindered to-morrow. "One to-day is worth two to-morrows," as Poor Richard says, and farther, "Never leave that till to-morrow, which you can do to-day."—If you were a servant, would you not be ashamed that a good master should catch you idle? Are you then your own master? be ashamed to catch yourself idle, when there is so much to be done for yourself, your family, your country, and your king. Handle your tools without mittens: remember, that "The cat in gloves catches no mice," as Poor Richard says. It is true, there is much to be done, and, perhaps, you are weak-handed: but stick to it steadily, and you will see great effects; for "Constant dropping wears away stones; and by diligence and patience the mouse ate in two the cable; and little strokes fell great oaks."

'Methinks I hear some of you say, "Must a man afford himself no leisure?" I will tell thee, my friend, what Poor Richard says, "Employ thy time well, if thou meanest to gain leisure; and, since thou art not sure of a minute, throw not away an hour." Leisure is time for doing something useful; this leisure the diligent man will obtain, but the lazy man never; for "A life of leisure and a life of laziness are two things. Many, without labour, would live by their wits only, but they break for want of stock;" whereas industry gives comfort, and plenty, and respect. "Fly pleasures and they will follow you. The diligent spinner has a large shift; and now I have a sheep and a cow, every body bids me good-morrow."

II. 'But with our industry we must likewise be steady, settled, and careful, and oversee our own affairs with our own eyes, and not trust too much to others: for, as Poor Richard says,

"I never saw an oft-removed tree,
Nor yet an oft-removed family,
That throve so well as those that settled be."

And again, "Three removes are as bad as a fire," and again, "Keep thy shop, and thy shop will keep thee:" and again, "If you would have your business done, go; if not, send." And again,

"He that by the plow would thrive,
Himself must either hold or drive."

'And again, "The eye of the master will do more work than both his hands:" and again, "Want of care does us more damage than want of knowledge;" and again, "Not to oversee workmen, is to leave them your purse open."

'Trusting too much to others' care is the ruin of many; for, "In the affairs of this world, men are saved, not by faith, but by the want of it:" but a man's own care is profitable; for, "If you would have a faithful servant, and one that you like,—serve yourself. A little neglect may breed great mischief; for want of a nail the shoe was lost; for want of a shoe the horse was lost; and for want of a horse the rider was lost;" being overtaken and slain by the enemy; all for want of a little care about a horse-shoe nail.

III. 'So much for industry, my friends, and attention to one's own business; but to these we must add frugality, if we would make our industry more certainly successful. A man may if he knows not how to save as he gets, "keep his nose all his life to the grindstone, and die not worth a groat at last. A fat kitchen makes a lean will;" and,

"Many estates are spent in the getting,
Since women for tea forsook spinning and knitting,
And men for punch forsook hewing and splitting."

"If you would be wealthy, think of saving, as well as of getting. The Indies have not made Spain rich, because her out-goes are greater than her incomes."

'Away, then, with your expensive follies, and you will not then have so much cause to complain of hard times, heavy taxes, and chargeable families; for,

"Women and wine, game and deceit,
Make the wealth small, and the want great."

And farther, "What maintains one vice, would bring up two children." You may think perhaps, that a little tea, or a little punch now and then, diet a little more costly, clothes a little finer, and a little entertainment now and then, can be no great matter; but remember, "Many a little makes a mickle." Beware of little expences; "A small leak will sink a great ship," as Poor Richard says; and again, "Who dainties love shall beggars prove;" and moreover, "Fools make feasts, and wise men eat them." Here you are all got together to this sale of fineries and nick-nacks. You call them goods; but, if you do not take care, they will prove evils to some of you. You expect they will be sold cheap, and, perhaps, they may for less than they cost; but, if you have no occasion for them, they must be dear to you. Remember what poor Richard says, "Buy what thou hast no need of, and ere long thou shalt sell thy necessaries." And again, "At a great pennyworth pause a while:" he means, that perhaps the cheapness is apparent only, and not real; or the bargain, by straitening thee in thy business, may do thee more harm than good. For, in another place, he says, "Many have been ruined by buying good pennyworths." Again, "It is foolish to lay out money in a purchase of repentance;" and yet this folly is practised every day at auctions, for want of minding the Almanack. Many a one, for the sake of finery on the back, have gone with a hungry belly, and half starved their families; "Silks and satins, scarlet and velvets, put out the kitchen fire," as Poor Richard says. These are not the necessaries of life; they can scarcely be called the conveniences: and yet only because they look pretty, how many want to have them?—By these, and other extravagancies, the genteel are reduced to poverty, and forced to borrow of those whom they formerly despised, but who, through industry and frugality, have maintained their standing; in which case it appears plainly, that "A ploughman on his legs is higher than a gentleman on his knees," as Poor Richard says. Perhaps they have had a small estate left them, which they knew not the getting of; they think "it is day, and will never be night:" that a little to be spent out of so much is not worth minding; but "Always taking out of the meal-tub, and never putting in, soon comes to the bottom," as Poor Richard says; and then, "When the well is dry, they know the worth of water." But this they might have known before, if they had taken his advice. "If you would know the value of money, go and try to borrow some; for he that goes a borrowing, goes a sorrowing," as Poor Richard says; and, indeed, so does he that lends to such people, when he goes to get it in again. Poor Dick farther advises, and says,

"Fond pride of dress is sure a very curse,
Ere fancy you consult, consult your purse."

'And again, "Pride is as loud a beggar as Want, and a great deal more saucy." When you have bought one fine thing, you must buy ten more, that your appearance may be all of a piece; but[28] Poor Dick says, "It is easier to suppress the first desire, than to satisfy all that follow it." And it is as truly folly for the poor to ape the rich, as for the frog to swell, in order to equal the ox.

"Vessels large may venture more,
But little boats should keep near shore."

It is, however, a folly soon punished: for, as Poor Richard says, "Pride that dines on vanity, sups on contempt;—Pride breakfasted with Plenty, dined with Poverty and supped with Infamy." And, after all, of what use is this pride of appearance, for which so much is risked, so much is suffered? It cannot promote health, nor ease pain; it makes no increase of merit in the person, it creates envy, it hastens misfortune.

'But what madness it must be to run in debt for these superfluities? We are offered, by the terms of this sale, six months credit; and that, perhaps, has induced some of us to attend it, because we cannot spare the ready money, and hope now to be fine without it. But, ah! think what you do when you run in debt; you give to another power over your liberty, If you cannot pay at the time, you will be ashamed to see your creditor; you will be in fear when you speak to him; you will make poor pitiful sneaking excuses, and, by degrees, come to lose your veracity, and sink into base, downright lying; for, "The second vice is lying, the first is running in debt," as Poor Richard says; and again, to the same purpose, "Lying rides upon Debt's back:" whereas a free-born Englishman ought not to be ashamed nor afraid to see or speak to any man living. But poverty often deprives a man of all spirit and virtue. "It is hard for an empty bag to stand upright."—What would you think of that prince, or of that government, who should issue an edict forbidding you to dress like a gentleman or gentlewoman, on pain of imprisonment or servitude? Would you not say that you were free, have a right to dress as you please, and that such an edict would be a breach of your privileges, and such a government tyrannical? And yet you are about to put yourself under that tyranny, when you run in debt for such dress! Your creditor has authority, at his pleasure, to deprive you of your liberty, by confining you in gaol for life, or by selling you for a servant, if you should not be able to pay him. When you have got your bargain, you may, perhaps, think little of payment; but, as Poor Richard says, "Creditors have better memories than debtors; creditors are a superstitious sect, great observers of set days and times." The day comes round before you are aware, and the demand is made before you are prepared to satisfy it; or, if you bear your debt in mind, the term, which at first seemed so long, will, as it lessens, appear extremely short: "Time will seem to have added wings to his heels as well as his shoulders. Those have a short Lent, who owe money to be paid at Easter." At present, perhaps, you may think yourselves in thriving circumstances, and that you can bear a little extravagance without injury; but

"For age and want save while you may,
No morning sun lasts a whole day."

'Gain may be temporary and uncertain; but ever, while you live, expense is constant and certain; and "It is easier to build two chimneys, than to keep one in fuel," as Poor Richard says: so, "Rather go to bed supper-less, than rise in debt,"

Get what you can, and what you get hold,
'Tis the stone that will turn all your lead into gold.

And when you have got the Philosopher's stone, sure you will no longer complain of bad times, or the difficulty of paying taxes.

IV. 'This doctrine, my friends, is reason and wisdom; but, after all, do not depend too much upon your own industry, and frugality, and prudence, though excellent things; for they may all be blasted without the blessing of Heaven; and therefore, ask that blessing humbly, and be not uncharitable to those that at present seem to want it, but comfort and help them. Remember, Job suffered, and was afterwards prosperous.

'And now to conclude, "Experience keeps a dear school, but fools will learn in no other," as Poor Richard says, and scarce in that; for it is true, "We may give advice, but we cannot give conduct." However, remember this, "They that will not be counselled cannot be helped;" and farther, that "If you will not hear Reason, she will surely rap your knuckles," as Poor Richard says.'

Thus the old gentleman ended his harangue. The people heard it, and approved the doctrine, and immediately practised the contrary, just as if it had been a common sermon; for the auction opened, and they began to buy extravagantly.—I found the good man had thoroughly studied my Almanacks, and digested all I had dropt on those topics during the course of twenty-five years. The frequent mention he made of me must have tired any one else; but my vanity was wonderfully delighted with it, though I was conscious that not a tenth part of the wisdom was my own, which he ascribed to me; but rather the gleanings that I had made of the sense of all ages and nations. However, I resolved to be the better for the echo of it; and, though I had at first determined to buy stuff for a new coat, I went away, resolved to wear my old one a little longer. Reader, if thou wilt do the same, thy profit will be as great as mine.—I am, as ever, thine to serve thee,

RICHARD SAUNDERS.

3.4.2 "An Edict by the King of Prussia" (1773)

For the Public Advertiser.

The SUBJECT of the following Article of FOREIGN INTELLIGENCE being exceeding EXTRAORDINARY, is the Reason of its being separated from the usual Articles of *Foreign News.*

Dantzick, September 5.

WE have long wondered here at the Supineness of the English Nation, under the Prussian Impositions upon its Trade entering our Port. We did not till lately know the *Claims*, antient and modern, that hang over that Nation, and therefore could not suspect that it might submit to those Impositions from a Sense of *Duty*, or from Principles of *Equity*. The following *Edict*, just made public, may, if serious, throw some Light upon this Matter.

"FREDERICK, by the Grace of God, King of Prussia, &c. &c. &c. to all present and to come, HEALTH. The Peace now enjoyed throughout our Dominions, having afforded us Leisure to apply ourselves to the Regulation of Commerce, the Improvement of our Finances, and at the same Time the easing our *Domestic Subjects* in their Taxes: For these Causes, and other good Considerations us thereunto moving, We hereby make known, that after having deliberated these Affairs in our Council, present our dear Brothers, and other great Officers of the State, Members of the same, WE, of our certain Knowledge, full Power and Authority Royal, have made and issued this present Edict, viz.

WHEREAS it is well known to all the World, that the first German Settlements made in the Island of Britain, were by Colonies of People, Subjects to our renowned Ducal Ancestors, and drawn from *their* Dominions, under the Conduct of Hengist, Horsa, Hella, Uffa, Cerdicus, Ida, and others; and that the said Colonies have flourished under the Protection of our august House, for Ages past, have never been *emancipated* therefrom, and yet have hitherto yielded little Profit to the same. And whereas We Ourself have in the last War fought for and defended the said Colonies against the Power of France, and thereby enabled them to make Conquests from the said Power in America, for which we have not yet received adequate Compensation. And whereas it is just and expedient that a Revenue should be raised from the said Colonies in Britain towards our Indemnification; and that those who are Descendants of our antient Subjects, and thence still owe us due Obedience, should contribute to the replenishing of our Royal Coffers, as they must have done had their Ancestors remained in the Territories now to us appertaining: We do therefore hereby ordain and command, That from and after the Date of these Presents, there shall be levied and paid to our Officers of the Customs, on all Goods, Wares and Merchandizes, and on all Grain and other Produce of the Earth exported from the said Island of Britain, and on all Goods of whatever Kind imported into the same, a *Duty of Four and an Half* per Cent. *ad Valorem*, for the Use of us and our Successors. And that the said Duty may more effectually be collected, We do hereby ordain, that all Ships or Vessels bound from Great Britain to any other Part of the World, or from any other Part of the World to Great Britain, shall in their respective Voyages touch at our Port of KONINGSBERG, there to be unladen, searched, and charged with the said Duties.

AND WHEREAS there have been from Time to Time discovered in the said Island of Great Britain by our Colonists there, many Mines or Beds of Iron Stone; and sundry Subjects of our antient Dominion, skilful in converting the said Stone into Metal, have in Times past transported themselves thither, carrying with them and communicating that Art; and the Inhabitants of the said Island, *presuming* that they had a natural Right to make the best Use they could of the natural Productions of their Country for their own Benefit, have not only built Furnaces for smelting the said Stone into Iron, but have erected Plating Forges, Slitting Mills, and Steel Furnaces, for the more convenient manufacturing of the same, thereby endangering a Diminution of the said Manufacture in our antient Dominion. WE do *therefore* hereby farther ordain, that from and after the Date hereof, no Mill or other Engine for Slitting or Rolling of Iron, or any Plating Forge to work with a Tilt-Hammer, or any Furnace for making Steel, shall be erected or continued in the said Island of Great Britain: And the Lord Lieutenant of every County in the said Island is hereby commanded, on Information of any such Erection within his County, to order and by Force to cause the same to be abated and destroyed, as he shall answer the Neglect thereof to Us at his Peril. But We are nevertheless graciously pleased to permit the Inhabitants of the said Island to transport their Iron into Prussia, there to be manufactured, and to them returned, they paying our Prussian Subjects for the Workmanship, with all the Costs of Commission, Freight and Risque coming and returning, any Thing herein contained to the contrary notwithstanding.

WE do not however think fit to extend this our Indulgence to the Article of *Wool*, but meaning to encourage not only the manufacturing of woollen Cloth, but also the raising of Wool in our antient Dominions, and to prevent *both*, as much as may be, in our said Island, We do hereby absolutely forbid the Transportation of Wool from thence even to the Mother Country Prussia; and that those Islanders may be farther and more effectually restrained in making any Advantage of their own Wool in the Way of Manufacture, We command that none shall be carried *out of one County into another*, nor shall any Worsted-Bay, or Woollen-Yarn, Cloth, Says, Bays, Kerseys, Serges, Frizes, Druggets, Cloth-Serges, Shalloons, or any other Drapery Stuffs, or Woollen Manufactures whatsoever, made up or mixt with Wool in any of the said Counties, be carried into any other County, or be Waterborne even across the smallest River or Creek, on Penalty of Forfeiture of the same, together with the Boats, Carriages, Horses, &c. that shall be employed in removing them. *Nevertheless* Our loving Subjects there are hereby permitted, (if they think proper) to use all their Wool as *Manure for the Improvement of their Lands.*

AND WHEREAS the Art and Mystery of making *Hats* hath arrived at great Perfection in Prussia, and the making of Hats by our remote Subjects ought to be as much as possible restrained. And forasmuch as the Islanders before-mentioned, being in Possession of Wool, Beaver, and other Furs, have *presumptuously* conceived they had a Right to make some Advantage thereof, by manufacturing the same into Hats, to the Prejudice of our domestic Manufacture, We do therefore hereby strictly command and ordain, that no Hats or Felts whatsoever, dyed or undyed, finished or unfinished, shall be loaden or put into or upon any Vessel, Cart, Carriage or Horse, to be transported or conveyed *out of one County* in the said Island *into another County*, or to *any other Place whatsoever*, by any Person or Persons whatsoever, on Pain of forfeiting the same, with a Penalty of *Five Hundred Pounds* Sterling for every Offence. Nor shall any Hat-maker in any of the said Counties employ more than two Apprentices, on Penalty of *Five Pounds* Sterling per Month: We intending hereby that such Hat-makers, being so restrained both in the Production and Sale of their Commodity, may find no Advantage in continuing their Business. But lest the said Islanders should suffer Inconveniency by the Want of Hats, We are farther graciously pleased to permit them to send their Beaver Furs to Prussia; and We also permit Hats made thereof to be exported from Prussia to Britain, the People thus favoured to pay all Costs and Charges of Manufacturing, Interest, Commission to Our Merchants, Insurance and Freight going and returning, as in the Case of Iron.

And lastly, Being willing farther to favour Our said Colonies in Britain, We do hereby also ordain and command, that all the Thieves, Highway and Street-Robbers, House-breakers, Forgerers, Murderers, So[domi]tes, and Villains of every Denomination, who have forfeited their Lives to the Law in Prussia, but whom We, in Our great Clemency, do not think fit here to hang, shall be emptied out of our Gaols into the said Island of Great Britain *for the* BETTER PEOPLING *of that Country*.

We flatter Ourselves that these Our Royal Regulations and Commands will be thought *just* and *reasonable* by Our much-favoured Colonists in England, the said Regulations being copied from their own Statutes of 10 and 11 Will. iii. C. 10, 5 Geo. ii. C. 22, 23 Geo. ii. C. 29, 4 Geo. i. C. 11, and from other equitable Laws made by their Parliaments, or from Instructions given by their Princes, or from Resolutions of both Houses entered into for the GOOD *Government* of their own Colonies in Ireland and America.

And all Persons in the said Island are hereby cautioned not to oppose in any wise the Execution of this Our Edict, or any Part thereof, such Opposition being HIGH TREASON, of which all who are *suspected* shall be transported in Fetters from Britain to Prussia, there to be tried and executed according to the *Prussian Law*.

Such is our Pleasure.

Given at Potsdam this twenty-fifth Day of the Month of August, One Thousand Seven Hundred and Seventy-three, and in the Thirty-third Year of our Reign.

By the KING in his Council

RECHTMAESSIG, *Secr*."

Some take this Edict to be merely one of the King's *Jeux d'Esprit*: Others suppose it serious, and that he means a Quarrel with England: But all here think the Assertion it concludes with, "that these Regulations are copied from Acts of the English Parliament respecting their Colonies," a very *injurious* one: it being impossible to believe, that a People distinguish'd for their *Love of Liberty*, a Nation so *wise*, so *liberal in its Sentiments*, so *just and equitable* towards its *Neighbours*, should, from mean and *injudicious* Views of *petty immediate Profit*, treat *its own Children* in a Manner so *arbitrary* and TYRANNICAL!

3.4.3 "Rules by Which a Great Empire May Be Reduced to a Small One"

(1773)

For the Public Advertiser.

RULES *by which a* GREAT EMPIRE *may be reduced to a* SMALL ONE. [Presented privately to a *late Minister*, when he entered upon his Administration; and now first published.]

An ancient Sage valued himself upon this, that tho' he could not fiddle, he knew how to make a *great City* of a *little one*. The Science that I, a modern Simpleton, am about to communicate is the very reverse.

I address myself to all Ministers who have the Management of extensive Dominions, which from their very Greatness are become troublesome to govern, because the Multiplicity of their Affairs leaves no Time for *fiddling*.

I. In the first Place, Gentlemen, you are to consider, that a great Empire, like a great Cake, is most easily diminished at the Edges. Turn your Attention therefore first to your remotest Provinces; that as you get rid of them, the next may follow in Order.

II. That the Possibility of this Separation may always exist, take special Care the Provinces are never incorporated with the Mother Country, that they do not enjoy the same common Rights, the same Privileges in Commerce, and that they are governed by *severer* Laws, all of *your enacting*, without allowing them any

Share in the Choice of the Legislators. By carefully making and preserving such Distinctions, you will (to keep to my Simile of the Cake) act like a wise Gingerbread Baker, who, to facilitate a Division, cuts his Dough half through in those Places, where, when bak'd, he would have it *broken to Pieces.*

III. These remote Provinces have perhaps been acquired, purchas'd, or conquer'd, at the sole Expence of the Settlers or their Ancestors, without the Aid of the Mother Country. If this should happen to increase her *Strength* by their growing Numbers ready to join in her Wars, her *Commerce* by their growing Demand for her Manufactures, or her *Naval Power* by greater Employment for her Ships and Seamen, they may probably suppose some Merit in this, and that it entitles them to some Favour; you are therefore to *forget it all*, or resent it as if they had done you Injury. If they happen to be zealous Whigs, Friends of Liberty, nurtur'd in Revolution Principles, *remember all that* to their Prejudice, and contrive to punish it: For such Principles, after a Revolution is thoroughly established, are of *no more Use*, they are even *odious* and *abominable.*

IV. However peaceably your Colonies have submitted to your Government, shewn their Affection to your Interest, and patiently borne their Grievances, you are to *suppose* them always inclined to revolt, and treat them accordingly. Quarter Troops among them, who by their Insolence may *provoke* the rising of Mobs, and by their Bullets and Bayonets *suppress* them. By this Means, like the Husband who uses his Wife ill *from Suspicion*, you may in Time convert your *Suspicions* into *Realities.*

V. Remote Provinces must have *Governors*, and *Judges*, to represent the Royal Person, and execute every where the delegated Parts of his Office and Authority. You Ministers know, that much of the Strength of Government depends on the Opinion of the People; and much of that Opinion on the Choice of Rulers placed immediately over them. If you send them wise and good Men for Governors, who study the Interest of the Colonists, and advance their Prosperity, they will think their King wise and good, and that he wishes the Welfare of his Subjects. If you send them learned and upright Men for judges, they will think him a Lover of Justice. This may attach your Provinces more to his Government. You are therefore to be careful who you recommend for those Offices. If you can find Prodigals who have ruined their Fortunes, broken Gamesters or Stock-Jobbers, these may do well as *Governors*; for they will probably be rapacious, and provoke the People by their Extortions. Wrangling Proctors and petty-fogging Lawyers too are not amiss, for they will be for ever disputing and quarrelling with their little Parliaments, if withal they should be ignorant, wrong-headed and insolent, so much the better. Attorneys Clerks and Newgate Solicitors will do for *Chief-Justices*, especially if they hold their Places *during your Pleasure*: And all will contribute to impress those ideas of your Government that are proper for a People *you would wish to renounce it.*

VI. To confirm these Impressions, and strike them deeper, whenever the Injured come to the Capital with Complaints of Mal-administration, Oppression, or Injustice, punish such Suitors with long Delay, enormous Expence, and a final Judgment in Favour of the Oppressor. This will have an admirable Effect every Way. The Trouble of future Complaints will be prevented, and Governors and Judges will be encouraged to farther Acts of Oppression and Injustice; and thence the People may become more disaffected, *and at length desperate*.

VII. When such Governors have crammed their Coffers, and made themselves so odious to the People that they can no longer remain among them with Safety to their Persons, recall and *reward* them with Pensions. You may make them Baronets too, if that respectable Order should not think fit to resent it. All will contribute to encourage new Governors in the same Practices, and make the supreme Government *detestable*.

VIII. If when you are engaged in War, your Colonies should vie in liberal Aids of Men and Money against the common Enemy, upon your simple Requisition, and give far beyond their Abilities, reflect, that a Penny taken from them by your Power is more honourable to you than a Pound presented by their Benevolence. Despise therefore their voluntary Grants, and resolve to harrass them with novel Taxes. They will probably complain to your Parliaments that they are taxed by a Body in which they have no Representative, and that this is contrary to common Right. They will petition for Redress. Let the Parliaments flout their Claims, reject their Petitions, refuse even to suffer the reading of them, and treat the Petitioners with the utmost Contempt. Nothing can have a better Effect, in producing the Alienation proposed; for though many can forgive Injuries, *none ever forgave Contempt*.

IX. In laying these Taxes, never regard the heavy Burthens those remote People already undergo, in defending their own Frontiers, supporting their own provincial Governments, making new Roads, building Bridges, Churches and other public Edifices, which in old Countries have been done to your Hands by your Ancestors, but which occasion constant Calls and Demands on the Purses of a new People. Forget the *Restraints* you lay on their Trade for *your own* Benefit, and the Advantage a *Monopoly* of this Trade gives your exacting Merchants. Think nothing of the Wealth those Merchants and your Manufacturers acquire by the Colony Commerce; their encreased Ability thereby to pay Taxes at home; their accumulating, in the Price of their Commodities, most of those Taxes, and so levying them from their consuming Customers: All this, and the Employment and Support of thousands of your Poor by the Colonists, you are *intirely to forget*. But remember to make your arbitrary Tax more grievous to your Provinces, by public Declarations importing that your Power of taxing them has no limits, so that when you take from them without their Consent a Shilling in the Pound, you have a clear Right to the other nineteen. This will probably weaken every Idea of *Security in their Property*, and convince them that under such a Government *they have nothing they can call their own*; which can scarce fail of producing *the happiest Consequences*!

X. Possibly indeed some of them might still comfort themselves, and say, "Though we have no Property, we have yet *something* left that is valuable; we have constitutional *Liberty* both of Person and of Conscience. This King, these Lords, and these Commons, who it seems are too remote from us to know us and feel for us, cannot take from us our *Habeas Corpus* Right, or our Right of Trial *by a Jury of our Neighbours*: They cannot deprive us of the Exercise of our Religion, alter our ecclesiastical Constitutions, and compel us to be Papists if they please, or Mahometans." To annihilate this Comfort, begin by Laws to perplex their Commerce with infinite Regulations impossible to be remembered and observed; ordain Seizures of their Property for every Failure; take away the Trial of such Property by Jury, and give it to arbitrary Judges of your own appointing, and of the lowest Characters in the Country, whose Salaries and Emoluments are to arise out of the Duties or Condemnations, and whose Appointments are *during Pleasure*. Then let there be a formal Declaration of both Houses, that Opposition to your Edicts is *Treason*, and that Persons suspected of Treason in the Provinces may, according to some obsolete Law, be seized and sent to the Metropolis of the Empire for Trial; and pass an Act that those there charged with certain other Offences shall be sent away in Chains from their Friends and Country to be tried in the same Manner for Felony. Then erect a new Court of Inquisition among them, accompanied by an armed Force, with Instructions to transport all such suspected Persons, to be ruined by the Expence if they bring over Evidences to prove their Innocence, or be found guilty and hanged if they can't afford it. And lest the People should think you cannot possibly go any farther, pass another solemn declaratory Act, that "King, Lords, and Commons had, hath, and of Right ought to have, full Power and Authority to make Statutes of sufficient Force and Validity to bind the unrepresented Provinces IN ALL CASES WHATSOEVER." This will include *Spiritual* with temporal; and taken together, must operate wonderfully to your Purpose, by convincing them, that they are at present under a Power something like that spoken of in the Scriptures, which can not only *kill their Bodies*, but *damn their Souls* to all Eternity, by compelling them, if it pleases, *to worship the Devil.*

XI. To make your Taxes more odious, and more likely to procure Resistance, send from the Capital a Board of Officers to superintend the Collection, composed of the most *indiscreet, ill-bred* and *insolent* you can find. Let these have large Salaries out of the extorted Revenue, and live in open grating Luxury upon the Sweat and Blood of the Industrious, whom they are to worry continually with groundless and expensive Prosecutions before the above-mentioned arbitrary Revenue-Judges, all *at the Cost of the Party prosecuted* tho' acquitted, because *the King is to pay no Costs*. Let these Men *by your Order* be exempted from all the common Taxes and Burthens of the Province, though they and their Property are protected by its Laws. If any Revenue Officers are *suspected* of the least Tenderness for the People, discard them. If others are justly complained of, protect and reward them. If any of the Under-officers behave so as to provoke the People to drub them, promote those to better Offices: This will encourage others to procure for themselves such profitable Drubbings, by multiplying and enlarging such Provocations, and *all with work towards the End you aim at*.

XII. Another Way to make your Tax odious, is to misapply the Produce of it. If it was originally appropriated for the *Defence* of the Provinces and the better Support of Government, and the Administration of Justice where it may be *necessary*, then apply none of it to that *Defence*, but bestow it where it is *not necessary*, in augmented Salaries or Pensions to every Governor who has distinguished himself by his Enmity to the People, and by calumniating them to their Sovereign. This will make them pay it more unwillingly, and be more apt to quarrel with those that collect it, and those that imposed it, who will quarrel again with them, and all shall contribute to your *main Purpose* of making them *weary of your Government.*

XIII. If the People of any Province have been accustomed to support their own Governors and Judges to Satisfaction, you are to apprehend that such Governors and Judges may be thereby influenced to treat the People kindly, and to do them Justice. This is another Reason for applying Part of that Revenue in larger Salaries to such Governors and Judges, given, as their Commissions are, *during your Pleasure* only, forbidding them to take any Salaries from their Provinces; that thus the People may no longer hope any Kindness from their Governors, or (in Crown Cases) any Justice from their Judges. And as the Money thus mis-applied in one Province is extorted from all, probably *all will resent the Misapplication.*

XIV. If the Parliaments of your Provinces should dare to claim Rights or complain of your Administration, order them to be harass'd with repeated *Dissolutions.* If the same Men are continually return'd by new Elections, adjourn their Meetings to some Country Village where they cannot be accommodated, and there keep them *during Pleasure*; for this, you know, is your PREROGATIVE; and an excellent one it is, as you may manage it, to promote Discontents among the People, diminish their Respect, and *increase their Disaffection.*

XV. Convert the brave honest Officers of your Navy into pimping Tide-waiters and Colony Officers of the Customs. Let those who in Time of War fought gallantly in Defence of the Commerce of their Countrymen, in Peace be taught to prey upon it. Let them learn to be corrupted by great and real Smugglers; but (to shew their Diligence) scour with armed Boats every Bay, Harbour, River, Creek, Cove or Nook throughout the Coast of your Colonies, stop and detain every Coaster, every Wood-boat, every Fisherman, tumble their Cargoes, and even their Ballast, inside out and upside down; and if a Penn'orth of Pins is found un-entered, let the Whole be seized and confiscated. Thus shall the Trade of your Colonists suffer more from their Friends in Time of Peace, than it did from their Enemies in War. Then let these Boats Crews land upon every Farm in their Way, rob the Orchards, steal the Pigs and Poultry, and insult the Inhabitants. If the injured and exasperated Farmers, unable to procure other Justice, should attack the Agressors, drub them and burn their Boats, you are to call this *High Treason* and *Rebellion*, order Fleets and Armies into their Country, and threaten to carry all the Offenders three thousand Miles to be hang'd, drawn and quartered. *O! this will work admirably!*

XVI. If you are told of Discontents in your Colonies, never believe that they are general, or that you have given Occasion for them; therefore do not think of applying any Remedy, or of changing any offensive Measure. Redress no Grievance, lest they should be encouraged to demand the Redress of some other Grievance. Grant no Request that is just and reasonable, lest they should make another that is unreasonable. Take all your Informations of the State of the Colonies from your Governors and Officers in Enmity with them. Encourage and reward these *Leasing-makers*; secrete their lying Accusations lest they should be confuted; but act upon them as the clearest Evidence, and believe nothing you hear from the Friends of the People. Suppose all their Complaints to be invented and promoted by a few factious Demagogues, whom if you could catch and hang, all would be quiet. Catch and hang a few of them accordingly; and the *Blood of the Martyrs* shall *work Miracles* in favour of your Purpose.

XVII. If you see *rival Nations* rejoicing at the Prospect of your Disunion with your Provinces, and endeavouring to promote it: If they translate, publish and applaud all the Complaints of your discontented Colonists,5 at the same Time privately stimulating you to severer Measures; let not that *alarm* or offend you. Why should it? since you all mean *the same Thing*.

XVIII. If any Colony should at their own Charge erect a Fortress to secure their Port against the Fleets of a foreign Enemy, get your Governor to betray that Fortress into your Hands. Never think of paying what it cost the Country, for that would *look*, at least, like some Regard for Justice; but turn it into a Citadel to awe the Inhabitants and curb their Commerce. If they should have lodged in such Fortress the very Arms they bought and used to aid you in your Conquests, seize them all, 'twill provoke like *Ingratitude* added to *Robbery*. One admirable Effect of these Operations will be, to discourage every other Colony from erecting such Defences, and so their and your Enemies may more easily invade them, to the great Disgrace of your Government, and of course *the Furtherance of your Project*.

XIX. Send Armies into their Country under Pretence of protecting the Inhabitants; but instead of garrisoning the Forts on their Frontiers with those Troops, to prevent Incursions, demolish those Forts, and order the Troops into the Heart of the Country, that the Savages may be encouraged to attack the Frontiers, and that the Troops may be protected by the Inhabitants: This will seem to proceed from your Ill will or your Ignorance, and contribute farther to produce and strengthen an Opinion among them, *that you are no longer fit to govern them*.

XX. Lastly, Invest the General of your Army in the Provinces with great and unconstitutional Powers, and free him from the Controul of even your own Civil Governors. Let him have Troops enow under his Command, with all the Fortresses in his Possession; and who knows but (like some provincial Generals in the Roman Empire, and encouraged by the universal Discontent you have produced) he may take it into his Head to set up for himself. If he should, and you have carefully practised these few *excellent Rules* of mine, take my Word for it, all the Provinces will immediately join him, and you will that Day (if you have not done it sooner) get rid of the Trouble of governing them, and all the *Plagues* attending their *Commerce* and Connection from thenceforth and for ever.

Q.E.D.

3.4.4 *The Autobiography of Benjamin Franklin* (1789)

Part I

Twyford, at the Bishop of St. Asaph's, 1771.

DEAR SON: I have ever had pleasure in obtaining any little anecdotes of my ancestors. You may remember the inquiries I made among the remains of my relations when you were with me in England, and the journey I undertook for that purpose. Imagining it may be equally agreeable to you to know the circumstances of my life, many of which you are yet unacquainted with, and expecting the enjoyment of a week's uninterrupted leisure in my present country retirement, I sit down to write them for you. To which I have besides some other inducements. Having emerged from the poverty and obscurity in which I was born and bred, to a state of affluence and some degree of reputation in the world, and having gone so far through life with a considerable share of felicity, the conducing means I made use of, which with the blessing of God so well succeeded, my posterity may like to know, as they may find some of them suitable to their own situations, and therefore fit to be imitated.

That felicity, when I reflected on it, has induced me sometimes to say, that were it offered to my choice, I should have no objection to a repetition of the same life from its beginning, only asking the advantages authors have in a second edition to correct some faults of the first. So I might, besides correcting the faults, change some sinister accidents and events of it for others more favorable. But though this were denied, I should still accept the offer. Since such a repetition is not to be expected, the next thing most like living one's life over again seems to be a recollection of that life, and to make that recollection as durable as possible by putting it down in writing.

Hereby, too, I shall indulge the inclination so natural in old men, to be talking of themselves and their own past actions; and I shall indulge it without being tiresome to others, who, through respect to age, might conceive themselves obliged to give me a hearing, since this may be read or not as any one pleases. And, lastly (I may as well confess it, since my denial of it will be believed by nobody), perhaps I shall a good deal gratify my own *vanity*. Indeed, I scarce ever heard or saw the introductory words, "*Without vanity I may say*," &c., but some vain thing immediately followed. Most people dislike vanity in others, whatever share they have of it themselves; but I give it fair quarter wherever I meet with it, being persuaded that it is often productive of good to the possessor, and to others that are within his sphere of action; and therefore, in many cases, it would not be altogether absurd if a man were to thank God for his vanity among the other comforts of life.

And now I speak of thanking God, I desire with all humility to acknowledge that I owe the mentioned happiness of my past life to His kind providence, which lead me to the means I used and gave them success. My belief of this induces me to *hope*, though I must not *presume*, that the same goodness will still be exercised toward me, in continuing that happiness, or enabling me to bear a fatal reverse, which I may experience as others have done: the complexion of my future fortune being known to Him only in whose power it is to bless to us even our afflictions.

The notes one of my uncles (who had the same kind of curiosity in collecting family anecdotes) once put into my hands, furnished me with several particulars relating to our ancestors. From these notes I learned that the family had lived in the same village, Ecton, in Northamptonshire, for three hundred years, and how much longer he knew not (perhaps from the time when the name of Franklin, that before was the name of an order of people, was assumed by them as a surname when others took surnames all over the kingdom), on a freehold of about thirty acres, aided by the smith's business, which had continued in the family till his time, the eldest son being always bred to that business; a custom which he and my father followed as to their eldest sons. When I searched the registers at Ecton, I found an account of their births, marriages and burials from the year 1555 only, there being no registers kept in that parish at any time preceding. By that register I perceived that I was the youngest son of the youngest son for five generations back. My grandfather Thomas, who was born in 1598, lived at Ecton till he grew too old to follow business longer, when he went to live with his son John, a dyer at Banbury, in Oxfordshire, with whom my father served an apprenticeship. There my grandfather died and lies buried. We saw his gravestone in 1758. His eldest son Thomas lived in the house at Ecton, and left it with the land to his only child, a daughter, who, with her husband, one Fisher, of Wellingborough, sold it to Mr. Isted, now lord of the manor there. My grandfather had four sons that grew up, viz.: Thomas, John, Benjamin and Josiah. I will give you what account I can of them, at this distance from my papers, and if these are not lost in my absence, you will among them find many more particulars.

Thomas was bred a smith under his father; but, being ingenious, and encouraged in learning (as all my brothers were) by an Esquire Palmer, then the principal gentleman in that parish, he qualified himself for the business of scrivener; became a considerable man in the county; was a chief mover of all public-spirited undertakings for the county or town of Northampton, and his own village, of which many instances were related of him; and much taken notice of and patronized by the then Lord Halifax. He died in 1702, January 6, old style, just four years to a day before I was born. The account we received of his life and character from some old people at Ecton, I remember, struck you as something extraordinary, from its similarity to what you knew of mine. "Had he died on the same day," you said, "one might have supposed a transmigration."

John was bred a dyer, I believe of woolens. Benjamin was bred a silk dyer, serving an apprenticeship at London. He was an ingenious man. I remember him well, for when I was a boy he came over to my father in Boston, and lived in the house with us some years. He lived to a great age. His grandson, Samuel Franklin, now lives in Boston. He left behind him two quarto volumes, MS., of his own poetry, consisting of little occasional pieces addressed to his friends and relations, of which the following, sent to me, is a specimen. He had formed a short-hand of his own, which he taught me, but, never practising it, I have now forgot it. I was named after this uncle, there being a particular affection between him and my father. He was very pious, a great attender of sermons of the best preachers, which he took down in his short-hand, and had with him many volumes of them. He was also much of a politician; too much, perhaps, for his station. There fell lately into my hands, in London, a collection he had made of all the principal pamphlets, relating to public affairs, from 1641 to 1717; many of the volumes are wanting as appears by the numbering, but there still remain eight volumes in folio, and twenty-four in quarto and in octavo. A dealer in old books met with them, and knowing me by my sometimes buying of him, he brought them to me. It seems my uncle must have left them here, when he went to America, which was about fifty years since. There are many of his notes in the margins.

This obscure family of ours was early in the Reformation, and continued Protestants through the reign of Queen Mary, when they were sometimes in danger of trouble on account of their zeal against popery. They had got an English Bible, and to conceal and secure it, it was fastened open with tapes under and within the cover of a joint-stool. When my great-great-grandfather read it to his family, he turned up the joint-stool upon his knees, turning over the leaves then under the tapes. One of the children stood at the door to give notice if he saw the apparitor coming, who was an officer of the spiritual court. In that case the stool was turned down again upon its feet, when the Bible remained concealed under it as before. This anecdote I had from my uncle Benjamin. The family continued all of the Church of England till about the end of Charles the Second's reign, when some of the ministers that had been outed for nonconformity holding conventicles in Northamptonshire, Benjamin and Josiah adhered to them, and so continued all their lives: the rest of the family remained with the Episcopal Church.

Josiah, my father, married young, and carried his wife with three children into New England, about 1682. The conventicles having been forbidden by law, and frequently disturbed, induced some considerable men of his acquaintance to remove to that country, and he was prevailed with to accompany them thither, where they expected to enjoy their mode of religion with freedom. By the same wife he had four children more born there, and by a second wife ten more, in all seventeen; of which I remember thirteen sitting at one time at his table, who all grew up to be men and women, and married; I was the youngest son, and the youngest child but two, and was born in Boston, New England. My mother, the second wife, was Abiah Folger, daughter of Peter Folger, one of the first settlers of New England, of whom honorable mention is made by Cotton Mather, in his church history of that country, entitled Magnalia Christi Americana, as "*a godly, learned Englishman*," if I remember the words rightly. I have heard that he wrote sundry small occasional pieces, but only one of them was printed, which I saw now many years since. It was written in 1675, in the home-spun verse of that time and people, and addressed to those then concerned in the government there. It was in favor of liberty of conscience, and in behalf of the Baptists, Quakers, and other sectaries that had been under persecution, ascribing the Indian wars, and other distresses that had befallen the country, to that persecution, as so many judgments of God to punish so heinous an offense, and exhorting a repeal of those uncharitable laws. The whole appeared to me as written with a good deal of decent plainness and manly freedom. The six concluding lines I remember, though I have forgotten the two first of the stanza; but the purport of them was, that his censures proceeded from good-will, and, therefore, he would be known to be the author.

"Because to be a libeller (says he)
  I hate it with my heart;
From Sherburne town, where now I dwell
  My name I do put here;
Without offense your real friend,
  It is Peter Folgier."

My elder brothers were all put apprentices to different trades. I was put to the grammar-school at eight years of age, my father intending to devote me, as the tithe of his sons, to the service of the Church. My early readiness in learning to read (which must have been very early, as I do not remember when I could not read), and the opinion of all his friends, that I should certainly make a good scholar, encouraged him in this purpose of his. My uncle Benjamin, too, approved of it, and proposed to give me all his short-hand volumes of sermons, I suppose as a stock to set up with, if I would learn his character. I continued, however, at the grammar-school not quite one year, though in that time I had risen gradually from the middle of the class of that year to be the head of it, and farther was removed into the next class above it, in order to go with that into the third at the end of the year. But my father, in the meantime, from a view of the expense of a college education, which having so large a family he could not well afford, and the mean living many so educated were afterwards able to obtain—reasons that he gave to his friends in my hearing—altered his first intention, took me from the grammar-school, and sent me to a school for writing and arithmetic, kept by a then famous man, Mr. George Brownell, very successful in his profession generally, and that by mild, encouraging methods. Under him I acquired fair writing pretty soon, but I failed in the arithmetic, and made no progress in it. At ten years old I was taken home to assist my father in his business, which was that of a tallow-chandler and sope-boiler; a business [11] he was not bred to, but had assumed on his arrival in New England, and on finding his dying trade would not maintain his family, being in little request. Accordingly, I was employed in cutting wick for the candles, filling the dipping mold and the molds for cast candles, attending the shop, going of errands, etc.

I disliked the trade, and had a strong inclination for the sea, but my father declared against it; however, living near the water, I was much in and about it, learnt early to swim well, and to manage boats; and when in a boat or canoe with other boys, I was commonly allowed to govern, especially in any case of difficulty; and upon other occasions I was generally a leader among the boys, and sometimes led them into scrapes, of which I will mention one instance, as it shows an early projecting public spirit, tho' not then justly conducted.

There was a salt-marsh that bounded part of the mill-pond, on the edge of which, at high water, we used to stand to fish for minnows. By much trampling, we had made it a mere quagmire. My proposal was to build a wharff there fit for us to stand upon, and I showed my comrades a large heap of stones, which were intended for a new house near the marsh, and which would very well suit our purpose. Accordingly, in the evening, when the workmen were gone, I assembled a number of my play-fellows, and working with them diligently like so many emmets, sometimes two or three to a stone, we brought them all away and built our little wharff. The next morning the workmen were surprised at missing the stones, which were found in our wharff. Inquiry was made after the removers; we were discovered and complained of; several of us were corrected by our fathers; and though I pleaded the usefulness of the work, mine convinced me that nothing was useful which was not honest.

I think you may like to know something of his person and character. He had an excellent constitution of body, was of middle stature, but well set, and very strong; he was ingenious, could draw prettily, was skilled a little in music, and had a clear pleasing voice, so that when he played psalm tunes on his violin and sung withal, as he sometimes 12 did in an evening after the business of the day was over, it was extremely agreeable to hear. He had a mechanical genius too, and, on occasion, was very handy in the use of other tradesmen's tools; but his great excellence lay in a sound understanding and solid judgment in prudential matters, both in private and publick affairs. In the latter, indeed, he was never employed, the numerous family he had to educate and the straitness of his circumstances keeping him close to his trade; but I remember well his being frequently visited by leading people, who consulted him for his opinion in affairs of the town or of the church he belonged to, and showed a good deal of respect for his judgment and advice: he was also much consulted by private persons about their affairs when any difficulty occurred, and frequently chosen an arbitrator between contending parties.

At his table he liked to have, as often as he could, some sensible friend or neighbor to converse with, and always took care to start some ingenious or useful topic for discourse, which might tend to improve the minds of his children. By this means he turned our attention to what was good, just, and prudent in the conduct of life; and little or no notice was ever taken of what related to the victuals on the table, whether it was well or ill dressed, in or out of season, of good or bad flavor, preferable or inferior to this or that other thing of the kind, so that I was bro't up in such a perfect inattention to those matters as to be quite indifferent what kind of food was set before me, and so unobservant of it, that to this day if I am asked I can scarce tell a few hours after dinner what I dined upon. This has been a convenience to me in travelling, where my companions have been sometimes very unhappy for want of a suitable gratification of their more delicate, because better instructed, tastes and appetites.

My mother had likewise an excellent constitution: she suckled all her ten children. I never knew either my father or mother to have any sickness but that of which they dy'd, he at 89, and she at 85 years of age. They lie buried together at Boston, where I some years since placed a marble over their grave, with this inscription:

JOSIAH FRANKLIN,
and
ABIAH his wife,
lie here interred.
They lived lovingly together in wedlock fifty-five years.
Without an estate, or any gainful employment,
By constant labor and industry,
with God's blessing,
They maintained a large family comfortably,
and brought up thirteen children
and seven grandchildren reputably.
From this instance, reader,
Be encouraged to diligence in thy calling,
And distrust not Providence.
He was a pious and prudent man;
She, a discreet and virtuous woman.
Their youngest son,
In filial regard to their memory,
Places this stone.
J.F. born 1655, died 1744, Ætat 89.
A.F. born 1667, died 1752,———85.

By my rambling digressions I perceive myself to be grown old. I us'd to write more methodically. But one does not dress for private company as for a publick ball. 'Tis perhaps only negligence.

To return: I continued thus employed in my father's business for two years, that is, till I was twelve years old; and my brother John, who was bred to that business, having left my father, married, and set up for himself at Rhode Island, there was all appearance that I was destined to supply his place, and become a tallow-chandler. But my dislike to the trade continuing, my father was under apprehensions that if he did not find one for me more agreeable, I should break away and get to sea, as his son Josiah had done, to his great vexation. He therefore sometimes took me to walk with him, and see joiners, bricklayers, turners, braziers, etc., at their work, that he might observe my inclination, and endeavor to fix it on some trade or other on land. It has ever since been a pleasure to me to see good workmen handle their tools; and it has been useful to me, having learnt so much by it as to be able to do little jobs myself in my house when a workman could not readily be got, and to construct little machines for my experiments, while the intention of making the experiment was fresh and warm in my mind. My father at last fixed upon the cutler's trade, and my uncle Benjamin's son Samuel, who was bred to that business in London, being about that time established in Boston, I was sent to be with him some time on liking. But his expectations of a fee with me displeasing my father, I was taken home again.

From a child I was fond of reading, and all the little money that came into my hands was ever laid out in books. Pleased with the Pilgrim's Progress, my first collection was of John Bunyan's works in separate little volumes. I afterward sold them to enable me to buy R. Burton's Historical Collections; they were small chapmen's books, and cheap, 40 or 50 in all. My father's little library consisted chiefly of books in polemic divinity, most of which I read, and have since often regretted that, at a time when I had such a thirst for knowledge, more proper books had not fallen in my way since it was now resolved I should not be a clergyman. Plutarch's Lives there was in which I read abundantly, and I still think that time spent to great advantage. There was also a book of De Foe's, called an Essay on Projects, and another of Dr. Mather's, called Essays to do Good, which perhaps gave me a turn of thinking that had an influence on some of the principal future events of my life.

This bookish inclination at length determined my father to make me a printer, though he had already one son (James) of that profession. In 1717 my brother James returned from England with a press and letters to set up his business in Boston. I liked it much better than that of my father, but still had a hankering for the sea. To prevent the apprehended effect of such an inclination, my father was impatient to have me bound to my brother. I stood out some time, but at last was persuaded, and signed the indentures when I was yet but twelve years old. I was to serve as an apprentice till I was twenty-one years of age, only I was to be allowed journeyman's wages during the last year. In a little time I made great proficiency in the 15 business, and became a useful hand to my brother. I now had access to better books. An acquaintance with the apprentices of booksellers enabled me sometimes to borrow a small one, which I was careful to return soon and clean. Often I sat up in my room reading the greatest part of the night, when the book was borrowed in the evening and to be returned early in the morning, lest it should be missed or wanted.

And after some time an ingenious tradesman, Mr. Matthew Adams, who had a pretty collection of books, and who frequented our printing-house, took notice of me, invited me to his library, and very kindly lent me such books as I chose to read. I now took a fancy to poetry, and made some little pieces; my brother, thinking it might turn to account, encouraged me, and put me on composing occasional ballads. One was called *The Lighthouse Tragedy*, and contained an account of the drowning of Captain Worthilake, with his two daughters: the other was a sailor's song, on the taking of *Teach* (or Blackbeard) the pirate. They were wretched stuff, in the Grub-street-ballad style; and when they were printed he sent me about the town to sell them. The first sold wonderfully, the event being recent, having made a great noise. This flattered my vanity; but my father discouraged me by ridiculing my performances, and telling me verse-makers were generally beggars. So I escaped being a poet, most probably a very bad one; but as prose writing had been of great use to me in the course of my life, and was a principal means of my advancement, I shall tell you how, in such a situation, I acquired what little ability I have in that way.

There was another bookish lad in the town, John Collins by name, with whom I was intimately acquainted. We sometimes disputed, and very fond we were of argument, and very desirous of confuting one another, which disputatious turn, by the way, is apt to become a very bad habit, making people often extremely disagreeable in company by the contradiction that is necessary to bring it into practice; and thence, besides souring and spoiling the conversation, is productive of disgusts and, perhaps enmities where you may have occasion for friendship. I had caught it by reading my father's books of dispute about religion. Persons of good sense, I have since observed, seldom fall into it, except lawyers, university men, and men of all sorts that have been bred at Edinborough.

A question was once, somehow or other, started between Collins and me, of the propriety of educating the female sex in learning, and their abilities for study. He was of opinion that it was improper, and that they were naturally unequal to it. I took the contrary side, perhaps a little for dispute's sake. He was naturally more eloquent, had a ready plenty of words; and sometimes, as I thought, bore me down more by his fluency than by the strength of his reasons. As we parted without settling the point, and were not to see one another again for some time, I sat down to put my arguments in writing, which I copied fair and sent to him. He answered, and I replied. Three or four letters of a side had passed, when my father happened to find my papers and read them. Without entering into the discussion, he took occasion to talk to me about the manner of my writing; observed that, though I had the advantage of my antagonist in correct spelling and pointing (which I ow'd to the printing-house), I fell far short in elegance of expression, in method and in perspicuity, of which he convinced me by several instances. I saw the justice of his remark, and thence grew more attentive to the manner in writing, and determined to endeavor at improvement.

About this time I met with an odd volume of the *Spectator*. It was the third. I had never before seen any of them. I bought it, read it over and over, and was much delighted with it. I thought the writing excellent, and wished, if possible, to imitate it. With this view I took some of the papers, and, making short hints of the sentiment in each sentence, laid them by a few days, and then, without looking at the book, try'd to compleat the papers again, by expressing each hinted sentiment at length, and as fully as it had been expressed before, in any suitable words that should come to hand. Then I compared my *Spectator* with the original, discovered some of my faults, and corrected them. But I found I wanted a stock of words, or a readiness in recollecting and using them, which I thought I should have acquired before that time if I had gone on making verses; since the continual occasion for words of the same import, but of different length, to suit the measure, or of different sound for the rhyme, would have laid me under a constant necessity of searching for variety, and also have tended to fix that variety in my mind, and make me master of it. Therefore I took some of the tales and turned them into verse; and, after a time, when I had pretty well forgotten the prose, turned them back again. I also sometimes jumbled my collections of hints into confusion, and after some weeks endeavored to reduce them into the best order, before I began to form the full sentences and compleat the paper. This was to teach me method in the arrangement of thoughts. By comparing my work afterwards with the original, I discovered many faults and amended them; but I sometimes had the pleasure of fancying that, in certain particulars of small import, I had been lucky enough to improve the method or the language, and this encouraged me to think I might possibly in time come to be a tolerable English writer, of which I was extremely ambitious. My time for these exercises and for reading was at night, after work or before it began in the morning, or on Sundays, when I contrived to be in the printing-house alone, evading as much as I could the common attendance on public worship which my father used to exact on me when I was under his care, and which indeed I still thought a duty, though I could not, as it seemed to me, afford time to practise it.

When about 16 years of age I happened to meet with a book, written by one Tryon, recommending a vegetable diet. I determined to go into it. My brother, being yet unmarried, did not keep house, but boarded himself and his apprentices in another family. My refusing to eat flesh occasioned an inconveniency, and I was frequently chid for my singularity. I made myself acquainted with Tryon's manner of preparing some of his dishes, such as boiling potatoes or rice, making hasty pudding, and a few others, and then proposed to my brother, that if he would give me, weekly, half the money he paid for my board, I would board myself. He instantly agreed to it, and I presently found that I could save half what he paid me. This was an additional fund for buying books. But I had another advantage in it. My brother and the rest going from the printing-house to their meals, I remained there alone, and, despatching presently my light repast, which often was no more than a bisket or a slice of bread, a handful of raisins or a tart from the pastry-cook's, and a glass of water, had the rest of the time till their return for study, in which I made the greater progress, from that greater clearness of head and quicker apprehension which usually attend temperance in eating and drinking.

And now it was that, being on some occasion made asham'd of my ignorance in figures, which I had twice failed in learning when at school, I took Cocker's book of Arithmetick, and went through the whole by myself with great ease. I also read Seller's and Shermy's books of Navigation, and became acquainted with the little geometry they contain; but never proceeded far in that science. And I read about this time Locke *On Human Understanding*, and the *Art of Thinking*, by Messrs. du Port Royal.

While I was intent on improving my language, I met with an English grammar (I think it was Greenwood's), at the end of which there were two little sketches of the arts of rhetoric and logic, the latter finishing with a specimen of a dispute in the Socratic method; and soon after I procur'd Xenophon's Memorable Things of Socrates, wherein there are many instances of the same method. I was charm'd with it, adopted it, dropt my abrupt contradiction and positive argumentation, and put on the humble inquirer and doubter. And being then, from reading Shaftesbury and Collins, become a real doubter in many points of our religious doctrine, I found this method safest for myself and very embarrassing to those against whom I used it; therefore I took a delight in it, practis'd it continually, and grew very artful and expert in drawing people, even of superior knowledge, into concessions, the consequences of which they did not foresee, entangling them in difficulties out of which they could not extricate themselves, and so obtaining victories that neither myself nor my cause always deserved. I continu'd this method some few years, but gradually left it, retaining only the habit of expressing myself in terms of modest diffidence; never using, when I advanced any thing that may possibly be disputed, the words *certainly, undoubtedly*, or any others that give the air of positiveness to an opinion; but rather say, I conceive or apprehend a thing to be so and so; it appears to me, or *I should think it so or so*, for such and such reasons; or *I imagine it to be so*; or *it is so, if I am not mistaken.* This habit, I believe, has been of great advantage to me when I have had occasion to inculcate my opinions, and persuade men into measures that I have been from time to time engag'd in promoting; and, as the chief ends of conversation are to *inform* or to be *informed*, to *please* or to *persuade*, I wish well-meaning, sensible men would not lessen their power of doing good by a positive, assuming manner, that seldom fails to disgust, tends to create opposition, and to defeat every one of those purposes for which speech was given to us, to wit, giving or receiving information or pleasure. For, if you would inform, a positive and dogmatical manner in advancing your sentiments may provoke contradiction and prevent a candid attention. If you wish information and improvement from the knowledge of others, and yet at the same time express yourself as firmly fix'd in your present opinions, modest, sensible men, who do not love disputation, will probably leave you undisturbed in the possession of your error. And by such a manner, you can seldom hope to recommend yourself in *pleasing* your hearers, or to persuade those whose concurrence you desire. Pope says, judiciously:

> *"Men should be taught as if you taught them not,*
> *And things unknown propos'd as things forgot;"*

farther recommending to us

"To speak, tho' sure, with seeming diffidence."

And he might have coupled with this line that which he has coupled with another, I think, less properly,

"For want of modesty is want of sense."

If you ask, Why less properly? I must repeat the lines,

"Immodest words admit of no defense,
For want of modesty is want of sense."

Now, is not *want of sense* (where a man is so unfortunate as to want it) some apology for his *want of modesty*? and would not the lines stand more justly thus?

"Immodest words admit *but* this defense,
That want of modesty is want of sense."

This, however, I should submit to better judgments.

My brother had, in 1720 or 1721, begun to print a newspaper. It was the second that appeared in America, and was called the New England Courant. The only one before it was the Boston News-Letter. I remember his being dissuaded by some of his friends from the undertaking, as not likely to succeed, one newspaper being, in their judgment, enough for America. At this time (1771) there are not less than five-and-twenty. He went on, however, with the undertaking, and after having worked in composing the types and printing off the sheets, I was employed to carry the papers thro' the streets to the customers.

He had some ingenious men among his friends, who amus'd themselves by writing little pieces for this paper, which gain'd it credit and made it more in demand, and these gentlemen often visited us. Hearing their conversations, and their accounts of the approbation their papers were received with, I was excited to try my hand among them; but, being still a boy, and suspecting that my brother would object to printing anything of mine in his paper if he knew it to be mine, I contrived to disguise my hand, and, writing an anonymous paper, I put it in at night under the door of the printing-house. It was found in the morning, and communicated to his writing friends when they call'd in as usual. They read it, commented on it in my hearing, and I had the exquisite pleasure of finding it met with their approbation, and that, in their different guesses at the author, none were named but men of some character among us for learning and ingenuity. I suppose now that I was rather lucky in my judges, and that perhaps they were not really so very good ones as I then esteem'd them.

Encourag'd, however, by this, I wrote and convey'd in the same way to the press several more papers which were equally approv'd; and I kept my secret till my small fund of sense for such performances was pretty well exhausted and then I discovered it, when I began to be considered a little more by my brother's acquaintance, and in a manner that did not quite please him, as he thought, probably with reason, that it tended to make me too vain. And, perhaps, this might be one occasion of the differences that we began to have about this time. Though a brother, he considered himself as my master, and me as his apprentice, and accordingly, expected the same services from me as he would from another, while I thought he demean'd me too much in some he requir'd of me, who from a brother expected more indulgence. Our disputes were often brought before our father, and I fancy I was either generally in the right, or else a better pleader, because the judgment was generally in my favor. But my brother was passionate, and had often beaten me, which I took extreamly amiss; and, thinking my apprenticeship very tedious, I was continually wishing for some opportunity of shortening it, which at length offered in a manner unexpected.

One of the pieces in our newspaper on some political point, which I have now forgotten, gave offense to the Assembly. He was taken up, censur'd, and imprison'd for a month, by the speaker's warrant, I suppose, because he would not discover his author. I too was taken up and examin'd before the council; but, tho' I did not give them any satisfaction, they content'd themselves with admonishing me, and dismissed me, considering me, perhaps, as an apprentice, who was bound to keep his master's secrets.

During my brother's confinement, which I resented a good deal, notwithstanding our private differences, I had the management of the paper; and I made bold to give our rulers some rubs in it, which my brother took very kindly, while others began to consider me in an unfavorable light, as a young genius that had a turn for libelling and satyr. My brother's discharge was accompany'd with an order of the House (a very odd one), that "*James Franklin should no longer print the paper called the New England Courant.*"

There was a consultation held in our printing-house among his friends, what he should do in this case. Some proposed to evade the order by changing the name of the paper; but my brother, seeing inconveniences in that, it was finally concluded on as a better way, to let it be printed for the future under the name of BENJAMIN FRANKLIN; and to avoid the censure of the Assembly, that might fall on him as still printing it by his apprentice, the contrivance was that my old indenture should be return'd to me, with a full discharge on the back of it, to be shown on occasion, but to secure to him the benefit of my service, I was to sign new indentures for the remainder of the term, which were to be kept private. A very flimsy scheme it was; however, it was immediately executed, and the paper went on accordingly, under my name for several months.

At length, a fresh difference arising between my brother and me, I took upon me to assert my freedom, presuming that he would not venture to produce the new indentures. It was not fair in me to take this advantage, and this I therefore reckon one of the first errata of my life; but the unfairness of it weighed little with me, when under the impressions of resentment for the blows his passion too often urged him to bestow upon me, though he was otherwise not an ill-natur'd man: perhaps I was too saucy and provoking.

When he found I would leave him, he took care to prevent my getting employment in any other printing-house of the town, by going round and speaking to every master, who accordingly refus'd to give me work. I then thought of going to New York, as the nearest place where there was a printer; and I was rather inclin'd to leave Boston when I reflected that I had already made myself a little obnoxious to the governing party, and, from the arbitrary proceedings of the Assembly in my brother's case, it was likely I might, if I stay'd, soon bring myself into scrapes; and farther, that my indiscrete disputations about religion began to make me pointed at with horror by good people as an infidel or atheist. I determin'd on the point, but my father now siding with my brother, I was sensible that, if I attempted to go openly, means would be used to prevent me. My friend Collins, therefore, undertook to manage a little for me. He agreed with the captain of a New York sloop for my passage, under the notion of my being a young acquaintance of his, that had got a naughty girl with child, whose friends would compel me to marry her, and therefore I could not appear or come away publicly. So I sold some of my books to raise a little money, was taken on board privately, and as we had a fair wind, in three days I found myself in New York, near 300 miles from home, a boy of but 17, without the least recommendation to, or knowledge of any person in the place, and with very little money in my pocket.

My inclinations for the sea were by this time worne out, or I might now have gratify'd them. But, having a trade, and supposing myself a pretty good workman, I offer'd my service to the printer in the place, old Mr. William Bradford, who had been the first printer in Pennsylvania, but removed from thence upon the quarrel of George Keith. He could give me no employment, having little to do, and help enough already; but says he, "My son at Philadelphia has lately lost his principal hand, Aquila Rose, by death; if you go thither, I believe he may employ you." Philadelphia was a hundred miles further; I set out, however, in a boat for Amboy, leaving my chest and things to follow me round by sea.

In crossing the bay, we met with a squall that tore our rotten sails to pieces, prevented our getting into the Kill, and drove us upon Long Island. In our way, a drunken Dutchman, who was a passenger too, fell overboard; when he was sinking, I reached through the water to his shock pate, and drew him up, so that we got him in again. His ducking sobered him a little, and he went to sleep, taking first out of his pocket a book, which he desir'd I would dry for him. It proved to be my old favorite author, Bunyan's Pilgrim's Progress, in Dutch, finely printed on good paper, with copper cuts, a dress better than I had ever seen it wear in its own language. I have since found that it has been translated into most of the languages of Europe, and suppose it has been more generally read than any other book, except perhaps the Bible. Honest John was the first that I know of who mix'd narration and dialogue; a method of writing very engaging to the reader, who in the most interesting parts finds himself, as it were, brought into the company and present at the discourse. De Foe in his Cruso, his Moll Flanders, Religious Courtship, Family Instructor, and other pieces, has imitated it with success; and Richardson has done the same in his Pamela, etc.

When we drew near the island, we found it was at a place where there could be no landing, there being a great surff on the stony beach. So we dropt anchor, and swung round towards the shore. Some people came down to the water edge and hallow'd to us, as we did to them; but the wind was so high, and the surff so loud, that we could not hear so as to understand each other. There were canoes on the shore, and we made signs, and hallow'd that they should fetch us; but they either did not understand us, or thought it impracticable, so they went away, and night coming on, we had no remedy but to wait till the wind should abate; and, in the meantime, the boatman and I concluded to sleep, if we could; and so crowded into the scuttle, with the Dutchman, who was still wet, and the spray beating over the head of our boat, leak'd thro' to us, so that we were soon almost as wet as he. In this manner we lay all night, with very little rest; but, the wind abating the next day, we made a shift to reach Amboy before night, having been thirty hours on the water, without victuals, or any drink but a bottle of filthy rum, and the water we sail'd on being salt.

In the evening I found myself very feverish, and went in to bed; but, having read somewhere that cold water drank plentifully was good for a fever, I follow'd the prescription, sweat plentiful most of the night, my fever left me, and in the morning, crossing the ferry, I proceeded on my journey on foot, having fifty miles to Burlington, where I was told I should find boats that would carry me the rest of the way to Philadelphia.

It rained very hard all the day; I was thoroughly soak'd, and by noon a good deal tired; so I stopt at a poor inn, where I staid all night, beginning now to wish that I had never left home. I cut so miserable a figure, too, that I found, by the questions ask'd me, I was suspected to be some runaway servant, and in danger of being taken up on that suspicion. However, I proceeded the next day, and got in the evening to an inn, within eight or ten miles of Burlington, kept by one Dr. Brown. He entered into conversation with me while I took some refreshment, and, finding I had read a little, became very sociable and friendly. Our acquaintance continu'd as long as he liv'd. He had been, I imagine, an itinerant doctor, for there was no town in England, or country in Europe, of which he could not give a very particular account. He had some letters, and was ingenious, but much of an unbeliever, and wickedly undertook, some years after, to travestie the Bible in doggrel verse, as Cotton had done Virgil. By this means he set many of the facts in a very ridiculous light, and might have hurt weak minds if his work had been published; but it never was.

At his house I lay that night, and the next morning reach'd Burlington, but had the mortification to find that the regular boats were gone a little before my coming, and no other expected to go before Tuesday, this being Saturday; wherefore I returned to an old woman in the town, of whom I had bought gingerbread to eat on the water, and ask'd her advice. She invited me to lodge at her house till a passage by water should offer; and being tired with my foot travelling, I accepted the invitation. She understanding I was a printer, would have had me stay at that town and follow my business, being ignorant of the stock necessary to begin with. She was very hospitable, gave me a dinner of ox-cheek with great good will, accepting only a pot of ale in return; and I thought myself fixed till Tuesday should come. However, walking in the evening by the side of the river, a boat came by, which I found was going towards Philadelphia, with several people in her. They took me in, and, as there was no wind, we row'd all the way; and about midnight, not having yet seen the city, some of the company were confident we must have passed it, and would row no farther; the others knew not where we were; so we put toward the shore, got into a creek, landed near an old fence, with the rails of which we made a fire, the night being cold, in October, and there we remained till daylight. Then one of the company knew the place to be Cooper's Creek, a little above Philadelphia, which we saw as soon as we got out of the creek, and arriv'd there about eight or nine o'clock on the Sunday morning, and landed at the Market-street wharf.

I have been the more particular in this description of my journey, and shall be so of my first entry into that city, that you may in your mind compare such unlikely beginnings with the figure I have since made there. I was in my working dress, my best cloaths being to come round by sea. I was dirty from my journey; my pockets were stuff'd out with shirts and stockings, and I knew no soul nor where to look for lodging. I was fatigued with travelling, rowing, and want of rest, I was very hungry; and my whole stock of cash consisted of a Dutch dollar, and about a shilling in copper. The latter I gave the people of the boat for my passage, who at first refus'd it, on account of my rowing; but I insisted on their taking it. A man being sometimes more generous when he has but a little money than when he has plenty, perhaps thro' fear of being thought to have but little.

Then I walked up the street, gazing about till near the market-house I met a boy with bread. I had made many a meal on bread, and, inquiring where he got it, I went immediately to the baker's he directed me to, in Second-street, and ask'd for bisket, intending such as we had in Boston; but they, it seems, were not made in Philadelphia. Then I asked for a three-penny loaf, and was told they had none such. So not considering or knowing the difference of money, and the greater cheapness nor the names of his bread, I made him give me three-penny worth of any sort. He gave me, accordingly, three great puffy rolls. I was surpriz'd at the quantity, but took it, and, having no room in my pockets, walk'd off with a roll under each arm, and eating the other. Thus I went up Market-street as far as Fourth-street, passing by the door of Mr. Read, my future wife's father; when she, standing at the door, saw me, and thought I made, as I certainly did, a most awkward, ridiculous appearance. Then I turned and went down Chestnut-street and part of Walnut-street, eating my roll all the way, and, coming round, found myself again at Market-street wharf, near the boat I came in, to which I went for a draught of the river water; and, being filled with one of my rolls, gave the other two to a woman and her child that came down the river in the boat with us, and were waiting to go farther.

Thus refreshed, I walked again up the street, which by this time had many clean-dressed people in it, who were all walking the same way. I joined them, and thereby was led into the great meeting-house of the Quakers near the market. I sat down among them, and, after looking round awhile and hearing nothing said, being very drowsy thro' labor and want of rest the preceding night, I fell fast asleep, and continued so till the meeting broke up, when one was kind enough to rouse me. This was, therefore, the first house I was in, or slept in, in Philadelphia.

Walking down again toward the river, and, looking in the faces of people, I met a young Quaker man, whose countenance I lik'd, and, accosting him, requested he would tell me where a stranger could get lodging. We were then near the sign of the Three Mariners. "Here," says he, "is one place that entertains strangers, but it is not a reputable house; if thee wilt walk with me, I'll show thee a better." He brought me to the Crooked Billet in Water-street. Here I got a dinner; and, while I was eating it, several sly questions were asked me, as it seemed to be suspected from my youth and appearance, that I might be some runaway.

After dinner, my sleepiness return'd, and being shown to a bed, I lay down without undressing, and slept till six in the evening, was call'd to supper, went to bed again very early, and slept soundly till next morning. Then I made myself as tidy as I could, and went to Andrew Bradford the printer's. I found in the shop the old man his father, whom I had seen at New York, and who, travelling on horseback, had got to Philadelphia before me. He introduc'd me to his son, who receiv'd me civilly, gave me a breakfast, but told me he did not at present want a hand, being lately suppli'd with one; but there was another printer in town, lately set up, one Keimer, who, perhaps, might employ me; if not, I should be welcome to lodge at his house, and he would give me a little work to do now and then till fuller business should offer.

The old gentleman said he would go with me to the new printer; and when we found him, "Neighbor," says Bradford, "I have brought to see you a young man of your business; perhaps you may want such a one." He ask'd me a few questions, put a composing stick in my hand to see how I work'd, and then said he would employ me soon, though he had just then nothing for me to do; and, taking old Bradford, whom he had never seen before, to be one of the town's people that had a good will for him, enter'd into a conversation on his present undertaking and prospects; while Bradford, not discovering that he was the other printer's father, on Keimer's saying he expected soon to get the greatest part of the business into his own hands, drew him on by artful questions, and starting little doubts, to explain all his views, what interests he reli'd on, and in what manner he intended to proceed. I, who stood by and heard all, saw immediately that one of them was a crafty old sophister, and the other a mere novice. Bradford left me with Keimer, who was greatly surpris'd when I told him who the old man was.

Keimer's printing-house, I found, consisted of an old shatter'd press, and one small, worn-out font of English which he was then using himself, composing an Elegy on Aquila Rose, before mentioned, an ingenious young man, of excellent character, much respected in the town, clerk of the Assembly, and a pretty poet. Keimer made verses too, but very indifferently. He could not be said to write them, for his manner was to compose them in the types directly out of his head. So there being no copy, but one pair of cases, and the Elegy likely to require all the letter, no one could help him. I endeavor'd to put his press (which he had not yet us'd, and of which he understood nothing) into order fit to be work'd with; and, promising to come and print off his Elegy as soon as he should have got it ready, I return'd to Bradford's, who gave me a little job to do for the present, and there I lodged and dieted. A few days after, Keimer sent for me to print off the Elegy. And now he had got another pair of cases, and a pamphlet to reprint, on which he set me to work.

These two printers I found poorly qualified for their business. Bradford had not been bred to it, and was very illiterate; and Keimer, tho' something of a scholar, was a mere compositor, knowing nothing of presswork. He had been one of the French prophets, and could act their enthusiastic agitations. At this time he did not profess any particular religion, but something of all on occasion; was very ignorant of the world, and had, as I afterward found, a good deal of the knave in his composition. He did not like my lodging at Bradford's while I work'd with him. He had a house, indeed, but without furniture, so he could not lodge me; but he got me a lodging at Mr. Read's, before mentioned, who was the owner of his house; and, my chest and clothes being come by this time, I made rather a more respectable appearance in the eyes of Miss Read than I had done when she first happen'd to see me eating my roll in the street.

I began now to have some acquaintance among the young people of the town, that were lovers of reading, with whom I spent my evenings very pleasantly; and gaining money by my industry and frugality, I lived very agreeably, forgetting Boston as much as I could, and not desiring that any there should know where I resided, except my friend Collins, who was in my secret, and kept it when I wrote to him. At length, an incident happened that sent me back again much sooner than I had intended. I had a brother-in-law, Robert Holmes, master of a sloop that traded between Boston and Delaware. He being at Newcastle, forty miles below Philadelphia, heard there of me, and wrote me a letter mentioning the concern of my friends in Boston at my abrupt departure, assuring me of their good will to me, and that every thing would be accommodated to my mind if I would return, to which he exhorted me very earnestly. I wrote an answer to his letter, thank'd him for his advice, but stated my reasons for quitting Boston fully and in such a light as to convince him I was not so wrong as he had apprehended.

Sir William Keith, governor of the province, was then at Newcastle, and Captain Holmes, happening to be in company with him when my letter came to hand, spoke to him of me, and show'd him the letter. The governor read it, and seem'd surpris'd when he was told my age. He said I appear'd a young man of promising parts, and therefore should be encouraged; the printers at Philadelphia were wretched ones; and, if I would set up there, he made no doubt I should succeed; for his part, he would procure me the public business, and do me every other service in his power. This my brother-in-law afterwards told me in Boston, but I knew as yet nothing of it; when, one day, Keimer and I being at work together near the window, we saw the governor and another gentleman (which proved to be Colonel French, of Newcastle), finely dress'd, come directly across the street to our house, and heard them at the door.

Keimer ran down immediately, thinking it a visit to him; but the governor inquir'd for me, came up, and with a condescension of politeness I had been quite unus'd to, made me many compliments, desired to be acquainted with me, blam'd me kindly for not having made myself known to him when I first came to the place, and would have me away with him to the tavern, where he was going with Colonel French to taste, as he said, some excellent Madeira. I was not a little surprised, and Keimer star'd like a pig poison'd. I went, however, with the governor and Colonel French to a tavern, at the corner of Third-street, and over the Madeira he propos'd my setting up my business, laid before me the probabilities of success, and both he and Colonel French assur'd me I should have their interest and influence in procuring the public business of both governments. On my doubting whether my father would assist me in it, Sir William said he would give me a letter to him, in which he would state the advantages, and he did not doubt of prevailing with him. So it was concluded I should return to Boston in the first vessel, with the governor's letter recommending me to my father. In the mean time the intention was to be kept a secret, and I went on working with Keimer as usual, the governor sending for me now and then to dine with him, a very great honor I thought it, and conversing with me in the most affable, familiar, and friendly manner imaginable.

About the end of April, 1724, a little vessel offer'd for Boston. I took leave of Keimer as going to see my friends. The governor gave me an ample letter, saying many flattering things of me to my father, and strongly recommending the project of my setting up at Philadelphia as a thing that must make my fortune. We struck on a shoal in going down the bay, and sprung a leak; we had a blustering time at sea, and were oblig'd to pump almost continually, at which I took my turn. We arriv'd safe, however, at Boston in about a fortnight. I had been absent seven months, and my friends had heard nothing of me; for my br. Holmes was not yet return'd, and had not written about me. My unexpected appearance surpriz'd the family; all were, however, very glad to see me, and made me welcome, except my brother. I went to see him at his printing-house. I was better dress'd than ever while in his service, having a genteel new suit from head to foot, a watch, and my pockets lin'd with near five pounds sterling in silver. He receiv'd me not very frankly, look'd me all over, and turn'd to his work again.

The journeymen were inquisitive where I had been, what sort of a country it was, and how I lik'd it. I prais'd it much, the happy life I led in it, expressing strongly my intention of returning to it; and, one of them asking what kind of money we had there, I produc'd a handful of silver, and spread it before them, which was a kind of raree-show they had not been us'd to, paper being the money of Boston. Then I took an opportunity of letting them see my watch; and, lastly (my brother still grum and sullen), I gave them a piece of eight to drink, and took my leave. This visit of mine offended him extreamly; for, when my mother some time after spoke to him of a reconciliation, and of her wishes to see us on good terms together, and that we might live for the future as brothers, he said I had insulted him in such a manner before his people that he could never forget or forgive it. In this, however, he was mistaken.

My father received the governor's letter with some apparent surprise, but said little of it to me for some days, when Capt. Holmes returning he showed it to him, ask'd him if he knew Keith, and what kind of man he was; adding his opinion that he must be of small discretion to think of setting a boy up in business who wanted yet three years of being at man's estate. Holmes said what he could in favor of the project, but my father was clear in the impropriety of it, and at last gave a flat denial to it. Then he wrote a civil letter to Sir William, thanking him for the patronage he had so kindly offered me, but declining to assist me as yet in setting up, I being, in his opinion, too young to be trusted with the management of a business so important, and for which the preparation must be so expensive.

My friend and companion Collins, who was a clerk in the post-office, pleas'd with the account I gave him of my new country, determined to go thither also; and, while I waited for my father's determination, he set out before me by land to Rhode Island, leaving his books, which were a pretty collection of mathematicks and natural philosophy, to come with mine and me to New York, where he propos'd to wait for me.

My father, tho' he did not approve Sir William's proposition, was yet pleas'd that I had been able to obtain so advantageous a character from a person of such note where I had resided, and that I had been so industrious and careful as to equip myself so handsomely in so short a time; therefore, seeing no prospect of an accommodation between my brother and me, he gave his consent to my returning again to Philadelphia, advis'd me to behave respectfully to the people there, endeavor to obtain the general esteem, and avoid lampooning and libeling, to which he thought I had too much inclination; telling me, that by steady industry and a prudent parsimony I might save enough by the time I was one-and-twenty to set me up; and that, if I came near the matter, he would help me out with the rest. This was all I could obtain, except some small gifts as tokens of his and my mother's love, when I embark'd again for New York, now with their approbation and their blessing.

The sloop putting in at Newport, Rhode Island, I visited my brother John, who had been married and settled there some years. He received me very affectionately, for he always lov'd me. A friend of his, one Vernon, having some money due to him in Pensilvania, about thirty-five pounds currency, desired I would receive it for him, and keep it till I had his directions what to remit it in. Accordingly, he gave me an order. This afterwards occasion'd me a good deal of uneasiness.

At Newport we took in a number of passengers for New York, among which were two young women, companions, and a grave, sensible, matron-like Quaker woman, with her attendants. I had shown an obliging readiness to do her some little services, which impress'd her I suppose with a degree of good will toward me; therefore, when she saw a daily growing familiarity between me and the two young women, which they appear'd to encourage, she took me aside, and said: "Young man, I am concern'd for thee, as thou has no friend with thee, and seems not to know much of the world, or of the snares youth is expos'd to; depend upon it, those are very bad women; I can see it in all their actions; and if thee art not upon thy guard, they will draw thee into some danger; they are strangers to thee, and I advise thee, in a friendly concern for thy welfare, to have no acquaintance with them." As I seem'd at first not to think so ill of them as she did, she mentioned some things she had observ'd and heard that had escap'd my notice, but now convinc'd me she was right. I thank'd her for her kind advice, and promis'd to follow it. When we arriv'd at New York, they told me where they liv'd, and invited me to come and see them; but I avoided it, and it was well I did; for the next day the captain miss'd a silver spoon and some other things, that had been taken out of his cabbin, and, knowing that these were a couple of strumpets, he got a warrant to search their lodgings, found the stolen goods, and had the thieves punish'd. So, tho' we had escap'd a sunken rock, which we scrap'd upon in the passage, I thought this escape of rather more importance to me.

At New York I found my friend Collins, who had arriv'd there some time before me. We had been intimate from children, and had read the same books together; but he had the advantage of more time for reading and studying, and a wonderful genius for mathematical learning, in which he far outstript me. While I liv'd in Boston most of my hours of leisure for conversation were spent with him, and he continu'd a sober as well as an industrious lad; was much respected for his learning by several of the clergy and other gentlemen, and seemed to promise making a good figure in life. But, during my absence, he had acquir'd a habit of sotting with brandy; and I found by his own account, and what I heard from others, that he had been drunk every day since his arrival at New York, and behav'd very oddly. He had gam'd, too, and lost his money, so that I was oblig'd to discharge his lodgings, and defray his expenses to and at Philadelphia, which prov'd extremely inconvenient to me.

The then governor of New York, Burnet (son of Bishop Burnet), hearing from the captain that a young man, one of his passengers, had a great many books, desir'd he would bring me to see him. I waited upon him accordingly, and should have taken Collins with me but that he was not sober. The gov'r. treated me with great civility, show'd me his library, which was a very large one, and we had a good deal of conversation about books and authors. This was the second governor who had done me the honor to take notice of me; which, to a poor boy like me, was very pleasing.

We proceeded to Philadelphia. I received on the way Vernon's money, without which we could hardly have finish'd our journey. Collins wished to be employ'd in some counting-house, but, whether they discover'd his dramming by his breath, or by his behaviour, tho' he had some recommendations, he met with no success in any application, and continu'd lodging and boarding at the same house with me, and at my expense. Knowing I had that money of Vernon's, he was continually borrowing of me, still promising repayment as soon as he should be in business. At length he had got so much of it that I was distress'd to think what I should do in case of being call'd on to remit it.

His drinking continu'd, about which we sometimes quarrell'd; for, when a little intoxicated, he was very fractious. Once, in a boat on the Delaware with some other young men, he refused to row in his turn. "I will be row'd home," says he. "We will not row you," says I. "You must, or stay all night on the water," says he, "just as you please." The others said, "Let us row; what signifies it?" But, my mind being soured with his other conduct, I continu'd to refuse. So he swore he would make me row, or throw me overboard; and coming along, stepping on the thwarts, toward me, when he came up and struck at me, I clapped my hand under his crutch, and, rising, pitched him head-foremost into the river. I knew he was a good swimmer, and so was under little concern about him; but before he could get round to lay hold of the boat, we had with a few strokes pull'd her out of his reach; and ever when he drew near the boat, we ask'd if he would row, striking a few strokes to slide her away from him. He was ready to die with vexation, and obstinately would not promise to row. However, seeing him at last beginning to tire, we lifted him in and brought him home dripping wet in the evening. We hardly exchang'd a civil word afterwards, and a West India captain, who had a commission to procure a tutor for the sons of a gentleman at Barbadoes, happening to meet with him, agreed to carry him thither. He left me then, promising to remit me the first money he should receive in order to discharge the debt; but I never heard of him after.

The breaking into this money of Vernon's was one of the first great errata of my life; and this affair show'd that my father was not much out in his judgment when he suppos'd me too young to manage business of importance. But Sir William, on reading his letter, said he was too prudent. There was great difference in persons; and discretion did not always accompany years, nor was youth always without it. "And since he will not set you up," says he, "I will do it myself. Give me an inventory of the things necessary to be had from England, and I will send for them. You shall repay me when you are able; I am resolv'd to have a good printer here, and I am sure you must succeed." This was spoken with such an appearance of cordiality, that I had not the least doubt of his meaning what he said. I had hitherto kept the proposition of my setting up, a secret in Philadelphia, and I still kept it. Had it been known that I depended on the governor, probably some friend, that knew him better, would have advis'd me not to rely on him, as I afterwards heard it as his known character to be liberal of promises which he never meant to keep. Yet, unsolicited as he was by me, how could I think his generous offers insincere? I believ'd him one of the best men in the world.

I presented him an inventory of a little print'g-house, amounting by my computation to about one hundred pounds sterling. He lik'd it, but ask'd me if my being on the spot in England to chuse the types, and see that every thing was good of the kind, might not be of some advantage. "Then," says he, "when there, you may make acquaintances, and establish correspondences in the bookselling and stationery way." I agreed that this might be advantageous. "Then," says he, "get yourself ready to go with Annis;" which was the annual ship, and the only one at that time usually passing between London and Philadelphia. But it would be some months before Annis sail'd, so I continu'd working with Keimer, fretting about the money Collins had got from me, and in daily apprehensions of being call'd upon by Vernon, which, however, did not happen for some years after.

I believe I have omitted mentioning that, in my first voyage from Boston, being becalm'd off Block Island, our people set about catching cod, and hauled up a great many. Hitherto I had stuck to my resolution of not eating animal food, and on this occasion consider'd, with my master Tryon, the taking every fish as a kind of unprovoked murder, since none of them had, or ever could do us any injury that might justify the slaughter. All this seemed very reasonable. But I had formerly been a great lover of fish, and, when this came hot out of the frying-pan, it smelt admirably well. I balanc'd some time between principle and inclination, till I recollected that, when the fish were opened, I saw smaller fish taken out of their stomachs; then thought I, "If you eat one another, I don't see why we mayn't eat you." So I din'd upon cod very heartily, and continued to eat with other people, returning only now and then occasionally to a vegetable diet. So convenient a thing it is to be a *reasonable creature*, since it enables one to find or make a reason for everything one has a mind to do.

Keimer and I liv'd on a pretty good familiar footing, and agreed tolerably well, for he suspected nothing of my setting up. He retained a great deal of his old enthusiasms and lov'd argumentation. We therefore had many disputations. I used to work him so with my Socratic method, and had trepann'd him so often by questions apparently so distant from any point we had in hand, and yet by degrees lead to the point, and brought him into difficulties and contradictions, that at last he grew ridiculously cautious, and would hardly answer me the most common question, without asking first, "*What do you intend to infer from that*?" However, it gave him so high an opinion of my abilities in the confuting way, that he seriously proposed my being his colleague in a project he had of setting up a new sect. He was to preach the doctrines, and I was to confound all opponents. When he came to explain with me upon the doctrines, I found several conundrums which I objected to, unless I might have my way a little too, and introduce some of mine.

Keimer wore his beard at full length, because somewhere in the Mosaic law it is said, "*Thou shalt not mar the corners of thy beard.*" He likewise kept the Seventh day, Sabbath; and these two points were essentials with him. I dislik'd both; but agreed to admit them upon condition of his adopting the doctrine of using no animal food. "I doubt," said he, "my constitution will not bear that." I assur'd him it would, and that he would be the better for it. He was usually a great glutton, and I promised myself some diversion in half starving him. He agreed to try the practice, if I would keep him company. I did so, and we held it for three months. We had our victuals dress'd, and brought to us regularly by a woman in the neighborhood, who had from me a list of forty dishes to be prepar'd for us at different times, in all which there was neither fish, flesh, nor fowl, and the whim suited me the better at this time from the cheapness of it, not costing us above eighteenpence sterling each per week. I have since kept several Lents most strictly, leaving the common diet for that, and that for the common, abruptly, without the least inconvenience, so that I think there is little in the advice of making those changes by easy gradations. I went on pleasantly, but poor Keimer suffered grievously, tired of the project, long'd for the flesh-pots of Egypt, and order'd a roast pig. He invited me and two women friends to dine with him; but, it being brought too soon upon table, he could not resist the temptation, and ate the whole before we came.

I had made some courtship during this time to Miss Read. I had a great respect and affection for her, and had some reason to believe she had the same for me; but, as I was about to take a long voyage, and we were both very young, only a little above eighteen, it was thought most prudent by her mother to prevent our going too far at present, as a marriage, if it was to take place, would be more convenient after my return, when I should be, as I expected, set up in my business. Perhaps, too, she thought my expectations not so well founded as I imagined them to be.

My chief acquaintances at this time were Charles Osborne, Joseph Watson, and James Ralph, all lovers of reading. The two first were clerks to an eminent scrivener or conveyancer in the town, Charles Brogden; the other was clerk to a merchant. Watson was a pious, sensible young man, of great integrity; the others rather more lax in their principles of religion, particularly Ralph, who, as well as Collins, had been unsettled by me, for which they both made me suffer. Osborne was sensible, candid, frank; sincere and affectionate to his friends; but, in literary matters, too fond of criticising. Ralph was ingenious, genteel in his manners, and extremely eloquent; I think I never knew a prettier talker. Both of them great admirers of poetry, and began to try their hands in little pieces. Many pleasant walks we four had together on Sundays into the woods, near Schuylkill, where we read to one another, and conferr'd on what we read.

Ralph was inclin'd to pursue the study of poetry, not doubting but he might become eminent in it, and make his fortune by it, alleging that the best poets must, when they first began to write, make as many faults as he did. Osborne dissuaded him, assur'd him he had no genius for poetry, and advis'd him to think of nothing beyond the business he was bred to; that, in the mercantile way, tho' he had no stock, he might, by his diligence and punctuality, recommend himself to employment as a factor, and in time acquire wherewith to trade on his own account. I approv'd the amusing one's self with poetry now and then, so far as to improve one's language, but no farther.

On this it was propos'd that we should each of us, at our next meeting, produce a piece of our own composing, in order to improve by our mutual observations, criticisms, and corrections. As language and expression were what we had in view, we excluded all considerations of invention 39 by agreeing that the task should be a version of the eighteenth Psalm, which describes the descent of a Deity. When the time of our meeting drew nigh, Ralph called on me first, and let me know his piece was ready. I told him I had been busy, and, having little inclination, had done nothing. He then show'd me his piece for my opinion, and I much approv'd it, as it appear'd to me to have great merit. "Now," says he, "Osborne never will allow the least merit in any thing of mine, but makes 1000 criticisms out of mere envy. He is not so jealous of you; I wish, therefore, you would take this piece, and produce it as yours; I will pretend not to have had time, and so produce nothing. We shall then see what he will say to it." It was agreed, and I immediately transcrib'd it, that it might appear in my own hand.

We met; Watson's performance was read; there were some beauties in it, but many defects. Osborne's was read; it was much better; Ralph did it justice; remarked some faults, but applauded the beauties. He himself had nothing to produce. I was backward; seemed desirous of being excused; had not had sufficient time to correct, etc.; but no excuse could be admitted; produce I must. It was read and repeated; Watson and Osborne gave up the contest, and join'd in applauding it. Ralph only made some criticisms, and propos'd some amendments; but I defended my text. Osborne was against Ralph, and told him he was no better a critic than poet, so he dropt the argument. As they two went home together, Osborne expressed himself still more strongly in favor of what he thought my production; having restrain'd himself before, as he said, lest I should think it flattery. "But who would have imagin'd," said he, "that Franklin had been capable of such a performance; such painting, such force, such fire! He has even improv'd the original. In his common conversation he seems to have no choice of words; he hesitates and blunders; and yet, good God! how he writes!" When we next met, Ralph discovered the trick we had plaid him, and Osborne was a little laught at.

This transaction fixed Ralph in his resolution of becoming a poet. I did all I could to dissuade him from it, but he continued scribbling verses till *Pope* cured him. He became, however, a pretty good prose writer. More of him hereafter. But, as I may not have occasion again to mention the other two, I shall just remark here, that Watson died in my arms a few years after, much lamented, being the best of our set. Osborne went to the West Indies, where he became an eminent lawyer and made money, but died young. He and I had made a serious agreement, that the one who happen'd first to die should, if possible, make a friendly visit to the other, and acquaint him how he found things in that separate state. But he never fulfill'd his promise.

The governor, seeming to like my company, had me frequently to his house, and his setting me up was always mention'd as a fixed thing. I was to take with me letters recommendatory to a number of his friends, besides the letter of credit to furnish me with the necessary money for purchasing the press and types, paper, etc. For these letters I was appointed to call at different times, when they were to be ready, but a future time was still named. Thus he went on till the ship, whose departure too had been several times postponed, was on the point of sailing. Then, when I call'd to take my leave and receive the letters, his secretary, Dr. Bard, came out to me and said the governor was extremely busy in writing, but would be down at Newcastle before the ship, and there the letters would be delivered to me.

Ralph, though married, and having one child, had determined to accompany me in this voyage. It was thought he intended to establish a correspondence, and obtain goods to sell on commission; but I found afterwards, that, thro' some discontent with his wife's relations, he purposed to leave her on their hands, and never return again. Having taken leave of my friends, and interchang'd some promises with Miss Read, I left Philadelphia in the ship, which anchor'd at Newcastle. The governor was there; but when I went to his lodging, the secretary came to me from him with the civillest message in the world, that he could not then see me, being engaged in business of the utmost importance, but should send the letters to me on board, wish'd me heartily a good voyage and a speedy return, etc. I returned on board a little puzzled, but still not doubting.

Mr. Andrew Hamilton, a famous lawyer of Philadelphia, had taken passage in the same ship for himself and son, and with Mr. Denham, a Quaker merchant, and Messrs. Onion and Russel, masters of an iron work in Maryland, had engag'd the great cabin; so that Ralph and I were forced to take up with a berth in the steerage, and none on board knowing us, were considered as ordinary persons. But Mr. Hamilton and his son (it was James, since governor) return'd from Newcastle to Philadelphia, the father being recall'd by a great fee to plead for a seized ship; and, just before we sail'd, Colonel French coming on board, and showing me great respect, I was more taken notice of, and, with my friend Ralph, invited by the other gentlemen to come into the cabin, there being now room. Accordingly, we remov'd thither.

Understanding that Colonel French had brought on board the governor's despatches, I ask'd the captain for those letters that were to be under my care. He said all were put into the bag together and he could not then come at them; but, before we landed in England, I should have an opportunity of picking them out; so I was satisfied for the present, and we proceeded on our voyage. We had a sociable company in the cabin, and lived uncommonly well, having the addition of all Mr. Hamilton's stores, who had laid in plentifully. In this passage Mr. Denham contracted a friendship for me that continued during his life. The voyage was otherwise not a pleasant one, as we had a great deal of bad weather.

When we came into the Channel, the captain kept his word with me, and gave me an opportunity of examining the bag for the governor's letters. I found none upon which my name was put as under my care. I picked out six or seven, that, by the handwriting, I thought might be the promised letters, especially as one of them was directed to Basket, the king's printer, and another to some stationer. We arriv'd in London the 24th of December, 1724. I waited upon the stationer, who came first in my way, delivering the letter as from Governor Keith. "I don't know such a person," says he; but, opening the letter, "O! this is from Riddlesden. I have lately found him to be a compleat rascal, and I will have nothing to do with him, nor receive any letters from him." So, putting the letter into my hand, he turn'd on his heel and left me to serve some customer. I was surprized to find these were not the governor's letters; and, after recollecting and comparing circumstances, I began to doubt his sincerity. I found my friend Denham, and opened the whole affair to him. He let me into Keith's character; told me there was not the least probability that he had written any letters for me; that no one, who knew him, had the smallest dependence on him; and he laught at the notion of the governor's giving me a letter of credit, having, as he said, no credit to give. On my expressing some concern about what I should do, he advised me to endeavor getting some employment in the way of my business. "Among the printers here," said he, "you will improve yourself, and when you return to America, you will set up to greater advantage."

We both of us happen'd to know, as well as the stationer, that Riddlesden, the attorney, was a very knave. He had half ruin'd Miss Read's father by persuading him to be bound for him. By this letter it appear'd there was a secret scheme on foot to the prejudice of Hamilton (suppos'd to be then coming over with us); and that Keith was concerned in it with Riddlesden. Denham, who was a friend of Hamilton's thought he ought to be acquainted with it; so, when he arriv'd in England, which was soon after, partly from resentment and ill-will to Keith and Riddlesden, and partly from good-will to him, I waited on him, and gave him the letter. He thank'd me cordially, the information being of importance to him; and from that time he became my friend, greatly to my advantage afterwards on many occasions.

But what shall we think of a governor's playing such pitiful tricks, and imposing so grossly on a poor ignorant boy! It was a habit he had acquired. He wish'd to please everybody; and, having little to give, he gave expectations. He was otherwise an ingenious, sensible man, a pretty good writer, and a good governor for the people, tho' not for his constituents, the proprietaries, whose instructions he sometimes disregarded. Several of our best laws were of his planning and passed during his administration.

Ralph and I were inseparable companions. We took lodgings together in Little Britain at three shillings and sixpence a week—as much as we could then afford. He found some relations, but they were poor, and unable to assist him. He now let me know his intentions of remaining in London, and that he never meant to return to Philadelphia. He had brought no money with him, the whole he could muster having been expended in paying his passage. I had fifteen pistoles; so he borrowed occasionally of me to subsist, while he was looking out for business. He first endeavored to get into the playhouse, believing himself qualify'd for an actor; but Wilkes, to whom he apply'd, advis'd him candidly not to think of that employment, as it was impossible he should succeed in it. Then he propos'd to Roberts, a publisher in Paternoster Row, to write for him a weekly paper like the Spectator, on certain conditions, which Roberts did not approve. Then he endeavored to get employment as a hackney writer, to copy for the stationers and lawyers about the Temple, but could find no vacancy.

I immediately got into work at Palmer's, then a famous printing-house in Bartholomew Close, and here I continu'd near a year. I was pretty diligent, but spent with Ralph a good deal of my earnings in going to plays and other places of amusement. We had together consumed all my pistoles, and now just rubbed on from hand to mouth. He seem'd quite to forget his wife and child, and I, by degrees, my engagements with Miss Read, to whom I never wrote more than one letter, and that was to let her know I was not likely soon to return. This was another of the great errata of my life, which I should wish to correct if I were to live it over again. In fact, by our expenses, I was constantly kept unable to pay my passage.

At Palmer's I was employed in composing for the second edition of Wollaston's "Religion of Nature." Some of his reasonings not appearing to me well founded, I wrote a little metaphysical piece in which I made remarks on them. It was entitled "A Dissertation on Liberty and Necessity, Pleasure and Pain." I inscribed it to my friend Ralph; I printed a small number. It occasion'd my being more consider'd by Mr. Palmer as a young man of some ingenuity, tho' he seriously expostulated with me upon the principles of my pamphlet, which to him appear'd abominable. My printing this pamphlet was another erratum. While I lodg'd in Little Britain, I made an acquaintance with one Wilcox, a bookseller, whose shop was at the next door. He had an immense collection of second-hand books. Circulating libraries were not then in use; but we agreed that, on certain reasonable terms, which I have now forgotten, I might take, read, and return any of his books. This I esteem'd a great advantage, and I made as much use of it as I could.

My pamphlet by some means falling into the hands of one Lyons, a surgeon, author of a book entitled "The Infallibility of Human Judgment," it occasioned an acquaintance between us. He took great notice of me, called on me often to converse on those subjects, carried me to the Horns, a pale alehouse in ——— Lane, Cheapside, and introduced me to Dr. Mandeville, author of the "Fable of the Bees," who had a club there, of which he was the soul, being a most facetious, entertaining companion. Lyons, too, introduced me to Dr. Pemberton, at Batson's Coffee-house, who promis'd to give me an opportunity, some time or other, of seeing Sir Isaac Newton, of which I was extreamely desirous; but this never happened.

I had brought over a few curiosities, among which the principal was a purse made of the asbestos, which purifies by fire. Sir Hans Sloane heard of it, came to see me, and invited me to his house in Bloomsbury Square, where he show'd me all his curiosities, and persuaded me to let him add that to the number, for which he paid me handsomely.

In our house there lodg'd a young woman, a milliner, who, I think, had a shop in the Cloisters. She had been genteelly bred, was sensible and lively, and of most pleasing conversation. Ralph read plays to her in the evenings, they grew intimate, she took another lodging, and he followed her. They liv'd together some time; but, he being still out of business, and her income not sufficient to maintain them with her child, he took a resolution of going from London, to try for a country school, which he thought himself well qualified to undertake, as he wrote an excellent hand, and was a master of arithmetic and accounts. This, however, he deemed a business below him, and confident of future better fortune, when he should be unwilling to have it known that he once was so meanly employed, he changed his name, and did me the honor to assume mine; for I soon after had a letter from him, acquainting me that he was settled in a small village (in Berkshire, I think it was, where he taught reading and writing to ten or a dozen boys, at sixpence each per week), recommending Mrs. T——— to my care, and desiring me to write to him, directing for Mr. Franklin, schoolmaster, at such a place.

He continued to write frequently, sending me large specimens of an epic poem which he was then composing, and desiring my remarks and corrections. These I gave him from time to time, but endeavor'd rather to discourage his proceeding. One of Young's Satires was then just published. I copy'd and sent him a great part of it, which set in a strong light the folly of pursuing the Muses with any hope of advancement by them. All was in vain; sheets of the poem continued to come by every post. In the mean time, Mrs. T———, having on his account lost her friends and business, was often in distresses, and us'd to send for me, and borrow what I could spare to help her out of them. I grew fond of her company, and, being at that time under no religious restraint, and presuming upon my importance to her, I attempted familiarities (another erratum) which she repuls'd with a proper resentment, and acquainted him with my behaviour. This made a breach between us; and, when he returned again to London, he let me know he thought I had cancell'd all the obligations he had been under to me. So I found I was never to expect his repaying me what I lent to him, or advanc'd for him. This, however, was not then of much consequence, as he was totally unable; and in the loss of his friendship I found myself relieved from a burthen. I now began to think of getting a little money beforehand, and, expecting better work, I left Palmer's to work at Watts's, near Lincoln's Inn Fields, a still greater printing-house. Here I continued all the rest of my stay in London.

At my first admission into this printing-house I took to working at press, imagining I felt a want of the bodily exercise I had been us'd to in America, where presswork is mix'd with composing. I drank only water; the other workmen, near fifty in number, were great guzzlers of beer. On occasion, I carried up and down stairs a large form of types in each hand, when others carried but one in both hands. They wondered to see, from this and several instances, that the *Water-American*, as they called me, was *stronger* than themselves, who drank *strong* beer! We had an alehouse boy who attended always in the house to supply the workmen. My companion at the press drank every day a pint before breakfast, a pint at breakfast with his bread and cheese, a pint between breakfast and dinner, a pint at dinner, a pint in the afternoon about six o'clock, and another when he had done his day's work. I thought it a detestable custom; but it was necessary, he suppos'd, to drink *strong* beer, that he might be *strong* to labor. I endeavored to convince him that the bodily strength afforded by beer could only be in proportion to the grain or flour of the barley dissolved in the water of which it was made; that there was more flour in a pennyworth of bread; and therefore, if he would eat that with a pint of water, it would give him more strength than a quart of beer. He drank on, however, and had four or five shillings to pay out of his wages every Saturday night for that muddling liquor; an expense I was free from. And thus these poor devils keep themselves always under.

Watts, after some weeks, desiring to have me in the composing-room, I left the pressmen; a new bien venu or sum for drink, being five shillings, was demanded of me by the compositors. I thought it an imposition, as I had paid below; the master thought so too, and forbad my paying it. I stood out two or three weeks, was accordingly considered as an excommunicate, and had so many little pieces of private mischief done me, by mixing my sorts, transposing my pages, breaking my matter, etc., etc., if I were ever so little out of the room, and all ascribed to the chappel ghost, which they said ever haunted those not regularly admitted, that, notwithstanding the master's protection, I found myself oblig'd to comply and pay the money, convinc'd of the folly of being on ill terms with those one is to live with continually.

I was now on a fair footing with them, and soon acquir'd considerable influence. I propos'd some reasonable alterations in their chappel laws, and carried them against all opposition. From my example, a great part of them left their muddling breakfast of beer, and bread, and cheese, finding they could with me be suppli'd from a neighboring house with a large porringer of hot water-gruel, sprinkled with pepper, crumbl'd with bread, and a bit of butter in it, for the price of a pint of beer, viz., three half-pence. This was a more comfortable as well as cheaper breakfast, and kept their heads clearer. Those who continued sotting with beer all day, were often, by not paying, out of credit at the alehouse, and us'd to make interest with me to get beer; their *light*, as they phrased it, *being out*. I watch'd the pay-table on Saturday night, and collected what I stood engag'd for them, having to pay sometimes near thirty shillings a week on their account. This, and my being esteem'd a pretty good *riggite*, that is, a jocular verbal satirist, supported my consequence in the society. My constant attendance (I never making a St. Monday) recommended me to the master; and my uncommon quickness at composing occasioned my being put upon all work of dispatch, which was generally better paid. So I went on now very agreeably.

My lodging in Little Britain being too remote, I found another in Duke-street, opposite to the Romish Chapel. It was two pair of stairs backwards, at an Italian warehouse. A widow lady kept the house; she had a daughter, and a maid servant, and a journeyman who attended the warehouse, but lodg'd abroad. After sending to inquire my character at the house where I last lodg'd she agreed to take me in at the same rate, 3s. 6d. per week; cheaper, as she said, from the protection she expected in having a man lodge in the house. She was a widow, an elderly woman; had been bred a Protestant, being a clergyman's daughter, but was converted to the Catholic religion by her husband, whose memory she much revered; had lived much among people of distinction, and knew a thousand anecdotes of them as far back as the times of Charles the Second. She was lame in her knees with the gout, and, therefore, seldom stirred out of her room, so sometimes wanted company; and hers was so highly amusing to me, that I was sure to spend an evening with her whenever she desired it. Our supper was only half an anchovy each, on a very little strip of bread and butter, and half a pint of ale between us; but the entertainment was in her conversation. My always keeping good hours, and giving little trouble in the family, made her unwilling to part with me; so that, when I talk'd of a lodging I had heard of, nearer my business, for two shillings a week, which, intent as I now was on saving money, made some difference, she bid me not think of it, for she would abate me two shillings a week for the future; so I remained with her at one shilling and sixpence as long as I staid in London.

In a garret of her house there lived a maiden lady of seventy, in the most retired manner, of whom my landlady gave me this account: that she was a Roman Catholic, had been sent abroad when young, and lodg'd in a nunnery with an intent of becoming a nun; but, the country not agreeing with her, she returned to England, where, there being no nunnery, she had vow'd to lead the life of a nun, as near as might be done in those circumstances. Accordingly, she had given all her estate to charitable uses, reserving only twelve pounds a year to live on, and out of this sum she still gave a great deal in charity, living herself on water-gruel only, and using no fire but to boil it. She had lived many years in that garret, being permitted to remain there gratis by successive Catholic tenants of the house below, as they deemed it a blessing to have her there. A priest visited her to confess her every day. "I have ask'd her," says my landlady, "how she, as she liv'd, could possibly find so much employment for a confessor?" "Oh," said she, "it is impossible to avoid *vain thoughts*." I was permitted once to visit her. She was chearful and polite, and convers'd pleasantly. The room was clean, but had no other furniture than a matras, a table with a crucifix and book, a stool which she gave me to sit on, and a picture over the chimney of Saint Veronica displaying her handkerchief, with the miraculous figure of Christ's bleeding face on it, which she explained to me with great seriousness. She look'd pale, but was never sick; and I give it as another instance on how small an income life and health may be supported.

At Watts's printing-house I contracted an acquaintance with an ingenious young man, one Wygate, who, having wealthy relations, had been better educated than most printers; was a tolerable Latinist, spoke French, and lov'd reading. I taught him and a friend of his to swim at twice going into the river, and they soon became good swimmers. They introduc'd me to some gentlemen from the country, who went to Chelsea by water to see the College and Don Saltero's curiosities. In our return, at the request of the company, whose curiosity Wygate had excited, I stripped and leaped into the river, and swam from near Chelsea to Blackfryar's, performing on the way many feats of activity, both upon and under water, that surpris'd and pleas'd those to whom they were novelties.

I had from a child been ever delighted with this exercise, had studied and practis'd all Thevenot's motions and positions, added some of my own, aiming at the graceful and easy as well as the useful. All these I took this occasion of exhibiting to the company, and was much flatter'd by their admiration; and Wygate, who was desirous of becoming a master, grew more and more attach'd to me on that account, as well as from the similarity of our studies. He at length proposed to me travelling all over Europe together, supporting ourselves everywhere by working at our business. I was once inclined to it; but, mentioning it to my good friend Mr. Denham, with whom I often spent an hour when I had leisure, he dissuaded me from it, advising me to think only of returning to Pennsilvania, which he was now about to do.

I must record one trait of this good man's character. He had formerly been in business at Bristol, but failed in debt to a number of people, compounded and went to America. There, by a close application to business as a merchant, he acquir'd a plentiful fortune in a few years. Returning to England in the ship with me, he invited his old creditors to an entertainment, at which he thank'd them for the easy composition they had favored him with, and, when they expected nothing but the treat, every man at the first remove found under his plate an order on a banker for the full amount of the unpaid remainder with interest.

He now told me he was about to return to Philadelphia, and should carry over a great quantity of goods in order to open a store there. He propos'd to take me over as his clerk, to keep his books, in which he would instruct me, copy his letters, and attend the store. He added that, as soon as I should be acquainted with mercantile business, he would promote me by sending me with a cargo of flour and bread, etc., to the West Indies, and procure me commissions from others which would be profitable; and, if I manag'd well, would establish me handsomely. The thing pleas'd me; for I was grown tired of London, remembered with pleasure the happy months I had spent in Pennsylvania, and wish'd again to see it; therefore I immediately agreed on the terms of fifty pounds a year, Pennsylvania money; less, indeed, than my present gettings as a compositor, but affording a better prospect.

I now took leave of printing, as I thought, for ever, and was daily employed in my new business, going about with Mr. Denham among the tradesmen to purchase various articles, and seeing them pack'd up, doing errands, calling upon workmen to dispatch, etc.; and, when all was on board, I had a few days' leisure. On one of these days, I was, to my surprise, sent for by a great man I knew only by name, a Sir William Wyndham, and I waited upon him. He had heard by some means or other of my swimming from Chelsea to Blackfriar's, and of my teaching Wygate and another young man to swim in a few hours. He had two sons, about to set out on their travels; he wish'd to have them first taught swimming, and proposed to gratify me handsomely if I would teach them. They were not yet come to town, and my stay was uncertain, so I could not undertake it; but, from this incident, I thought it likely that, if I were to remain in England and open a swimming-school, I might get a good deal of money; and it struck me so strongly, that, had the overture been sooner made me, probably I should not so soon have returned to America. After many years, you and I had something of more importance to do with one of these sons of Sir William Wyndham, become Earl of Egremont, which I shall mention in its place.

Thus I spent about eighteen months in London; most part of the time I work'd hard at my business, and spent but little upon myself except in seeing plays and in books. My friend Ralph had kept me poor; he owed me about twenty-seven pounds, which I was now never likely to receive; a great sum out of my small earnings! I lov'd him, notwithstanding, for he had many amiable qualities. I had by no means improv'd my fortune; but I had picked up some very ingenious acquaintance, whose conversation was of great advantage to me; and I had read considerably.

We sail'd from Gravesend on the 23d of July, 1726. For the incidents of the voyage, I refer you to my Journal, where you will find them all minutely related. Perhaps the most important part of that journal is the *plan* to be found in it, which I formed at sea, for regulating my future conduct in life. It is the more remarkable, as being formed when I was so young, and yet being pretty faithfully adhered to quite thro' to old age.

We landed in Philadelphia on the 11th of October, where I found sundry alterations. Keith was no longer governor, being superseded by Major Gordon. I met him walking the streets as a common citizen. He seem'd a little asham'd at seeing me, but pass'd without saying anything. I should have been as much asham'd at seeing Miss Read, had not her friends, despairing with reason of my return after the receipt of my letter, persuaded her to marry another, one Rogers, a potter, which was done in my absence. With him, however, she was never happy, and soon parted from him, refusing to cohabit with him or bear his name, it being now said that he had another wife. He was a worthless fellow, tho' an excellent workman, which was the temptation to her friends. He got into debt, ran away in 1727 or 1728, went to the West Indies, and died there. Keimer had got a better house, a shop well supply'd with stationery, plenty of new types, a number of hands, tho' none good, and seem'd to have a great deal of business.

Mr. Denham took a store in Water-street, where we open'd our goods; I attended the business diligently, studied accounts, and grew, in a little time, expert at selling. We lodg'd and boarded together; he counsell'd me as a father, having a sincere regard for me. I respected and lov'd him, and we might have gone on together very happy; but, in the beginning of February, 1726-7, when I had just pass'd my twenty-first year, we both were taken ill. My distemper was a pleurisy, which very nearly carried me off. I suffered a good deal, gave up the point in my own mind, and was rather disappointed when I found myself recovering, regretting, in some degree, that I must now, some time or other, have all that disagreeable work to do over again. I forget what his distemper was; it held him a long time, and at length carried him off. He left me a small legacy in a nuncupative will, as a token of his kindness for me, and he left me once more to the wide world; for the store was taken into the care of his executors, and my employment under him ended.

My brother-in-law, Holmes, being now at Philadelphia, advised my return to my business; and Keimer tempted me, with an offer of large wages by the year, to come and take the management of his printing-house, that he might better attend his stationer's shop. I had heard a bad character of him in London from his wife and her friends, and was not fond of having any more to do with him. I tri'd for farther employment as a merchant's clerk; but, not readily meeting with any, I clos'd again with Keimer. I found in his house these hands: Hugh Meredith, a Welsh Pensilvanian, thirty years of age, bred to country work; honest, sensible, had a great deal of solid observation, was something of a reader, but given to drink. Stephen Potts, a young countryman of full age, bred to the same, of uncommon natural parts, and great wit and humor, but a little idle. These he had agreed with at extream low wages per week, to be rais'd a shilling every three months, as they would deserve by improving in their business; and the expectation of these high wages, to come on hereafter, was what he had drawn them in with. Meredith was to work at press, Potts at book-binding, which he, by agreement, was to teach them, though he knew neither one nor t'other. John ———, a wild Irishman, brought up to no business, whose service, for four years, Keimer had purchased from the captain of a ship; he, too, was to be made a pressman. George Webb, an Oxford scholar, whose time for four years he had likewise bought, intending him for a compositor, of whom more presently; and David Harry, a country boy, whom he had taken apprentice.

I soon perceiv'd that the intention of engaging me at wages so much higher than he had been us'd to give, was, to have these raw, cheap hands form'd thro' me; and, as soon as I had instructed them, then they being all articled to him, he should be able to do without me. I went on, however, very cheerfully, put his printing-house in order, which had been in great confusion, and brought his hands by degrees to mind their business and to do it better.

It was an odd thing to find an Oxford scholar in the situation of a bought servant. He was not more than eighteen years of age, and gave me this account of himself; that he was born in Gloucester, educated at a grammar-school there, had been distinguish'd among the scholars for some apparent superiority in performing his part, when they exhibited plays; belong'd to the Witty Club there, and had written some pieces in prose and verse, which were printed in the Gloucester newspapers; thence he was sent to Oxford; where he continued about a year, but not well satisfi'd, wishing of all things to see London, and become a player. At length, receiving his quarterly allowance of fifteen guineas, instead of discharging his debts he walk'd out of town, hid his gown in a furze bush, and footed it to London, where, having no friend to advise him, he fell into bad company, soon spent his guineas, found no means of being introduc'd among the players, grew necessitous, pawn'd his cloaths, and wanted bread. Walking the street very hungry, and not knowing what to do with himself, a crimp's bill was put into his hand, offering immediate entertainment and encouragement to such as would bind themselves to serve in America. He went directly, sign'd the indentures, was put into the ship, and came over, never writing a line to acquaint his friends what was become of him. He was lively, witty, good-natur'd, and a pleasant companion, but idle, thoughtless, and imprudent to the last degree.

John, the Irishman, soon ran away; with the rest I began to live very agreeably, for they all respected me the more, as they found Keimer incapable of instructing them, and that from me they learned something daily. We never worked on Saturday, that being Keimer's Sabbath, so I had two days for reading. My acquaintance with ingenious people in the town increased. Keimer himself treated me with great civility and apparent regard, and nothing now made me uneasy but my debt to Vernon, which I was yet unable to pay, being hitherto but a poor œconomist. He, however, kindly made no demand of it.

Our printing-house often wanted sorts, and there was no letter-founder in America; I had seen types cast at James's in London, but without much attention to the manner; however, I now contrived a mould, made use of the letters we had as puncheons, struck the matrices in lead, and thus supply'd in a pretty tolerable way all deficiencies. I also engrav'd several things on occasion; I made the ink; I was warehouseman, and everything, and, in short, quite a factotum.

But, however serviceable I might be, I found that my services became every day of less importance, as the other hands improv'd in the business; and, when Keimer paid my second quarter's wages, he let me know that he felt them too heavy, and thought I should make an abatement. He grew by degrees less civil, put on more of the master, frequently found fault, was captious, and seem'd ready for an outbreaking. I went on, nevertheless, with a good deal of patience, thinking that his encumber'd circumstances were partly the cause. At length a trifle snapt our connections; for, a great noise happening near the court-house, I put my head out of the window to see what was the matter. Keimer, being in the street, look'd up and saw me, call'd out to me in a loud voice and angry tone to mind my business, adding some reproachful words, that nettled me the more for their publicity, all the neighbors who were looking out on the same occasion being witnesses how I was treated. He came up immediately into the printing-house, continu'd the quarrel, high words pass'd on both sides, he gave me the quarter's warning we had stipulated, expressing a wish that he had not been oblig'd to so long a warning. I told him his wish was unnecessary, for I would leave him that instant; and so, taking my hat, walk'd out of doors, desiring Meredith, whom I saw below, to take care of some things I left, and bring them to my lodgings.

Meredith came accordingly in the evening, when we talked my affair over. He had conceiv'd a great regard for me, and was very unwilling that I should leave the house while he remain'd in it. He dissuaded me from returning to my native country, which I began to think of; he reminded me that Keimer was in debt for all he possess'd; that his creditors began to be uneasy; that he kept his shop miserably, sold often without profit for ready money, and often trusted without keeping accounts; that he must therefore fall, which would make a vacancy I might profit of. I objected my want of money. He then let me know that his father had a high opinion of me, and, from some discourse that had pass'd between them, he was sure would advance money to set us up, if I would enter into partnership with him. "My time," says he, "will be out with Keimer in the spring; by that time we may have our press and types in from London. I am sensible I am no workman; if you like it, your skill in the business shall be set against the stock I furnish, and we will share the profits equally."

The proposal was agreeable, and I consented; his father was in town and approv'd of it; the more as he saw I had great influence with his son, had prevail'd on him to abstain long from dram-drinking, and he hop'd might break him off that wretched habit entirely, when we came to be so closely connected. I gave an inventory to the father, who carry'd it to a merchant; the things were sent for, the secret was to be kept till they should arrive, and in the mean time I was to get work, if I could, at the other printing-house. But I found no vacancy there, and so remain'd idle a few days, when Keimer, on a prospect of being employ'd to print some paper money in New Jersey, which would require cuts and various types that I only could supply, and apprehending Bradford might engage me and get the jobb from him, sent me a very civil message, that old friends should not part for a few words, the effect of sudden passion, and wishing me to return. Meredith persuaded me to comply, as it would give more opportunity for his improvement under my daily instructions; so I return'd, and we went on more smoothly than for some time before. The New Jersey jobb was obtain'd, I contriv'd a copperplate press for it, the first that had been seen in the country; I cut several ornaments and checks for the bills. We went together to Burlington, where I executed the whole to satisfaction; and he received so large a sum for the work as to be enabled thereby to keep his head much longer above water.

At Burlington I made an acquaintance with many principal people of the province. Several of them had been appointed by the Assembly a committee to attend the press, and take care that no more bills were printed than the law directed. They were therefore, by turns, constantly with us, and generally he who attended, brought with him a friend or two for company. My mind having been much more improv'd by reading than Keimer's, I suppose it was for that reason my conversation seem'd to be more valu'd. They had me to their houses, introduced me to their friends, and show'd me much civility; while he, tho' the master, was a little neglected. In truth, he was an odd fish; ignorant of common life, fond of rudely opposing receiv'd opinions, slovenly to extream dirtiness, enthusiastic in some points of religion, and a little knavish withal.

We continu'd there near three months; and by that time I could reckon among my acquired friends, Judge Allen, Samuel Bustill, the secretary of the Province, Isaac Pearson, Joseph Cooper, and several of the Smiths, members of Assembly, and Isaac Decow, the surveyor-general. The latter was a shrewd, sagacious old man, who told me that he began for himself, when young, by wheeling clay for the brick-makers, learned to write after he was of age, carri'd the chain for surveyors, who taught him surveying, and he had now by his industry, acquir'd a good estate;

and says he, "I foresee that you will soon work this man out of business, and make a fortune in it at Philadelphia." He had not then the least intimation of my intention to set up there or anywhere. These friends were afterwards of great use to me, as I occasionally was to some of them. They all continued their regard for me as long as they lived.

Before I enter upon my public appearance in business, it may be well to let you know the then state of my mind with regard to my principles and morals, that you may see how far those influenc'd the future events of my life. My parents had early given me religious impressions, and brought me through my childhood piously in the Dissenting way. But I was scarce fifteen, when, after doubting by turns of several points, as I found them disputed in the different books I read, I began to doubt of Revelation itself. Some books against Deism fell into my hands; they were said to be the substance of sermons preached at Boyle's Lectures. It happened that they wrought an effect on me quite contrary to what was intended by them; for the arguments of the Deists, which were quoted to be refuted, appeared to me much stronger than the refutations; in short, I soon became a thorough Deist. My arguments perverted some others, particularly Collins and Ralph; but, each of them having afterwards wrong'd me greatly without the least compunction, and recollecting Keith's conduct towards me (who was another freethinker), and my own towards Vernon and Miss Read, which at times gave me great trouble, I began to suspect that this doctrine, tho' it might be true, was not very useful. My London pamphlet, which had for its motto these lines of Dryden:

"Whatever is, is right. Though purblind man
Sees but a part o' the chain, the nearest link:
His eyes not carrying to the equal beam,
That poises all above;"

and from the attributes of God, his infinite wisdom, goodness and power, concluded that nothing could possibly be wrong in the world, and that vice and virtue were empty distinctions, no such things existing, appear'd now not so clever a performance as I once thought it; and I doubted whether some 58 error had not insinuated itself unperceiv'd into my argument, so as to infect all that follow'd, as is common in metaphysical reasonings.

I grew convinc'd that *truth*, *sincerity* and *integrity* in dealings between man and man were of the utmost importance to the felicity of life; and I form'd written resolutions, which still remain in my journal book, to practice them ever while I lived. Revelation had indeed no weight with me, as such; but I entertain'd an opinion that, though certain actions might not be bad *because* they were forbidden by it, or good *because* it commanded them, yet probably these actions might be forbidden *because* they were bad for us, or commanded *because* they were beneficial to us, in their own natures, all the circumstances of things considered. And this persuasion, with the kind hand of Providence, or some guardian angel, or accidental favorable circumstances and situations, or all together, preserved me, thro' this dangerous time of youth, and the hazardous situations I was sometimes in among strangers, remote from the eye and advice of my father, without any willful gross immorality or injustice, that might have been expected from my want of religion. I say willful, because the instances I have mentioned had something of *necessity* in them, from my youth, inexperience, and the knavery of others. I had therefore a tolerable character to begin the world with; I valued it properly, and determin'd to preserve it.

We had not been long return'd to Philadelphia before the new types arriv'd from London. We settled with Keimer, and left him by his consent before he heard of it. We found a house to hire near the market, and took it. To lessen the rent, which was then but twenty-four pounds a year, tho' I have since known it to let for seventy, we took in Thomas Godfrey, a glazier, and his family, who were to pay a considerable part of it to us, and we to board with them. We had scarce opened our letters and put our press in order, before George House, an acquaintance of mine, brought a countryman to us, whom he had met in the street inquiring for a printer. All our cash was now expended in the variety of particulars we had been obliged to procure, and this countryman's five shillings, being our first-fruits, and coming so seasonably, gave me more pleasure than any crown I have since earned; and the gratitude I felt toward House has made me often more ready than perhaps I should otherwise have been to assist young beginners.

There are croakers in every country, always boding its ruin. Such a one then lived in Philadelphia; a person of note, an elderly man, with a wise look and a very grave manner of speaking; his name was Samuel Mickle. This gentleman, a stranger to me, stopt one day at my door, and asked me if I was the young man who had lately opened a new printing-house. Being answered in the affirmative, he said he was sorry for me, because it was an expensive undertaking, and the expense would be lost; for Philadelphia was a sinking place, the people already half-bankrupts, or near being so; all appearances to the contrary, such as new buildings and the rise of rents, being to his certain knowledge fallacious; for they were, in fact, among the things that would soon ruin us. And he gave me such a detail of misfortunes now existing, or that were soon to exist, that he left me half melancholy. Had I known him before I engaged in this business, probably I never should have done it. This man continued to live in this decaying place, and to declaim in the same strain, refusing for many years to buy a house there, because all was going to destruction; and at last I had the pleasure of seeing him give five times as much for one as he might have bought it for when he first began his croaking.

I should have mentioned before, that, in the autumn of the preceding year, I had form'd most of my ingenious acquaintance into a club of mutual improvement, which we called the Junto; we met on Friday evenings. The rules that I drew up required that every member, in his turn, should produce one or more queries on any point of Morals, Politics, or Natural Philosophy, to be discuss'd by the company; and once in three months produce and read an essay of his own writing, on any subject he pleased. Our debates were to be under the direction of a president, and to be conducted in the sincere spirit of inquiry after truth, without fondness for dispute, or desire of victory; and, to prevent warmth, all expressions of positiveness in opinions, or direct contradiction, were after some time made contraband, and prohibited under small pecuniary penalties.

The first members were Joseph Breintnal, a copyer of deeds for the scriveners, a good-natur'd, friendly, middle-ag'd man, a great lover of poetry, reading all he could meet with, and writing some that was tolerable; very ingenious in many little Nicknackeries, and of sensible conversation.

Thomas Godfrey, a self-taught mathematician, great in his way, and afterward inventor of what is now called Hadley's Quadrant. But he knew little out of his way, and was not a pleasing companion; as, like most great mathematicians I have met with, he expected universal precision in everything said, or was for ever denying or distinguishing upon trifles, to the disturbance of all conversation. He soon left us.

Nicholas Scull, a surveyor, afterwards surveyor-general, who lov'd books, and sometimes made a few verses.

William Parsons, bred a shoemaker, but loving reading, had acquir'd a considerable share of mathematics, which he first studied with a view to astrology, that he afterwards laught at it. He also became surveyor-general.

William Maugridge, a joiner, a most exquisite mechanic, and a solid, sensible man.

Hugh Meredith, Stephen Potts, and George Webb I have characteriz'd before.

Robert Grace, a young gentleman of some fortune, generous, lively, and witty; a lover of punning and of his friends.

And William Coleman, then a merchant's clerk, about my age, who had the coolest, clearest head, the best heart, and the exactest morals of almost any man I ever met with. He became afterwards a merchant of great note, and one of our provincial judges. Our friendship continued without interruption to his death, upward of forty years; and the club continued almost as long, and was the best school of philosophy, morality, and politics that then existed in the province; for our queries, which were read the week preceding their discussion, put us upon reading with attention upon the several subjects, that we might speak more to the purpose; and here, too, we acquired better habits of conversation, every thing being studied in our rules which might prevent our disgusting each other. From hence the long continuance of the club, which I shall have frequent occasion to speak further of hereafter.

But my giving this account of it here is to show something of the interest I had, every one of these exerting themselves in recommending business to us. Breintnal particularly procur'd us from the Quakers the printing forty sheets of their history, the rest being to be done by Keimer; and upon this we work'd exceedingly hard, for the price was low. It was a folio, pro patria size, in pica, with long primer notes. I compos'd of it a sheet a day, and Meredith worked it off at press; it was often eleven at night, and sometimes later, before I had finished my distribution for the next day's work, for the little jobbs sent in by our other friends now and then put us back. But so determin'd I was to continue doing a sheet a day of the folio, that one night, when, having impos'd my forms, I thought my day's work over, one of them by accident was broken, and two pages reduced to pi, I immediately distributed and compos'd it over again before I went to bed; and this industry, visible to our neighbors, began to give us character and credit; particularly, I was told, that mention being made of the new printing-office at the merchants' Every-night club, the general opinion was that it must fail, there being already two printers in the place, Keimer and Bradford; but Dr. Baird (whom you and I saw many years after at his native place, St. Andrew's in Scotland) gave a contrary opinion: "For the industry of that Franklin," says he, "is superior to any thing I ever saw of the kind; I see him still at work when I go home from club, and he is at work again before his neighbors are out of bed." This struck the rest, and we soon after had offers from one of them to supply us with stationery; but as yet we did not chuse to engage in shop business.

I mention this industry the more particularly and the more freely, tho' it seems to be talking in my own praise, that those of my posterity, who shall read it, may know the use of that virtue, when they see its effects in my favour throughout this relation.

George Webb, who had found a female friend that lent him wherewith to purchase his time of Keimer, now came to offer himself as a journeyman to us. We could not then imploy him; but I foolishly let him know as a secret that I soon intended to begin a newspaper, and might then have work for him. My hopes of success, as I told him, were founded on this, that the then only newspaper, printed by Bradford, was a paltry thing, wretchedly manag'd, no way entertaining, and yet was profitable to him; I therefore thought a good paper would scarcely fail of good encouragement. I requested Webb not to mention it; but he told it to Keimer, who immediately, to be beforehand with me, published proposals for printing one himself, on which Webb was to be employ'd. I resented this; and, to counteract them, as I could not yet begin our paper, I wrote several pieces of entertainment for Bradford's paper, under the title of the Busy Body, which Breintnal continu'd some months. By this means the attention of the publick was fixed on that paper, and Keimer's proposals, which we burlesqu'd and ridicul'd, were disregarded. He began his paper, however, and, after carrying it on three quarters of a year, with at most only ninety subscribers, he offered it to me for a trifle; and I, having been ready some time to go on with it, took it in hand directly; and it prov'd in a few years extremely profitable to me.

I perceive that I am apt to speak in the singular number, though our partnership still continu'd; the reason may be that, in fact, the whole management of the business lay upon me. Meredith was no compositor, a poor pressman, and seldom sober. My friends lamented my connection with him, but I was to make the best of it.

Our first papers made a quite different appearance from any before in the province; a better type, and better printed; but some spirited remarks of my writing, on the dispute then going on between Governor Burnet and the Massachusetts

Assembly, struck the principal people, occasioned the paper and the manager of it to be much talk'd of, and in a few weeks brought them all to be our subscribers.

Their example was follow'd by many, and our number went on growing continually. This was one of the first good effects of my having learnt a little to scribble; another was, that the leading men, seeing a newspaper now in the hands of one who could also handle a pen, thought it convenient to oblige and encourage me. Bradford still printed the votes, and laws, and other publick business. He had printed an address of the House to the governor, in a coarse, blundering manner, we reprinted it elegantly and correctly, and sent one to every member. They were sensible of the difference: it strengthened the hands of our friends in the House, and they voted us their printers for the year ensuing.

Among my friends in the House I must not forget Mr. Hamilton, before mentioned, who was then returned from England, and had a seat in it. He interested himself for me strongly in that instance, as he did in many others afterward, continuing his patronage till his death.

Mr. Vernon, about this time, put me in mind of the debt I ow'd him, but did not press me. I wrote him an ingenuous letter of acknowledgment, crav'd his forbearance a little longer, which he allow'd me, and as soon as I was able, I paid the principal with interest, and many thanks; so that erratum was in some degree corrected.

But now another difficulty came upon me which I had never the least reason to expect. Mr. Meredith's father, who was to have paid for our printing-house, according to the expectations given me, was able to advance only one hundred pounds currency, which had been paid; and a hundred more was due to the merchant, who grew impatient, and su'd us all. We gave bail, but saw that, if the money could not be rais'd in time, the suit must soon come to a judgment and execution, and our hopeful prospects must, with us, be ruined, as the press and letters must be sold for payment, perhaps at half price.

In this distress two true friends, whose kindness I have never forgotten, nor ever shall forget while I can remember any thing, came to me separately, unknown to each other, and, without any application from me, offering each of them to advance me all the money that should be necessary to enable me to take the whole business upon myself, if that should be practicable; but they did not like my continuing the partnership with Meredith, who, as they said, was often seen drunk in the streets, and playing at low games in alehouses, much to our discredit. These two friends were William Coleman and Robert Grace. I told them I could not propose a separation while any prospect remain'd of the Merediths' fulfilling their part of our agreement, because I thought myself under great obligations to them for what they had done, and would do if they could; but, if they finally fail'd in their performance, and our partnership must be dissolv'd, I should then think myself at liberty to accept the assistance of my friends.

Thus the matter rested for some time, when I said to my partner, "Perhaps your father is dissatisfied at the part you have undertaken in this affair of ours, and is unwilling to advance for you and me what he would for you alone. If that is the case, tell me, and I will resign the whole to you, and go about my business." "No," said he, "my father has really been disappointed, and is really unable; and I am unwilling to distress him farther. I see this is a business I am not fit for. I was bred a farmer, and it was a folly in me to come to town, and put myself, at thirty years of age, an apprentice to learn a new trade. Many of our Welsh people are going to settle in North Carolina, where land is cheap. I am inclin'd to go with them, and follow my old employment. You may find friends to assist you. If you will take the debts of the company upon you; return to my father the hundred pound he has advanced; pay my little personal debts, and give me thirty pounds and a new saddle, I will relinquish the partnership, and leave the whole in your hands." I agreed to this proposal: it was drawn up in writing, sign'd, and seal'd immediately. I gave him what he demanded, and he went soon after to Carolina, from whence he sent me next year two long letters, containing the best account that had been given of that country, the climate, the soil, husbandry, etc., for in those matters he was very judicious. I printed them in the papers, and they gave great satisfaction to the publick.

As soon as he was gone, I recurr'd to my two friends; and because I would not give an unkind preference to either, I took half of what each had offered and I wanted of one, 65 and half of the other; paid off the company's debts, and went on with the business in my own name, advertising that the partnership was dissolved. I think this was in or about the year 1729.

About this time there was a cry among the people for more paper money, only fifteen thousand pounds being extant in the province, and that soon to be sunk. The wealthy inhabitants oppos'd any addition, being against all paper currency, from an apprehension that it would depreciate, as it had done in New England, to the prejudice of all creditors. We had discuss'd this point in our Junto, where I was on the side of an addition, being persuaded that the first small sum struck in 1723 had done much good by increasing the trade, employment, and number of inhabitants in the province, since I now saw all the old houses inhabited, and many new ones building: whereas I remembered well, that when I first walk'd about the streets of Philadelphia, eating my roll, I saw most of the houses in Walnut-street, between Second and Front streets, with bills on their doors, "To be let"; and many likewise in Chestnut-street and other streets, which made me then think the inhabitants of the city were deserting it one after another.

Our debates possess'd me so fully of the subject, that I wrote and printed an anonymous pamphlet on it, entitled "*The Nature and Necessity of a Paper Currency*." It was well receiv'd by the common people in general; but the rich men dislik'd it, for it increas'd and strengthen'd the clamor for more money, and they happening to have no writers among them that were able to answer it, their opposition slacken'd, and the point was carried by a majority in the House. My friends there, who conceiv'd I had been of some service, thought fit to reward me by employing me in printing the money; a very profitable jobb and a great help to me. This was another advantage gain'd by my being able to write.

The utility of this currency became by time and experience so evident as never afterwards to be much disputed; so that it grew soon to fifty-five thousand pounds, and in 1739 to eighty thousand pounds, since which it arose during war to upwards of three hundred and fifty thousand pounds, trade, building, and inhabitants all the while increasing, tho' I now think there are limits beyond which the quantity may be hurtful.

I soon after obtain'd, thro' my friend Hamilton, the printing of the Newcastle paper money, another profitable jobb as I then thought it; small things appearing great to those in small circumstances; and these, to me, were really great advantages, as they were great encouragements. He procured for me, also, the printing of the laws and votes of that government, which continu'd in my hands as long as I follow'd the business.

I now open'd a little stationer's shop. I had in it blanks of all sorts, the correctest that ever appear'd among us, being assisted in that by my friend Breintnal. I had also paper, parchment, chapmen's books, etc. One Whitemash, a compositor I had known in London, an excellent workman, now came to me, and work'd with me constantly and diligently; and I took an apprentice, the son of Aquila Rose.

I began now gradually to pay off the debt I was under for the printing-house. In order to secure my credit and character as a tradesman, I took care not only to be in *reality* industrious and frugal, but to avoid all appearances to the contrary. I drest plainly; I was seen at no places of idle diversion. I never went out a fishing or shooting; a book, indeed, sometimes debauch'd me from my work, but that was seldom, snug, and gave no scandal; and, to show that I was not above my business, I sometimes brought home the paper I purchas'd at the stores thro' the streets on a wheelbarrow. Thus being esteem'd an industrious, thriving young man, and paying duly for what I bought, the merchants who imported stationery solicited my custom; others proposed supplying me with books, and I went on swimmingly. In the mean time, Keimer's credit and business declining daily, he was at last forc'd to sell his printing-house to satisfy his creditors. He went to Barbadoes, and there lived some years in very poor circumstances.

His apprentice, David Harry, whom I had instructed while I work'd with him, set up in his place at Philadelphia, having bought his materials. I was at first apprehensive of a powerful rival in Harry, as his friends were very able, and had a good deal of interest. I therefore propos'd a partnership to him which he, fortunately for me, rejected with scorn. He was very proud, dress'd like a gentleman, liv'd expensively, took much diversion and pleasure abroad, ran in debt, and neglected his business; upon which, all business left him; and, finding nothing to do, he followed Keimer to Barbadoes, taking the printing-house with him. There this apprentice employ'd his former master as a journeyman; they quarrel'd often; Harry went continually behindhand, and at length was forc'd to sell his types and return to his country work in Pensilvania. The person that bought them employ'd Keimer to use them, but in a few years he died.

There remained now no competitor with me at Philadelphia but the old one, Bradford; who was rich and easy, did a little printing now and then by straggling hands, but was not very anxious about the business. However, as he kept the post-office, it was imagined he had better opportunities of obtaining news; his paper was thought a better distributer of advertisements than mine, and therefore had many more, which was a profitable thing to him, and a disadvantage to me; for, tho' I did indeed receive and send papers by the post, yet the publick opinion was otherwise, for what I did send was by bribing the riders, who took them privately, Bradford being unkind enough to forbid it, which occasion'd some resentment on my part; and I thought so meanly of him for it, that, when I afterward came into his situation, I took care never to imitate it.

I had hitherto continu'd to board with Godfrey, who lived in part of my house with his wife and children, and had one side of the shop for his glazier's business, tho' he worked little, being always absorbed in his mathematics. Mrs. Godfrey projected a match for me with a relation's daughter, took opportunities of bringing us often together, till a serious courtship on my part ensu'd, the girl being in herself very deserving. The old folks encourag'd me by continual invitations to supper, and by leaving us together, till at length it was time to explain. Mrs. Godfrey manag'd our little treaty. I let her know that I expected as much money with their daughter as would pay off my remaining debt for the printing-house, which I believe was not then above a hundred pounds. She brought me word they had no such sum to spare; I said they might mortgage their house in the loan-office. The answer to this, after some days, was, that they did not approve the match; that, on inquiry of Bradford, they had been inform'd the printing business was not a profitable one; the types would soon be worn out, and more wanted; that S. Keimer and D. Harry had failed one after the other, and I should probably soon follow them; and, therefore, I was forbidden the house, and the daughter shut up.

Whether this was a real change of sentiment or only artifice, on a supposition of our being too far engaged in affection to retract, and therefore that we should steal a marriage, which would leave them at liberty to give or withhold what they pleas'd, I know not; but I suspected the latter, resented it, and went no more. Mrs. Godfrey brought me afterward some more favorable accounts of their disposition, and would have drawn me on again; but I declared absolutely my resolution to have nothing more to do with that family. This was resented by the Godfreys; we differ'd, and they removed, leaving me the whole house, and I resolved to take no more inmates.

But this affair having turned my thoughts to marriage, I look'd round me and made overtures of acquaintance in other places; but soon found that, the business of a printer being generally thought a poor one, I was not to expect money with a wife, unless with such a one as I should not otherwise think agreeable. In the mean time, that hard-to-be-governed passion of youth hurried me frequently into intrigues with low women that fell in my way, which were attended with some expense and great inconvenience, besides a continual risque to my health by a distemper which of all things I dreaded, though by great good luck I escaped it. A friendly correspondence as neighbors and old acquaintances had continued between me and Mrs. Read's family, who all had a regard for me from the time of my first lodging in their house. I was often invited there and consulted in their affairs, wherein I sometimes was of service. I piti'd poor Miss Read's unfortunate situation, who was generally dejected, seldom cheerful, and avoided company. I considered my giddiness and inconstancy when in London as in a great degree the cause of her unhappiness, tho' the mother was good enough to think the fault more her own than mine, as she had prevented our marrying before I went thither, and persuaded the other match in my absence. Our mutual affection was revived, but there were now great objections to our union. The match was indeed looked upon as invalid, a preceding wife being said to be living in England; but this could not easily be prov'd, because of the distance; and, tho' there was a report of his death, it was not certain. Then, tho' it should be true, he had left many debts, which his successor might be call'd upon to pay. We ventured, however, over all these difficulties, and I took her to wife, September 1st, 1730. None of the inconveniences happened that we had apprehended; she proved a good and faithful helpmate, assisted me much by attending the shop; we throve together, and have ever mutually endeavored to make each other happy. Thus I corrected that great erratum as well as I could.

About this time, our club meeting, not at a tavern, but in a little room of Mr. Grace's, set apart for that purpose, a proposition was made by me, that, since our books were often referr'd to in our disquisitions upon the queries, it might be convenient to us to have them altogether where we met, that upon occasion they might be consulted; and by thus clubbing our books to a common library, we should, while we lik'd to keep them together, have each of us the advantage of using the books of all the other members, which would be nearly as beneficial as if each owned the whole. It was lik'd and agreed to, and we fill'd one end of the room with such books as we could best spare. The number was not so great as we expected; and tho' they had been of great use, yet some inconveniences occurring for want of due care of them, the collection, after about a year, was separated, and each took his books home again.

And now I set on foot my first project of a public nature, that for a subscription library. I drew up the proposals, got them put into form by our great scrivener, Brockden, and, by the help of my friends in the Junto, procured fifty subscribers of forty shillings each to begin with, and ten shillings a year for fifty years, the term our company was to continue. We afterwards obtain'd a charter, the company being increased to one hundred: this was the mother of all the North American subscription libraries, now so numerous. It is become a great thing itself, and continually increasing. These libraries have improved the general conversation of the Americans, made the common tradesmen and farmers as intelligent as most gentlemen from other countries, and perhaps have contributed in some degree to the stand so generally made throughout the colonies in defense of their privileges.

Memo. Thus far was written with the intention express'd in the beginning and therefore contains several little family anecdotes of no importance to others. What follows was written many years after in compliance with the advice contain'd in these letters, and accordingly intended for the public. The affairs of the Revolution occasion'd the interruption.

Part II

Letter from Mr. Abel James, with Notes of my Life (received in Paris).

"MY DEAR AND HONORED FRIEND: I have often been desirous of writing to thee, but could not be reconciled to the thought that the letter might fall into the hands of the British, lest some printer or busy-body should publish some part of the contents, and give our friend pain, and myself censure.

"Some time since there fell into my hands, to my great joy, about twenty-three sheets in thy own handwriting, containing an account of the parentage and life of thyself, directed to thy son, ending in the year 1730, with which there were notes, likewise in thy writing; a copy of which I inclose, in hopes it may be a means, if thou continued it up to a later period, that the first and latter part may be put together; and if it is not yet continued, I hope thee will not delay it. Life is uncertain, as the preacher tells us; and what will the world say if kind, humane, and benevolent Ben. Franklin should leave his friends and the world deprived of so pleasing and profitable a work; a work which would be useful and entertaining not only to a few, but to millions? The influence writings under that class have on the minds of youth is very great, and has nowhere appeared to me so plain, as in our public friend's journals. It almost insensibly leads the youth into the resolution of endeavoring to become as good and eminent as the journalist. Should thine, for instance, when published (and I think it could not fail of it), lead the youth to equal the industry and temperance of thy early youth, what a blessing with that class would such a work be! I know of no character living, nor many of them put together, who has so much in his power as thyself to promote a greater spirit of industry and early attention to business, frugality, and temperance with the American youth. Not that I think the work would have no other merit and use in the world, far from it; but the first is of such vast importance that I know nothing that can equal it."

The foregoing letter and the minutes accompanying it being shown to a friend, I received from him the following:

Letter from Mr. Benjamin Vaughan.

"Paris, January 31, 1783.

"My Dearest Sir: When I had read over your sheets of minutes of the principal incidents of your life, recovered for you by your Quaker acquaintance, I told you I would send you a letter expressing my reasons why I thought it would be useful to complete and publish it as he desired. Various concerns have for some time past prevented this letter being written, and I do not know whether it was worth any expectation; happening to be at leisure, however, at present, I shall by writing, at least interest and instruct myself; but as the terms I am inclined to use may tend to offend a person of your manners, I shall only tell you how I would address any other person, who was as good and as great as yourself, but less diffident. I would say to him, Sir, I solicit the history of your life from the following motives: Your history is so remarkable, that if you do not give it, somebody else will certainly give it; and perhaps so as nearly to do as much harm, as your own management of the thing might do good. It will moreover present a table of the internal circumstances of your country, which will very much tend to invite to it settlers of virtuous and manly minds. And considering the eagerness with which such information is sought by them, and the extent of your reputation, I do not know of a more efficacious advertisement than your biography would give. All that has happened to you is also connected with the detail of the manners and situation of a rising people; and in this respect I do not think that the writings of Cæsar and Tacitus can be more interesting to a true judge of human nature and society. But these, sir, are small reasons, in my opinion, compared with the chance which your life will give for the forming of future great men; and in conjunction with your Art of Virtue (which you design to publish) of improving the features of private character, and consequently of aiding all happiness, both public and domestic. The two works I allude to, sir, will in particular give a noble rule and example of self-education. School and other education constantly proceed upon false principles, and show a clumsy apparatus pointed at a false mark; but your apparatus is simple, and the mark a true one; and while parents and young persons are left destitute of other just means of estimating and becoming prepared for a reasonable course in life, your discovery that the thing is in many a man's private power, will be invaluable! Influence upon the private character, late in life, is not only an influence late in life, but a weak influence. It is in youth that we plant our chief habits and prejudices; it is in youth that we take our party as to profession, pursuits and matrimony. In youth, therefore, the turn is given; in youth the education even of the next generation is given; in youth the private and public character is determined; and the term of life extending but from youth to age, life ought to begin well from youth, and more especially before we take our party as to our principal objects. But your biography will not merely teach self-education, but the education of a wise man; and the wisest man will receive lights and improve his progress, by seeing detailed the conduct of another wise man. And why are weaker men to be deprived of such helps, when we see our race has been blundering on in the dark, almost without a guide in this particular, from the farthest trace of time? Show then, sir, how much is to be done, both to sons and fathers; and invite all wise men to become like yourself, and other men to become wise. When we see how cruel statesmen and warriors can be to the human race, and how absurd distinguished men can be to their acquaintance, it will be instructive to observe the instances multiply of pacific, acquiescing manners; and to find how compatible it is to be great and domestic, enviable and yet good-humored.

"The little private incidents which you will also have to relate, will have considerable use, as we want, above all things, rules of prudence in ordinary affairs; and it will be curious to see how you have acted in these. It will be so far a sort of key to life, and explain many things that all men ought to have once explained to them, to give them a chance of becoming wise by foresight. The nearest thing to having experience of one's own, is to have other people's affairs brought before us in a shape that is interesting; this is sure to happen from your pen; our affairs and management will have an air of simplicity or importance that will not fail to strike; and I am convinced you have conducted them with as much originality as if you had been conducting discussions in politics or philosophy; and what more worthy of experiments and system (its importance and its errors considered) than human life?

"Some men have been virtuous blindly, others have speculated fantastically, and others have been shrewd to bad purposes; but you, sir, I am sure, will give under your hand, nothing but what is at the same moment, wise, practical and good. Your account of yourself (for I suppose the parallel I am drawing for Dr. Franklin, will hold not only in point of character, but of private history) will show that you are ashamed of no origin; a thing the more important, as you prove how little necessary all origin is to happiness, virtue, or greatness. As no end likewise happens without a means, so we shall find, sir, that even you yourself framed a plan by which you became considerable; but at the same time we may see that though the event is flattering, the means are as simple as wisdom could make them; that is, depending upon nature, virtue, thought and habit. Another thing demonstrated will be the propriety of every man's waiting for his time for appearing upon the stage of the world. Our sensations being very much fixed to the moment, we are apt to forget that more moments are to follow the first, and consequently that man should arrange his conduct so as to suit the whole of a life. Your attribution appears to have been applied to your life, and the passing moments of it have been enlivened with content and enjoyment, instead of being tormented with foolish impatience or regrets. Such a conduct is easy for those who make virtue and themselves in countenance by examples of other truly great men, of whom patience is so often the characteristic. Your Quaker correspondent, sir (for here again I will suppose the subject of my letter resembling Dr. Franklin), praised your frugality, diligence and temperance, which he considered as a pattern for all youth; but it is singular that he should have forgotten your modesty and your disinterestedness, without which you never could have waited for your advancement, or found your situation in the mean time comfortable; which is a strong lesson to show the poverty of glory and the importance of regulating our minds. If this correspondent had known the nature of your reputation as well as I do, he would have said, Your former writings and measures would secure attention to your Biography, and Art of Virtue; and your Biography and Art of Virtue, in return, would secure attention to them. This is an advantage attendant upon a various character, and which brings all that belongs to it into greater play; and it is the more useful, as perhaps more persons are at a loss for the means of improving their minds and characters, than they are for the time or the inclination to do it. But there is one concluding reflection, sir, that will shew the use of your life as a mere piece of biography. This style of writing seems a little gone out of vogue, and yet it is a very useful one; and your specimen of it may be particularly serviceable, as it will make a subject of comparison with the lives of various public cutthroats and intriguers, and with absurd monastic self-tormentors or vain literary triflers. If it encourages more writings of the same kind with your own, and induces more men to spend lives fit to be written, it will be worth all Plutarch's Lives put together. But being tired of figuring to myself a character of which every feature suits only one man in the world, without giving him the praise of it, I shall end my letter, my dear Dr. Franklin, with a personal application to your proper self. I am earnestly desirous, then, my dear sir, that you should let the world into the traits of your genuine character, as civil broils may otherwise tend to disguise or traduce it. Considering your great age, the caution of your character, and your peculiar style of thinking, it is not likely that any one besides yourself can be sufficiently master of the facts of your life, or the intentions of your mind. Besides all this, the immense revolution of the present period, will necessarily turn our attention towards the author of it, and when virtuous principles have been pretended in it, it will be highly important to shew that such have really influenced; and, as your own character will be the principal one to receive a scrutiny, it is proper (even for its effects upon your vast and rising country, as well as upon England and upon Europe) that it should stand respectable and eternal. For the furtherance of human happiness, I have always maintained that it is necessary to prove that man is not even at present a vicious and detestable animal; and still more to prove that good management may greatly amend him; and it is for much the same reason, that I am anxious to see the opinion established, that there are fair characters existing among the individuals of the race; for the moment that all men, without exception, shall be conceived abandoned, good people will cease efforts deemed to be hopeless, and perhaps think of taking their share in the scramble of life, or at least of making it comfortable principally for themselves. Take then, my dear sir, this work most speedily into hand: shew yourself good as you are good; temperate as you are temperate; and above all things, prove yourself as one, who from your infancy have loved justice, liberty and concord, in a way that has made it natural and consistent for you to have acted, as we have seen you act in the last seventeen years of your life. Let Englishmen be made not only to respect, but even to love you. When they think well of individuals in your native country, they will go nearer to thinking well of your country; and when your countrymen see themselves well thought of by Englishmen, they will go nearer to thinking well of England. Extend your views even further; do not stop at those who speak the English tongue, but after having settled so many points in nature and politics, think of bettering the whole race of men. As I have not read any part of the life in question, but know only the character that lived it, I write somewhat at hazard. I am sure, however, that the life and the treatise I allude to (on the Art of Virtue) will necessarily fulfil the chief of my expectations; and still more so if you take up the measure of suiting these performances to the several views above stated. Should they even prove unsuccessful in all that a sanguine admirer of yours hopes from them, you will at least have framed pieces to interest the human mind; and whoever gives a feeling of pleasure that is innocent to man, has added so much to the fair side of a life otherwise too much darkened by anxiety and too much injured by pain. In the hope, therefore, that you will listen to the prayer addressed to you in this letter, I beg to subscribe myself, my dearest sir, etc., etc.,

"Signed, BENJ. VAUGHAN."

Continuation of the Account of my Life, begun at Passy, near Paris, 1784.

It is some time since I receiv'd the above letters, but I have been too busy till now to think of complying with the request they contain. It might, too, be much better done if I were at home among my papers, which would aid my memory, and help to ascertain dates; but my return being uncertain and having just now a little leisure, I will endeavor to recollect and write what I can; if I live to get home, it may there be corrected and improv'd.

Not having any copy here of what is already written, I know not whether an account is given of the means I used to establish the Philadelphia public library, which, from a small beginning, is now become so considerable, though I remember to have come down to near the time of that transaction (1730). I will therefore begin here with an account of it, which may be struck out if found to have been already given.

At the time I establish'd myself in Pennsylvania, there was not a good bookseller's shop in any of the colonies to the southward of Boston. In New York and Philad'a the printers were indeed stationers; they sold only paper, etc., almanacs, ballads, and a few common school-books. Those who lov'd reading were oblig'd to send for their books from England; the members of the Junto had each a few. We had left the alehouse, where we first met, and hired a room to hold our club in. I propos'd that we should all of us bring our books to that room, where they would not only be ready to consult in our conferences, but become a common benefit, each of us being at liberty to borrow such as he wish'd to read at home. This was accordingly done, and for some time contented us.

Finding the advantage of this little collection, I propos'd to render the benefit from books more common, by commencing a public subscription library. I drew a sketch of the plan and rules that would be necessary, and got a skilful conveyancer, Mr. Charles Brockden, to put the whole in form of articles of agreement to be subscribed, by which each subscriber engag'd to pay a certain sum down for the first purchase of books, and an annual contribution for increasing them. So few were the readers at that time in Philadelphia, and the majority of us so poor, that I was not able, with great industry; to find more than fifty persons, mostly young tradesmen, willing to pay down for this purpose forty shillings each, and ten shillings per annum. On this little fund we began. The books were imported; the library was opened one day in the week for lending to the subscribers, on their promissory notes to pay double the value if not duly returned. The institution soon manifested its utility, was imitated by other towns, and in other provinces. The libraries were augmented by donations; reading became fashionable; and our people, having no publick amusements to divert their attention from study, became better acquainted with books, and in a few years were observ'd by strangers to be better instructed and more intelligent than people of the same rank generally are in other countries.

When we were about to sign the above-mentioned articles, which were to be binding upon us, our heirs, etc., for fifty years, Mr. Brockden, the scrivener, said to us, "You are young men, but it is scarcely probable that any of you will live to see the expiration of the term fix'd in the instrument." A number of us, however, are yet living; but the instrument was after a few years rendered null by a charter that incorporated and gave perpetuity to the company.

The objections and reluctances I met with in soliciting the subscriptions, made me soon feel the impropriety of presenting one's self as the proposer of any useful project, that might be suppos'd to raise one's reputation in the smallest degree above that of one's neighbors, when one has need of their assistance to accomplish that project. I therefore put myself as much as I could out of sight, and stated it as a scheme of a number of friends, who had requested me to go about and propose it to such as they thought lovers of reading. In this way my affair went on more smoothly, and I ever after practis'd it on such occasions; and, from my frequent successes, can heartily recommend it. The present little sacrifice of your vanity will afterwards be amply repaid. If it remains a while uncertain to whom the merit belongs, some one more vain than yourself will be encouraged to claim it, and then even envy will be disposed to do you justice by plucking those assumed feathers, and restoring them to their right owner.

This library afforded me the means of improvement by constant study, for which I set apart an hour or two each day, and thus repair'd in some degree the loss of the learned education my father once intended for me. Reading was the only amusement I allow'd myself. I spent no time in taverns, games, or frolicks of any kind; and my industry in my business continu'd as indefatigable as it was necessary. I was indebted for my printing-house; I had a young family coming on to be educated, and I had to contend with for business two printers, who were established in the place before me. My circumstances, however, grew daily easier. My original habits of frugality continuing, and my father having, among his instructions to me when a boy, frequently repeated a proverb of Solomon, "Seest thou a man diligent in his calling, he shall stand before kings, he shall not stand before mean men," I from thence considered industry as a means of obtaining wealth and distinction, which encourag'd me, tho' I did not think that I should ever literally stand before kings, which, however, has since happened; for I have stood before five, and even had the honor of sitting down with one, the King of Denmark, to dinner.

We have an English proverb that says, "He that would thrive, must ask his wife." It was lucky for me that I had one as much dispos'd to industry and frugality as myself. She assisted me cheerfully in my business, folding and stitching pamphlets, tending shop, purchasing old linen rags for the papermakers, etc., etc. We kept no idle servants, our table was plain and simple, our furniture of the cheapest. For instance, my breakfast was a long time bread and milk (no tea), and I ate it out of a twopenny earthen porringer, with a pewter spoon. But mark how luxury will enter families, and make a progress, in spite of principle: being call'd one morning to breakfast, I found it in a China bowl, with a spoon of silver! They had been bought for me without my knowledge by my wife, and had cost her the enormous sum of three-and-twenty shillings, for which she had no other excuse or apology to make, but that she thought her husband deserv'd a silver spoon and China bowl as well as any of his neighbors. This was the first appearance of plate and China in our house, which afterward, in a course of years, as our wealth increas'd, augmented gradually to several hundred pounds in value.

I had been religiously educated as a Presbyterian; and tho' some of the dogmas of that persuasion, such as the eternal decrees of God, election, reprobation, etc., appeared to me unintelligible, others doubtful, and I early absented myself from the public assemblies of the sect, Sunday being my studying day, I never was without some religious principles. I never doubted, for instance, the existence of the Deity; that he made the world, and govern'd it by his Providence; that the most acceptable service of God was the doing good to man; that our souls are immortal; and that all crime will be punished, and virtue rewarded, either here or hereafter. These I esteem'd the essentials of every religion; and, being to be found in all the religions we had in our country, I respected them all, tho' with different degrees of respect, as I found them more or less mix'd with other articles, which, without any tendency to inspire, promote, or confirm morality, serv'd principally to divide us, and make us unfriendly to one another. This respect to all, with an opinion that the worst had some good effects, induc'd me to avoid all discourse that might tend to lessen the good opinion another might have of his own religion; and as our province increas'd in people, and new places of worship were continually wanted, and generally erected by voluntary contributions, my mite for such purpose, whatever might be the sect, was never refused.

Tho' I seldom attended any public worship, I had still an opinion of its propriety, and of its utility when rightly conducted, and I regularly paid my annual subscription for the support of the only Presbyterian minister or meeting we had in Philadelphia. He us'd to visit me sometimes as a friend, and admonish me to attend his administrations, and I was now and then prevail'd on to do so, once for five Sundays successively. Had he been in my opinion a good preacher, perhaps I might have continued, notwithstanding the occasion I had for the Sunday's leisure in my course of study; but his discourses were chiefly either polemic arguments, or explications of the peculiar doctrines of our sect, and were all to me very dry, uninteresting, and unedifying, since not a single moral principle was inculcated or enforc'd, their aim seeming to be rather to make us Presbyterians than good citizens.

At length he took for his text that verse of the fourth chapter of Philippians, "*Finally, brethren, whatsoever things are true, honest, just, pure, lovely, or of good report, if there be any virtue, or any praise, think on these things.*" And I imagin'd, in a sermon on such a text, we could not miss of having some morality. But he confin'd himself to five points only, as meant by the apostle, viz.: 1. Keeping holy the Sabbath day. 2. Being diligent in reading the holy Scriptures. 3. Attending duly the publick worship. 4. Partaking of the Sacrament. 5. Paying a due respect to God's ministers. These might be all good things; but, as they were not the kind of good things that I expected from that text, I despaired of ever meeting with them from any other, was disgusted, and attended his preaching no more. I had some years before compos'd a little Liturgy, or form of prayer, for my own private use (viz., in 1728), entitled, *Articles of Belief and Acts of Religion.* I return'd to the use of this, and went no more to the public assemblies. My conduct might be blameable, but I leave it, without attempting further to excuse it; my present purpose being to relate facts, and not to make apologies for them.

It was about this time I conceiv'd the bold and arduous project of arriving at moral perfection. I wish'd to live without committing any fault at any time; I would conquer all that either natural inclination, custom, or company might lead me into. As I knew, or thought I knew, what was right and wrong, I did not see why I might not always do the one and avoid the other. But I soon found I had undertaken a task of more difficulty than I had imagined. While my care was employ'd in guarding against one fault, I was often surprised by another; habit took the advantage of inattention; inclination was sometimes too strong for reason. I concluded, at length, that the mere speculative conviction that it was our interest to be completely virtuous, was not sufficient to prevent our slipping; and that the contrary habits must be broken, and good ones acquired and established, before we can have any dependence on a steady, uniform rectitude of conduct. For this purpose I therefore contrived the following method.

In the various enumerations of the moral virtues I had met with in my reading, I found the catalogue more or less numerous, as different writers included more or fewer ideas under the same name. Temperance, for example, was by some confined to eating and drinking, while by others it was extended to mean the moderating every other pleasure, appetite, inclination, or passion, bodily or mental, even to our avarice and ambition. I propos'd to myself, for the sake of clearness, to use rather more names, with fewer ideas annex'd to each, than a few names with more ideas; and I included under thirteen names of virtues all that at that time occurr'd to me as necessary or desirable, and annexed to each a short precept, which fully express'd the extent I gave to its meaning.

These names of virtues, with their precepts, were:

1. Temperance.
   Eat not to dullness; drink not to elevation.
2. Silence.
   Speak not but what may benefit others or yourself; avoid trifling conversation.

3. Order.

    Let all your things have their places; let each part of your business have its time.

4. Resolution.

    Resolve to perform what you ought; perform without fail what you resolve.

5. Frugality.

    Make no expense but to do good to others or yourself; i.e., waste nothing.

6. Industry.

    Lose no time; be always employ'd in something useful; cut off all unnecessary actions.

7. Sincerity.

    Use no hurtful deceit; think innocently and justly, and, if you speak, speak accordingly.

8. Justice.

    Wrong none by doing injuries, or omitting the benefits that are your duty.

9. Moderation.

    Avoid extreams; forbear resenting injuries so much as you think they deserve.

10. Cleanliness. 84

    Tolerate no uncleanliness in body, cloaths, or habitation.

11. Tranquillity.

    Be not disturbed at trifles, or at accidents common or unavoidable.

12. Chastity.

    Rarely use venery but for health or offspring, never to dulness, weakness, or the injury of your own or another's peace or reputation.

13. Humility.

    Imitate Jesus and Socrates.

My intention being to acquire the *habitude* of all these virtues, I judg'd it would be well not to distract my attention by attempting the whole at once, but to fix it on one of them at a time; and, when I should be master of that, then to proceed to another, and so on, till I should have gone thro' the thirteen; and, as the previous acquisition of some might facilitate the acquisition of certain others, I arrang'd them with that view, as they stand above. Temperance first, as it tends to procure that coolness and clearness of head, which is so necessary where constant vigilance was to be kept up, and guard maintained against the unremitting attraction of ancient habits, and the force of perpetual temptations. This being acquir'd and establish'd, Silence would be more easy; and my desire being to gain knowledge at the same time that I improv'd in virtue, and considering that in conversation it was obtain'd rather by the use of the ears than of the tongue, and therefore wishing to break a habit I was getting into of prattling, punning, and joking, which only made me acceptable to trifling company, I gave *Silence* the second place. This and the next, *Order*, I expected would allow me more time for attending to my project and my studies. *Resolution*, once become habitual, would keep me firm in my endeavors to obtain all the subsequent virtues; *Frugality* and Industry freeing me from my remaining debt, and producing affluence and independence, would make more easy the practice of Sincerity and Justice, etc., etc. Conceiving then, that, agreeably to the advice of Pythagoras in his Golden Verses, daily examination would be necessary, I contrived the following method for conducting that examination.

I made a little book, in which I allotted a page for each of the virtues. I rul'd each page with red ink, so as to have seven columns, one for each day of the week, marking each column with a letter for the day. I cross'd these columns with thirteen red lines, marking the beginning of each line with the first letter of one of the virtues, on which line, and in its proper column, I might mark, by a little black spot, every fault I found upon examination to have been committed respecting that virtue upon that day.

Form of the pages.

TEMPERANCE.							
EAT NOT TO DULNESS; DRINK NOT TO ELEVATION.							
	S.	**M.**	**T.**	**W.**	**T.**	**F.**	**S.**
T.							
S.	•	•		•		•	
O.	••	•	•		•	•	•
R.			•			•	
F.		•			•		
I.			•				
S.							
J.							
M.							
C.							
T.							
C.							
H.							

I determined to give a week's strict attention to each of the virtues successively. Thus, in the first week, my great guard was to avoid every the least offence against *Temperance*, leaving the other virtues to their ordinary chance, only marking every evening the faults of the day. Thus, if in the first week I could keep my first line, marked T, clear of spots, I suppos'd the habit of that virtue so much strengthen'd, and its opposite weaken'd, that I might venture extending my attention to include the next, and for the following week keep both lines clear of spots. Proceeding thus to the last, I could go thro' a course compleat in thirteen weeks, and four courses in a year. And like him who, having a garden to weed, does not attempt to eradicate all the bad herbs at once, which would exceed his reach and his strength, but works on one of the beds at a time, and, having accomplish'd the first, proceeds to a second, so I should have, I hoped, the encouraging pleasure of seeing on my pages the progress I made in virtue, by clearing successively my lines of their spots, till in the end, by a number of courses, I should be happy in viewing a clean book, after a thirteen weeks' daily examination.

This my little book had for its motto these lines from Addison's *Cato*:

> "Here will I hold. If there's a power above us
> (And that there is, all nature cries aloud
> Thro' all her works), He must delight in virtue;
> And that which he delights in must be happy."

Another from Cicero,

> "O vitæ Philosophia dux! O virtutum indagatrix expultrixque vitiorum! Unus dies, bene et ex præceptis tuis actus, peccanti immortalitati est anteponendus."

Another from the Proverbs of Solomon, speaking of wisdom or virtue:

> "Length of days is in her right hand, and in her left hand riches and honour. Her ways are ways of pleasantness, and all her paths are peace." iii. 16, 17.

And conceiving God to be the fountain of wisdom, I thought it right and necessary to solicit his assistance for obtaining it; to this end I formed the following little prayer, which was prefix'd to my tables of examination, for daily use.

> *"O powerful Goodness! bountiful Father! merciful Guide! Increase in me that wisdom which discovers my truest interest. Strengthen my resolutions to perform what that wisdom dictates. Accept my kind offices to thy other children as the only return in my power for thy continual favors to me."*

I used also sometimes a little prayer which I took from Thomson's Poems, viz.:

"Father of light and life, thou Good Supreme!
O teach me what is good; teach me Thyself!
Save me from folly, vanity, and vice,
From every low pursuit; and fill my soul
With knowledge, conscious peace, and virtue pure;
Sacred, substantial, never-fading bliss!"

The precept of *Order* requiring that *every part of my business should have its allotted time,* one page in my little book contain'd the following scheme of employment for the twenty-four hours of a natural day:

<table>
<tr><td>The Morning.
Question.
What good shall I do this day?</td><td>5
6

7</td><td>Rise, wash, and address *Powerful Goodness!* Contrive day's business, and take the resolution of the day; prosecute the present study, and breakfast.</td></tr>
<tr><td></td><td>8
9
10
11</td><td>Work.</td></tr>
<tr><td>Noon.</td><td>12
1</td><td>Read, or overlook my accounts, and dine.</td></tr>
<tr><td></td><td>2
3
4
5</td><td>Work.</td></tr>
<tr><td>Evening.
Question.
What good have I done to-day?</td><td>6
7
8
9</td><td>Put things in their places. Supper. Music or diversion, or conversation. Examination of the day.</td></tr>
<tr><td>Night.</td><td>10
11
12
1
2
3
4</td><td>Sleep.</td></tr>
</table>

I enter'd upon the execution of this plan for self-examination, and continu'd it with occasional intermissions for some time. I was surpris'd to find myself so much fuller of faults than I had imagined; but I had the satisfaction of seeing them diminish. To avoid the trouble of renewing now and then my little book, which, by scraping out the marks on the paper of old faults to make room for new ones in a new course, became full of holes, I transferr'd my tables and precepts to the ivory leaves of a memorandum book, on which the lines were drawn with red ink, that made a durable stain, and on those lines I mark'd my faults with a black-lead pencil, which marks I could easily wipe out with a wet sponge. After a while I went thro' one course only in a year, and afterward only one in several years, till at length I omitted them entirely, being employ'd in voyages and business abroad, with a multiplicity of affairs that interfered; but I always carried my little book with me.

My scheme of ORDER gave me the most trouble; and I found that, tho' it might be practicable where a man's business was such as to leave him the disposition of his time, that of a journeyman printer, for instance, it was not possible to be exactly observed by a master, who must mix with the world, and often receive people of business at their own hours. *Order*, too, with regard to places for things, papers, etc., I found extreamly difficult to acquire. I had not been early accustomed to it, and, having an exceeding good memory, I was not so sensible of the inconvenience attending want of method. This article, therefore, cost me so much painful attention, and my faults in it vexed me so much, and I made so little progress in amendment, and had such frequent relapses, that I was almost ready to give up the attempt, and content myself with a faulty character in that respect, like the man who, in buying an ax of a smith, my neighbour, desired to have the whole of its surface as bright as the edge. The smith consented to grind it bright for him if he would turn the wheel; he turn'd, while the smith press'd the broad face of the ax hard and heavily on the stone, which made the turning of it very fatiguing. The man came every now and then from the wheel to see how the work went on, and at length would take his ax as it was, without farther grinding. "No," said the smith, "turn on, turn on; we shall have it bright by-and-by; as yet, it is only speckled." "Yes," said the man, "*but I think I like a speckled ax best.*" And I believe this may have been the case with many, who, having, for want of some such means as I employ'd, found the difficulty of obtaining good and breaking bad habits in other points of vice and virtue, have given up the struggle, and concluded that "*a speckled ax was best*"; for something, that pretended to be reason, was every now and then suggesting to me that such extream nicety as I exacted of myself might be a kind of foppery in morals, which, if it were known, would make me ridiculous; that a perfect character might be attended with the inconvenience of being envied and hated; and that a benevolent man should allow a few faults in himself, to keep his friends in countenance.

In truth, I found myself incorrigible with respect to Order; and now I am grown old, and my memory bad, I feel very sensibly the want of it. But, on the whole, tho' I never arrived at the perfection I had been so ambitious of obtaining, but fell far short of it, yet I was, by the endeavour, a better and a happier man than I otherwise should have been if I had not attempted it; as those who aim at perfect writing by imitating the engraved copies, tho' they never reach the wish'd-for excellence of those copies, their hand is mended by the endeavor, and is tolerable while it continues fair and legible.

It may be well my posterity should be informed that to this little artifice, with the blessing of God, their ancestor ow'd the constant felicity of his life, down to his 79th year, in which this is written. What reverses may attend the remainder is in the hand of Providence; but, if they arrive, the reflection on past happiness enjoy'd ought to help his bearing them with more resignation. To Temperance he ascribes his long-continued health, and what is still left to him of a good constitution; to Industry and Frugality, the early easiness of his circumstances and acquisition of his fortune, with all that knowledge that enabled him to be a useful citizen, and obtained for him some degree of reputation among the learned; to Sincerity and Justice, the confidence of his country, and the honorable employs it conferred upon him; and to the joint influence of the whole mass of the virtues, even in the imperfect state he was able to acquire them, all that evenness of temper, and that cheerfulness in conversation, which makes his company still sought for, and agreeable even to his younger acquaintance. I hope, therefore, that some of my descendants may follow the example and reap the benefit.

It will be remark'd that, tho' my scheme was not wholly without religion, there was in it no mark of any of the distinguishing tenets of any particular sect. I had purposely avoided them; for, being fully persuaded of the utility and excellency of my method, and that it might be serviceable to people in all religions, and intending some time or other to publish it, I would not have any thing in it that should prejudice any one, of any sect, against it. I purposed writing a little comment on each virtue, in which I would have shown the advantages of possessing it, and the mischiefs attending its opposite vice; and I should have called my book The Art of Virtue, because it would have shown the means and manner of obtaining virtue, which would have distinguished it from the mere exhortation to be good, that does not instruct and indicate the means, but is like the apostle's man of verbal charity, who only without showing to the naked and hungry how or where they might get clothes or victuals, exhorted them to be fed and clothed.—James ii. 15, 16.

But it so happened that my intention of writing and publishing this comment was never fulfilled. I did, indeed, from time to time, put down short hints of the sentiments, reasonings, etc., to be made use of in it, some of which I have still by me; but the necessary close attention to private business in the earlier part of my life, and public business since, have occasioned my postponing it; for, it being connected in my mind with a *great and extensive project*, that required the whole man to execute, and which an unforeseen succession of employs prevented my attending to, it has hitherto remain'd unfinish'd.

In this piece it was my design to explain and enforce this doctrine, that vicious actions are not hurtful because they are forbidden, but forbidden because they are hurtful, the nature of man alone considered; that it was, therefore, every one's interest to be virtuous who wish'd to be happy even in this world; and I should, from this circumstance (there being always in the world a number of rich merchants, nobility, states, and princes, who have need of honest instruments for the management of their affairs, and such being so rare), have endeavored to convince young persons that no qualities were so likely to make a poor man's fortune as those of probity and integrity.

My list of virtues contain'd at first but twelve; but a Quaker friend having kindly informed me that I was generally thought proud; that my pride show'd itself frequently in conversation; that I was not content with being in the right when discussing any point, but was overbearing, and rather insolent, of which he convinc'd me by mentioning several instances; I determined endeavouring to cure myself, if I could, of this vice or folly among the rest, and I added *Humility* to my list, giving an extensive meaning to the word.

I cannot boast of much success in acquiring the reality of this virtue, but I had a good deal with regard to the *appearance* of it. I made it a rule to forbear all direct contradiction to the sentiments of others, and all positive assertion of my own. I even forbid myself, agreeably to the old laws of our Junto, the use of every word or expression in the language that imported a fix'd opinion, such as *certainly*, *undoubtedly*, etc., and I adopted, instead of them, *I conceive*, *I apprehend*, or *I imagine* a thing to be so or so; or it *so appears to me at present*. When another asserted something that I thought an error, I deny'd myself the pleasure of contradicting him abruptly, and of showing immediately some absurdity in his proposition; and in answering I began by observing that in certain cases or circumstances his opinion would be right, but in the present case there *appear'd* or *seem'd* to me some difference, etc. I soon found the advantage of this change in my manner; the conversations I engag'd in went on more pleasantly. The modest way in which I propos'd my opinions procur'd them a readier reception and less contradiction; I had less mortification when I was found to be in the wrong, and I more easily prevail'd with others to give up their mistakes and join with me when I happened to be in the right.

And this mode, which I at first put on with some violence to natural inclination, became at length so easy, and so habitual to me, that perhaps for these fifty years past no one has ever heard a dogmatical expression escape me. And to this habit (after my character of integrity) I think it principally owing that I had early so much weight with my fellow-citizens when I proposed new institutions, or alterations in the old, and so much influence in public councils when I became a member; for I was but a bad speaker, never eloquent, subject to much hesitation in my choice of words, hardly correct in language, and yet I generally carried my points.

In reality, there is, perhaps, no one of our natural passions so hard to subdue as *pride*. Disguise it, struggle with it, beat it down, stifle it, mortify it as much as one pleases, it is still alive, and will every now and then peep out and show itself; you will see it, perhaps, often in this history; for, even if I could conceive that I had compleatly overcome it, I should probably be proud of my humility.

[Thus far written at Passy, 1784.]

3.4.5 Reading and Review Questions

1. In *The Way to Wealth*, what comfort does Franklin derive from his works being preferred not by critics and other writers but by common people? Why?
2. In "An Edict by the King of Prussia," what faults of the British Crown does Franklin attribute to the King of Prussia? Why does he deflect criticism in this way?
1. What complaints against the British Crown are shared by the "Rules by Which a Great Empire May be Reduced to a Small One" and the Declaration of Independence? Why does Franklin use this means to make these complaints, do you think?
2. In *The Autobiography of Benjamin Franklin*, what literary works does Franklin cite as important to the shaping of his mind? What, if anything, do these works have in common? What power does Franklin attribute to the written word?
3. What human behaviors and qualities does Franklin list in his virtues and precepts? What, if anything, do they have in common? How do they compare to Puritan virtues? How do they contrast?

3.5 SAMSON OCCOM

(1723–1792)

Samson Occom was born in New London, Connecticut into the Mohegan tribe. Occom's youth coincided with the tail end of the Great Awakening, a revivalist and evangelical movement that stressed the equality of all people in the eyes of God. Moved by hearing evangelical sermons with this message, Occom converted to Christianity at the age of sixteen.

Image 3.5 |The Reverend Samuel Occom
Artist | Unknown
Source | Wikimedia Commons
License | Public Domain

A few years later, his mother asked the Reverend Eleazar Wheelock (1711–1779) to accept Occom as his pupil. Wheelock, an evangelical minister, hoped to spread Christianity among Native Americans by training young Native Americans to serve as missionaries to their own people. In 1754, Wheelock, through teaching Occom, transformed his English school into the Moor's Indian Charity School in Lebanon, Connecticut. Girls and boys were taught such skills as husbandry and the domestic arts. Boys were also taught Greek, Latin, and Hebrew in order to interpret the Bible themselves.

From 1749 to 1764, Occom worked as a missionary for the Montauks at Montauk, Long Island. He taught reading and spread the word of God; for his efforts, he received twenty pounds a year from the London Society for the Propagation of the Gospel, a stipend less than what was given to whites. Occom also married Mary Fowler, who was a Montauk; together they raised a family.

In 1759, Occom was ordained as a Presbyterian minister by the Presbytery of Suffolk. He fulfilled several missions among the Oneida tribe before accompanying the Reverend Nathaniel Whitaker to England to raise money for Moor's Indian Charity School. Wheelock promised to take care of Occom's family during his absence. Occom remained in England for two years, successfully raising twelve thousand pounds. He returned home to find his family neglected and the money he raised being used by Wheelock to move the Indian School to Hanover, New Hampshire, where it eventually became Dartmouth College. Wheelock now intended to introduce white missionaries among Native Americans through the groundwork laid by Native American ministers like Occom. Anticipating a diversion of funds and activities away from Native Americans, Occom broke with Wheelock.

Occom became an impoverished itinerant preacher among the New England Native Americans. In 1768, he described his ministry and life in a ten-page manuscript that remained unpublished in the Dartmouth archives until 1982. In it, he describes his life as a minister and teacher, particularly his efforts to encourage learning among the young. He also notes his difficulty in straddling the differing cultures of the whites and Native Americans. He assesses his marginalized position as due to the whites always seeing him as an Indian rather than as a Christian preacher. The poor conditions of his life both fulfilled and reflected his being viewed by whites as a poor Indian and a despised creature.

During the American Revolution, Occom encouraged Native Americans to remain neutral. In 1798, he established Brothertown for Christian Indians among the Oneida and served as a minister there for the remainder of his life.

3.5.1 *A Short Narrative of My Life*

https://collections.dartmouth.edu/occom/html/normalized/768517-normalized.html

3.5.2 Reading and Review Questions

1. What, if any, are the rhetorical benefits of Occom's referring to himself and other Native Americans as heathen—until his conversion to Christianity?
2. What are features of Mohegan life that distinguish it from that of white Christians? What is significant about these differences?

3. How does Occom reconcile his spiritual needs with his physical needs when teaching the Mohegans?
4. Why does Occom go into such detail on his teaching methods and schedules, as well as his religious meetings routine? How do you know?
5. How and why does Occom defend himself against the gentlemen of Boston's (the group working to propagating the Gospel in New England) assumption of Occom's "extravagance?" What attitude towards Native Americans do the Boston gentlemen seem to hold, do you think? How fairly do they treat Occom? Why?

3.6 J. HECTOR ST. JOHN DE CRÈVECŒUR

(1735–1813)

Crevecoeur was born Michel-Guillaume Jean de Crevecoeur in Caen, Normandy. Only after he was in America did he change his name to J. Hector St. John de Crevecoeur. He came to North America in 1755, enlisting in the Canadian militia during the French and Indian War; he served as a surveyor and cartographer. After leaving the military, he traveled through New York, Pennsylvania, and the southern colonies, making a living as a surveyor and trader with Native Americans.

Image 3.6 | J. Hector St. John de Crèvecœur
Artist | Unknown
Source | Wikimedia Commons
License | Public Domain

In 1769, he bought farmland in Orange County, New York, married, and raised a family. The American Revolution disrupted this idyllic pastoral life. A Tory sympathizer, Crevecoeur left for France ostensibly to recover family lands, and returned to post-war America as French consul for New York, New Jersey, and Connecticut. During his absence, his wife had died, his farm was burned in a Native American raid, and his children relocated with strangers. He continued for some years as a successful diplomat before returning to France in 1780. Two years later, he published his *Letters from an American Farmer*, recording his observations of America, from Pennsylvania to Charles Town and the western frontier. Using the persona of Farmer James—who hailed from a farm not in Orange County, New York but near Carlisle, Pennsylvania—and suppressing his Tory sympathies, Crevecoeur praised the agrarian life. He noted extensive fields and decent houses in a land that only one hundred years previously had been all wilderness. He expressed optimism for continued positive change through humanitarian action yet also noted the cruelty of slavery in the southern states and lawless behaviors in the western frontier. His book documented the transformation of colonial America to the American Republic. He asked the important question, "What is an American?" And he defined one of the shaping characteristics of the future nature: as a melting pot of peoples and cultures.

The book's topicality contributed to its remarkable success. Its success certainly helped popularize the idea of America as a classless society, rich with opportunity. After 1790, Crevecoeur himself never returned to America but lived the remainder of his life in France.

3.6.1 From *Letters from an American Farmer* (1782)

Letter III

WHAT IS AN AMERICAN

I wish I could be acquainted with the feelings and thoughts which must agitate the heart and present themselves to the mind of an enlightened Englishman, when he first lands on this continent. He must greatly rejoice that he lived at a time to see this fair country discovered and settled; he must necessarily feel a share of national pride, when he views the chain of settlements which embellishes these extended shores. When he says to himself, this is the work of my countrymen, who, when convulsed by factions, afflicted by a variety of miseries and wants, restless and impatient, took refuge here. They brought along with them their national genius, to which they principally owe what liberty they enjoy, and what substance they possess. Here he sees the industry of his native country displayed in a new manner, and traces in their works the embryos of all the arts, sciences, and ingenuity which nourish in Europe. Here he beholds fair cities, substantial villages, extensive fields, an immense country filled with decent houses, good roads, orchards,

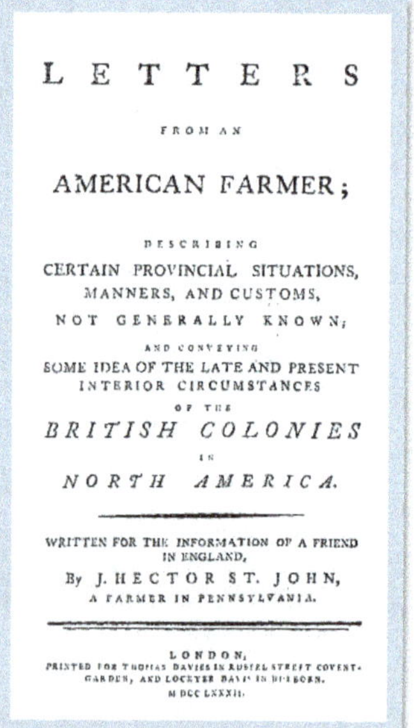

LETTERS

FROM AN

AMERICAN FARMER;

DESCRIBING

CERTAIN PROVINCIAL SITUATIONS,
MANNERS, AND CUSTOMS,
NOT GENERALLY KNOWN;

AND CONVEYING

SOME IDEA OF THE LATE AND PRESENT
INTERIOR CIRCUMSTANCES

OF THE

BRITISH COLONIES

IN

NORTH AMERICA.

WRITTEN FOR THE INFORMATION OF A FRIEND
IN ENGLAND,

By J. HECTOR ST. JOHN,
A FARMER IN PENNSYLVANIA.

LONDON,
PRINTED FOR THOMAS DAVIES IN RUSSEL STREET COVENT-GARDEN, AND LOCKYER DAVIS IN HOLBORN.
M DCC LXXXII.

Image 3.7 | *Letters from an American Farmer*
Author | J. Hector St. John de Crèvecœur
Source | Wikimedia Commons
License | Public Domain

meadows, and bridges, where an hundred years ago all was wild, woody, and uncultivated! What a train of pleasing ideas this fair spectacle must suggest; it is a prospect which must inspire a good citizen with the most heartfelt pleasure. The difficulty consists in the manner of viewing so extensive a scene. He is arrived on a new continent; a modern society offers itself to his contemplation, different from what he had hitherto seen. It is not composed, as in Europe, of great lords who possess everything, and of a herd of people who have nothing. Here are no aristocratical families, no courts, no kings, no bishops, no ecclesiastical dominion, no invisible power giving to a few a very visible one; no great manufacturers employing thousands, no great refinements of luxury. The rich and the poor are not so far removed from each other as they are in Europe. Some few towns excepted, we are all tillers of the earth, from Nova Scotia to West Florida. We are a people of cultivators, scattered over an immense territory, communicating with each other by means of good roads and navigable rivers, united by the silken bands of mild government, all respecting the laws, without dreading their power, because they are equitable. We are all animated with the spirit of an industry which is unfettered and unrestrained, because each person works for himself. If he travels through our rural districts he views not the hostile castle, and the haughty mansion, contrasted with the clay- built hut and miserable cabin, where cattle and men help to keep each other warm, and dwell in meanness, smoke, and indigence. A pleasing uniformity of decent competence appears throughout our habitations. The meanest of our log-houses is a dry and comfortable habitation. Lawyer or merchant are the fairest titles our towns afford; that of a farmer is the only appellation of the rural inhabitants of our country. It must take some time ere he can reconcile himself to our dictionary, which is but short in words of dignity, and names of honour. There, on a Sunday, he sees a congregation of respectable farmers and their wives, all clad in neat homespun, well mounted, or riding in their own humble waggons. There is not among them an esquire, saving the unlettered magistrate. There he sees a parson as simple as his flock, a farmer who does not riot on the labour of others. We have no princes, for whom we toil, starve, and bleed: we are the most perfect society now existing in the world. Here man is free as he ought to be; nor is this pleasing equality so transitory as many others are. Many ages will not see the shores of our great lakes replenished with inland nations, nor the unknown bounds of North America entirely peopled. Who can tell how far it extends? Who can tell the millions of men whom it will feed and contain? for no European foot has as yet travelled half the extent of this mighty continent!

The next wish of this traveller will be to know whence came all these people? they are a mixture of English, Scotch, Irish, French, Dutch, Germans, and Swedes. From this promiscuous breed, that race now called Americans have arisen. The eastern provinces must indeed be excepted, as being the unmixed descendants of Englishmen. I have heard many wish that they had been more intermixed also: for my part, I am no wisher, and think it much better as it has happened. They exhibit a most conspicuous figure in this great and variegated picture; they too enter for a great share in the pleasing perspective displayed in these thirteen provinces. I know it is fashionable to reflect on them, but I respect them for what they have done; for the accuracy and wisdom with which they have settled their territory; for the decency of their manners; for their early love of letters; their ancient college, the first in this hemisphere; for their industry; which to me who am but a farmer, is the criterion of everything. There never was a people, situated as they are, who with so ungrateful a soil have done more in so short a time. Do you think that the monarchical ingredients which are more prevalent in other governments, have purged them from all foul stains? Their histories assert the contrary.

In this great American asylum, the poor of Europe have by some means met together, and in consequence of various causes; to what purpose should they ask one another what countrymen they are? Alas, two thirds of them had no country. Can a wretch who wanders about, who works and starves, whose life is a continual scene of sore affliction or pinching penury; can that man call England or any other kingdom his country? A country that had no bread for him, whose fields procured him no harvest, who met with nothing but the frowns of the rich, the severity of the laws, with jails and punishments; who owned not a single foot of the extensive surface of this planet? No! urged by a variety of motives, here they came. Every thing has tended to regenerate them; new laws, a new mode of living, a new social system; here they are become men: in Europe they were as so many useless plants, wanting vegetative mould, and refreshing showers; they withered, and were mowed down by want, hunger, and war; but now by the power of transplantation, like all other plants they have taken root and flourished! Formerly they were not numbered in any civil lists of their country, except in those of the poor; here they rank as citizens. By what invisible power has this surprising metamorphosis been performed? By that of the laws and that of their industry. The laws, the indulgent laws, protect them as they arrive, stamping on them the symbol of adoption; they receive ample rewards for their labours; these accumulated rewards procure them lands; those lands confer on them the title of freemen, and to that title every benefit is affixed which men can possibly require. This is the great operation daily performed by our laws. From whence proceed these laws? From our government. Whence the government? It is derived from the original genius and strong desire of the people ratified and confirmed by the crown. This is the great chain which links us all, this is the picture which every province exhibits, Nova Scotia excepted.

There the crown has done all; either there were no people who had genius, or it was not much attended to: the consequence is, that the province is very thinly inhabited indeed; the power of the crown in conjunction with the musketos has prevented men from settling there. Yet some parts of it flourished once, and it contained a mild harmless set of people. But for the fault of a few leaders, the whole were banished. The greatest political error the crown ever committed in America, was to cut off men from a country which wanted nothing but men!

What attachment can a poor European emigrant have for a country where he had nothing? The knowledge of the language, the love of a few kindred as poor as himself, were the only cords that tied him: his country is now that which gives him land, bread, protection, and consequence: Ubi panis ibi patria, is the motto of all emigrants. What then is the American, this new man? He is either an European, or the descendant of an European, hence that strange mixture of blood, which you will find in no other country. I could point out to you a family whose grandfather was an Englishman, whose wife was Dutch, whose son married a French woman, and whose present four sons have now four wives of different nations. He is an American, who, leaving behind him all his ancient prejudices and manners, receives new ones from the new mode of life he has embraced, the new government he obeys, and the new rank he holds. He becomes an American by being received in the broad lap of our great Alma Mater. Here individuals of all nations are melted into a new race of men, whose labours and posterity will one day cause great changes in the world. Americans are the western pilgrims, who are carrying along with them that great mass of arts, sciences, vigour, and industry which began long since in the east; they will finish the great circle. The Americans were once scattered all over Europe; here they are incorporated into one of the finest systems of population which has ever appeared, and which will hereafter become distinct by the power of the different climates they inhabit. The American ought therefore to love this country much better than that wherein either he or his forefathers were born. Here the rewards of his industry follow with equal steps the progress of his labour; his labour is founded on the basis of nature, SELF-INTEREST: can it want a stronger allurement? Wives and children, who before in vain demanded of him a morsel of bread, now, fat and frolicsome, gladly help their father to clear those fields whence exuberant crops are to arise to feed and to clothe them all; without any part being claimed, either by a despotic prince, a rich abbot, or a mighty lord. Here religion demands but little of him; a small voluntary salary to the minister, and gratitude to God; can he refuse these? The American is a new man, who acts upon new principles; he must therefore entertain new ideas, and form new opinions. From involuntary idleness, servile dependence, penury, and useless labour, he has passed to toils of a very different nature, rewarded by ample subsistence.—This is an American.

British America is divided into many provinces, forming a large association, scattered along a coast 1500 miles extent and about 200 wide. This society I would fain examine, at least such as it appears in the middle provinces; if it does not afford that variety of tinges and gradations which may be observed in Europe, we have colours peculiar to ourselves. For instance, it is natural to conceive that those who live near the sea, must be very different from those who live in the woods; the intermediate space will afford a separate and distinct class.

Men are like plants; the goodness and flavour of the fruit proceeds from the peculiar soil and exposition in which they grow. We are nothing but what we derive from the air we breathe, the climate we inhabit, the government we obey, the system of religion we profess, and the nature of our employment. Here you will find but few crimes; these have acquired as yet no root among us. I wish I was able to trace all my ideas; if my ignorance prevents me from describing them properly, I hope I shall be able to delineate a few of the outlines, which are all I propose.

Those who live near the sea, feed more on fish than on flesh, and often encounter that boisterous element. This renders them more bold and enterprising; this leads them to neglect the confined occupations of the land. They see and converse with a variety of people, their intercourse with mankind becomes extensive. The sea inspires them with a love of traffic, a desire of transporting produce from one place to another; and leads them to a variety of resources which supply the place of labour. Those who inhabit the middle settlements, by far the most numerous, must be very different; the simple cultivation of the earth purifies them, but the indulgences of the government, the soft remonstrances of religion, the rank of independent freeholders, must necessarily inspire them with sentiments, very little known in Europe among people of the same class. What do I say? Europe has no such class of men; the early knowledge they acquire, the early bargains they make, give them a great degree of sagacity. As freemen they will be litigious; pride and obstinacy are often the cause of law suits; the nature of our laws and governments may be another. As citizens it is easy to imagine, that they will carefully read the newspapers, enter into every political disquisition, freely blame or censure governors and others. As farmers they will be careful and anxious to get as much as they can, because what they get is their own. As northern men they will love the cheerful cup. As Christians, religion curbs them not in their opinions; the general indulgence leaves every one to think for themselves in spiritual matters; the laws inspect our actions, our thoughts are left to God. Industry, good living, selfishness, litigiousness, country politics, the pride of freemen, religious indifference, are their characteristics. If you recede still farther from the sea, you will come into more modern settlements; they exhibit the same strong lineaments, in a ruder appearance. Religion seems to have still less influence, and their manners are less improved.

Now we arrive near the great woods, near the last inhabited districts; there men seem to be placed still farther beyond the reach of government, which in some measure leaves them to themselves. How can it pervade every corner; as they were driven there by misfortunes, necessity of beginnings, desire of acquiring large tracts of land, idleness, frequent want of economy, ancient debts; the re-union of such people does not afford a very pleasing spectacle. When discord, want of unity and friendship; when either drunkenness or idleness prevail in such remote districts; contention, inactivity, and wretchedness must ensue. There are not the same remedies to these evils as in a long established community. The few magistrates they have, are in general little better than the rest; they are often in a perfect state of war; that of man against man, sometimes decided by blows, sometimes by means of the law; that of man against every wild inhabitant of these venerable woods, of which they are come to dispossess them. There men appear to be no better than carnivorous animals of a superior rank, living on the flesh of wild animals when they can catch them, and when they are not able, they subsist on grain. He who would wish to see America in its proper light, and have a true idea of its feeble beginnings and barbarous rudiments, must visit our extended line of frontiers where the last settlers dwell, and where he may see the first labours of settlement, the mode of clearing the earth, in all their different appearances; where men are wholly left dependent on their native tempers, and on the spur of uncertain industry, which often fails when not sanctified by the efficacy of a few moral rules. There, remote from the power of example and check of shame, many families exhibit the most hideous parts of our society. They are a kind of forlorn hope, preceding by ten or twelve years the most respectable army of veterans which come after them. In that space, prosperity will polish some, vice and the law will drive off the rest, who uniting again with others like themselves will recede still farther; making room for more industrious people, who will finish their improvements, convert the loghouse into a convenient habitation, and rejoicing that the first heavy labours are finished, will change in a few years that hitherto barbarous country into a fine fertile, well regulated district. Such is our progress, such is the march of the Europeans toward the interior parts of this continent. In all societies there are off-casts; this impure part serves as our precursors or pioneers; my father himself was one of that class, but he came upon honest principles, and was therefore one of the few who held fast; by good conduct and temperance, he transmitted to me his fair inheritance, when not above one in fourteen of his contemporaries had the same good fortune.

Forty years ago this smiling country was thus inhabited; it is now purged, a general decency of manners prevails throughout, and such has been the fate of our best countries.

Exclusive of those general characteristics, each province has its own, founded on the government, climate, mode of husbandry, customs, and peculiarity of circumstances. Europeans submit insensibly to these great powers, and become, in the course of a few generations, not only Americans in general, but either Pennsylvanians, Virginians, or provincials under some other name. Whoever traverses the continent must easily observe those strong differences, which will grow more evident in time. The inhabitants of Canada, Massachusetts, the middle provinces, the southern ones will be as different as their climates; their only points of unity will be those of religion and language.

As I have endeavoured to show you how Europeans become Americans; it may not be disagreeable to show you likewise how the various Christian sects introduced, wear out, and how religious indifference becomes prevalent. When any considerable number of a particular sect happen to dwell contiguous to each other, they immediately erect a temple, and there worship the Divinity agreeably to their own peculiar ideas. Nobody disturbs them. If any new sect springs up in Europe it may happen that many of its professors will come and settle in American. As they bring their zeal with them, they are at liberty to make proselytes if they can, and to build a meeting and to follow the dictates of their consciences; for neither the government nor any other power interferes. If they are peaceable subjects, and are industrious, what is it to their neighbours how and in what manner they think fit to address their prayers to the Supreme Being? But if the sectaries are not settled close together, if they are mixed with other denominations, their zeal will cool for want of fuel, and will be extinguished in a little time. Then the Americans become as to religion, what they are as to country, allied to all. In them the name of Englishman, Frenchman, and European is lost, and in like manner, the strict modes of Christianity as practised in Europe are lost also. This effect will extend itself still farther hereafter, and though this may appear to you as a strange idea, yet it is a very true one. I shall be able perhaps hereafter to explain myself better; in the meanwhile, let the following example serve as my first justification.

Let us suppose you and I to be travelling; we observe that in this house, to the right, lives a Catholic, who prays to God as he has been taught, and believes in transubstantiation; he works and raises wheat, he has a large family of children, all hale and robust; his belief, his prayers offend nobody. About one mile farther on the same road, his next neighbour may be a good honest plodding German Lutheran, who addresses himself to the same God, the God of all, agreeably to the modes he has been educated in, and believes in consubstantiation; by so doing he scandalises nobody; he also works in his fields, embellishes the earth, clears swamps, etc. What has the world to do with his Lutheran principles? He persecutes nobody, and nobody persecutes him, he visits his neighbours, and his neighbours visit him. Next to him lives a seceder, the most enthusiastic of all sectaries; his zeal is hot and fiery, but separated as he is from others of the same complexion, he has no congregation of his own to resort to, where he might cabal and mingle religious pride with worldly obstinacy. He likewise raises good crops, his house is handsomely painted, his orchard is one of the fairest in the neighbourhood. How does it concern the welfare of the country, or of the province at large, what this man's religious sentiments are, or really whether he has any at all? He is a good farmer, he is a sober, peaceable, good citizen: William Penn himself would not wish for more. This is the visible character, the invisible one is only guessed at, and is nobody's business. Next again lives a Low Dutchman, who implicitly believes the rules laid down by the synod of Dort. He conceives no other idea of a clergyman than that of an hired man; if he does his work well he will pay him the stipulated sum; if not he will dismiss him, and do without his sermons, and let his church be shut up for years. But notwithstanding this coarse idea, you will find his house and farm to be the neatest in all the country; and you will judge by his waggon and fat horses, that he thinks more of the affairs of this world than of those of the next. He is sober and laborious, therefore he is all he ought to be as to the affairs of this life; as for those of the next, he must trust to the great Creator. Each of these people instruct their children as well as they can, but these instructions are feeble compared to those which are given to the youth of the poorest class in Europe. Their children will therefore grow up less zealous and more indifferent in matters of religion than their parents. The foolish vanity, or rather the fury of making Proselytes, is unknown here; they have no time, the seasons call for all their attention, and thus in a few years, this mixed neighbourhood will exhibit a strange religious medley, that will be neither pure Catholicism nor pure Calvinism.

A very perceptible indifference even in the first generation, will become apparent; and it may happen that the daughter of the Catholic will marry the son of the seceder, and settle by themselves at a distance from their parents. What religious education will they give their children? A very imperfect one. If there happens to be in the neighbourhood any place of worship, we will suppose a Quaker's meeting; rather than not show their fine clothes, they will go to it, and some of them may perhaps attach themselves to that society. Others will remain in a perfect state of indifference; the children of these zealous parents will not be able to tell what their religious principles are, and their grandchildren still less. The neighbourhood of a place of worship generally leads them to it, and the action of going thither, is the strongest evidence they can give of their attachment to any sect. The Quakers are the only people who retain a fondness for their own mode of worship; for be they ever so far separated from each other, they hold a sort of communion with the society, and seldom depart from its rules, at least in this country. Thus all sects are mixed as well as all nations; thus religious indifference is imperceptibly disseminated from one end of the continent to the other; which is at present one of the strongest characteristics of the Americans. Where this will reach no one can tell, perhaps it may leave a vacuum fit to receive other systems. Persecution, religious pride, the love of contradiction, are the food of what the world commonly calls religion. These motives have ceased here; zeal in Europe is confined; here it evaporates in the great distance it has to travel; there it is a grain of powder inclosed, here it burns away in the open air, and consumes without effect.

But to return to our back settlers. I must tell you, that there is something in the proximity of the woods, which is very singular. It is with men as it is with the plants and animals that grow and live in the forests; they are entirely different from those that live in the plains. I will candidly tell you all my thoughts but you are not to expect that I shall advance any reasons. By living in or near the woods, their actions are regulated by the wildness of the neighbourhood. The deer often come to eat their grain, the wolves to destroy their sheep, the bears to kill their hogs, the foxes to catch their poultry. This surrounding hostility immediately puts the gun into their hands; they watch these animals, they kill some; and thus by defending their property, they soon become professed hunters; this is the progress; once hunters, farewell to the plough. The chase renders them ferocious, gloomy, and unsociable; a hunter wants no neighbour, he rather hates them, because he dreads the competition. In a little time their success in the woods makes them neglect their tillage. They trust to the natural fecundity of the earth, and therefore do little; carelessness in fencing often exposes what little they sow to destruction; they are not at home to watch; in order therefore to make up the deficiency, they go oftener to the woods. That new mode of life brings along with it a new set of manners, which I cannot easily describe. These new manners being grafted on the old stock, produce a strange sort of lawless profligacy, the impressions of which are indelible. The manners of the Indian natives are respectable, compared with this European medley. Their wives and children live in sloth and inactivity; and having no proper pursuits, you may judge what education the latter receive. Their tender minds have nothing else to contemplate but the example of their parents; like them they grow up a mongrel breed, half civilised, half savage, except nature stamps on them some constitutional propensities. That rich, that voluptuous sentiment is gone that struck them so forcibly; the possession of their freeholds no longer conveys to their minds the same pleasure and pride. To all these reasons you must add, their lonely situation, and you cannot imagine what an effect on manners the great distances they live from each other has! Consider one of the last settlements in its first view: of what is it composed? Europeans who have not that sufficient share of knowledge they ought to have, in order to prosper; people who have suddenly passed from oppression, dread of government, and fear of laws, into the unlimited freedom of the woods. This sudden change must have a very great effect on most men, and on that class particularly. Eating of wild meat, whatever you may think, tends to alter their temper: though all the proof I can adduce, is, that I have seen it: and having no place of worship to resort to, what little society this might afford is denied them. The Sunday meetings, exclusive of religious benefits, were the only social bonds that might have inspired them with some degree of emulation in neatness. Is it then surprising to see men thus situated, immersed in great and heavy labours, degenerate a little? It is rather a wonder the effect is not more diffusive. The Moravians and the Quakers are the only instances in exception to what I have advanced. The first never settle singly, it is a colony of the society which emigrates; they carry with them their forms, worship, rules, and decency: the others never begin so hard, they are always able to buy improvements, in which there is a great advantage, for by that time the country is recovered from its first barbarity. Thus our bad people are those who are half cultivators and half hunters; and the worst of them are those who have degenerated altogether into the hunting state. As old ploughmen and new men of the woods, as Europeans and new made Indians, they contract the vices of both; they adopt the moroseness and ferocity of a native, without his mildness, or even his industry at home. If manners are not refined, at least they are rendered simple and inoffensive by tilling the earth; all our wants are supplied by it, our time is divided between labour and rest, and leaves none for the commission of great misdeeds. As hunters it is divided between the toil of the chase, the idleness of repose, or the indulgence of inebriation. Hunting is but a licentious idle life, and if it does not always pervert good dispositions; yet, when it is united with bad luck, it leads to want: want stimulates that propensity to rapacity and injustice, too natural to needy men, which is the fatal gradation. After this explanation of the effects which follow by living in the woods, shall we yet vainly flatter ourselves with the hope of converting the Indians? We should rather begin with converting our back- settlers; and now if I dare mention the name of religion, its sweet accents would be lost in the immensity of these woods. Men thus placed are not fit either to receive or remember its mild instructions; they want temples and ministers, but as soon as men cease to remain at home, and begin to lead an erratic life, let them be either tawny or white, they cease to be its disciples.

Thus have I faintly and imperfectly endeavoured to trace our society from the sea to our woods! yet you must not imagine that every person who moves back, acts upon the same principles, or falls into the same degeneracy. Many families carry with them all their decency of conduct, purity of morals, and respect of religion; but these are scarce, the power of example is sometimes irresistible. Even among these back-settlers, their depravity is greater or less, according to what nation or province they belong. Were I to adduce proofs of this, I might be accused of partiality. If there happens to be some rich intervals, some fertile bottoms, in those remote districts, the people will there prefer tilling the land to hunting, and will attach themselves to it; but even on these fertile spots you may plainly perceive the inhabitants to acquire a great degree of rusticity and selfishness.

It is in consequence of this straggling situation, and the astonishing power it has on manners, that the back-settlers of both the Carolinas, Virginia, and many other parts, have been long a set of lawless people; it has been even dangerous to travel among them. Government can do nothing in so extensive a country, better it should wink at these irregularities, than that it should use means inconsistent with its usual mildness. Time will efface those stains: in proportion as the great body of population approaches them they will reform, and become polished and subordinate. Whatever has been said of the four New England provinces, no such degeneracy of manners has ever tarnished their annals; their back-settlers have been kept within the bounds of decency, and government, by means of wise laws, and by the influence of religion. What a detestable idea such people must have given to the natives of the Europeans! They trade with them, the worst of people are permitted to do that which none but persons of the best characters should be employed in. They get drunk with them, and often defraud the Indians. Their avarice, removed from the eyes of their superiors, knows no bounds; and aided by the little superiority of knowledge, these traders deceive them, and even sometimes shed blood. Hence those shocking violations, those sudden devastations which have so often stained our frontiers, when hundreds of innocent people have been sacrificed for the crimes of a few. It was in consequence of such behaviour, that the Indians took the hatchet against the Virginians in 1774. Thus are our first steps trod, thus are our first trees felled, in general, by the most vicious of our people; and thus the path is opened for the arrival of a second and better class, the true American freeholders; the most respectable set of people in this part of the world: respectable for their industry, their happy independence, the great share of freedom they possess, the good regulation of their families, and for extending the trade and the dominion of our mother country.

Europe contains hardly any other distinctions but lords and tenants; this fair country alone is settled by freeholders, the possessors of the soil they cultivate, members of the government they obey, and the framers of their own laws, by means of their representatives. This is a thought which you have taught me to cherish; our difference from Europe, far from diminishing, rather adds to our usefulness and consequence as men and subjects. Had our forefathers remained there, they would only have crowded it, and perhaps prolonged those convulsions which had shook it so long. Every industrious European who transports himself here, may be compared to a sprout growing at the foot of a great tree; it enjoys and draws but a little portion of sap; wrench it from the parent roots, transplant it, and it will become a tree bearing fruit also. Colonists are therefore entitled to the consideration due to the most useful subjects; a hundred families barely existing in some parts of Scotland, will here in six years, cause an annual exportation of 10,000 bushels of wheat: 100 bushels being but a common quantity for an industrious family to sell, if they cultivate good land. It is here then that the idle may be employed, the useless become useful, and the poor become rich; but by riches I do not mean gold and silver, we have but little of those metals; I mean a better sort of wealth, cleared lands, cattle, good houses, good clothes, and an increase of people to enjoy them.

There is no wonder that this country has so many charms, and presents to Europeans so many temptations to remain in it. A traveller in Europe becomes a stranger as soon as he quits his own kingdom; but it is otherwise here. We know, properly speaking, no strangers; this is every person's country; the variety of our soils, situations, climates, governments, and produce, hath something which must please everybody. No sooner does an European arrive, no matter of what condition, than his eyes are opened upon the fair prospect; he hears his language spoke, he retraces many of his own country manners, he perpetually hears the names of families and towns with which he is acquainted; he sees happiness and prosperity in all places disseminated; he meets with hospitality, kindness, and plenty everywhere; he beholds hardly any poor, he seldom hears of punishments and executions; and he wonders at the elegance of our towns, those miracles of industry and freedom. He cannot admire enough our rural districts, our convenient roads, good taverns, and our many accommodations; he involuntarily loves a country where everything is so lovely. When in England, he was a mere Englishman; here he stands on a larger portion of the globe, not less than its fourth part, and may see the productions of the north, in iron and naval stores; the provisions of Ireland, the grain of Egypt, the indigo, the rice of China. He does not find, as in Europe, a crowded society, where every place is over-stocked; he does not feel that perpetual collision of parties, that difficulty of beginning, that contention which oversets so many. There is room for everybody in America; has he any particular talent, or industry? he exerts it in order to procure a livelihood, and it succeeds. Is he a merchant? the avenues of trade are infinite; is he eminent in any respect? he will be employed and respected. Does he love a country life? pleasant farms present themselves; he may purchase what he wants, and thereby become an American farmer. Is he a labourer, sober and industrious? he need not go many miles, nor receive many informations before he will be hired, well fed at the table of his employer, and paid four or five times more than he can get in Europe. Does he want uncultivated lands? thousands of acres present themselves, which he may purchase cheap. Whatever be his talents or inclinations, if they are moderate, he may satisfy them. I do not mean that every one who comes will grow rich in a little time; no, but he may procure an easy, decent maintenance, by his industry. Instead of starving he will be fed, instead of being idle he will have employment; and these are riches enough for such men as come over here. The rich stay in Europe, it is only the middling and the poor that emigrate. Would you wish to travel in independent idleness, from north to south, you will find easy access, and the most cheerful reception at every house; society without ostentation, good cheer without pride, and every decent diversion which the country affords, with little expense. It is no wonder that the European who has lived here a few years, is desirous to remain; Europe with all its pomp, is not to be compared to this continent, for men of middle stations, or labourers.

An European, when he first arrives, seems limited in his intentions, as well as in his views; but he very suddenly alters his scale; two hundred miles formerly appeared a very great distance, it is now but a trifle; he no sooner breathes our air than he forms schemes, and embarks in designs he never would have thought of in his own country. There the plenitude of society confines many useful ideas, and often extinguishes the most laudable schemes which here ripen into maturity. Thus Europeans become Americans.

But how is this accomplished in that crowd of low, indigent people, who flock here every year from all parts of Europe? I will tell you; they no sooner arrive than they immediately feel the good effects of that plenty of provisions we possess: they fare on our best food, and they are kindly entertained; their talents, character, and peculiar industry are immediately inquired into; they find countrymen everywhere disseminated, let them come from whatever part of Europe. Let me select one as an epitome of the rest; he is hired, he goes to work, and works moderately; instead of being employed by a haughty person, he finds himself with his equal, placed at the substantial table of the farmer, or else at an inferior one as good; his wages are high, his bed is not like that bed of sorrow on which he used to lie: if he behaves with propriety, and is faithful, he is caressed, and becomes as it were a member of the family. He begins to feel the effects of a sort of resurrection; hitherto he had not lived, but simply vegetated; he now feels himself a man, because he is treated as such; the laws of his own country had overlooked him in his insignificancy; the laws of this cover him with their mantle. Judge what an alteration there must arise in the mind and thoughts of this man; he begins to forget his former servitude and dependence, his heart involuntarily swells and glows; this first swell inspires him with those new thoughts which constitute an American. What love can he entertain for a country where his existence was a burthen to him; if he is a generous good man, the love of this new adoptive parent will sink deep into his heart. He looks around, and sees many a prosperous person, who but a few years before was as poor as himself. This encourages him much, he begins to form some little scheme, the first, alas, he ever formed in his life. If he is wise he thus spends two or three years, in which time he acquires knowledge, the use of tools, the modes of working the lands, felling trees, etc. This prepares the foundation of a good name, the most useful acquisition he can make. He is encouraged, he has gained friends; he is advised and directed, he feels bold, he purchases some land; he gives all the money he has brought over, as well as what he has earned, and trusts to the God of harvests for the discharge of the rest. His good name procures him credit. He is now possessed of the deed, conveying to him and his posterity the fee simple and absolute property of two hundred acres of land, situated on such a river. What an epocha in this man's life! He is become a freeholder, from perhaps a German boor—he is now an American, a Pennsylvanian, an English subject. He is naturalised, his name is enrolled with those of the other citizens of the province. Instead of being a vagrant, he has a place of residence; he is called the inhabitant of such a county, or of such a district, and for the first time in his life counts for something; for hitherto he has been a cypher. I only repeat what I have heard many say, and no wonder their hearts should glow, and be agitated with a multitude of feelings, not easy to describe. From nothing to start into being; from a servant to the rank of a master; from being the slave of some despotic prince, to become a free man, invested with lands, to which every municipal blessing is annexed! What a change indeed! It is in consequence of that change that he becomes an American. This great metamorphosis has a double effect, it extinguishes all his European prejudices, he forgets that mechanism of subordination, that servility of disposition which poverty had taught him; and sometimes he is apt to forget too much, often passing from one extreme to the other. If he is a good man, he forms schemes of future prosperity, he proposes to educate his children better than he has been educated himself; he thinks of future modes of conduct, feels an ardour to labour he never felt before. Pride steps in and leads him to everything that the laws do not forbid: he respects them; with a heart-felt gratitude he looks toward the east, toward that insular government from whose wisdom all his new felicity is derived, and under whose wings and protection he now lives. These reflections constitute him the good man and the good subject. Ye poor Europeans, ye, who sweat, and work for the great— ye, who are obliged to give so many sheaves to the church, so many to your lords, so many to your government, and have hardly any left for yourselves—ye, who are held in less estimation than favourite hunters or useless lap-dogs—ye, who only breathe the air of nature, because it cannot be withheld from you; it is here that ye can conceive the possibility of those feelings I have been describing; it is here the laws of naturalisation invite every one to partake of our great labours and felicity, to till unrented, untaxed lands! Many, corrupted beyond the power of amendment, have brought with them all their vices, and disregarding the advantages held to them, have gone on in their former career of iniquity, until they have been overtaken and punished by our laws. It is not every emigrant who succeeds; no, it is only the sober, the honest, and industrious: happy those to whom this transition has served as a powerful spur to labour, to prosperity, and to the good establishment of children, born in the days of their poverty; and who had no other portion to expect but the rags of their parents, had it not been for their happy emigration. Others again, have been led astray by this enchanting scene; their new pride, instead of leading them to the fields, has kept them in idleness; the idea of possessing lands is all that satisfies them—though surrounded with fertility, they have mouldered away their time in inactivity, misinformed husbandry, and ineffectual endeavours. How much wiser, in general, the honest Germans than almost all other Europeans; they hire themselves to some of their wealthy landsmen, and in that apprenticeship learn everything that is necessary. They attentively consider the prosperous industry of others, which imprints in their minds a strong desire of possessing the same advantages. This forcible idea never quits them, they launch forth, and by dint of sobriety, rigid parsimony, and the most persevering industry, they commonly succeed. Their astonishment at their first arrival from Germany is very great—it is to them a dream; the contrast must be powerful indeed; they observe their countrymen flourishing in every place; they travel through whole counties where not a word of English is spoken; and in the names and the language of the people, they retrace Germany. They have been an useful acquisition to this continent, and to Pennsylvania in particular; to them it owes some share of its prosperity: to their mechanical knowledge and patience it owes the finest mills in all America, the best teams of horses, and many other advantages. The recollection of their former poverty and slavery never quits them as long as they live.

The Scotch and the Irish might have lived in their own country perhaps as poor, but enjoying more civil advantages, the effects of their new situation do not strike them so forcibly, nor has it so lasting an effect. From whence the difference arises I know not, but out of twelve families of emigrants of each country, generally seven Scotch will succeed, nine German, and four Irish. The Scotch are frugal and laborious, but their wives cannot work so hard as German women, who on the contrary vie with their husbands, and often share with them the most severe toils of the field, which they understand better. They have therefore nothing to struggle against, but the common casualties of nature. The Irish do not prosper so well; they love to drink and to quarrel; they are litigious, and soon take to the gun, which is the ruin of everything; they seem beside to labour under a greater degree of ignorance in husbandry than the others; perhaps it is that their industry had less scope, and was less exercised at home. I have heard many relate, how the land was parcelled out in that kingdom; their ancient conquest has been a great detriment to them, by over-setting their landed property. The lands possessed by a few, are leased down ad infinitum, and the occupiers often pay five guineas an acre. The poor are worse lodged there than anywhere else in Europe; their potatoes, which are easily raised, are perhaps an inducement to laziness: their wages are too low, and their whisky too cheap.

There is no tracing observations of this kind, without making at the same time very great allowances, as there are everywhere to be found, a great many exceptions. The Irish themselves, from different parts of that kingdom, are very different. It is difficult to account for this surprising locality, one would think on so small an island an Irishman must be an Irishman: yet it is not so, they are different in their aptitude to, and in their love of labour.

The Scotch on the contrary are all industrious and saving; they want nothing more than a field to exert themselves in, and they are commonly sure of succeeding. The only difficulty they labour under is, that technical American knowledge which requires some time to obtain; it is not easy for those who seldom saw a tree, to conceive how it is to be felled, cut up, and split into rails and posts.

As I am fond of seeing and talking of prosperous families, I intend to finish this letter by relating to you the history of an honest Scotch Hebridean, who came here in 1774, which will show you in epitome what the Scotch can do, wherever they have room for the exertion of their industry. Whenever I hear of any new settlement, I pay it a visit once or twice a year, on purpose to observe the different steps each settler takes, the gradual improvements, the different tempers of each family, on which their prosperity in a great nature depends; their different modifications of industry, their ingenuity, and contrivance; for being all poor, their life requires sagacity and prudence. In the evening I love to hear them tell their stories, they furnish me with new ideas; I sit still and listen to their ancient misfortunes, observing in many of them a strong degree of gratitude to God, and the government. Many a well meant sermon have I preached to some of them. When I found laziness and inattention to prevail, who could refrain from wishing well to these new countrymen, after having undergone so many fatigues. Who could withhold good advice? What a happy change it must be, to descend from the high, sterile, bleak lands of Scotland, where everything is barren and cold, to rest on some fertile farms in these middle provinces! Such a transition must have afforded the most pleasing satisfaction.

The following dialogue passed at an out-settlement, where I lately paid a visit:

Well, friend, how do you do now; I am come fifty odd miles on purpose to see you; how do you go on with your new cutting and slashing? Very well, good Sir, we learn the use of the axe bravely, we shall make it out; we have a belly full of victuals every day, our cows run about, and come home full of milk, our hogs get fat of themselves in the woods: Oh, this is a good country! God bless the king, and William Penn; we shall do very well by and by, if we keep our healths. Your loghouse looks neat and light, where did you get these shingles? One of our neighbours is a New-England man, and he showed us how to split them out of chestnut-trees. Now for a barn, but all in good time, here are fine trees to build with. Who is to frame it, sure you don't understand that work yet? A countryman of ours who has been in America these ten years, offers to wait for his money until the second crop is lodged in it. What did you give for your land? Thirty-five shillings per acre, payable in seven years. How many acres have you got? An hundred and fifty. That is enough to begin with; is not your land pretty hard to clear? Yes, Sir, hard enough, but it would be harder still if it were ready cleared, for then we should have no timber, and I love the woods much; the land is nothing without them. Have not you found out any bees yet? No, Sir; and if we had we should not know what to do with them. I will tell you by and by. You are very kind. Farewell, honest man, God prosper you; whenever you travel toward——, inquire for J.S. He will entertain you kindly, provided you bring him good tidings from your family and farm. In this manner I often visit them, and carefully examine their houses, their modes of ingenuity, their different ways; and make them all relate all they know, and describe all they feel. These are scenes which I believe you would willingly share with me. I well remember your philanthropic turn of mind. Is it not better to contemplate under these humble roofs, the rudiments of future wealth and population, than to behold the accumulated bundles of litigious papers in the office of a lawyer? To examine how the world is gradually settled, how the howling swamp is converted into a pleasing meadow, the rough ridge into a fine field; and to hear the cheerful whistling, the rural song, where there was no sound heard before, save the yell of the savage, the screech of the owl or the hissing of the snake? Here an European, fatigued with luxury, riches, and pleasures, may find a sweet relaxation in a series of interesting scenes, as affecting as they are new. England, which now contains so many domes, so many castles, was once like this; a place woody and marshy; its inhabitants, now the favourite nation for arts and commerce, were once painted like our neighbours. The country will nourish in its turn, and the same observations will be made which I have just delineated. Posterity will look back with avidity and pleasure, to trace, if possible, the era of this or that particular settlement.

Pray, what is the reason that the Scots are in general more religious, more faithful, more honest, and industrious than the Irish? I do not mean to insinuate national reflections, God forbid! It ill becomes any man, and much less an American; but as I know men are nothing of themselves, and that they owe all their different modifications either to government or other local circumstances, there must be some powerful causes which constitute this great national difference.

Agreeable to the account which several Scotchmen have given me of the north of Britain, of the Orkneys, and the Hebride Islands, they seem, on many accounts, to be unfit for the habitation of men; they appear to be calculated only for great sheep pastures. Who then can blame the inhabitants of these countries for transporting themselves hither? This great continent must in time absorb the poorest part of Europe; and this will happen in proportion as it becomes better known; and as war, taxation, oppression, and misery increase there. The Hebrides appear to be fit only for the residence of malefactors, and it would be much better to send felons there than either to Virginia or Maryland. What a strange compliment has our mother country paid to two of the finest provinces in America! England has entertained in that respect very mistaken ideas; what was intended as a punishment, is become the good fortune of several; many of those who have been transported as felons, are now rich, and strangers to the stings of those wants that urged them to violations of the law: they are become industrious, exemplary, and useful citizens. The English government should purchase the most northern and barren of those islands; it should send over to us the honest, primitive Hebrideans, settle them here on good lands, as a reward for their virtue and ancient poverty; and replace them with a colony of her wicked sons. The severity of the climate, the inclemency of the seasons, the sterility of the soil, the tempestuousness of the sea, would afflict and punish enough. Could there be found a spot better adapted to retaliate the injury it had received by their crimes? Some of those islands might be considered as the hell of Great Britain, where all evil spirits should be sent. Two essential ends would be answered by this simple operation. The good people, by emigration, would be rendered happier; the bad ones would be placed where they ought to be. In a few years the dread of being sent to that wintry region would have a much stronger effect than that of transportation.—This is no place of punishment; were I a poor hopeless, breadless Englishman, and not restrained by the power of shame, I should be very thankful for the passage. It is of very little importance how, and in what manner an indigent man arrives; for if he is but sober, honest, and industrious, he has nothing more to ask of heaven. Let him go to work, he will have opportunities enough to earn a comfortable support, and even the means of procuring some land; which ought to be the utmost wish of every person who has health and hands to work. I knew a man who came to this country, in the literal sense of the expression, stark naked; I think he was a Frenchman, and a sailor on board an English man-of-war. Being discontented, he had stripped himself and swam ashore; where, finding clothes and friends, he settled afterwards at Maraneck, in the county of Chester, in the province of New York: he married and left a good farm to each of his sons. I knew another person who was but twelve years old when he was taken on the frontiers of Canada, by the Indians; at his arrival at Albany he was purchased by a gentleman, who generously bound him apprentice to a tailor. He lived to the age of ninety, and left behind him a fine estate and a numerous family, all well settled; many of them I am acquainted with.—Where is then the industrious European who ought to despair?

After a foreigner from any part of Europe is arrived, and become a citizen; let him devoutly listen to the voice of our great parent, which says to him, "Welcome to my shores, distressed European; bless the hour in which thou didst see my verdant fields, my fair navigable rivers, and my green mountains!—If thou wilt work, I have bread for thee; if thou wilt be honest, sober, and industrious, I have greater rewards to confer on thee—ease and independence. I will give thee fields to feed and clothe thee; a comfortable fireside to sit by, and tell thy children by what means thou hast prospered; and a decent bed to repose on. I shall endow thee beside with the immunities of a freeman. If thou wilt carefully educate thy children, teach them gratitude to God, and reverence to that government, that philanthropic government, which has collected here so many men and made them happy. I will also provide for thy progeny; and to every good man this ought to be the most holy, the most powerful, the most earnest wish he can possibly form, as well as the most consolatory prospect when he dies. Go thou and work and till; thou shalt prosper, provided thou be just, grateful, and industrious."

HISTORY OF ANDREW, THE HEBRIDEAN

Let historians give the detail of our charters, the succession of our several governors, and of their administrations; of our political struggles, and of the foundation of our towns: let annalists amuse themselves with collecting anecdotes of the establishment of our modern provinces: eagles soar high—I, a feebler bird, cheerfully content myself with skipping from bush to bush, and living on insignificant insects. I am so habituated to draw all my food and pleasure from the surface of the earth which I till, that I cannot, nor indeed am I able to quit it—I therefore present you with the short history of a simple Scotchman; though it contain not a single remarkable event to amaze the reader; no tragical scene to convulse the heart, or pathetic narrative to draw tears from sympathetic eyes. All I wish to delineate is, the progressive steps of a poor man, advancing from indigence to ease; from oppression to freedom; from obscurity and contumely to some degree of consequence—not by virtue of any freaks of fortune, but by the gradual operation of sobriety, honesty, and emigration. These are the limited fields, through which I love to wander; sure to find in some parts, the smile of new-born happiness, the glad heart, inspiring the cheerful song, the glow of manly pride excited by vivid hopes and rising independence. I always return from my neighbourly excursions extremely happy, because there I see good living almost under every roof, and prosperous endeavours almost in every field. But you may say, why don't you describe some of the more ancient, opulent settlements of our country, where even the eye of an European has something to admire? It is true, our American fields are in general pleasing to behold, adorned and intermixed as they are with so many substantial houses, flourishing orchards, and copses of woodlands; the pride of our farms, the source of every good we possess. But what I might observe there is but natural and common; for to draw comfortable subsistence from well fenced cultivated fields, is easy to conceive. A father dies and leaves a decent house and rich farm to his son; the son modernises the one, and carefully tills the other; marries the daughter of a friend and neighbour: this is the common prospect; but though it is rich and pleasant, yet it is far from being so entertaining and instructive as the one now in my view.

I had rather attend on the shore to welcome the poor European when he arrives, I observe him in his first moments of embarrassment, trace him throughout his primary difficulties, follow him step by step, until he pitches his tent on some piece of land, and realises that energetic wish which has made him quit his native land, his kindred, and induced him to traverse a boisterous ocean. It is there I want to observe his first thoughts and feelings, the first essays of an industry, which hitherto has been suppressed. I wish to see men cut down the first trees, erect their new buildings, till their first fields, reap their first crops, and say for the first time in their lives, "This is our own grain, raised from American soil—on it we shall feed and grow fat, and convert the rest into gold and silver." I want to see how the happy effects of their sobriety, honesty, and industry are first displayed: and who would not take a pleasure in seeing these strangers settling as new countrymen, struggling with arduous difficulties, overcoming them, and becoming happy.

Landing on this great continent is like going to sea, they must have a compass, some friendly directing needle; or else they will uselessly err and wander for a long time, even with a fair wind: yet these are the struggles through which our forefathers have waded; and they have left us no other records of them, but the possession of our farms. The reflections I make on these new settlers recall to my mind what my grandfather did in his days; they fill me with gratitude to his memory as well as to that government, which invited him to come, and helped him when he arrived, as well as many others. Can I pass over these reflections without remembering thy name, O Penn! thou best of legislators; who by the wisdom of thy laws hast endowed human nature, within the bounds of thy province, with every dignity it can possibly enjoy in a civilised state; and showed by thy singular establishment, what all men might be if they would follow thy example!

In the year 1770, I purchased some lands in the county of——, which I intended for one of my sons; and was obliged to go there in order to see them properly surveyed and marked out: the soil is good, but the country has a very wild aspect. However I observed with pleasure, that land sells very fast; and I am in hopes when the lad gets a wife, it will be a well-settled decent country. Agreeable to our customs, which indeed are those of nature, it is our duty to provide for our eldest children while we live, in order that our homesteads may be left to the youngest, who are the most helpless. Some people are apt to regard the portions given to daughters as so much lost to the family; but this is selfish, and is not agreeable to my way of thinking; they cannot work as men do; they marry young: I have given an honest European a farm to till for himself, rent free, provided he clears an acre of swamp every year, and that he quits it whenever my daughter shall marry. It will procure her a substantial husband, a good farmer—and that is all my ambition.

Whilst I was in the woods I met with a party of Indians; I shook hands with them, and I perceived they had killed a cub; I had a little Peach brandy, they perceived it also, we therefore joined company, kindled a large fire, and ate an hearty supper. I made their hearts glad, and we all reposed on good beds of leaves. Soon after dark, I was surprised to hear a prodigious hooting through the woods; the Indians laughed heartily. One of them, more skilful than the rest, mimicked the owls so exactly, that a very large one perched on a high tree over our fire. We soon brought him down; he measured five feet seven inches from one extremity of the wings to the other. By Captain——I have sent you the talons, on which I have had the heads of small candlesticks fixed. Pray keep them on the table of your study for my sake.

Contrary to my expectation, I found myself under the necessity of going to Philadelphia, in order to pay the purchase money, and to have the deeds properly recorded. I thought little of the journey, though it was above two hundred miles, because I was well acquainted with many friends, at whose houses I intended to stop. The third night after I left the woods, I put up at Mr.——'s, the most worthy citizen I know; he happened to lodge at my house when you was there.—He kindly inquired after your welfare, and desired I would make a friendly mention of him to you. The neatness of these good people is no phenomenon, yet I think this excellent family surpasses everything I know. No sooner did I lie down to rest than I thought myself in a most odoriferous arbour, so sweet and fragrant were the sheets. Next morning I found my host in the orchard destroying caterpillars. I think, friend B., said I, that thee art greatly departed from the good rules of the society; thee seemeth to have quitted that happy simplicity for which it hath hitherto been so remarkable. Thy rebuke, friend James, is a pretty heavy one; what motive canst thee have for thus accusing us? Thy kind wife made a mistake last evening, I said; she put me on a bed of roses, instead of a common one; I am not used to such delicacies. And is that all, friend James, that thee hast to reproach us with?—Thee wilt not call it luxury I hope? thee canst but know that it is the produce of our garden; and friend Pope sayeth, that "to enjoy is to obey." This is a most learned excuse indeed, friend B., and must be valued because it is founded upon truth. James, my wife hath done nothing more to thy bed than what is done all the year round to all the beds in the family; she sprinkles her linen with rose-water before she puts it under the press; it is her fancy, and I have nought to say. But thee shalt not escape so, verily I will send for her; thee and she must settle the matter, whilst I proceed on my work, before the sun gets too high.—Tom, go thou and call thy mistress Philadelphia. What. said I, is thy wife called by that name? I did not know that before. I'll tell thee, James, how it came to pass: her grandmother was the first female child born after William Penn landed with the rest of our brethren; and in compliment to the city he intended to build, she was called after the name he intended to give it; and so there is always one of the daughters of her family known by the name of Philadelphia. She soon came, and after a most friendly altercation, I gave up the point; breakfasted, departed, and in four days reached the city.

A week after news came that a vessel was arrived with Scotch emigrants. Mr. C. and I went to the dock to see them disembark. It was a scene which inspired me with a variety of thoughts; here are, said I to my friend, a number of people, driven by poverty, and other adverse causes, to a foreign land, in which they know nobody. The name of a stranger, instead of implying relief, assistance, and kindness, on the contrary, conveys very different ideas. They are now distressed; their minds are racked by a variety of apprehensions, fears, and hopes. It was this last powerful sentiment which has brought them here. If they are good people, I pray that heaven may realise them. Whoever were to see them thus gathered again in five or six years, would behold a more pleasing sight, to which this would serve as a very powerful contrast. By their honesty, the vigour of their arms, and the benignity of government, their condition will be greatly improved; they will be well clad, fat, possessed of that manly confidence which property confers; they will become useful citizens. Some of the posterity may act conspicuous parts in our future American transactions. Most of them appeared pale and emaciated, from the length of the passage, and the indifferent provision on which they had lived. The number of children seemed as great as that of the people; they had all paid for being conveyed here. The captain told us they were a quiet, peaceable, and harmless people, who had never dwelt in cities. This was a valuable cargo; they seemed, a few excepted, to be in the full vigour of their lives. Several citizens, impelled either by spontaneous attachments, or motives of humanity, took many of them to their houses; the city, agreeable to its usual wisdom and humanity, ordered them all to be lodged in the barracks, and plenty of provisions to be given them. My friend pitched upon one also and led him to his house, with his wife, and a son about fourteen years of age. The majority of them had contracted for land the year before, by means of an agent; the rest depended entirely upon chance; and the one who followed us was of this last class. Poor man, he smiled on receiving the invitation, and gladly accepted it, bidding his wife and son do the same, in a language which I did not understand. He gazed with uninterrupted attention on everything he saw; the houses, the inhabitants, the negroes, and carriages: everything appeared equally new to him; and we went slow, in order to give him time to feed on this pleasing variety. Good God! said he, is this Philadelphia, that blessed city of bread and provisions, of which we have heard so much? I am told it was founded the same year in which my father was born; why, it is finer than Greenock and Glasgow, which are ten times as old. It is so, said my friend to him, and when thee hast been here a month, thee will soon see that it is the capital of a fine province, of which thee art going to be a citizen: Greenock enjoys neither such a climate nor such a soil. Thus we slowly proceeded along, when we met several large Lancaster six-horse waggons, just arrived from the country. At this stupendous sight he stopped short, and with great diffidence asked us what was the use of these great moving houses, and where those big horses came from? Have you none such at home, I asked him? Oh, no; these huge animals would eat all the grass of our island! We at last reached my friend's house, who in the glow of well-meant hospitality, made them all three sit down to a good dinner, and gave them as much cider as they could drink. God bless this country, and the good people it contains, said he; this is the best meal's victuals I have made a long time.—I thank you kindly.

What part of Scotland dost thee come from, friend Andrew, said Mr. C.? Some of us come from the main, some from the island of Barra, he answered—I myself am a Barra man. I looked on the map, and by its latitude, easily guessed that it must be an inhospitable climate. What sort of land have you got there, I asked him? Bad enough, said he; we have no such trees as I see here, no wheat, no kine, no apples. Then, I observed, that it must be hard for the poor to live. We have no poor, he answered, we are all alike, except our laird; but he cannot help everybody. Pray what is the name of your laird? Mr. Neiel, said Andrew; the like of him is not to be found in any of the isles; his forefathers have lived there thirty generations ago, as we are told. Now, gentlemen, you may judge what an ancient family estate it must be. But it is cold, the land is thin, and there were too many of us, which are the reasons that some are come to seek their fortunes here. Well, Andrew, what step do you intend to take in order to become rich? I do not know, Sir; I am but an ignorant man, a stranger besides—I must rely on the advice of good Christians, they would not deceive me, I am sure. I have brought with me a character from our Barra minister, can it do me any good here? Oh, yes; but your future success will depend entirely on your own conduct; if you are a sober man, as the certificate says, laborious, and honest, there is no fear but that you will do well. Have you brought any money with you, Andrew? Yes, Sir, eleven guineas and an half. Upon my word it is a considerable sum for a Barra man; how came you by so much money? Why seven years ago I received a legacy of thirty-seven pounds from an uncle, who loved me much; my wife brought me two guineas, when the laird gave her to me for a wife, which I have saved ever since. I have sold all I had; I worked in Glasgow for some time. I am glad to hear you are so saving and prudent; be so still; you must go and hire yourself with some good people; what can you do? I can thresh a little, and handle the spade. Can you plough? Yes, Sir, with the little breast plough I have brought with me. These won't do here, Andrew; you are an able man; if you are willing you will soon learn. I'll tell you what I intend to do; I'll send you to my house, where you shall stay two or three weeks, there you must exercise yourself with the axe, that is the principal tool the Americans want, and particularly the back- settlers. Can your wife spin? Yes, she can. Well then as soon as you are able to handle the axe, you shall go and live with Mr. P. R., a particular friend of mine, who will give you four dollars per month, for the first six, and the usual price of five as long as you remain with him. I shall place your wife in another house, where she shall receive half a dollar a week for spinning; and your son a dollar a month to drive the team. You shall have besides good victuals to eat, and good beds to lie on; will all this satisfy you, Andrew? He hardly understood what I said; the honest tears of gratitude fell from his eyes as he looked at me, and its expressions seemed to quiver on his lips.—Though silent, this was saying a great deal; there was besides something extremely moving to see a man six feet high thus shed tears; and they did not lessen the good opinion I had entertained of him. At last he told me, that my offers were more than he deserved, and that he would first begin to work for his victuals. No, no, said I, if you are careful and sober, and do what you can, you shall receive what I told you, after you have served a short apprenticeship at my house. May God repay you for all your kindnesses, said Andrew; as long as I live I shall thank you, and do what I can for you. A few days after I sent them all three to——, by the return of some waggons, that he might have an opportunity of viewing, and convincing himself of the utility of those machines which he had at first so much admired.

The further descriptions he gave us of the Hebrides in general, and of his native island in particular; of the customs and modes of living of the inhabitants; greatly entertained me. Pray is the sterility of the soil the cause that there are no trees, or is it because there are none planted? What are the modern families of all the kings of the earth, compared to the date of that of Mr. Neiel? Admitting that each generation should last but forty years, this makes a period of 1200; an extraordinary duration for the uninterrupted descent of any family! Agreeably to the description he gave us of those countries, they seem to live according to the rules of nature, which gives them but bare subsistence; their constitutions are uncontaminated by any excess or effeminacy, which their soil refuses. If their allowance of food is not too scanty, they must all be healthy by perpetual temperance and exercise; if so, they are amply rewarded for their poverty. Could they have obtained but necessary food, they would not have left it; for it was not in consequence of oppression, either from their patriarch or the government, that they had emigrated. I wish we had a colony of these honest people settled in some parts of this province; their morals, their religion, seem to be as simple as their manners. This society would present an interesting spectacle could they be transported on a richer soil. But perhaps that soil would soon alter everything; for our opinions, vices, and virtues, are altogether local: we are machines fashioned by every circumstance around us.

Andrew arrived at my house a week before I did, and I found my wife, agreeable to my instructions, had placed the axe in his hands, as his first task. For some time he was very awkward, but he was so docile, so willing, and grateful, as well as his wife, that I foresaw he would succeed. Agreeably to my promise, I put them all with different families, where they were well liked, and all parties were pleased. Andrew worked hard, lived well, grew fat, and every Sunday came to pay me a visit on a good horse, which Mr. P. R. lent him. Poor man, it took him a long time ere he could sit on the saddle and hold the bridle properly. I believe he had never before mounted such a beast, though I did not choose to ask him that question, for fear it might suggest some mortifying ideas. After having been twelve months at Mr. P. R.'s, and having received his own and his family's wages, which amounted to eighty-four dollars; he came to see me on a week-day, and told me, that he was a man of middle age, and would willingly have land of his own, in order to procure him a home, as a shelter against old age: that whenever this period should come, his son, to whom he would give his land, would then maintain him, and thus live altogether; he therefore required my advice and assistance. I thought his desire very natural and praiseworthy, and told him that I should think of it, but that he must remain one month longer with Mr. P. R., who had 3000 rails to split. He immediately consented. The spring was not far advanced enough yet for Andrew to begin clearing any land even supposing that he had made a purchase; as it is always necessary that the leaves should be out, in order that this additional combustible may serve to burn the heaps of brush more readily.

A few days after, it happened that the whole family of Mr. P. R. went to meeting, and left Andrew to take care of the house. While he was at the door, attentively reading the Bible, nine Indians just come from the mountains, suddenly made their appearance, and unloaded their packs of furs on the floor of the piazza. Conceive, if you can, what was Andrew's consternation at this extraordinary sight! From the singular appearance of these people, the honest Hebridean took them for a lawless band come to rob his master's house. He therefore, like a faithful guardian, precipitately withdrew and shut the doors, but as most of our houses are without locks, he was reduced to the necessity of fixing his knife over the latch, and then flew upstairs in quest of a broadsword he had brought from Scotland. The Indians, who were Mr. P. R.'s particular friends, guessed at his suspicions and fears; they forcibly lifted the door, and suddenly took possession of the house, got all the bread and meat they wanted, and sat themselves down by the fire. At this instant Andrew, with his broadsword in his hand, entered the room; the Indians earnestly looking at him, and attentively watching his motions. After a very few reflections, Andrew found that his weapon was useless, when opposed to nine tomahawks; but this did not diminish his anger, on the contrary; it grew greater on observing the calm impudence with which they were devouring the family provisions. Unable to resist, he called them names in broad Scotch, and ordered them to desist and be gone; to which the Indians (as they told me afterwards) replied in their equally broad idiom. It must have been a most unintelligible altercation between this honest Barra man, and nine Indians who did not much care for anything he could say. At last he ventured to lay his hands on one of them, in order to turn him out of the house. Here Andrew's fidelity got the better of his prudence; for the Indian, by his motions, threatened to scalp him, while the rest gave the war hoop. This horrid noise so effectually frightened poor Andrew, that, unmindful of his courage, of his broadsword, and his intentions, he rushed out, left them masters of the house, and disappeared. I have heard one of the Indians say since, that he never laughed so heartily in his life. Andrew at a distance, soon recovered from the fears which had been inspired by this infernal yell, and thought of no other remedy than to go to the meeting-house, which was about two miles distant. In the eagerness of his honest intentions, with looks of affright still marked on his countenance, he called Mr. P. R. out, and told him with great vehemence of style, that nine monsters were come to his house—some blue, some red, and some black; that they had little axes in their hands out of which they smoked; and that like highlanders, they had no breeches; that they were devouring all his victuals, and that God only knew what they would do more. Pacify yourself, said Mr. P. R., my house is as safe with these people, as if I was there myself; as for the victuals, they are heartily welcome, honest Andrew; they are not people of much ceremony; they help themselves thus whenever they are among their friends; I do so too in their wigwams, whenever I go to their village: you had better therefore step in and hear the remainder of the sermon, and when the meeting is over we will all go back in the waggon together.

At their return, Mr. P. R., who speaks the Indian language very well, explained the whole matter; the Indians renewed their laugh, and shook hands with honest Andrew, whom they made to smoke out of their pipes; and thus peace was made, and ratified according to the Indian custom, by the calumet.

Soon after this adventure, the time approached when I had promised Andrew my best assistance to settle him; for that purpose I went to Mr. A. V. in the county of——, who, I was informed, had purchased a tract of land, contiguous to—— settlement. I gave him a faithful detail of the progress Andrew had made in the rural arts; of his honesty, sobriety, and gratitude, and pressed him to sell him an hundred acres. This I cannot comply with, said Mr. A. V., but at the same time I will do better; I love to encourage honest Europeans as much as you do, and to see them prosper: you tell me he has but one son; I will lease them an hundred acres for any term of years you please, and make it more valuable to your Scotchman than if he was possessed of the fee simple. By that means he may, with what little money he has, buy a plough, a team, and some stock; he will not be incumbered with debts and mortgages; what he raises will be his own; had he two or three sons as able as himself, then I should think it more eligible for him to purchase the fee simple. I join with you in opinion, and will bring Andrew along with me in a few days.

Well, honest Andrew, said Mr. A. V., in consideration of your good name, I will let you have an hundred acres of good arable land, that shall be laid out along a new road; there is a bridge already erected on the creek that passes through the land, and a fine swamp of about twenty acres. These are my terms, I cannot sell, but I will lease you the quantity that Mr. James, your friend, has asked; the first seven years you shall pay no rent, whatever you sow and reap, and plant and gather, shall be entirely your own; neither the king, government, nor church, will have any claim on your future property: the remaining part of the time you must give me twelve dollars and an half a year; and that is all you will have to pay me. Within the three first years you must plant fifty apple trees, and clear seven acres of swamp within the first part of the lease; it will be your own advantage: whatever you do more within that time, I will pay you for it, at the common rate of the country. The term of the lease shall be thirty years; how do you like it, Andrew? Oh, Sir, it is very good, but I am afraid, that the king or his ministers, or the governor, or some of our great men, will come and take the land from me; your son may say to me, by and by, this is my father's land, Andrew, you must quit it. No, no, said Mr. A. V., there is no such danger; the king and his ministers are too just to take the labour of a poor settler; here we have no great men, but what are subordinate to our laws; but to calm all your fears, I will give you a lease, so that none can make you afraid. If ever you are dissatisfied with the land, a jury of your own neighbourhood shall value all your improvements, and you shall be paid agreeably to their verdict. You may sell the lease, or if you die, you may previously dispose of it, as if the land was your own. Expressive, yet inarticulate joy, was mixed in his countenance, which seemed impressed with astonishment and confusion. Do you understand me well, said Mr. A. V.? No, Sir, replied Andrew, I know nothing of what you mean about lease, improvement, will, jury, etc. That is honest, we will explain these things to you by and by. It must be confessed that those were hard words, which he had never heard in his life; for by his own account, the ideas they convey would be totally useless in the island of Barra. No wonder, therefore, that he was embarrassed; for how could the man who had hardly a will of his own since he was born, imagine he could have one after his death? How could the person who never possessed anything, conceive that he could extend his new dominion over this land, even after he should be laid in his grave? For my part, I think Andrew's amazement did not imply any extraordinary degree of ignorance; he was an actor introduced upon a new scene, it required some time ere he could reconcile himself to the part he was to perform. However he was soon enlightened, and introduced into those mysteries with which we native Americans are but too well acquainted.

Here then is honest Andrew, invested with every municipal advantage they confer; become a freeholder, possessed of a vote, of a place of residence, a citizen of the province of Pennsylvania. Andrew's original hopes and the distant prospects he had formed in the island of Barra, were at the eve of being realised; we therefore can easily forgive him a few spontaneous ejaculations, which would be useless to repeat. This short tale is easily told; few words are sufficient to describe this sudden change of situation; but in his mind it was gradual, and took him above a week before he could be sure, that without disturbing any money he could possess lands. Soon after he prepared himself; I lent him a barrel of pork, and 200 lb. weight of meal, and made him purchase what was necessary besides.

He set out, and hired a room in the house of a settler who lived the most contiguous to his own land. His first work was to clear some acres of swamp, that he might have a supply of hay the following year for his two horses and cows. From the first day he began to work, he was indefatigable; his honesty procured him friends, and his industry the esteem of his new neighbours. One of them offered him two acres of cleared land, whereon he might plant corn, pumpkins, squashes, and a few potatoes, that very season. It is astonishing how quick men will learn when they work for themselves. I saw with pleasure two months after, Andrew holding a two-horse plough and tracing his furrows quite straight; thus the spade man of the island of Barra was become the tiller of American soil. Well done, said I, Andrew, well done; I see that God speeds and directs your works; I see prosperity delineated in all your furrows and head lands. Raise this crop of corn with attention and care, and then you will be master of the art.

As he had neither mowing nor reaping to do that year, I told him that the time was come to build his house; and that for the purpose I would myself invite the neighbourhood to a frolic; that thus he would have a large dwelling erected, and some upland cleared in one day. Mr. P. R., his old friend, came at the time appointed, with all his hands, and brought victuals in plenty: I did the same. About forty people repaired to the spot; the songs, and merry stories, went round the woods from cluster to cluster, as the people had gathered to their different works; trees fell on all sides, bushes were cut up and heaped; and while many were thus employed, others with their teams hauled the big logs to the spot which Andrew had pitched upon for the erection of his new dwelling. We all dined in the woods; in the afternoon the logs were placed with skids, and the usual contrivances: thus the rude house was raised, and above two acres of land cut up, cleared, and heaped.

Whilst all these different operations were performing, Andrew was absolutely incapable of working; it was to him the most solemn holiday he had ever seen; it would have been sacrilegious in him to have denied it with menial labour. Poor man, he sanctified it with joy and thanksgiving, and honest libations—he went from one to the other with the bottle in his hand, pressing everybody to drink, and drinking himself to show the example. He spent the whole day in smiling, laughing, and uttering monosyllables: his wife and son were there also, but as they could not understand the language, their pleasure must have been altogether that of the imagination. The powerful lord, the wealthy merchant, on seeing the superb mansion finished, never can feel half the joy and real happiness which was felt and enjoyed on that day by this honest Hebridean: though this new dwelling, erected in the midst of the woods, was nothing more than a square inclosure, composed of twenty-four large clumsy logs, let in at the ends. When the work was finished, the company made the woods resound with the noise of their three cheers, and the honest wishes they formed for Andrew's prosperity. He could say nothing, but with thankful tears he shook hands with them all. Thus from the first day he had landed, Andrew marched towards this important event: this memorable day made the sun shine on that land on which he was to sow wheat and other grain. What swamp he had cleared lay before his door; the essence of future bread, milk, and meat, were scattered all round him. Soon after he hired a carpenter, who put on a roof and laid the floors; in a week more the house was properly plastered, and the chimney finished. He moved into it, and purchased two cows, which found plenty of food in the woods—his hogs had the same advantage. That very year, he and his son sowed three bushels of wheat, from which he reaped ninety-one and a half; for I had ordered him to keep an exact account of all he should raise. His first crop of other corn would have been as good, had it not been for the squirrels, which were enemies not to be dispersed by the broadsword. The fourth year I took an inventory of the wheat this man possessed, which I send you. Soon after, further settlements were made on that road, and Andrew, instead of being the last man towards the wilderness, found himself in a few years in the middle of a numerous society. He helped others as generously as others had helped him; and I have dined many times at his table with several of his neighbours. The second year he was made overseer of the road, and served on two petty juries, performing as a citizen all the duties required of him. The historiographer of some great prince or general, does not bring his hero victorious to the end of a successful campaign, with one half of the heart-felt pleasure with which I have conducted Andrew to the situation he now enjoys: he is independent and easy. Triumph and military honours do not always imply those two blessings. He is unencumbered with debts, services, rents, or any other dues; the successes of a campaign, the laurels of war, must be purchased at the dearest rate, which makes every cool reflecting citizen to tremble and shudder. By the literal account hereunto annexed, you will easily be made acquainted with the happy effects which constantly flow, in this country, from sobriety and industry, when united with good land and freedom.

The account of the property he acquired with his own hands and those of his son, in four years, is under:

Dollars	
The value of his improvements and lease	225
Six cows, at 13 dollars	78
Two breeding mares	50
The rest of the stock	100
Seventy-three bushels of wheat	66
Money due to him on notes	43
Pork and beef in his cellar	28
Wool and flax	19
Ploughs and other utensils of husbandry	31
240 pounds Pennsylvania currency—dollars	640

Letter IX

DESCRIPTION OF CHARLES-TOWN; THOUGHTS ON SLAVERY; ON PHYSICAL EVIL; A MELANCHOLY SCENE

Charles-town is, in the north, what Lima is in the south; both are Capitals of the richest provinces of their respective hemispheres: you may therefore conjecture, that both cities must exhibit the appearances necessarily resulting from riches. Peru abounding in gold, Lima is filled with inhabitants who enjoy all those gradations of pleasure, refinement, and luxury, which proceed from wealth. Carolina produces commodities, more valuable perhaps than gold, because they are gained by greater industry; it exhibits also on our northern stage, a display of riches and luxury, inferior indeed to the former, but far superior to what are to be seen in our northern towns. Its situation is admirable, being built at the confluence of two large rivers, which receive in their course a great number of inferior streams; all navigable in the spring, for flat boats. Here the produce of this extensive territory concentres; here therefore is the seat of the most valuable exportation; their wharfs, their docks, their magazines, are extremely convenient to facilitate this great commercial business. The inhabitants are the gayest in America; it is called the centre of our beau monde, and is always filled with the richest planters of the province, who resort hither in quest of health and pleasure. Here are always to be seen a great number of valetudinarians from the West Indies, seeking for the renovation of health, exhausted by the debilitating nature of their sun, air, and modes of living. Many of these West Indians have I seen, at thirty, loaded with the infirmities of old age; for nothing is more common in those countries of wealth, than for persons to lose the abilities of enjoying the comforts of life, at a time when we northern men just begin to taste the fruits of our labour and prudence. The round of pleasure, and the expenses of those citizens' tables, are much superior to what you would imagine: indeed the growth of this town and province has been astonishingly rapid. It is pity that the narrowness of the neck on which it stands prevents it from increasing; and which is the reason why houses are so dear. The heat of the climate, which is sometimes very great in the interior parts of the country, is always temperate in Charles-Town; though sometimes when they have no sea breezes the sun is too powerful. The climate renders excesses of all kinds very dangerous, particularly those of the table; and yet, insensible or fearless of danger, they live on, and enjoy a short and a merry life: the rays of their sun seem to urge them irresistibly to dissipation and pleasure: on the contrary, the women, from being abstemious, reach to a longer period of life, and seldom die without having had several husbands. An European at his first arrival must be greatly surprised when he sees the elegance of their houses, their sumptuous furniture, as well as the magnificence of their tables. Can he imagine himself in a country, the establishment of which is so recent?

The three principal classes of inhabitants are, lawyers, planters, and merchants; this is the province which has afforded to the first the richest spoils, for nothing can exceed their wealth, their power, and their influence. They have reached the ne plus ultra of worldly felicity; no plantation is secured, no title is good, no will is valid, but what they dictate, regulate, and approve. The whole mass of provincial property is become tributary to this society; which, far above priests and bishops, disdain to be satisfied with the poor Mosaical portion of the tenth. I appeal to the many inhabitants, who, while contending perhaps for their right to a few hundred acres, have lost by the mazes of the law their whole patrimony. These men are more properly law givers than interpreters of the law; and have united here, as well as in most other provinces, the skill and dexterity of the scribe with the power and ambition of the prince: who can tell where this may lead in a future day? The nature of our laws, and the spirit of freedom, which often tends to make us litigious, must necessarily throw the greatest part of the property of the colonies into the hands of these gentlemen. In another century, the law will possess in the north, what now the church possesses in Peru and Mexico.

While all is joy, festivity, and happiness in Charles-Town, would you imagine that scenes of misery overspread in the country? Their ears by habit are become deaf, their hearts are hardened; they neither see, hear, nor feel for the woes of their poor slaves, from whose painful labours all their wealth proceeds. Here the horrors of slavery, the hardship of incessant toils, are unseen; and no one thinks with compassion of those showers of sweat and of tears which from the bodies of Africans, daily drop, and moisten the ground they till. The cracks of the whip urging these miserable beings to excessive labour, are far too distant from the gay Capital to be heard. The chosen race eat, drink, and live happy, while the unfortunate one grubs up the ground, raises indigo, or husks the rice; exposed to a sun full as scorching as their native one; without the support of good food, without the cordials of any cheering liquor. This great contrast has often afforded me subjects of the most conflicting meditation. On the one side, behold a people enjoying all that life affords most bewitching and pleasurable, without labour, without fatigue, hardly subjected to the trouble of wishing. With gold, dug from Peruvian mountains, they order vessels to the coasts of Guinea; by virtue of that gold, wars, murders, and devastations are committed in some harmless, peaceable African neighbourhood, where dwelt innocent people, who even knew not but that all men were black. The daughter torn from her weeping mother, the child from the wretched parents, the wife from the loving husband; whole families swept away and brought through storms and tempests to this rich metropolis! There, arranged like horses at a fair, they are branded like cattle, and then driven to toil, to starve, and to languish for a few years on the different plantations of these citizens. And for whom must they work? For persons they know not, and who have no other power over them than that of violence, no other right than what this accursed metal has given them! Strange order of things! Oh, Nature, where art thou?—Are not these blacks thy children as well as we? On the other side, nothing is to be seen but the most diffusive misery and wretchedness, unrelieved even in thought or wish! Day after day they drudge on without any prospect of ever reaping for themselves; they are obliged to devote their lives, their limbs, their will, and every vital exertion to swell the wealth of masters; who look not upon them with half the kindness and affection with which they consider their dogs and horses. Kindness and affection are not the portion of those who till the earth, who carry the burdens, who convert the logs into useful boards. This reward, simple and natural as one would conceive it, would border on humanity; and planters must have none of it!

If negroes are permitted to become fathers, this fatal indulgence only tends to increase their misery: the poor companions of their scanty pleasures are likewise the companions of their labours; and when at some critical seasons they could wish to see them relieved, with tears in their eyes they behold them perhaps doubly oppressed, obliged to bear the burden of nature—a fatal present—as well as that of unabated tasks. How many have I seen cursing the irresistible propensity, and regretting, that by having tasted of those harmless joys, they had become the authors of double misery to their wives. Like their masters, they are not permitted to partake of those ineffable sensations with which nature inspires the hearts of fathers and mothers; they must repel them all, and become callous and passive. This unnatural state often occasions the most acute, the most pungent of their afflictions; they have no time, like us, tenderly to rear their helpless off-spring, to nurse them on their knees, to enjoy the delight of being parents. Their paternal fondness is embittered by considering, that if their children live, they must live to be slaves like themselves; no time is allowed them to exercise their pious office, the mothers must fasten them on their backs, and, with this double load, follow their husbands in the fields, where they too often hear no other sound than that of the voice or whip of the taskmaster, and the cries of their infants, broiling in the sun. These unfortunate creatures cry and weep like their parents, without a possibility of relief; the very instinct of the brute, so laudable, so irresistible, runs counter here to their master's interest; and to that god, all the laws of nature must give way. Thus planters get rich; so raw, so unexperienced am I in this mode of life, that were I to be possessed of a plantation, and my slaves treated as in general they are here, never could I rest in peace; my sleep would be perpetually disturbed by a retrospect of the frauds committed in Africa, in order to entrap them; frauds surpassing in enormity everything which a common mind can possibly conceive. I should be thinking of the barbarous treatment they meet with on ship-board; of their anguish, of the despair necessarily inspired by their situation, when torn from their friends and relations; when delivered into the hands of a people differently coloured, whom they cannot understand; carried in a strange machine over an ever agitated element, which they had never seen before; and finally delivered over to the severities of the whippers, and the excessive labours of the field. Can it be possible that the force of custom should ever make me deaf to all these reflections, and as insensible to the injustice of that trade, and to their miseries, as the rich inhabitants of this town seem to be? What then is man; this being who boasts so much of the excellence and dignity of his nature, among that variety of unscrutable mysteries, of unsolvable problems, with which he is surrounded? The reason why man has been thus created, is not the least astonishing! It is said, I know that they are much happier here than in the West Indies; because land being cheaper upon this continent than in those islands, the fields allowed them to raise their subsistence from, are in general more extensive. The only possible chance of any alleviation depends on the humour of the planters, who, bred in the midst of slaves, learn from the example of their parents to despise them; and seldom conceive either from religion or philosophy, any ideas that tend to make their fate less calamitous; except some strong native tenderness of heart, some rays of philanthropy, overcome the obduracy contracted by habit.

I have not resided here long enough to become insensible of pain for the objects which I every day behold. In the choice of my friends and acquaintance, I always endeavour to find out those whose dispositions are somewhat congenial with my own. We have slaves likewise in our northern provinces; I hope the time draws near when they will be all emancipated: but how different their lot, how different their situation, in every possible respect! They enjoy as much liberty as their masters, they are as well clad, and as well fed; in health and sickness they are tenderly taken care of; they live under the same roof, and are, truly speaking, a part of our families. Many of them are taught to read and write, and are well instructed in the principles of religion; they are the companions of our labours, and treated as such; they enjoy many perquisites, many established holidays, and are not obliged to work more than white people. They marry where inclination leads them; visit their wives every week; are as decently clad as the common people; they are indulged in educating, cherishing, and chastising their children, who are taught subordination to them as to their lawful parents: in short, they participate in many of the benefits of our society, without being obliged to bear any of its burdens. They are fat, healthy, and hearty, and far from repining at their fate; they think themselves happier than many of the lower class whites: they share with their masters the wheat and meat provision they help to raise; many of those whom the good Quakers have emancipated have received that great benefit with tears of regret, and have never quitted, though free, their former masters and benefactors.

But is it really true, as I have heard it asserted here, that those blacks are incapable of feeling the spurs of emulation, and the cheerful sound of encouragement? By no means; there are a thousand proofs existing of their gratitude and fidelity: those hearts in which such noble dispositions can grow, are then like ours, they are susceptible of every generous sentiment, of every useful motive of action; they are capable of receiving lights, of imbibing ideas that would greatly alleviate the weight of their miseries. But what methods have in general been made use of to obtain so desirable an end? None; the day in which they arrive and are sold, is the first of their labours; labours, which from that hour admit of no respite; for though indulged by law with relaxation on Sundays, they are obliged to employ that time which is intended for rest, to till their little plantations. What can be expected from wretches in such circumstances? Forced from their native country, cruelly treated when on board, and not less so on the plantations to which they are driven; is there anything in this treatment but what must kindle all the passions, sow the seeds of inveterate resentment, and nourish a wish of perpetual revenge? They are left to the irresistible effects of those strong and natural propensities; the blows they receive, are they conducive to extinguish them, or to win their affections? They are neither soothed by the hopes that their slavery will ever terminate but with their lives; or yet encouraged by the goodness of their food, or the mildness of their treatment. The very hopes held out to mankind by religion, that consolatory system, so useful to the miserable, are never presented to them; neither moral nor physical means are made use of to soften their chains; they are left in their original and untutored state; that very state wherein the natural propensities of revenge and warm passions are so soon kindled. Cheered by no one single motive that can impel the will, or excite their efforts; nothing but terrors and punishments are presented to them; death is denounced if they run away; horrid delaceration if they speak with their native freedom; perpetually awed by the terrible cracks of whips, or by the fear of capital punishments, while even those punishments often fail of their purpose.

A clergyman settled a few years ago at George-Town, and feeling as I do now, warmly recommended to the planters, from the pulpit, a relaxation of severity; he introduced the benignity of Christianity, and pathetically made use of the admirable precepts of that system to melt the hearts of his congregation into a greater degree of compassion toward their slaves than had been hitherto customary; "Sir," said one of his hearers, "we pay you a genteel salary to read to us the prayers of the liturgy, and to explain to us such parts of the Gospel as the rule of the church directs; but we do not want you to teach us what we are to do with our blacks." The clergyman found it prudent to withhold any farther admonition. Whence this astonishing right, or rather this barbarous custom, for most certainly we have no kind of right beyond that of force? We are told, it is true, that slavery cannot be so repugnant to human nature as we at first imagine, because it has been practised in all ages, and in all nations: the Lacedemonians themselves, those great assertors of liberty, conquered the Helotes with the design of making them their slaves; the Romans, whom we consider as our masters in civil and military policy, lived in the exercise of the most horrid oppression; they conquered to plunder and to enslave. What a hideous aspect the face of the earth must then have exhibited! Provinces, towns, districts, often depopulated! their inhabitants driven to Rome, the greatest market in the world, and there sold by thousands! The Roman dominions were tilled by the hands of unfortunate people, who had once been, like their victors, free, rich, and possessed of every benefit society can confer; until they became subject to the cruel right of war, and to lawless force. Is there then no superintending power who conducts the moral operations of the world, as well as the physical? The same sublime hand which guides the planets round the sun with so much exactness, which preserves the arrangement of the whole with such exalted wisdom and paternal care, and prevents the vast system from falling into confusion; doth it abandon mankind to all the errors, the follies, and the miseries, which their most frantic rage, and their most dangerous vices and passions can produce?

The history of the earth! doth it present anything but crimes of the most heinous nature, committed from one end of the world to the other? We observe avarice, rapine, and murder, equally prevailing in all parts. History perpetually tells us of millions of people abandoned to the caprice of the maddest princes, and of whole nations devoted to the blind fury of tyrants. Countries destroyed; nations alternately buried in ruins by other nations; some parts of the world beautifully cultivated, returned again to the pristine state; the fruits of ages of industry, the toil of thousands in a short time destroyed by a few! If one corner breathes in peace for a few years, it is, in turn subjected, torn, and levelled; one would almost believe the principles of action in man, considered as the first agent of this planet, to be poisoned in their most essential parts. We certainly are not that class of beings which we vainly think ourselves to be; man an animal of prey, seems to have rapine and the love of bloodshed implanted in his heart; nay, to hold it the most honourable occupation in society: we never speak of a hero of mathematics, a hero of knowledge of humanity; no, this illustrious appellation is reserved for the most successful butchers of the world. If Nature has given us a fruitful soil to inhabit, she has refused us such inclinations and propensities as would afford us the full enjoyment of it. Extensive as the surface of this planet is, not one half of it is yet cultivated, not half replenished; she created man, and placed him either in the woods or plains, and provided him with passions which must for ever oppose his happiness; everything is submitted to the power of the strongest; men, like the elements, are always at war; the weakest yield to the most potent; force, subtlety, and malice, always triumph over unguarded honesty and simplicity. Benignity, moderation, and justice, are virtues adapted only to the humble paths of life: we love to talk of virtue and to admire its beauty, while in the shade of solitude and retirement; but when we step forth into active life, if it happen to be in competition with any passion or desire, do we observe it to prevail? Hence so many religious impostors have triumphed over the credulity of mankind, and have rendered their frauds the creeds of succeeding generations, during the course of many ages; until worn away by time, they have been replaced by new ones. Hence the most unjust war, if supported by the greatest force, always succeeds; hence the most just ones, when supported only by their justice, as often fail. Such is the ascendancy of power; the supreme arbiter of all the revolutions which we observe in this planet: so irresistible is power, that it often thwarts the tendency of the most forcible causes, and prevents their subsequent salutary effects, though ordained for the good of man by the Governor of the universe. Such is the perverseness of human nature; who can describe it in all its latitude?

In the moments of our philanthropy we often talk of an indulgent nature, a kind parent, who for the benefit of mankind has taken singular pains to vary the genera of plants, fruits, grain, and the different productions of the earth; and has spread peculiar blessings in each climate. This is undoubtedly an object of contemplation which calls forth our warmest gratitude; for so singularly benevolent have those parental intentions been, that where barrenness of soil or severity of climate prevail, there she has implanted in the heart of man, sentiments which overbalance every misery, and supply the place of every want. She has given to the inhabitants of these regions, an attachment to their savage rocks and wild shores, unknown to those who inhabit the fertile fields of the temperate zone. Yet if we attentively view this globe, will it not appear rather a place of punishment, than of delight? And what misfortune! that those punishments should fall on the innocent, and its few delights be enjoyed by the most unworthy. Famine, diseases, elementary convulsions, human feuds, dissensions, etc., are the produce of every climate; each climate produces besides, vices, and miseries peculiar to its latitude. View the frigid sterility of the north, whose famished inhabitants hardly acquainted with the sun, live and fare worse than the bears they hunt: and to which they are superior only in the faculty of speaking. View the arctic and antarctic regions, those huge voids, where nothing lives; regions of eternal snow: where winter in all his horrors has established his throne, and arrested every creative power of nature. Will you call the miserable stragglers in these countries by the name of men? Now contrast this frigid power of the north and south with that of the sun; examine the parched lands of the torrid zone, replete with sulphureous exhalations; view those countries of Asia subject to pestilential infections which lay nature waste; view this globe often convulsed both from within and without; pouring forth from several mouths, rivers of boiling matter, which are imperceptibly leaving immense subterranean graves, wherein millions will one day perish! Look at the poisonous soil of the equator, at those putrid slimy tracks, teeming with horrid monsters, the enemies of the human race; look next at the sandy continent, scorched perhaps by the fatal approach of some ancient comet, now the abode of desolation. Examine the rains, the convulsive storms of those climates, where masses of sulphur, bitumen, and electrical fire, combining their dreadful powers, are incessantly hovering and bursting over a globe threatened with dissolution. On this little shell, how very few are the spots where man can live and flourish? even under those mild climates which seem to breathe peace and happiness, the poison of slavery, the fury of despotism, and the rage of superstition, are all combined against man! There only the few live and rule, whilst the many starve and utter ineffectual complaints: there, human nature appears more debased, perhaps than in the less favoured climates. The fertile plains of Asia, the rich low lands of Egypt and of Diarbeck, the fruitful fields bordering on the Tigris and the Euphrates, the extensive country of the East Indies in all its separate districts; all these must to the geographical eye, seem as if intended for terrestrial paradises: but though surrounded with the spontaneous riches of nature, though her kindest favours seem to be shed on those beautiful regions with the most profuse hand; yet there in general we find the most wretched people in the world. Almost everywhere, liberty so natural to mankind is refused, or rather enjoyed but by their tyrants;

the word slave, is the appellation of every rank, who adore as a divinity, a being worse than themselves; subject to every caprice, and to every lawless rage which unrestrained power can give. Tears are shed, perpetual groans are heard, where only the accents of peace, alacrity, and gratitude should resound. There the very delirium of tyranny tramples on the best gifts of nature, and sports with the fate, the happiness, the lives of millions: there the extreme fertility of the ground always indicates the extreme misery of the inhabitants!

Everywhere one part of the human species are taught the art of shedding the blood of the other; of setting fire to their dwellings; of levelling the works of their industry: half of the existence of nations regularly employed in destroying other nations.—"What little political felicity is to be met with here and there, has cost oceans of blood to purchase; as if good was never to be the portion of unhappy man. Republics, kingdoms, monarchies, founded either on fraud or successful violence, increase by pursuing the steps of the same policy, until they are destroyed in their turn, either by the influence of their own crimes, or by more successful but equally criminal enemies."

If from this general review of human nature, we descend to the examination of what is called civilised society; there the combination of every natural and artificial want, makes us pay very dear for what little share of political felicity we enjoy. It is a strange heterogeneous assemblage of vices and virtues, and of a variety of other principles, for ever at war, for ever jarring, for ever producing some dangerous, some distressing extreme. Where do you conceive then that nature intended we should be happy? Would you prefer the state of men in the woods, to that of men in a more improved situation? Evil preponderates in both; in the first they often eat each other for want of food, and in the other they often starve each other for want of room. For my part, I think the vices and miseries to be found in the latter, exceed those of the former; in which real evil is more scarce, more supportable, and less enormous. Yet we wish to see the earth peopled; to accomplish the happiness of kingdoms, which is said to consist in numbers. Gracious God! to what end is the introduction of so many beings into a mode of existence in which they must grope amidst as many errors, commit as many crimes, and meet with as many diseases, wants, and sufferings!

The following scene will I hope account for these melancholy reflections, and apologise for the gloomy thoughts with which I have filled this letter: my mind is, and always has been, oppressed since I became a witness to it. I was not long since invited to dine with a planter who lived three miles from——, where he then resided. In order to avoid the heat of the sun, I resolved to go on foot, sheltered in a small path, leading through a pleasant wood. I was leisurely travelling along, attentively examining some peculiar plants which I had collected, when all at once I felt the air strongly agitated, though the day was perfectly calm and sultry. I immediately cast my eyes toward the cleared ground, from which I was but at a small distance, in order to see whether it was not occasioned by a sudden shower; when at that instant a sound resembling a deep rough voice, uttered, as I thought, a few inarticulate monosyllables. Alarmed and surprised, I precipitately looked all round, when I perceived at about six rods distance something resembling a cage, suspended to the limbs of a tree; all the branches of which appeared covered with large birds of prey, fluttering about, and anxiously endeavouring to perch on the cage. Actuated by an involuntary motion of my hands, more than by any design of my mind, I fired at them; they all flew to a short distance, with a most hideous noise: when, horrid to think and painful to repeat, I perceived a negro, suspended in the cage, and left there to expire! I shudder when I recollect that the birds had already picked out his eyes, his cheek bones were bare; his arms had been attacked in several places, and his body seemed covered with a multitude of wounds. From the edges of the hollow sockets and from the lacerations with which he was disfigured, the blood slowly dropped, and tinged the ground beneath. No sooner were the birds flown, than swarms of insects covered the whole body of this unfortunate wretch, eager to feed on his mangled flesh and to drink his blood. I found myself suddenly arrested by the power of affright and terror; my nerves were convoked; I trembled, I stood motionless, involuntarily contemplating the fate of this negro, in all its dismal latitude. The living spectre, though deprived of his eyes, could still distinctly hear, and in his uncouth dialect begged me to give him some water to allay his thirst. Humanity herself would have recoiled back with horror; she would have balanced whether to lessen such reliefless distress, or mercifully with one blow to end this dreadful scene of agonising torture! Had I had a ball in my gun, I certainly should have despatched him; but finding myself unable to perform so kind an office, I sought, though trembling, to relieve him as well as I could. A shell ready fixed to a pole, which had been used by some negroes, presented itself to me; filled it with water, and with trembling hands I guided it to the quivering lips of the wretched sufferer. Urged by the irresistible power of thirst, he endeavoured to meet it, as he instinctively guessed its approach by the noise it made in passing through the bars of the cage. "Tanke, you white man, tanke you, pute some poison and give me." "How long have you been hanging there?" I asked him. "Two days, and me no die; the birds, the birds; aaah me!" Oppressed with the reflections which this shocking spectacle afforded me, I mustered strength enough to walk away, and soon reached the house at which I intended to dine. There I heard that the reason for this slave being thus punished, was on account of his having killed the overseer of the plantation. They told me that the laws of self-preservation rendered such executions necessary; and supported the doctrine of slavery with the arguments generally made use of to justify the practice; with the repetition of which I shall not trouble you at present.—Adieu.

Letter XII

DISTRESSES OF A FRONTIER MAN

I wish for a change of place; the hour is come at last, that I must fly from my house and abandon my farm! But what course shall I steer, inclosed as I am? The climate best adapted to my present situation and humour would be the polar regions, where six months day and six months night divide the dull year: nay, a simple Aurora Borealis would suffice me, and greatly refresh my eyes, fatigued now by so many disagreeable objects. The severity of those climates, that great gloom, where melancholy dwells, would be perfectly analogous to the turn of my mind. Oh, could I remove my plantation to the shores of the Oby, willingly would I dwell in the hut of a Samoyede; with cheerfulness would I go and bury myself in the cavern of a Laplander. Could I but carry my family along with me, I would winter at Pello, or Tobolsky, in order to enjoy the peace and innocence of that country. But let me arrive under the pole, or reach the antipodes, I never can leave behind me the remembrance of the dreadful scenes to which I have been a witness; therefore never can I be happy! Happy, why would I mention that sweet, that enchanting word? Once happiness was our portion; now it is gone from us, and I am afraid not to be enjoyed again by the present generation! Whichever way I look, nothing but the most frightful precipices present themselves to my view, in which hundreds of my friends and acquaintances have already perished: of all animals that live on the surface of this planet, what is man when no longer connected with society; or when he finds himself surrounded by a convulsed and a half dissolved one? He cannot live in solitude, he must belong to some community bound by some ties, however imperfect. Men mutually support and add to the boldness and confidence of each other; the weakness of each is strengthened by the force of the whole. I had never before these calamitous times formed any such ideas; I lived on, laboured and prospered, without having ever studied on what the security of my life and the foundation of my prosperity were established: I perceived them just as they left me. Never was a situation so singularly terrible as mine, in every possible respect, as a member of an extensive society, as a citizen of an inferior division of the same society, as a husband, as a father, as a man who exquisitely feels for the miseries of others as well as for his own! But alas! so much is everything now subverted among us, that the very word misery, with which we were hardly acquainted before, no longer conveys the same ideas; or rather tired with feeling for the miseries of others, every one feels now for himself alone. When I consider myself as connected in all these characters, as bound by so many cords, all uniting in my heart, I am seized with a fever of the mind, I am transported beyond that degree of calmness which is necessary to delineate our thoughts. I feel as if my reason wanted to leave me, as if it would burst its poor weak tenement: again I try to compose myself, I grow cool, and preconceiving the dreadful loss, I endeavour to retain the useful guest.

You know the position of our settlement; I need not therefore describe it. To the west it is inclosed by a chain of mountains, reaching to——; to the east, the country is as yet but thinly inhabited; we are almost insulated, and the houses are at a considerable distance from each other. From the mountains we have but too much reason to expect our dreadful enemy; the wilderness is a harbour where it is impossible to find them. It is a door through which they can enter our country whenever they please; and, as they seem determined to destroy the whole chain of frontiers, our fate cannot be far distant: from Lake Champlain, almost all has been conflagrated one after another. What renders these incursions still more terrible is, that they most commonly take place in the dead of the night; we never go to our fields but we are seized with an involuntary fear, which lessens our strength and weakens our labour. No other subject of conversation intervenes between the different accounts, which spread through the country, of successive acts of devastation; and these told in chimney-corners, swell themselves in our affrighted imaginations into the most terrific ideas! We never sit down either to dinner or supper, but the least noise immediately spreads a general alarm and prevents us from enjoying the comfort of our meals. The very appetite proceeding from labour and peace of mind is gone; we eat just enough to keep us alive: our sleep is disturbed by the most frightful dreams; sometimes I start awake, as if the great hour of danger was come; at other times the howling of our dogs seems to announce the arrival of the enemy: we leap out of bed and run to arms; my poor wife with panting bosom and silent tears, takes leave of me, as if we were to see each other no more; she snatches the youngest children from their beds, who, suddenly awakened, increase by their innocent questions the horror of the dreadful moment. She tries to hide them in the cellar, as if our cellar was inaccessible to the fire. I place all my servants at the windows, and myself at the door, where I am determined to perish. Fear industriously increases every sound; we all listen; each communicates to the other his ideas and conjectures. We remain thus sometimes for whole hours, our hearts and our minds racked by the most anxious suspense: what a dreadful situation, a thousand times worse than that of a soldier engaged in the midst of the most severe conflict! Sometimes feeling the spontaneous courage of a man, I seem to wish for the decisive minute; the next instant a message from my wife, sent by one of the children, puzzling me beside with their little questions, unmans me: away goes my courage, and I descend again into the deepest despondency. At last finding that it was a false alarm, we return once more to our beds; but what good can the kind sleep of nature do to us when interrupted by such scenes! Securely placed as you are, you can have no idea of our agitations, but by hear-say; no relation can be equal to what we suffer and to what we feel. Every morning my youngest children are sure to have frightful dreams to relate: in vain I exert my authority to keep them silent, it is not in my power; and these images of their disturbed imagination, instead of being frivolously looked upon as in the days of our happiness, are on the contrary considered as warnings and sure prognostics of our future fate. I am not a superstitious man, but since our misfortunes, I am grown more timid, and less disposed to treat the doctrine of omens with contempt.

Though these evils have been gradual, yet they do not become habitual like other incidental evils. The nearer I view the end of this catastrophe, the more I shudder. But why should I trouble you with such unconnected accounts; men secure and out of danger are soon fatigued with mournful details: can you enter with me into fellowship with all these afflictive sensations; have you a tear ready to shed over the approaching ruin of a once opulent and substantial family? Read this I pray with the eyes of sympathy; with a tender sorrow, pity the lot of those whom you once called your friends; who were once surrounded with plenty, ease, and perfect security; but who now expect every night to be their last, and who are as wretched as criminals under an impending sentence of the law.

As a member of a large society which extends to many parts of the world, my connection with it is too distant to be as strong as that which binds me to the inferior division in the midst of which I live. I am told that the great nation, of which we are a part, is just, wise, and free, beyond any other on earth, within its own insular boundaries; but not always so to its distant conquests: I shall not repeat all I have heard, because I cannot believe half of it. As a citizen of a smaller society, I find that any kind of opposition to its now prevailing sentiments, immediately begets hatred: how easily do men pass from loving, to hating and cursing one another! I am a lover of peace, what must I do? I am divided between the respect I feel for the ancient connection, and the fear of innovations, with the consequence of which I am not well acquainted; as they are embraced by my own countrymen. I am conscious that I was happy before this unfortunate Revolution. I feel that I am no longer so; therefore I regret the change. This is the only mode of reasoning adapted to persons in my situation. If I attach myself to the Mother Country, which is 3000 miles from me, I become what is called an enemy to my own region; if I follow the rest of my countrymen, I become opposed to our ancient masters: both extremes appear equally dangerous to a person of so little weight and consequence as I am, whose energy and example are of no avail. As to the argument on which the dispute is founded, I know little about it. Much has been said and written on both sides, but who has a judgment capacious and clear enough to decide? The great moving principles which actuate both parties are much hid from vulgar eyes, like mine; nothing but the plausible and the probable are offered to our contemplation.

The innocent class are always the victim of the few; they are in all countries and at all times the inferior agents, on which the popular phantom is erected; they clamour, and must toil, and bleed, and are always sure of meeting with oppression and rebuke. It is for the sake of the great leaders on both sides, that so much blood must be spilt; that of the people is counted as nothing. Great events are not achieved for us, though it is by us that they are principally accomplished; by the arms, the sweat, the lives of the people. Books tell me so much that they inform me of nothing. Sophistry, the bane of freemen, launches forth in all her deceiving attire! After all, most men reason from passions; and shall such an ignorant individual as I am decide, and say this side is right, that side is wrong? Sentiment and feeling are the only guides I know. Alas, how should I unravel an argument, in which reason herself hath given way to brutality and bloodshed! What then must I do? I ask the wisest lawyers, the ablest casuists, the warmest patriots; for I mean honestly. Great Source of wisdom! inspire me with light sufficient to guide my benighted steps out of this intricate maze! Shall I discard all my ancient principles, shall I renounce that name, that nation which I held once so respectable? I feel the powerful attraction;

the sentiments they inspired grew with my earliest knowledge, and were grafted upon the first rudiments of my education. On the other hand, shall I arm myself against that country where I first drew breath, against the play-mates of my youth, my bosom friends, my acquaintance?—the idea makes me shudder! Must I be called a parricide, a traitor, a villain, lose the esteem of all those whom I love, to preserve my own; be shunned like a rattlesnake, or be pointed at like a bear? I have neither heroism not magnanimity enough to make so great a sacrifice. Here I am tied, I am fastened by numerous strings, nor do I repine at the pressure they cause; ignorant as I am, I can pervade the utmost extent of the calamities which have already overtaken our poor afflicted country. I can see the great and accumulated ruin yet extending itself as far as the theatre of war has reached; I hear the groans of thousands of families now ruined and desolated by our aggressors. I cannot count the multitude of orphans this war has made; nor ascertain the immensity of blood we have lost. Some have asked, whether it was a crime to resist; to repel some parts of this evil. Others have asserted, that a resistance so general makes pardon unattainable, and repentance useless: and dividing the crime among so many, renders it imperceptible. What one party calls meritorious, the other denominates flagitious. These opinions vary, contract, or expand, like the events of the war on which they are founded. What can an insignificant man do in the midst of these jarring contradictory parties, equally hostile to persons situated as I am? And after all who will be the really guilty?—Those most certainly who fail of success. Our fate, the fate of thousands, is then necessarily involved in the dark wheel of fortune. Why then so many useless reasonings; we are the sport of fate. Farewell education, principles, love of our country, farewell; all are become useless to the generality of us: he who governs himself according to what he calls his principles, may be punished either by one party or the other, for those very principles. He who proceeds without principle, as chance, timidity, or self-preservation directs, will not perhaps fare better; but he will be less blamed. What are we in the great scale of events, we poor defenceless frontier inhabitants? What is it to the gazing world, whether we breathe or whether we die? Whatever virtue, whatever merit and disinterestedness we may exhibit in our secluded retreats, of what avail?

We are like the pismires destroyed by the plough; whose destruction prevents not the future crop. Self-preservation, therefore, the rule of nature, seems to be the best rule of conduct; what good can we do by vain resistance, by useless efforts? The cool, the distant spectator, placed in safety, may arraign me for ingratitude, may bring forth the principles of Solon or Montesquieu; he may look on me as wilfully guilty; he may call me by the most opprobrious names. Secure from personal danger, his warm imagination, undisturbed by the least agitation of the heart, will expatiate freely on this grand question; and will consider this extended field, but as exhibiting the double scene of attack and defence. To him the object becomes abstracted, the intermediate glares, the perspective distance and a variety of opinions unimpaired by affections, presents to his mind but one set of ideas. Here he proclaims the high guilt of the one, and there the right of the other; but let him come and reside with us one single month, let him pass with us through all the successive hours of necessary toil, terror and affright, let him watch with us, his musket in his hand, through tedious, sleepless nights, his imagination furrowed by the keen chisel of every passion; let his wife and his children become exposed to the most dreadful hazards of death; let the existence of his property depend on a single spark, blown by the breath of an enemy; let him tremble with us in our fields, shudder at the rustling of every leaf; let his heart, the seat of the most affecting passions, be powerfully wrung by hearing the melancholy end of his relations and friends; let him trace on the map the progress of these desolations; let his alarmed imagination predict to him the night, the dreadful night when it may be his turn to perish, as so many have perished before. Observe then, whether the man will not get the better of the citizen, whether his political maxims will not vanish! Yes, he will cease to glow so warmly with the glory of the metropolis; all his wishes will be turned toward the preservation of his family! Oh, were he situated where I am, were his house perpetually filled, as mine is, with miserable victims just escaped from the flames and the scalping knife, telling of barbarities and murders that make human nature tremble; his situation would suspend every political reflection, and expel every abstract idea. My heart is full and involuntarily takes hold of any notion from whence it can receive ideal ease or relief. I am informed that the king has the most numerous, as well as the fairest, progeny of children, of any potentate now in the world: he may be a great king, but he must feel as we common mortals do, in the good wishes he forms for their lives and prosperity. His mind no doubt often springs forward on the wings of anticipation, and contemplates us as happily settled in the world. If a poor frontier inhabitant may be allowed to suppose this great personage the first in our system, to be exposed but for one hour, to the exquisite pangs we so often feel, would not the preservation of so numerous a family engross all his thoughts; would not the ideas of dominion and other felicities attendant on royalty all vanish in the hour of danger? The regal character, however sacred, would be superseded by the stronger, because more natural one of man and father. Oh! did he but know the circumstances of this horrid war, I am sure he would put a stop to that long destruction of parents and children. I am sure that while he turned his ears to state policy, he would attentively listen also to the dictates of nature, that great parent; for, as a good king, he no doubt wishes to create, to spare, and to protect, as she does. Must I then, in order to be called a faithful subject, coolly, and philosophically say, it is necessary for the good of Britain, that my children's brains should be dashed against the walls of the house in which they were reared; that my wife should be stabbed and scalped before my face; that I should be either murdered or captivated; or that for greater expedition we should all be locked up and burnt to ashes as the family of the B—- -n was? Must I with meekness wait for that last pitch of desolation, and receive with perfect resignation so hard a fate, from ruffians, acting at such a distance from the eyes of any superior; monsters, left to the wild impulses of the wildest nature. Could the lions of Africa be transported here and let loose, they would no doubt kill us in order to prey upon our carcasses! but their appetites would not require so many victims.

Shall I wait to be punished with death, or else to be stripped of all food and raiment, reduced to despair without redress and without hope. Shall those who may escape, see everything they hold dear destroyed and gone. Shall those few survivors, lurking in some obscure corner, deplore in vain the fate of their families, mourn over parents either captivated, butchered, or burnt; roam among our wilds, and wait for death at the foot of some tree, without a murmur, or without a sigh, for the good of the cause? No, it is impossible! so astonishing a sacrifice is not to be expected from human nature, it must belong to beings of an inferior or superior order, actuated by less, or by more refined principles. Even those great personages who are so far elevated above the common ranks of men, those, I mean, who wield and direct so many thunders; those who have let loose against us these demons of war, could they be transported here, and metamorphosed into simple planters as we are, they would, from being the arbiters of human destiny, sink into miserable victims; they would feel and exclaim as we do, and be as much at a loss what line of conduct to prosecute. Do you well comprehend the difficulties of our situation? If we stay we are sure to perish at one time or another; no vigilance on our part can save us; if we retire, we know not where to go; every house is filled with refugees as wretched as ourselves; and if we remove we become beggars. The property of farmers is not like that of merchants; and absolute poverty is worse than death. If we take up arms to defend ourselves, we are denominated rebels; should we not be rebels against nature, could we be shamefully passive? Shall we then, like martyrs, glory in an allegiance, now become useless, and voluntarily expose ourselves to a species of desolation which, though it ruin us entirely, yet enriches not our ancient masters. By this inflexible and sullen attachment, we shall be despised by our countrymen, and destroyed by our ancient friends; whatever we may say, whatever merit we may claim, will not shelter us from those indiscriminate blows, given by hired banditti, animated by all those passions which urge men to shed the blood of others; how bitter the thought! On the contrary, blows received by the hands of those from whom we expected protection, extinguish ancient respect, and urge us to self-defence- -perhaps to revenge; this is the path which nature herself points out, as well to the civilised as to the uncivilised. The Creator of hearts has himself stamped on them those propensities at their first formation; and must we then daily receive this treatment from a power once so loved? The Fox flies or deceives the hounds that pursue him; the bear, when overtaken, boldly resists and attacks them; the hen, the very timid hen, fights for the preservation of her chickens, nor does she decline to attack, and to meet on the wing even the swift kite. Shall man, then, provided both with instinct and reason, unmoved, unconcerned, and passive, see his subsistence consumed, and his progeny either ravished from him or murdered? Shall fictitious reason extinguish the unerring impulse of instinct? No; my former respect, my former attachment vanishes with my safety; that respect and attachment was purchased by protection, and it has ceased. Could not the great nation we belong to have accomplished her designs by means of her numerous armies, by means of those fleets which cover the ocean? Must those who are masters of two thirds of the trade of the world; who have in their hands the power which almighty gold can give; who possess a species of wealth that increases with their desires; must they establish their conquest with our insignificant innocent blood!

Must I then bid farewell to Britain, to that renowned country? Must I renounce a name so ancient and so venerable? Alas, she herself, that once indulgent parent, forces me to take up arms against her. She herself, first inspired the most unhappy citizens of our remote districts, with the thoughts of shedding the blood of those whom they used to call by the name of friends and brethren. That great nation which now convulses the world; which hardly knows the extent of her Indian kingdoms; which looks toward the universal monarchy of trade, of industry, of riches, of power: why must she strew our poor frontiers with the carcasses of her friends, with the wrecks of our insignificant villages, in which there is no gold? When, oppressed by painful recollection, I revolve all these scattered ideas in my mind, when I contemplate my situation, and the thousand streams of evil with which I am surrounded; when I descend into the particular tendency even of the remedy I have proposed, I am convulsed— convulsed sometimes to that degree, as to be tempted to exclaim—Why has the master of the world permitted so much indiscriminate evil throughout every part of this poor planet, at all times, and among all kinds of people? It ought surely to be the punishment of the wicked only. I bring that cup to my lips, of which I must soon taste, and shudder at its bitterness. What then is life, I ask myself, is it a gracious gift? No, it is too bitter; a gift means something valuable conferred, but life appears to be a mere accident, and of the worst kind: we are born to be victims of diseases and passions, of mischances and death: better not to be than to be miserable.—Thus impiously I roam, I fly from one erratic thought to another, and my mind, irritated by these acrimonious reflections, is ready sometimes to lead me to dangerous extremes of violence. When I recollect that I am a father, and a husband, the return of these endearing ideas strikes deep into my heart. Alas! they once made it to glow with pleasure and with every ravishing exultation; but now they fill it with sorrow. At other times, my wife industriously rouses me out of these dreadful meditations, and soothes me by all the reasoning she is mistress of; but her endeavours only serve to make me more miserable, by reflecting that she must share with all these calamities, the bare apprehensions of which I am afraid will subvert her reason. Nor can I with patience think that a beloved wife, my faithful help-mate, throughout all my rural schemes, the principal hand which has assisted me in rearing the prosperous fabric of ease and independence I lately possessed, as well as my children, those tenants of my heart, should daily and nightly be exposed to such a cruel fate. Selfpreservation is above all political precepts and rules, and even superior to the dearest opinions of our minds; a reasonable accommodation of ourselves to the various exigencies of the time in which we live, is the most irresistible precept. To this great evil I must seek some sort of remedy adapted to remove or to palliate it; situated as I am, what steps should I take that will neither injure nor insult any of the parties, and at the same time save my family from that certain destruction which awaits it, if I remain here much longer. Could I insure them bread, safety, and subsistence, not the bread of idleness, but that earned by proper labour as heretofore; could this be accomplished by the sacrifice of my life, I would willingly give it up. I attest before heaven, that it is only for these I would wish to live and to toil: for these whom I have brought into this miserable existence. I resemble, methinks, one of the stones of a ruined arch, still retaining that pristine form that anciently fitted the place I occupied, but the centre is tumbled down; I can be nothing until I am replaced, either in the former circle, or in some stronger one. I see one on a smaller scale, and at a considerable distance, but it is within my power to reach it: and since I have ceased to consider myself as a member of the ancient state now convulsed, I willingly descend into an inferior one. I will revert into a state approaching nearer to that of nature, unencumbered either with voluminous laws, or contradictory codes, often galling the very necks of those whom they protect; and at the same time sufficiently remote from the brutality of unconnected savage nature. Do you, my friend, perceive the path I have found out? it is that which leads to the tenants of the great———village of———, where, far removed from the accursed neighbourhood of Europeans, its inhabitants live with more ease, decency, and peace, than you imagine: where, though governed by no laws, yet find, in uncontaminated simple manners all that laws can afford. Their system is sufficiently complete to answer all the primary wants of man, and to constitute him a social being, such as he ought to be in the great forest of nature. There it is that I have resolved at any rate to transport myself and family: an eccentric thought, you may say, thus to cut asunder all former connections, and to form new ones with a people whom nature has stamped with such different characteristics! But as the happiness of my family is the only object of my wishes, I care very little where we be, or where we go, provided that we are safe, and all united together. Our new calamities being shared equally by all, will become lighter; our mutual affection for each other, will in this great transmutation become the strongest link of our new society, will afford us every joy we can receive on a foreign soil, and preserve us in unity, as the gravity and coherency of matter prevents the world from dissolution. Blame me not, it would be cruel in you, it would beside be entirely useless; for when you receive this we shall be on the wing. When we think all hopes are gone, must we, like poor pusillanimous wretches, despair and die? No; I perceive before me a few resources, though through many dangers, which I will explain to you hereafter. It is not, believe me, a disappointed ambition which leads me to take this step, it is the bitterness of my situation, it is the impossibility of knowing what better measure to adopt: my education fitted me for nothing more than the most simple occupations of life; I am but a feller of trees, a cultivator of land, the most honourable title an American can have. I have no exploits, no discoveries, no inventions to boast of; I have cleared about 370 acres of land, some for the plough, some for the scythe; and this has occupied many years of my life. I have never possessed, or wish to possess anything more than what could be earned or produced by the united industry of my family. I wanted nothing more than to live at home independent and tranquil, and to teach my children how to provide the means of a future ample subsistence, founded on labour, like that of their father, This is the career of life I have pursued, and that which I had marked out for them and for which they seemed to be so well calculated by their inclinations, and by their constitutions. But now these pleasing expectations are gone, we must abandon the accumulated industry of nineteen years, we must fly we hardly know whither, through the most impervious paths, and become members of a new and strange community. Oh, virtue! is this all the reward thou hast to confer on thy votaries? Either thou art only a chimera, or thou art a timid useless being; soon affrighted, when ambition, thy great adversary, dictates, when war re-echoes the dreadful sounds, and poor helpless individuals are mowed down by its cruel reapers like useless grass. I have at all times generously relieved what few distressed people I have met with; I have encouraged the industrious; my house has always been opened to travellers; I have not lost a month in illness since I have been a man; I have caused upwards of an hundred and twenty families to remove hither. Many of them I have led by the hand in the days of their first trial; distant as I am from any places of worship or school of education, I have been the pastor of my family, and the teacher of many of my neighbours. I have learnt them as well as I could, the gratitude they owe to God, the father of harvests; and their duties to man: I have been as useful a subject; ever obedient to the laws, ever vigilant to see them respected and observed. My wife hath faithfully followed the same line within her province; no woman was ever a better economist, or spun or wove better linen; yet we must perish, perish like wild beasts, included within a ring of fire!

Yes, I will cheerfully embrace that resource, it is an holy inspiration; by night and by day, it presents itself to my mind: I have carefully revolved the scheme; I have considered in all its future effects and tendencies, the new mode of living we must pursue, without salt, without spices, without linen and with little other clothing; the art of hunting, we must acquire, the new manners we must adopt, the new language we must speak; the dangers attending the education of my children we must endure. These changes may appear more terrific at a distance perhaps than when grown familiar by practice: what is it to us, whether we eat well made pastry, or pounded alagriches; well roasted beef, or smoked venison; cabbages, or squashes? Whether we wear neat home-spun or good beaver; whether we sleep on feather-beds, or on bear-skins? The difference is not worth attending to. The difficulty of the language, fear of some great intoxication among the Indians; finally, the apprehension lest my younger children should be caught by that singular charm, so dangerous at their tender years; are the only considerations that startle me. By what power does it come to pass, that children who have been adopted when young among these people, can never be prevailed on to readopt European manners? Many an anxious parent I have seen last war, who at the return of the peace, went to the Indian villages where they knew their children had been carried in captivity; when to their inexpressible sorrow, they found them so perfectly Indianised, that many knew them no longer, and those whose more advanced ages permitted them to recollect their fathers and mothers, absolutely refused to follow them, and ran to their adopted parents for protection against the effusions of love their unhappy real parents lavished on them! Incredible as this may appear, I have heard it asserted in a thousand instances, among persons of credit. In the village of———, where I purpose to go, there lived, about fifteen years ago, an Englishman and a Swede, whose history would appear moving, had I time to relate it. They were grown to the age of men when they were taken; they happily escaped the great punishment of war captives, and were obliged to marry the Squaws who had saved their lives by adoption. By the force of habit, they became at last thoroughly naturalised to this wild course of life. While I was there, their friends sent them a considerable sum of money to ransom themselves with. The Indians, their old masters, gave them their choice, and without requiring any consideration, told them, that they had been long as free as themselves. They chose to remain; and the reasons they gave me would greatly surprise you: the most perfect freedom, the ease of living, the absence of those cares and corroding solicitudes which so often prevail with us; the peculiar goodness of the soil they cultivated, for they did not trust altogether to hunting; all these, and many more motives, which I have forgot, made them prefer that life, of which we entertain such dreadful opinions. It cannot be, therefore, so bad as we generally conceive it to be; there must be in their social bond something singularly captivating, and far superior to anything to be boasted of among us; for thousands of Europeans are Indians, and we have no examples of even one of those Aborigines having from choice become Europeans! There must be something more congenial to our native dispositions, than the fictitious society in which we live; or else why should children, and even grown persons, become in a short time so invincibly attached to it? There must be something very bewitching in their manners, something very indelible and marked by the very hands of nature. For, take a young Indian lad, give him the best education you possibly can, load him with your bounty, with presents, nay with riches; yet he will secretly long for his native woods, which you would imagine he must have long since forgot; and on the first opportunity he can possibly find, you will see him voluntarily leave behind him all you have given him, and return with inexpressible joy to lie on the mats of his fathers. Mr.——, some years ago, received from a good old Indian, who died in his house, a young lad, of nine years of age, his grandson. He kindly educated him with his children, and bestowed on him the same care and attention in respect to the memory of his venerable grandfather, who was a worthy man. He intended to give him a genteel trade, but in the spring season when all the family went to the woods to make their maple sugar, he suddenly disappeared; and it was not until seventeen months after, that his benefactor heard he had reached the village of Bald Eagle, where he still dwelt. Let us say what we will of them, of their inferior organs, of their want of bread, etc., they are as stout and well made as the Europeans. Without temples, without priests, without kings, and without laws, they are in many instances superior to us; and the proofs of what I advance, are, that they live without care, sleep without inquietude, take life as it comes, bearing all its asperities with unparalleled patience, and die without any kind of apprehension for what they have done, or for what they expect to meet with hereafter. What system of philosophy can give us so many necessary qualifications for happiness? They most certainly are much more closely connected with nature than we are; they are her immediate children, the inhabitants of the woods are her undefiled off-spring: those of the plains are her degenerated breed, far, very far removed from her primitive laws, from her original design. It is therefore resolved on. I will either die in the attempt or succeed; better perish all together in one fatal hour, than to suffer what we daily endure. I do not expect to enjoy in the village of———an uninterrupted happiness; it cannot be our lot, let us live where we will; I am not founding my future prosperity on golden dreams. Place mankind where you will, they must always have adverse circumstances to struggle with; from nature, accidents, constitution; from seasons, from that great combination of mischances which perpetually lead us to new diseases, to poverty, etc. Who knows but I may meet in this new situation, some accident from whence may spring up new sources of unexpected prosperity? Who can be presumptuous enough to predict all the good? Who can foresee all the evils, which strew the paths of our lives? But after all, I cannot but recollect what sacrifice I am going to make, what amputation I am going to suffer, what transition I am going to experience. Pardon my repetitions, my wild, my trifling reflections, they proceed from the agitations of my mind, and the fulness of my heart; the action of thus retracing them seems to lighten the burden, and to exhilarate my spirits; this is besides the last letter you will receive from me; I would fain tell you all, though I hardly know how. Oh! in the hours, in the moments of my greatest anguish, could I intuitively represent to you that variety of thought which crowds on my mind, you would have reason to be surprised, and to doubt of their possibility. Shall we ever meet again? If we should, where will it be? On the wild shores of——. If it be my doom to end my days there, I will greatly improve them; and perhaps make room for a few more families, who will choose to retire from the fury of a storm, the agitated billows of which will yet roar for many years on our extended shores. Perhaps I may repossess my house, if it be not burnt down; but how will my improvements look? why, half defaced, bearing the strong marks of abandonment, and of the ravages of war. However, at present I give everything over for lost; I will bid a long farewell to what I leave behind. If ever I repossess it, I shall receive it as a gift, as a reward for my conduct and fortitude. Do not imagine, however, that I am a stoic—by no means: I must, on the contrary, confess to you, that I feel the keenest regret, at abandoning an house which I have in some measure reared with my own hands. Yes, perhaps I may never revisit those fields which I have cleared, those trees which I have planted, those meadows which, in my youth, were a hideous wilderness, now converted by my industry into rich pastures and pleasant lawns. If in Europe it is praise-worthy to be attached to paternal inheritances, how much more natural, how much more powerful must the tie be with us, who, if I may be permitted the expression, are the founders, the creators of our own farms! When I see my table surrounded with my blooming offspring, all united in the bonds of the strongest affection, it kindles in my paternal heart a variety of tumultuous sentiments, which none but a father and a husband in my situation can feel or describe. Perhaps I may see my wife, my children, often distressed, involuntarily recalling to their minds the ease and abundance which they enjoyed under the paternal roof. Perhaps I may see them want that bread which I now leave behind; overtaken by diseases and penury, rendered more bitter by the recollection of former days of opulence and plenty. Perhaps I may be assailed on every side by unforeseen accidents, which I shall not be able to prevent or to alleviate. Can I contemplate such images without the most unutterable emotions? My fate is determined; but I have not determined it, you may assure yourself, without having undergone the most painful conflicts of a variety of passions;— interest, love of ease, disappointed views, and pleasing expectations frustrated;—I shuddered at the review! Would to God I was master of the stoical tranquillity of that magnanimous sect; oh, that I were possessed of those sublime lessons which Appollonius of Chalcis gave to the Emperor Antoninus! I could then with much more propriety guide the helm of my little bark, which is soon to be freighted with all that I possess most dear on earth, through this stormy passage to a safe harbour; and when there, become to my fellow passengers, a surer guide, a brighter example, a pattern more worthy of imitation, throughout all the new scenes they must pass, and the new career they must traverse. I have observed notwithstanding, the means hitherto made use of, to arm the principal nations against our frontiers. Yet they have not, they will not take up the hatchet against a people who have done them no harm. The passions necessary to urge these people to war, cannot be roused, they cannot feel the stings of vengeance, the thirst of which alone can compel them to shed blood: far superior in their motives of action to the Europeans, who for sixpence per day, may be engaged to shed that of any people on earth. They know nothing of the nature of our disputes, they have no ideas of such revolutions as this; a civil division of a village or tribe, are events which have never been recorded in their traditions: many of them know very well that they have too long been the dupes and the victims of both parties; foolishly arming for our sakes, sometimes against each other, sometimes against our white enemies. They consider us as born on the same land, and, though they have no reasons to love us, yet they seem carefully to avoid entering into this quarrel, from whatever motives. I am speaking of those nations with which I am best acquainted, a few hundreds of the worst kind mixed with whites, worse than themselves, are now hired by Great Britain, to perpetuate those dreadful incursions. In my youth I traded with the——, under the conduct of my uncle, and always traded justly and equitably; some of them remember it to this day. Happily their village is far removed from the dangerous neighbourhood of the whites; I sent a man last spring to it, who understands the woods extremely well, and who speaks their language; he is just returned, after several weeks absence, and has brought me, as I had flattered myself, a string of thirty purple wampum, as a token that their honest chief will spare us half of his wigwam until we have time to erect one. He has sent me word that they have land in plenty, of which they are not so covetous as the whites; that we may plant for ourselves, and that in the meantime he will procure for us some corn and some meat; that fish is plenty in the waters of—-, and that the village to which he had laid open my proposals, have no objection to our becoming dwellers with them. I have not yet communicated these glad tidings to my wife, nor do I know how to do it; I tremble lest she should refuse to follow me; lest the sudden idea of this removal rushing on her mind, might be too powerful. I flatter myself I shall be able to accomplish it, and to prevail on her; I fear nothing but the effects of her strong attachment to her relations. I will willingly let you know how I purpose to remove my family to so great a distance, but it would become unintelligible to you, because you are not acquainted with the geographical situation of this part of the country. Suffice it for you to know, that with about twenty-three miles land carriage, I am enabled to perform the rest by water; and when once afloat, I care not whether it be two or three hundred miles. I propose to send all our provisions, furniture, and clothes to my wife's father, who approves of the scheme, and to reserve nothing but a few necessary articles of covering; trusting to the furs of the chase for our future apparel. Were we imprudently to encumber ourselves too much with baggage, we should never reach to the waters of—-, which is the most dangerous as well as the most difficult part of our journey; and yet but a trifle in point of distance. I intend to say to my negroes—In the name of God, be free, my honest lads, I thank you for your past services; go, from henceforth, and work for yourselves; look on me as your old friend, and fellow labourer; be sober, frugal, and industrious, and you need not fear earning a comfortable subsistence.—Lest my countrymen should think that I am gone to join the incendiaries of our frontiers, I intend to write a letter to Mr.—-, to inform him of our retreat, and of the reasons that have urged me to it. The man whom I sent to——village, is to accompany us also, and a very useful companion he will be on every account.

You may therefore, by means of anticipation, behold me under the Wigwam; I am so well acquainted with the principal manners of these people, that I entertain not the least apprehension from them. I rely more securely on their strong hospitality, than on the witnessed compacts of many Europeans. As soon as possible after my arrival, I design to build myself a wigwam, after the same manner and size with the rest, in order to avoid being thought singular, or giving occasion for any railleries; though these people are seldom guilty of such European follies. I shall erect it hard by the lands which they propose to allot me, and will endeavour that my wife, my children, and myself may be adopted soon after our arrival. Thus becoming truly inhabitants of their village, we shall immediately occupy that rank within the pale of their society, which will afford us all the amends we can possibly expect for the loss we have met with by the convulsions of our own. According to their customs we shall likewise receive names from them, by which we shall always be known. My youngest children shall learn to swim, and to shoot with the bow, that they may acquire such talents as will necessarily raise them into some degree of esteem among the Indian lads of their own age; the rest of us must hunt with the hunters. I have been for several years an expert marksman; but I dread lest the imperceptible charm of Indian education, may seize my younger children, and give them such a propensity to that mode of life, as may preclude their returning to the manners and customs of their parents. I have but one remedy to prevent this great evil; and that is, to employ them in the labour of the fields, as much as I can; I am even resolved to make their daily subsistence depend altogether on it. As long as we keep ourselves busy in tilling the earth, there is no fear of any of us becoming wild; it is the chase and the food it procures, that have this strange effect. Excuse a simile—those hogs which range in the woods, and to whom grain is given once a week, preserve their former degree of tameness; but if, on the contrary, they are reduced to live on ground nuts, and on what they can get, they soon become wild and fierce. For my part, I can plough, sow, and hunt, as occasion may require; but my wife, deprived of wool and flax, will have no room for industry; what is she then to do? like the other squaws, she must cook for us the nasaump, the ninchicke, and such other preparations of corn as are customary among these people. She must learn to bake squashes and pumpkins under the ashes; to slice and smoke the meat of our own killing, in order to preserve it; she must cheerfully adopt the manners and customs of her neighbours, in their dress, deportment, conduct, and internal economy, in all respects. Surely if we can have fortitude enough to quit all we have, to remove so far, and to associate with people so different from us; these necessary compliances are but part of the scheme. The change of garments, when those they carry with them are worn out, will not be the least of my wife's and daughter's concerns: though I am in hopes that self-love will invent some sort of reparation. Perhaps you would not believe that there are in the woods looking-glasses, and paint of every colour; and that the inhabitants take as much pains to adorn their faces and their bodies, to fix their bracelets of silver, and plait their hair, as our forefathers the Picts used to do in the time of the Romans. Not that I would wish to see either my wife or daughter adopt those savage customs; we can live in great peace and harmony with them without descending to every article; the interruption of trade hath, I hope, suspended this mode of dress. My wife understands inoculation perfectly well, she inoculated all our children one after another, and has successfully performed the operation on several scores of people, who, scattered here and there through our woods, were too far removed from all medical assistance. If we can persuade but one family to submit to it, and it succeeds, we shall then be as happy as our situation will admit of; it will raise her into some degree of consideration, for whoever is useful in any society will always be respected. If we are so fortunate as to carry one family through a disorder, which is the plague among these people, I trust to the force of example, we shall then become truly necessary, valued, and beloved; we indeed owe every kind office to a society of men who so readily offer to assist us into their social partnership, and to extend to my family the shelter of their village, the strength of their adoption, and even the dignity of their names. God grant us a prosperous beginning, we may then hope to be of more service to them than even missionaries who have been sent to preach to them a Gospel they cannot understand.

As to religion, our mode of worship will not suffer much by this removal from a cultivated country, into the bosom of the woods; for it cannot be much simpler than that which we have followed here these many years: and I will with as much care as I can, redouble my attention, and twice a week, retrace to them the great outlines of their duty to God and to man. I will read and expound to them some part of the decalogue, which is the method I have pursued ever since I married.

Half a dozen of acres on the shores of—-, the soil of which I know well, will yield us a great abundance of all we want; I will make it a point to give the over-plus to such Indians as shall be most unfortunate in their huntings; I will persuade them, if I can, to till a little more land than they do, and not to trust so much to the produce of the chase. To encourage them still farther, I will give a quirn to every six families; I have built many for our poor back settlers, it being often the want of mills which prevents them from raising grain. As I am a carpenter, I can build my own plough, and can be of great service to many of them; my example alone, may rouse the industry of some, and serve to direct others in their labours. The difficulties of the language will soon be removed; in my evening conversations, I will endeavour to make them regulate the trade of their village in such a manner as that those pests of the continent, those Indian traders, may not come within a certain distance; and there they shall be obliged to transact their business before the old people. I am in hopes that the constant respect which is paid to the elders, and shame, may prevent the young hunters from infringing this regulation. The son of——will soon be made acquainted with our schemes, and I trust that the power of love, and the strong attachment he professes for my daughter, may bring him along with us: he will make an excellent hunter; young and vigorous, he will equal in dexterity the stoutest man in the village. Had it not been for this fortunate circumstance, there would have been the greatest danger; for however I respect the simple, the inoffensive society of these people in their villages, the strongest prejudices would make me abhor any alliance with them in blood: disagreeable no doubt, to nature's intentions which have strongly divided us by so many indelible characters. In the days of our sickness, we shall have recourse to their medical knowledge, which is well calculated for the simple diseases to which they are subject. Thus shall we metamorphose ourselves, from neat, decent, opulent planters, surrounded with every conveniency which our external labour and internal industry could give, into a still simpler people divested of everything beside hope, food, and the raiment of the woods: abandoning the large framed house, to dwell under the wigwam; and the featherbed, to lie on the mat, or bear's skin. There shall we sleep undisturbed by fruitful dreams and apprehensions; rest and peace of mind will make us the most ample amends for what we shall leave behind. These blessings cannot be purchased too dear; too long have we been deprived of them. I would cheerfully go even to the Mississippi, to find that repose to which we have been so long strangers. My heart sometimes seems tired with beating, it wants rest like my eye-lids, which feel oppressed with so many watchings.

These are the component parts of my scheme, the success of each of which appears feasible; from whence I flatter myself with the probable success of the whole. Still the danger of Indian education returns to my mind, and alarms me much; then again I contrast it with the education of the times; both appear to be equally pregnant with evils. Reason points out the necessity of choosing the least dangerous, which I must consider as the only good within my reach; I persuade myself that industry and labour will be a sovereign preservative against the dangers of the former; but I consider, at the same time, that the share of labour and industry which is intended to procure but a simple subsistence, with hardly any superfluity, cannot have the same restrictive effects on our minds as when we tilled the earth on a more extensive scale. The surplus could be then realised into solid wealth, and at the same time that this realisation rewarded our past labours, it engrossed and fixed the attention of the labourer, and cherished in his mind the hope of future riches. In order to supply this great deficiency of industrious motives, and to hold out to them a real object to prevent the fatal consequences of this sort of apathy; I will keep an exact account of all that shall be gathered, and give each of them a regular credit for the amount of it to be paid them in real property at the return of peace. Thus, though seemingly toiling for bare subsistence on a foreign land, they shall entertain the pleasing prospect of seeing the sum of their labours one day realised either in legacies or gifts, equal if not superior to it. The yearly expense of the clothes which they would have received at home, and of which they will then be deprived, shall likewise be added to their credit; thus I flatter myself that they will more cheerfully wear the blanket, the matchcoat, and the Moccasins. Whatever success they may meet with in hunting or fishing, shall only be considered as recreation and pastime; I shall thereby prevent them from estimating their skill in the chase as an important and necessary accomplishment. I mean to say to them: "You shall hunt and fish merely to show your new companions that you are not inferior to them in point of sagacity and dexterity." Were I to send them to such schools as the interior parts of our settlements afford at present, what can they learn there? How could I support them there? What must become of me; am I to proceed on my voyage, and leave them? That I never could submit to. Instead of the perpetual discordant noise of disputes so common among us, instead of those scolding scenes, frequent in every house, they will observe nothing but silence at home and abroad: a singular appearance of peace and concord are the first characteristics which strike you in the villages of these people. Nothing can be more pleasing, nothing surprises an European so much as the silence and harmony which prevails among them, and in each family; except when disturbed by that accursed spirit given them by the wood rangers in exchange for their furs. If my children learn nothing of geometrical rules, the use of the compass, or of the Latin tongue, they will learn and practise sobriety, for rum can no longer be sent to these people; they will learn that modesty and diffidence for which the young Indians are so remarkable; they will consider labour as the most essential qualification; hunting as the second. They will prepare themselves in the prosecution of our small rural schemes, carried on for the benefit of our little community, to extend them further when each shall receive his inheritance. Their tender minds will cease to be agitated by perpetual alarms; to be made cowards by continual terrors: if they acquire in the village of—-, such an awkwardness of deportment and appearance as would render them ridiculous in our gay capitals, they will imbibe, I hope, a confirmed taste for that simplicity, which so well becomes the cultivators of the land. If I cannot teach them any of those professions which sometimes embellish and support our society, I will show them how to hew wood, how to construct their own ploughs; and with a few tools how to supply themselves with every necessary implement, both in the house and in the field. If they are hereafter obliged to confess, that they belong to no one particular church, I shall have the consolation of teaching them that great, that primary worship which is the foundation of all others. If they do not fear God according to the tenets of any one seminary, they shall learn to worship him upon the broad scale of nature. The Supreme Being does not reside in peculiar churches or communities; he is equally the great Manitou of the woods and of the plains; and even in the gloom, the obscurity of those very woods, his justice may be as well understood and felt as in the most sumptuous temples. Each worship with us, hath, you know, its peculiar political tendency; there it has none but to inspire gratitude and truth: their tender minds shall receive no other idea of the Supreme Being, than that of the father of all men, who requires nothing more of us than what tends to make each other happy. We shall say with them, Soungwaneha, esa caurounkyawga, nughwonshauza neattewek, nesalanga.—Our father, be thy will done in earth as it is in great heaven.

Perhaps my imagination gilds too strongly this distant prospect; yet it appears founded on so few, and simple principles, that there is not the same probability of adverse incidents as in more complex schemes. These vague rambling contemplations which I here faithfully retrace, carry me sometimes to a great distance; I am lost in the anticipation of the various circumstances attending this proposed metamorphosis! Many unforeseen accidents may doubtless arise. Alas! it is easier for me in all the glow of paternal anxiety, reclined on my bed, to form the theory of my future conduct, than to reduce my schemes into practice. But when once secluded from the great society to which we now belong, we shall unite closer together; and there will be less room for jealousies or contentions. As I intend my children neither for the law nor the church, but for the cultivation of the land, I wish them no literary accomplishments; I pray heaven that they may be one day nothing more than expert scholars in husbandry: this is the science which made our continent to flourish more rapidly than any other. Were they to grow up where I am now situated, even admitting that we were in safety; two of them are verging toward that period in their lives, when they must necessarily take up the musket, and learn, in that new school, all the vices which are so common in armies. Great God! close my eyes for ever, rather than I should live to see this calamity! May they rather become inhabitants of the woods.

Thus then in the village of—-, in the bosom of that peace it has enjoyed ever since I have known it, connected with mild hospitable people, strangers to OUR political disputes, and having none among themselves; on the shores of a fine river, surrounded with woods, abounding with game; our little society united in perfect harmony with the new adoptive one, in which we shall be incorporated, shall rest I hope from all fatigues, from all apprehensions, from our perfect terrors, and from our long watchings. Not a word of politics shall cloud our simple conversation; tired either with the chase or the labour of the field, we shall sleep on our mats without any distressing want, having learnt to retrench every superfluous one: we shall have but two prayers to make to the Supreme Being, that he may shed his fertilising dew on our little crops, and that he will be pleased to restore peace to our unhappy country. These shall be the only subject of our nightly prayers, and of our daily ejaculations: and if the labour, the industry, the frugality, the union of men, can be an agreeable offering to him, we shall not fail to receive his paternal blessings. There I shall contemplate nature in her most wild and ample extent; I shall carefully study a species of society, of which I have at present but very imperfect ideas; I will endeavour to occupy with propriety that place which will enable me to enjoy the few and sufficient benefits it confers. The solitary and unconnected mode of life I have lived in my youth must fit me for this trial, I am not the first who has attempted it; Europeans did not, it is true, carry to the wilderness numerous families; they went there as mere speculators; I, as a man seeking a refuge from the desolation of war. They went there to study the manner of the aborigines; I to conform to them, whatever they are; some went as visitors, as travellers; I as a sojourner, as a fellow hunter and labourer, go determined industriously to work up among them such a system of happiness as may be adequate to my future situation, and may be a sufficient compensation for all my fatigues and for the misfortunes I have borne: I have always found it at home, I may hope likewise to find it under the humble roof of my wigwam.

O Supreme Being! if among the immense variety of planets, inhabited by thy creative power, thy paternal and omnipotent care deigns to extend to all the individuals they contain; if it be not beneath thy infinite dignity to cast thy eye on us wretched mortals; if my future felicity is not contrary to the necessary effects of those secret causes which thou hast appointed, receive the supplications of a man, to whom in thy kindness thou hast given a wife and an offspring: View us all with benignity, sanctify this strong conflict of regrets, wishes, and other natural passions; guide our steps through these unknown paths, and bless our future mode of life. If it is good and well meant, it must proceed from thee; thou knowest, O Lord, our enterprise contains neither fraud, nor malice, nor revenge. Bestow on me that energy of conduct now become so necessary, that it may be in my power to carry the young family thou hast given me through this great trial with safety and in thy peace. Inspire me with such intentions and such rules of conduct as may be most acceptable to thee. Preserve, O God, preserve the companion of my bosom, the best gift thou hast given me: endue her with courage and strength sufficient to accomplish this perilous journey. Bless the children of our love, those portions of our hearts; I implore thy divine assistance, speak to their tender minds, and inspire them with the love of that virtue which alone can serve as the basis of their conduct in this world, and of their happiness with thee. Restore peace and concord to our poor afflicted country; assuage the fierce storm which has so long ravaged it. Permit, I beseech thee, O Father of nature, that our ancient virtues, and our industry, may not be totally lost: and that as a reward for the great toils we have made on this new land, we may be restored to our ancient tranquillity, and enabled to fill it with successive generations, that will constantly thank thee for the ample subsistence thou hast given them.

The unreserved manner in which I have written must give you a convincing proof of that friendship and esteem, of which I am sure you never yet doubted. As members of the same society, as mutually bound by the ties of affection and old acquaintance, you certainly cannot avoid feeling for my distresses; you cannot avoid mourning with me over that load of physical and moral evil with which we are all oppressed. My own share of it I often overlook when I minutely contemplate all that hath befallen our native country.

The End

3.6.2 Reading and Review Questions

1. In Letter III, how does Crevecoeur distinguish what defines identify in the Old World from what defines identify in America? Why?
2. Unlike Europe, what opportunities and ideal benefits does America offer?
3. In Letter IX, what evidence does Crevecoeur offer in support of the fair treatment of blacks? Why?
4. Why does Crevecoeur rank slavery with Old World despotism and superstition, do you think?
5. How do the narrator's views of America and American life change from Letter III to Letter XII? Why do you think?

3.7 JOHN ADAMS AND ABIGAIL ADAMS

(1735–1826) & (1744–1818)

John Adams was born in Braintree (now Quincey), Massachusetts, situated ten miles from Boston. He attended Harvard then practiced law in Braintree. His opposition to the Stamp Act and the Intolerable Acts led to his serving as delegate to the intercolonial congress; the First Continental Congress (that adapted his "Declaration of Rights"); and the Second Continental Congress. Accepting the need for armed resistance, Adams helped delegates join together to declare independence against England. He also helped negotiate the Treaty of Paris that ended the Revolutionary War; served as America's first constitutional vice president (under George Washington); and its second president.

Image 3.8 | John Adams
Artist | Gilbert Stuart
Source | Wikimedia Commons
License | Public Domain

Abigail Adams née Smith was also born in Braintree, Massachusetts. She received no formal education, instead being guided by her mother in the domestic arts expected of women in that era. She fulfilled her expected role as wife when she married John in 1764 and as mother when she bore five children in seven years. During the early years of their marriage, Abigail moved from one household to another in order to remain close to John. The two were separated, however, starting in 1775 as he served in the congresses leading to the American Revolution. Abigail remained in Braintree, managing their farm, enduring many privations and witnessing terrifying battles—experiences from which John was, to some degree, insulated. After the war, John and Abigail would live separately and together in America and abroad

Image 3.1 | Abigail Adams
Artist | Benjamin Blyth
Source | Wikimedia Commons
License | Public Domain

until John retired from politics and returned permanently to Braintree. In 1818, Abigail died of typhoid fever, predeceasing John by eight years.

Their correspondence comprises 1,100 letters, giving glimpses into their frugalities, friendships, illnesses, parenting, and griefs—especially through the early death of their daughter and their last child being stillborn. Their letters also provide glimpses into a time of momentous upheaval and change in American life, as John and Abigail were active participants in these changes. The March 31, 1776 letter from Abigail to John expresses the hope for a universal democracy, liberating women from the legal tyranny of their husbands, and suggesting a more equitable relationship between friends who are spouses. John's letters on independence vault even beyond these hopes to an almost millennial vision of America and its great experiment in freedom and democracy.

3.7.1 From *Familiar Letters of John Adams and his Wife Abigail Adams, During the Revolution*

A. Adams to J. Adams, March 31, 1776

Braintree, 31 March, 1776.

I wish you would ever write me a letter half as long as I write you, and tell me, if you may, where your fleet are gone; what sort of defense Virginia can make against our common enemy; whether it is so situated as to make an able defense. Are not the gentry lords, and the common people vassals? Are they not like the uncivilized vassals Britain represents us to be? I hope their riflemen, who have shown themselves very savage and even blood-thirsty, are not a specimen of the generality of the people. I am willing to allow the colony great merit for having produced a Washington; but they have been shamefully duped by a Dunmore.

I have sometimes been ready to think that the passion for liberty cannot be equally strong in the breasts of those who have been accustomed to deprive their fellow-creatures of theirs. Of this I am certain, that it is not founded upon that generous and Christian principle of doing to others as we would that others should do unto us.

Do not you want to see Boston? I am fearful of the small-pox, or I should have been in before this time. I got Mr. Crane to go to our house and see what state it was in. I find it has been occupied by one of the doctors of a regiment; very dirty, but no other damage has been done to it. The few things which were left in it are all gone. I look upon it as a new acquisition of property—a property which one month ago I did not value at a single shilling, and would with pleasure have seen it in flames.

The town in general is left in a better state than we expected; more owing to a precipitate flight than any regard to the inhabitants; though some individuals discovered a sense of honor and justice, and have left the rent of the houses in which they were, for the owners, and the furniture unhurt, or, if damaged, sufficient to make it good. Others have committed abominable ravages. The mansion-house of your President is safe, and the furniture unhurt; while the house and furniture of the Solicitor General have fallen a prey to their own merciless party. Surely the very fiends feel a reverential awe for virtue and patriotism, whilst they detest the parricide and traitor.

I feel very differently at the approach of spring from what I did a month ago. We knew not then whether we could plant or sow with safety, whether where we had tilled we could reap the fruits of our own industry, whether we could rest in our own cottages or whether we should be driven from the seacoast to seek shelter in the wilderness; but now we feel a temporary peace, and the poor fugitives are returning to their deserted habitations.

Though we felicitate ourselves, we sympathize with those who are trembling lest the lot of Boston should be theirs. But they cannot be in similar circumstances unless pusillanimity and cowardice should take possession of them. They have time and warning given them to see the evil and shun it.

I long to hear that you have declared an independency. And, by the way, in the new code of laws which I suppose it will be necessary for you to make, I desire you would remember the ladies and be more generous and favorable to them than your ancestors. Do not put such unlimited power into the hands of the husbands. Remember, all men would be tyrants if they could. If particular care and attention is not paid to the ladies, we are determined to foment a rebellion, and will not hold ourselves bound by any laws in which we have no voice or representation.

That your sex are naturally tyrannical is a truth so thoroughly established as to admit of no dispute; but such of you as wish to be happy willingly give up the harsh title of master for the more tender and endearing one of friend. Why, then, not put it out of the power of the vicious and the lawless to use us with cruelty and indignity with impunity? Men of sense in all ages abhor those customs which treat us only as the vassals of your sex; regard us then as beings placed by Providence under your protection, and in imitation of the Supreme Being make use of that power only for our happiness.

J. Adams to A. Adams, April 14, 1776

14 April.

You justly complain of my short letters, but the critical state of things and the multiplicity of avocations must plead my excuse. You ask where the fleet is? The inclosed papers will inform you. You ask what sort of defense Virginia can make? I believe they will make an able defense. Their militia and minute-men have been some time employed in training themselves, and they have nine battalions of regulars, as they call them, maintained among them, under good officers, at the Continental expense. They have set up a number of manufactories of firearms, which are busily employed. They are tolerably supplied with powder, and are successful and assiduous in making saltpetre. Their neighboring sister, or rather daughter colony of North Carolina, which is a warlike colony, and has several battalions at the Continental expense, as well as a pretty good militia, are ready to assist them, and they are in very good spirits and seem determined to make a brave resistance. The gentry are very rich, and the common people very poor. This inequality of property gives an aristocratical turn to all their proceedings, and occasions a strong aversion in their patricians to "Common Sense." But the spirit of these Barons is coming down, and it must submit. It is very true, as you observe, they have been duped by Dunmore. But this is a common case. All the colonies are duped, more or less, at one time and another. A more egregious bubble was never blown up than the story of Commissioners coming to treat with the Congress, yet it has gained credit like a charm, not only with, but against the clearest evidence. I never shall forget the delusion which seized our best and most sagacious friends, the dear inhabitants of Boston, the winter before last. Credulity and the want of foresight are imperfections in the human character, that no politician can sufficiently guard against.

You give me some pleasure by your account of a certain house in Queen Street. I had burned it long ago in imagination. It rises now to my view like a phœnix. What shall I say of the Solicitor General? I pity his pretty children. I pity his father and his sisters. I wish I could be clear that it is no moral evil to pity him and his lady. Upon repentance, they will certainly have a large share in [155]the compassions of many. But let us take warning, and give it to our children. Whenever vanity and gayety, a love of pomp and dress, furniture, equipage, buildings, great company, expensive diversions, and elegant entertainments get the better of the principles and judgments of men or women, there is no knowing where they will stop, nor into what evils, natural, moral, or political, they will lead us.

Your description of your own *gaieté de cœur* charms me. Thanks be to God, you have just cause to rejoice, and may the bright prospect be obscured by no cloud. As to declarations of independency, be patient. Read our privateering laws and our commercial laws. What signifies a word?

As to your extraordinary code of laws, I cannot but laugh. We have been told that our struggle has loosened the bonds of government everywhere; that children and apprentices were disobedient; that schools and colleges were grown turbulent; that Indians slighted their guardians, and negroes grew insolent to their masters. But your letter was the first intimation that another tribe, more numerous and powerful than all the rest, were grown discontented. This is rather too coarse a compliment, but you are so saucy, I won't blot it out. Depend upon it, we know better than to repeal our masculine systems. Although they are in full force, you know they are little more than theory. We dare not exert our power in its full latitude. We are obliged to go fair and softly, and, in practice, you know we are the subjects. We have only the name of masters, and rather than give up this, which would completely subject us to the despotism of the petticoat, I hope General Washington and all our brave heroes would fight; I am sure every good politician would plot, as long as he would against despotism, empire, monarchy, aristocracy, oligarchy, or ochlocracy. A fine story, indeed! I begin to think the ministry as deep as they are wicked. After stirring up Tories, land-jobbers, trimmers, bigots, Canadians, Indians, negroes, Hanoverians, Hessians, Russians, Irish Roman Catholics, Scotch renegadoes, at last they have stimulated the——to demand new privileges and threaten to rebel.

J. Adams to A. Adams, July 3, 1776 (Letter 1)

3 July, 1776.

Your favor of 17 June, dated at Plymouth, was handed me by yesterday's post. I was much pleased to find that you had taken a journey to Plymouth, to see your friends, in the long absence of one whom you may wish to see. The excursion will be an amusement, and will serve your health. How happy would it have made me to have taken this journey with you!

I was informed, a day or two before the receipt of your letter, that you was gone to Plymouth, by Mrs. Polly Palmer, who was obliging enough, in your absence, to send me the particulars of the expedition to the lower harbor against the men-of-war. Her narration is executed with a precision and perspicuity, which would have become the pen of an accomplished historian.

I am very glad you had so good an opportunity of seeing one of our little American men-of-war. Many ideas new to you must have presented themselves in such a scene; and you will, in future, better understand the relations of sea engagements.

I rejoice extremely at Dr. Bulfinch's petition to open a hospital. But I hope the business will be done upon a larger scale. I hope that one hospital will be licensed in every county, if not in every town. I am happy to find you resolved to be with the children in the first class. Mr. Whitney and Mrs. Katy Quincy are cleverly through inoculation in this city.

The information you give me of our friend's refusing his appointment has given me much pain, grief, and anxiety. I believe I shall be obliged to follow his example. I have not fortune enough to support my family, and, what is of more importance, to support the dignity of that exalted station. It is too high and lifted up for me, who delight in nothing so much as retreat, solitude, silence, and obscurity. In private life, no one has a right to censure me for following my own inclinations in retirement, simplicity, and frugality. In public life, every man has a right to remark as he pleases. At least he thinks so.

Yesterday, the greatest question was decided which ever was debated in America, and a greater, perhaps, never was nor will be decided among men. A Resolution was passed without one dissenting Colony "that these United Colonies are, and of right ought to be, free and independent States, and as such they have, and of right ought to have, full power to make war, conclude peace, establish commerce, and to do all other acts and things which other States may rightfully do." You will see, in a few days, a Declaration setting forth the causes which have impelled us to this mighty revolution, and the reasons which will justify it in the sight of God and man. A plan of confederation will be taken up in a few days.

When I look back to the year 1761, and recollect the argument concerning writs of assistance in the superior court, which I have hitherto considered as the commencement of this controversy between Great Britain and America, and run through the whole period from that time to this, and recollect the series of political events, the chain of causes and effects, I am surprised at the suddenness as well as greatness of this revolution. Britain has been filled with folly, and America with wisdom; at least, this is my judgment. Time must determine. It is the will of Heaven that the two countries should be sundered forever. It may be the will of Heaven that America shall suffer calamities still more wasting, and distresses yet more dreadful. If this is to be the case, it will have this good effect at least. It will inspire us with many virtues which we have not, and correct many errors, follies, and vices which threaten to disturb, dishonor, and destroy us. The furnace of affliction produces refinement in states as well as individuals. And the new Governments we are assuming in every part will require a purification from our vices, and an augmentation of our virtues, or they will be no blessings. The people will have unbounded power, and the people are extremely addicted to corruption and venality, as well as the great. But I must submit all my hopes and fears to an overruling Providence, in which, unfashionable as the faith may be, I firmly believe.

J. Adams to A. Adams, July 3, 1776 (Letter 2)

Philadelphia, 3 July, 1776.

Had a Declaration of Independency been made seven months ago, it would have been attended with many great and glorious effects. We might, before this hour, have formed alliances with foreign states. We should have mastered Quebec, and been in possession of Canada. You will perhaps wonder how such a declaration would have influenced our affairs in Canada, but if I could write with freedom, I could easily convince you that it would, and explain to you the manner how. Many gentlemen in high stations, and of great influence, have been duped by the ministerial bubble of Commissioners to treat. And in real, sincere expectation of this event, which they so fondly wished, they have been slow and languid in promoting measures for the reduction of that province. Others there are in the Colonies who really wished that our enterprise in Canada would be defeated, that the Colonies might be brought into danger and distress between two fires, and be thus induced to submit. Others really wished to defeat the expedition to Canada, lest the conquest of it should elevate the minds of the people too much to hearken to those terms of reconciliation which, they believed, would be offered us. These jarring views, wishes, and designs occasioned an opposition to many salutary measures which were proposed for the support of that expedition, and caused obstructions, embarrassments, and studied delays, which have finally lost us the province.

All these causes, however, in conjunction would not have disappointed us, if it had not been for a misfortune which could not be foreseen, and perhaps could not have been prevented; I mean the prevalence of the small-pox among our troops. This fatal pestilence completed our destruction. It is a frown of Providence upon us, which we ought to lay to heart.

But, on the other hand, the delay of this Declaration to this time has many great advantages attending it. The hopes of reconciliation which were fondly entertained by multitudes of honest and well-meaning, though weak and mistaken people, have been gradually, and at last totally extinguished. Time has been given for the whole people maturely to consider the great question of independence, and to ripen their judgment, dissipate their fears, and allure their hopes, by discussing it in newspapers and pamphlets, by debating it in assemblies, conventions, committees of safety and inspection, in town and county meetings, as well as in private conversations, so that the whole people, in every colony of the thirteen, have now adopted it as their own act. This will cement the union, and avoid those heats, and perhaps convulsions, which might have been occasioned by such a Declaration six months ago.

But the day is past. The second day of July, 1776, will be the most memorable epocha in the history of America. I am apt to believe that it will be celebrated by succeeding generations as the great anniversary festival. It ought to be commemorated as the day of deliverance, by solemn acts of devotion to God Almighty. It ought to be solemnized with pomp and parade, with shows, games, sports, guns, bells, bonfires, and illuminations, from one end of this continent to the other, from this time forward forevermore.

You will think me transported with enthusiasm, but I am not. I am well aware of the toil and blood and treasure that it will cost us to maintain this Declaration and support and defend these States. Yet, through all the gloom, I can see the rays of ravishing light and glory. I can see that the end is more than worth all the means. And that posterity will triumph in that day's transaction, even although we should rue it, which I trust in God we shall not.

3.7.2 Reading and Review Questions

1. In her March 31, 1776 letter, how does Abigail use Christian principles to advise John against perpetuating tyrannies against blacks and women? What threats against such tyrannies, especially on the part of women, does she promise to make?
2. In his April 14, 1776 letter, how does John answer Abigail's call for a more equal code of law? What political and philosophical (versus religious) language does he use? How, if at all, does he equate the tyranny of petticoats with those of wealthy slave-holders and land-owners? Why?
3. In his July 3, 1776 (Letter 1), what does John believe would have been obtained had the Declaration of Independence been signed seven months earlier? Why? To what does he attribute the delay? What benefits, if any, does he attribute to the delay? Why?
4. In their letters, what unconventional views of women's intellect do both John and Abigail express? Consider their exchanges on politics, society, family, and religion as well as their sharing of information with each other.
5. What import does John give to both the Declaration of Independence and its signing by all the colonies? How does he support it both concretely, through quotes, and abstractly, through predictions of the future and the use of religious tropes?

3.8 THOMAS PAINE

(1737–1826)

Thomas Paine was born in England and was apprenticed to his father, a maker of corsets. When he was nineteen, he ran away to sea but returned two years later to take up his apprenticeship work. He did not stay in that profession but instead became an excise officer, collecting taxes on goods. Through this work, he witnessed the misery of the poor and the limitations placed on lower-class working men. In 1773, he petitioned Parliament for a living wage on behalf of excise workers. For that reason, or perhaps for negligence in inspecting goods, Paine was dismissed from the excise. During these years, he also lost his first wife to early death and his second wife to separation.

Image 3.10 | Thomas Paine
Artist | Laurent Dabos
Source | Wikimedia Commons
License | Public Domain

In 1774, he overcame these setbacks when he arrived in America, carrying a letter from Benjamin Franklin who declared Paine to be "an ingenious worthy young man." He soon found a position in Philadelphia editing the *Pennsylvania Magazine*. Immersed in the news, events, and ideas of these years, Paine published the famous pamphlet *Common Sense* (1776). In stirring terms, he moved for a Declaration of Independence from England. He later claimed that his work helped America stand her ground against tyranny. It certainly was an influential work, selling 120,000 copies in two months. Once the Revolutionary War began, Paine enlisted and was appointed aide-de-camp to General Nathanael Greene (1742–1786). Although he saw action in New York, New Jersey, and Pennsylvania, Paine's greatest contribution to the war was *Crisis* (1776–1783), a series of sixteen pamphlets applauding America's actions and lifting soldiers' morale. The very first pamphlet, with the resonating statement that "These are the times that try men's souls," was read to George Washington's troops soon after their retreat across New Jersey.

After the war, Paine was lauded as a great patriot but failed to take advantage of the political offices given to him for his services to the American cause. He invented an iron bridge and, to obtain its patent, he returned to England in 1787. There, he published his *Rights of Man* (1791–1792), a work that advocated overthrowing the monarchy. He was indicted for treason and was forced to flee to France, which was deep in the throes of overthrowing its own monarchy. Hailed at first as one of their revolutionary number, Paine was later arrested and imprisoned when he protested the execution of King Louis XIV. Through the offices of James Monroe (1758–1831), then America's ambassador to France, Paine was released. He lived for a few months at Monroe's home where he completed *The Age of Reason* (1794–1795), a work that expressed his deistic views and that was vehemently criticized as atheist. In 1802, he returned to America, living out the remainder of his life in obscurity mainly at a farm in New Rochelle.

As a writer, he offered in plain language the shared wisdom of his day, helping others to see self-evident truths about human rights and the responsibilities of each person to themselves and to others.

3.8.1 Common Sense

(1776)

INTRODUCTION

PERHAPS the sentiments contained in the following pages, are not *yet* sufficiently fashionable to procure them general favor; a long habit of not thinking a thing *wrong*, gives it a superficial appearance of being *right*, and raises at first a formidable outcry in defense of custom. But the tumult soon subsides. Time makes more converts than reason.

As a long and violent abuse of power, is generally the Means of calling the right of it in question (and in Matters too which might never have been thought of, had not the Sufferers been aggravated into the inquiry) and as the King of England hath undertaken in his *own Right*, to support the Parliament in what he calls *Theirs*, and as the good people of this country are grievously oppressed by the combination, they have an undoubted privilege to inquire into the pretensions of both, and equally to reject the usurpation of either.

In the following sheets, the author hath studiously avoided every thing which is personal among ourselves. Compliments as well as censure to individuals make no part thereof. The wise, and the worthy, need not the triumph of a pamphlet; and those whose sentiments are injudicious, or unfriendly, will cease of themselves unless too much pains are bestowed upon their conversion.

The cause of America is in a great measure the cause of all mankind. Many circumstances hath, and will arise, which are not local, but universal, and through which the principles of all Lovers of Mankind are affected, and in the Event of which, their Affections are interested. The laying a Country desolate with Fire and Sword, declaring War against the natural rights of all Mankind, and extirpating the Defenders thereof from the Face of the Earth, is the Concern of every Man to whom Nature hath given the Power of feeling; of which Class, regardless of Party Censure, is the

AUTHOR

P.S. The Publication of this new Edition hath been delayed, with a View of taking notice (had it been necessary) of any Attempt to refute the Doctrine of

Independance: As no Answer hath yet appeared, it is now presumed that none will, the Time needful for getting such a Performance ready for the Public being considerably past.

Who the Author of this Production is, is wholly unnecessary to the Public, as the Object for Attention is the *Doctrine itself,* not the *Man*. Yet it may not be unnecessary to say, That he is unconnected with any Party, and under no sort of Influence public or private, but the influence of reason and principle.

Philadelphia, February 14, 1776

OF THE ORIGIN AND DESIGN OF GOVERNMENT IN GENERAL, WITH CONCISE REMARKS ON THE ENGLISH CONSTITUTION.

SOME writers have so confounded society with government, as to leave little or no distinction between them; whereas they are not only different, but have different origins. Society is produced by our wants, and government by our wickedness; the former promotes our happiness *positively* by uniting our affections, the latter *negatively* by restraining our vices. The one encourages intercourse, the other creates distinctions. The first a patron, the last a punisher.

Society in every state is a blessing, but government even in its best state is but a necessary evil; in its worst state an intolerable one; for when we suffer, or are exposed to the same miseries *by a government*, which we might expect in a country *without government*, our calamity is heightened by reflecting that we furnish the means by which we suffer. Government, like dress, is the badge of lost innocence; the palaces of kings are built on the ruins of the bowers of paradise. For were the impulses of conscience clear, uniform, and irresistibly obeyed, man would need no other lawgiver; but that not being the case, he finds it necessary to surrender up a part of his property to furnish means for the protection of the rest; and this he is induced to do by the same prudence which in every other case advises him out of two evils to choose the least. *Wherefore*, security being the true design and end of government, it unanswerably follows that whatever *form* thereof appears most likely to ensure it to us, with the least expence and greatest benefit, is preferable to all others.

In order to gain a clear and just idea of the design and end of government, let us suppose a small number of persons settled in some sequestered part of the earth, unconnected with the rest, they will then represent the first peopling of any country, or of the world. In this state of natural liberty, society will be their first thought. A thousand motives will excite them thereto, the strength of one man is so unequal to his wants, and his mind so unfitted for perpetual solitude, that he is soon obliged to seek assistance and relief of another, who in his turn requires the same. Four or five united would be able to raise a tolerable dwelling in the midst of a wilderness, but *one* man might labour out of the common period of life without accomplishing any thing; when he had felled his timber he could not remove it, nor erect it after it was removed; hunger in the mean time would urge him from his work, and every different want call him a different way. Disease, nay even misfortune would be death, for though neither might be mortal, yet either would disable him from living, and reduce him to a state in which he might rather be said to perish than to die.

Thus necessity, like a gravitating power, would soon form our newly arrived emigrants into society, the reciprocal blessings of which, would supersede, and render the obligations of law and government unnecessary while they remained perfectly just to each other; but as nothing but heaven is impregnable to vice, it will unavoidably happen, that in proportion as they surmount the first difficulties of emigration, which bound them together in a common cause, they will begin to relax in their duty and attachment to each other; and this remissness, will point out the necessity, of establishing some form of government to supply the defect of moral virtue.

Some convenient tree will afford them a State-House, under the branches of which, the whole colony may assemble to deliberate on public matters. It is more than probable that their first laws will have the title only of REGULATIONS, and be enforced by no other penalty than public disesteem. In this first parliament every man, by natural right, will have a seat.

But as the colony increases, the public concerns will increase likewise, and the distance at which the members may be separated, will render it too inconvenient for all of them to meet on every occasion as at first, when their number was small, their habitations near, and the public concerns few and trifling. This will point out the convenience of their consenting to leave the legislative part to be managed by a select number chosen from the whole body, who are supposed to have the same concerns at stake which those who appointed them, and who will act in the same manner as the whole body would act were they present. If the colony continue increasing, it will become necessary to augment the number of the representatives, and that the interest of every part of the colony may be attended to, it will be found best to divide the whole into convenient parts, each part sending its proper number; and that the *elected* might never form to themselves an interest separate from the *electors*, prudence will point out the propriety of having elections often; because as the *elected* might by that means return and mix again with the general body of the *electors* in a few months, their fidelity to the public will be secured by the prudent reflexion of not making a rod for themselves. And as this frequent interchange will establish a common interest with every part of the community, they will mutually and naturally support each other, and on this (not on the unmeaning name of king) depends the *strength of government, and the happiness of the governed.*

Here then is the origin and rise of government; namely, a mode rendered necessary by the inability of moral virtue to govern the world; here too is the design and end of government, viz. freedom and security. And however our eyes may be dazzled with show, or our ears deceived by sound; however prejudice may warp our wills, or interest darken our understanding, the simple voice of nature and of reason will say, it is right.

I draw my idea of the form of government from a principle in nature, which no art can overturn, viz. that the more simple any thing is, the less liable it is to be disordered; and the easier repaired when disordered; and with this maxim in view, I offer a few remarks on the so much boasted constitution of England. That it was noble for the dark and slavish times in which it was erected, is granted. When the world was over run with tyranny the least remove therefrom was a glorious rescue. But that it is imperfect, subject to convulsions, and incapable of producing what it seems to promise, is easily demonstrated.

Absolute governments (tho' the disgrace of human nature) have this advantage with them, that they are simple; if the people suffer, they know the head from which their suffering springs, know likewise the remedy, and are not bewildered by a variety of causes and cures. But the constitution of England is so exceedingly complex, that the nation may suffer for years together without being able to discover in which part the fault lies, some will say in one and some in another, and every political physician will advise a different medicine.

I know it is difficult to get over local or long standing prejudices, yet if we will suffer ourselves to examine the component parts of the English constitution, we shall find them to be the base remains of two ancient tyrannies, compounded with some new republican materials.

First.—The remains of monarchical tyranny in the person of the king.

Secondly.—The remains of aristocratical tyranny in the persons of the peers.

Thirdly.—The new republican materials, in the persons of the commons, on whose virtue depends the freedom of England.

The two first, by being hereditary, are independent of the people; wherefore in a *constitutional* sense they contribute nothing towards the freedom of the state.

To say that the constitution of England is a *union* of three powers reciprocally checking each other, is farcical, either the words have no meaning, or they are flat contradictions.

To say that the commons is a check upon the king, presupposes two things:

First.—That the king is not to be trusted without being looked after, or in other words, that a thirst for absolute power is the natural disease of monarchy.

Secondly.—That the commons, by being appointed for that purpose, are either wiser or more worthy of confidence than the crown.

But as the same constitution which gives the commons a power to check the king by withholding the supplies, gives afterwards the king a power to check the commons, by empowering him to reject their other bills; it again supposes that the king is wiser than those whom it has already supposed to be wiser than him. A mere absurdity!

There is something exceedingly ridiculous in the composition of monarchy; it first excludes a man from the means of information, yet empowers him to act in cases where the highest judgment is required. The state of a king shuts him from the world, yet the business of a king requires him to know it thoroughly; wherefore the different parts, by unnaturally opposing and destroying each other, prove the whole character to be absurd and useless.

Some writers have explained the English constitution thus; the king, say they, is one, the people another; the peers are an house in behalf of the king; the commons in behalf of the people; but this hath all the distinctions of a house divided against itself; and though the expressions be pleasantly arranged, yet when examined they appear idle and ambiguous; and it will always happen, that the nicest construction that words are capable of, when applied to the description of some thing which either cannot exist, or is too incomprehensible to be within the compass of description, will be words of sound only, and though they may amuse the ear, they cannot inform the mind, for this explanation includes a previous question, viz. *How came the king by a power which the people are afraid to trust, and always obliged to check*? Such a power could not be the gift of a wise people, neither can any power, which needs checking, be from God; yet the provision, which the constitution makes, supposes such a power to exist.

But the provision is unequal to the task; the means either cannot or will not accomplish the end, and the whole affair is a felo de se; for as the greater weight will always carry up the less, and as all the wheels of a machine are put in motion by one, it only remains to know which power in the constitution has the most weight, for that will govern; and though the others, or a part of them, may clog, or, as the phrase is, check the rapidity of its motion, yet so long as they cannot stop it, their endeavors will be ineffectual; the first moving power will at last have its way, and what it wants in speed is supplied by time.

That the crown is this overbearing part in the English constitution needs not be mentioned, and that it derives its whole consequence merely from being the giver of places and pensions is self-evident, wherefore, though we have been wise enough to shut and lock a door against absolute monarchy, we at the same time have been foolish enough to put the crown in possession of the key.

The prejudice of Englishmen, in favour of their own government by king, lords and commons, arises as much or more from national pride than reason. Individuals are undoubtedly safer in England than in some other countries, but the *will* of the king is as much the law of the land in Britain as in France, with this difference, that instead of proceeding directly from his mouth, it is handed to the people under the more formidable shape of an act of parliament. For the fate of Charles the first, hath only made kings more subtle—not more just.

Wherefore, laying aside all national pride and prejudice in favour of modes and forms, the plain truth is, that *it is wholly owing to the constitution of the people, and not to the constitution of the government* that the crown is not as oppressive in England as in Turkey.

An inquiry into the *constitutional errors* in the English form of government is at this time highly necessary, for as we are never in a proper condition of doing justice to others, while we continue under the influence of some leading partiality, so neither are we capable of doing it to ourselves while we remain fettered by any obstinate prejudice. And as a man, who is attached to a prostitute, is unfitted to choose or judge of a wife, so any prepossession in favour of a rotten constitution of government will disable us from discerning a good one.

OF MONARCHY AND HEREDITARY SUCCESSION.

MANKIND being originally equals in the order of creation, the equality could only be destroyed by some subsequent circumstance; the distinctions of rich, and poor, may in a great measure be accounted for, and that without having recourse to the harsh ill sounding names of oppression and avarice. Oppression is often the *consequence*, but seldom or never the *means* of riches; and though avarice will preserve a man from being necessitously poor, it generally makes him too timorous to be wealthy.

But there is another and greater distinction for which no truly natural or religious reason can be assigned, and that is, the distinction of men into KINGS and SUBJECTS. Male and female are the distinctions of nature, good and bad the distinctions of heaven; but how a race of men came into the world so exalted above the rest, and distinguished like some new species, is worth enquiring into, and whether they are the means of happiness or of misery to mankind.

In the early ages of the world, according to the scripture chronology, there were no kings; the consequence of which was there were no wars; it is the pride of kings which throw mankind into confusion. Holland without a king hath enjoyed more peace for this last century than any of the monarchial governments in Europe. Antiquity favors the same remark; for the quiet and rural lives of the first patriarchs hath a happy something in them, which vanishes away when we come to the history of Jewish royalty.

Government by kings was first introduced into the world by the Heathens, from whom the children of Israel copied the custom. It was the most prosperous invention the Devil ever set on foot for the promotion of idolatry. The Heathens paid divine honors to their deceased kings, and the christian world hath improved on the plan by doing the same to their living ones. How impious is the title of sacred majesty applied to a worm, who in the midst of his splendor is crumbling into dust!

As the exalting one man so greatly above the rest cannot be justified on the equal rights of nature, so neither can it be defended on the authority of scripture; for the will of the Almighty, as declared by Gideon and the prophet Samuel, expressly disapproves of government by kings. All anti-monarchical parts of scripture have been very smoothly glossed over in monarchical governments, but they undoubtedly merit the attention of countries which have their governments yet to form. "*Render unto Cæsar the things which are Cæsar's*" is the scripture doctrine of courts, yet it is no support of monarchical government, for the Jews at that time were without a king, and in a state of vassalage to the Romans.

Near three thousand years passed away from the Mosaic account of the creation, till the Jews under a national delusion requested a king. Till then their form of government (except in extraordinary cases, where the Almighty interposed) was a kind of republic administred by a judge and the elders of the tribes. Kings they had none, and it was held sinful to acknowledge any being under that title but the Lord of Hosts. And when a man seriously reflects on the idolatrous homage which is paid to the persons of Kings, he need not wonder, that the Almighty ever jealous of his honor, should disapprove of a form of government which so impiously invades the prerogative of heaven.

Monarchy is ranked in scripture as one of the sins of the Jews, for which a curse in reserve is denounced against them. The history of that transaction is worth attending to.

The children of Israel being oppressed by the Midianites, Gideon marched against them with a small army, and victory, thro' the divine interposition, decided in his favour. The Jews elate with success, and attributing it to the generalship of Gideon, proposed making him a king, saying, *Rule thou over us, thou and thy son and thy son's son.* Here was temptation in its fullest extent; not a kingdom only, but an hereditary one, but Gideon in the piety of his soul replied, *I will not rule over you, neither shall my son rule over you.* THE LORD SHALL RULE OVER YOU. Words need not be more explicit; Gideon doth not *decline* the honor, but denieth their right to give it; neither doth he compliment them with invented declarations of his thanks, but in the positive stile of a prophet charges them with disaffection to their proper Sovereign, the King of heaven.

About one hundred and thirty years after this, they fell again into the same error. The hankering which the Jews had for the idolatrous customs of the Heathens, is something exceedingly unaccountable; but so it was, that laying hold of the misconduct of Samuel's two sons, who were entrusted with some secular concerns, they came in an abrupt and clamorous manner to Samuel, saying, *Behold thou art old, and thy sons walk not in thy ways, now make us a king to judge us like all other nations.* And here we cannot but observe that their motives were bad, viz. that they might be *like* unto other nations, i.e. the Heathens, whereas their true glory laid in being as much *unlike* them as possible. *But the thing displeased Samuel when they said, Give us a king to judge us; and Samuel prayed unto the Lord, and the Lord said unto Samuel, Hearken unto the voice of the people in all that they say unto thee, for they have not rejected thee, but they have rejected me,* THAT I SHOULD NOT REIGN OVER THEM. *According to all the works which they have done since the day that I brought them up out of Egypt, even unto this day; wherewith they have forsaken me and served other Gods; so do they also unto thee. Now therefore hearken unto their voice, howbeit, protest solemnly unto them and shew them the manner of the king that shall reign over them, i.e.* not of any particular king, but the general manner of the kings of the earth, whom Israel was so eagerly copying after. And notwithstanding the great distance of time and difference of manners, the character is still in fashion. *And Samuel told all the words of the Lord unto the people, that asked of him a king. And he said, This shall be the manner of the king that shall reign over you; he will take your sons and appoint them for himself, for his chariots, and to be his horsemen, and some shall run before his chariots* (this description agrees with the present mode of impressing men) *and he will appoint him captains over thousands and captains over fifties, and will set them to ear his ground and to reap his harvest, and to make his instruments of war, and instruments of his chariots; and he will take your daughters to be confectionaries, and to be cooks and to be bakers* (this describes the expence and luxury as well as the oppression of kings) *and he will take your fields and your olive yards, even the best of them, and give them to his servants; and he will take the tenth of your feed, and of your vineyards, and give them to his officers and to his servants* (by which we see that bribery, corruption and favoritism are the standing vices of kings) *and he will take the tenth of your men servants, and your maid servants, and your goodliest young men and your asses, and put them to his work; and he will take the tenth of your sheep, and ye shall be his servants, and ye shall cry out in that day because of your king which ye shall have chosen,* AND THE LORD WILL NOT HEAR YOU IN THAT DAY. This accounts for the continuation of monarchy; neither do the characters of the few good kings which have lived since, either sanctify the title, or blot out the sinfulness of the origin; the high encomium given of David takes no notice of him *officially as a king*, but only as a *man* after God's own heart. *Nevertheless the People refused to obey the voice of Samuel, and they said, Nay, but we will have a king over us, that we may be like all the nations, and that our king may judge us, and go out before us, and fight our battles.* Samuel continued to reason with them, but to no purpose; he set before them their ingratitude, but all would not avail; and seeing them fully bent on their folly, he cried out, *I will call unto the Lord, and he shall send thunder and rain* (which then was a punishment, being in the time of wheat harvest) *that ye may perceive and see that your wickedness is great which ye have done in the sight of the Lord,* IN ASKING YOU A KING. *So Samuel called unto the Lord, and the Lord sent thunder and rain that day, and all the people greatly feared the Lord and Samuel. And all the people said unto Samuel, Pray for thy servants unto the Lord thy God that we die not, for* WE HAVE ADDED UNTO OUR SINS THIS EVIL, TO ASK A KING. These portions of scripture are direct and positive. They admit of no equivocal construction. That the Almighty hath here entered his protest against monarchical government is true, or the scripture is false. And a man hath good reason to believe that there is as much of king-craft, as priest-craft, in withholding the scripture from the public in Popish countries. For monarchy in every instance is the Popery of government.

To the evil of monarchy we have added that of hereditary succession; and as the first is a degradation and lessening of ourselves, so the second, claimed as a matter of right, is an insult and an imposition on posterity. For all men being originally equals, no *one* by *birth* could have a right to set up his own family in perpetual preference to all others for ever, and though himself might deserve *some* decent degree of honors of his cotemporaries, yet his descendants might be far too unworthy to inherit them. One of the strongest *natural* proofs of the folly of hereditary right in kings, is, that nature disapproves it, otherwise she would not so frequently turn it into ridicule by giving mankind an *ass for a lion*.

Secondly, as no man at first could possess any other public honors than were bestowed upon him, so the givers of those honors could have no power to give away the right of posterity, and though they might say "We choose you for *our* head," they could not, without manifest injustice to their children, say "that your children and your children's children shall reign over *ours* for ever." Because such an unwise, unjust, unnatural compact might (perhaps) in the next succession put them under the government of a rogue or a fool. Most wise men, in their private sentiments, have ever treated hereditary right with contempt; yet it is one of those evils, which when once established is not easily removed; many submit from fear, others from superstition, and the more powerful part shares with the king the plunder of the rest.

This is supposing the present race of kings in the world to have had an honorable origin; whereas it is more than probable, that could we take off the dark covering of antiquity, and trace them to their first rise, that we should find the first of them nothing better than the principal ruffian of some restless gang, whose savage manners or pre-eminence in subtility obtained him the title of chief among plunderers; and who by increasing in power, and extending his depredations, overawed the quiet and defenceless to purchase their safety by frequent contributions. Yet his electors could have no idea of giving hereditary right to his descendants, because such a perpetual exclusion of themselves was incompatible with the free and unrestrained principles they professed to live by. Wherefore, hereditary succession in the early ages of monarchy could not take place as a matter of claim, but as something casual or complimental; but as few or no records were extant in those days, and traditional history stuffed with fables, it was very easy, after the lapse of a few generations, to trump up some superstitious tale, conveniently timed, Mahomet like, to cram hereditary right down the throats of the vulgar. Perhaps the disorders which threatened, or seemed to threaten, on the decease of a leader and the choice of a new one (for elections among ruffians could not be very orderly) induced many at first to favor hereditary pretensions; by which means it happened, as it hath happened since, that what at first was submitted to as a convenience, was afterwards claimed as a right.

England, since the conquest, hath known some few good monarchs, but groaned beneath a much larger number of bad ones; yet no man in his senses can say that their claim under William the Conqueror is a very honorable one. A French bastard landing with an armed banditti, and establishing himself king of England against the consent of the natives, is in plain terms a very paltry rascally original.—It certainly hath no divinity in it. However, it is needless to spend much time in exposing the folly of hereditary right; if there are any so weak as to believe it, let them promiscuously worship the ass and lion, and welcome. I shall neither copy their humility, nor disturb their devotion.

Yet I should be glad to ask how they suppose kings came at first? The question admits but of three answers, viz. either by lot, by election, or by usurpation. If the first king was taken by lot, it establishes a precedent for the next, which excludes hereditary succession. Saul was by lot, yet the succession was not hereditary, neither does it appear from that transaction there was any intention it ever should. If the first king of any country was by election, that likewise establishes a precedent for the next; for to say, that the *right* of all future generations is taken away, by the act of the first electors, in their choice not only of a king, but of a family of kings for ever, hath no parrallel in or out of scripture but the doctrine of original sin, which supposes the free will of all men lost in Adam; and from such comparison, and it will admit of no other, hereditary succession can derive no glory. For as in Adam all sinned, and as in the first electors all men obeyed; as in the one all mankind were subjected to Satan, and in the other to Sovereignty; as our innocence was lost in the first, and our authority in the last; and as both disable us from reassuming some former state and privilege, it unanswerably follows that original sin and hereditary succession are parellels. Dishonorable rank! Inglorious connexion! Yet the most subtile sophist cannot produce a juster simile.

As to usurpation, no man will be so hardy as to defend it; and that William the Conqueror was an usurper is a fact not to be contradicted. The plain truth is, that the antiquity of English monarchy will not bear looking into.

But it is not so much the absurdity as the evil of hereditary succession which concerns mankind. Did it ensure a race of good and wise men it would have the seal of divine authority, but as it opens a door to the *foolish*, the *wicked*, and the *improper*, it hath in it the nature of oppression. Men who look upon themselves born to reign, and others to obey, soon grow insolent; selected from the rest of mankind their minds are early poisoned by importance; and the world they act in differs so materially from the world at large, that they have but little opportunity of knowing its true interests, and when they succeed to the government are frequently the most ignorant and unfit of any throughout the dominions.

Another evil which attends hereditary succession is, that the throne is subject to be possessed by a minor at any age; all which time the regency, acting under the cover of a king, have every opportunity and inducement to betray their trust. The same national misfortune happens, when a king worn out with age and infirmity, enters the last stage of human weakness. In both these cases the public becomes a prey to every miscreant, who can tamper successfully with the follies either of age or infancy.

The most plausible plea, which hath ever been offered in favour of hereditary succession, is, that it preserves a nation from civil wars; and were this true, it would be weighty; whereas, it is the most barefaced falsity ever imposed upon mankind. The whole history of England disowns the fact. Thirty kings and two minors have reigned in that distracted kingdom since the conquest, in which time there have been (including the Revolution) no less than eight civil wars and nineteen rebellions. Wherefore instead of making for peace, it makes against it, and destroys the very foundation it seems to stand on.

The contest for monarchy and succession, between the houses of York and Lancaster, laid England in a scene of blood for many years. Twelve pitched battles, besides skirmishes and sieges, were fought between Henry and Edward. Twice was Henry prisoner to Edward, who in his turn was prisoner to Henry. And so uncertain is the fate of war and the temper of a nation, when nothing but personal matters are the ground of a quarrel, that Henry was taken in triumph from a prison to a palace, and Edward obliged to fly from a palace to a foreign land; yet, as sudden transitions of temper are seldom lasting, Henry in his turn was driven from the throne, and Edward recalled to succeed him. The parliament always following the strongest side.

This contest began in the reign of Henry the Sixth, and was not entirely extinguished till Henry the Seventh, in whom the families were united. Including a period of 67 years, viz. from 1422 to 1489.

In short, monarchy and succession have laid (not this or that kingdom only) but the world in blood and ashes. 'Tis a form of government which the word of God bears testimony against, and blood will attend it.

If we inquire into the business of a king, we shall find that in some countries they have none; and after sauntering away their lives without pleasure to themselves or advantage to the nation, withdraw from the scene, and leave their successors to tread the same idle round. In absolute monarchies the whole weight of business, civil and military, lies on the king; the children of Israel in their request for a king, urged this plea "that he may judge us, and go out before us and fight our battles." But in countries where he is neither a judge nor a general, as in England, a man would be puzzled to know what is his business.

The nearer any government approaches to a republic the less business there is for a king. It is somewhat difficult to find a proper name for the government of England. Sir William Meredith calls it a republic; but in its present state it is unworthy of the name, because the corrupt influence of the crown, by having all the places in its disposal, hath so effectually swallowed up the power, and eaten out the virtue of the house of commons (the republican part in the constitution) that the government of England is nearly as monarchical as that of France or Spain. Men fall out with names without understanding them. For it is the republican and not the monarchical part of the constitution of England which Englishmen glory in, viz. the liberty of choosing a house of commons from out of their own body—and it is easy to see that when republican virtue fails, slavery ensues. Why is the constitution of England sickly, but because monarchy hath poisoned the republic, the crown hath engrossed the commons?

In England a king hath little more to do than to make war and give away places; which in plain terms, is to impoverish the nation and set it together by the ears.

A pretty business indeed for a man to be allowed eight hundred thousand sterling a year for, and worshipped into the bargain! Of more worth is one honest man to society and in the sight of God, than all the crowned ruffians that ever lived.

THOUGHTS ON THE PRESENT STATE OF AMERICAN AFFAIRS.

In the following pages I offer nothing more than simple facts, plain arguments, and common sense; and have no other preliminaries to settle with the reader, than that he will divest himself of prejudice and prepossession, and suffer his reason and his feelings to determine for themselves; that he will put on, or rather that he will not put off, the true character of a man, and generously enlarge his views beyond the present day.

Volumes have been written on the subject of the struggle between England and America. Men of all ranks have embarked in the controversy, from different motives, and with various designs; but all have been ineffectual, and the period of debate is closed. Arms, as the last resource, decide the contest; the appeal was the choice of the king, and the continent hath accepted the challenge.

It hath been reported of the late Mr. Pelham (who tho' an able minister was not without his faults) that on his being attacked in the house of commons, on the score, that his measures were only of a temporary kind, replied "*they will last my time.*" Should a thought so fatal and unmanly possess the colonies in the present contest, the name of ancestors will be remembered by future generations with detestation.

The sun never shined on a cause of greater worth. 'Tis not the affair of a city, a country, a province, or a kingdom, but of a continent—of at least one eighth part of the habitable globe. 'Tis not the concern of a day, a year, or an age; posterity are virtually involved in the contest, and will be more or less affected, even to the end of time, by the proceedings now. Now is the seed time of continental union, faith and honor. The least fracture now will be like a name engraved with the point of a pin on the tender rind of a young oak; the wound will enlarge with the tree, and posterity read it in full grown characters.

By referring the matter from argument to arms, a new æra for politics is struck; a new method of thinking hath arisen. All plans, proposals, &c. prior to the nineteenth of April, i.e. to the commencement of hostilities, are like the almanacks of the last year; which, though proper then, are superseded and useless now. Whatever was advanced by the advocates on either side of the question then, terminated in one and the same point, viz. a union with Great-Britain; the only difference between the parties was the method of effecting it; the one proposing force, the other friendship; but it hath so far happened that the first hath failed, and the second hath withdrawn her influence.

As much hath been said of the advantages of reconciliation, which, like an agreeable dream, hath passed away and left us as we were, it is but right, that we should examine the contrary side of the argument, and inquire into some of the many material injuries which these colonies sustain, and always will sustain, by being connected with, and dependant on Great-Britain. To examine that connexion and dependance, on the principles of nature and common sense, to see what we have to trust to, if separated, and what we are to expect, if dependant.

I have heard it asserted by some, that as America hath flourished under her former connexion with Great-Britain, that the same connexion is necessary towards her future happiness, and will always have the same effect. Nothing can be more fallacious than this kind of argument. We may as well assert that because a child has thrived upon milk, that it is never to have meat, or that the first twenty years of our lives is to become a precedent for the next twenty. But even this is admitting more than is true, for I answer roundly, that America would have flourished as much, and probably much more, had no European power had any thing to do with her. The commerce, by which she hath enriched herself are the necessaries of life, and will always have a market while eating is the custom of Europe.

But she has protected us, say some. That she has engrossed us is true, and defended the continent at our expence as well as her own is admitted, and she would have defended Turkey from the same motive, viz. the sake of trade and dominion.

Alas, we have been long led away by ancient prejudices, and made large sacrifices to superstition. We have boasted the protection of Great-Britain, without considering, that her motive was *interest* not *attachment*; that she did not protect us from *our enemies* on *our account*, but from *her enemies* on *her own account*, from those who had no quarrel with us on any *other account*, and who will always be our enemies on the *same account*. Let Britain wave her pretensions to the continent, or the continent throw off the dependance, and we should be at peace with France and Spain were they at war with Britain. The miseries of Hanover last war ought to warn us against connexions.

It has lately been asserted in parliament, that the colonies have no relation to each other but through the parent country, i.e. that Pennsylvania and the Jerseys, and so on for the rest, are sister colonies by the way of England; this is certainly a very round-about way of proving relationship, but it is the nearest and only true way of proving enemyship, if I may so call it. France and Spain never were, nor perhaps ever will be our enemies as *Americans*, but as our being the *subjects of Great-Britain*.

But Britain is the parent country, say some. Then the more shame upon her conduct. Even brutes do not devour their young, nor savages make war upon their families; wherefore the assertion, if true, turns to her reproach; but it happens not to be true, or only partly so, and the phrase *parent* or *mother country* hath been jesuitically adopted by the king and his parasites, with a low papistical design of gaining an unfair bias on the credulous weakness of our minds. Europe, and not England, is the parent country of America. This new world hath been the asylum for the persecuted lovers of civil and religious liberty from *every part* of Europe. Hither have they fled, not from the tender embraces of the mother, but from the cruelty of the monster; and it is so far true of England, that the same tyranny which drove the first emigrants from home, pursues their descendants still.

In this extensive quarter of the globe, we forget the narrow limits of three hundred and sixty miles (the extent of England) and carry our friendship on a larger scale; we claim brotherhood with every European christian, and triumph in the generosity of the sentiment.

It is pleasant to observe by what regular gradations we surmount the force of local prejudice, as we enlarge our acquaintance with the world. A man born in any town in England divided into parishes, will naturally associate most with his fellow parishioners (because their interests in many cases will be common) and distinguish him by the name of *neighbour*; if he meet him but a few miles from home, he drops the narrow idea of a street, and salutes him by the name of *townsman*; if he travel out of the county, and meet him in any other, he forgets the minor divisions of street and town, and calls him *countryman*, i.e. *county-man*; but if in their foreign excursions they should associate in France or any other part of *Europe*, their local remembrance would be enlarged into that of *Englishmen*. And by a just parity of reasoning, all Europeans meeting in America, or any other quarter of the globe, are *countrymen*; for England, Holland, Germany, or Sweden, when compared with the whole, stand in the same places on the larger scale, which the divisions of street, town, and county do on the smaller ones; distinctions too limited for continental minds. Not one third of the inhabitants, even of this province, are of English descent. Wherefore I reprobate the phrase of parent or mother country applied to England only, as being false, selfish, narrow and ungenerous.

But admitting, that we were all of English descent, what does it amount to? Nothing. Britain, being now an open enemy, extinguishes every other name and title: And to say that reconciliation is our duty, is truly farcical. The first king of England, of the present line (William the Conqueror) was a Frenchman, and half the Peers of England are descendants from the same country; therefore, by the same method of reasoning, England ought to be governed by France.

Much hath been said of the united strength of Britain and the colonies, that in conjunction they might bid defiance to the world. But this is mere presumption; the fate of war is uncertain, neither do the expressions mean any thing; for this continent would never suffer itself to be drained of inhabitants, to support the British arms in either Asia, Africa, or Europe.

Besides what have we to do with setting the world at defiance? Our plan is commerce, and that, well attended to, will secure us the peace and friendship of all Europe; because, it is the interest of all Europe to have America a *free port*. Her trade will always be a protection, and her barrenness of gold and silver secure her from invaders.

I challenge the warmest advocate for reconciliation, to shew, a single advantage that this continent can reap, by being connected with Great Britain. I repeat the challenge, not a single advantage is derived. Our corn will fetch its price in any market in Europe, and our imported goods must be paid for buy them where we will.

But the injuries and disadvantages we sustain by that connection, are without number; and our duty to mankind at large, as well as to ourselves, instruct us to renounce the alliance: Because, any submission to, or dependance on Great-Britain, tends directly to involve this continent in European wars and quarrels;

and sets us at variance with nations, who would otherwise seek our friendship, and against whom, we have neither anger nor complaint. As Europe is our market for trade, we ought to form no partial connection with any part of it. It is the true interest of America to steer clear of European contentions, which she never can do, while by her dependence on Britain, she is made the make-weight in the scale of British politics.

Europe is too thickly planted with kingdoms to be long at peace, and whenever a war breaks out between England and any foreign power, the trade of America goes to ruin, *because of her connection with Britain*. The next war may not turn out like the last, and should it not, the advocates for reconciliation now will be wishing for separation then, because, neutrality in that case, would be a safer convoy than a man of war. Every thing that is right or natural pleads for separation. The blood of the slain, the weeping voice of nature cries, 'Tis time to part. Even the distance at which the Almighty hath placed England and America, is a strong and natural proof, that the authority of the one, over the other, was never the design of Heaven. The time likewise at which the continent was discovered, adds weight to the argument, and the manner in which it was peopled encreases the force of it. The reformation was preceded by the discovery of America, as if the Almighty graciously meant to open a sanctuary to the persecuted in future years, when home should afford neither friendship nor safety.

The authority of Great-Britain over this continent, is a form of government, which sooner or later must have an end: And a serious mind can draw no true pleasure by looking forward, under the painful and positive conviction, that what he calls "the present constitution" is merely temporary. As parents, we can have no joy, knowing that *this government* is not sufficiently lasting to ensure any thing which we may bequeath to posterity: And by a plain method of argument, as we are running the next generation into debt, we ought to do the work of it, otherwise we use them meanly and pitifully. In order to discover the line of our duty rightly, we should take our children in our hand, and fix our station a few years farther into life; that eminence will present a prospect, which a few present fears and prejudices conceal from our sight.

Though I would carefully avoid giving unnecessary offence, yet I am inclined to believe, that all those who espouse the doctrine of reconciliation, may be included within the following descriptions. Interested men, who are not to be trusted; weak men, who *cannot* see; prejudiced men, who *will not* see; and a certain set of moderate men, who think better of the European world than it deserves; and this last class, by an ill-judged deliberation, will be the cause of more calamities to this continent, than all the other three.

It is the good fortune of many to live distant from the scene of sorrow; the evil is not sufficient brought to *their* doors to make *them* feel the precariousness with which all American property is possessed. But let our imaginations transport us for a few moments to Boston, that seat of wretchedness will teach us wisdom, and instruct us for ever to renounce a power in whom we can have no trust. The inhabitants of that unfortunate city, who but a few months ago were in ease and affluence, have now, no other alternative than to stay and starve, or turn out to beg. Endangered by the fire of their friends if they continue within the city, and plundered by the soldiery if they leave it. In their present condition they are prisoners without the hope of redemption, and in a general attack for their relief, they would be exposed to the fury of both armies.

Men of passive tempers look somewhat lightly over the offences of Britain, and, still hoping for the best, are apt to call out, "*Come, come, we shall be friends again, for all this.*" But examine the passions and feelings of mankind, Bring the doctrine of reconciliation to the touchstone of nature, and then tell me, whether you can hereafter love, honour, and faithfully serve the power that hath carried fire and sword into your land? If you cannot do all these, then are you only deceiving yourselves, and by your delay bringing ruin upon posterity. Your future connection with Britain, whom you can neither love nor honour, will be forced and unnatural, and being formed only on the plan of present convenience, will in a little time fall into a relapse more wretched than the first. But if you say, you can still pass the violations over, then I ask, Hath your house been burnt? Hath your property been destroyed before your face? Are your wife and children destitute of a bed to lie on, or bread to live on? Have you lost a parent or a child by their hands, and yourself the ruined and wretched survivor? If you have not, then are you not a judge of those who have. But if you have, and still can shake hands with the murderers, then are you unworthy of the name of husband, father, friend, or lover, and whatever may be your rank or title in life, you have the heart of a coward, and the spirit of a sycophant.

This is not inflaming or exaggerating matters, but trying them by those feelings and affections which nature justifies, and without which, we should be incapable of discharging the social duties of life, or enjoying the felicities of it. I mean not to exhibit horror for the purpose of provoking revenge, but to awaken us from fatal and unmanly slumbers, that we may pursue determinately some fixed object. It is not in the power of Britain or of Europe to conquer America, if she do not conquer herself by *delay* and *timidity*. The present winter is worth an age if rightly employed, but if lost or neglected, the whole continent will partake of the misfortune; and there is no punishment which that man will not deserve, be he who, or what, or where he will, that may be the means of sacrificing a season so precious and useful.

It is repugnant to reason, to the universal order of things to all examples from former ages, to suppose, that this continent can longer remain subject to any external power. The most sanguine in Britain does not think so. The utmost stretch of human wisdom cannot, at this time, compass a plan short of separation, which can promise the continent even a year's security. Reconciliation is *now* a fallacious dream. Nature hath deserted the connexion, and Art cannot supply her place. For, as Milton wisely expresses, "never can true reconcilement grow where wounds of deadly hate have pierced so deep."

Every quiet method for peace hath been ineffectual. Our prayers have been rejected with disdain; and only tended to convince us, that nothing flatters vanity, or confirms obstinacy in Kings more than repeated petitioning—and nothing hath contributed more than that very measure to make the Kings of Europe absolute: Witness Denmark and Sweden. Wherefore, since nothing but blows will do, for God's sake, let us come to a final separation, and not leave the next generation to be cutting throats, under the violated unmeaning names of parent and child.

To say, they will never attempt it again is idle and visionary, we thought so at the repeal of the stamp-act, yet a year or two undeceived us; as well may we suppose that nations, which have been once defeated, will never renew the quarrel.

As to government matters, it is not in the power of Britain to do this continent justice: The business of it will soon be too weighty, and intricate, to be managed with any tolerable degree of convenience, by a power, so distant from us, and so very ignorant of us; for if they cannot conquer us, they cannot govern us. To be always running three or four thousand miles with a tale or a petition, waiting four or five months for an answer, which when obtained requires five or six more to explain it in, will in a few years be looked upon as folly and childishness—There was a time when it was proper, and there is a proper time for it to cease.

Small islands not capable of protecting themselves, are the proper objects for kingdoms to take under their care; but there is something very absurd, in supposing a continent to be perpetually governed by an island. In no instance hath nature made the satellite larger than its primary planet, and as England and America, with respect to each other, reverses the common order of nature, it is evident they belong to different systems: England to Europe, America to itself.

I am not induced by motives of pride, party, or resentment to espouse the doctrine of separation and independance; I am clearly, positively, and conscientiously persuaded that it is the true interest of this continent to be so; that every thing short of *that* is mere patchwork, that it can afford no lasting felicity,—that it is leaving the sword to our children, and shrinking back at a time, when, a little more, a little farther, would have rendered this continent the glory of the earth.

As Britain hath not manifested the least inclination towards a compromise, we may be assured that no terms can be obtained worthy the acceptance of the continent, or any ways equal to the expence of blood and treasure we have been already put to.

The object, contended for, ought always to bear some just proportion to the expence. The removal of North, or the whole detestable junto, is a matter unworthy the millions we have expended. A temporary stoppage of trade, was an inconvenience, which would have sufficiently ballanced the repeal of all the acts complained of, had such repeals been obtained; but if the whole continent must take up arms, if every man must be a soldier, it is scarcely worth our while to fight against a contemptible ministry only. Dearly, dearly, do we pay for the repeal of the acts, if that is all we fight for; for in a just estimation, it is as great a folly to pay a Bunker-hill price for law, as for land. As I have always considered the independancy of this continent, as an event, which sooner or later must arrive, so from the late rapid progress of the continent to maturity, the event could not be far off. Wherefore, on the breaking out of hostilities, it was not worth the while to have disputed a matter, which time would have finally redressed, unless we meant to be in earnest; otherwise, it is like wasting an estate on a suit at law, to regulate the trespasses of a tenant, whose lease is just expiring. No man was a warmer wisher for reconciliation than myself, before the fatal nineteenth of April 1775, but the moment the event of that day was made known, I rejected the hardened, sullen tempered Pharaoh of England for ever; and disdain the wretch, that with the pretended title of FATHER OF HIS PEOPLE can unfeelingly hear of their slaughter, and composedly sleep with their blood upon his soul.

But admitting that matters were now made up, what would be the event? I answer, the ruin of the continent. And that for several reasons.

First. The powers of governing still remaining in the hands of the king, he will have a negative over the whole legislation of this continent. And as he hath shewn himself such an inveterate enemy to liberty, and discovered such a thirst for arbitrary power; is he, or is he not, a proper man to say to these colonies, "*You shall make no laws but what I please.*" And is there any inhabitant in America so ignorant, as not to know, that according to what is called the *present constitution*, that this continent can make no laws but what the king gives leave to; and is there any man so unwise, as not to see, that (considering what has happened) he will suffer no law to be made here, but such as suit his purpose. We may be as effectually enslaved by the want of laws in America, as by submitting to laws made for us in England. After matters are made up (as it is called) can there be any doubt, but the whole power of the crown will be exerted, to keep this continent as low and humble as possible? Instead of going forward we shall go backward, or be perpetually quarrelling or ridiculously petitioning.—We are already greater than the king wishes us to be, and will he not hereafter endeavour to make us less? To bring the matter to one point. Is the power who is jealous of our prosperity, a proper power to govern us? Whoever says *No* to this question is an *independant*, for independancy means no more, than, whether we shall make our own laws, or whether the king, the greatest enemy this continent hath, or can have, shall tell us "*there shall be no laws but such as I like.*"

But the king you will say has a negative in England; the people there can make no laws without his consent. In point of right and good order, there is something very ridiculous, that a youth of twenty-one (which hath often happened) shall say to several millions of people, older and wiser than himself, I forbid this or that act of yours to be law. But in this place I decline this sort of reply, though I will never cease to expose the absurdity of it, and only answer, that England being the King's residence, and America not so, makes quite another case. The king's negative *here* is ten times more dangerous and fatal than it can be in England, for *there* he will scarcely refuse his consent to a bill for putting England into as strong a state of defence as possible, and in America he would never suffer such a bill to be passed.

America is only a secondary object in the system of British politics, England consults the good of *this* country, no farther than it answers her *own* purpose. Wherefore, her own interest leads her to suppress the growth of *ours* in every case which doth not promote her advantage, or in the least interferes with it. A pretty state we should soon be in under such a second-hand government, considering what has happened! Men do not change from enemies to friends by the alteration of a name: And in order to shew that reconciliation *now* is a dangerous doctrine, I affirm, *that it would be policy in the king at this time, to repeal the acts for the sake of reinstating himself in the government of the provinces*; in order, that HE MAY ACCOMPLISH BY CRAFT AND SUBTILTY, IN THE LONG RUN, WHAT HE CANNOT DO BY FORCE AND VIOLENCE IN THE SHORT ONE. Reconciliation and ruin are nearly related.

Secondly. That as even the best terms, which we can expect to obtain, can amount to no more than a temporary expedient, or a kind of government by guardianship, which can last no longer than till the colonies come of age, so the general face and state of things, in the interim, will be unsettled and unpromising. Emigrants of property will not choose to come to a country whose form of government hangs but by a thread, and who is every day tottering on the brink of commotion and disturbance; and numbers of the present inhabitants would lay hold of the interval, to dispense of their effects, and quit the continent.

But the most powerful of all arguments, is, that nothing but independance, i.e. a continental form of government, can keep the peace of the continent and preserve it inviolate from civil wars. I dread the event of a reconciliation with Britain now, as it is more than probable, that it will be followed by a revolt somewhere or other, the consequences of which may be far more fatal than all the malice of Britain.

Thousands are already ruined by British barbarity; (thousands more will probably suffer the same fate) Those men have other feelings than us who have nothing suffered. *All* they now possess is liberty, what they before enjoyed is sacrificed to its service, and having nothing more to lose, they disdain submission. Besides, the general temper of the colonies, towards a British government, will be like that of a youth, who is nearly out of his time; they will care very little about her. And a government which cannot preserve the peace, is no government at all, and in that case we pay our money for nothing; and pray what is it that Britain can do, whose power will be wholly on paper, should a civil tumult break out the very day after reconciliation? I have heard some men say, many of whom I believe spoke without thinking, that they dreaded an independance, fearing that it would produce civil wars. It is but seldom that our first thoughts are truly correct, and that is the case here; for there are ten times more to dread from a patched up connexion than from independance. I make the sufferers case my own, and I protest, that were I driven from house and home, my property destroyed, and my circumstances ruined, that as man, sensible of injuries, I could never relish the doctrine of reconciliation, or consider myself bound thereby.

The colonies have manifested such a spirit of good order and obedience to continental government, as is sufficient to make every reasonable person easy and happy on that head. No man can assign the least pretence for his fears, on any other grounds, than such as are truly childish and ridiculous, viz. that one colony will be striving for superiority over another.

Where there are no distinctions there can be no superiority, perfect equality affords no temptation. The republics of Europe are all (and we may say always) in peace. Holland and Swisserland are without wars, foreign or domestic: Monarchical governments, it is true, are never long at rest; the crown itself is a temptation to enterprizing ruffians at *home*; and that degree of pride and insolence ever attendant on regal authority, swells into a rupture with foreign powers, in instances, where a republican government, by being formed on more natural principles, would negociate the mistake.

If there is any true cause of fear respecting independance, it is because no plan is yet laid down. Men do not see their way out—Wherefore, as an opening into that business, I offer the following hints; at the same time modestly affirming, that I have no other opinion of them myself, than that they may be the means of giving rise to something better. Could the straggling thoughts of individuals be collected, they would frequently form materials for wise and able men to improve into useful matter.

Let the assemblies be annual, with a President only. The representation more equal. Their business wholly domestic, and subject to the authority of a Continental Congress.

Let each colony be divided into six, eight, or ten, convenient districts, each district to send a proper number of delegates to Congress, so that each colony send at least thirty. The whole number in Congress will be at least 390. Each Congress to sit and to choose a president by the following method. When the delegates are met, let a colony be taken from the whole thirteen colonies by lot, after which, let the whole Congress choose (by ballot) a president from out of the delegates of *that* province. In the next Congress, let a colony be taken by lot from twelve only, omitting that colony from which the president was taken in the former Congress, and so proceeding on till the whole thirteen shall have had their proper rotation. And in order that nothing may pass into a law but what is satisfactorily just, not less than three fifths of the Congress to be called a majority.—He that will promote discord, under a government so equally formed as this, would have joined Lucifer in his revolt.

But as there is a peculiar delicacy, from whom, or in what manner, this business must first arise, and as it seems most agreeable and consistent that it should come from some intermediate body between the governed and the governors, that is, between the Congress and the people, let a CONTINENTAL CONFERENCE be held, in the following manner, and for the following purpose.

A committee of twenty-six members of Congress, viz. two for each colony. Two members from each House of Assembly, or Provincial Convention; and five representatives of the people at large, to be chosen in the capital city or town of each province, for, and in behalf of the whole province, by as many qualified voters as shall think proper to attend from all parts of the province for that purpose; or, if more convenient, the representatives may be chosen in two or three of the most populous parts thereof. In this conference, thus assembled, will be united, the two grand principles of business, *knowledge* and *power*. The members of Congress, Assemblies, or Conventions, by having had experience in national concerns, will be able and useful counsellors, and the whole, being impowered by the people, will have a truly legal authority.

The conferring members being met, let their business be to frame a CONTINENTAL CHARTER, or Charter of the United Colonies; (answering to what is called the Magna Charta of England) fixing the number and manner of choosing members of Congress, members of Assembly, with their date of sitting, and drawing the line of business and jurisdiction between them: (Always remembering, that our strength is continental, not provincial:) Securing freedom and property to all men, and above all things, the free exercise of religion, according to the dictates of conscience; with such other matter as is necessary for a charter to contain. Immediately after which, the said Conference to dissolve, and the bodies which shall be chosen comformable to the said charter, to be the legislators and governors of this continent for the time being: Whose peace and happiness, may God preserve, Amen.

Should any body of men be hereafter delegated for this or some similar purpose, I offer them the following extracts from that wise observer on governments *Dragonetti*. "The science" says he "of the politician consists in fixing the true point of happiness and freedom. Those men would deserve the gratitude of ages, who should discover a mode of government that contained the greatest sum of individual happiness, with the least national expense.

Dragonetti on virtue and rewards."

But where says some is the King of America? I'll tell you Friend, he reigns above, and doth not make havoc of mankind like the Royal Brute of Britain. Yet that we may not appear to be defective even in earthly honors, let a day be solemnly set apart for proclaiming the charter; let it be brought forth placed on the divine law, the word of God; let a crown be placed thereon, by which the world may know, that so far as we approve of monarchy, that in America THE LAW IS KING. For as in absolute governments the King is law, so in free countries the law ought to be King; and there *ought* to be no other. But lest any ill use should afterwards arise, let the crown at the conclusion of the ceremony be demolished, and scattered among the people whose right it is.

A government of our own is our natural right: And when a man seriously reflects on the precariousness of human affairs, he will become convinced, that it is infinitely wiser and safer, to form a constitution of our own in a cool deliberate manner, while we have it in our power, than to trust such an interesting event to time and chance. If we omit it now, some Massanello may hereafter arise, who laying hold of popular disquietudes, may collect together the desperate and the discontented, and by assuming to themselves the powers of government, may sweep away the liberties of the continent like a deluge. Should the government of America return again into the hands of Britain, the tottering situation of things, will be a temptation for some desperate adventurer to try his fortune; and in such a case, what relief can Britain give? Ere she could hear the news, the fatal business might be done; and ourselves suffering like the wretched Britons under the oppression of the Conqueror. Ye that oppose independance now, ye know not what ye do; ye are opening a door to eternal tyranny, by keeping vacant the seat of government. There are thousands, and tens of thousands, who would think it glorious to expel from the continent, that barbarous and hellish power, which hath stirred up the Indians and Negroes to destroy us, the cruelty hath a double guilt, it is dealing brutally by us, and treacherously by them.

To talk of friendship with those in whom our reason forbids us to have faith, and our affections wounded through a thousand pores instruct us to detest, is madness and folly. Every day wears out the little remains of kindred between us and them, and can there be any reason to hope, that as the relationship expires, the affection will increase, or that we shall agree better, when we have ten times more and greater concerns to quarrel over than ever?

Ye that tell us of harmony and reconciliation, can ye restore to us the time that is past? Can ye give to prostitution its former innocence? Neither can ye reconcile Britain and America. The last cord now is broken, the people of England are presenting addresses against us. There are injuries which nature cannot forgive; she would cease to be nature if she did. As well can the lover forgive the ravisher of his mistress, as the continent forgive the murders of Britain. The Almighty hath implanted in us these unextinguishable feelings for good and wise purposes. They are the guardians of his image in our hearts. They distinguish us from the herd of common animals. The social compact would dissolve, and justice be extirpated the earth, or have only a casual existence were we callous to the touches of affection. The robber, and the murderer, would often escape unpunished, did not the injuries which our tempers sustain, provoke us into justice.

O ye that love mankind! Ye that dare oppose, not only the tyranny, but the tyrant, stand forth! Every spot of the old world is overrun with oppression. Freedom hath been hunted round the globe. Asia, and Africa, have long expelled her—Europe regards her like a stranger, and England hath given her warning to depart. O! receive the fugitive, and prepare in time an asylum for mankind.

OF THE PRESENT ABILITY OF AMERICA, WITH SOME MISCELLANEOUS REFLEXIONS.

I HAVE never met with a man, either in England or America, who hath not confessed his opinion, that a separation between the countries, would take place one time or other: And there is no instance, in which we have shewn less judgment, than in endeavouring to describe, what we call, the ripeness or fitness of the Continent for independance.

As all men allow the measure, and vary only in their opinion of the time, let us, in order to remove mistakes, take a general survey of things, and endeavour, if possible, to find out the *very* time. But we need not go far, the inquiry ceases at once, for, the *time hath found us*. The general concurrence, the glorious union of all things prove the fact.

It is not in numbers, but in unity, that our great strength lies; yet our present numbers are sufficient to repel the force of all the world. The Continent hath, at this time, the largest body of armed and disciplined men of any power under Heaven; and is just arrived at that pitch of strength, in which no single colony is able to support itself, and the whole, when united, can accomplish the matter, and either more, or, less than this, might be fatal in its effects. Our land force is already sufficient, and as to naval affairs, we cannot be insensible, that Britain would never suffer an American man of war to be built, while the continent remained in her hands. Wherefore, we should be no forwarder an hundred years hence in that branch, than we are now; but the truth is, we should be less so, because the timber of the country is every day diminishing, and that, which will remain at last, will be far off and difficult to procure.

Were the continent crowded with inhabitants, her sufferings under the present circumstances would be intolerable. The more sea port towns we had, the more should we have both to defend and to lose. Our present numbers are so happily proportioned to our wants, that no man need be idle. The diminution of trade affords an army, and the necessities of an army create a new trade.

Debts we have none; and whatever we may contract on this account will serve as a glorious memento of our virtue. Can we but leave posterity with a settled form of government, an independant constitution of its own, the purchase at any price will be cheap. But to expend millions for the sake of getting a few vile acts repealed, and routing the present ministry only, is unworthy the charge, and is using posterity with the utmost cruelty; because it is leaving them the great work to do, and a debt upon their backs, from which they derive no advantage. Such a thought is unworthy a man of honor, and is the true characteristic of a narrow heart and a pedling politician.

The debt we may contract doth not deserve our regard if the work be but accomplished. No nation ought to be without a debt. A national debt is a national bond; and when it bears no interest, is in no case a grievance. Britain is oppressed with a debt of upwards of one hundred and forty millions sterling, for which she pays upwards of four millions interest. And as a compensation for her debt, she has a large navy; America is without a debt, and without a navy; yet for the twentieth part of the English national debt, could have a navy as large again. The navy of England is not worth, at this time, more than three millions and an half sterling.

The first and second editions of this pamphlet were published without the following calculations, which are now given as a proof that the above estimation of the navy is just. *See Entic's naval history, intro.* page 56.

The charge of building a ship of each rate, and furnishing her with masts, yards, sails and rigging, together with a proportion of eight months boatswain's and carpenter's sea-stores, as calculated by Mr. Burchett, Secretary to the navy.

		£ [pounds sterling]
For a ship of 100 guns	=	35,553
90	=	29,886
80	=	23,638
70	=	17,785
60	=	14,197
50	=	10,606
40	=	7,558
30	=	5,846
20	=	3,710

And from hence it is easy to sum up the value, or cost rather, of the whole British navy, which in the year 1757, when it was at its greatest glory consisted of the following ships and guns:

Ships.	Guns.	Cost of one.	Cost of all.
		Cost in £ [pounds sterling]	
6	100	35,553	213,318
12	90	29,886	358,632
12	80	23,638	283,656
43	70	17,785	764,755
35	60	14,197	496,895
40	50	10,606	424,240
45	40	7,558	340,110
58	20	3,710	215,180
85	Sloops, bombs and fireships, one with another, at	2,000	170,000
Cost			3,266,786
Remains for Guns			233,214
			3,500,000

No country on the globe is so happily situated, or so internally capable of raising a fleet as America. Tar, timber, iron, and cordage are her natural produce. We need go abroad for nothing. Whereas the Dutch, who make large profits by hiring out their ships of war to the Spaniards and Portuguese, are obliged to import most of the materials they use. We ought to view the building a fleet as an article of commerce, it being the natural manufactory of this country. It is the best money we can lay out. A navy when finished is worth more than it cost. And is that nice point in national policy, in which commerce and protection are united. Let us build; if we want them not, we can sell; and by that means replace our paper currency with ready gold and silver.

In point of manning a fleet, people in general run into great errors; it is not necessary that one fourth part should be sailors. The Terrible privateer, Captain Death, stood the hottest engagement of any ship last war, yet had not twenty sailors on board, though her complement of men was upwards of two hundred. A few able and social sailors will soon instruct a sufficient number of active landmen in the common work of a ship. Wherefore, we never can be more capable to begin on maritime matters than now, while our timber is standing, our fisheries blocked up, and our sailors and shipwrights out of employ. Men of war, of seventy and eighty guns were built forty years ago in New-England, and why not the same now? Ship-building is America's greatest pride, and in which, she will in time excel the whole world. The great empires of the east are mostly inland, and consequently excluded from the possibility of rivalling her. Africa is in a state of barbarism; and no power in Europe, hath either such an extent of coast, or such an internal supply of materials. Where nature hath given the one, she has withheld the other; to America only hath she been liberal of both. The vast empire of Russia is almost shut out from the sea; wherefore, her boundless forests, her tar, iron, and cordage are only articles of commerce.

In point of safety, ought we to be without a fleet? We are not the little people now, which we were sixty years ago; at that time we might have trusted our property in the streets, or fields rather; and slept securely without locks or bolts to our doors or windows. The case now is altered, and our methods of defence, ought to improve with our increase of property. A common pirate, twelve months ago, might have come up the Delaware, and laid the city of Philadelphia under instant contribution, for what sum he pleased; and the same might have happened to other places. Nay, any daring fellow, in a brig of fourteen or sixteen guns, might have robbed the whole Continent, and carried off half a million of money. These are circumstances which demand our attention, and point out the necessity of naval protection.

Some, perhaps, will say, that after we have made it up with Britain, she will protect us. Can we be so unwise as to mean, that she shall keep a navy in our harbours for that purpose? Common sense will tell us, that the power which hath endeavoured to subdue us, is of all others, the most improper to defend us. Conquest may be effected under the pretence of friendship; and ourselves, after a long and brave resistance, be at last cheated into slavery. And if her ships are not to be admitted into our harbours, I would ask, how is she to protect us? A navy three or four thousand miles off can be of little use, and on sudden emergencies, none at all. Wherefore, if we must hereafter protect ourselves, why not do it for ourselves? Why do it for another?

The English list of ships of war, is long and formidable, but not a tenth part of them are at any one time fit for service, numbers of them not in being; yet their names are pompously continued in the list, if only a plank be left of the ship: and not a fifth part, of such as are fit for service, can be spared on any one station at one time. The East and West Indies, Mediterranean, Africa, and other parts over which Britain extends her claim, make large demands upon her navy. From a mixture of prejudice and inattention, we have contracted a false notion respecting the navy of England, and have talked as if we should have the whole of it to encounter at once, and for that reason, supposed, that we must have one as large; which not being instantly practicable, have been made use of by a set of disguised Tories to discourage our beginning thereon. Nothing can be farther from truth than this; for if America had only a twentieth part of the naval force of Britain, she would be by far an over match for her; because, as we neither have, nor claim any foreign dominion, our whole force would be employed on our own coast, where we should, in the long run, have two to one the advantage of those who had three or four thousand miles to sail over, before they could attack us, and the same distance to return in order to refit and recruit. And although Britain by her fleet, hath a check over our trade to Europe, we have as large a one over her trade to the West-Indies, which, by laying in the neighbourhood of the Continent, is entirely at its mercy.

Some method might be fallen on to keep up a naval force in time of peace, if we should not judge it necessary to support a constant navy. If premiums were to be given to merchants, to build and employ in their service ships mounted with twenty, thirty, forty or fifty guns, (the premiums to be in proportion to the loss of bulk to the merchants) fifty or sixty of those ships, with a few guardships on constant duty, would keep up a sufficient navy, and that without burdening ourselves with the evil so loudly complained of in England, of suffering their fleet, in time of peace to lie rotting in the docks. To unite the sinews of commerce and defense is sound policy; for when our strength and our riches play into each other's hand, we need fear no external enemy.

In almost every article of defense we abound. Hemp flourishes even to rankness, so that we need not want cordage. Our iron is superior to that of other countries. Our small arms equal to any in the world. Cannon we can cast at pleasure. Saltpetre and gunpowder we are every day producing. Our knowledge is hourly improving. Resolution is our inherent character, and courage hath never yet forsaken us. Wherefore, what is it that we want? Why is it that we hesitate? From Britain we can expect nothing but ruin. If she is once admitted to the government of America again, this Continent will not be worth living in. Jealousies will be always arising; insurrections will be constantly happening; and who will go forth to quell them? Who will venture his life to reduce his own countrymen to a foreign obedience?

The difference between Pennsylvania and Connecticut, respecting some unlocated lands, shews the insignificance of a British government, and fully proves, that nothing but Continental authority can regulate Continental matters.

Another reason why the present time is preferable to all others, is, that the fewer our numbers are, the more land there is yet unoccupied, which instead of being lavished by the king on his worthless dependants, may be hereafter applied, not only to the discharge of the present debt, but to the constant support of government. No nation under heaven hath such an advantage as this.

The infant state of the Colonies, as it is called, so far from being against, is an argument in favour of independance. We are sufficiently numerous, and were we more so, we might be less united. It is a matter worthy of observation, that the more a country is peopled, the smaller their armies are. In military numbers, the ancients far exceeded the moderns: and the reason is evident. For trade being the consequence of population, men become too much absorbed thereby to attend to anything else. Commerce diminishes the spirit, both of patriotism and military defence. And history sufficiently informs us, that the bravest achievements were always accomplished in the non-age of a nation. With the increase of commerce, England hath lost its spirit. The city of London, notwithstanding its numbers, submits to continued insults with the patience of a coward. The more men have to lose, the less willing are they to venture. The rich are in general slaves to fear, and submit to courtly power with the trembling duplicity of a Spaniel.

Youth is the seed time of good habits, as well in nations as in individuals. It might be difficult, if not impossible, to form the Continent into one government half a century hence. The vast variety of interests, occasioned by an increase of trade and population, would create confusion. Colony would be against colony. Each being able might scorn each other's assistance: and while the proud and foolish gloried in their little distinctions, the wise would lament, that the union had not been formed before. Wherefore, the *present time* is the *true time* for establishing it. The intimacy which is contracted in infancy, and the friendship which is formed in misfortune, are, of all others, the most lasting and unalterable. Our present union is marked with both these characters: we are young and we have been distressed; but our concord hath withstood our troubles, and fixes a memorable area for posterity to glory in.

The present time, likewise, is that peculiar time, which never happens to a nation but once, viz. the time of forming itself into a government. Most nations have let slip the opportunity, and by that means have been compelled to receive laws from their conquerors, instead of making laws for themselves. First, they had a king, and then a form of government; whereas, the articles or charter of government, should be formed first, and men delegated to execute them afterward: but from the errors of other nations, let us learn wisdom, and lay hold of the present opportunity—*To begin government at the right end.*

When William the Conqueror subdued England, he gave them law at the point of the sword; and until we consent, that the seat of government, in America, be legally and authoritatively occupied, we shall be in danger of having it filled by some fortunate ruffian, who may treat us in the same manner, and then, where will be our freedom? where our property?

As to religion, I hold it to be the indispensable duty of all government, to protect all conscientious professors thereof, and I know of no other business which government hath to do therewith. Let a man throw aside that narrowness of soul, that selfishness of principle, which the niggards of all professions are so unwilling to part with, and he will be at once delivered of his fears on that head. Suspicion is the companion of mean souls, and the bane of all good society. For myself, I fully and conscientiously believe, that it is the will of the Almighty, that there should be diversity of religious opinions among us: It affords a larger field for our Christian kindness. Were we all of one way of thinking, our religious dispositions would want matter for probation; and on this liberal principle, I look on the various denominations among us, to be like children of the same family, differing only, in what is called, their Christian names.

In page forty, I threw out a few thoughts on the propriety of a Continental Charter, (for I only presume to offer hints, not plans) and in this place, I take the liberty of re-mentioning the subject, by observing, that a charter is to be understood as a bond of solemn obligation, which the whole enters into, to support the right of every separate part, whether of religion, personal freedom, or property. A firm bargain and a right reckoning make long friends.

In a former page I likewise mentioned the necessity of a large and equal representation; and there is no political matter which more deserves our attention. A small number of electors, or a small number of representatives, are equally dangerous. But if the number of the representatives be not only small, but unequal, the danger is increased. As an instance of this, I mention the following; when the Associators petition was before the House of Assembly of Pennsylvania; twenty-eight members only were present, all the Bucks county members, being eight, voted against it, and had seven of the Chester members done the same, this whole province had been governed by two counties only, and this danger it is always exposed to. The unwarrantable stretch likewise, which that house made in their last sitting, to gain an undue authority over the delegates of that province, ought to warn the people at large, how they trust power out of their own hands. A set of instructions for the Delegates were put together, which in point of sense and business would have dishonoured a schoolboy, and after being approved by a few, a very few without doors, were carried into the House, and there passed *in behalf of the whole colony*; whereas, did the whole colony know, with what ill-will that House hath entered on some necessary public measures, they would not hesitate a moment to think them unworthy of such a trust.

Immediate necessity makes many things convenient, which if continued would grow into oppressions. Expedience and right are different things. When the calamities of America required a consultation, there was no method so ready, or at that time so proper, as to appoint persons from the several Houses of Assembly for that purpose; and the wisdom with which they have proceeded hath preserved this continent from ruin. But as it is more than probable that we shall never be without a CONGRESS, every well wisher to good order, must own, that the mode for choosing members of that body, deserves consideration. And I put it as a question to those, who make a study of mankind, whether *representation and election* is not too great a power for one and the same body of men to possess? When we are planning for posterity, we ought to remember, that virtue is not hereditary.

It is from our enemies that we often gain excellent maxims, and are frequently surprised into reason by their mistakes. Mr. Cornwall (one of the Lords of the Treasury) treated the petition of the New-York Assembly with contempt, because *that* House, he said, consisted but of twenty-six members, which trifling number, he argued, could not with decency be put for the whole. We thank him for his involuntary honesty.

TO CONCLUDE, however strange it may appear to some, or however unwilling they may be to think so, matters not, but many strong and striking reasons may be given, to shew, that nothing can settle our affairs so expeditiously as an open and determined declaration for independance. Some of which are,

First.—It is the custom of nations, when any two are at war, for some other powers, not engaged in the quarrel, to step in as mediators, and bring about the preliminaries of a peace: but while America calls herself the Subject of Great-Britain, no power, however well disposed she may be, can offer her mediation. Wherefore, in our present state we may quarrel on for ever.

Secondly.—It is unreasonable to suppose, that France or Spain will give us any kind of assistance, if we mean only, to make use of that assistance for the purpose of repairing the breach, and strengthening the connection between Britain and America; because, those powers would be sufferers by the consequences.

Thirdly.—While we profess ourselves the subjects of Britain, we must, in the eye of foreign nations, be considered as rebels. The precedent is somewhat dangerous to their peace, for men to be in arms under the name of subjects; we, on the spot, can solve the paradox: but to unite resistance and subjection, requires an idea much too refined for common understanding.

Fourthly.—Were a manifesto to be published, and despatched to foreign courts, setting forth the miseries we have endured, and the peaceable methods we have ineffectually used for redress; declaring, at the same time, that not being able, any longer, to live happily or safely under the cruel disposition of the British court, we had been driven to the necessity of breaking off all connections with her; at the same time, assuring all such courts of our peaceable disposition towards them, and of our desire of entering into trade with them: Such a memorial would produce more good effects to this Continent, than if a ship were freighted with petitions to Britain.

Under our present denomination of British subjects, we can neither be received nor heard abroad: The custom of all courts is against us, and will be so, until, by an independance, we take rank with other nations.

These proceedings may at first appear strange and difficult; but, like all other steps which we have already passed over, will in a little time become familiar and agreeable; and, until an independance is declared, the Continent will feel itself like a man who continues putting off some unpleasant business from day to day, yet knows it must be done, hates to set about it, wishes it over, and is continually haunted with the thoughts of its necessity.

APPENDIX.

SINCE the publication of the first edition of this pamphlet, or rather, on the same day on which it came out, the King's Speech made its appearance in this city. Had the spirit of prophecy directed the birth of this production, it could not have brought it forth, at a more seasonable juncture, or a more necessary time. The bloody mindedness of the one, shew the necessity of pursuing the doctrine of the other. Men read by way of revenge. And the Speech, instead of terrifying, prepared a way for the manly principles of Independance.

Ceremony, and even, silence, from whatever motive they may arise, have a hurtful tendency, when they give the least degree of countenance to base and wicked performances; wherefore, if this maxim be admitted, it naturally follows, that the King's Speech, as being a piece of finished villainy, deserved, and still deserves, a general execration both by the Congress and the people. Yet, as the domestic tranquillity of a nation, depends greatly, on the *chastity* of what may properly be called NATIONAL MANNERS, it is often better, to pass some things over in silent disdain, than to make use of such new methods of dislike, as might introduce the least innovation, on that guardian of our peace and safety. And, perhaps, it is chiefly owing to this prudent delicacy, that the King's Speech, hath not, before now, suffered a public execution. The Speech if it may be called one, is nothing better than a wilful audacious libel against the truth, the common good, and the existence of mankind; and is a formal and pompous method of offering up human sacrifices to the pride of tyrants. But this general massacre of mankind, is one of the privileges, and the certain consequence of Kings; for as nature knows them *not*, they know *not her*, and although they are beings of our *own* creating, they know not us, and are become the gods of their creators. The Speech hath one good quality, which is, that it is not calculated to deceive, neither can we, even if we would, be deceived by it. Brutality and tyranny appear on the face of it. It leaves us at no loss: And every line convinces, even in the moment of reading, that He, who hunts the woods for prey, the naked and untutored Indian, is less a Savage than the King of Britain.

Sir John Dalrymple, the putative father of a whining jesuitical piece, fallaciously called, "*The Address of the people of* ENGLAND *to the inhabitants of* AMERICA," hath, perhaps, from a vain supposition, that the people *here* were to be frightened at the pomp and description of a king, given, (though very unwisely on his part) the real character of the present one: "But" says this writer, "if you are inclined to pay compliments to an administration, which we do not complain of," (meaning the Marquis of Rockingham's at the repeal of the Stamp Act) "it is very unfair in you to withhold them from that prince, *by whose* NOD ALONE *they were permitted to do any thing*." This is toryism with a witness! Here is idolatry even without a mask: And he who can calmly hear, and digest such doctrine, hath forfeited his claim to rationality—an apostate from the order of manhood; and ought to be considered—as one, who hath not only given up the proper dignity of man, but sunk himself beneath the rank of animals, and contemptibly crawls through the world like a worm.

However, it matters very little now, what the king of England either says or does; he hath wickedly broken through every moral and human obligation, trampled nature and conscience beneath his feet; and by a steady and constitutional spirit of insolence and cruelty, procured for himself an universal hatred. It is *now* the interest of America to provide for herself. She hath already a large and young family, whom it is more her duty to take care of, than to be granting away her property, to support a power who is become a reproach to the names of men and christians—Ye, whose office it is to watch over the morals of a nation, of whatsoever sect or denomination ye are of, as well as ye, who are more immediately the guardians of the public liberty, if ye wish to preserve your native country uncontaminated by European corruption, ye must in secret wish a separation—But leaving the moral part to private reflection, I shall chiefly confine my farther remarks to the following heads.

First. That it is the interest of America to be separated from Britain.

Secondly. Which is the easiest and most practicable plan, RECONCILIATION or INDEPENDANCE? with some occasional remarks.

In support of the first, I could, if I judged it proper, produce the opinion of some of the ablest and most experienced men on this continent; and whose sentiments, on that head, are not yet publicly known. It is in reality a self-evident position: For no nation in a state of foreign dependance, limited in its commerce, and cramped and fettered in its legislative powers, can ever arrive at any material eminence. America doth not yet know what opulence is; and although the progress which she hath made stands unparalleled in the history of other nations, it is but childhood, compared with what she would be capable of arriving at, had she, as she ought to have, the legislative powers in her own hands. England is, at this time, proudly coveting what would do her no good, were she to accomplish it; and the Continent hesitating on a matter, which will be her final ruin if neglected. It is the commerce and not the conquest of America, by which England is to be benefited, and that would in a great measure continue, were the countries as independant of each other as France and Spain; because in many articles, neither can go to a better market. But it is the independance of this country of Britain or any other, which is now the main and only object worthy of contention, and which, like all other truths discovered by necessity, will appear clearer and stronger every day.

First. Because it will come to that one time or other.

Secondly. Because, the longer it is delayed the harder it will be to accomplish.

I have frequently amused myself both in public and private companies, with silently remarking, the specious errors of those who speak without reflecting. And among the many which I have heard, the following seems the most general, viz. that had this rupture happened forty or fifty years hence, instead of *now*, the Continent would have been more able to have shaken off the dependance. To which I reply, that our military ability, *at this time*, arises from the experience gained in the last war, and which in forty or fifty years time, would have been totally extinct. The Continent, would not, by that time, have had a General, or even a military officer left; and we, or those who may succeed us, would have been as ignorant of martial matters as the ancient Indians: And this single position, closely attended to, will unanswerably prove, that the present time is preferable to all others. The argument turns thus—at the conclusion of the last war, we had experience, but wanted numbers; and forty or fifty years hence, we should have numbers, without experience; wherefore, the proper point of time, must be some particular point between the two extremes, in which a sufficiency of the former remains, and a proper increase of the latter is obtained: And that point of time is the present time.

The reader will pardon this digression, as it does not properly come under the head I first set out with, and to which I again return by the following position, viz.

Should affairs be patched up with Britain, and she to remain the governing and sovereign power of America, (which, as matters are now circumstanced, is giving up the point intirely) we shall deprive ourselves of the very means of sinking the debt we have, or may contract. The value of the back lands which some of the provinces are clandestinely deprived of, by the unjust extention of the limits of Canada, valued only at five pounds sterling per hundred acres, amount to upwards of twenty-five millions, Pennsylvania currency; and the quit-rents at one penny sterling per acre, to two millions yearly.

It is by the sale of those lands that the debt may be sunk, without burthen to any, and the quit-rent reserved thereon, will always lessen, and in time, will wholly support the yearly expence of government. It matters not how long the debt is in paying, so that the lands when sold be applied to the discharge of it, and for the execution of which, the Congress for the time being, will be the continental trustees.

I proceed now to the second head, viz. Which is the easiest and most practicable plan, RECONCILIATION or INDEPENDANCE; with some occasional remarks.

He who takes nature for his guide is not easily beaten out of his argument, and on that ground, I answer *generally—That* INDEPENDANCE *being a* SINGLE SIMPLE LINE, *contained within ourselves; and reconciliation, a matter exceedingly perplexed and complicated, and in which, a treacherous capricious court is to interfere, gives the answer without a doubt.*

The present state of America is truly alarming to every man who is capable of reflexion. Without law, without government, without any other mode of power than what is founded on, and granted by courtesy. Held together by an unexampled concurrence of sentiment, which, is nevertheless subject to change, and which every secret enemy is endeavouring to dissolve. Our present condition, is, Legislation without law; wisdom without a plan; constitution without a name; and, what is strangely astonishing, perfect Independance contending for dependance. The instance is without a precedent; the case never existed before; and who can tell what may be the event? The property of no man is secure in the present unbraced system of things. The mind of the multitude is left at random, and seeing no fixed object before them, they pursue such as fancy or opinion starts. Nothing is criminal; there is no such thing as treason; wherefore, every one thinks himself at liberty to act as he pleases. The Tories dared not have assembled offensively, had they known that their lives, by that act, were forfeited to the laws of the state. A line of distinction should be drawn, between, English soldiers taken in battle, and inhabitants of America taken in arms. The first are prisoners, but the latter traitors. The one forfeits his liberty, the other his head.

Notwithstanding our wisdom, there is a visible feebleness in some of our proceedings which gives encouragement to dissensions. The Continental Belt is too loosely buckled. And if something is not done in time, it will be too late to do any thing, and we shall fall into a state, in which, neither *Reconciliation* nor *Independance* will be practicable. The king and his worthless adherents are got at their old game of dividing the Continent, and there are not wanting among us, Printers, who will be busy in spreading specious falsehoods. The artful and hypocritical letter which appeared a few months ago in two of the New-York papers, and likewise in two others, is an evidence that there are men who want either judgment or honesty.

It is easy getting into holes and corners and talking of reconciliation: But do such men seriously consider, how difficult the task is, and how dangerous it may prove, should the Continent divide thereon. Do they take within their view, all the various orders of men whose situation and circumstances, as well as their own, are to be considered therein. Do they put themselves in the place of the sufferer whose *all* is *already* gone, and of the soldier, who hath quitted *all* for the defence of his country. If their ill judged moderation be suited to their own private situations *only*, regardless of others, the event will convince them, that "they are reckoning without their Host."

Put us, say some, on the footing we were on in sixty-three: To which I answer, the request is not *now* in the power of Britain to comply with, neither will she propose it; but if it were, and even should be granted, I ask, as a reasonable question, By what means is such a corrupt and faithless court to be kept to its engagements? Another parliament, nay, even the present, may hereafter repeal the obligation, on the pretence, of its being violently obtained, or unwisely granted; and in that case, Where is our redress?—No going to law with nations; cannon are the barristers of Crowns; and the sword, not of justice, but of war, decides the suit. To be on the footing of sixty-three, it is not sufficient, that the laws only be put on the same state, but, that our circumstances, likewise, be put on the same state; Our burnt and destroyed towns repaired or built up, our private losses made good, our public debts (contracted for defence) discharged; otherwise, we shall be millions worse than we were at that enviable period. Such a request, had it been complied with a year ago, would have won the heart and soul of the Continent—but now it is too late, "The Rubicon is passed."

Besides, the taking up arms, merely to enforce the repeal of a pecuniary law, seems as unwarrantable by the divine law, and as repugnant to human feelings, as the taking up arms to enforce obedience thereto. The object, on either side, doth not justify the means; for the lives of men are too valuable to be cast away on such trifles. It is the violence which is done and threatened to our persons; the destruction of our property by an armed force; the invasion of our country by fire and sword, which conscientiously qualifies the use of arms: And the instant, in which such a mode of defence became necessary, all subjection to Britain ought to have ceased; and the independancy of America, should have been considered, as dating its æra from, and published by, the *first musket that was fired against her*. This line is a line of consistency; neither drawn by caprice, nor extended by ambition; but produced by a chain of events, of which the colonies were not the authors.

I shall conclude these remarks, with the following timely and well intended hints. We ought to reflect, that there are three different ways, by which an independancy may hereafter be effected; and that *one* of those *three*, will one day or other, be the fate of America, viz. By the legal voice of the people in Congress; by a military power; or by a mob: It may not always happen that our soldiers are citizens, and the multitude a body of reasonable men; virtue, as I have already remarked, is not hereditary, neither is it perpetual. Should an independancy be brought about by the first of those means, we have every opportunity and every encouragement before us, to form the noblest purest constitution on the face of the earth. We have it in our power to begin the world over again. A situation, similar to the present, hath not happened since the days of Noah until now. The birthday of a new world is at hand, and a race of men, perhaps as numerous as all Europe contains, are to receive their portion of freedom from the event of a few months. The Reflexion is awful—and in this point of view, How trifling, how ridiculous, do the little, paltry cavellings, of a few weak or interested men appear, when weighed against the business of a world.

Should we neglect the present favorable and inviting period, and an Independance be hereafter effected by any other means, we must charge the consequence to ourselves, or to those rather, whose narrow and prejudiced souls, are habitually opposing the measure, without either inquiring or reflecting. There are reasons to be given in support of Independance, which men should rather privately think of, than be publicly told of. We ought not now to be debating whether we shall be independant or not, but, anxious to accomplish it on a firm, secure, and honorable basis, and uneasy rather that it is not yet began upon. Every day convinces us of its necessity. Even the Tories (if such beings yet remain among us) should, of all men, be the most solicitous to promote it; for, as the appointment of committees at first, protected them from popular rage, so, a wise and well established form of government, will be the only certain means of continuing it securely to them. *Wherefore*, if they have not virtue enough to be Whigs, they ought to have prudence enough to wish for Independance.

In short, Independance is the only Bond that can tye and keep us together. We shall then see our object, and our ears will be legally shut against the schemes of an intriguing, as well, as a cruel enemy. We shall then too, be on a proper footing, to treat with Britain; for there is reason to conclude, that the pride of that court, will be less hurt by treating with the American states for terms of peace, than with those, whom she denominates, "rebellious subjects," for terms of accommodation. It is our delaying it that encourages her to hope for conquest, and our backwardness tends only to prolong the war. As we have, without any good effect therefrom, withheld our trade to obtain a redress of our grievances, let us *now* try the alternative, by *independantly* redressing them ourselves, and then offering to open the trade. The mercantile and reasonable part in England, will be still with us; because, peace *with* trade, is preferable to war *without* it. And if this offer be not accepted, other courts may be applied to.

On these grounds I rest the matter. And as no offer hath yet been made to refute the doctrine contained in the former editions of this pamphlet, it is a negative proof, that either the doctrine cannot be refuted, or, that the party in favour of it are too numerous to be opposed. WHEREFORE, instead of gazing at each other with suspicious or doubtful curiosity; let each of us, hold out to his neighbour the hearty hand of friendship, and unite in drawing a line, which, like an act of oblivion shall bury in forgetfulness every former dissension. Let the names of Whig and Tory be extinct; and let none other be heard among us, than those of *a good citizen, an open and resolute friend, and a virtuous supporter of the* RIGHTS *of MANKIND and of the* FREE AND INDEPENDANT STATES OF AMERICA.

To the Representatives of the Religious Society of the People called Quakers, or to so many of them as were concerned in publishing the late piece, entitled "THE ANCIENT TESTIMONY AND PRINCIPLES of the People called QUAKERS renewed, with Respect to the KING and GOVERNMENT, and touching the COMMOTIONS now prevailing in these and other parts of AMERICA addressed to the PEOPLE IN GENERAL."

The Writer of this, is one of those few, who never dishonours religion either by ridiculing, or cavilling at any denomination whatsoever. To God, and not to man, are all men accountable on the score of religion. Wherefore, this epistle is not so properly addressed to you as a religious, but as a political body, dabbling in matters, which the professed Quietude of your Principles instruct you not to meddle with.

As you have, without a proper authority for so doing, put yourselves in the place of the whole body of the Quakers, so, the writer of this, in order to be on an equal rank with yourselves, is under the necessity, of putting himself in the place of all those, who, approve the very writings and principles, against which your testimony is directed: And he hath chosen this singular situation, in order, that you might discover in him that presumption of character which you cannot see in yourselves. For neither he nor you can have any claim or title to *Political Representation*.

When men have departed from the right way, it is no wonder that they stumble and fall. And it is evident from the manner in which ye have managed your testimony, that politics, (as a religious body of men) is not your proper Walk; for however well adapted it might appear to you, it is, nevertheless, a jumble of good and bad put unwisely together, and the conclusion drawn therefrom, both unnatural and unjust.

The two first pages, (and the whole doth not make four) we give you credit for, and expect the same civility from you, because the love and desire of peace is not confined to Quakerism, it is the natural, as well the religious wish of all denominations of men. And on this ground, as men labouring to establish an Independant Constitution of our own, do we exceed all others in our hope, end, and aim. *Our plan is peace for ever*. We are tired of contention with Britain, and can see no real end to it but in a final separation. We act consistently, because for the sake of introducing an endless and uninterrupted peace, do we bear the evils and burthens of the present day. We are endeavoring, and will steadily continue to endeavour, to separate and dissolve a connexion which hath already filled our land with blood; and which, while the name of it remains, will be the fatal cause of future mischiefs to both countries.

We fight neither for revenge nor conquest; neither from pride nor passion; we are not insulting the world with our fleets and armies, nor ravaging the globe for plunder. Beneath the shade of our own vines are we attacked; in our own houses, and on our own lands, is the violence committed against us. We view our enemies in the character of Highwaymen and Housebreakers, and having no defence for ourselves in the civil law, are obliged to punish them by the military one, and apply the sword, in the very case, where you have before now, applied the halter—Perhaps we feel for the ruined and insulted sufferers in all and every part of the continent, with a degree of tenderness which hath not yet made its way into some of your bosoms. But be ye sure that ye mistake not the cause and ground of your Testimony. Call not coldness of soul, religion; nor put the *Bigot* in the place of the *Christian*.

O ye partial ministers of your own acknowledged principles. If the bearing arms be sinful, the first going to war must be more so, by all the difference between wilful attack and unavoidable defence. Wherefore, if ye really preach from conscience, and mean not to make a political hobby-horse of your religion, convince the world thereof, by proclaiming your doctrine to our enemies, *for they likewise bear* ARMS. Give us proof of your sincerity by publishing it at St. James's, to the commanders in chief at Boston, to the Admirals and Captains who are piratically ravaging our coasts, and to all the murdering miscreants who are acting in authority under HIM whom ye profess to serve. Had ye the honest soul of *Barclay* ye would preach repentance to *your* king; Ye would tell the Royal Wretch his sins, and warn him of eternal ruin. Ye would not spend your partial invectives against the injured and the insulted only, but, like faithful ministers, would cry aloud and *spare none*. Say not that ye are persecuted, neither endeavour to make us the authors of that reproach, which, ye are bringing upon yourselves; for we testify unto all men, that we do not complain against you because ye are *Quakers*, but because ye pretend to *be* and are NOT Quakers.

Alas! it seems by the particular tendency of some part of your testimony, and other parts of your conduct, as if, all sin was reduced to, and comprehended in, *the act of bearing arms*, and that by the *people* only. Ye appear to us, to have mistaken party for conscience; because, the general tenor of your actions wants uniformity: And it is exceedingly difficult to us to give credit to many of your pretended scruples; because, we see them made by the same men, who, in the very instant that they are exclaiming against the mammon of this world, are nevertheless, hunting after it with a step as steady as Time, and an appetite as keen as Death.

The quotation which ye have made from Proverbs, in the third page of your testimony, that, "when a man's ways please the Lord, he maketh even his enemies to be at peace with him"; is very unwisely chosen on your part; because, it amounts to a proof, that the king's ways (whom ye are desirous of supporting) do *not* please the Lord, otherwise, his reign would be in peace.

I now proceed to the latter part of your testimony, and that, for which all the foregoing seems only an introduction, viz.

"It hath ever been our judgment and principle, since we were called to profess the light of Christ Jesus, manifested in our consciences unto this day, that the setting up and putting down kings and governments, is God's peculiar prerogative; for causes best known to himself: And that it is not our business to have any hand or contrivance therein; nor to be busy bodies above our station, much less to plot and contrive the ruin, or overturn of any of them, but to pray for the king, and safety of our nation, and good of all men: That we may live a peaceable and quiet life, in all godliness and honesty; *under the government which God is pleased to set over us*."—If these are *really* your principles why do ye not abide by them? Why do ye not leave that, which ye call God's Work, to be managed by himself? These very principles instruct you to wait with patience and humility, for the event of all public measures, and to receive *that event* as the divine will towards you. *Wherefore*, what occasion is there for your *political testimony* if you fully believe what it contains: And the very publishing it proves, that either, ye do not believe what ye profess, or have not virtue enough to practise what ye believe.

The principles of Quakerism have a direct tendency to make a man the quiet and inoffensive subject of any, and every government *which is set over him*. And if the setting up and putting down of kings and governments is God's peculiar prerogative, he most certainly will not be robbed thereof by us; wherefore, the principle itself leads you to approve of every thing, which ever happened, or may happen to kings as being his work. OLIVER CROMWELL thanks you. CHARLES, then, died not by the hands of man; and should the present Proud Imitator of him, come to the same untimely end, the writers and publishers of the Testimony, are bound, by the doctrine it contains, to applaud the fact. Kings are not taken away by miracles, neither are changes in governments brought about by any other means than such as are common and human; and such as we are now using. Even the dispersion of the Jews, though foretold by our Saviour, was effected by arms. Wherefore, as ye refuse to be the means on one side, ye ought not to be meddlers on the other; but to wait the issue in silence; and unless ye can produce divine authority, to prove, that the Almighty who hath created and placed this *new* world, at the greatest distance it could possibly stand, east and west, from every part of the old, doth, nevertheless, disapprove of its being independant of the corrupt and abandoned court of Britain, unless I say, ye can shew this, how can ye on the ground of your principles, justify the exciting and stirring up the people "firmly to unite in the *abhorrence* of all such *writings*, and *measures*, as evidence a desire and design to break off the *happy* connexion we have hitherto enjoyed, with the kingdom of Great-Britain, and our just and necessary subordination to the king, and those who are lawfully placed in authority under him." What a slap of the face is here! the men, who in the very paragraph before, have quietly and passively resigned up the ordering, altering, and disposal of kings and governments, into the hands of God, are now, recalling their principles, and putting in for a share of the business. Is it possible, that the conclusion, which is here justly quoted, can any ways follow from the doctrine laid down? The inconsistency is too glaring not to be seen; the absurdity too great not to be laughed at; and such as could only have been made by those, whose understandings were darkened by the narrow and crabby spirit of a despairing political party; for ye are not to be considered as the whole body of the Quakers but only as a factional and fractional part thereof.

Here ends the examination of your testimony; (which I call upon no man to abhor, as ye have done, but only to read and judge of fairly;) to which I subjoin the following remark; "That the setting up and putting down of kings," most certainly mean, the making him a king, who is yet not so, and the making him no king who is already one. And pray what hath this to do in the present case? We neither mean to *set up* nor to *put down*, neither to *make* nor to *unmake*, but to have nothing to *do* with them. Wherefore, your testimony in whatever light it is viewed serves only to dishonor your judgement, and for many other reasons had better have been let alone than published.

First, Because it tends to the decrease and reproach of all religion whatever, and is of the utmost danger to society, to make it a party in political disputes.

Secondly, Because it exhibits a body of men, numbers of whom disavow the publishing political testimonies, as being concerned therein and approvers thereof.

Thirdly, Because it hath a tendency to undo that continental harmony and friendship which yourselves by your late liberal and charitable donations hath lent a hand to establish; and the preservation of which, is of the utmost consequence to us all.

And here without anger or resentment I bid you farewell. Sincerely wishing, that as men and christians, ye may always fully and uninterruptedly enjoy every civil and religious right; and be, in your turn, the means of securing it to others;

but that the example which ye have unwisely set, of mingling religion with politics, *may be disavowed and reprobated by every inhabitant of* AMERICA.

3.8.2 Reading and Review Questions

1. How does Paine present himself in *Common Sense*? In other words, what is his persona? What sort of relationship does his persona seem to have with the intended audience? Why?
2. Why, and to what effect, do you think Paine uses religious language and scriptural authority?
3. How does Paine use logic? As a logician, is his argument fallible or convincing? Why, either way?
4. How does Paine use emotions, or sensibility, and affections? How and on what terms does he use emotions to represent the Revolution?
5. What benefits does Paine point to in perfect equality among humankind? Why?

3.9 THOMAS JEFFERSON

(1743–1826)

Following the tenets of the Enlightenment, Thomas Jefferson's mind ranged amid such disparate fields of knowledge as law, philosophy, government, architecture, education, religion, science, and agriculture. Jefferson acquired understanding of law and government through the works of others—including Sir Isaac Newton (1643–1727), the classic republican theorist James Harrington (1611–1677), political philosopher Thomas Hobbes (1588–1679), Locke, and enlightenment writer Voltaire (1694–1778). Later, his library, comprising thousands of books, served as the foundation for the Library of Congress. He put this understanding to practical use in his public life devoted to the American democracy, delineating through his writing a clear and fair social contract that protects the rights of the individual.

Image 3.11 | Thomas Jefferson
Artist | Rembrandt Peale
Source | Wikimedia Commons
License | Public Domain

He was born in Albemarle County, Virginia. He was educated first at home and then at the College of William and Mary in Williamsburg, Virginia. In 1769, he was elected to the Virginia House of Burgesses and thereafter devoted much of his public life to that state, including representing Virginia in the Second Continental Congress. He also served in the Virginia legislature, codifying its laws to accord with ideas of religious freedom and tolerance. From 1779 to 1781, he was the governor of Virginia. He also served as its delegate to the Congress of the Confederation.

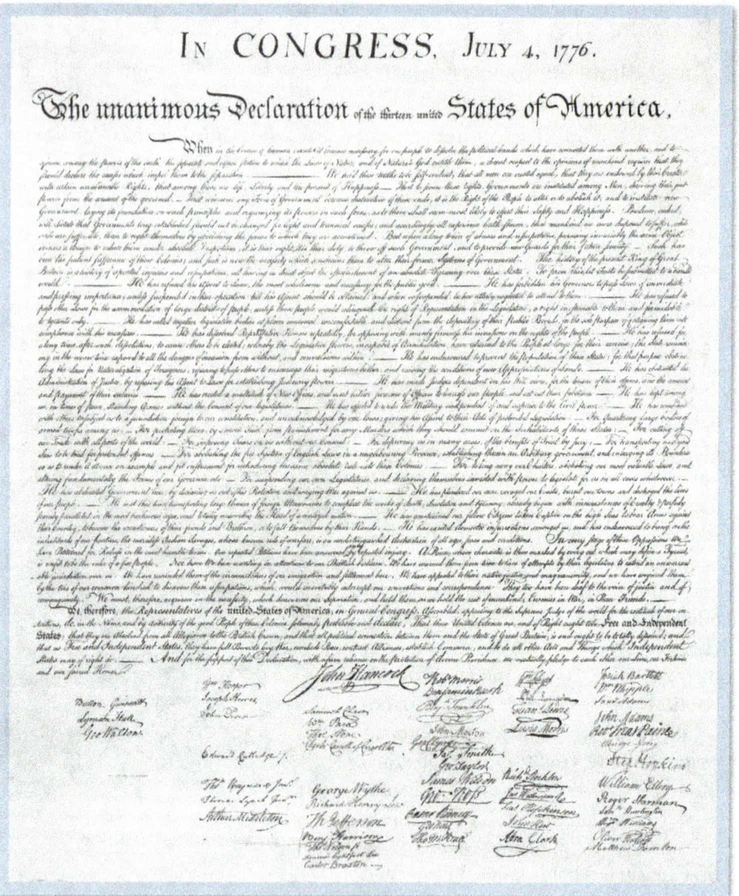

IN CONGRESS, JULY 4, 1776.

The unanimous Declaration of the thirteen united States of America,

Image 3.12 | The Declaration of Independence
Authors | Second Continental Congress
Source | Wikimedia Commons
License | Public Domain

After the Revolutionary War, he helped negotiate the Treaty of Paris then remained in France as the American Minister (1785–1789). Returning to America, he devoted his public life to national affairs. He served as the first secretary of state (under George Washington), the second vice president (under John Adams), and then the third president. The Louisiana Purchase (1803) was made during his presidency, and he funded the exploratory expedition of Lewis and Clark (1803–1806).

In 1793, he retired from political life to live at Monticello, the home he designed. Although he had hoped to include a statement against slavery in the Declaration of Independence, he nevertheless held slaves at Monticello, fathered children there by his slave Sally Hemmings, and ultimately advocated for the colonization of blacks outside of America. He also founded the University of Virginia upon Enlightenment tenets of education. The buildings he designed for this university make it to this day one of the most beautiful campuses in America.

He had put on his gravestone at Monticello the accomplishments for which he most wanted to be remembered: Author of the Declaration of American Independence, of the Statute of Virginia for religious freedom, and Father of the University of Virginia.

Image 3.13 | Thomas Jefferson's Monticello
Photographer | Martin Falbisoner
Source | Wikimedia Commons
License | CC BY-SA 3.0

3.9.1 From *Notes on the State of Virginia* (1785)

Query VI

A notice of its Mountains?

For the particular geography of our mountains I must refer to Fry and Jefferson's map of Virginia; and to Evans's analysis of his map of America for a more philosophical view of them than is to be found in any other work. It is worthy notice, that our mountains are not solitary and scattered confusedly over the face of the country; but that they commence at about 150 miles from the sea-coast, are disposed in ridges one behind another, running nearly parallel with the sea-coast, though rather approaching it as they advance north-eastwardly. To the south-west, as the tract of country between the sea-coast and the Missisipi becomes narrower, the mountains converge into a single ridge, which, as it approaches the Gulph of Mexico, subsides into plain country, and gives rise to some of the waters of that Gulph, and particularly to a river called the Apalachicola, probably from the Apalachies, an Indian nation formerly residing on it. Hence the mountains giving rise to that river, and seen from its various parts, were called the Apalachian mountains, being in fact the end or termination only of the great ridges passing through the continent. European geographers however extended the name northwardly as far as the mountains extended; some giving it, after their separation into different ridges, to the Blue ridge, others to the North mountain, others to the Alleghaney, others to the Laurel ridge, as may be seen in their different maps. But the fact I believe is, that none of these ridges were ever known by that name to the inhabitants, either native or emigrant, but as they saw them so called in European maps. In the same direction generally are the veins of lime-stone, coal and other minerals hitherto discovered; and so range the falls of our great rivers. But the courses of the great rivers are at right angles with these. James and Patowmac penetrate through all the ridges of mountains eastward of the Alleghaney, that is broken by no water course. It is in fact the spine of the country between the Atlantic on one side, and the Missisipi and St. Laurence on the other. The passage of the Patowmac through the Blue ridge is perhaps one of the most stupendous scenes in nature. You stand on a very high point of land. On your right comes up the Shenandoah, having ranged along the foot of the mountain an hundred miles to seek a vent. On your left approaches the Patowmac, in quest of a passage also. In the moment of their junction they rush together against the mountain, rend it asunder, and pass off to the sea. The first glance of this scene hurries our senses into the opinion, that this earth has been created in time, that the mountains were formed first, that the rivers began to flow afterwards, that in this place particularly they have been dammed up by the Blue ridge of mountains, and have formed an ocean which filled the whole valley; that continuing to rise they have at length broken over at this spot, and have torn the mountain down from its summit to its base. The piles of rock on each hand, but particularly on the Shenandoah, the evident marks of their disrupture and avulsion from their beds by the most powerful agents of nature, corroborate the impression. But the distant finishing which nature has given to the picture is of a very different character. It is a true contrast to the foreground. It is as placid and delightful, as that is wild and tremendous. For the mountain being cloven asunder, she presents to your eye, through the cleft, a small catch of smooth blue horizon, at an infinite distance in the plain country, inviting you, as it were, from the riot and tumult roaring around, to pass through the breach and participate of the calm below. Here the eye ultimately composes itself; and that way too the road happens actually to lead. You cross the Patowmac above the junction, pass along its side through the base of the mountain for three miles, its terrible precipices hanging in fragments over you, and within about 20 miles reach Frederick town and the fine country round that. This scene is worth a voyage across the Atlantic. Yet here, as in the neighbourhood of the natural bridge, are people who have passed their lives within half a dozen miles, and have never been to survey these monuments of a war between rivers and mountains, which must have shaken the earth itself to its centre.—The height of our mountains has not yet been estimated with any degree of exactness. The Alleghaney being the great ridge which divides the waters of the Atlantic from those of the Missisipi, its summit is doubtless more elevated above the ocean than that of any other mountain. But its relative height, compared with the base on which it stands, is not so great as that of some others, the country rising behind the successive ridges like the steps of stairs. The mountains of the Blue ridge, and of these the Peaks of Otter, are thought to be of a greater height, measured from their base, than any others in our country, and perhaps in North America. From data, which may found a tolerable conjecture, we suppose the highest peak to be about 4000 feet perpendicular, which is not a fifth part of the height of the mountains of South America, nor one third of the height which would be necessary in our latitude to preserve ice in the open air unmelted through the year. The ridge of mountains next beyond the Blue ridge, called by us the North mountain, is of the greatest extent; for which reason they were named by the Indians the Endless mountains.

A substance supposed to be pumice, found floating on the Missisipi, has induced a conjecture, that there is a volcano on some of its waters: and as these are mostly known to their sources, except the Missouri, our expectations of verifying the conjecture would of course be led to the mountains which divide the waters of the Mexican Gulph from those of the South Sea; but no volcano having ever yet been known at such a distance from the sea, we must rather suppose that this floating substance has been erroneously deemed pumice.

Query XIV

The administration of justice and description of the laws?

The state is divided into counties. In every county are appointed magistrates, called justices of the peace, usually from eight to thirty or forty in number, in proportion to the size of the county, of the most discreet and honest inhabitants. They are nominated by their fellows, but commissioned by the governor, and act without reward. These magistrates have jurisdiction both criminal and civil. If the question before them be a question of law only, they decide on it themselves: but if it be of fact, or of fact and law combined, it must be referred to a jury. In the latter case, of a combination of law and fact, it is usual for the jurors to decide the fact, and to refer the law arising on it to the decision of the judges. But this division of the subject lies with their discretion only. And if the question relate to any point of public liberty, or if it be one of those in which the judges may be suspected of bias, the jury undertake to decide both law and fact. If they be mistaken, a decision against right, which is casual only, is less dangerous to the state, and less afflicting to the loser, than one which makes part of a regular and uniform system. In truth, it is better to toss up cross and pile in a cause, than to refer it to a judge whose mind is warped by any motive whatever, in that particular case. But the common sense of twelve honest men gives still a better chance of just decision, than the hazard of cross and pile. These judges execute their process by the sheriff or coroner of the county, or by constables of their own appointment. If any free person commit an offence against the commonwealth, if it be below the degree of felony, he is bound by a justice to appear before their court, to answer it on indictment or information. If it amount to felony, he is committed to jail, a court of these justices is called; if they on examination think him guilty, they send him to the jail of the general court, before which court he is to be tried first by a grand jury of 24, of whom 13 must concur in opinion: if they find him guilty, he is then tried by a jury of 12 men of the county where the offence was committed, and by their verdict, which must be unanimous, he is acquitted or condemned without appeal. If the criminal be a slave the trial by the county court is final. In every case however, except that of high treason, there resides in the governor a power of pardon. In high treason, the pardon can only flow from the general assembly. In civil matters these justices have jurisdiction in all cases of whatever value, not appertaining to the department of the admiralty. This jurisdiction is twofold. If the matter in dispute be of less value than four dollars and one-sixth, a single member may try it at any time and place within his county, and may award execution on the goods of the party cast. If it be of that or greater value, it is determinable before the county court, which consists of four at the least of those justices, and assembles at the court-house of the county on a certain day in every month. From their determination, if the matter be of the value of ten pounds sterling, or concern the title or bounds of lands, an appeal lies to one of the superior courts.

There are three superior courts, to wit, the high-court of chancery, the general court, and court of admiralty. The first and second of these receive appeals from the county courts, and also have original jurisdiction where the subject of controversy is of the value of ten pounds sterling, or where it concerns the title or bounds of land. The jurisdiction of the admiralty is original altogether. The high-court of chancery is composed of three judges, the general court of five, and the court of admiralty of three. The two first hold their sessions at Richmond at stated times, the chancery twice in the year, and the general court twice for business civil and criminal, and twice more for criminal only. The court of admiralty sits at Williamsburgh whenever a controversy arises.

There is one supreme court, called the court of appeals, composed of the judges of the three superior courts, assembling twice a year at stated times at Richmond. This court receives appeals in all civil cases from each of the superior courts, and determines them finally. But it has no original jurisdiction.

If a controversy arise between two foreigners of a nation in alliance with the United States, it is decided by the Consul for their state, or, if both parties chuse it, by the ordinary courts of justice. If one of the parties only be such a foreigner, it is triable before the courts of justice of the country. But if it shall have been instituted in a county court, the foreigner may remove it into the general court, or court of chancery, who are to determine it at their first sessions, as they must also do if it be originally commenced before them. In cases of life and death, such foreigners have a right to be tried by a jury, the one half foreigners, the other natives.

All public accounts are settled with a board of auditors, consisting of three members, appointed by the general assembly, any two of whom may act. But an individual, dissatisfied with the determination of that board, may carry his case into the proper superior court.

A description of the laws.

The general assembly was constituted, as has been already shewn, by letters-patent of March the 9th, 1607, in the 4th year of the reign of James the First. The laws of England seem to have been adopted by consent of the settlers, which might easily enough be done whilst they were few and living all together. Of such adoption however we have no other proof than their practice, till the year 1661, when they were expressly adopted by an act of the assembly, except so far as 'a difference of condition' rendered them inapplicable. Under this adoption, the rule, in our courts of judicature was, that the common law of England, and the general statutes previous to the 4th of James, were in force here; but that no subsequent statutes were, *unless we were named in them*, said the judges and other partisans of the crown, *but named or not named*, said those who reflected freely. It will be unnecessary to attempt a description of the laws of England, as that may be found in English publications. To those which were established here, by the adoption of the legislature, have been since added a number of acts of assembly passed during the monarchy, and ordinances of convention and acts of assembly enacted since the establishment of the republic. The following variations from the British model are perhaps worthy of being specified.

Debtors unable to pay their debts, and making faithful delivery of their whole effects, are released from confinement, and their persons for ever discharged from restraint for such previous debts: but any property they may afterwards acquire will be subject to their creditors.

The poor, unable to support themselves, are maintained by an assessment on the tytheable persons in their parish. This assessment is levied and administered by twelve persons in each parish, called vestrymen, originally chosen by the housekeepers of the parish, but afterwards filling vacancies in their own body by their own choice. These are usually the most discreet farmers, so distributed through their parish, that every part of it may be under the immediate eye of some one of them. They are well acquainted with the details and œconomy of private life, and they find sufficient inducements to execute their charge well, in their philanthropy, in the approbation of their neighbours, and the distinction which that gives them.

The poor who have neither property, friends, nor strength to labour, are boarded in the houses of good farmers, to whom a stipulated sum is annually paid. To those who are able to help themselves a little, or have friends from whom they derive some succours, inadequate however to their full maintenance, supplementary aids are given, which enable them to live comfortably in their own houses, or in the houses of their friends. Vagabonds, without visible property or vocation, are placed in workhouses, where they are well cloathed, fed, lodged, and made to labour. Nearly the same method of providing for the poor prevails through all our states; and from Savannah to Portsmouth you will seldom meet a beggar. In the larger towns indeed they sometimes present themselves. These are usually foreigners, who have never obtained a settlement in any parish. I never yet saw a native American begging in the streets or highways. A subsistence is easily gained here: and if, by misfortunes, they are thrown on the charities of the world, those provided by their own country are so comfortable and so certain, that they never think of relinquishing them to become strolling beggars. Their situation too, when sick, in the family of a good farmer, where every member is emulous to do them kind offices, where they are visited by all the neighbours, who bring them the little rarities which their sickly appetites may crave, and who take by rotation the nightly watch over them, when their condition requires it, is without comparison better than in a general hospital, where the sick, the dying, and the dead are crammed together, in the same rooms, and often in the same beds. The disadvantages, inseparable from general hospitals, are such as can never be counterpoised by all the regularities of medicine and regimen. Nature and kind nursing save a much greater proportion in our plain way, at a smaller expence, and with less abuse. One branch only of hospital institution is wanting with us; that is, a general establishment for those labouring under difficult cases of chirurgery. The aids of this art are not equivocal. But an able chirurgeon cannot be had in every parish. Such a receptacle should therefore be provided for those patients: but no others should be admitted.

Marriages must be solemnized either on special licence, granted by the first magistrate of the county, on proof of the consent of the parent or guardian of either party under age, or after solemn publication, on three several Sundays, at some place of religious worship, in the parishes where the parties reside. The act of solemnization may be by the minister of any society of Christians, who shall have been previously licensed for this purpose by the court of the county. Quakers and Menonists however are exempted from all these conditions, and marriage among them is to be solemnized by the society itself.

A foreigner of any nation, not in open war with us, becomes naturalized by removing to the state to reside, and taking an oath of fidelity: and thereupon acquires every right of a native citizen: and citizens may divest themselves of that character, by declaring, by solemn deed, or in open court, that they mean to expatriate themselves, and no longer to be citizens of this state.

Conveyances of land must be registered in the court of the county wherein they lie, or in the general court, or they are void, as to creditors, and subsequent purchasers.

Slaves pass by descent and dower as lands do. Where the descent is from a parent, the heir is bound to pay an equal share of their value in money to each of his brothers and sisters.

Slaves, as well as lands, were entailable during the monarchy: but, by an act of the first republican assembly, all donees in tail, present and future, were vested with the absolute dominion of the entailed subject.

Bills of exchange, being protested, carry 10 per cent. interest from their date.

No person is allowed, in any other case, to take more than five per cent. per annum simple interest, for the loan of monies.

Gaming debts are made void, and monies actually paid to discharge such debts (if they exceeded 40 shillings) may be recovered by the payer within three months, or by any other person afterwards.

Tobacco, flour, beef, pork, tar, pitch, and turpentine, must be inspected by persons publicly appointed, before they can be exported.

The erecting iron-works and mills is encouraged by many priviledges; with necessary cautions however to prevent their dams from obstructing the navigation of the water-courses. The general assembly have on several occasions shewn a great desire to encourage the opening the great falls of James and Patowmac rivers. As yet, however, neither of these have been effected.

The laws have also descended to the preservation and improvement of the races of useful animals, such as horses, cattle, deer; to the extirpation of those which are noxious, as wolves, squirrels, crows, blackbirds; and to the guarding our citizens against infectious disorders, by obliging suspected vessels coming into the state, to perform quarantine, and by regulating the conduct of persons having such disorders within the state.

The mode of acquiring lands, in the earliest times of our settlement, was by petition to the general assembly. If the lands prayed for were already cleared of the Indian title, and the assembly thought the prayer reasonable, they passed the property by their vote to the petitioner. But if they had not yet been ceded by the Indians, it was necessary that the petitioner should previously purchase their right. This purchase the assembly verified, by inquiries of the Indian proprietors; and being satisfied of its reality and fairness, proceeded further to examine the reasonableness of the petition, and its consistence with policy; and, according to the result, either granted or rejected the petition. The company also sometimes, though very rarely, granted lands, independently of the general assembly. As the colony increased, and individual applications for land multiplied, it was found to give too much occupation to the general assembly to inquire into and execute the grant in every special case. They therefore thought it better to establish general rules, according to which all grants should be made, and to leave to the governor the execution of them, under these rules. This they did by what have been usually called the land laws, amending them from time to time, as their defects were developed. According to these laws, when an individual wished a portion of unappropriated land, he was to locate and survey it by a public officer, appointed for that purpose: its breadth was to bear a certain proportion to its length: the grant was to be executed by the governor: and the lands were to be improved in a certain manner, within a given time. From these regulations there resulted to the state a sole and exclusive power of taking conveyances of the Indian right of soil: since, according to them, an Indian conveyance alone could give no right to an individual, which the laws would acknowledge. The state, or the crown, thereafter, made general purchases of the Indians from time to time, and the governor parcelled them out by special grants, conformed to the rules before described, which it was not in his power, or in that of the crown, to dispense with. Grants, unaccompanied by their proper legal circumstances, were set aside regularly by scire facias, or by bill in chancery. Since the establishment of our new government, this order of things is but little changed. An individual, wishing to appropriate to himself lands still unappropriated by any other, pays to the public treasurer a sum of money proportioned to the quantity he wants. He carries the treasurer's receipt to the auditors of public accompts, who thereupon debit the treasurer with the sum, and order the register of the land-office to give the party a warrant for his land. With this warrant from the register, he goes to the surveyor of the county where the land lies on which he has cast his eye. The surveyor lays it off for him, gives him its exact description, in the form of a certificate, which certificate he returns to the land-office, where a grant is made out, and is signed by the governor. This vests in him a perfect dominion in his lands, transmissible to whom he pleases by deed or will, or by descent to his heirs if he die intestate.

Many of the laws which were in force during the monarchy being relative merely to that form of government, or inculcating principles inconsistent with republicanism, the first assembly which met after the establishment of the commonwealth appointed a committee to revise the whole code, to reduce it into proper form and volume, and report it to the assembly. This work has been executed by three gentlemen, and reported; but probably will not be taken up till a restoration of peace shall leave to the legislature leisure to go through such a work.

The plan of the revisal was this. The common law of England, by which is meant, that part of the English law which was anterior to the date of the oldest statutes extant, is made the basis of the work. It was thought dangerous to attempt to reduce it to a text: it was therefore left to be collected from the usual monuments of it. Necessary alterations in that, and so much of the whole body of the British statutes, and of acts of assembly, as were thought proper to be retained, were digested into 126 new acts, in which simplicity of style was aimed at, as far as was safe. The following are the most remarkable alterations proposed:

To change the rules of descent, so as that the lands of any person dying intestate shall be divisible equally among all his children, or other representatives, in equal degree.

To make slaves distributable among the next of kin, as other moveables.

To have all public expences, whether of the general treasury, or of a parish or county, (as for the maintenance of the poor, building bridges, court-houses, &c.) supplied by assessments on the citizens, in proportion to their property.

To hire undertakers for keeping the public roads in repair, and indemnify individuals through whose lands new roads shall be opened.

To define with precision the rules whereby aliens should become citizens, and citizens make themselves aliens.

To establish religious freedom on the broadest bottom.

To emancipate all slaves born after passing the act. The bill reported by the revisors does not itself contain this proposition; but an amendment containing it was prepared, to be offered to the legislature whenever the bill should be taken up, and further directing, that they should continue with their parents to a certain age, then be brought up, at the public expence, to tillage, arts or sciences, according to their geniusses, till the females should be eighteen, and the males twenty-one years of age, when they should be colonized to such place as the circumstances of the time should render most proper, sending them out with arms, implements of houshold and of the handicraft arts, seeds, pairs of the useful domestic animals, &c. to declare them a free and independent people, and extend to them our alliance and protection, till they have acquired strength; and to send vessels at the same time to other parts of the world for an equal number of white inhabitants; to induce whom to migrate hither, proper encouragements were to be proposed. It will probably be asked, Why not retain and incorporate the blacks into the state, and thus save the expence of supplying, by importation of white settlers, the vacancies they will leave? Deep rooted prejudices entertained by the whites; ten thousand recollections, by the blacks, of the injuries they have sustained; new provocations; the real distinctions which nature has made; and many other circumstances, will divide us into parties, and produce convulsions which will probably never end but in the extermination of the one or the other race.—To these objections, which are political, may be added others, which are physical and moral. The first difference which strikes us is that of colour. Whether the black of the negro resides in the reticular membrane between the skin and scarfskin, or in the scarf-skin itself; whether it proceeds from the colour of the blood, the colour of the bile, or from that of some other secretion, the difference is fixed in nature, and is as real as if its seat and cause were better known to us. And is this difference of no importance? Is it not the foundation of a greater or less share of beauty in the two races? Are not the fine mixtures of red and white, the expressions of every passion by greater or less suffusions of colour in the one, preferable to that eternal monotony, which reigns in the countenances, that immoveable veil of black which covers all the emotions of the other race? Add to these, flowing hair, a more elegant symmetry of form, their own judgment in favour of the whites, declared by their preference of them, as uniformly as is the preference of the Oranootan for the black women over those of his own species. The circumstance of superior beauty, is thought worthy attention in the propagation of our horses, dogs, and other domestic animals; why not in that of man? Besides those of colour, figure, and hair, there are other physical distinctions proving a difference of race. They have less hair on the face and body. They secrete less by the kidnies, and more by the glands of the skin, which gives them a very strong and disagreeable odour. This greater degree of transpiration renders them more tolerant of heat, and less so of cold, than the whites. Perhaps too a difference of structure in the pulmonary apparatus, which a late ingenious experimentalist has discovered to be the principal regulator of animal heat, may have disabled them from extricating, in the act of inspiration, so much of that fluid from the outer air, or obliged them in expiration, to part with more of it.

They seem to require less sleep. A black after hard labour through the day, will be induced by the slightest amusemements to sit up till midnight, or later, though knowing he must be out with the first dawn of the morning. They are at least as brave, and more adventuresome. But this may perhaps proceed from a want of fore-thought, which prevents their seeing a danger till it be present. When present, they do not go through it with more coolness or steadiness than the whites. They are more ardent after their female: but love seems with them to be more an eager desire, than a tender delicate mixture of sentiment and sensation. Their griefs are transient. Those numberless afflictions, which render it doubtful whether heaven has given life to us in mercy or in wrath, are less felt, and sooner forgotten with them. In general, their existence appears to participate more of sensation than reflection. To this must be ascribed their disposition to sleep when abstracted from their diversions, and unemployed in labour. An animal whose body is at rest, and who does not reflect, must be disposed to sleep of course. Comparing them by their faculties of memory, reason, and imagination, it appears to me, that in memory they are equal to the whites; in reason much inferior, as I think one could scarcely be found capable of tracing and comprehending the investigations of Euclid; and that in imagination they are dull, tasteless, and anomalous. It would be unfair to follow them to Africa for this investigation. We will consider them here, on the same stage with the whites, and where the facts are not apocryphal on which a judgment is to be formed. It will be right to make great allowances for the difference of condition, of education, of conversation, of the sphere in which they move. Many millions of them have been brought to, and born in America. Most of them indeed have been confined to tillage, to their own homes, and their own society: yet many have been so situated, that they might have availed themselves of the conversation of their masters; many have been brought up to the handicraft arts, from that circumstance have always been associated with the whites. Some have been liberally educated, and all have lived in countries where the arts and sciences are cultivated to a considerable degree, and have had before their eyes samples of the best works from abroad. The Indians, with no advantages of this kind, will often carve figures on their pipes not destitute of design and merit. They will crayon out an animal, a plant, or a country, so as to prove the existence of a germ in their minds which only wants cultivation. They astonish you with strokes of the most sublime oratory; such as prove their reason and sentiment strong, their imagination glowing and elevated. But never yet could I find that a black had uttered a thought above the level of plain narration; never see even an elementary trait of painting or sculpture. In music they are more generally gifted than the whites with accurate ears for tune and time, and they have been found capable of imagining a small catch.

Whether they will be equal to the composition of a more extensive run of melody, or of complicated harmony, is yet to be proved. Misery is often the parent of the most affecting touches in poetry.—Among the blacks is misery enough, God knows, but no poetry. Love is the peculiar œstrum of the poet. Their love is ardent, but it kindles the senses only, not the imagination. Religion indeed has produced a Phyllis Whately; but it could not produce a poet. The compositions published under her name are below the dignity of criticism. The heroes of the Dunciad are to her, as Hercules to the author of that poem. Ignatius Sancho has approached nearer to merit in composition; yet his letters do more honour to the heart than the head. They breathe the purest effusions of friendship and general philanthropy, and shew how great a degree of the latter may be compounded with strong religious zeal. He is often happy in the turn of his compliments, and his style is easy and familiar, except when he affects a Shandean fabrication of words. But his imagination is wild and extravagant, escapes incessantly from every restraint of reason and taste, and, in the course of its vagaries, leaves a tract of thought as incoherent and eccentric, as is the course of a meteor through the sky. His subjects should often have led him to a process of sober reasoning: yet we find him always substituting sentiment for demonstration. Upon the whole, though we admit him to the first place among those of his own colour who have presented themselves to the public judgment, yet when we compare him with the writers of the race among whom he lived, and particularly with the epistolary class, in which he has taken his own stand, we are compelled to enroll him at the bottom of the column. This criticism supposes the letters published under his name to be genuine, and to have received amendment from no other hand; points which would not be of easy investigation. The improvement of the blacks in body and mind, in the first instance of their mixture with the whites, has been observed by every one, and proves that their inferiority is not the effect merely of their condition of life. We know that among the Romans, about the Augustan age especially, the condition of their slaves was much more deplorable than that of the blacks on the continent of America. The two sexes were confined in separate apartments, because to raise a child cost the master more than to buy one. Cato, for a very restricted indulgence to his slaves in this particular, took from them a certain price.

But in this country the slaves multiply as fast as the free inhabitants. Their situation and manners place the commerce between the two sexes almost without restraint.—The same Cato, on a principle of œconomy, always sold his sick and superannuated slaves. He gives it as a standing precept to a master visiting his farm, to sell his old oxen, old waggons, old tools, old and diseased servants, and every thing else become useless. 'Vendat boves vetulos, plaustrum vetus, ferramenta vetera, servum senem, servum morbosum, & si quid aliud supersit vendat.' Cato de re rusticâ. c. 2. The American slaves cannot enumerate this among the injuries and insults they receive. It was the common practice to expose in the island of Æsculapius, in the Tyber, diseased slaves, whose cure was like to become tedious.

The emperor Claudius, by an edict, gave freedom to such of them as should recover, and first declared, that if any person chose to kill rather than to expose them, it should be deemed homicide. The exposing them is a crime of which no instance has existed with us; and were it to be followed by death, it would be punished capitally. We are told of a certain Vedius Pollio, who, in the presence of Augustus, would have given a slave as food to his fish, for having broken a glass. With the Romans, the regular method of taking the evidence of their slaves was under torture. Here it has been thought better never to resort to their evidence. When a master was murdered, all his slaves, in the same house, or within hearing, were condemned to death. Here punishment falls on the guilty only, and as precise proof is required against him as against a freeman. Yet notwithstanding these and other discouraging circumstances among the Romans, their slaves were often their rarest artists. They excelled too in science, insomuch as to be usually employed as tutors to their master's children. Epictetus, Terence, and Phædrus, were slaves. But they were of the race of whites. It is not their condition then, but nature, which has produced the distinction.—Whether further observation will or will not verify the conjecture, that nature has been less bountiful to them in the endowments of the head, I believe that in those of the heart she will be found to have done them justice. That disposition to theft with which they have been branded, must be ascribed to their situation, and not to any depravity of the moral sense. The man, in whose favour no laws of property exist, probably feels himself less bound to respect those made in favour of others. When arguing for ourselves, we lay it down as a fundamental, that laws, to be just, must give a reciprocation of right: that, without this, they are mere arbitrary rules of conduct, founded in force, and not in conscience: and it is a problem which I give to the master to solve, whether the religious precepts against the violation of property were not framed for him as well as his slave? And whether the slave may not as justifiably take a little from one, who has taken all from him, as he may slay one who would slay him? That a change in the relations in which a man is placed should change his ideas of moral right and wrong, is neither new, nor peculiar to the colour of the blacks. Homer tells us it was so 2600 years ago.

'Emisu, gar t' areles apoainutai euruopa Zeus
Haneros, eut' an min kata doulion ema elesin. Od. 17. 323.

Jove fix'd it certain, that whatever day
Makes man a slave, takes half his worth away.

But the slaves of which Homer speaks were whites. Notwithstanding these considerations which must weaken their respect for the laws of property, we find among them numerous instances of the most rigid integrity, and as many as among their better instructed masters, of benevolence, gratitude, and unshaken fidelity.— The opinion, that they are inferior in the faculties of reason and imagination, must be hazarded with great dissidence. To justify a general conclusion, requires many observations, even where the subject may be submitted to the anatomical knife, to optical glasses, to analysis by fire, or by solvents. How much more then where it is a faculty, not a substance, we are examining; where it eludes the research of all the senses; where the conditions of its existence are various and variously combined; where the effects of those which are present or absent bid defiance to calculation; let me add too, as a circumstance of great tenderness, where our conclusion would degrade a whole race of men from the rank in the scale of beings which their Creator may perhaps have given them. To our reproach it must be said, that though for a century and a half we have had under our eyes the races of black and of red men, they have never yet been viewed by us as subjects of natural history. I advance it therefore as a suspicion only, that the blacks, whether originally a distinct race, or made distinct by time and circumstances, are inferior to the whites in the endowments both of body and mind. It is not against experience to suppose, that different species of the same genus, or varieties of the same species, may posses different qualifications. Will not a lover of natural history then, one who views the gradations in all the races of animals with the eye of philosophy, excuse an effort to keep those in the department of man as distinct as nature has formed them? This unfortunate difference of colour, and perhaps of faculty, is a powerful obstacle to the emancipation of these people. Many of their advocates, while they wish to vindicate the liberty of human nature, are anxious also to preserve its dignity and beauty. Some of these, embarrassed by the question 'What further is to be done with them?' join themselves in opposition with those who are actuated by sordid avarice only. Among the Romans emancipation required but one effort. The slave, when made free, might mix with, without staining the blood of his master. But with us a second is necessary, unknown to history. When freed, he is to be removed beyond the reach of mixture.

The revised code further proposes to proportion crimes and punishments. This is attempted on the following scale.

I. Crimes whose punishment extends to LIFE.

1. High treason.		Death by hanging.
		Forfeiture of lands and goods to the commonwealth.
2. Petty treason.		Death by hanging. Dissection.
		Forfeiture of half the lands and goods to the representatives of the party slain.
3. Murder.	1. by poison.	Death by poison.
		Forfeiture of one-half as before.

	2. in duel.	Death by hanging. Gibbeting, if the challenger.
		Forfeiture of one-half as before, unless it be the party challenged, then the forfeiture is to the commonwealth.
	3. in any other way.	Death by hanging.
		Forfeiture of one-half as before.
	4. Manslaughter.	The second offence is murder.

II. Crimes whose punishment goes to LIMB.

1. Rape.	Dismemberment.
2. Sodomy.	
3. Maiming.	Retaliation, and the forfeiture of half the lands and goods to the sufferer.
4. Disfiguring.	

III. Crimes punishable by LABOUR.

1. Manslaughter, 1st offence.	Labour VII. years for the public.	Forfeiture of half as in murder.	
2. Counterfeiting money.	Labour VI. years.	Forfeiture of lands and goods to the commonwealth.	
3. Arson.	Labour V. years.	Reparation threefold.	
4. Asportation of vessels.	Labour V. years.	Reparation threefold.	
5. Robbery.	Labour IV. years.	Reparation double.	
6. Burglary.	Labour IV. years.	Reparation double.	
7. House-breaking.	Labour III. years.	Reparation.	
8. Horse-stealing.	Labour III. years.	Reparation.	
9. Grand larceny.	Labour II. years.	Reparation.	Pillory.
10. Petty larceny.	Labour I. year.	Reparation.	Pillory.
11. Pretensions to witchcraft, &c.	Ducking.	Stripes.	
12. Excusable homicide.	To be pitied, not punished.		
13. Suicide.	To be pitied, not punished.		
14. Apostacy. Heresy.	To be pitied, not punished.		

Pardon and privilege of clergy are proposed to be abolished: but if the verdict be against the defendant, the court in their discretion, may allow a new trial. No attainder to cause a corruption of blood, or forfeiture of dower. Slaves guilty of offences punishable in others by labour, to be transported to Africa, or elsewhere, as the circumstance of the time admit, there to be continued in slavery. A rigorous regimen proposed for those condemned to labour.

Another object of the revisal is, to diffuse knowledge more generally through the mass of the people. This bill proposes to lay off every county into small districts of five or six miles square, called hundreds, and in each of them to establish a school for teaching reading, writing, and arithmetic. The tutor to be supported by the hundred, and every person in it entitled to send their children three years gratis, and as much longer as they please, paying for it. These schools to be under a visitor, who is annually to chuse the boy, of best genius in the school, of those whose parents are too poor to give them further education, and to send him forward to one of the grammar schools, of which twenty are proposed to be erected in different parts of the country, for teaching Greek, Latin, geography, and the higher branches of numerical arithmetic. Of the boys thus sent in any one year, trial is to be made at the grammar schools one or two years, and the best genius of the whole selected, and continued six years, and the residue dismissed. By this means twenty of the best geniusses will be raked from the rubbish annually, and be instructed, at the public expence, so far as the grammar schools go. At the end of six years instruction, one half are to be discontinued (from among whom the grammar schools will probably be supplied with future masters); and the other half, who are to be chosen for the superiority of their parts and disposition, are to be sent and continued three years in the study of such sciences as they shall chuse, at William and Mary college, the plan of which is proposed to be enlarged, as will be hereafter explained, and extended to all the useful sciences. The ultimate result of the whole scheme of education would be the teaching all the children of the state reading, writing and common arithmetic: turning out ten annually of superior genius, well taught in Greek, Latin, geography, and the higher branches of arithmetic: turning out ten others annually, of still superior parts, who, to those branches of learning, shall have added such of the sciences as their genius shall have led them to: the furnishing to the wealthier part of the people convenient schools, at which their children may be educated at their own expence.—The general objects of this law are to provide an education adapted to the years, to the capacity, and the condition of every one, and directed to their freedom and happiness. Specific details were not proper for the law. These must be the business of the visitors entrusted with its execution. The first stage of this education being the schools of the hundreds, wherein the great mass of the people will receive their instruction, the principal foundations of future order will be laid here. Instead therefore of putting the Bible and Testament into the hands of the children, at an age when their judgments are not sufficiently matured for religious inquiries, their memories may here be stored with the most useful facts from Grecian, Roman,

European and American history. The first elements of morality too may be instilled into their minds; such as, when further developed as their judgments advance in strength, may teach them how to work out their own greatest happiness, by shewing them that it does not depend on the condition of life in which chance has placed them, but is always the result of a good conscience, good health, occupation, and freedom in all just pursuits.—Those whom either the wealth of their parents or the adoption of the state shall destine to higher degrees of learning, will go on to the grammar schools, which constitute the next stage, there to be instructed in the languages. The learning Greek and Latin, I am told, is going into disuse in Europe. I know not what their manners and occupations may call for: but it would be very ill-judged in us to follow their example in this instance. There is a certain period of life, say from eight to fifteen or sixteen years of age, when the mind, like the body, is not yet firm enough for laborious and close operations. If applied to such, it falls an early victim to premature exertion; exhibiting indeed at first, in these young and tender subjects, the flattering appearance of their being men while they are yet children, but ending in reducing them to be children when they should be men. The memory is then most susceptible and tenacious of impressions; and the learning of languages being chiefly a work of memory, it seems precisely fitted to the powers of this period, which is long enough too for acquiring the most useful languages ancient and modern. I do not pretend that language is science. It is only an instrument for the attainment of science. But that time is not lost which is employed in providing tools for future operation: more especially as in this case the books put into the hands of the youth for this purpose may be such as will at the same time impress their minds with useful facts and good principles. If this period be suffered to pass in idleness, the mind becomes lethargic and impotent, as would the body it inhabits if unexercised during the same time. The sympathy between body and mind during their rise, progress and decline, is too strict and obvious to endanger our being misled while we reason from the one to the other.—As soon as they are of sufficient age, it is supposed they will be sent on from the grammar schools to the university, which constitutes our third and last stage, there to study those sciences which may be adapted to their views.—By that part of our plan which prescribes the selection of the youths of genius from among the classes of the poor, we hope to avail the state of those talents which nature has sown as liberally among the poor as the rich, but which perish without use, if not sought for and cultivated.—but of all the views of this law none is more important, none more legitimate, than that of rendering the people the safe, as they are the ultimate, guardians of their own liberty. For this purpose the reading in the first stage, where they will receive their whole education, is proposed, as has been said, to be chiefly historical. History by apprising them of the past will enable them to judge of the future; it will avail them of the experience of other times and other nations; it will qualify them as judges of the actions and designs of men; it will enable them to know ambition under every disguise it may assume; and knowing it, to defeat its views. In every government on earth is some trace of human weakness, some germ of corruption and degeneracy, which cunning will discover, and wickedness insensibly open, cultivate and improve. Every government degenerates when trusted to the rulers of the people alone. The people themselves therefore are its only safe depositories. And to render even them safe their minds must be improved to a certain degree. This indeed is not all that is necessary, though it be essentially necessary. An amendment of our constitution must here come in aid of the public education. The influence over government must be shared among all the people. If every individual which composes their mass participates of the ultimate authority, the government will be safe; because the corrupting the whole mass will exceed any private resources of wealth: and public ones cannot be provided but by levies on the people. In this case every man would have to pay his own price. The government of Great-Britain has been corrupted, because but one man in ten has a right to vote for members of parliament. The sellers of the government therefore get nine-tenths of their price clear. It has been thought that corruption is restrained by confining the right of suffrage to a few of the wealthier of the people: but it would be more effectually restrained by an extension of that right to such numbers as would bid defiance to the means of corruption.

Lastly, it is proposed, by a bill in this revisal, to begin a public library and gallery, by laying out a certain sum annually in books, paintings, and statues.

Query XVII

The different religions received into that state?

The first settlers in this country were emigrants from England, of the English church, just at a point of time when it was flushed with complete victory over the religious of all other persuasions. Possessed, as they became, of the powers of making, administering, and executing the laws, they shewed equal intolerance in this country with their Presbyterian brethren, who had emigrated to the northern government. The poor Quakers were flying from persecution in England. They cast their eyes on these new countries as asylums of civil and religious freedom; but they found them free only for the reigning sect. Several acts of the Virginia assembly of 1659, 1662, and 1693, had made it penal in parents to refuse to have their children baptized; had prohibited the unlawful assembling of Quakers; had made it penal for any master of a vessel to bring a Quaker into the state; had ordered those already here, and such as should come thereafter, to be imprisoned till they should abjure the country; provided a milder punishment for their first and second return, but death for their third; had inhibited all persons from suffering their meetings in or near their houses, entertaining them individually, or disposing of books which supported their tenets. If no capital execution took place here, as did in New-England, it was not owing to the moderation of the church, or spirit of the legislature, as may be inferred from the law itself; but to historical circumstances which have not been handed down to us. The Anglicans retained full possession of the country about a century. Other opinions began then to creep in, and the great care of the government to support their own church, having begotten an equal degree of indolence in its clergy, two-thirds of the people had become dissenters at the commencement of the present revolution. The laws indeed were still oppressive on them, but the spirit of the one party had subsided into moderation, and of the other had risen to a degree of determination which commanded respect.

The present state of our laws on the subject of religion is this. The convention of May 1776, in their declaration of rights, declared it to be a truth, and a natural right, that the exercise of religion should be free; but when they proceeded to form on that declaration the ordinance of government, instead of taking up every principle declared in the bill of rights, and guarding it by legislative sanction, they passed over that which asserted our religious rights, leaving them as they found them. The same convention, however, when they met as a member of the general assembly in October 1776, repealed all acts of parliament which had rendered criminal the maintaining any opinions in matters of religion, the forbearing to repair to church, and the exercising any mode of worship; and suspended the laws giving salaries to the clergy, which suspension was made perpetual in October 1779. Statutory oppressions in religion being thus wiped away, we remain at present under those only imposed by the common law, or by our own acts of assembly. At the common law, heresy was a capital offence, punishable by burning. Its definition was left to the ecclesiastical judges, before whom the conviction was, till the statute of the 1 El. c. 1. circumscribed it, by declaring, that nothing should be deemed heresy, but what had been so determined by authority of the canonical scriptures, or by one of the four first general councils, or by some other council having for the grounds of their declaration the express and plain words of the scriptures. Heresy, thus circumscribed, being an offence at the common law, our act of assembly of October 1777, c. 17. gives cognizance of it to the general court, by declaring, that the jurisdiction of that court shall be general in all matters at the common law. The execution is by the writ de hœritico comburendo. By our own act of assembly of 1705, c. 30. if a person brought up in the Christian religion denies the being of a God, or the Trinity, or asserts there are more gods than one, or denies the Christian religion to be true, or the scriptures to be of divine authority, he is punishable on the first offence by incapacity to hold any office or employment ecclesiastical, civil, or military; on the second by disability to sue, to take any gift or legacy, to be guardian, executor, or administrator, and by three years imprisonment, without bail. A father's right to the custody of his own children being founded in law on his right of guardianship, this being taken away, they may of course be severed from him, and put, by the authority of a court, into more orthodox hands. This is a summary view of that religious slavery, under which a people have been willing to remain, who have lavished their lives and fortunes for the establishment of their civil freedom.

The error seems not sufficiently eradicated, that the operations of the mind, as well as the acts of the body, are subject to the coercion of the laws. But our rulers can have authority over such natural rights only as we have submitted to them. The rights of conscience we never submitted, we could not submit. We are answerable for them to our God. The legitimate powers of government extend to such acts only as are injurious to others. But it does me no injury for my neighbour to say there are twenty gods, or no god. It neither picks my pocket nor breaks my leg. If it be said, his testimony in a court of justice cannot be relied on, reject it then, and be the stigma on him. Constraint may make him worse by making him a hypocrite, but it will never make him a truer man. It may fix him obstinately in his errors, but will not cure them. Reason and free inquiry are the only effectual agents against error. Give a loose to them, they will support the true religion, by bringing every false one to their tribunal, to the test of their investigation. They are the natural enemies of error, and of error only. Had not the Roman government permitted free inquiry, Christianity could never have been introduced. Had not free inquiry been indulged, at the æra of the reformation, the corruptions of Christianity could not have been purged away. If it be restrained now, the present corruptions will be protected, and new ones encouraged. Was the government to prescribe to us our medicine and diet, our bodies would be in such keeping as our souls are now. Thus in France the emetic was once forbidden as a medicine, and the potatoe as an article of food. Government is just as infallible too when it fixes systems in physics. Galileo was sent to the inquisition for affirming that the earth was a sphere: the government had declared it to be as flat as a trencher, and Galileo was obliged to abjure his error. This error however at length prevailed, the earth became a globe, and Descartes declared it was whirled round its axis by a vortex. The government in which he lived was wise enough to see that this was no question of civil jurisdiction, or we should all have been involved by authority in vortices. In fact, the vortices have been exploded, and the Newtonian principle of gravitation is now more firmly established, on the basis of reason, than it would be were the government to step in, and to make it an article of necessary faith. Reason and experiment have been indulged, and error has fled before them. It is error alone which needs the support of government. Truth can stand by itself. Subject opinion to coercion: whom will you make your inquisitors? Fallible men; men governed by bad passions, by private as well as public reasons. And why subject it to coercion? To produce uniformity. But is uniformity of opinion desireable? No more than of face and stature. Introduce the bed of Procrustes then, and as there is danger that the large men may beat the small, make us all of a size, by lopping the former and stretching the latter. Difference of opinion is advantageous in religion. The several sects perform the office of a Censor morum over each other. Is uniformity attainable? Millions of innocent men, women, and children, since the introduction of Christianity, have been burnt, tortured, fined, imprisoned; yet we have not advanced one inch towards uniformity. What has been the effect of coercion? To make one half the world fools, and the other half hypocrites. To support roguery and error all over the earth. Let us reflect that it is inhabited by a thousand millions of people. That these profess probably a thousand different systems of religion. That ours is but one of that thousand. That if there be but one right, and ours that one, we should wish to see the 999 wandering sects gathered into the fold of truth. But against such a majority we cannot effect this by force. Reason and persuasion are the only practicable instruments. To make way for these, free inquiry must be indulged; and how can we wish others to indulge it while we refuse it ourselves. But every state, says an inquisitor, has established some religion. No two, say I, have established the same. Is this a proof of the infallibility of establishments? Our sister states of Pennsylvania and New York, however, have long subsisted without any establishment at all. The experiment was new and doubtful when they made it. It has answered beyond conception. They flourish infinitely. Religion is well supported; of various kinds, indeed, but all good enough; all sufficient to preserve peace and order: or if a sect arises, whose tenets would subvert morals, good sense has fair play, and reasons and laughs it out of doors, without suffering the state to be troubled with it. They do not hang more malefactors than we do. They are not more disturbed with religious dissensions. On the contrary, their harmony is unparalleled, and can be ascribed to nothing but their unbounded tolerance, because there is no other circumstance in which they differ from every nation on earth. They have made the happy discovery, that the way to silence religious disputes, is to take no notice of them. Let us too give this experiment fair play, and get rid, while we may, of those tyrannical laws. It is true, we are as yet secured against them by the spirit of the times. I doubt whether the people of this country would suffer an execution for heresy, or a three years imprisonment for not comprehending the the mysteries of the Trinity. But is the spirit of the people an infallible, a permanent reliance? Is it government? Is this the kind of protection we receive in return for the rights we give up? Besides, the spirit of the times may alter, will alter. Our rulers will become corrupt, our people careless. A single zealot may commence persecutor, and better men be his victims. It can never be too often repeated, that the time for fixing every essential right on a legal basis is while our rulers are honest, and ourselves united. From the conclusion of this war we shall be going down hill. It will not then be necessary to resort every moment to the people for support. They will be forgotten, therefore, and their rights disregarded. They will forget themselves, but in the sole faculty of making money, and will never think of uniting to effect a due respect for their rights. The shackles, therefore, which shall not be knocked off at the conclusion of this war, will remain on us long, will be made heavier and heavier, till our rights shall revive or expire in a convulsion.

Query XIX

The present state of manufactures, commerce, interior and exterior trade?

We never had an interior trade of any importance. Our exterior commerce has suffered very much from the beginning of the present contest. During this time we have manufactured within our families the most necessary articles of cloathing. Those of cotton will bear some comparison with the same kinds of manufacture in Europe; but those of wool, flax and hemp are very coarse, unsightly, and unpleasant: and such is our attachment to agriculture, and such our preference for foreign manufactures, that be it wise or unwise, our people will certainly return as soon as they can, to the raising raw materials, and exchanging them for finer manufactures than they are able to execute themselves.

The political œconomists of Europe have established it as a principle that every state should endeavour to manufacture for itself: and this principle, like many others, we transfer to America, without calculating the difference of circumstance which should often produce a difference of result. In Europe the lands are either cultivated, or locked up against the cultivator. Manufacture must therefore be resorted to of necessity not of choice, to support the surplus of their people. But we have an immensity of land courting the industry of the husbandman. It is best then that all our citizens should be employed in its improvement, or that one half should be called off from that to exercise manufactures and handicraft arts for the other? Those who labour in the earth are the chosen people of God, if ever he had a chosen people, whose breasts he has made his peculiar deposit for substantial and genuine virtue. It is the focus in which he keeps alive that sacred fire, which otherwise might escape from the face of the earth. Corruption of morals in the mass of cultivators is a phænomenon of which no age nor nation has furnished an example. It is the mark set on those, who not looking up to heaven, to their own soil and industry, as does the husbandman, for their subsistance, depend for it on the casualties and caprice of customers. Dependance begets subservience and venality, suffocates the germ of virtue, and prepares fit tools for the designs of ambition. This, the natural progress and consequence of the arts, has sometimes perhaps been retarded by accidental circumstances: but, generally speaking, the proportion which the aggregate of the other classes of citizens bears in any state to that of its husbandmen, is the proportion of its unfound to its healthy parts, and is a good-enough barometer whereby to measure its degree of corruption. While we have land to labour then, let us never wish to see our citizens occupied at a work-bench, or twirling a distaff. Carpenters, masons, smiths, are wanting in husbandry: but, for the general operations of manufacture, let our work-shops remain in Europe. It is better to carry provisions and materials to workmen there, than bring them to the provisions and materials, and with them their manners and principles. The loss by the transportation of commodities across the Atlantic will be made up in happiness and permanence of government. The mobs of great cities add just so much to the support of pure government, as sores do to the strength of the human body. It is the manners and spirit of a people which preserve a republic in vigour. A degeneracy in these is a canker which soon eats to the heart of its laws and constitution.

3.9.2 *Autobiography of Thomas Jefferson* (1821)

JANUARY 6, 1821.

At the age of 77, I begin to make some memoranda, and state some recollections of dates and facts concerning myself, for my own more ready reference, and for the information of my family.

The tradition in my father's family was, that their ancestor came to this country from Wales, and from near the mountain of Snowdon, the highest in Great Britain. I noted once a case from Wales, in the law reports, where a person of our name was either plaintiff or defendant; and one of the same name was secretary to the Virginia Company. These are the only instances in which I have met with the name in that country. I have found it in our early records; but the first particular information I have of any ancestor was of my grandfather, who lived at the place in Chesterfield called Ozborne's, and owned the lands afterwards the glebe of the parish. He had three sons; Thomas who died young, Field who settled on the waters of Roanoke and left numerous descendants, and Peter, my father, who settled on the lands I still own, called Shadwell, adjoining my present residence. He was born February 29, 1707-8, and intermarried 1739, with Jane Randolph, of the age of 19, daughter of Isham Randolph, one of the seven sons of that name and family, settled at Dungeoness in Goochland. They trace their pedigree far back in England and Scotland, to which let every one ascribe the faith and merit he chooses.

My father's education had been quite neglected; but being of a strong mind, sound judgment, and eager after information, he read much and improved himself, insomuch that he was chosen, with Joshua Fry, Professor of Mathematics in William and Mary college, to continue the boundary line between Virginia and North Carolina, which had been begun by Colonel Byrd; and was afterwards employed with the same Mr. Fry, to make the first map of Virginia which had ever been made, that of Captain Smith being merely a conjectural sketch. They possessed excellent materials for so much of the country as is below the Blue Ridge; little being then known beyond that ridge. He was the third or fourth settler, about the year 1737, of the part of the country in which I live. He died, August 17th, 1757, leaving my mother a widow, who lived till 1776, with six daughters and two sons, myself the elder. To my younger brother he left his estate on James River, called Snowdon, after the supposed birth-place of the family: to myself, the lands on which I was born and live.

He placed me at the English school at five years of age; and at the Latin at nine, where I continued until his death. My teacher, Mr. Douglas, a clergyman from Scotland, with the rudiments of the Latin and Greek languages, taught me the French; and on the death of my father, I went to the Reverend James Maury, a correct classical scholar, with whom I continued two years; and then, to wit, in the spring of 1760, went to William and Mary College, where I continued two years. It was my great good fortune, and what probably fixed the destinies of my life, that Dr. William Small of Scotland, was then Professor of Mathematics, a man profound in most of the useful branches of science, with a happy talent of communication, correct and gentlemanly manners, and an enlarged and liberal mind. He, most happily for me, became soon attached to me, and made me his daily companion when not engaged in the school; and from his conversation I got my first views of the expansion of science, and of the system of things in which we are placed. Fortunately, the philosophical chair became vacant soon after my arrival at college, and he was appointed to fill it per interim: and he was the first who ever gave, in that college, regular lectures in Ethics, Rhetoric and Belles Letters. He returned to Europe in 1762, having previously filled up the measure of his goodness to me, by procuring for me, from his most intimate friend, George Wythe, a reception as a student of law, under his direction, and introduced me to the acquaintance and familiar table of Governor Fauquier, the ablest man who had ever filled that office. With him, and at his table, Dr. Small and Mr. Wythe, his amici omnium horarum, and myself, formed a partie quarrée, and to the habitual conversations on these occasions I owed much instruction. Mr. Wythe continued to be my faithful and beloved mentor in youth, and my most affectionate friend through life. In 1767, he led me into the practice of the law at the bar of the General court, at which I continued until the Revolution shut up the courts of justice.

In 1769, I became a member of the legislature by the choice of the county in which I live, and so continued until it was closed by the Revolution. I made one effort in that body for the permission of the emancipation of slaves, which was rejected: and indeed, during the regal government, nothing liberal could expect success. Our minds were circumscribed within narrow Iimits, by an habitual belief that it was our duty to be subordinate to the mother country in all matters of government, to direct all our labors in subservience to her interests, and even to observe a bigoted intolerance for all religions but hers. The difficulties with our representatives were of habit and despair, not of reflection and conviction. Experience soon proved that they could bring their minds to rights, on the first summons of their attention. But the King's Council, which acted as another house of legislature, held their places at will, and were in most humble obedience to that will: the Governor too, who had a negative on our laws, held by the same tenure, and with still greater devotedness to it: and, last of all, the Royal negative closed the last door to every hope of amelioration.

On the 1st of January, 1772, I was married to Martha Skelton, widow of Bathurst Skelton, and daughter of John Wayles, then twenty-three years old. Mr. Wayles was a lawyer of much practice, to which he was introduced more by his great industry, punctuality, and practical readiness, than by eminence in the science of his profession. He was a most agreeable companion, full of pleasantry and good humor, and welcomed in every society. He acquired a handsome fortune, and died in May, 1773, leaving three daughters: the portion which came on that event to Mrs. Jefferson, after the debts should be paid, which were very considerable, was about equal to my own patrimony, and consequently doubled the ease of our circumstances.

When the famous Resolutions of 1765, against the Stamp Act, were proposed, I was yet a student of law in Williamsburg. I attended the debate, however, at the door of the lobby of the House of Burgesses, and heard the splendid display of Mr. Patrick Henry's talents as a popular orator. They were great indeed; such as I have never heard from any other man. He appeared to me to speak as Homer wrote. Mr. Johnson, a lawyer, and member from the Northern Neck, seconded the resolutions, and by him the learning and the logic of the case were chiefly maintained. My recollections of these transactions may be seen page 60 of the life of Patrick Henry, by Wirt, to whom I furnished them.

In May, 1769, a meeting of the General Assembly was called by the Governor, Lord Botetourt. I had then become a member; and to that meeting became known the joint resolutions and address of the Lords and Commons, of 1768-9, on the proceedings in Massachusetts. Counter-resolutions , and an address to the King by the House of Burgesses, were agreed to with little opposition, and a spirit manifestly displayed itself of considering the cause of Massachusetts as a common one. The Governor dissolved us: but we met the next day in the Apollo of the Raleigh tavern, formed ourselves into a voluntary convention, drew up articles of association against the use of any merchandise imported from Great Britain, signed and recommended them to the people, repaired to our several counties, and were re-elected without any other exception than of the very few who had declined assent to our proceedings.

Nothing of particular excitement occurring for a considerable time, our countrymen seemed to fall into a state of insensibility to our situation; the duty on tea, not yet repealed, and the declaratory act of a right in the British Parliament to bind us by their laws in all cases whatsoever, still suspended over us. But a court of inquiry held in Rhode Island in 1762, with a power to send persons to England to be tried for offences committed here, was considered, at our session of the spring of 1773, as demanding attention. Not thinking our old and leading members up to the point of forwardness and zeal which the times required, Mr. Henry, Richard Henry Lee, Francis L. Lee, Mr. Carr and myself agreed to meet in the evening, in a private room of the Raleigh, to consult on the state of things. There may have been a member or two more whom I do not recollect. We were all sensible that the most urgent of all measures was that of coming to an understanding with all the other colonies, to consider the British claims as a common cause to all, and to produce a unity of action: and, for this purpose, that a committee of correspondence in each colony would be the best instrument for intercommunication : and that their first measure would probably be, to propose a meeting of deputies from every colony, at some central place, who should be charged with the direction of the measures which should be taken by all. We, therefore, drew up the resolutions which may be seen in Wirt, page 87. The consulting members proposed to me to move them, but I urged that it should be done by Mr. Dabney Carr, my friend and brother-in-law, then a new member, to whom I wished an opportunity should be given of making known to the house his great worth and talents. It was so agreed; he moved them, they were agreed to nem. con. and a committee of correspondence appointed, of whom Peyton Randolph, the speaker; was chairman. The Governor (then Lord Dunmore) dissolved us, but the committee met the next day, prepared a circular letter to the speakers of the other colonies, inclosing to each a copy of the resolutions, and left it in charge with their chairman to forward them by expresses.

The origination of these committees of correspondence between the colonies has been since claimed for Massachusetts, and Marshall has given into this error, although the very note of his appendix to which he refers, shows that their establishment was confined to their own towns. This matter will be seen clearly stated in a letter of Samuel Adams Wells to me of April 2nd, 1819, and my answer of May 12th. I was corrected by the letter of Mr. Wells in the information I had given Mr. Wirt, as stated in his note, page 87, that the messengers of Massachusetts and Virginia crossed each other on the way, bearing similar propositions; for Mr. Wells shows that Massachusetts did not adopt the measure, but on the receipt of our proposition, delivered at their next session. Their message, therefore, which passed ours, must have related to something else, for I well remember Peyton Randolph's informing me of the crossing of our messengers.

The next event which excited our sympathies for Massachusetts, was the Boston port bill, by which that port was to be shut up on the 1st of June, 1774. This arrived while we were in session in the spring of that year. The lead in the House, on these subjects, being no longer left to the old members, Mr. Henry, R. H. Lee, Fr. L. Lee, three or four other members, whom I do not recollect, and myself, agreeing that we must boldly take an unequivocal stand in the line with Massachusetts, determined to meet and consult on the proper measures, in the council-chamber, for the benefit of the library in that room. We were under conviction of the necessity *of arousing our people from the lethargy into which they had fallen, as to passing events*; and thought that the appointment of a day of general fasting and prayer would be most likely to call up and alarm their attention. No example of such a solemnity had existed since the days of our distresses in the war of '55, since which a new generation had grown up. With the help, therefore, of Rushworth, whom we rummaged over for the revolutionary precedents and forms of the Puritans of that day, preserved by him, we cooked up a resolution, somewhat modernizing their phrases, for appointing the 1st day of June, on which the portbill was to commence, for a day of fasting, humiliation, and prayer, to implore Heaven to avert from us the evils of civil war, to inspire us with firmness in support of our rights, and to turn the hearts of the King and Parliament to moderation and justice. To give greater emphasis to our proposition, we agreed to wait the next morning on Mr. Nicholas, whose grave and religious character was more in unison with the tone of our resolution, and to solicit him to move it. We accordingly went to him in the morning. He moved it the same day; the 1st of June was proposed; and it passed without opposition. The Governor dissolved us, as usual. We retired to the Apollo, as before, agreed to an association, and instructed the committee of correspondence to propose to the corresponding committees of the other colonies, to appoint deputies to meet in Congress at such place, annually, as should be convenient, to direct, from time to time, the measures required by the general interest: and we declared that an attack on any one colony, should be considered as an attack on the whole. This was in May. We further recommended to the several counties to elect deputies to meet at Williamsburg, the 1st of August ensuing, to consider the state of the colony, and particularly to appoint delegates to a general Congress, should that measure be acceded to by the committees of correspondence generally. It was acceded to; Philadelphia was appointed for the place, and the 5th of September for the time of meeting. We returned home, and in our several counties invited the clergy to meet assemblies of the people on the 1st of June, to perform the ceremonies of the day, and to address to them discourses suited to the occasion. The people met generally, with anxiety and alarm in their countenances, and the effect of the day, through the whole colony, was like a shock of electricity, arousing every man, and placing him erect and solidly on his centre. They chose, universally, delegates for the convention. Being elected one for my own county, I prepared a draught of instructions to be given to the delegates whom we should send to the Congress, which I meant to propose at our meeting. In this I took the ground that, from the beginning, I had thought the only one orthodox or tenable, which was, that the relation between Great Britain and these colonies was exactly the same as that of England and Scotland, after the accession of James, and until the union, and the same as her present relations with Hanover, having the same executive chief, but no other necessary political connection; and that our emigration from England to this country gave her no more rights over us, than the emigrations of the Danes and Saxons gave to the present authorities of the mother country, over England. In this doctrine, however, I had never been able to get any one to agree with me but Mr. Withe. He concurred in it from the first dawn of the question, What was the political relation between us and England? Our other patriots, Randolph, the Lees, Nicholas, Pendleton, stopped at the half-way house of John Dickinson, who admitted that England had a right-to regulate our commerce, and to lay duties on it for the purposes of regulation, but not of raising revenue. But for this ground there was no foundation in compact, in any acknowledged principles of colonization, nor in reason: expatriation being a natural right, and acted on as such, by all nations, in all ages. I set out for Williamsburg some days before that appointed for our meeting, but was taken ill of a dysentery on the road, and was unable to proceed. I sent on, therefore, to Williamsburg two copies of my draught, the one under cover to Peyton Randolph, who I knew would be in the chair of the convention, the other to Patrick Henry. Whether Mr. Henry disapproved the ground taken, or was too lazy to read it (for he was the laziest man in reading I ever knew) I never learned: but he communicated it to nobody. Peyton Randolph informed the convention he had received such a paper from a member, prevented by sickness from offering it in his place, and he laid it on the table for perusal.

It was read generally by the members approved by many, though thought too bold for the present state of things; but they printed it in pamphlet form, under the title of *A Summary View of the Rights of British America*. It found its way to England, was taken up by the opposition, interpolated a little by Mr. Burke so as to make it answer opposition purposes, and in that form ran rapidly through several editions. This information I had from Parson Hurt, who happened at the time to be in London, whither he had gone to receive clerical orders; and I was informed afterwards by Peyton Randolph, that it had procured me the honor of having my name inserted in a long list of proscriptions, enrolled in a bill of attainder commenced in one of the Houses of Parliament, but suppressed in embryo by the hasty step of events, which warned them to be a little cautious. Montague, agent of the House of Burgesses in England, made extracts from the bill, copied the names, and sent them to Peyton Randolph. The names, I think, were about twenty, which he repeated to me, but I recollect those only of Hancock, the two Adamses, Peyton Randolph himself, Patrick Henry, and myself. The convention met on the 1st of August, renewed their association, appointed delegates to the Congress, gave them instructions very temperately and properly expressed, both as to style and matter; and they repaired to Philadelphia at the time appointed. The splendid proceedings of that Congress, at their first session, belong to general history, are known to every one, and need not therefore be noted here. They terminated their session on the 26th of October, to meet again on the 10th of May ensuing. The convention, at their ensuing session of March, approved of the proceedings of Congress, thanked their delegates, and reappointed the same persons to represent the colony at the meeting to be held in May: and foreseeing the probability that Peyton Randolph, their president, and speaker also of the House of Burgesses, might be called off, they added me, in that event, to the delegation.

Mr. Randolph was, according to expectation, obliged to leave the chair of Congress, to attend the General Assembly summoned by Lord Dunmore, to meet on the 1st day of June, 1775. Lord North's conciliatory propositions, as they were called, had been received by the Governor, and furnished the subject for which this assembly was convened. Mr. Randolph accordingly attended, and the tenor of these propositions being generally known, as having been addressed to all the governors, he was anxious that the answer of our Assembly, likely to be the first, should harmonize with what he knew to be the sentiments and wishes of the body he had recently left. He feared that Mr. Nicholas, whose mind was not yet up to the mark of the times, would undertake the answer, and therefore pressed me to prepare it. I did so, and, with his aid, carried it through the House, with long and doubtful scruples from Mr. Nicholas and James Mercer, and a dash of cold water on it here and there, enfeebling it somewhat, but finally with unanimity, or a vote approaching it. This being passed, I repaired immediately to Philadelphia, and conveyed to Congress the first notice they had of it. It was entirely approved there. I took my seat with them on the 21st of June. On the 24th, a committee which had been appointed to prepare a declaration of the causes of taking up arms, brought in their report (drawn I believe by J. Rutledge) which, not being liked, the House recommitted it, on the 26th, and added Mr. Dickinson and myself to the committee. On the rising of the House, the committee having not yet met, I happened to find myself near Governor W. Livingston, and proposed to him to draw the paper. He excused himself and proposed that. I should draw it. On my pressing him with urgency, *we are as yet but new acquaintances, sir*, said he, *why are you so earnest for my doing it? Because*, said I, *I have been informed that you drew the Address to the people of Great Britain, a production, certainly, of the finest pen in America. On that,* says he, *perhaps, sir, you may not have been correctly informed.* I had received the information in Virginia from Colonel Harrison on his return from that Congress. Lee, Livingston, and Jay had been the committee for that draught. The first, prepared by Lee, had been disapproved and recommitted. The second was drawn by Jay, but being presented by Governor Livingston, had led Colonel Harrison into the error. The next morning, walking in the hall of Congress, many members being assembled, but the House not yet formed, I observed Mr. Jay speaking to R. H. Lee, and leading him by the button of his coat to me. *I understand, sir,* said he to me, *that this gentleman informed you, that Governor Livingston drew the Address to the people of Great Britain.* I assured him, at once, that I had not received that information from Mr. Lee, and that not a word had ever passed on the subject between Mr. Lee and myself; and after some explanations the subject was dropped. These gentlemen had had some sparrings in debate before, and continued ever very hostile to each other.

I prepared a draught of the declaration committed to us. It was too strong for Mr. Dickinson. He still retained the hope of reconciliation with the mother country, and was unwilling it should be Lessened by offensive statements. He was so honest a man, and so able a one, that he was greatly indulged even by those who could not feel his scruples. We therefore requested him to take the paper, and put it into a form he could approve. He did so, preparing an entire new statement, and preserving of the former only the last four paragraphs and half of the preceding one. We approved and reported it to Congress, who accepted it. Congress gave a signal proof of their indulgence to Mr. Dickinson, and of their great desire not to go too fast for any respectable part of our body, in permitting him to draw their second petition to the King according to his own ideas, and passing it with scarcely any amendment. The disgust against this numility was general; and Mr. Dickinson's delight at its passage was the only circumstance which reconciled them to it. The vote being passed, although further observation on it was out of order, he could not refrain from rising and expressing his satisfaction, and concluded by saying, *there is but one word, Mr. President, in the paper which I disapprove, and that is the word Congress*; on which Ben Harrison rose and said, *There is but one word in the paper, Mr. President, of which I approve, and that is the word Congress.*

On the 22d of July, Dr. Franklin, Mr. Adams, R. H. Lee, and myself, were appointed a committee to consider and report on Lord North's conciliatory resolution. The answer of the Virginia Assembly on that subject having been approved, I was requested by the committee to prepare this report, which will account for the similarity of feature in the two instruments.

On the 15th of May, 1776, the convention of Virginia instructed their delegates in Congress, to propose to that body to declare the colonies independent of Great Britain, and appointed a committee to prepare a declaration of rights and plan of government.

In Congress, Friday, June 7, 1776. The delegates from Virginia moved, in obedience to instructions from their constituents, that the Congress should declare that these United colonies are, and of right ought to be, free and independent states, that they are absolved from all allegiance to the British crown, and that all political connection between them and the state of Great Britain is, and ought to be, totally dissolved; that measures should be immediately taken for procuring the assistance of foreign powers, and a Confederation be formed to bind the colonies more closely together.

The House being obliged to attend at that time to some other business, the proposition was referred to the next day, when the members were ordered to attend punctually at ten o'clock.

Saturday, June 8. They proceeded to take it into consideration, and referred it to a committee of the whole, into which they immediately resolved themselves, and passed that day and Monday, the loth, in debating on the subject. It was argued by Wilson, Robert R. Livingston, E. Rutledge, Dickinson, and others that, though they were friends to the measures themselves, and saw the impossibility that we should ever again be united with Great Britain, yet they were against adopting them at this time : That the conduct we had formerly observed was wise and proper now, of deferring to take any capital step till the voice of the people drove us into it:

That they were our power, and without them our declarations could not be carried into effect:

That the people of the middle colonies (Maryland, Delaware, Pennsylvania, the Jerseys and New York) were not yet ripe for bidding adieu to British connection, but that they were fast ripening, and, in a short time, would join in the general voice of America:

That the resolution, entered into by this House on the l5th of May, for suppressing the exercise of all powers derived from the crown, had shown, by the ferment into which it had thrown these middle colonies, that they had not yet accommodated their minds to a separation from the mother country:

That some of them had expressly forbidden their delegates to consent to such a declaration, and others had given no instructions, and consequently no powers to give such consent:

That if the delegates of any particular colony had no power to declare such colony independent, certain they were, the others could not declare it for them; the colonies being as yet perfectly independent of each other:

That the assembly of Pennsylvania was now sitting above stairs, their convention would sit within a few days, the convention of New York was now sitting, and those of the Jerseys and Delaware counties would meet on the Monday following, and it was probable these bodies would take up the question of Independence, and would declare to their delegates the voice of their state:

That if such a declaration should now be agreed to, these delegates must retire, and possibly their colonies might secede from the Union:

That such a secession would weaken us more than could be compensated by any foreign alliance:

That in the event of such a division, foreign powers would either refuse to join themselves to our fortunes, or, having us so much in their power as that desperate declaration would place us, they would insist on terms proportionably more hard and prejudicial

That we had little reason to expect an alliance with those to whom alone, as yet, we had cast our eyes:

That France and Spain had reason to be jealous of that rising power, which would one day certainly strip them of all their American possessions:

That it was more likely they should form a connection with the British court, who, if they should find themselves unable otherwise to extricate themselves from their difficulties, would agree to a partition of our territories, restoring Canada to France, and the Floridas to Spain, to accomplish for themselves a recovery of these colonies.

That it would not be long before we should receive certain information of the disposition of the French court, from the agent whom we had sent to Paris for that purpose:

That if this disposition should be favorable, by waiting the event of the present campaign, which we all hoped would be successful, we should have reason to expect an alliance on better terms:

That this would in fact work no delay of any effectual aid from such ally, as, from the advance of the season and distance of our situation, it was impossible we could receive any assistance during this campaign:

That it was prudent to fix among ourselves the terms on which we should form alliance, before we declared we would form one at all events:

And that if these were agreed on, and our Declaration of Independence ready by the time our Ambassador should be prepared to sail, it would be as well as to go into that Declaration at this day.

On the other side, it was urged by J. Adams, Lee, Withe, and others, that no gentleman had argued against the policy or the right of separation from Britain, nor had supposed it possible we should ever renew our connection; that they had only opposed its being now declared:

That the question was not whether, by a Declaration of Independence, we should make ourselves what we are not; but whether we should declare a fact which already exists:

That, as to the people or parliament of England, we had always been independent of them, their restraints on our trade deriving efficacy from our acquiescence only, and not from any rights they possessed of imposing them, and that so far, our connection had been federal only, and was now dissolved by the commencement of hostilities:

That, as to the King, we had been bound to him by allegiance, but that this bond was now dissolved by his assent to the last act of Parliament, by which he declares us out of his protection, and by his levying war on us, a fact which had long ago proved us out of his protection; it being a certain position in law, that allegiance and protection are reciprocal, the one ceasing when the other is withdrawn:

That James the Second never declared the people of England out of his protection, yet his actions proved it, and the Parliament declared it: No delegates then can be denied, or ever want, a power of declaring an existing truth: That the delegates from the Delaware counties having declared their constituents ready to join, there are only two colonies, Pennsylvania and Maryland, whose delegates are absolutely tied up, and that these had, by their instructions, only reserved a right of confirming or rejecting the measure:

That the instructions from Pennsylvania might be accounted for from the times in which they were drawn, near a twelvemonth ago,since which the face of affairs has totally changed:

That within that time, it had become apparent that Britain was determined to accept nothing less than a carte-blanche, and that the King's answer to the Lord Mayor, Aldermen and Common Council of London, which had come to hand four days ago, must have satisfied every one of this point:

That the people wait for us to lead the way:

That they are in favor of the measure, though the instructions given by some of their representatives are not:

That the voice of the representatives is not always consonant with the voice of the people, and that this is remarkably the case in these middle colonies:

That the effect of the resolution of the 15th of May has proved this, which, raising the murmurs of some in the colonies of Pennsylvania and Maryland, called forth the opposing voice of the freer part of the people, and proved them to be the majority even in these colonies:

That the backwardness of these two colonies might be ascribed, partly to the influence of proprietary power and connections, and partly, to their having not yet been attacked by the enemy:

That these causes were not likely to be soon removed, as there seemed no probability that the enemy would make either of these the seat of this summer's war:

That it would be vain to wait either weeks or months for perfect unanimity, since it was impossible that all men should ever become of one sentiment on any question:

That the conduct of some colonies, from the beginning of this contest, had given reason to suspect it was their settled policy to keep in the rear of the confederacy, that their particular prospect might be better, even in the worst event:

That, therefore, it was necessary for those colonies who had thrown themselves forward and hazarded all from the beginning, to come forward now also, and put all again to their own hazard:

That the history of the Dutch Revolution, of whom three states only confederated at first, proved that a secession of some colonies would not be so dangerous as some apprehended:

That a Declaration of Independence alone could render it consistent with European delicacy, for European powers to treat with us, or even to receive an Ambassador from us: That till this, they would not receive our vessels into their ports, nor acknowledge the adjudications of our courts of admiralty to be legitimate, in cases of capture of British vessels:

That though France and Spain may be jealous of our rising power, they must think it will be much more formidable with the addition of Great Britain; and will therefore see it their interest to prevent a coalition; but should they refuse, we shall be but where we are; whereas without trying, we shall never know whether they will aid us or not:

That the present campaign may be unsuccessful, and therefore we had better propose an alliance while our affairs wear a hopeful aspect:

That to wait the event of this campaign will certainly work delay, because, during the summer, France may assist us effectually, by cutting off those supplies of provisions from England and Ireland, on which the enemy's armies here are to depend; or by setting in motion the great power they have collected in the West Indies, and calling our enemy to the defense of the possessions they have there:

That it would be idle to lose time in settling the terms of alliance, till we had first determined we would enter into alliance:

That it is necessary to lose no time in opening a trade for our people, who will want clothes, and will want money too, for the payment of taxes:

And that the only misfortune is, that we did not enter into alliance with France six months sooner, as, besides opening her ports for the vent of our last year's produce, she might have marched an army into Germany, and prevented the petty princes there, from selling their unhappy subjects to subdue us.

It appearing in the course of these debates, that the colonies of New York, New Jersey, Pennsylvania, Delaware, Maryland, and South Carolina were not yet matured for falling from the parent stem, but that they were fast advancing to that state, it was thought most prudent to wait a while for them, and to postpone the final decision to July 1st; but, that this might occasion as little delay as possible, a committee was appointed to prepare a Declaration of Independence. The committee were John Adams, Dr. Franklin, Roger Sherman, Robert R. Livingston, and myself. Committees were also appointed, at the same time, to prepare a plan of confederation for the colonies, and to state the terms proper to be proposed for foreign alliance. The committee for drawing the Declaration of Independence, desired me to do it. It was accordingly done, and being approved by them, I reported it to the House on Friday, the 28th of June, when it was read, and ordered to lie on the table.

On Monday, the 1st of July, the House resolved itself into a committee of the whole, and resumed the consideration of the original motion made by the delegates of Virginia, which, being again debated through the day, was carried in the affirmative by the votes of New Hampshire, Connecticut, Massachusetts, Rhode Island, New Jersey, Maryland, Virginia, North Carolina and Georgia. South Carolina and

Pennsylvania voted against it. Delaware had but two members present, and they were divided. The delegates from New York declared they were for it themselves, and were assured their constituents were for it; but that their instructions having been drawn near a twelve month before, when reconciliation was still the general object, they were enjoined by them to do nothing which should impede that object. They, therefore, thought themselves not justifiable in voting on either side, and asked leave to withdraw from the question; which was given them. The committee rose and reported their resolution to the House. Mr. Edward Rutledge, of South Carolina, then requested the determination might be put off to the next day, as he believed his colleagues, though they disapproved of the resolution, would then join in it for the sake of unanimity. The ultimate question, whether the House would agree to the resolution of the committee, was accordingly postponed to the next day, when it was again moved, and South Carolina concurred in voting for it. In the meantime, a third member had come post from the Delaware counties, and turned the vote of that colony in favor of the resolution. Members of a different sentiment attending that morning from Pennsylvania also, her vote was changed, so that the whole twelve colonies who were authorized to vote at all, gave their voices for it; and, within a few days, the convention of New York approved of it, and thus supplied the void occasioned by the withdrawing of her delegates from the vote.

Congress proceeded the same day to consider the Declaration of Independence, which had been reported and lain on the table the Friday preceding, and on Monday referred to a committee of the whole. The pusillanimous idea that we had friends in England worth keeping terms with, still haunted the minds of many. For this reason, those passages which conveyed censures on the people of England were struck out, lest they should give them offence. The clause too, reprobating the enslaving the inhabitants of Africa, was struck out in complaisance to South Carolina and Georgia, who had never attempted to restrain the importation of slaves, and who, on the contrary, still wished to continue it. Our northern brethren also, I believe, felt a little tender under those censures; for though their people had very few slaves themselves, yet they had been pretty considerable carriers of them to others. The debates, having taken up the greater parts of the 2d, 3d, and 4th days of July, were, on the evening of the last, closed; the Declaration was reported by the committee, agreed to by the House, and signed by every member present, except Mr. Dickinson. As the sentiments of men are known not only by what they receive, but what they reject also, I will state the form of the Declaration as originally reported. The parts struck out by Congress shall be distinguished by a black line drawn under them; and those inserted by them shall be placed in the margin, or in a concurrent column.

3.9.3 Reading and Review Questions

1. In *Notes on the State of Virginia*, why does Jefferson believe that whites will treat Native Americans well, if the Native Americans surrender themselves to whites?

2. How does Silouee's defense of Colonel Byrd compare with Pocahontas's defense of John Smith (as Smith described it)?
3. In what ways are races of men unequal, according to Jefferson? Why? Why is the color of blacks' skin important? According to Jefferson, what does it signify?
4. According to Jefferson, why are Americans free from religious dissension? Are his views logical or logically expressed? Why?
5. According to his autobiography, what motivates most of the revisions to his draft of the Declaration of Independence? To what effect are they made, do you think?

3.10 THE FEDERALIST

(1788)

Upon securing their independence from Britain, the American colonies drew up the Articles of Confederation (1777) which stated their "firm league of friendship," a friendship uniting each colony to the rest but maintaining each state's separate sovereignty. Determining the need for a central authority to deal with their united problems, a Federal Convention met in Philadelphia in 1787 to draw up a new Constitution, one that delineated the powers of this centralized government. Those who supported such a government became known as Federalists.

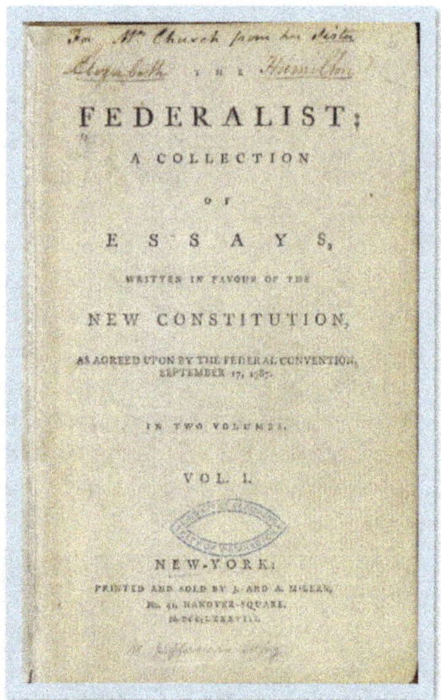

THE FEDERALIST:

A COLLECTION OF ESSAYS,

WRITTEN IN FAVOUR OF THE NEW CONSTITUTION,

AS AGREED UPON BY THE FEDERAL CONVENTION, SEPTEMBER 17, 1787.

IN TWO VOLUMES.

VOL. I.

NEW-YORK:

PRINTED AND SOLD BY J. AND A. M'LEAN, No. 41, HANOVER-SQUARE. M,DCC,LXXXVIII.

Image 3.14 | The Federalist
Author | "Publius" (Alexander Hamilton, John Jay, James Madison)
Source | Wikimedia Commons
License | Public Domain

Anti-federalists included states-rights advocates, those who perceived a bias in favor of cities over country, and those who feared the authority of a large government. To defend against its critics and encourage its adoption by each state, Alexander Hamilton (1757–1804) began to write a series of essays defending this new Constitution, describing the political theory on which it was founded. Hamilton was a New York lawyer who served as George Washington's secretary and aide-de-camp during the Revolution; a member of the Continental Congress; a delegate to the Constitutional Convention; and first secretary of the United States treasury. He was joined in this writing endeavor by James Madison (1751–1836), who represented the state of Virginia at both the Continental Congress and the Constitutional Convention and who later became the fourth president of the United States. John Jay (1745–1829), the third author, had been president of the Continental Congress and secretary of foreign affairs and would become the first chief justice of the United States. The three wrote under the pseudonym "Publius," publishing in New York newspapers a total of eighty-five essays between October 1787 and April 1788.

Although they were published anonymously, their authors became known; it is now the general belief that Hamilton wrote fifty-one essays. In 1788, the collected essays were published as *The Federalist*. Their influence led to the Constitution's ratification that same year. Their influence continues well beyond that year to this very day, in the definition they gave to this new government that secured individual rights, protected public good, and mitigated the potential dangers of majority rule.

3.10.1 Federalist #1

[Alexander Hamilton]

FOR THE INDEPENDENT JOURNAL.
SATURDAY, OCTOBER 27, 1787

Image 3.15 | Alexander Hamilton
Artist | John Trumbull
Source | Wikimedia Commons
License | Public Domain

To the People of the State of New York:

AFTER an unequivocal experience of the inefficacy of the subsisting federal government, you are called upon to deliberate on a new Constitution for the United States of America. The subject speaks its own importance; comprehending in its consequences nothing less than the existence of the UNION, the safety and welfare of the parts of which it is composed, the fate of an empire in many respects the most interesting in the world. It has been frequently remarked that it seems to have been reserved to the people of this country, by their conduct and example, to decide the important question, whether societies of men are really capable or not of establishing good government from reflection and choice, or whether they are forever destined to depend for their political constitutions on accident and force. If there be any truth in the remark, the crisis at which we are arrived may with propriety be regarded as the era in which that decision is to be made; and a wrong election of the part we shall act may, in this view, deserve to be considered as the general misfortune of mankind.

This idea will add the inducements of philanthropy to those of patriotism, to heighten the solicitude which all considerate and good men must feel for the event. Happy will it be if our choice should be directed by a judicious estimate of our true interests, unperplexed and unbiased by considerations not connected with the public good. But this is a thing more ardently to be wished than seriously to be expected. The plan offered to our deliberations affects too many particular interests, innovates upon too many local institutions, not to involve in its discussion a variety of objects foreign to its merits, and of views, passions and prejudices little favorable to the discovery of truth.

Among the most formidable of the obstacles which the new Constitution will have to encounter may readily be distinguished the obvious interest of a certain class of men in every State to resist all changes which may hazard a diminution of the power, emolument, and consequence of the offices they hold under the State establishments; and the perverted ambition of another class of men, who will either hope to aggrandize themselves by the confusions of their country, or will flatter themselves with fairer prospects of elevation from the subdivision of the empire into several partial confederacies than from its union under one government.

It is not, however, my design to dwell upon observations of this nature. I am well aware that it would be disingenuous to resolve indiscriminately the opposition of any set of men (merely because their situations might subject them to suspicion) into interested or ambitious views. Candor will oblige us to admit that even such men may be actuated by upright intentions; and it cannot be doubted that much of the opposition which has made its appearance, or may hereafter make its appearance, will spring from sources, blameless at least, if not respectable—the honest errors of minds led astray by preconceived jealousies and fears. So numerous indeed and so powerful are the causes which serve to give a false bias to the judgment, that we, upon many occasions, see wise and good men on the wrong as well as on the right side of questions of the first magnitude to society. This circumstance, if duly attended to, would furnish a lesson of moderation to those who are ever so much persuaded of their being in the right in any controversy. And a further reason for caution, in this respect, might be drawn from the reflection that we are not always sure that those who advocate the truth are influenced by purer principles than their antagonists. Ambition, avarice, personal animosity, party opposition, and many other motives not more laudable than these, are apt to operate as well upon those who support as those who oppose the right side of a question. Were there not even these inducements to moderation, nothing could be more ill-judged than that intolerant spirit which has, at all times, characterized political parties. For in politics, as in religion, it is equally absurd to aim at making proselytes by fire and sword. Heresies in either can rarely be cured by persecution.

And yet, however just these sentiments will be allowed to be, we have already sufficient indications that it will happen in this as in all former cases of great national discussion. A torrent of angry and malignant passions will be let loose. To judge from the conduct of the opposite parties, we shall be led to conclude that they will mutually hope to evince the justness of their opinions, and to increase the number of their converts by the loudness of their declamations and the bitterness of their invectives. An enlightened zeal for the energy and efficiency of government will be stigmatized as the offspring of a temper fond of despotic power and hostile to the principles of liberty. An over-scrupulous jealousy of danger to the rights of the people, which is more commonly the fault of the head than of the heart, will be represented as mere pretense and artifice, the stale bait for popularity at the expense of the public good. It will be forgotten, on the one hand, that jealousy is the usual concomitant of love, and that the noble enthusiasm of liberty is apt to be infected with a spirit of narrow and illiberal distrust. On the other hand, it will be equally forgotten that the vigor of government is essential to the security of liberty; that, in the contemplation of a sound and well-informed judgment, their interest can never be separated; and that a dangerous ambition more often lurks behind the specious mask of zeal for the rights of the people than under the forbidden appearance of zeal for the firmness and efficiency of government. History will teach us that the former has been found a much more certain road to the introduction of despotism than the latter, and that of those men who have overturned the liberties of republics, the greatest number have begun their career by paying an obsequious court to the people; commencing demagogues, and ending tyrants.

In the course of the preceding observations, I have had an eye, my fellow-citizens, to putting you upon your guard against all attempts, from whatever quarter, to influence your decision in a matter of the utmost moment to your welfare, by any impressions other than those which may result from the evidence of truth. You will, no doubt, at the same time, have collected from the general scope of them, that they proceed from a source not unfriendly to the new Constitution. Yes, my countrymen, I own to you that, after having given it an attentive consideration, I am clearly of opinion it is your interest to adopt it. I am convinced that this is the safest course for your liberty, your dignity, and your happiness. I affect not reserves which I do not feel. I will not amuse you with an appearance of deliberation when I have decided. I frankly acknowledge to you my convictions, and I will freely lay before you the reasons on which they are founded. The consciousness of good intentions disdains ambiguity. I shall not, however, multiply professions on this head. My motives must remain in the depository of my own breast. My arguments will be open to all, and may be judged of by all. They shall at least be offered in a spirit which will not disgrace the cause of truth.

I propose, in a series of papers, to discuss the following interesting particulars:

THE UTILITY OF THE UNION TO YOUR POLITICAL PROSPERITY THE INSUFFICIENCY OF THE PRESENT CONFEDERATION TO PRESERVE THAT UNION THE NECESSITY OF A GOVERNMENT AT LEAST EQUALLY ENERGETIC WITH THE ONE PROPOSED, TO THE ATTAINMENT OF THIS OBJECT THE CONFORMITY OF THE PROPOSED CONSTITUTION TO THE

TRUE PRINCIPLES OF REPUBLICAN GOVERNMENT ITS ANALOGY TO YOUR OWN STATE CONSTITUTION and lastly, THE ADDITIONAL SECURITY WHICH ITS ADOPTION WILL AFFORD TO THE PRESERVATION OF THAT SPECIES OF GOVERNMENT, TO LIBERTY, AND TO PROPERTY.

In the progress of this discussion I shall endeavor to give a satisfactory answer to all the objections which shall have made their appearance, that may seem to have any claim to your attention.

It may perhaps be thought superfluous to offer arguments to prove the utility of the UNION, a point, no doubt, deeply engraved on the hearts of the great body of the people in every State, and one, which it may be imagined, has no adversaries. But the fact is, that we already hear it whispered in the private circles of those who oppose the new Constitution, that the thirteen States are of too great extent for any general system, and that we must of necessity resort to separate confederacies of distinct portions of the whole. This doctrine will, in all probability, be gradually propagated, till it has votaries enough to countenance an open avowal of it. For nothing can be more evident, to those who are able to take an enlarged view of the subject, than the alternative of an adoption of the new Constitution or a dismemberment of the Union. It will therefore be of use to begin by examining the advantages of that Union, the certain evils, and the probable dangers, to which every State will be exposed from its dissolution. This shall accordingly constitute the subject of my next address.

PUBLIUS

3.10.2 Federalist #10

[James Madison]

FROM THE DAILY ADVERTISER. THURSDAY, NOVEMBER 22, 1787.

To the People of the State of New York:

AMONG the numerous advantages promised by a well constructed Union, none deserves to be more accurately developed than its tendency to break and control the violence of faction. The friend of popular governments never finds himself so much alarmed for their character and fate, as when he contemplates their propensity to this dangerous vice. He will not fail, therefore, to set a due value on any plan which, without violating the principles to which he is attached, provides a proper cure for it. The instability,

Image 3.16 | James Madison
Artist | John Vanderlyn
Source | Wikimedia Commons
License | Public Domain

injustice, and confusion introduced into the public councils, have, in truth, been the mortal diseases under which popular governments have everywhere perished; as they continue to be the favorite and fruitful topics from which the adversaries to liberty derive their most specious declamations. The valuable improvements made by the American constitutions on the popular models, both ancient and modern, cannot certainly be too much admired; but it would be an unwarrantable partiality, to contend that they have as effectually obviated the danger on this side, as was wished and expected. Complaints are everywhere heard from our most considerate and virtuous citizens, equally the friends of public and private faith, and of public and personal liberty, that our governments are too unstable, that the public good is disregarded in the conflicts of rival parties, and that measures are too often decided, not according to the rules of justice and the rights of the minor party, but by the superior force of an interested and overbearing majority. However anxiously we may wish that these complaints had no foundation, the evidence, of known facts will not permit us to deny that they are in some degree true. It will be found, indeed, on a candid review of our situation, that some of the distresses under which we labor have been erroneously charged on the operation of our governments; but it will be found, at the same time, that other causes will not alone account for many of our heaviest misfortunes; and, particularly, for that prevailing and increasing distrust of public engagements, and alarm for private rights, which are echoed from one end of the continent to the other. These must be chiefly, if not wholly, effects of the unsteadiness and injustice with which a factious spirit has tainted our public administrations.

By a faction, I understand a number of citizens, whether amounting to a majority or a minority of the whole, who are united and actuated by some common impulse of passion, or of interest, adversed to the rights of other citizens, or to the permanent and aggregate interests of the community.

There are two methods of curing the mischiefs of faction: the one, by removing its causes; the other, by controlling its effects.

There are again two methods of removing the causes of faction: the one, by destroying the liberty which is essential to its existence; the other, by giving to every citizen the same opinions, the same passions, and the same interests.

It could never be more truly said than of the first remedy, that it was worse than the disease. Liberty is to faction what air is to fire, an aliment without which it instantly expires. But it could not be less folly to abolish liberty, which is essential to political life, because it nourishes faction, than it would be to wish the annihilation of air, which is essential to animal life, because it imparts to fire its destructive agency.

The second expedient is as impracticable as the first would be unwise. As long as the reason of man continues fallible, and he is at liberty to exercise it, different opinions will be formed. As long as the connection subsists between his reason and his self-love, his opinions and his passions will have a reciprocal influence on each other; and the former will be objects to which the latter will attach themselves.

The diversity in the faculties of men, from which the rights of property originate, is not less an insuperable obstacle to a uniformity of interests. The protection of these faculties is the first object of government. From the protection of different and unequal faculties of acquiring property, the possession of different degrees and kinds of property immediately results; and from the influence of these on the sentiments and views of the respective proprietors, ensues a division of the society into different interests and parties.

The latent causes of faction are thus sown in the nature of man; and we see them everywhere brought into different degrees of activity, according to the different circumstances of civil society. A zeal for different opinions concerning religion, concerning government, and many other points, as well of speculation as of practice; an attachment to different leaders ambitiously contending for pre-eminence and power; or to persons of other descriptions whose fortunes have been interesting to the human passions, have, in turn, divided mankind into parties, inflamed them with mutual animosity, and rendered them much more disposed to vex and oppress each other than to co-operate for their common good. So strong is this propensity of mankind to fall into mutual animosities, that where no substantial occasion presents itself, the most frivolous and fanciful distinctions have been sufficient to kindle their unfriendly passions and excite their most violent conflicts. But the most common and durable source of factions has been the various and unequal distribution of property. Those who hold and those who are without property have ever formed distinct interests in society. Those who are creditors, and those who are debtors, fall under a like discrimination. A landed interest, a manufacturing interest, a mercantile interest, a moneyed interest, with many lesser interests, grow up of necessity in civilized nations, and divide them into different classes, actuated by different sentiments and views. The regulation of these various and interfering interests forms the principal task of modern legislation, and involves the spirit of party and faction in the necessary and ordinary operations of the government.

No man is allowed to be a judge in his own cause, because his interest would certainly bias his judgment, and, not improbably, corrupt his integrity. With equal, nay with greater reason, a body of men are unfit to be both judges and parties at the same time; yet what are many of the most important acts of legislation, but so many judicial determinations, not indeed concerning the rights of single persons, but concerning the rights of large bodies of citizens? And what are the different classes of legislators but advocates and parties to the causes which they determine? Is a law proposed concerning private debts? It is a question to which the creditors are parties on one side and the debtors on the other. Justice ought to hold the balance between them. Yet the parties are, and must be, themselves the judges; and the most numerous party, or, in other words, the most powerful faction must be expected to prevail. Shall domestic manufactures be encouraged, and in what degree, by restrictions on foreign manufactures? are questions which would be differently decided by the landed and the manufacturing classes, and probably by neither with a sole regard to justice and the public good. The apportionment of taxes on the various descriptions of property is an act which seems to require the most exact impartiality; yet there is, perhaps, no legislative act in which greater opportunity and temptation are given to a predominant party to trample on the rules of justice. Every shilling with which they overburden the inferior number, is a shilling saved to their own pockets.

It is in vain to say that enlightened statesmen will be able to adjust these clashing interests, and render them all subservient to the public good. Enlightened statesmen will not always be at the helm. Nor, in many cases, can such an adjustment be made at all without taking into view indirect and remote considerations, which will rarely prevail over the immediate interest which one party may find in disregarding the rights of another or the good of the whole.

The inference to which we are brought is, that the CAUSES of faction cannot be removed, and that relief is only to be sought in the means of controlling its EFFECTS.

If a faction consists of less than a majority, relief is supplied by the republican principle, which enables the majority to defeat its sinister views by regular vote. It may clog the administration, it may convulse the society; but it will be unable to execute and mask its violence under the forms of the Constitution. When a majority is included in a faction, the form of popular government, on the other hand, enables it to sacrifice to its ruling passion or interest both the public good and the rights of other citizens. To secure the public good and private rights against the danger of such a faction, and at the same time to preserve the spirit and the form of popular government, is then the great object to which our inquiries are directed. Let me add that it is the great desideratum by which this form of government can be rescued from the opprobrium under which it has so long labored, and be recommended to the esteem and adoption of mankind.

By what means is this object attainable? Evidently by one of two only. Either the existence of the same passion or interest in a majority at the same time must be prevented, or the majority, having such coexistent passion or interest, must be rendered, by their number and local situation, unable to concert and carry into effect schemes of oppression. If the impulse and the opportunity be suffered to coincide, we well know that neither moral nor religious motives can be relied on as an adequate control. They are not found to be such on the injustice and violence of individuals, and lose their efficacy in proportion to the number combined together, that is, in proportion as their efficacy becomes needful.

From this view of the subject it may be concluded that a pure democracy, by which I mean a society consisting of a small number of citizens, who assemble and administer the government in person, can admit of no cure for the mischiefs of faction. A common passion or interest will, in almost every case, be felt by a majority of the whole; a communication and concert result from the form of government itself; and there is nothing to check the inducements to sacrifice the weaker party or an obnoxious individual. Hence it is that such democracies have ever been spectacles of turbulence and contention; have ever been found incompatible with personal security or the rights of property; and have in general been as short in their lives as they have been violent in their deaths. Theoretic politicians, who have patronized this species of government, have erroneously supposed that by reducing mankind to a perfect equality in their political rights, they would, at the same time, be perfectly equalized and assimilated in their possessions, their opinions, and their passions.

A republic, by which I mean a government in which the scheme of representation takes place, opens a different prospect, and promises the cure for which we are seeking. Let us examine the points in which it varies from pure democracy, and we shall comprehend both the nature of the cure and the efficacy which it must derive from the Union.

The two great points of difference between a democracy and a republic are: first, the delegation of the government, in the latter, to a small number of citizens elected by the rest; secondly, the greater number of citizens, and greater sphere of country, over which the latter may be extended.

The effect of the first difference is, on the one hand, to refine and enlarge the public views, by passing them through the medium of a chosen body of citizens, whose wisdom may best discern the true interest of their country, and whose patriotism and love of justice will be least likely to sacrifice it to temporary or partial considerations. Under such a regulation, it may well happen that the public voice, pronounced by the representatives of the people, will be more consonant to the public good than if pronounced by the people themselves, convened for the purpose. On the other hand, the effect may be inverted. Men of factious tempers, of local prejudices, or of sinister designs, may, by intrigue, by corruption, or by other means, first obtain the suffrages, and then betray the interests, of the people. The question resulting is, whether small or extensive republics are more favorable to the election of proper guardians of the public weal; and it is clearly decided in favor of the latter by two obvious considerations:

In the first place, it is to be remarked that, however small the republic may be, the representatives must be raised to a certain number, in order to guard against the cabals of a few; and that, however large it may be, they must be limited to a certain number, in order to guard against the confusion of a multitude. Hence, the number of representatives in the two cases not being in proportion to that of the two constituents, and being proportionally greater in the small republic, it follows that, if the proportion of fit characters be not less in the large than in the small republic, the former will present a greater option, and consequently a greater probability of a fit choice.

In the next place, as each representative will be chosen by a greater number of citizens in the large than in the small republic, it will be more difficult for unworthy candidates to practice with success the vicious arts by which elections are too often carried; and the suffrages of the people being more free, will be more likely to centre in men who possess the most attractive merit and the most diffusive and established characters.

It must be confessed that in this, as in most other cases, there is a mean, on both sides of which inconveniences will be found to lie. By enlarging too much the number of electors, you render the representatives too little acquainted with all their local circumstances and lesser interests; as by reducing it too much, you render him unduly attached to these, and too little fit to comprehend and pursue great and national objects. The federal Constitution forms a happy combination in this respect; the great and aggregate interests being referred to the national, the local and particular to the State legislatures.

The other point of difference is, the greater number of citizens and extent of territory which may be brought within the compass of republican than of democratic government; and it is this circumstance principally which renders factious combinations less to be dreaded in the former than in the latter. The smaller the society, the fewer probably will be the distinct parties and interests composing it; the fewer the distinct parties and interests, the more frequently will a majority be found of the same party; and the smaller the number of individuals composing a majority, and the smaller the compass within which they are placed, the more easily will they concert and execute their plans of oppression. Extend the sphere, and you take in a greater variety of parties and interests; you make it less probable that a majority of the whole will have a common motive to invade the rights of other citizens; or if such a common motive exists, it will be more difficult for all who feel it to discover their own strength, and to act in unison with each other. Besides other impediments, it may be remarked that, where there is a consciousness of unjust or dishonorable purposes, communication is always checked by distrust in proportion to the number whose concurrence is necessary.

Hence, it clearly appears, that the same advantage which a republic has over a democracy, in controlling the effects of faction, is enjoyed by a large over a small republic,—is enjoyed by the Union over the States composing it. Does the advantage consist in the substitution of representatives whose enlightened views and virtuous sentiments render them superior to local prejudices and schemes of injustice? It will not be denied that the representation of the Union will be most likely to possess these requisite endowments. Does it consist in the greater security afforded by a greater variety of parties, against the event of any one party being able to outnumber and oppress the rest? In an equal degree does the increased variety of parties comprised within the Union, increase this security. Does it, in fine, consist in the greater obstacles opposed to the concert and accomplishment of the secret wishes of an unjust and interested majority? Here, again, the extent of the Union gives it the most palpable advantage.

The influence of factious leaders may kindle a flame within their particular States, but will be unable to spread a general conflagration through the other States. A religious sect may degenerate into a political faction in a part of the Confederacy; but the variety of sects dispersed over the entire face of it must secure the national councils against any danger from that source. A rage for paper money, for an abolition of debts, for an equal division of property, or for any other improper or wicked project, will be less apt to pervade the whole body of the Union than a particular member of it; in the same proportion as such a malady is more likely to taint a particular county or district, than an entire State.

In the extent and proper structure of the Union, therefore, we behold a republican remedy for the diseases most incident to republican government. And according to the degree of pleasure and pride we feel in being republicans, ought to be our zeal in cherishing the spirit and supporting the character of Federalists.

PUBLIUS

3.10.3 Reading and Review Questions

1. In Federalist #1, against what propensities of human nature does a viable constitution need to work, according to Hamilton? Why?
2. Why does Hamilton appeal to an attitude of moderation in regards to establishing the union and constitution?
3. Is Hamilton himself moderate in his views and statements here? Why?
4. In Federalist #10, why does Madison caution against factions, or rival parties, in a government?
5. According to Madison, how can governments avoid factionalism? Why do you think Madison focuses on controlling the effects, versus the causes, of factionalism?

3.11 OLAUDAH EQUIANO

(c. 1745–1797)

Born in Essaka, Kingdom of Benin (now in Nigeria) to an Igbo tribe elder, Olaudah Equiano (at the age of eleven) and his sister were kidnapped, separated, and sold to slave traders. He was transported across the Atlantic to Barbados. Along with other captured Africans, he was put up for auction. Although he was not purchased there, he was sent to Virginia. He was sold in 1754 to Michael Henry Pascal (d. 1786), a British Royal Navy lieutenant.

Image 3.17 | Oaudah Equiano
Artist | Unknown
Source | Wikimedia Commons
License | Public Domain

For the next ten years, Equiano, now called Gustavas Vassa, worked on various ships, including the military warships *Roebuck* and *Namur* and did service as Pascal's valet and by hauling gunpowder during the Seven Years' War with France. Equiano was sent by Pascal to his sister in

England, where Equiano learned to read and write in school. He also converted to Christianity in 1759 and was baptized in St. Margaret's, Westminster. His godparents, Pascal's cousins Mary Guerin and Maynard Guerin, later attested to details in Equiano's autobiography, including his learning English only after coming to England.

Pascal sold Equiano to Captain James Doran who transported Equiano to Montserrat. There Equiano was sold to Robert King, an American Quaker. Equiano assisted King in his business ventures and was allowed to engage in trade for his own profit. In 1767, Equiano bought his freedom from King for forty pounds, the amount King paid to purchase Equiano. Even as a freedman, he was almost captured as a "runaway slave" and sent to Georgia.

Equiano traveled on scientific expeditions to the Arctic and to Central America as well as on other sailing ventures. He eventually returned to England where he devoted himself to ending the slave trade and the Abolitionist cause. He exposed for examination and condemnation slave atrocities, including the *Zong* massacre (1781). Because this slave ship ran low on potable water, its crew threw slaves—who were insured as cargo—overboard in order to cash in on the insurance and save water for the rest of the ship's passengers. In 1789, Equiano published *The Interesting Narrative of the Life of Olaudah Equiano: Or, Gustavus Vassa, the African.* Now considered one of the first major slave autobiographies in English, it became a bestseller, running through nine editions during his lifetime. It gave firsthand details of slaves chained in ships, whipping, starvation, the division of families, and other horrors committed by so-called Christians. It became a forceful weapon in the fight against slavery, leading to the Slave Trade Act of 1807 which ended the African slave trade for Britain and its colonies. It directly influenced other slave narratives, such as Frederick Douglass's *Narrative of the Life of Frederick Douglass* and Harriet Jacobs's *Incidents in the Life of a Slave Girl.*

His narrative is characterized by its vivid imagery, humanity, and commitment to Christianity in the face of almost unbearable cruelty and struggle.

3.11.1 From *The Interesting Narrative of the Life of Olaudah Equiano: Or, Gustavus Vassa, the African, Written by Himself*

(1789)

Chapter I

The Author's account of his country, and their manners and customs—Administration of justice—Embrenché—Marriage ceremony, and public entertainments—Mode of living—Dress—Manufactures—Buildings—Commerce—Agriculture—War and Religion—Superstition of the natives—Funeral ceremonies of the priests or magicians—Curious mode of discovering poison—Some hints concerning the origin of the author's countrymen, with the opinions of different writers on that subject.

I BELIEVE it is difficult for those who publish their own memoirs to escape the imputation of vanity; nor is this the only disadvantage under which they labour; it is also their misfortune, that whatever is uncommon is rarely, if ever, believed; and what is obvious we are apt to turn from with disgust, and to charge the writer with impertinence. People generally think those memoirs only worthy to be read or remembered which abound in great or striking events; those, in short, which in a high degree excite either admiration or pity: all others they consign to contempt and oblivion. It is, therefore, I confess, not a little hazardous, in a private and obscure individual and a stranger too, thus to solicit the indulgent attention of the public; especially when I own I offer here the history of neither a saint, a hero, nor a tyrant. I believe there are a few events in my life which have not happened to many; it is true the incidents of it are numerous; and, did I consider myself an European, I might say my sufferings were great; but, when I compare my lot with that of most of my countrymen, I regard myself as a particular favourite of Heaven, and acknowledge the mercies of Providence in every occurrence of my life. If, then, the following narrative does not appear sufficiently interresting to engage general attention, let my motive be some excuse for its publication. I am not so foolishly vain as to expect from it either immortality or literary reputation. If it affords any satisfaction to my numerous friends, at whose request it has been written, or in the smallest degree promotes the interests of humanity, the ends for which it was undertaken will by fully attained, and every wish of my heart gratified. Let it therefore be remembered that, in wishing to avoid censure, I do not aspire to praise.

That part of Africa known by the name of Guinea, to which the trade for slaves is carried on, extends along the coast above 3400 miles, from Senegal to Angola, and includes a variety of kindoms. Of these the most considerable is the kingdom of Benin, both as to extent and wealth, the richness and cultivation of the soil, the power of its king, and the number and warlike disposition of the inhabitants. It is situated nearly under the lines, and extends along the coast above 170 miles, but runs back into the interior part of Africa, to a distance hitherto, I believe, unexplored by any traveller; and seems only terminated at length by the empire of Abyssinia, near 1500 miles from its beginning. This kingdom is divided into many provinces or districts: in one of the most remote and fertile of which I was born, in the year 1745, situated in a charming fruitful vale, named Essaka. The distance of this province from the capital of Benin and the sea coast must be very considerable; for I had never heard of white men or Europeans, nor of the sea; and our subjection to the king of Benin was little more than nominal; for every transaction of the government, as far as my slender observation extended, was conducted by the chiefs or elders of the place. The manners and government of a people who have little commerce with other countries are generally very simple; and the history of what passes in one family or village, may serve as a specimen of the whole nation. My father was one of those elders or chiefs I have spoken of, and was stiled Embrenché; a term, as I remember, importing the highest distinction, and signifying in our language a mark of grandeur. This mark is conferred on the person entitled to it, by cutting the skin across at the top of the forehead, and drawing it down to the eye-brows; and while it is in this situation, applying a warm hand, and rubbing it until it shrinks up into a thick weal across the lower part of the forehead. Most of the judges and senators were thus marked; my father had long borne it: I had seen it conferred on one of my brothers, and I also was destined to receive it by my parents. Those Embrenché, or chief men, decided disputes, and punished crimes; for which purpose they always assembled together. The proceedings were generally short; and in most cases the law of retaliation prevailed. I remember a man was brought before my father, and the other judges, for kidnapping a boy; and although he was the son of a chief, or senator, he was condemned to make recompense by a man and woman slave. Adultery, however, was sometimes punished with slavery or death; a punishment, which I believe is inflicted on it throughout most of the nations of Africa: so sacred among them is the honour of the marriage-bed, and so jealous are they of the fidelity of their wives. Of this I recollect an instance,—A woman was convicted before the judges of adultery, and delivered over, as the custom was, to her husband to be punished. Accordingly, he determined to put her to death; but, it being found, just before her execution, that she had an infant at her breast, and no woman being prevailed on to perform the part of a nurse, she was spared on account of the child. The men, however do not preserve the same constancy to their wives which they expect from them; for they indulge in a plurality, though seldom in more than two. Their mode of marriage is thus:—Both parties are usually betrothed when young by their parents (though I have known the males to betroth themselves). On this occasion a feast is prepared, and the bride and bridegroom stand up in the midst of all their friends, who are assembled for the purpose, while he declares she is thenceforth to be looked upon as his wife, and that no person is to pay any addresses to her. This is also immediately proclaimed in the vicinity, on which the bride retires from the assembly. Some time after she is brought home to her husband, and then another feast is made, to which the relations of both parties are invited: her parents then deliver her to the bridegroom, accompanied with a number of blessings; and at the same time they tie around her waist a cotton string, of the thickness of a goose quill, which none but married women are permitted to wear; she is now considered as completely his wife; and at this time the dowry is given to the new married pair, which generally consists of portions of land, slaves, and cattle, household goods, and implements of husbandry. These are offered by the friends of both parties; besides which the parents of the bridegroom present gifts to those of the bride, whose property she is looked upon before marriage; but, after it, she is esteemed the sole property of the husband. The ceremony being now ended, the festival begins, which is celebrated with bonfires, and loud acclamations of joy, accompanied with music and dancing.

We are almost a nation of dancers, musicians, and poets. Thus every great event, such as a triumphant return from battle, or other cause of public rejoicing, is celebrated in public dances, which are accompanied with songs and music suited to the occasion. The assembly is separated into four divisions, which dance either apart or is succession, and each with a character peculiar to itself. The first division contains the married men, who, in their dances frequently exhibit feats of arms, and the representation of a battle. To these suceed the married women, who dance in the second division. The young men occupy the third; and the maidens the fourth. Each represents some interesting scene of real life, such as a great achievement, doestic employment, a pathetic story, or some rural sport; and, as the subject is generally founded on some recent event, it is therefore ever new. This gives our dances a spirit and variety which I have scarcely seen elsewhere. We have many musical instruments, particularly drums of different kinds, a piece of music which resembles a guitar, and another much like a stickado. These last are chiefly used by betrothed virgins, who play on them on all grand festivals.

As our manners are simple, our luxuries are few. The dress of both sexes are nearly the same. It generally consists of a long piece of calico, or muslin, wrapped loosely round the body, somewhat in the form of a Highland plaid. This is usually dyed blue, which is our favourite colour. It is extracted from a berry, and is brighter and richer than any I have seen in Europe. Besides this, our women of distinction wear golden ornaments, which they dispose with some profusion on their arms and legs. When our women are not employed with the men in tillage, their usual occupation is spinning and weaving cotton, which they afterwards dye, and make into garments. They also manufacture earthen vessels, of which we have many kinds. Among the rest tobacco pipes, made after the same fashion, and used in the same manner, as those in Turkey.

Our manner of living is entirely plain; for as yet the natives are unacquainted with those refinements in cookery which debauch the taste: bullocks, goats, and poultry supply the greatest part of their food. These constitute likewise the principal wealth of the country, and the chief articles of its commerce. The flesh is usually stowed in a pan. To make is savory, we sometimes use also pepper and other spices; and we have salt made of wood ashes. Our vegetables are mostly plantains, eadas, yams, beans, and Indian corn. The head of the family usually eats alone; his wives and slaves have also their separate tables. Before we taste food, we always wash our hands; indeed our cleanliness on all occasions is extreme; but on this it is an indispensible ceremony. After washing, libation is made, by pouring out a small portion of the drink on the floor, and tossing a small quantity of the food in a certain place, for the spirits of departed relations, which the natives suppose to preside over their conduct, and guard them from evil. They are totally unacquainted with strong or spiritous liquors; and their principal beverage is palm wine. This is got from a tree of that name, by tapping it at the top, and fastening a large gourd to it; and sometimes one tree will yield three or four galloms in a night. When just drawn it is of a most delicious sweetness; but in a few days it acquires a tartish and more spiritous flavour: though I never saw any one intoxicated by it.The same tree also produces nuts and oil. Our principal luxury is in perfumes;

one sort of these is an odoriferous wood of delicious fragrance; the other a kind of earth; a small portion of which thrown into the fire diffuses a most powerful odour. We beat this wood into powder, and mix it with palm-oil; with which both men and women perfume themselves.

In our buildings we study convenience rather than ornament. Each master of a family has a large square piece of ground, surrounded with a moat or fence, or inclosed with a wall made of red earth tempered, which, when dry is as hard as brick. Within this are his houses to accommodate his family and slaves; which, if numerous, frequently present the appearance of a village. In the middle stands the principal building, appropriated to the sole use of the master, and consisting of two apartments; in one of which he fits in the day with his family, the other is left apart for the reception of his friends. He has besides these a distinct apartment, in which he sleeps, together with his male children. On each side are the apartments of his wives, who have also their separate day and night houses. The habitations of the slaves and their families are distributed throughout the rest of the inclosure. These houses never exceed one story in height; they are always built of wood, or stakes driven in to the ground, crossed with wattles, and neatly plastered within and without. The roof is thatched with reeds. Our day houses are left open at the sides; but those in which we sleep are always covered, and plastered in the inside with a composition mixed with cow-dung, to keep off the different insects which annoy us during the night. The walls and floors also of these aregenerally covered with mats. Our beds consist of a platform, raised three or four feet from the ground, on which are laid skins, and different parts of a spungy tree called plantain. Our covering is calico, or muslin, the same as our dress. The usual seats are a few logs of wood; but we have benches, which are generally perfumed, to accommodate strangers; these compose the greater part of our household furniture. Houses so constructed and furnished require but little skill to erect them. Every man is a sufficient architect for the purpose. The whole neighbourhood afford their unanimous assistance in building them, and, in return, receive and expect no other recompense than a feast.

As we live in a country where nature is prodigal of her favours, our wants are few, and easily supplied; of course we have few manufactures. They consist for the most part of calicoes, earthen ware, ornaments, and instruments of war and husbandry. But these make no part of our commerce, the principal articles of which, as I have observed, are provisions. In such a state money is of little use; however we have some small pieces of coin, if I may call them such. They are made something like an anchor; but I do not remember either their value or denomination. We have also markets, at which I have been frequently with my mother. These are sometimes visited by stout, mahogany-coloured men from the south-west of us: we call them Oye-Eboe, which term signifies red men living at a distance. They generally bring us fire-arms, gun-powder, hats, beads, and dried fish. The last we esteemed a great rarity, as our waters were only brooks and springs. These articles they barter with us for odoriferous woods and earth, and our salt of wood-ashes. They always carry slaves through our land, but the strictest account is exacted of their manner of procuring them before they are suffered to pass. Sometimes indeed we sold slaves to them, but they were only prisoners of war, or such among us as had been convicted of kidnapping, or adultery, and some other crimes which we esteemed heinous. This practice of kidnapping induces me to think, that, notwithstanding all our strictness, their principal business among us was to trepan our people. I remember too they carried great sacks along with them, which, not long after, I had an opportunity of fatally seeing applied to that infamous purpose.

Our land is uncommonly rich and fruitful, and produced all kinds of vegetables in great abundance. We have plenty of Indian corn, and vast quantities of cotton and tobacco. Our pine apples grow without culture; they are about the size of the largest sugar-loaf, and finely flavoured. We have also spices of different kinds, particularly of pepper; and a variety of delicious fruits which I have never seen in Europe; together with gums of various kinds, and honey in abundance. All our industry is exerted to improve those blessings of nature. Agriculture is our chief employment; and every one, even the children and women, are engaged in it. Thus we are all habituated to labour from our earliest years. Every one contributes something to the common stock; and, as we are unacquainted with idleness, we have no beggars. The benefits of such a mode of living are obvious. The West-India planters prefer he slaves of Benin or Eboe to those of any other part of Guinea, for their hardiness, intelligence, integrity, and zeal. Those benefits are felt by us in the general healthiness of the people, and in their vigour and activity; I might have added too in their comeliness. Deformity is indeed unknown amongst us, I mean that of shape. Numbers of the natives of Eboe, now in London, might be brought in support of this assertion; for, in regard to complexion, ideas of beauty are wholly relative. I remember while in Africa to have seen three negro children, who were tawny, and another quite white, who were universally regarded by myself and the natives in general, as far as related to their complexions, as deformed. Our women too were, in my eyes at least, uncommonly graceful, alert, and modest to a degree of bashfulness; nor do I remember to have ever heard of an instance of incontinence amongst them before marriage. They are also remarkably cheerful. Indeed cheerfulness and affability are two of the leading characteristics of our nation.

Our tillage is exercised in a large plain or common, some hours walk from our dwellings, and all the neighbours resort thither in a body. They use no beasts of husbandry; and their only instruments are hoes, axes, shovels, and beaks, or pointed iron, to dig with. Sometimes we are visited by locusts, which come in large clouds, so as to darken the air, and destroy our harvest. This however happens rarely, but when it does a famine is produced by it. I remember an instance or two wherein this happened. This common is oftimes the theatre of war; and therefore when our people go out to till their land, they not only go in a body, but generally take their arms with them, for fear of a surprise; and when they apprehend an invasion, they guard the avenues to their dwellings by driving sticks into the ground, which are so sharp at one end as to pierce the foot, and are generally dipt in poison. From what I can recollect of these battles, they appear to have been irruptions of one little state or district on the other, to obtain prisoners or booty. Perhaps they were incited to this by those traders who brought the European goods I mentioned amongst us. Such a mode of obtaining slaves in Africa is common; and I believe more are procured this way, and by kidnapping, than any other. When a trader wants slaves, he applies to a chief for them, and tempts him with his wares. It is not extraordinary, if on this occasion he yields to the temptation with as little firmness, and accepts the price of his fellow creature's liberty with as little reluctance, as the enlightened merchant. Accordingly, he falls on his neighbours, and a desperate battle ensues. If he prevails, and takes prisoners, he gratifies his avarice by selling them; but, if his party be vanquished, and he falls into the hands of the enemy, he is put to death: for, as he has been known to foment quarrels, it is thought dangerous to let him survive; and no ransom can save him, though all other prisoners may be redeemed. We have fire-arms, bows and arrows, broad two-edged swords and javelins; we have shields also, which cover a man from head to foot. All are taught the use of these weapons. Even our women are warriors, and march boldly out to fight along with the men. Our whole district is a kind of militia: On a certain signal given, such as the firing of a gun at night, they all rise in arms, and rush upon their enemy. It is perhaps something remarkable, that, when our people march to the field, a red flag or banner is borne before them. I was once a witness to a battle in our common. We had been all at work in it one day as usual, when our people were suddenly attacked. I climbed a tree at some distance, from which I beheld the fight. There were many women as well as men on both sides; among others my mother was there, armed with a broad sword. After the fighting for a considerable time with great fury, and many had been killed, our people obtained the victory, and took the enemy's Chief prisoner. He was carried off in great triumph; and, though he offered a large ransom for his life, he was put to death. A virgin of note among our enemies had been slain in the battle, and her arm was exposed in our market-place, where our trophies were always exhibited. The spoils were divided according to the merit of the warriors. Those prisoners which were not sold or redeemed we kept as slaves: but, how different was their condition from that of the slaves in the West Indies! With us they do no more work than other members of the community, even their master. Their food, cloathing, and lodging, were nearly the same as theirs, except that they were not permitted to eat with those who were free born; and there were scarce any other difference between them than a superior degree of importance which the head of a family possesses in our state, and that authority which, as such, he exercises over every part of his household. Some of these slaves have even slaves under them, as their own property, and for their own use.

As to religion, the natives believe that there is one Creator of all things, and that he lives in the sun, and is girded round with a belt, that he may never eat or drink; but according to some, he smokes a pipe, which is our own favourite luxury. They believe he governs events, especially our deaths or captivity; but, as for the doctrine of eternity, I do not remember to have ever heard of it: some however believe in the transmigration of souls to a certain degree. Those spirits, which are not transmigrated, such as their dear friends or relations, they believe always attend them, and guard them from the bad spirits of their foes. For this reason, they always, before eating, as I have observed, put some small portion of the meat, and pour some of their drink, on the ground for them; and they often make oblations of the blood of beasts or fowls at their graves. I was very fond of my mother, and almost constantly with her. When she went to make these oblations at her mother's tomb, which was a kind of small solitary thatched house, I sometimes attended her. There she made her libations, and spent most of the night in cries and lamentation. I have been often extremely terrified on these occasions. The loneliness of the place, the darkness of the night, and the ceremony of libation, naturally awful and gloomy, were heightened by my mother's lamentations; and these concorring with the doleful cries of birds, by which these places were frequented, gave an inexpressible terror to the scene.

We compute the year from the day on which the sun crosses the line; and, on its setting that evening, there is a general shout throughout the land; at least I can speak from my own knowledge throughout our vicinity. The people at the same time make a great noise with rattles not unlike the basket rattles used by children here, though much larger, and hold up their hands to heaven for a blessing. It is then the greatest offerings are made; and those children whom our wise men foretel will be fortunate are then presented to different people. I remember many used to come to see me, and I was carried about to others for that purpose. They have many offerings, particularly at full moons, generally two at harvest, before the fruits are taken out of the ground: and, when any young animals are killed, sometimes they offer up part of them as a sacrifice. These offerings, when made by one of the heads of a family, serve for the whole. I remember we often had them at my father's and my uncle's, and their families have been present. Some of our offerings are eaten with bitter herbs. We had a saying among us to any one of a cross temper, 'That if they were to be eaten, they should be eaten with bitter herbs.'

We practised circumcision like the Jews, and made offerings of feasts on that occasion in the same manner as they did. Like them also our children were named from some event, some circumstance, or fancied foreboding, at the time of their birth. I was named Olaudah, which in our language, signifies vicissitude, or fortunate also; one favoured, and having a loud voice, and well spoken. I remember we never polluted the name of the object of our adoration; on the contrary, it was always mentioned with the greatest reverence; and we were totally unacquainted with swearing, and all those terms of abuse and eproach which find their way so readily and copiously into the language of more civilized people. The only expressions of that kind I remember were, 'May you rot, or 'may you swell, or may a beast take you.'

I have before remarked, that the natives of this part of Africa are extremely cleanly. This necessary habit of decency was with us a part of religion, and therefore we had many purifications and washings; indeed almost as many, and used on the same occasions, if my recollection does not fail me, as the Jews. Those that touched the dead at any time were obliged to wash and purify themselves before they could enter a dwelling-house. Every woman too, at certain times was forbidden to come into a dwelling-house, or touch any person, or any thing we eat. I was so fond of my mother I could not keep from her, or avoid touching her at some of those periods, in consequence of which I was obliged to be kept out with her, in a little house made for that purpose, till offering was made, and then we were purified.

Though we had no places of public worship, we had priests and magicians, or wise men. I do not remember whether they had different offices, or whether they were united in the same persons, but they were held in great reverence by the people. They calculated our time, and foretold events, as their name imported, for we called them Ah-affoe-way-cah, which signifies calculators, or yearly men, our year being called Ah-Affoe. They wore their beards; and, when they died, they were succeeded by their sons. Most of their implements and things of value were interred along with them. Pipes and tobacco were also put into the grave with the corpse, which was always perfumed and ornamented; and animals were offered in sacrifice to them. None accompanied their funerals, but those of the same profession or tribe. These buried them after sunset, and always returned from the grave by a different way from that which they went.

These magicians were also our doctors or physicians. They prectised bleeding by cupping, and were very successful in healing wounds and expelling poisons. They had likewise some extraordinary method of discovering jealousy, theft, and poisoning; the success of which no doubt they derived from the unbounded influence over the credulity and superstition of the people. I do not remember what those methods were, except that as to poisoning. I recollect an instance or two, which I hope it will not be deemed impertinent here to insert, as it may serve as a kind of specimen of the rest, and is still used by the negroes in the West Indies. A young woman had been poisoned, but it was not known by whom; the doctors ordered the corpse to be taken up by some persons, and carried to the grave. As soon as the bearers had raised it on their shoulders, they seemed seized with some sudden impulse, and ran to and fro', unable to stop themselves. At last, after having passed through a number of thorns and prickly bushes unhurt, the corpse fell from them close to a house, and defaces it in the fall: and the owner being taken up, he immediately confessed the poisoning.

The natives are extremely cautious about poison. When they buy any eatable, the seller kisses it all round before the buyer, to shew him it is not poisoned; and the same is done when any meat or drink is presented, particularly to a stranger. We have serpents of different kinds, some of which are esteemed ominous when they appear in our houses, and there we never molest. I remember two of those ominous snakes, each of which was as thick as the calf of a man's leg, and in colour resembling a dolphin in the water, crept at different times into my mother's night-house, where I always lay with her, and coiled themselves into folds, and each time they crowed like a cock. I was desired by some of our wise men to touch these, that I might be interested in the good omens, which I did, for they are quite harmless, and would tamely suffer themselves to be handled; and then they were put into a large open earthen pan, and set on one side of the high-way. Some of our snakes, however, were poisonous. One of them crossed the road one day as I was standing on it, and passed between my feet, without offering to touch me, to the great surprise of many who saw it; and these incidents were accounted, by the wise men, and likewise by my mother and the rest of the people, as remarkable omens in my favour.

Such is the imperfect sketch my memory has furnished me with of the manners and customs of the people among whom I first drew my breath. And here I cannot forbear suggesting what has long struck me very forcibly, namely, the strong analogy which even by this sketch, imperfect as it is, appears to prevail in the manners and customs of my country-men, and those of the Jews, before they reached the Land of Promise, and particularly the patriarchs, while they were yet in that pastoral state which is described in Genesis —an analogy which alone would induce me to think that the one people had sprung from the other. Indeed this is the opinion of Dr. Gill, who, in his Commentary on Genesis very ably deduces the pedigree of the Africans from Aser and Afra, the descendants of Abraham by Keturah his wife and concubine, (for both these titles applied to her). It is also conformable to the sentiments of Dr. John Clarke, formerly Dean of Sarum, in his Truth of the Christian Religion: both these authors concur in ascribing to us this original. The reasonings of those gentlemen are still further confirmed by the Scripture Chronology of the Rev. Arthur Bedford and, if any further corroboration were required, this resemblance in so many respects, is a strong evidence in support of the opinion. Like the Israelites in their primitive state, our government was conducted by our chiefs, our judges, our wise men, and elders; and the head of a family with us enjoyed a similar authority over his household with that which is ascribed to Abraham and the other patriarchs. The law of retaliation obtained almost universally with us as with them: and even their religion appeared to have shed upon us a ray of its glory, though broken and spent in its passage, or eclipsed by the cloud with which time, tradition, and ignorance might have enveloped it; for we had our circumcision (a rule I believe peculiar to that people): we had also our sacrifices and burnt-offerings, our washings and purifications, on the same occasions as they had.

As to the difference of colour between the Eboan Africans and the modern Jews, I shall not presume to account for it. Is is a subject which has engaged the pens of men of both genius and learning, and is far above my strength. The most able and Reverend Mr. T. Clarkson, however, in his much-admired Essay on the Slavery and Commerce of the Human Species, has acertained the cause in a manner that at once solves every objection on that account, and, on my mind at least, has produced the fullest conviction, I shall therefore refer ot that performance for the theory, contenting myself with extracting a fact as related by Dr. Mitchel.

> "The Spaniards who have inhabited America under the torrid zone for any time, are become as dark coloured as our native Indians of Virginia, of which I myself have been a witness. There is also another instance of a Portuguese settlement at Mitomba, a river in Sierra Leona, where the inhabitants are bred from a mixture of the first Portuguese discoverers with the natives, and are now become, in their complexion, and in the woolly quality of their hair, perfect negroes, retaining, however, a smattering of the Portuguese language."

These instances, and a great many more which might be adduced, while they shew how the complexions of the same persons vary in different climates, it is hoped may tend also to remove the prejudice that some conceive against the natives of Africa on account of their colour. Surely the minds of the Spaniards did not change with their complexions! Are there not causes enough to which the apparent inferiority of an African may be ascribed, without limiting the goodness of God, and supposing he forebore to stamp understanding on certainly his own image, because "carved in ebony?" Might it not naturally be ascribed to their situation? When they come among Europeans, they are ignorant of their language, religion, manners, and customs. Are any pains taken to teach them these? Are they treated as men? Does not slavery itself depress the mind, and extinguish all its fire, and every noble sentiment? But, above all, what advantages do not a refined people possess over those who are rude and uncultivated? Let the polished and haughty European recollect, that his ancestors were once, like the Africans, uncivilized, and even barbarous. Did Nature make them inferior to their sons? and should they too have been made slaves? Every rational mind answers, No. Let such reflections as these melt the pride of their superiority into sympathy for the wants and miseries of their sable brethren, and compel them to acknowledge, that understanding is not confined to feature or colour. If, when they look round the world, they feel exultation, let it be tempered with benevolence to others, and gratitude to God, "who hath made of one blood all nations of me for to dwell on all the face of the earth; and whose wisdom is not our wisdom, neither are our ways his ways."

Chapter II

The Author's birth and parentage—His being kidnapped with his sister—Their separation—Surprise at meeting again—Are finally separated—Account of the different places and incidents the Author met with till his arrival on the coast—The effect the sight of a slave-ship had on him—He sails for the West-Indies—Horrors of a slave-ship—Arrives at Barbadoes, where the cargo is sold and dispersed.

I HOPE the reader will not think I have trespassed on his patience in introducing myself to him with some account of the manners and customs of my country. They had been implanted in me with great care, and made an impression on my mind which time could not erase, and which all the adversity and variety of fortune I have since experienced served only to rivet and record: for, whether the love of one's country be real or imaginary, or a lesson of reason, or an instinct of nature, I still look back with pleasure on the first scenes of my life, though that pleasure has been for the most part mingled with sorrow.

I have already acquainted the reader with the time and place of my birth. My father, besides many slaves, had a numerous family, of which seven lived to grow up, including myself and a sister, who was the only daughter. As I was the youngest of the sons, I became, of course, the greatest favourite with my mother, and was always with her; and she used to take particular pains to form my mind. I was trained up from my earliest years in the arts of agriculture and war: my daily exercise was shooting and throwing javelins; and my mother adorned me with emblems, after the manner of our greatest warriors. In this way I grew up till I was turned the age of eleven, when an end was put to my happiness in the following manner:—Generally, when the grown people in the neighbourhood were gone far in the fields to labour, the children assembled together in some of the neighbours premises to play, and commonly some of us used to get up a tree to look out for any assailant, or kidnapper that might come upon us; for they sometimes took these opportunities of our parents' absence, to attack and carry off as many as they could seize. One day, as I was watching at the top of a tree in our yard, I saw one of those people come into the yard of our next neighbour but one, to kidnap, there being many stout young people in it. Immediately, on this, I gave the alarm of the rogue, and he was surrounded by the stoutest of them, who entangled him with cords, so that he could not escape till some of the grown people came and secured him. But, alas! ere long it was my fate to be thus attacked, and to be carried off, when none of the grown people were nigh. One day, when all our people were gone out to their works as usual, and only I and my dear sister were left to mind the house, two men and a woman got over our walls, and in a moment seized us both; and, without giving us time to cry out, or make resitance, they stopped our mouths, tied our hands, and ran off with us into the nearest wood: and continued to carry us as far as they could, till night came on, when we reached a small house, where the robbers halted for refreshment, and spent the night. We were then unbound, but were unable to take any food; and being quite overpowered by fatigue and grief, our only relief was some slumber, which allayed our misfortune for a short time. The next morning we left the house, and continued travelling all the day. For a long time we had kept the woods, but at last we came into a road which I believed I knew. I had now some hopes of being delivered;; for we had advanced but a little way before I discovered some people at a distance, on which I began to cry out for their assistance; but my cries had no other effect than to make them tie me faster, and stop my mouth, and then they put me into a large sack. They also stopped my sister's mouth, and tied her hands; and in this manner we proceeded ill we were out of the sight of these people.—When we went to rest the following night they offered us some victuals; but we refused them; and the only comfort we had was in being in one another's arms all that night, and bathing each other with our tears. But, alas! we were soon deprived of even the smallest comfort of weeping together. The next day proved a day of greater sorrow than I had yet experienced; for my sister and I were then separated, while we lay clasped in each other's arms; it was in vain that we besought them not to part us: she was torn from me, and immediately carried away, while I was left in a state of distraction not to be described. I cried and grieved continually; and for several days did not eat any thing but what they forced into my mouth. At length, after many days travelling, during which I had often changed masters, I got into the hands of a chieftain, in a very pleasant country. This man had two wives and some children, and they all used me extremely well, and did all they could to comfort me; particularly the first wife, who was something like my mother. Although I was a great many days journey from my father's house, yet these people spoke exactly the same language with us. This first master of mine, as I may call him, was a smith, and my principal employment was working his bellows, which was the same kind as I had seen in my vicinity. They were in some respects not unlike the stoves here in gentlemens' kitchens; and were covered over with leather; and in the middle of that leather a stick was fixed, and a person stood up and worked it, in the same manner as is done to pump water out of a cask with a hand-pump. I believe it was gold he worked, for it was of a lovely bright yellow colour, and was worn by the women on their wrists and ancles. I was there I suppose about a month, and they at last used to trust me some little distance from the house. This liberty I used to inquire the way to my own home: and I also sometimes, for the same purpose, went with the maidens, in the cool of the evenings, to bring pitchers of water from the springs for the use of the house. I had also remarked where the sun rose in the morning, and set in the evening, as I had travelled along and I had observed that my father's house was towards the rising of the sun. I therefore determined to seize the first opportunity of making my escape, and to shape my course for that quarter, for I was quite oppressed and weighted down by grief after my mother and friends: and my love of liberty, ever great, was strengthened by the mortifying circumstance of not daring to eat with free-born children, although I was mostly their companion.

—While I was projecting my escape one day, an unlucky event happened, which quite disconcerted my plan, and put an end to my hopes. I used to be sometimes employed in assisting an elderly woman slave to cook and take care of the poulty; and one morning, while I was feeding some chickens, I happened to toss a small pebble at one of them, which hit it on the middle, and directly killed it. The old slave, having soon after missed the chicken, inquired after it; and on my relating the accident (for I told her the truth; because my mother would never suffer me to tell a lie) she flew into a violent passion, threatening that I should suffer for it; and, my master being out, she immediately went and told her mistress what I had done. This alarmed me very much, and I expected an instant correction, which to me was uncommonly dreadful; for I had seldom been beaten at home. I therefore resolved to fly; and accordingly I ran into a thicket that was hard by, and hid myself in the bushes. Soon afterwards my mistress and the slave returned, and, not seeing me, they searched all the house, but, not finding me, and I not making answer when they called to me, they though I had ran away, and the whole neighbourhood was raised in pursuit of me. In that part of the country (as well as ours) the houses and villages were skirted with woods or shrubberies, and the bushed were so thick, that a man could readily conceal himself in them, so as to elude the strictest search. The neighbours continued the whole day looking for me, and several times many of them came within a few yards of the place where I lay hid. I expected every moment, when I heard a rustling among the trees, to be found out, and punished by my master; but they never discovered me, though they were often so near that I even heard their conjectures as they were looking about for me; and I now learned from them that any attempt to return home would be hopeless. Most of them supposed I had fled towards home; but the distance was so great, and the way so intricate, that they thought I could never reach it, and that I should be lost in the woods. When I heard this I was seized with a violent panic, and abandoned myself to despair. Night too began to approach, and aggravated all my fears. I had before entertained hopes of getting home, and had determined when it should be dark to make the attempt; but I was now convinced it was fruitless, and began to consider that, if possibly I could escape all other animals, I could not those of the human kind; and that, not knowing the way, I must perish in the woods.—Thus was I like the hunted deer:

—"Ev'ry lead, and ev'ry whispering breath
"Convey'd a foe, and ev'ry foe a death."

I heard frequent rustlings among the leaves; and, being pretty sure they were snakes, I expected every instant to be stung by them.—This increased my anguish; and the horror of my situation became now quite insupportable. I at length quitted the thicket, very faint and hungry, for I had not eaten or drank any thing all the day, and crept to my master's kitchen, from whence I set out at first, and which was an open shed, and laid myself down in the ashes, with an anxious wish for death to relieve me from all my pains. I was scarcely awake in the morning when the old woman slave, who was the first up, came to light the fire, and saw me in the fire place. She was very much surprised to see me, and could scarcely believe her own eyes. She now promised to intercede for me, and went for her master, who soon after came, and, having slightly reprimanded me, ordered me to be taken care of, and not ill treated.

Soon after this my master's only daughter and child by his first wife sickened and died, which affected him so much that for some time he was almost frantic, and really would have killed himself had he not been watched and prevented. However, in a small time afterwards he recovered, and I was again sold. I was now carried to the left of the sun's rising, through many dreary wastes and dismal woods, amidst the hideous roarings of wild beasts.—The people I was sold to used to carry me very often, when I was tired, either on their shoulders or on their backs. I saw many convenient well-built sheds along the roads, at proper distances, to accommodate the merchants and travellers, who lay in those buildings along with their wives, who often accompany them; and they always go well armed.

From the time I left my own nation I always found someboy that understood me till I came to the sea coast. The languages of different nations did not totally differ, nor were they so copious as those of the Europeans, particularly the English. They were therefore easily learned; and, while I was journeying thus through Africa, I acquired two or three different tongues. In this manner I had been travelling for a considerable time, when one evening, to my great surprise, whom should I see brought to the house where I was but my dear sister. As soon as she saw me she gave a loud shriek, and ran into my arms.—I was quite overpowered; neither of us could speak, but, for a considerable time, clung to each other in mutual embraces, unable to do any thing but weep. Our meeting affected all who saw us; and indeed I must acknowledge, in honour of those sable destroyers of human rights that I never met with any ill treatment, or saw any offered to their slaves except tying them, when necessary, to keep them from running away. When thse people knew we were brother and sister, they indulged us to be together; and the man, to whom I supposed we belonged, lay with us, he in the middle, while she and I held one another by the hands across his breast all night; and thus for a while we forgot our misfortunes in the joy of being together; but even this small comfort was soon to have an end; for scarcely had the fatal morning appeared, when she was again torn from me for ever! I was now more miserable, if possible, than before. The small relief which her presence gave me from pain was gone, and the wretchedness of my situation was redoubled by my anxiety after her fate, and my apprehensions lest her sufferings should be greater than mine, when I could not be with her to alleviate them. Yes, thou dear partner of all my childish sports! thou sharer of my joys and sorrows! happy should I have ever esteemed myself to encounter every misery for you, and to procure your freedom by the sacrifice of my own! Though you were early forced from my arms, your image has been always rivetted in my heart, from which neither *time nor fortune* have been able to remove it: so that while the thoughts of your sufferings have damped my prosperity, they have mingled with adversity, and encreased its bitterness.—To that heaven which protects the weak from the strong, I commit the care of your innocence and virtues, if they have not already received their full reward; and if your youth and delicacy have not long since fallen victimsto the violence of the African trader, the the pestilential stench of a Guinea ship, the seasoning in the European colonies, or the lash and lust of a brutal and unrelenting overseer.

I did not long remain after my sister. I was again sold, and carried through a number of places, till, after travelling a considerable time, I came to a town called Timnah, in the most beautiful country I had yet seen in Africa. It was extremely rich, and there were many rivulets which flowed through it; and supplied a large pond in the center of the town, where the people washed. Here I first saw and tasted cocoa nuts, which I thought superior to any nuts I had ever tasted before; and the trees, which were loaded, were also interspersed amongst the houses, which had commodious shades adjoining, and were in the same manner as ours, the insides being neatly plastered and white-washed. Here I also saw and tasted for the first time sugar-cane. Their money consisted of little white shells, the size of the finger-nail: they are known in this country by the name of core. I was sold here for one hundred and seventy-two of them by a merchant who lived and brought me there. I had been about two or theree days at his house, when a wealthy widow, a neighbour of his, came there one evening, and brought with her an only son, a young gentleman about my own age and size. Here they saw me; and having taken a fancy to me, I was bought of the merchant, and went home with them. Her house and premises were situated close to one of those rivulets I have mentioned, and were the finest I ever saw in Africa: they were very extensive, and she had a number of slaves to attend her. The next day I was washed and perfumed, and when meal-time came, I was led into the presence of my mistress, and eat and drank before her with her son. This filled me with astonishment: and I could scarce help expressing my surprise that the young gentleman should suffer me, who was bound to eat with him who was free; and not only so, but that he would not at any time either eat or drink till I had taken first because I was the eldest, which was agreeable to our custom. Indeed every thing here, and all their treatment of me, made me forget that I was a slave. The language of these people resembled ours so nearly, that we understood each other perfectly. They had also the very same customs as we. There were likewise slaves daily to attend us, while my young master and I, with other boys sported with our darts and arrows, as I had been used to do at home. In this resemblance to my former happy fate, I passed about two months, and I now began to think I was to be adopted into the family, and was beginning to be reconciled to my situation, and to forget by degrees my misfortunes, when all at once the delusion vanished; for, without the least previous knowledge, one morning early, while my dear master and companion was still asleep, I was awakened out of my reverie to fresh sorrow, and hurried away even among the uncircumcised.

Thus, at the very moment I dreamed of the greatest happiness, I found myself most miserable: and seemed as if fortune wished to give me this taste of joy only to render the reverse more poignant. The change I now experienced was as painful as it was sudden and unexpected. It was a change indeed from a state of bliss to a scene which is inexpressible by me, as it discovered to me an element I had never before beheld, and till then had no idea of, and wherein such instances of hardship and fatigue continually occurred as I can never reflect on but with horror.

All the nations and people I had hitherto passed through ressembled our own in their manners, customs and language but I cam at length to a country, the inhabitants of which differed from us in all those particulars. I was very much struck with this difference, especially when I came among a people who did not circumcise, and eat without washing their hands. They cooked also in iron pots, and had European cutlasses and cross bows, which were unknown to us, and fought with their fists among themselves. Their women were not so modest as ours, for they eat, and drank, and slept with their men. But, above all, I was amazed to see no sacrifices or offerings among them. In some of those places the people ornamented themselves with scars, and likewise filed their teeth very sharp. They wanted sometimes to ornament me in the same manner, but I would not suffer them; hoping that I might some time be among a people who did not thus disfigure themselves, as I thought they did. At last, I came to the banks of a large river, which was covered with canoes, in which the people appeared to live with their household utensils and provisions of all kinds. I was beyond measure astonished at this, as I had never before seen any water larger than a pond or a rivulet; and my surprise was mingled with no small fear, when I was put into one of these canoes, and we began to paddle and move along the river. We continued going on thus till night; and, when we came to land, and made fires on the banks, each family by themselves, some dragged their canoes on shore, others staid and cooked in theirs, and lay in them all night. Those on the land had mats, of which they made tents, some in the shape of little houses: In these we slept; and, after the morning meal, we embarked again, and proceeded as before. I was often very much astonished to see some of the women, as well as the men, jump into the water, dive to the bottom, come up again, and swim about. Thus I continued to travel, sometimes by land sometimes by water, through different countries, and various nations, till, at the end of six or seven months after I had been kidnapped, I arrived at the sea coast. It would be tedious and uninteresting to relate all the incidents which befel me during this journey, and which I have not yet forgotten; of the various lands I passed through, and the manners and customs of all the different people among whom I lived: I shall therefore only observe, that, in all the places where I was, the soil was exceedingly rich; the pomkins, eadas, plantains, yams, &c. &c. were in great abundance, and of incredible size. There were also large quantities of different gums, though not used for any purpose; and every where a great deel of tobacco. The cotton even grew quite wild; and there was plenty of red wood. I saw no mechanics whatever in all the way, except such as I have mentioned. The chief employment in all these countries was agriculture, and both the males and females, as with us, were brought up to it, and trained in the arts of war.

The first object which saluted my eyes when I arrived on the coast was the sea, and a slave-ship, which was then riding at anchor, and waiting for its cargo. Thses filled me with astonishment, which was soon converted into terror, which I am yet at a loss to describe, nor the then feelings of my mind. When I was carried on board I was immediately handled, and tossed up, to see if I were sound, by some of the crew; and I was now persuaded that I had got into a world of bad spirits, and that they were going to kill me. Their complexions too differing so much from ours, their long hair, and the language they spoke, which was very different from any I had ever heard, united to confirm me in this belief. Indeed, such were the horrors of my views and fears at the moment, that, if ten thousand worlds had been my own, I would have freely parted with them all to have exchanged my condition with that of the meanest slave in my own country. When I looked round the ship too, and saw a large furnace or copper boiling, and a multitude of black people of every description changed together, every one of their countenances expressing dejection and sorrow, I no longer doubted my fate, and, quite overpowered with horror and anguish, I fell motionless on the deck and fainted. When I recovered a little, I found some black people about me, who I believed were some of those who brought me on board, and had been receiving their pay; they talked to me in order to cheer me, but all in vain. I asked them if we were not to be eaten by those white men with horrible looks, red faces, and long hair? They told me I was not; and one of the crew brought me a small portion of spiritous liqour in a wine glass; but, being afraid of him, I would not take it out of his hand. One of the blacks therefore took it from him and gave it to me, and I took a little down my palate, which, instead of reviving me, as they thought it would, threw me into the greatest consternation at the strange feeling it produced having never tasted any such liquor before. Soon after this, the blacks who brought me on board went off, and left me abandoned to despair. I now saw myself deprived of all chance of returning to my native country, or even the least glimpse of hope of aining the shore, which I now considered as friendly: and even wished for my former slavery, in preference to my present situation, which was filled with horrors of every kind, still heightened by my ignorance of what I was to undergo. I was not long suffered to indulge my grief; I was soon put down under the decks, and there I received such a salutation in my nostrils as I had never experienced in my life; so that with the loathsomeness of the stench, and crying together, I became so sick and low that I was not able to eat, nor had I the least desire to taste any thing. I now wished for the last friend, Death, to relieve me; but soon, to my grief, two of the white men offered me eatables; and, on my refusing to eat, one of them held me fast by the hands, and laid me across, I think, the windlass, and tied my feet, while the other flogged me severely. I had never experienced any thing of this kind before; and although not being used to the water, I naturally feared that element the first time I saw it; yet, nevertheless, could I have got over the nettings, I would have jumped over the side; but I could not; and, besides, the crew used to watch us very closely who were not chained down to the decks, lest we should leap into the water; and I have seen some of these poor African prisoners, most severely cut for attempting to do so, and hourly whipped for not eating. This indeed was often the case with myself. In a little time after, amongst the poor chained men, I found some of my own nation, which in a small degree gave ease to my mind. I inquired of them what was to be done with us? they give me to understand we were to be carried to these white people's country to work for them. I then was a little revived, and thought, if it were no worse than working, my situation was not so desperate: but still I feared I should be put to death, the white people looked and acted, as I thought, in so savage a manner; for I had never seen among any people such instances of brutal cruelty; and this not only shewn towards us blacks, but also to some of the whites themselves. One white man in particular I saw, when we were permitted to be on deck, flogged so unmercifully, with a large rope near the foremast, that he died in consequence of it; and they tossed him over the side as they would have done a brute. This made me fear these people the more; and I expected nothing less than to be treated in the same manner. I could not help expressing my fears and apprehensions to some of my countrymen: I asked them if these people had no country, but lived in this hollow place the ship? they told me they did not, but came from a distant one. 'Then,' said I, 'how comes it in all our country we never heard of them?' They told me, because they lived so very far off. I then asked, where were their women? had they any like themselves! I was told they had: 'Ande why,' said I, 'do we not see them?' they answered, because they were left behind. I asked how the vessel could go? they told me they could not tell; but that there were cloth put upon the mastsby the help of the ropes I saw, and then the vessel went on; and the white men had some spell or magic they put in the water when they liked in order to stop the vessel. I was exceedingly amazed at this account, and really thought they were spirits. I therefore wished much to be from amongst them, for I expected they would sacrifice me: but my wishes were vain; for we were so quartered that it was impossible for any of us to make our escape. While we staid on the coast I was mostly on deck; and one day, to my great astonishment, I saw one of these vessels coming in with the sails up. As soon as the whites saw it, they gave a great shout, at which we were amazed; and the more so as the vessel appeared larger by approaching nearer. At last she came to anchor in my sight, and when the anchor was let go, I and my countrymen who saw it were lost in astonishment to observe the vessel stop; and were now convinceced it was done by magic. Soon after this the other ship got her boats out, and they came on board of us, and the people of both ships seemed very glad to see each other. Several of the strangers also shook hands with us black people, and made motions with their hands, signifying, I suppose, we were to go to their country; but we did not understand them. At last, when the ship we were in had got in all her cargo they made ready with many fearful noises, and we were all put under deck, so that we could not see how they managed the vessel. But this disappointment was the least of my sorrow. The stench of the hold while we were on the coast was so intolerably loathsome, that it was dangerous to remain there for any time, and some of us had been permitted to stay on the deck for the fresh air; but now that the whole ship's cargo were confined together, it became absolutely pestilential. The closeness of the place, and the heat of the climate, added to the number in the ship, which was so crouded that each had scarcely room to turn himself, almost suffocated us. This produced copious perspiration, from a variety of loathsome smells, and brought on a sickness amongst the slaves, of which many died, thus falling victims to the improvident avarice, as I may call it, of their purchasers. This wretched situation was again aggravated by the galling of the chains, now become insupportable; and the filth of the necessary tubs, into which the children often fell, and were almost suffocated. The shrieks of the women, and the groans of the dying, rendered the whole a scene of horror almost inconceiveable. Happily perhaps for myself I was soon reduced so low here that it was thought necessary to keep me almost always on deck; and from my extreme youth I was not put in fetters. In this situation I expected every hour to share the fate of my companions, some of whom were almost daily brought upon deck at the point of death, which I began to hope would soon put an end to my miseries. Often did I think many of the inhabitants of the deep much more happy than myself; I envied them the freedom they enjoyed, and as often wished I could change my condition for theirs. Every circumstance I met with served only to render my state more painful, and heighten my apprehensions and my opinion of the cruelty of the whites. One day they had taken a number of fishes; and when they had killed and satisfied themselves with as many as they thought fit, to our astonishment who were on deck, rather than give any of them to us to eat, as we expected, they tossed the remaining fish into the sea again, although we begged and prayed for some as well as we could, but in vain; and some of my countrymen, being pressed by hunger, took an opportunity, when they thought no one saw them, of trying to get a little privately; but they were discovered, and the attempt procured them some very severe floggings.

One day, when we had a smooth sea, and moderate wind, two of my wearied countrymen, who were chained together (I was near them at the time), preferring death to such a life of misery, somehow made through the nettings, and jumped into the sea; immediately another quite dejected fellow, who, on account of his illness, was suffered to be out of irons, also followed their example; and I believe many more would very soon have done the same, if they had not been prevented by the ship's crew, who were instantly alarmed. Those of us that were the most active were, in a moment, put down under the deck; and there was such a noise and confusion amongst the people of the ship as I never heard before, to stop her, and get the boat out to go after the slaves. However, two of the wretches were drowned, but they got the other, and afterwards flogged him unmercifully, for thus attempting to prefer death to slavery. In this manner we continued to undergo more hardships than I can now relate; hardships which are inseparable from this accursed trade.—Many a time we were near suffocation, from the want of fresh air, which we were often without for whole days together. This, and the stench of the necessary tubs, carried off many. During our passage I first saw flying fishes, which surprised me very much: they used frequently to fly across the ship, and many of them fell on the deck. I also now first saw the use of the quadrant. I had often with astonishmentseen the mariners make observations with it, and I could not think what it meant. They at last took notice of my surprise; and one of them willing to increase it, as well as to gratify my curiosity, made me one day look through it. The clouds appeared to me to be land, which disappeared as they passed along. This heightened my wonder: and I was now more persuaded than ever that I was in another world, and that every thing about me was magic. At last, we came in sight of the island of Barbadoes, at which the whites on board gave a great shout, and made many signs of joy to us. We did not know what to think of this; but, as the vessel drew nearer, we plainly saw the harbour, and other ships of different kinds and sizes: and we soon anchored amongst them off Bridge Town. Many merchants and planters now came on board, though it was in the evening. They put us in separate parcels, and examined us attentively.—They also made us jump, and pointed to the land, signifying we were to go there. We thought by this we should be eaten by these ugly men, as they appeared to us; and when, soon after we were all put down under the deck again, there was much dread and trembling among us, and nothing but bitter cries to be heard all the night from these apprehensions, insomuch that at last the white people got some old slaves from the land to pacify us. They told us we were not to be eaten, but to work, and were soon to go on land, where we should see many of our country people. This report eased us much; and sure enough, soon after we landed, there came to us Africans of all languages. We were conducted immediately to the merchant's yard, where we were all pent up together like so many sheep in a fold, without regard to sex or age. As every object was new to me, every thing I saw filled me with surprise. What struck me first was, that the houses were built with bricks, in stories, and in every other respect different from those I have seen in Africa: but I was still more astonished on seeing people on horseback. I did not know what this could mean; and indeed I thought these people were full of nothing but magical arts. While I was in this astonishment, one of my fellow prisoners spoke to a countryman of his about the horses, who said they were the same kind they had in their country. I understood them, though they were from a distant part of Africa, and I thought it odd I had not seen any horses there; but afterwards, when I came to converse with different Africans I found they had many horses amongst them, and much larger than those I then saw. We were not many days in the merchant's custody before we were sold after their usual manner, which is this:—On a signal given, (as the beat of a drum), the buyers rush at once into the yard where the slaves are confined, and make choice of that parcel they like best. The noise and clamour with which this is attended, and the eagerness visible in the countenances of the buyers, serve not a little to increase the apprehension of the terrified Africans, who may well be supposed to consider them as the ministers of that destruction to which they think themselves devoted. In this manner, without scruple, are relations and friends separated, most of them never to see each other again. I remember in the vessel in which I was brought over, in the men's apartment, there were several brothers who, in the sale, were sold in different lots; and it was very moving on this occasion to see and hear their cries at parting. O, ye nominal Christians! might not an African ask you, learned you this from your God? who says unto you, Do unto all men as you would men should do unto you. Is it not enough that we are torn from our country and friends to toil for your luxury and lust of gain? Must every tender feeling be likewise sacrifices to your avarice? Are the dearest friends and relations, now rendered more dear by their separation from their kindred, still to be parted from each other, and thus prevented from cheering the gloom of slavery with the small comfort of being together, and mingling their suffering and sorrows? Why are parents to lose their children, brothers their sisters, or husbands their wives? Surely this is a new refinement in cruelty, which, while it has no advantage to atone for it, thus aggravates distress, and adds fresh horrors even to the wretchedness of slavery.

Chapter X

The author leaves Dr. Irving, and engages on board a Turkey ship—Account of a black man's being kidnapped on board, and sent to the West Indies, and the author's fruitless endeavours to procure his freedom—Some account of the manner of the author's conversion to the Faith of Jesus Christ.

OUR voyage to the North Pole being ended, I returned to London with Dr. Irving, with whom I continued for some time, during which I began seriously to reflect on the dangers I had escaped, particularly those of my last voyage, which made a lasting impression on my mind; and, by the grace of God, proved afterwards a mercy to me: it caused me to reflect deeply on my eternal slate, and to seek the Lord with full purpose of heart ere it be too late. I rejoice greatly; and heartily thanked the Lord for directing me to London, where I was determined to work out my own salvation, and, in so doing, procure a title to heaven; being the result of a mind blinded by ignorance and sin.

In process of time I left my master, Doctor Irving, the purifier of waters. I lodged in Coventry-court, Haymarket, where I was continually oppressed and much concerned about the salvation of my soul, and was determined (in my own strength) to be a first-rate Christian. I used every means for this purpose; and, not being able to find any person amongst those with whom I was then acquainted that acquiesced with me in point of religion, or, in scripture language, that would shew me any good, I was much dejected, and knew not where to seek relief; however, I first frequented the neighbouring churches, St. James's, and others, two or three times a day, for many weeks: still I came away dissatisfied: something was wanting that I could not obtain, and I really found more heart-felt relief in reading my bible at home than in attending the church; and, being resolved to be saved, I pursued other methods. First I went among the people called Quakers, whose meeting at times was in silence, and I remained as much in the dark as ever. I then searched into the Roman Catholic principles. but was not in the least edified. I, at length, had recourse to the Jews, which availed me nothing, as the fear of eternity daily harassed my mind and I knew not where to seek shelter from the wrath to come. However, this was my conclusion, at all events, to read the Four Evangelists, and whatever sect or party I found adhering thereto, such I would join. Thus I went on heavily without any guide to direct me the way that leadeth to eternal life. I asked different people questions about the manner of going to heaven, and was told different ways. Here I was much staggered, and could not find any at that time more righteous than myself, or indeed so much inclined to devotion. I thought we should not all be saved (this is agreeable to the holy scriptures), nor would all be damned. I found none among the circle of my acquaintance that kept holy the Ten Commandments. So righteous was I in my own eyes, that I was convinced I excelled many of them in that point, by keeping eight out of ten; and finding those, who in general termed themselves Christians, not so honest or so good in their morals as the Turks. I really thought the Turks were in a safer way of salvation than my neighbours; so that between hopes and fears I went on, and the chief comforts I enjoyed were in the musical French-horn, which I then practised, and also dressing of hair. Such was my situation some months, experiencing the dishonesty of many people here. I determined at last to set out for Turkey, and there to end my days. It was now early in the spring 1774. I sought for a master, and found a Captain, John Hughes, commander of a ship called Anglicania, fitting out in the river Thames, and bound to Smyrna in Turkey. I shipped myself with him as a steward; at the same time I recommended to him a very clever black man, John Annis, as a cook. This man was on board the ship near two months doing his duty; he had formerly lived many years with Mr. William Kirkpatrick, a gentleman of the island of St. Kitt's, from whom he parted by consent, though he afterwards tried many schemes to inveigle the poor man. He had applied to many captains, who traded to St. Kitt's to trepan him; and when all their attempts and schemes of kidnapping proved abortive, Mr. Kirkpatrick came to our ship at Union stairs, on Easter Monday, April the 4th, with two wherry-boats and six men, having learned that the man was on board; and tied, and forcibly took him away from the ship, in the presence of the crew and the chief mate, who had detained him after he had information to come away. I believe this was a combined piece of business; but, be that as it may, it certainly reflected great disgrace on the mate, and captain also, who, although they had desired the oppressed man to stay on board, yet notwithstanding this vile act on the man who had served him, he did not in the least assist to recover him, or pay me a farthing of his wages, which was about five pounds. I proved the only friend he had, who attempted to regain him his liberty, if possible, having known the want of liberty myself. I sent as soon as I could to Gravesend, and got knowledge of the ship in which he was; but unluckily she had sailed the first tide after he was put on board. My intention was then immediately to apprehend Mr. Kirkpatrick, who was about setting off for Scotland; and, having obtained a habeas corpus for him, and got a tipstaff to go with me to St. Paul's Church yard, where he lived, he, suspecting something of this kind, set a watch to look out. My being known to them obliged me to use the following deception: I whitened my face that they might not know me, and this had the desired effect. He did not go out of his house that night, and next morning I contrived a well-plotted stratagem, notwithstanding he had a gentleman in his house to personate him. My direction to the tipstaff had the desired effect; he got admittance into the house, and conducted him to a judge according to the writ. When he came there, his plea was, that he had not the body in custody, on which he was admitted to bail. I proceeded immediately to that well-known philanthropist, Granville Sharp, Esq. who received me with the utmost kindness, and gave me every instruction that was needful on the occasion. I left him in full hopes that I should gain the unhappy man his liberty, with the warmest sense of gratitude towards Mr. Sharp for his kindness; but, alas! my attorney proved unfaithful; he took my money, lost me many months employ, and did not do the least good in the cause; and when the poor man arrived at St. Kitt's, he was, according to custom, staked to the ground with four pins through a cord, two on his wrists, and two on his ancles, was cut and flogged most unmercifully, and afterwards loaded cruelly with irons about his neck. I had two very moving letters from him while he was in this situation; and I made attempts to go after him at a great hazard, but was sadly disappointed: I also was told of it by some very respectable families now in London, who saw him in St. Kitt's in the same state, in which he remained till kind death released him out of the hands of his tyrants. During this disagreeable business, I was under strong convictions of sin, and thought that my state was worse than any man's; my mind was unaccountable disturbed; I often wished for death, though, at the same time, convinced I was all together unprepared for that awful summons: suffering much by villains in the late cause, and being much concerned about the state of my soul, these things (but particularly the latter) brought me very low; so that I became a burden to myself, and viewed all things around me as emptiness and vanity, which could give no satisfaction to a troubled conscience. I was again determined to go to Turkey and resolved, at that time, never more to return to England. I engaged as steward on board a Turkeyman the Wester Hall, Capt. Lina), but was prevented by means of my late captain Mr. Hughes, and others. All this appeared to be against me, and the only comfort I then experienced was in reading the Holy Scriptures, where I saw that 'there is no new thing under the sun,' Eccles. i. 9. and what was appointed for me I must submit to. Thus I continued to travel in much heaviness, and frequen ly murmured against the Almighty, particularly in his providential dealings; and, awful to think! I began to blaspheme, and wished often to be any thing but a human being. In these severe conflicts the Lord answered me by awful 'visions of the night, when deep sleep fålleth upon men, in slumberings upon the bed,' Job xxxiii. 15. He was pleased, in much mercy, to give me to see, and in some measure understand, the great and awful scene of the Judgement-day, that 'no unclean person, no unholy thing, can enter into the kingdom of God,' Eph. v. 5. I would then, if it had been possible, have changed my nature with the meanest worm on the earth, and was ready to say to the mountains and rocks, 'fall on me," Rev. vi. 16. but all in vain. I then, in the greatest agony, requested the divine Creator, that he would grant me a small space of time to repent of my follies and vile iniquities, which I felt was grievous. The Lord, in his manifold mercies, was pleased to grant my request, and being yet in a state of time, my sense of God's mercies were so great on my mind when I awoke, that my strength entirely failed me for many minutes, and I was exceedingly weak. This was the first spiritual mercy I ever was sensible of, and being on praying ground, as soon as I recovered a little strength, and got out of bed and dressed myself I invoked heaven from my inmost soul, and fervently begged that God would never again permit me to blaspheme his most holy name. The Lord, who is long-suffering, and full of compassion to such poor rebels as we are, condescended to hear and answer. I felt that I was altogether unholy, and saw clearly what a bad use I had made of the faculties I was endowed with: they were given me to glorify God with; I though, therefore, I ha better want them here, and enter into life eternal, than abuse them and be cast unto hell fire. I prayed to be directed, if there were any holier persons than those with whom I was acquainted, that the Lord would point them out to me. I appealed to the searcher of hearts, whether I did not wish to love him more, and serve him better. Notwithstanding all this, the reader may easily discern, if a believer, that I was still in nature's darkness. At length I hated the house in which I lodged, because God's most holy name was blasphemed in it; then I saw the word of God verified, viz. 'Before they call, I will answer; and while they are yet speaking I will hear.'

I had a great desire to read the Bible the whole day at home; but nit having a convenient place for retirement, I left the house in the day, rather than stay amongst the wicked ones; and that day, as I was walking, it pleased God to direct me to a house, where there was an old sea-faring man, who experienced much of the love of God shed abrouad in his heart. He began to discourse with me; and, as I desired to love the Lord, his conversation rejoiced me greatly; and indeed I had never heard before the love of Christ to believers set forth in such a manner, and in so clear a point of view. Here I had more questions to put to the man than his time would permit him to answer: and in that memorable hour there came in a Dissenting Minister; he joined our discourse, and asked me some few questions; among others, where I heard the gospel preached? I knew not what he meant by hearing the gospel; I told him I head read the gospel: and he asked me where I went to church, or whether I went at all, or not? To which I replied, 'I attended St. James's, St. Martin's, and St. Ann's, Soho.'—'So,' said he, 'you are a churchman?' I answered, I was. He then invited me to a love feast at his chapel that evening. I accepted the offer, and thanked him; and soon after he went away. I had some further discourse with the old christian, added to some profitable reading, which made me exceedingly happy. When I left him he reminded me of coming to the feast; I assured him I would be there. Thus we parted, and I weighed over the heavenly conversation that had passed between these two men, which cheered my then heavy and drooping spirit more than any thing I had met with for many months. However, I thought the time long in going to my supposed banquet. I also wished much for the company of these friendly men; their company pleased me much; and I thought the gentleman very kind in asking me, a stranger, to a feast; but how singular did it appear to me, to have it in a chapel! When the wished for hour came I went, and happily the old man was there, who kindly seated me, as he belonged to the place. I was much astonished to see the place filled with people, and no signs of eating and drinking. There were many ministers in the company. At last they began by giving out hymns, and between the singing, the ministers engaged in prayer: in short, I knew not what to make of this sight, having never seen any thing of the kind in my life before now; Some of the guests began to speak their experience, agreeable to what I read in the Scriptures: much was said by every speaker of the providence of God, and his unspeakable mercies to each of them. This I knew in a great measure, and could most heartily join them. But when they spoke of a future state, they seemed to be altogether certain of their calling and election of God; and that no one could ever separate them from the love of Christ, or pluck them out of his hands. This filled me with utter consternation intermingled with admiration. I was so amazed as not to know what to think of the company; my heart was attracted, and my affections were enlarged; I wished to be as happy as them, and was persuaded in my mind that they were different from the world "that lieth in wickedness,' I John v. 19. Their language and singing, &c. did well harmonize; I was entirely overcome, and wished to live and die thus. Lastly, some persons in the place produced some neat baskets full of buns, which they distributed about; and each person communicated with his neighbour, and sipped water out of different mugs, which they handed about to all who were present. This kind of Christian fellowship I had never seen, nor ever thought of seeing on earth; it fully reminded me of what I had read in the Holy Scriptures of the primitive Christians, who loved each other and broke bread; in partaking of it, even from house to house. This entertainment (which lasted about four hours) ended in singing and prayer. It was the first soul-feast I ever was present at. This last twenty-four hours produced me things, spiritual and temporal, sleeping and waking, judgment and mercy, that I could not but admire the goodness of God, in directing the blind, blasphemous sinner in the path that he knew not, even among the just; and instead of judgment he has shewed mercy, and will hear and answer the prayers and supplications of every returning prodigal;

O! to grace how great a debtor
Daily I'm constrain'd to be.

After this I was resolved to win heaven, if possible; and if I perished, I thought it should be at the feet of Jesus, in praying to him for salvation. After having been an eye-witness to some of the happiness which attended those who feared God, I knew not how, with any propriety, to return to my lodgings, where the name of God was continually profaned, at which I felt the greatest horror; I paused in my mind for some time, not knowing what to do; whether to hire a bed elsewhere, or go home again. At last, fearing an evil report might arise, I went home, with a farewell to card-playing and vain-jesting, &c. I saw that time was very short, eternity long, and very near; and I viewed those persons alone blessed who were found ready at midnight-call, or when the Judge of all, both quick and dead, cometh.

The next day I took courage, and went to Holborn, to see my new and worthy acquaintance, the old man, Mr. C—; he, with his wife, a gracious woman, were at work at silk-weaving; they seemed mutually happy, and both quite glad to see me, and I more so to see them. I sat down, and we conversed much about soul matters, &c. Their discourse was amazingly delightful, edifying, and pleasant. I knew not at last how to leave this agreeable pair, till time summoned me away. As I was going they lent me a little book, entitled, "The Conversion of an Indian." It was in questians and answers. The poor man came over the sea to London, to enquire after the Christian's God, who (through rich mercy) he found, and had not his journey in vain. The above book was of great use to me, and at that time was a means of strengthening my faith; however, in parting, they both invited me to call on them when I pleased. This delighted me, and I took care to make all the improvement from it I could; and so far I thanked God for such company and desires. I prayed that the many evils I felt within might be done away, and that I might be weaned from my former carnal acquaintances. This was quickly heard and answered, and I was soon connected with those whom the Scripture calls the excellent of the earth. I heard the gospel preached, and the thoughts of my heart and actions were laid open by the preachers, and the way of salvation by Christ alone was evidently set forth. Thus I went on happily for near two months; and I once heard during this period, a reverend gentleman Mr. Green, speak of a man who had departed this life in full assurance of his going to glory. I was much astonished at the assertion; and did very deliberately inquire how he could get at this knowledge. I was answered fully, agreeably to what I read in the oracles of truth; and was told also, that if I did not experience the new birth, and the pardon of my sins, thro' the blood of Christ, before I died, I could not enter the kingdom of heaven. I knew not what to think of this report, as I thought I kept eight commandments out of ten; then my worthy interpreter told me I did not do it, nor could I; and he added, that no man ever did or could keep the commandments, without offending in one point. I thought this sounded very strange, and puzzled me much for many weeks; for I thought it a hard saying. I then asked my friend, Mr. L—d, who was a clerk of a chapel, why the commandments of God were given, if we could not be saved by them? To which he replied, 'The law is a school-master to bring us to Christ,' who alone could, and did keep the commandments, and fulfilled all their requirements for his elect people, even those to whom he had given a living faith, and the sins of those chosen vessels were already atoned for and forgiven them whilst living;[1] and if I did not experience the same before my exit, the Lord would say at that great day to me, 'Go, ye cursed,' &c. &c. for God would appear faithful in his judgments to the wicked, as he would be faithful in shewing mercy to those who were ordained to it before the world was; therefore Christ Jesus seemed to be all in all to that man's soul. I was much wounded at this discourse, and brought into such a dilemma as I never expected. I asked him, if he was to die that moment, whether he was sure to enter the kingdom of God; and added, 'Do you know that your sins are forgiven you?" he answered in the affirmative. Then confusion, anger, and discontent seized me, and I staggered much at this sort of doctrine; it brought me to a stand, not knowing which to believe, whether salvation by works, or by faith only in Christ. I requested him to tell me how I might know when my sins were forgiven me. He assured me he could not, and that none but God alone could do this. I told him it was very mysterious; but he said it was really matter of fact, and quoted many portions of Scripture immediately to the point, to which I could make no reply. He then desired me to pray to God to shew me these things. I answered that I prayed to God every day. He said, 'I perceive you are a churchman.' I answered, I was. He then entreated me to beg of God, to shew me what I was, and the true state of my soul. I though the prayer very short and odd; so we parted for that time. I weighed all these things well over, and could not help thinking how is was possible for a man to know that his sins were forgiven him in this life. I wished that God would reveal this self-same thing unto me. In a short time after this I went to Westminster chapel; the late Rev. Dr. Peckwell preached from Lam. iii. 39. It was a wonderful sermon; he clearly shewed that a living man had no cause to complain for the punishments of his sins; he evidently justified the Lord in all his dealings with the sons of men; he also shewed the justice of God in the eternal punishment of the wicked and impenitent. The discourse seemed to me like a two-edged sword cutting all ways; it afforded much joy, intermingled with many fears about my soul; and when it was ended, he gave it out that he intended, the ensuing week, to examine all those who meant to attend the Lord's table. Now I thought much of my good works, and, at the same time, was doubtful of my being a proper object to receive the sacrament: I was full of meditation till the day of examining. However, I went to the chapel, and, though much distressed, I addressed the reverend gentleman, thinking, if I was not right, he would endeavour to convince me of it. When I conversed with him, the first thing he asked me was, What I knew of Christ? I told him I believed in him, and had been baptized in his name. 'Then,' said he, 'when were you brought to the knowledge of God; and how were you convinced of sin? I knew not what he meant by these questions; I told him I kept eight commandments out of ten; but that I sometimes swore on board ship, and sometimes when on shore, and broke the sabbath. He then asked me if I could read; I answered, 'Yes.'—'Then,' said he, 'do you not read in the Bible, he that offends in one point is guilty of all?' I said, 'Yes.' Then he assured me, that one sin unattoned for was as sufficient to damn a soul, as one leak was to sink a ship. Here I was struck with awe; for the minister exhorted me much, and reminded me of the shortness of time, and the length of eternity, and that no unregenerate soul, or any thing unclean, could enter the kingdom of heaven.

He did not admit me as a communicant; but recommended me to read the scriptures, and hear the word preached; not to neglect fervent prayer to God, who has promised to hear the supplications of those who seek him, with many thanks, and resolved to follow his advice, so far as the Lord would condescend to enable me. During this time I was out of employ, nor was I likely to get a situation suitable for me, which obliged me to go once more to sea. I engaged as steward of a ship called the Hope, Captain Richard Str nge, bound from London to Cadiz in Spain. In a short time after I was on board, I heard the name of God much blasphemed, and I feared greatly lest I should catch the horrible infection. I thought if I sinned again, after having life and death set evidently before me, I should certainly go to hell. My mind was uncommonly chagrined, and I murmured much at God's providential dealings with me, and was discontented with the commandments, that I could not be saved by what I had done; I hated all things, and wished I had never been born; confusion seized me, and I wished to be annihilated. One day I was standing on the very edge of the stern of the ship, thinking to drown myself; but this scripture was instantly impressed on my mind, 'That no murderer hath eternal life abiding in him,' I John iii. 19. Then I paused, and thought myself the unhappiest man living. Again, I was convinced that the Lord was better to me than I deserved; and I was better of in the world than many. After this I began to fear death; I fretted, mourned, and prayed, till I became a burden to others, but more so to myself. At length I concluded to beg my bread on shore, rather than go again to sea amongst a people who feared not God, and I entreated the captain three different times to discharge me; he would not, but each time gave me greater and greater encouragement to continue with him, and all on board shewed me very great civility: notwithstanding all this, I was unwilling to embark again. At last some of my religious friends advised me, by saying it was my lawful calling, consequently it was my duty to obey, and that God was not confined to place, &c. particularly Mr. G. Smith, the governor of Tothill-fields Bridewell, who pitied my case, and read the eleventh chapter of the Hebrews to me, with exhortations. He prayed for me, and I believe that he prevailed on my behalf, as my burden was then greatly removed, and I found a heartfelt resignation to the will of God. The good man gave me a pocket Bible, and Alleine's Alarm to the Unconverted. We parted, and the next day I went on board again. We said for Spain, and I found favour with the captain. It was the fourth of the month of September when we sailed from London: we had a delightful voyage to Cadiz, where we arrived the twenty-third of the same month. The place is strong, commands a fine prospect, and is very rich. The Spanish galleons frequent that port, and some arrived whilst we were there. I had many opportunities of reading the Scriptures. I wrestled hard with God in fervent prayers, who had declared his word that he would hear the groanings and deep sighs of the poor is spirit. I found this verified to my utter astonishment and comfort in the following manner: On the morning of the 6th of October (I pray you to attend) all that day, I thought that I should either see or hear something supernatural. I had a secret impulse on my mind of something that was to take place,[2], which drove me continually for that time to a throne of grace. It pleased God to enable me to wrestle with him, as Jacob did: I prayed that if sudden death were to happen, and I perished, it might be at Christ's feet.

In the evening of the same day, as I was reading and meditating on the fourth chapter of the Acts, twelfth verse, under the solemn apprehensions of eternity, and reflecting on my past actions, I began to think I had lived a moral life, and that I had a proper ground to believe I had an interest in the divine favour; but still meditating on the subject, not knowing whether salvation was to be had partly for our own good deeds, or solely as the sovereign gift of God:—in this deep consternation the Lord was pleased to break in upon my soul with his bright beams of heavenly light; and in an instant, as it were, removing the veil, and letting light into a dark place, Isa. xxv. 7. I saw clearly, with the eye of faith, the crucified Saviour bleeding on the cross on Mount Calvary: the Scriptures became an unsealed book, I saw myself as a condemned criminal under the law, which came with its full force to my conscience, and when 'the commandment came sin revived, and I died.' I saw the Lord Jesus Christ in his humiliation, loaded and bearing my reproach, sin and shame. I then clearly perceived, that by the deed of the law no flesh living could be justified. I was then convinced, that by the first Adam sin came, and by the second Adam (the Lord Jesus Christ) all that are saved must be made alive. It was given me at that time to know what it was to be born again, John iii. 5. I saw the eighth chapter to the Romans, and the doctrines of God's decrees verified, agreeable to his eternal, everlasting and unchangeable purposes. The word of God was sweet to my taste, yea sweeter than honey and the honey comb. Christ was revealed to my soul as the chiefest among ten thousand. These heavenly moments were really as life to the dead, and what John calls an earnest of the Spirit.[3] This was indeed unspeakable, and, I firmly believe, undeniable by many. Now every leading providential circumstance that happened to me, from the day I was taken from my parents to that hour, was then, in my view, as if it had but just occurred. I was sensible of the invisible had of God, which guided and protected me when in truth I knew it not: still the Lord pursued me although I slighted and disregarded it; this mercy melted me down. When I considered my poor wretched state, I wept, seeing what a great debtor I was to sovereign free grace. Now the Ethiopian was willing to be saved by Jesus Christ, the sinner's only surety, and also to rely on none other person or thing for salvation. Self was obnoxious, and good works he had none; for it is God that works in us both to will and to do. Oh! the amazing things of that hour can never be told—it was joy in the Holy Ghost! I felt an astonishing change; the burden of sin, the gaping jaws of hell, the fears of death, that weighed me down before, now lost their horror; indeed I thought death would now be the best earthly friend I ever had. uch were my grief and joy, as, I believe, are seldom experienced. I was bathed in tears, and said, What am I, that God should thus look on the vilest of sinners? I felt a deep concern for my mother and friends, which occasioned me to pray with fresh ardour; and, in the abyss of thought, I viewed the unconverted people of the world in a very awful state, being without God and without hope.

It pleased God to pour out on me the spiri of prayer and the grace of supplication, so that in loud acclamations I was enabled to praise and glorify his most holy name. When I got out of the cabin, and told some of the people what the Lord had done for me, alas! who could understand me or believe my report! None but to whom the arm of the Lord was revealed. I became a barbarian to them in talking of the love of Christ: his name was to me as ointment poured forth; indeed it was sweet to my soul, but to them a rock of offence. I thought my case singular, and every hour a day until I came to London, for I much longed to be with some to whom I could tell of the wonders of God's love towards me, and join in prayer to him whom my soul loved and thirsted after. I had uncommon commotions within, such as few can tell aught[4] about. Now the Bible was my only companion and comfort; I prized it much, with many thanks to God that I could read it for myself, and was not lost to be tossed about or led by man's devices and notions. The worth of a soul cannot be told.—May the Lord give the reader an understanding in this. Whenever I looked into the Bible I saw things new, and many texts were immediately applied to me with great comfort; for I knew that to me was the word of salvation sent. Sure I was that the Spirit which indited the word opened my heart to receive the truth of it as it is in Jesus—that the same Spirit enabled me to act with faith upon the promises which were precious to me, and enabled me to believe to the salvation of my soul. By free grace I was persuaded that I had a part and lot in the first resurrection, and was enlightened with the 'light of the living,' Job xxxiii. 30. I wished for a man of God, with whom I might converse; my soul was like the chariots of Aminadab, Canticles vi. 12. These, among others, were the precious promises that were so powerfully applied to me:

> All thing whatsoever ye shall ask in prayer, believing, ye shall receive,
> —Matt. xxi. 22.

> Peace I leave with you, my peace I give unto you,
> —John xiv. 27.

I saw the blessed Redeemer to be the fountain of life, and the well of salvation. I experienced him to be all in all; he had brought me by a way that I knew not, and he had made crooked paths straight. Then in his name I set up his Ebenezer, saying, Hitherto he had helped me: and could say to the sinners about me, Behold what a Saviour I have! Thus I was, by the teaching of that all glorious Deity, the great One in Three, and Three in One, confirmed in the truths of the Bible; those oracles of everlasting truth, on which every soul living must stand or fall eternally, agreeable to Acts iv. 12.

> Neither is there salvation in any other, for there is no other name under heaven given among men whereby we must be saved, but only Jesus Christ.

May god give the reader a right understanding in these facts!

To him that believeth, all things are possible, but to them that are unbelieving, nothing is pure,
—Titus i. 15.

During this period we remained at Cadiz until our ship got laden. We sailed about the 4th of November; and having a good passage, we arrived in London the month following, to my comfort, with heart-felt gratitude to God, for his rich and unspeakable mercies.

On my return, I had but one text which puzzled me, or that the devil endeavoured to buffet me with, viz. Rom. xi. 6. and as I had heard of the Rev. Mr. Romaine, and his great knowledge in the Scriptures, I wished to hear him preach. One day I went to Blackfriars church, and, to my great satisfaction and surprise, he preached from that very text. He very clearly shewed the difference between human works and free election, which is according to God's sovereign will and pleasure. These glad tidings set me entirely at liberty, and I went out of the church rejoicing, seeing my spots were those of God's children. I went to Westminster chapel, and saw some of my old friends, who were glad when they perceived the wonderful change that the Lord had wrought in me, particularly Mr. G. Smith, my worthy acquaintance, who was a man of a choice spirit, and had great zeal for the Lord's service. I enjoyed his correspondence till he died in the year 1784. I was again examined in that same chapel, and was received into church-fellowship amongst them: I rejoiced in spirit, making melody in my heart to the God of all my mercies. Now my whole wish was to be dissolved, and to be with Christ—but, alas! I must wait mine appointed time.

3.11.2 Reading and Review Questions

1. How are Equiano's experiences as a slave unique to him? Do these differences qualify or diminish the significance of his autobiography in terms of Abolitionist efforts? Why or why not?
2. How, if at all, does Equiano accommodate himself to Western culture? What does he "gain" through this accommodation? What does he "lose?"
3. How does Equiano distinguish the way that whites treat each other from the way that whites treat blacks? What behaviors to whites repeat among both groups, and why? What behaviors are different, and why? What's the effect of this difference?
4. What comments does Equiano make on Western institutions, such as the law and Christianity? Why?
5. How, if at all, does life change for Equiano after he purchases his freedom? Why?

3.12 JUDITH SARGENT MURRAY

(1751–1820)

Hailing from a wealthy sea merchant family, Judith Sargent Murray received an education unusual for women of her era. Along with her brother Winslow, Murray was tutored by a clergyman in classical languages and mathematics. Like women of her era, though, she endured the joys and vicissitudes of marriage and childbirth. She married her first husband, Captain John Stevens, in 1769. A sailor who traded goods, Stevens suffered economic catastrophes from the Revolutionary War and died a debtor in the West Indies. Murray's second marriage, to the Reverend John Murray (1741–1815), proved a spiritual and intellectual partnership to which she remained devoted even after his death. They had two children, with only a daughter surviving infancy.

Image 3.18 | Judith Sargent Murray
Artist | John Singleton Copley
Source | Wikimedia Commons
License | Public Domain

Unlike women of her era, Murray wrote and published a number of works, including poems, essays, and plays. Her later writing activities remained primarily within the relative position of wife, as she edited her husband John Murray's letters, sermons, and autobiography. Yet her more enduring and influential writing uniquely focused on women as individuals with claim to rights equal to that of men. With logic, scientific method, and wit, Murray targeted societal constructs that both assumed and imposed on women their "inferiority," adversely affecting their spiritual and mental well-being. Murray advocated equal education as an important means to correcting these wrongs. She also took conviction from her universalist faith through which she advocated the need for women to hold themselves in reverence.

The Gleaner (1798) proved to be her most profitable work. She used various pseudonyms for her writing, including the male pseudonym of Vigilius, or the Gleaner, from which the title of this collection derived. At its conclusion, Murray put aside this pseudonym and presented her true self to her readers, pointing to gender biases when she explained her "deception" as due to her doubts of her works being taken seriously if known from the start as written by a woman. In 1820, she died in Natchez, Mississippi, in her daughter's home.

3.12.1 "On the Equality of the Sexes" (1790)

SIR: In the foregoing letter I have examined the theory of the connection between equality and justice, with the view of showing that the only real connection between the two ideas is to be found in the fact that, as justice implies general rules, it also implies an impartial application of those rules to all the particular cases to which they may apply. I also showed that when equality is spoken of as being just or unjust in any more general sense than this, the expression can mean nothing else than that it is or is not generally expedient. The doctrine upon this subject which I deny, and which I am disposed to think Mr. Mill affirms—though, if he does, it is with somewhat less than his usual transparent vigor and decision is that equality is in itself always expedient, or, to say the very least, presumably expedient, and that in every case of inequality the burden of proof lies on those who justify its maintenance.

If I had time to do so, I might give in proof or illustration of this the whole of his essay on the "Subjection of Women," a work from which I dissent from the first sentence to the last, but which I will consider on the present occasion only with reference to the particular topic of equality, and as the strongest distinct illustration known to me of what is perhaps one of the strongest, and what appears to me to be by far the most ignoble, contemptible, and mischievous of all the popular feelings of the age.

The object of Mr. Mill's essay is to explain the grounds of the opinion that "the principle which regulates the existing social relations between the two sexes, the legal subordination of one sex to the other, is wrong in itself, and now one of the chief hindrances to human improvement; and that it ought to he replaced by a principle of perfect equality, admitting no power or privilege on the one side, nor disability on the other."

Mr. Mill is fully aware of the difficulty of his task. He admits that he is arguing against "an almost universal opinion," but he urges that it and the practice founded on it is a relic of a by-gone state of things. "We now live—that is to say, one or two of the most advanced nations of the world now live—in a state in which the law of the strongest seems to be entirely abandoned as the regulating principle of the world's affairs. Nobody professes it, and, as regards most of the relations between human beings, nobody is permitted to practise it.... This being the ostensible state of things, people flatter themselves that the rule of mere force is ended." Still they do not know how hard it dies, and in particular they are unaware of the fact that it still regulates the relations between men and women. It is true that the actually existing generation of women do not dislike their position. The consciousness of this haunts Mr. Mill throughout the whole of his argument, and embarrasses him at every turn. He is driven to account for it by such assertions as that "each individual of the subject class is in a chronic state of bribery and intimidation combined," by reference to the affection which slaves in classical times felt for their masters in many cases, and by other suggestions of the same sort. His great argument against the present state of things is that it is opposed to what he calls "the modern conviction, the fruit of a thousand years of experience"—

> "That things in which the individual is the person directly interested never go right but as they are left to his own discretion, and that any regulation of them by authority except to protect the rights of others is sure to be mischievous . . . . The peculiar character of the modern world . . . is that human beings are no longer born to their place in life and chained down by an inexorable bond to the place they are born to, but are free to employ their faculties and such favorable chances as offer, to achieve the lot which may appear to them most desirable. Human society of old was constituted on a very different principle. All were born to a fixed social position, and were mostly kept in it by law or interdicted from any means by which they could emerge from it . . . . In consonance with this doctrine it is felt to be an overstepping of the proper bounds of authority to fix beforehand on some general presumption that certain persons are not fit to do certain things. It is now thoroughly known and admitted that if some such presumptions exist no such presumption is infallible . . . . Hence we ought not . . . to ordain that to be born a girl instead of a boy shall decide the person's position all through life."

The result is that "the social subordination of women thus stands out as an isolated fact in modern social institutions." It is in "radical opposition" to "the progressive movement, which is the boast of the modern world." This fact creates a "prima-facie presumption" against it, "far outweighing any which custom and usage could in such circumstances create" in its favor.

I will not follow Mr. Mill through the whole of his argument, much of which consists of matter not relevant to my present purpose, and not agreeable to discuss, though many of his assertions provoke reply. There is something—I hardly know what to call it, indecent is too strong a word, but I may say unpleasant in the direction of indecorum—in prolonged and minute discussions about the relations between men and women, and the characteristics of women as such. I will therefore pass over what Mr. Mill says on this subject with a mere general expression of dissent from nearly every word he says. The following extracts show the nature of that part of his theory which bears on the question of equality:

> "The equality of married persons before the law . . . is the only means of rendering the daily life of mankind in any high sense a school of moral cultivation. Though the truth may not be felt or generally acknowledged for generations to come, the only school of genuine moral sentiment is society between equals. The moral education of mankind has hitherto emanated chiefly from the law of force, and is adapted almost solely to the relations which force creates. In

> the less advanced states of society, people hardly recognize any relation with their equals. To be an equal is to be an enemy. Society, from its highest place to its lowest, is one long chain, or rather ladder, where every individual is either above or below his nearest neighbor, and wherever he does not command he must obey. Existing moralities, accordingly, are mainly fitted to a relation of command and obedience. Yet command and obedience are but unfortunate necessities of human life; society in equality is its normal state. Already in modern life, and more and more as it progressively improves, command and obedience become exceptional facts in life, equal association its general rule . . . . "We have had the morality of submission and the morality of chivalry and generosity; the time is now come for the morality of justice."

In another part of the book this doctrine is stated more fully in a passage of which it will be enough for my purpose to quote a very few lines:

> "There are many persons for whom it is not enough that the inequality" (between the sexes) "has no just or legitimate defence; they require to be told what express advantage would be obtained by abolishing it. To which let me first answer, the advantage of having all the most universal and pervading of all human relations regulated by justice instead of injustice. The vast amount of this gain to human nature it is hardly possible by any explanation or illustration to place in a stronger light than it is placed in by the bare statement to any one who attaches a moral meaning to words."

These passages show what Mr. Mill's doctrine of equality is, and how it forms the very root, the essence, so to speak, of his theory about the subjection of women. I consider it unsound in every respect. I think that it rests upon an unsound view of history, an unsound view of morals, and a grotesquely distorted view of facts, and I believe that its practical application would be as injurious as its theory is false.

The theory may be shortly restated in the following propositions, which I think are implied in or may be collected from the extracts given above. They are as follows:

1. Justice requires that all people should live in society as equals.
2. History shows that human progress has been a progress from a "law of force" to a condition in which command and obedience become exceptional.
3. The "law of the strongest" having in this and one or two other countries been "entirely abandoned" in all other relations of life, it may be presumed not to apply to the relation between the sexes.
4. The notorious facts as to the nature of that relation show that in this particular case the presumption is, in fact, well founded.

I dissent from each of these propositions. In the present letter I shall examine the first and the fourth, which may be regarded as an illustration of the first. On a subsequent occasion I shall consider the second and third. First, as to the proposition that justice requires that all people should live in society as equals. I have already shown that this is equivalent to the proposition that it is expedient that all people should live in society as equals. Can this be proved? for it is certainly not a self-evident proposition.

I think that if the rights and duties which laws create are to be generally advantageous, they ought to be adapted to the situation of the persons who enjoy or are subject to them. They ought to recognize both substantial equality and substantial inequality, and they should from time to time be so moulded and altered as always to represent fairly well the existing state of society. Government, in a word, ought to fit society as a man's clothes fit him. To establish by law rights and duties which assume that people are equal when they are not is like trying to make clumsy feet look handsome by the help of tight boots. No doubt it may be necessary to legislate in such a manner as to correct the vices of society, or to protect it against special dangers or diseases to which it is liable. Law in this case is analogous to surgery, and the rights and duties imposed by it might be compared to the irons which are sometimes contrived for the purpose of supporting a weak limb or keeping it in some particular position. As a rule, however, it is otherwise. Rights and duties should be so moulded as to clothe, protect, and sustain society in the position which it naturally assumes. The proposition, therefore, that justice demands that people should live in society as equals may be translated thus: "It is inexpedient that any law should recognize any inequality between human beings."

This appears to me to involve the assertion, "There are no inequalities between human beings of sufficient importance to influence the rights and duties which it is expedient to confer upon them." This proposition I altogether deny. I say that there are many such differences, some of which are more durable and more widely extended than others, and of which some are so marked and so important that, unless human nature is radically changed, we cannot even imagine their removal; and of these the differences of age and sex are the most important.

The difference of age is so distinct a case of inequality that even Mr. Mill does not object to its recognition. He admits, as every one must, that perhaps a third or more of the average term of human life—and that the portion of it in which the strongest, the most durable, and beyond all comparison the most important impressions are made on human beings, the period in which character is formed—must be passed by every one in a state of submission, dependence, and obedience to orders the objects of which are usually most imperfectly understood by the persons who receive them. Indeed, as I have pointed out in previous letters, Mr. Mill is disposed rather to exaggerate than to underrate the influence of education and the powers of educators. Is not this a clear case of inequality of the strongest kind, and does it not at all events afford a most instructive precedent in favor of the recognition by law of a marked natural distinction? If children were regarded by law as the equals of adults, the result would be something infinitely worse than barbarism. It would involve a degree of cruelty to the young which can hardly be realized even in imagination. The proceeding, in short, would be so utterly monstrous and irrational that I suppose it never entered into the head of the wildest zealot for equality to propose it. Upon the practical question all are agreed; but consider the consequences which it involves. It involves the consequence that, so far from being "unfortunate necessities," command and obedience stand at the very entrance to life, and preside over the most important part of it. It involves the consequence that the exertion of power and constraint is so important and so indispensable in the greatest of all matters that it is a less evil to invest with it every head of a family indiscriminately, however unfit he may be to exercise it, than to fail to provide for its exercise. It involves the consequence that, by mere lapse of time and by following the promptings of passion, men acquire over others a position of superiority and of inequality which all nations and ages, the most cultivated as well as the rudest, have done their best to surround with every association of awe and reverence. The title of Father is the one which the best part of the human race have given to God, as being the least inadequate and inappropriate means of indicating the union of love, reverence, and submission. Whoever first gave the command or uttered the maxim, "Honor thy father and thy mother, that thy days may be long in the land," had a far better conception of the essential conditions of permanent national existence and prosperity than the author of the motto "Liberty, Equality, and Fraternity."

Now, if society and government ought to recognize the inequality of age as the foundation of an inequality of rights of this importance, it appears to me at least equally clear that they ought to recognize the inequality of sex for the same purpose, if it is a real inequality. Is it one? There are some propositions which it is difficult to prove, because they are so plain, and this is one of them. The physical differences between the two sexes affect every part of the human body, from the hair of the head to the sole of the feet, from the size and density of the bones to the texture of the brain and the character of the nervous system. Ingenious people may argue about any thing, and Mr. Mill does say a great number of things about women which, as I have already observed, I will not discuss; but all the talk in the world will never shake the proposition that men are stronger than women in every shape. They have greater muscular and nervous force, greater intellectual force, greater vigor of character. This general truth, which has been observed under all sorts of circumstances and in every age and country, has also in every age and country led to a division of labor between men and women, the general outline of which is as familiar and as universal as the general outline of the differences between them. These are the facts, and the question is, whether the law and public opinion ought to recognize this difference. How it ought to recognize it, what difference it ought to make between men and women as such, is quite another question. The first point to consider is, whether it ought to treat them as equals, although, as I have shown, they are not equals, because men are the stronger. I will take one or two illustrations. Men, no one denies, may, and in some cases ought to, be liable to compulsory military service. No one, I suppose, would hesitate to admit that, if we were engaged in a great war, it might become necessary, or that if necessary it would be right, to have a conscription both for the land and for the sea service. Ought men and women to be subject to it indiscriminately? If any one says that they ought, I have no more to say, except that he has got into the region at which argument is useless. But if it is admitted that this ought not to be done, an inequality of treatment founded on a radical inequality between the two sexes is admitted, and, if this admission is once made, where are you to draw the line? Turn from the case of liability to military service to that of education, which in Germany is rightly regarded as the other great branch of state activity, and the same question presents itself in another shape. Are boys and girls to be educated indiscriminately, and to be instructed in the same things? Are boys to learn to sew, to keep house, and to cook, as girls unquestionably ought to be, and are girls to play at cricket, to row, and be drilled like boys? I cannot argue with a person who says Yes. A person who says No admits an inequality between the sexes on which education must be founded, and which it must therefore perpetuate and perhaps increase.

Follow the matter a step further to the vital point of the whole question—marriage. Marriage is one of the subjects with which it is absolutely necessary both for law and morals to deal in some way or other. All that I need consider in reference to the present purpose is the question whether the laws and moral rules which relate to it should regard it as a contract between equals, or as a contract between a stronger and a weaker person involving subordination for certain purposes on the part of the weaker to the stronger. I say that a law which proceeded on the former and not on the latter of these views would be founded on a totally false assumption, and would involve cruel injustice in the sense of extreme general inexpediency, especially to women. If the parties to a contract of marriage are treated as equals, it is impossible to avoid the inference that marriage, like other partnerships, may be dissolved at pleasure. The advocates of women's rights are exceedingly shy of stating this plainly. Mr. Mill says nothing about it in his book on the "Subjection of Women," though in one place he comes very near to saying so, but it is as clear an inference from his principles as any thing can possibly be, nor has he ever disavowed it. If this were the law, it would make women the slaves of their husbands. A woman loses the qualities which make her attractive to men much earlier than men lose those which make them attractive to women. The tie between a woman and young children is generally far closer than the tie between them and their father. A woman who is no longer young, and who is the mother of children, would thus be absolutely in her husband's power, in nine cases out of ten, if he might put an end to the marriage when he pleased. This is one inequality in the position of the parties which must be recognized and provided for beforehand if the contract is to be for their common good. A second inequality is this: When a man marries, it is generally because he feels himself established in life. He incurs, no doubt, a good deal of expense, but he does not in any degree impair his means of earning a living. When a woman marries, she practically renounces in all but the rarest cases the possibility of undertaking any profession but one, and the possibility of carrying on that one profession in the society of any man but one. Here is a second inequality. It would be easy to mention others of the deepest importance, but these are enough to show that to treat a contract of marriage as a contract between persons who are upon an equality in regard of strength and power to protect their interest is to treat it as being what it notoriously is not.

Again, the contract is one which involves subordination and obedience on the part of the weaker party to the stronger. The proof of this is, to my mind, as clear as that of a proposition in Euclid, and it is this:

1. Marriage is a contract, one of the principal ones of which is the government of a family.
2. This government must be vested either by law or by contract in the hands of one of the two married persons.
3. If the arrangement is made by contract, the remedy for breach of it must either be by law or by a dissolution of the partnership at the will of the contracting parties.
4. Law could give no remedy in such a case. Therefore the only remedy for breach of the contract would be dissolution of the marriage.
5. Therefore, if marriage is to be permanent, the government of the family must be put by law and by moral rules in the hands of the husband, for no one proposes to give it to the wife.

Mr. Mill is totally unable to meet this argument, and apparently embraces the alternative that marriage ought to be dissoluble at the pleasure of the parties. After much argument as to contracts which appear to be visionary, his words are these: "Things never come to an issue of downright power on one side and obedience on the other except where the connection has been altogether a mistake, and it would be a blessing to both parties to be relieved from it."

This appears to me to show a complete misapprehension of the nature of family government, and of the sort of cases in which the question of obedience and authority can arise between husband and wife. No one contends that a man ought to have power to order his wife about like a slave, and beat her if she disobeys him. Such conduct in the eye of the law would be cruelty, and ground for a separation. The question of obedience arises in quite another way. It may, and no doubt often does, arise between the very best and most affectionate married people, and it need no more interfere with their mutual affection than the absolute power of the captain of a ship need interfere with perfect friendship and confidence between himself and his first-lieutenant. Take the following set of questions: "Shall we live on this scale or that? Shall we associate with such and such persons? Shall

I, the husband, embark in such an undertaking, and shall we change our place of residence in order that I may do so? Shall we send our son to college? Shall we send our daughters to school or have a governess? For what profession shall we train our sons?" On these and a thousand other such questions the wisest and the most affectionate people might arrive at opposite conclusions. What is to be done in such a case? for something must be done. I say the wife ought to give way. She ought to obey her husband, and carry out the view at which he deliberately arrives, just as, when the captain gives the word to cut away the masts, the lieutenant carries out his orders at once, though he may be a better seaman and may disapprove them. I also say that, to regard this as a humiliation, as a wrong, or as an evil in itself, is a mark not of spirit and courage, but of a base, unworthy, mutinous disposition—a disposition utterly subversive of all that is most worth having in life. The tacit assumption involved in it is that it is a degradation ever to give up one's own will to the will of another, and to me this appears the root of all evil, the negation of that which renders any combined efforts possible. No case can be specified in which people unite for a common object, from making a pair of shoes up to governing an empire, in which the power to decide does not rest somewhere; and what is this but command and obedience? Of course the person who for the time being is in command is of all fools the greatest if he deprives himself of the advantage of advice, if he is obstinate in his own opinion, if he does not hear as well as determine; but it is also practically certain that his inclination to hear will be proportioned to the degree of importance which he has been led to attach to the function of determining.

To sum the matter up, it appears to me that all the laws and moral rules by which the relation between the sexes is regulated should proceed upon the principle that their object is to provide for the common good of two great divisions of mankind who are connected together by the closest and most durable of all bonds, and who can no more have really conflicting interests than the different members of the same body, but who are not and never can be equals in any of the different forms of strength.

This problem law and morals have solved by monogamy, indissoluble marriage on the footing of the obedience of the wife to the husband, and a division of labor with corresponding differences in the matters of conduct, manners, and dress. Substantially this solution appears to me to be right and true; but I freely admit that in many particulars the stronger party has in this, as in other cases, abused his strength, and made rules for his supposed advantage, which, in fact, are greatly to the injury of both parties. It is, needless to say any thing in detail of the stupid coarseness of the laws about the effects of marriage on property—laws which might easily be replaced by a general statutory marriage settlement analogous to those which every prudent person makes who has any thing to settle. As to acts of violence against women, by all means make the law on this head as severe as it can be made without defeating itself.

As to throwing open to women the one or two employments from which they are at present excluded, it is rather a matter of sentiment than of practical importance.

I need not revive in this place a trite discussion. My object at present is simply to establish the general proposition that men and women are not equals, and that the laws which affect their relations ought to recognize that fact.

In my next letter I shall examine the opinion that laws which recognize any sort of inequality between human beings are mere vestiges of the past, against which as such there lies the strongest of all presumptions.—I am, sir, your obedient servant,

"F."

3.12.2 Reading and Review Questions

1. Why do you think Murray begin her essay with a poem?
2. How and on what grounds does Murray ask her readers to consider observed fact as opposed to societal constructs and stereotypes?
3. To what causes does Murray attribute female "inferiority"?
4. What opportunities would equal education afford women?
5. Why does Murray consider the effects of the Bible, or 'sacred oracles,' on society's views of women's equality (or lack thereof)?

3.13 PHILIP FRENEAU

(1752–1832)

Born in New York into a well-to-do family, Philip Freneau was tutored at home before entering the College of New Jersey (now Princeton University). The two important focuses of his future work—that is, politics and literature—might be discerned in two important friendships he made there, with James Madison, a future president, and Hugh Henry Brackenridge (1748–1816), a future novelist. He and Brackenridge collaborated on a commencement poem entitled *The Rising Glory of America.* A humanist and deistic optimist, Freneau thus early on in his writing expressed hope for America as a separate, democratic—and utopian—nation.

Image 3.19 | Philip Freneau
Artist | Frederick Halpin
Source | Wikimedia Commons
License | Public Domain

After graduating, Freneau taught briefly then traveled in 1776 to the West Indies to work as secretary on a plantation. His poem "The Beauties of Santa Cruz" reveals both the beauties of nature there and the misery of the impoverished and enslaved; indeed, it curses the ship that brought slaves to that island. After leaving the West Indies in 1778, Freneau took to the seas himself, serving as a seaman on a blockade runner. While on an American ship, he was captured and taken prisoner by the British. His poem "The British Prison Ship" (1781) describes his brutal treatment by the British while their prisoner.

With harsh invective, he continued to attack the British and support the Revolution, most particularly through his work as journalist and editor of *The Freeman's Journal*, an anti-British newspaper. During this time, he became known as the Poet of the Revolution. After the war, Freneau edited *The New York Daily Advertiser* and established and edited the anti-Federalist journal *TThe National Gazette*. In 1791, he worked as translating clerk in the Department of State of Thomas Jefferson, an avowed Democratic-Republican and then secretary of state. During that time, Freneau also vigorously attacked the *Gazette of the United States*, a Federalist vehicle edited by John Fenno (1751–1798) and supported by Alexander Hamilton, an avowed Federalist and opponent of Jefferson's. Through these critical pieces, Freneau became known as a powerful political satirist and is now considered a forerunner in satirical journalism. Coinciding with Jefferson's withdrawal from politics in 1793, Freneau's *National Gazette* folded.

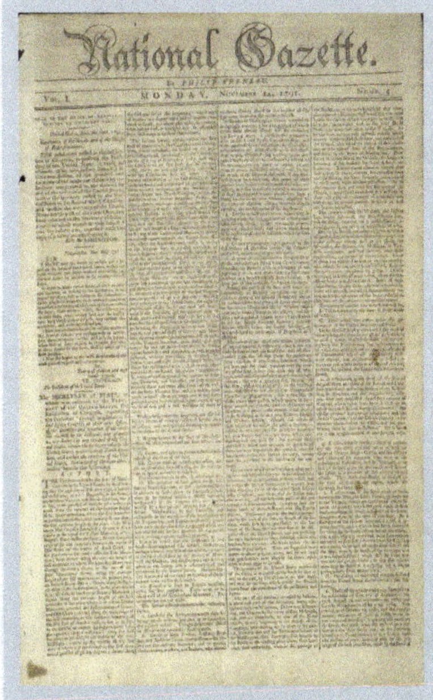

National Gazette.

Image 3.20 | *The National Gazette*
Author | Philip Freneau
Source | Wikimedia Commons
License | Public Domain

Freneau subsequently supported himself through captaining trading vessels and farming. He also wrote and published—by his own hand, with his own printing press—various poems and essays, with collections of his work appearing in 1795 and 1799. The love of nature and focus on the personal in his poetry strikes an early Romantic note in American literature. He offset the corruption of developing urbanism through what he described as the simplicity of Native American life. His poetry remains remarkable for its concreteness, sensuality, and intensity, qualities that herald the work of James Fenimore Cooper,

Ralph Waldo Emerson, and Herman Melville. Freneau died in 1832 from exposure during a blizzard.

3.13.1 To Sir Toby

(1795)

A Sugar Planter in the interior parts of Jamaica, near the City of San Jago de la Vega, (Spanish Town) 1784

"The motions of his spirit are black as night,
And his affections dark as Erebus."

—Shakespeare.

If there exists a hell—the case is clear—
Sir Toby's slaves enjoy that portion here:
Here are no blazing brimstone lakes—'tis true;
But kindled Rum too often burns as blue;
In which some fiend, whom nature must detest,
Steeps Toby's brand, and marks poor Cudjoe's breast.
Here whips on whips excite perpetual fears,
And mingled howlings vibrate on my ears:
Here nature's plagues abound, to fret and teaze,
Snakes, scorpions, despots, lizards, centipees—
No art, no care escapes the busy lash;
All have their dues—and all are paid in cash—
The eternal driver keeps a steady eye
On a black herd, who would his vengeance fly,
But chained, imprisoned, on a burning soil,
For the mean avarice of a tyrant, toil!
The lengthy cart-whip guards this monster's reign—
And cracks, like pistols, from the fields of cane.
Ye powers! who formed these wretched tribes, relate,
What had they done, to merit such a fate!
Why were they brought from Eboe's sultry waste,
To see that plenty which they must not taste—
Food, which they cannot buy, and dare not steal;
Yams and potatoes—many a scanty meal!—
One, with a gibbet wakes his negro's fears,
One to the windmill nails him by the ears;
One keeps his slave in darkened dens, unfed,
One puts the wretch in pickle ere he's dead:

This, from a tree suspends him by the thumbs,
That, from his table grudges even the crumbs!
O'er yond' rough hills a tribe of females go,
Each with her gourd, her infant, and her hoe;
Scorched by a sun that has no mercy here,
Driven by a devil, whom men call overseer—
In chains, twelve wretches to their labours haste;
Twice twelve I saw, with iron collars graced!—
Are such the fruits that spring from vast domains?
Is wealth, thus got, Sir Toby, worth your pains!—
Who would your wealth on terms, like these, possess,
Where all we see is pregnant with distress—
Angola's natives scourged by ruffian hands,
And toil's hard product shipp'd to foreign lands.
Talk not of blossoms, and your endless spring;
What joy, what smile, can scenes of misery bring?—
Though Nature, here, has every blessing spread,
Poor is the labourer—and how meanly fed!—
Here Stygian paintings light and shade renew,
Pictures of hell, that Virgil's[C] pencil drew:
Here, surly Charons make their annual trip,
And ghosts arrive in every Guinea ship,
To find what beasts these western isles afford,
Plutonian scourges, and despotic lords:—
Here, they, of stuff determined to be free,
Must climb the rude cliffs of the Liguanee;
Beyond the clouds, in sculking haste repair,
And hardly safe from brother traitors there.—

3.13.2 "The Indian Burying Ground" (1788)

In spite of all the learned have said,
I still my old opinion keep;
The posture, that we give the dead,
Points out the soul's eternal sleep.

Not so the ancients of these lands—
The Indian, when from life released,
Again is seated with his friends,
And shares again the joyous feast.

His imaged birds, and painted bowl,
And venison, for a journey dressed,
Bespeak the nature of the soul,
Activity, that knows no rest.

His bow, for action ready bent,
And arrows, with a head of stone,
Can only mean that life is spent,
And not the old ideas gone.

Thou, stranger, that shalt come this way,
No fraud upon the dead commit—
Observe the swelling turf, and say
They do not lie, but here they sit.

Here still a lofty rock remains,
On which the curious eye may trace
(Now wasted, half, by wearing rains)
The fancies of a ruder race.

Here still an aged elm aspires,
Beneath whose far-projecting shade
(And which the shepherd still admires)
The children of the forest played!

There oft a restless Indian queen
(Pale Shebah, with her braided hair)
And many a barbarous form is seen
To chide the man that lingers there.

By midnight moons, o'er moistening dews;
In habit for the chase arrayed,
The hunter still the deer pursues,
The hunter and the deer, a shade![364]

And long shall timorous fancy see
The painted chief, and pointed spear,
And Reason's self shall bow the knee
To shadows and delusions here.

"Bright as the bow that spans the storm
    In Erin's yellow vesture clad,
A son of light—a lovely form
    He comes and makes her glad;
Now on the grass-green turf he sits,
    His tassel'd horn beside him laid;
Now o'er the hills in chase he flits,
    The hunter and the deer a shade!"

3.13.3 "On Mr. Paine's Rights of Man" (1795)

Thus briefly sketch'd the sacred Rights of Man,
How inconsistent with the Royal Plan!
Which for itself exclusive honour craves,
Where some are masters born, and millions slaves.
With what contempt must every eye look down
On that base, childish bauble call'd a crown,
The gilded bait, that lures the crowd, to come,
Bow down their necks, and meet a slavish doom;
The source of half the miseries men endure,
The quack that kills them, while it seems to cure.
Rous'd by the Reason of his manly page,
Once more shall Paine a listening world engage:
From Reason's source, a bold reform he brings,
In raising up mankind, he pulls down kings,
Who, source of discord, patrons of all wrong,
On blood and murder have been fed too long:
Hid from the world, and tutor'd to be base,
The curse, the scourge, the ruin of our race,
Theirs was the task, a dull designing few,
To shackle beings that they scarcely knew,
Who made this globe the residence of slaves,
And built their thrones on systems form'd by knaves—
Advance, bright years, to work their final fall,
And haste the period that shall crush them all.
Who, that has read and scann'd the historic page
But glows, at every line, with kindling rage,
To see by them the rights of men aspers'd,
Freedom restrain'd, and Nature's law revers'd,
Men, rank'd with beasts, by monarchs will'd away,
And bound young fools, or madmen to obey:

Now driven to wars, and now oppress'd at home,
Compell'd in crowds o'er distant seas to roam,
From India's climes the plundered prize to bring
To glad the strumpet, or to glut the king.
    Columbia, hail! immortal be thy reign:
Without a king, we till the smiling plain;
Without a king, we trace the unbounded sea,
And traffic round the globe, through each degree;
Each foreign clime our honour'd flag reveres,
Which asks no monarch, to support the Stars:
Without a king, the Laws maintain their sway,
While honour bids each generous heart obey.
Be ours the task the ambitious to restrain,
And this great lesson teach—that kings are vain;
That warring realms to certain ruin haste,
That kings subsist by war, and wars are waste:
So shall our nation, form'd on Virtue's plan,
Remain the guardian of the Rights of Man,
A vast Republic, fam'd through every clime,
Without a king, to see the end of time.

3.13.4 "A Political Litany"

(1775)

Libera Nos, Domine.—Deliver us, O Lord, not only from British dependence, but also

From a junto that labour with absolute power,
Whose schemes disappointed have made them look sour,
From the lords of the council, who fight against freedom,
Who still follow on where delusion shall lead them.

From the group at St. James's, who slight our petitions,
And fools that are waiting for further submissions—
From a nation whose manners are rough and severe,
From scoundrels and rascals,—do keep us all clear.

From pirates sent out by command of the king
To murder and plunder, but never to swing.
From Wallace and Greaves, and Vipers and Roses,
Whom, if heaven pleases, we'll give bloody noses.

From the valiant Dunmore, with his crew of banditti,
Who plunder Virginians at Williamsburg city,
From hot-headed Montague, mighty to swear,
The little fat man with his pretty white hair.

From bishops in Britain, who butchers are grown,
From slaves that would die for a smile from the throne,
From assemblies that vote against Congress proceedings,
(Who now see the fruit of their stupid misleadings.)

From Tryon the mighty, who flies from our city,
And swelled with importance disdains the committee:
(But since he is pleased to proclaim us his foes,
What the devil care we where the devil he goes.)

From the caitiff, lord North, who would bind us in chains,
From a royal king Log, with his tooth-full of brains,
Who dreams, and is certain (when taking a nap)
He has conquered our lands, as they lay on his map.

From a kingdom that bullies, and hectors, and swears,
We send up to heaven our wishes and prayers
That we, disunited, may freemen be still,
And Britain go on—to be damned if she will.

3.13.5 Reading and Review Questions

1. In "To Sir Toby," why does Freneau group "despots" with such other of "nature's plagues" as "Snakes, scorpions. . . lizards, centipees?"
2. In "To Sir Toby," what are some of the atrocities perpetrated on slaves that Freneau lists? How do these atrocities connect with the poem's opening declaration that Sir Toby's slaves suffer hell on earth?
3. What actual knowledge about Native American culture does Freneau display in "The Indian Burying Ground?" What is his attitude towards Native Americans? How do you know?
4. Despite being "unnatural," according to Freneau in "On Mr Paine's Rights of Man," why have monarchs managed to rule "this globe?"
5. By what means, and why, does Freneau destroy the "heroism" of such figures as Wallace, Greaves, Dunmore, and Montague? What does his doing so suggest about American democratic ideals?

3.14 PHILLIS WHEATLEY

(c. 1753–1784)

Born in Africa (probably in Senegal or Gambia), Phillis Wheatley was enslaved at the age of seven or eight when she was bought by John Wheatley (1703–1778) of Boston to serve as his wife Susannah's companion. Susannah fostered Wheatley's intellectual avidity by having her daughter Mary oversee Wheatley's education. Wheatley became well-read in the Bible; classical literature, including some of the classics in their original Latin; and English literature, responding especially to the works of Alexander Pope (1688–1744), master of the heroic couplet, and John Milton. She also converted to Christianity, becoming a member of the Old South Congregational Church.

Image 3.21 | Phillis Wheatley
Artist | Unknown
Source | Wikimedia Commons
License | Public Domain

Her first poem, "On Messrs. Hussey and Coffin" (1767), was published in the *Newport Mercury*. What brought her attention as a writer—let alone an articulate black female slave—was her 1771 broadside elegy on George Whitefield (1714–1770), a famous evangelist minister. Touted thenceforth as a prodigy, Wheatley traveled to London for the publication of her *Poems on Various Subjects, Religious and Moral* (1773). There she became a minor celebrity, meeting the lord mayor of London, Benjamin Franklin, and William Legge, the 2nd Earl of Dartmouth (1731–1801). To the latter, she appealed for justice for those "snatched" from Africa, taken from their "parent's breast" and deprived of freedom.

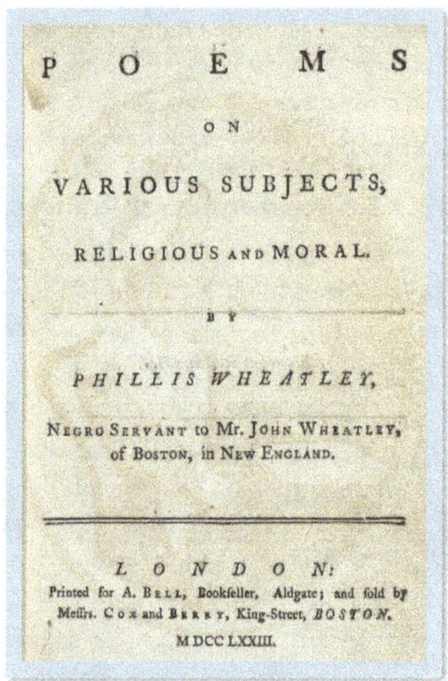

POEMS
ON
VARIOUS SUBJECTS,
RELIGIOUS AND MORAL.
BY
PHILLIS WHEATLEY,
NEGRO SERVANT to Mr. JOHN WHEATLEY, of BOSTON, in NEW ENGLAND.

LONDON:
Printed for A. BELL, Bookſeller, Aldgate; and ſold by Meſſrs. COX and BERRY, King-Street, BOSTON.
MDCCLXXIII.

Image 3.1 | Title Page for Phillis Wheatley's *Poems on Various Subjects*
Author | Phillis Wheatley
Source | Wikimedia Commons
License | Public Domain

The same year that her *Poems* were published, Wheatley was freed from slavery. She was with Susannah when she died a year later. Wheatley married

John Peters, a free black man, in 1778, the same year John Wheatley died. Wheatley and her husband lived in poverty. In 1779, a proposal for a second volume of her poetry appeared, promising several letters and thirty-three poems, but the promise was never fulfilled. None of the projected poems have been discovered, either. Over the course of her marriage, Wheatley lost two children and died in 1784 soon after the birth of her third. She and her infant were buried together in an unmarked grave.

In the past, her poetry was deemed unoriginal, as giving little sense of Africa, her race, or her life as a slave. This reading attests to Wheatley's strategic success in opposing prevalent views of women, blacks, and slaves during her era. Her poems are now recognized for their strong assertion of equality among all humankind and their strong-minded expression of self to contemporary readers who denied that selfhood.

3.14.1 "On Being Brought from Africa to America" (1773)

'Twas mercy brought me from my *Pagan* land,
Taught my benighted soul to understand
That there's a God, that there's a *Saviour* too:
Once I redemption neither sought nor knew.
Some view our sable race with scornful eye,
"Their colour is a diabolic die."
Remember, *Christians, Negros*, black as *Cain*,
May be refin'd, and join th' angelic train.

3.14.2 "To the Right Honorable William, Earl of Dartmouth" (1773)

HAIL, happy day, when, smiling like the morn,
Fair *Freedom* rose *New-England* to adorn:
The northern clime beneath her genial ray,
Dartmouth, congratulates thy blissful sway:
Elate with hope her race no longer mourns,
Each soul expands, each grateful bosom burns,
While in thine hand with pleasure we behold
The silken reins, and *Freedom's* charms unfold.
Long lost to realms beneath the northern sides
She shines supreme, while hated faction dies:
Soon as appear'd the *Goddess* long desir'd,
Sick at the view, she languish'd and expir'd;
Thus from the splendors of the morning light
The owl in sadness seeks the caves of night.

No more, *America*, in mournful strain
Of wrongs, and grievance unredress'd complain,
No longer shall thou dread the iron chain,
Which wanton *Tyranny* with lawless hand
Had made, and with it meant t' enslave the land.

Should you, my lord, while you peruse my song,
Wonder from whence my love of *Freedom* sprung,
Whence flow these wishes for the common good,
By feeling hearts alone best understood,
I, young in life, by seeming cruel fate
Was snatch'd from *Afric's* fancy'd happy seat:
What pangs excruciating must molest,
What sorrows labour in my parent's breast?
Steel'd was that soul and by no misery mov'd
That from a father seiz'd his babe belov'd:
Such, such my case. And can I then but pray
Others may never feel tyrannic sway?

For favours past, great Sir, our thanks are due,
And thee we ask thy favours to renew,
Since in thy pow'r, as in thy will before,

To sooth the griefs, which thou did'st once deplore.
May heav'nly grace the sacred sanction give
To all thy works, and thou for ever live
Not only on the wings of fleeting *Fame*,
Though praise immortal crowns the patriot's name,
But to conduct to heav'ns refulgent fane,
May fiery coursers sweep th' ethereal plain,
And bear thee upwards to that blest abode,
Where, like the prophet, thou shalt find thy God.

3.14.3 "On the Death of Rev. Mr. George Whitefield. 1770" (1771, 1773)

Hail, happy saint, on thine immortal throne,
Possest of glory, life, and bliss unknown;
We hear no more the music of thy tongue,
Thy wonted auditories cease to throng.
Thy sermons in unequall'd accents flow'd,
And ev'ry bosom with devotion glow'd;
Thou didst in strains of eloquence refin'd

Inflame the heart, and captivate the mind.
Unhappy we the setting sun deplore,
So glorious once, but ah! it shines no more.

Behold the prophet in his tow'ring flight
He leaves the earth for heav'n's unmeasur'd height,
And worlds unknown receive him from our sight.
There *Whitefield* wings with rapid course his way,
And sails to Zion through vast seas of day.
Thy pray'rs, great saint, and thine incessant cries
Have pierc'd the bosom cf thy native skies.
Thou moon hast seen, and all the stars of light,
How he has wrestled with his God by night.
He pray'd that grace in ev'ry heart might dwell,
He long'd to see *America* excel;
He charg'd its youth that ev'ry grace divine
Should with full lustre in their conduct shine;
That Saviour, which his soul did first receive,
The greatest gift that ev'n a God can give,
He freely offer'd to the num'rous throng,
That on his lips with list'ning pleasure hung,

"Take him, ye wretched, for your only good,
"Take him ye starving sinners, for your food;
"Ye thirsty, come to this life-giving stream,
"Ye preachers, take him for your joyful theme;
"Take him my dear *Americans*, he said,
"Be your complaints on his kind bosom laid:
"Take him, ye *Africans*, he longs for you,
"*Impartial Saviour* is his title due:
"Wash'd in the fountain of redeeming blood,
"You shall be sons, and kings, and priests to God."
Great Countess, we Americans revere
Thy name, and mingle in thy grief sincere;
New England deeply feels, the Orphans mourn,
Their more than father will no more return.

But, though arrested by the hand of death,
Whitefield no more exerts his lab'ring breath,
Yet let us view him in th' eternal skies,
Let ev'ry heart to this bright vision rise;
While the tomb safe retains its sacred trust,
Till life divine re-animates his dust.

3.14.4 "To S. M., a Young *African* Painter, on Seeing his Works" (1773)

To show the lab'ring bosom's deep intent,
And thought in living characters to paint,
When first thy pencil did those beauties give,
And breathing figures learnt from thee to live,
How did those prospects give my soul delight,
A new creation rushing on my sight?
Still, wond'rous youth! each noble path pursue,
On deathless glories fix thine ardent view:
Still may the painter's and the poet's fire
To aid thy pencil, and thy verse conspire!
And may the charms of each seraphic theme
Conduct thy footsteps to immortal fame!
High to the blissful wonders of the skies
Elate thy soul, and raise thy wishful eyes.
Thrice happy, when exalted to survey
That splendid city, crown'd with endless day,
Whose twice fix gates on radiant hinges ring:
Celestial *Salem* blooms in endless spring.

Calm and serene thy moments glide along,
And may the muse inspire each future song!
Still, with the sweets of contemplation bless'd,
May peace with balmy wings your soul invest!
But when these shades of time are chas'd away,
And darkness ends in everlasting day,
On what seraphic pinions shall we move,
And view the landscapes in the realms above?
There shall thy tongue in heav'nly murmurs flow,
And there my muse with heav'nly transport glow:
No more to tell of *Damon's* tender sighs,
Or rising radiance of *Aurora's* eyes,
For nobler themes demand a nobler strain,
And purer language on th' ethereal plain.
Cease, gentle muse! the solemn gloom of night
Now seals the fair creation from my sight.

3.14.5 "Letter to Rev. Samson Occom" (1773)

The Connecticut Gazette, March 11, 1774

Rev'd and honor'd Sir,

I have this Day received your obliging kind Epistle, and am greatly satisfied with your Reasons respecting the Negroes, and think highly reasonable what you offer in Vindication of their natural Rights: Those that invade them cannot be insensible that the divine Light is chasing away the thick Darkness which broods over the Land of Africa; and the Chaos which has reign'd so long, is converting into beautiful Order, and [r]eveals more and more clearly, the glorious Dispensation of civil and religious Liberty, which are so inseparably Limited, that there is little or no Enjoyment of one Without the other: Otherwise, perhaps, the Israelites had been less solicitous for their Freedom from Egyptian slavery; I do not say they would have been contented without it, by no means, for in every human Breast, God has implanted a Principle, which we call Love of Freedom; it is impatient of Oppression, and pants for Deliverance; and by the Leave of our modern Egyptians I will assert, that the same Principle lives in us. God grant Deliverance in his own Way and Time, and get him honour upon all those whose Avarice impels them to countenance and help forward tile Calamities of their fellow Creatures. This I desire not for their Hurt, but to convince them of the strange Absurdity of their Conduct whose Words and Actions are so diametrically, opposite. How well the Cry for Liberty, and the reverse Disposition for the exercise of oppressive Power over others agree,—

I humbly think it does not require the Penetration of a Philosopher to determine.—

3.14.6 Reading and Review Questions

1. What racial prejudices—on her own or on her audience's part—is Wheatley displaying in "On Being Brought from Africa to America?"
2. What images of slavery does Wheatley use in "To the Right Honorable William, Earl of Dartmouth" that could apply equally to black slaves and white colonists? What's the effect of this transfer?
3. How does Wheatley reveal her attitudes towards Christ and Christianity through her depiction of the Rev. Mr. Whitefield?
4. What does "To S. M. a Young *African* Painter, on Seeing his Works" reveal about Wheatley's attitude towards art and the artist? In other words, what is the role and purpose of art, according to this poem?
5. How does Wheatley counter implied arguments for slavery in her "Letter to Rev. Samson Occom?" To what hypocrisies does she draw attention, and why?

3.15 ROYALL TYLER

(1757–1826)

Royall Tyler was born and educated in Boston. His studies at Harvard were often interrupted by the events preceding the American Revolution. Indeed, in 1776, Harvard administered its classes outside of Cambridge in the comparative safety of Concord. Tyler earned his BA that same year then served in the colonial army during the American Revolution. In 1779, he earned his MA and was admitted to the bar the following year. He later served in the army again in the suppression of Shays' Rebellion (1786–1787), a Massachusetts uprising against unfair tax and debt collection.

Image 3.23 | Royall Tyler
Artist | Unknown
Source | Wikimedia Commons
License | Public Domain

Tyler practiced law in Maine and later in Massachusetts. After 1790, he practiced in Vermont where he was chief justice of the Supreme Court (1807–1813) and professor of jurisprudence at the University of Vermont (1811–1814). Tyler was a prolific author in various genres. He wrote legal papers, poems, and an epistolary travel book. He projected books on cosmography and the nature of religious intolerance. He also wrote plays and a satiric novel, *The Algerine Captive* (1797).

The work for which he is remembered today is his play *The Contrast* (1787), the first American comedy produced by a professional company. *The Contrast* is modeled after Restoration comedies, or comedies of manners, with their topical subject matter and intricate plots. Richard Brinsley Sheridan's (1751–1816) *The School for Scandal,* first performed in 1777, likely served as inspiration. *The Contrast* wittily satirizes hypocrisy and corruption, both of which vices Tyler locates in British culture, a culture that stains the more ethical and upright American culture.

3.15.1 *The Contrast*

(1787)

PROLOGUE

WRITTEN BY A YOUNG GENTLEMAN OF NEW-YORK, AND SPOKEN BY MR. WIGNELL

EXULT, each patriot heart!—this night is shewn
A piece, which we may fairly call our own;
Where the proud titles of "My Lord! Your Grace!"
To humble Mr. and plain Sir give place.
Our Author pictures not from foreign climes
The fashions or the follies of the times;
But has confin'd the subject of his work
To the gay scenes—the circles of New-York.
On native themes his Muse displays her pow'rs;
If ours the faults, the virtues too are ours.
Why should our thoughts to distant countries roam,
When each refinement may be found at home?
Who travels now to ape the rich or great,
To deck an equipage and roll in state;
To court the graces, or to dance with ease,
Or by hypocrisy to strive to please?
Our free-born ancestors such arts despis'd;
Genuine sincerity alone they pris'd;
Their minds, with honest emulation fir'd;
To solid good—not ornament—aspir'd;
Or, if ambition rous'd a bolder flame,
Stern virtue throve, where indolence was shame.

But modern youths, with imitative sense,
Deem taste in dress the proof of excellence;
And spurn the meanness of your homespun arts,
Since homespun habits would obscure their parts;
Whilst all, which aims at splendour and parade,
Must come from Europe, and be ready made.
Strange! We should thus our native worth disclaim,
And check the progress of our rising fame.
Yet one, whilst imitation bears the sway,
Aspires to nobler heights, and points the way.
Be rous'd, my friends! his bold example view;
Let your own Bards be proud to copy you!
Should rigid critics reprobate our play,
At least the patriotic heart will say,
"Glorious our fall, since in a noble cause.
"The bold attempt alone demands applause."
Still may the wisdom of the Comic Muse
Exalt your merits, or your faults accuse.
But think not, tis her aim to be severe;—
We all are mortals, and as mortals err.

If candour pleases, we are truly blest;
Vice trembles, when compell'd to stand confess'd.
Let not light Censure on your faults offend,
Which aims not to expose them, but amend.
Thus does our Author to your candour trust;
Conscious, the free are generous, as just.

Characters

New-York Maryland

Col. MANLY, Mr Henry. Mr Hallam.
DIMPLE, Mr Hallam. Mr Harper.
VANROUGH, Mr Morris. Mr Morris.
JESSAMY, Mr Harper. Mr Biddle.
JONATHAN, Mr Wignell. Mr Wignell.
CHARLOTTE, Mrs Morris. Mrs Morris.
MARIA, Mrs Harper. Mrs Harper.
LETITIA, Mrs Kenna. Mrs Williamson.
JENNY, Miss Tuke. Miss W. Tuke.
SERVANTS

SCENE, NEW-YORK.

ACT I. SCENE I.

Scene, an Apartment at CHARLOTTE'S.
CHARLOTTE and LETITIA discovered.

LETITIA
And so, Charlotte, you really think the pocket-hoop unbecoming.

CHARLOTTE
No, I don't say so. It may be very becoming to saunter round the house of a rainy day; to visit my grand-mamma, or to go to Quakers' meeting: but to swim in a minuet, with the eyes of fifty well-dressed beaux upon me, to trip it in the Mall, or walk on the battery, give me the luxurious, jaunty, flowing, bell-hoop. It would have delighted you to have seen me the last evening, my charming girl! I was dangling o'er the battery with Billy Dimple; a knot of young fellows were upon the platform; as I passed them I faultered with one of the most bewitching false steps you ever saw, and then recovered myself with such a pretty confusion, flirting my hoop to discover a jet black shoe and brilliant buckle. Gad! how my little heart thrilled to hear the confused raptures of—"Demme, Jack, what a delicate foot!" "Ha! General, what a well-turned—"

LETITIA

Fie! fie! Charlotte [stopping her mouth], I protest you are quite a libertine.

CHARLOTTE

Why, my dear little prude, are we not all such libertines? Do you think, when I sat tortured two hours under the hands of my friseur, and an hour more at my toilet, that I had any thoughts of my aunt Susan, or my cousin Betsey? though they are both allowed to be critical judges of dress.

LETITIA

Why, who should we dress to please, but those are judges of its merit?

CHARLOTTE

Why, a creature who does not know Buffon from Souflee—Man!—my Letitia—Man! for whom we dress, walk, dance, talk, lisp, languish, and smile. Does not the grave Spectator assure us that even our much bepraised diffidence, modesty, and blushes are all directed to make ourselves good wives and mothers as fast as we can? Why, I'll undertake with one flirt of this hoop to bring more beaux to my feet in one week than the grave Maria, and her sentimental circle, can do, by sighing sentiment till their hairs are grey.

LETITIA

Well, I won't argue with you; you always out-talk me; let us change the subject. I hear that Mr. Dimple and Maria are soon to be married.

CHARLOTTE

You hear true. I was consulted in the choice of the wedding clothes. She is to be married in a delicate white sattin, and has a monstrous pretty brocaded lutestring for the second day. It would have done you good to have seen with what an affected indifference the dear sentimentalist turned over a thousand pretty things, just as if her heart did not palpitate with her approaching happiness, and at last made her choice and arranged her dress with such apathy as if she did not know that plain white sattin and a simple blond lace would shew her clear skin and dark hair to the greatest advantage.

LETITIA

But they say her indifference to dress, and even to the gentleman himself, is not entirely affected.

CHARLOTTE

How?

LETITIA

It is whispered that if Maria gives her hand to Mr. Dimple, it will be without her heart.

CHARLOTTE

Though the giving the heart is one of the last of all laughable considerations in the marriage of a girl of spirit, yet I should like to hear what antiquated notions the dear little piece of old-fashioned prudery has got in her head.

LETITIA

Why, you know that old Mr. John-Richard-Robert-Jacob-Isaac-Abraham-Cornelius Van Dumpling, Billy Dimple's father (for he has thought fit to soften his name, as well as manners, during his English tour), was the most intimate friend of Maria's father. The old folks, about a year before Mr. Van Dumpling's death, proposed this match: the young folks were accordingly introduced, and told they must love one another. Billy was then a good-natured, decent-dressing young fellow, with a little dash of the coxcomb, such as our young fellows of fortune usually have. At this time, I really believe she thought she loved him; and had they been married, I doubt not they might have jogged on, to the end of the chapter, a good kind of a sing-song lack-a-daysaical life, as other honest married folks do.

CHARLOTTE

Why did they not then marry?

LETITIA

Upon the death of his father, Billy went to England to see the world and rub off a little of the patroon rust. During his absence, Maria, like a good girl, to keep herself constant to her nown true-love, avoided company, and betook herself, for her amusement, to her books, and her dear Billy's letters. But, alas! how many ways has the mischievous demon of inconstancy of stealing into a woman's heart! Her love was destroyed by the very means she took to support it.

CHARLOTTE

How?—Oh! I have it—some likely young beau found the way to her study.

LETITIA

Be patient, Charlotte; your head so runs upon beaux. Why, she read Sir Charles Grandison, Clarissa Harlow, Shenstone, and the Sentimental Journey; and between whiles, as I said, Billy's letters. But, as her taste improved, her love declined. The contrast was so striking betwixt the good sense of her books and the flimsiness of her love-letters, that she discovered she had unthinkingly engaged her hand without her heart; and then the whole transaction, managed by the old folks, now appeared so unsentimental, and looked so like bargaining for a bale of goods, that she found she ought to have rejected, according to every rule of romance, even the man of her choice, if imposed upon her in that manner. Clary Harlow would have scorned such a match.

CHARLOTTE

Well, how was it on Mr. Dimple's return? Did he meet a more favourable reception than his letters?

LETITIA

Much the same. She spoke of him with respect abroad, and with contempt in her closet. She watched his conduct and conversation, and found that he had by travelling, acquired the wickedness of Lovelace without his wit, and the politeness of Sir Charles Grandison without his generosity. The ruddy youth, who washed his face at the cistern every morning, and swore and looked eternal love and constancy, was now metamorphosed into a flippant, palid, polite beau, who devotes the morning to his toilet, reads a few pages of Chesterfield's letters, and then minces out, to put the infamous principles in practice upon every woman he meets.

CHARLOTTE

But, if she is so apt at conjuring up these sentimental bugbears, why does she not discard him at once?

LETITIA

Why, she thinks her word too sacred to be trifled with. Besides, her father, who has a great respect for the memory of his deceased friend, is ever telling her how he shall renew his years in their union, and repeating the dying injunctions of old Van Dumpling.

CHARLOTTE

A mighty pretty story! And so you would make me believe that the sensible Maria would give up Dumpling manor, and the all-accomplished Dimple as a husband, for the absurd, ridiculous reason, forsooth, because she despises and abhors him. Just as if a lady could not be privileged to spend a man's fortune, ride in his carriage, be called after his name, and call him her nown dear lovee when she wants money, without loving and respecting the great he-creature. Oh! my dear girl, you are a monstrous prude.

LETITIA

I don't say what I would do; I only intimate how I suppose she wishes to act.

CHARLOTTE

No, no, no! A fig for sentiment. If she breaks, or wishes to break, with Mr. Dimple, depend upon it, she has some other man in her eye. A woman rarely discards one lover until she is sure of another. Letitia little thinks what a clue I have to Dimple's conduct. The generous man submits to render himself disgusting to Maria, in order that she may leave him at liberty to address me. I must change the subject. [Aside, and rings a bell.

Enter SERVANT.

Frank, order the horses to.—Talking of marriage, did you hear that Sally Bloomsbury is going to be married next week to Mr. Indigo, the rich Carolinian?

LETITIA

Sally Bloomsbury married!—why, she is not yet in her teens.

CHARLOTTE

I do not know how that is, but you may depend upon it, 'tis a done affair. I have it from the best authority. There is my aunt Wyerly's Hannah. You know Hannah; though a black, she is a wench that was never caught in a lie in her life. Now, Hannah has a brother who courts Sarah, Mrs. Catgut the milliner's girl, and she told Hannah's brother, and Hannah, who, as I said before, is a girl of undoubted veracity, told it directly to me, that Mrs. Catgut was making a new cap for Miss Bloomsbury, which, as it was very dressy, it is very probable is designed for a wedding cap. Now, as she is to be married, who can it be to but to Mr. Indigo? Why, there is no other gentleman that visits at her papa's.

LETITIA

Say not a word more, Charlotte. Your intelligence is so direct and well grounded, it is almost a pity that it is not a piece of scandal.

CHARLOTTE

Oh! I am the pink of prudence. Though I cannot charge myself with ever having discredited a tea-party by my silence, yet I take care never to report any thing of my acquaintance, especially if it is to their credit,—discredit, I mean,—until I have searched to the bottom of it. It is true, there is infinite pleasure in this charitable pursuit. Oh! how delicious to go and condole with the friends of some backsliding sister, or to retire with some old dowager or maiden aunt of the family, who love scandal so well that they cannot forbear gratifying their appetite at the expense of the reputation of their nearest relations! And then to return full fraught with a rich collection of circumstances, to retail to the next circle of our acquaintance under the strongest injunctions of secrecy,—ha, ha, ha!—interlarding the melancholy tale with so many doleful shakes of the head, and more doleful "Ah! who would have thought it! so amiable, so prudent a young lady, as we all thought her, what a monstrous pity! well, I have nothing to charge myself with; I acted the part of a friend, I warned her of the principles of that rake, I told her what would be the consequence; I told her so, I told her so."—Ha, ha, ha!

LETITIA

Ha, ha, ha! Well, but, Charlotte, you don't tell me what you think of Miss Bloomsbury's match.

CHARLOTTE

Think! why I think it is probable she cried for a plaything, and they have given her a husband. Well, well, well, the puling chit shall not be deprived of her plaything: 'tis only exchanging London dolls for American babies.—Apropos, of babies, have you heard what Mrs. Affable's high-flying notions of delicacy have come to?

LETITIA

Who, she that was Miss Lovely?

CHARLOTTE

The same; she married Bob Affable of Schenectady. Don't you remember?

Enter SERVANT.

SERVANT

Madam, the carriage is ready.

LETITIA

Shall we go to the stores first, or visiting?

CHARLOTTE

I should think it rather too early to visit, especially Mrs. Prim; you know she is so particular.

LETITIA

Well, but what of Mrs. Affable?

CHARLOTTE

Oh, I'll tell you as we go; come, come, let us hasten. I hear Mrs. Catgut has some of the prettiest caps arrived you ever saw. I shall die if I have not the first sight of them. [Exeunt.]

SCENE II.

A Room in VAN ROUGH'S House

MARIA sitting disconsolate at a Table, with Books, &c.

SONG.

I.

The sun sets in night, and the stars shun the day;
But glory remains when their lights fade away!
Begin, ye tormentors! your threats are in vain,
For the son of Alknomook shall never complain.

II.

Remember the arrows he shot from his bow;
Remember your chiefs by his hatchet laid low:
Why so slow?—do you wait till I shrink from the pain?
No—the son of Alknomook will never complain.

III.

Remember the wood where in ambush we lay,
And the scalps which we bore from your nation away:
Now the flame rises fast, you exult in my pain;
But the son of Alknomook can never complain.

IV.

I go to the land where my father is gone;
His ghost shall rejoice in the fame of his son:
Death comes like a friend, he relieves me from pain;
And thy son, Oh Alknomook! has scorn'd to complain.

There is something in this song which ever calls forth my affections. The manly virtue of courage, that fortitude which steels the heart against the keenest misfortunes, which interweaves the laurel of glory amidst the instruments of torture and death, displays something so noble, so exalted, that in despite of the prejudices of education I cannot but admire it, even in a savage. The prepossession which our sex is supposed to entertain for the character of a soldier is, I know, a standing piece of raillery among the wits. A cockade, a lapell'd coat, and a feather, they will tell you, are irresistible by a female heart. Let it be so. Who is it that considers the helpless situation of our sex, that does not see that we each moment stand in need of a protector, and that a brave one too? Formed of the more delicate materials of nature, endowed only with the softer passions, incapable, from our ignorance of the world, to guard against the wiles of mankind, our security for happiness often depends upon their generosity and courage. Alas! how little of the former do we find! How inconsistent! that man should be leagued to destroy that honour upon which solely rests his respect and esteem. Ten thousand temptations allure us, ten thousand passions betray us; yet the smallest deviation from the path of rectitude is followed by the contempt and insult of man, and the more remorseless pity of woman; years of penitence and tears cannot wash away the stain, nor a life of virtue obliterate its remembrance. Reputation is the life of woman; yet courage to protect it is masculine and disgusting; and the only safe asylum a woman of delicacy can find is in the arms of a man of honour. How naturally, then, should we love the brave and the generous; how gratefully should we bless the arm raised for our protection, when nerv'd by virtue and directed by honour! Heaven grant that the man with whom I may be connected—may be connected! Whither has my imagination transported me—whither does it now lead me? Am I not indissolubly engaged, "by every obligation of honour which my own consent and my father's approbation can give," to a man who can never share my affections, and whom a few days hence it will be criminal for me to disapprove—to disapprove! would to heaven that were all—to despise. For, can the most frivolous manners, actuated by the most depraved heart, meet, or merit, anything but contempt from every woman of delicacy and sentiment?

[VAN ROUGH without. Mary!]

Ha! my father's voice—Sir!—

Enter VAN ROUGH.

VAN ROUGH

What, Mary, always singing doleful ditties, and moping over these plaguy books.

MARIA

I hope, Sir, that it is not criminal to improve my mind with books, or to divert my melancholy with singing, at my leisure hours.

VAN ROUGH

Why, I don't know that, child; I don't know that. They us'd to say, when I was a young man, that if a woman knew how to make a pudding, and to keep herself out of fire and water, she knew enough for a wife. Now, what good have these books done you? have they not made you melancholy? as you call it. Pray, what right has a girl of your age to be in the dumps? haven't you everything your heart can wish; an't you going to be married to a young man of great fortune; an't you going to have the quit-rent of twenty miles square?

MARIA

One-hundredth part of the land, and a lease for life of the heart of a man I could love, would satisfy me.

VAN ROUGH

Pho, pho, pho! child; nonsense, downright nonsense, child. This comes of your reading your storybooks; your Charles Grandisons, your Sentimental Journals, and your Robinson Crusoes, and such other trumpery. No, no, no! child; it is money makes the mare go; keep your eye upon the main chance, Mary.

MARIA

Marriage, Sir, is, indeed, a very serious affair.

VAN ROUGH

You are right, child; you are right. I am sure I found it so, to my cost.

MARIA

I mean, Sir, that as marriage is a portion for life, and so intimately involves our happiness, we cannot be too considerate in the choice of our companion.

VAN ROUGH

Right, child; very right. A young woman should be very sober when she is making her choice, but when she has once made it, as you have done, I don't see why she should not be as merry as a grig; I am sure she has reason enough to be so. Solomon says that "there is a time to laugh, and a time to weep." Now, a time for a young woman to laugh is when she has made sure of a good rich husband. Now, a time to cry, according to you, Mary, is when she is making choice of him; but I should think that a young woman's time to cry was when she despaired of getting one. Why, there was your mother, now: to be sure, when I popp'd the question to her she did look a little silly; but when she had once looked down on her apron-strings, as all modest young women us'd to do, and drawled out ye-s, she was as brisk and as merry as a bee.

MARIA

My honoured mother, Sir, had no motive to melancholy; she married the man of her choice.

VAN ROUGH

The man of her choice! And pray, Mary, an't you going to marry the man of your choice—what trumpery notion is this? It is these vile books [throwing them away]. I'd have you to know, Mary, if you won't make young Van Dumpling the man of your choice, you shall marry him as the man of my choice.

MARIA

You terrify me, Sir. Indeed, Sir, I am all submission. My will is yours.

VAN ROUGH

Why, that is the way your mother us'd to talk. "My will is yours, my dear Mr. Van Rough, my will is yours"; but she took special care to have her own way, though, for all that.

MARIA

Do not reflect upon my mother's memory, Sir—

VAN ROUGH

Why not, Mary, why not? She kept me from speaking my mind all her life, and do you think she shall henpeck me now she is dead too? Come, come; don't go to sniveling; be a good girl, and mind the main chance. I'll see you well settled in the world.

MARIA

I do not doubt your love, Sir, and it is my duty to obey you. I will endeavour to make my duty and inclination go hand in hand.

VAN ROUGH

Well, Well, Mary; do you be a good girl, mind the main chance, and never mind inclination. Why, do you know that I have been down in the cellar this very morning to examine a pipe of Madeira which I purchased the week you were born, and mean to tap on your wedding day?—That pipe cost me fifty pounds sterling. It was well worth sixty pounds; but I over-reach'd Ben Bulkhead, the supercargo. I'll tell you the whole story. You must know that—

Enter SERVANT.

SERVANT

Sir, Mr. Transfer, the broker is below. [Exit.]

VAN ROUGH

Well, Mary, I must go. Remember, and be a good girl, and mind the main chance. [Exit.

MARIA, alone.

How deplorable is my situation! How distressing for a daughter to find her heart militating with her filial duty! I know my father loves me tenderly; why then do I reluctantly obey him? Heaven knows! with what reluctance I should oppose the will of a parent, or set an example of filial disobedience; at a parent's command, I could wed awkwardness and deformity. Were the heart of my husband good, I would so magnify his good qualities with the eye of conjugal affection, that the defects of his person and manners should be lost in the emanation of his virtues. At a father's command, I could embrace poverty. Were the poor man my husband, I would learn resignation to my lot; I would enliven our frugal meal with good humour, and chase away misfortune from our cottage with a smile. At a father's command, I could almost submit to what every female heart knows to be the most mortifying, to marry a weak man, and blush at my husband's folly in every company I visited. But to marry a depraved wretch, whose only virtue is a polished exterior; who is actuated by the unmanly ambition of conquering the defenceless; whose heart, insensible to the emotions of patriotism, dilates at the plaudits of every unthinking girl; whose laurels are the sighs and tears of the miserable victims of his specious behaviour,—can he, who has no regard for the peace and happiness of other families, ever have a due regard for the peace and happiness of his own? Would to heaven that my father were not so hasty in his temper? Surely, if I were to state my reasons for declining this match, he would not compel me to marry a man, whom, though my lips may solemnly promise to honour, I find my heart must ever despise. [Exit.

END OF THE FIRST ACT.

ACT II. SCENE I.

Enter CHARLOTTE and LETITIA.

CHARLOTTE [at entering]

Betty, take those things out of the carriage and carry them to my chamber; see that you don't tumble them. My dear, I protest, I think it was the homeliest of the whole. I declare I was almost tempted to return and change it.

LETITIA

Why would you take it?

CHARLOTTE

Didn't Mrs. Catgut say it was the most fashionable?

LETITIA

But, my dear, it will never fit becomingly on you.

CHARLOTTE

I know that; but did you not hear Mrs. Catgut say it was fashionable?

LETITIA

Did you see that sweet airy cap with the white sprig?

CHARLOTTE

Yes, and I longed to take it; but, my dear, what could I do? Did not Mrs. Catgut say it was the most fashionable; and if I had not taken it, was not that awkward, gawky, Sally Slender, ready to purchase it immediately?

LETITIA

Did you observe how she tumbled over the things at the next shop, and then went off without purchasing anything, nor even thanking the poor man for his trouble? But, of all the awkward creatures, did you see Miss Blouze endeavouring to thrust her unmerciful arm into those small kid gloves?

CHARLOTTE

Ha, ha, ha, ha!

LETITIA

Then did you take notice with what an affected warmth of friendship she and Miss Wasp met? when all their acquaintance know how much pleasure they take in abusing each other in every company.

CHARLOTTE

Lud! Letitia, is that so extraordinary? Why, my dear, I hope you are not going to turn sentimentalist. Scandal, you know, is but amusing ourselves with the faults, foibles, follies, and reputations of our friends; indeed, I don't know why we should have friends, if we are not at liberty to make use of them. But no person is so ignorant of the world as to suppose, because I amuse myself with a lady's faults, that I am obliged to quarrel with her person every time we meet: believe me, my dear, we should have very few acquaintance at that rate.

SERVANT enters and delivers a letter to CHARLOTTE, and—[Exit.]

CHARLOTTE

You'll excuse me, my dear.

[Opens and reads to herself.]

LETITIA

Oh, quite excusable.

CHARLOTTE

As I hope to be married, my brother Henry is in the city.

LETITIA

What, your brother, Colonel Manly?

CHARLOTTE

Yes, my dear; the only brother I have in the world.

LETITIA

Was he never in this city?

CHARLOTTE

Never nearer than Harlem Heights, where he lay with his regiment.

LETITIA

What sort of a being is this brother of yours? If he is as chatty, as pretty, as sprightly as you, half the belles in the city will be pulling caps for him.

CHARLOTTE

My brother is the very counterpart and reverse of me: I am gay, he is grave; I am airy, he is solid; I am ever selecting the most pleasing objects for my laughter, he has a tear for every pitiful one. And thus, whilst he is plucking the briars and thorns from the path of the unfortunate, I am strewing my own path with roses.

LETITIA

My sweet friend, not quite so poetical, and a little more particular.

CHARLOTTE

Hands off, Letitia. I feel the rage of simile upon me; I can't talk to you in any other way. My brother has a heart replete with the noblest sentiments, but then, it is like—it is like—Oh! you provoking girl, you have deranged all my ideas—it is like—Oh! I have it—his heart is like an old maiden lady's bandbox; it contains many costly things, arranged with the most scrupulous nicety, yet the misfortune is that they are too delicate, costly, and antiquated for common use.

LETITIA

By what I can pick out of your flowery description, your brother is no beau.

CHARLOTTE

No, indeed; he makes no pretension to the character. He'd ride, or rather fly, an hundred miles to relieve a distressed object, or to do a gallant act in the service of his country; but should you drop your fan or bouquet in his presence, it is ten to one that some beau at the farther end of the room would have the honour of presenting it to you before he had observed that it fell. I'll tell you one of his antiquated, anti-gallant notions. He said once in my presence, in a room full of company,—would you believe it?—in a large circle of ladies, that the best evidence a gentleman could give a young lady of his respect and affection was to endeavour in a friendly manner to rectify her foibles. I protest I was crimson to the eyes, upon reflecting that I was known as his sister.

LETITIA

Insupportable creature! tell a lady of her faults! if he is so grave, I fear I have no chance of captivating him.

CHARLOTTE

His conversation is like a rich, old-fashioned brocade,—it will stand alone; every sentence is a sentiment. Now you may judge what a time I had with him, in my twelve months' visit to my father. He read me such lectures, out of pure brotherly affection, against the extremes of fashion, dress, flirting, and coquetry, and all the other dear things which he knows I doat upon, that I protest his conversation made me as melancholy as if I had been at church; and heaven knows, though I never prayed to go there but on one occasion, yet I would have exchanged his conversation for a psalm and a sermon. Church is rather melancholy, to be sure; but then I can ogle the beaux, and be regaled with "here endeth the first lesson," but his brotherly here, you would think had no end. You captivate him! Why, my dear, he would as soon fall in love with a box of Italian flowers. There is Maria, now, if she were not engaged, she might do something. Oh! how I should like to see that pair of pensorosos together, looking as grave as two sailors' wives of a stormy night, with a flow of sentiment meandering through their conversation like purling streams in modern poetry.

LETITIA

Oh! my dear fanciful—

CHARLOTTE

Hush! I hear some person coming through the entry.

Enter SERVANT.

SERVANT

Madam, there's a gentleman below who calls himself Colonel Manly; do you chuse to be at home?

CHARLOTTE

Shew him in. [Exit Servant.] Now for a sober face.

Enter Colonel MANLY.

MANLY

My dear Charlotte, I am happy that I once more enfold you within the arms of fraternal affection. I know you are going to ask (amiable impatience!) how our parents do,—the venerable pair transmit you their blessing by me. They totter on the verge of a well-spent life, and wish only to see their children settled in the world, to depart in peace.

CHARLOTTE

I am very happy to hear that they are well. [Coolly.] Brother, will you give me leave to introduce you to our uncle's ward, one of my most intimate friends?

MANLY [saluting Letitia]

I ought to regard your friends as my own.

CHARLOTTE

Come, Letitia, do give us a little dash of your vivacity; my brother is so sentimental and so grave, that I protest he'll give us the vapours.

MANLY

Though sentiment and gravity, I know, are banished the polite world, yet I hoped they might find some countenance in the meeting of such near connections as brother and sister.

CHARLOTTE

Positively, brother, if you go one step further in this strain, you will set me crying, and that, you know, would spoil my eyes; and then I should never get the husband which our good papa and mamma have so kindly wished me—never be established in the world.

MANLY

Forgive me, my sister,—I am no enemy to mirth; I love your sprightliness; and I hope it will one day enliven the hours of some worthy man; but when I mention the respectable authors of my existence,—the cherishers and protectors of my helpless infancy, whose hearts glow with such fondness and attachment that they would willingly lay down their lives for my welfare,—you will excuse me if I am so unfashionable as to speak of them with some degree of respect and reverence.

CHARLOTTE

Well, well, brother; if you won't be gay, we'll not differ; I will be as grave as you wish. [Affects gravity.] And so, brother, you have come to the city to exchange some of your commutation notes for a little pleasure?

MANLY

Indeed you are mistaken; my errand is not of amusement, but business; and as I neither drink nor game, my expenses will be so trivial, I shall have no occasion to sell my notes.

CHARLOTTE

Then you won't have occasion to do a very good thing. Why, here was the Vermont General—he came down some time since, sold all his musty notes at one stroke, and then laid the cash out in trinkets for his dear Fanny. I want a dozen pretty things myself; have you got the notes with you?

MANLY

I shall be ever willing to contribute, as far as it is in my power, to adorn or in any way to please my sister; yet I hope I shall never be obliged for this to sell my notes. I may be romantic, but I preserve them as a sacred deposit. Their full amount is justly due to me, but as embarrassments, the natural consequences of a long war, disable my country from supporting its credit, I shall wait with patience until it is rich enough to discharge them. If that is not in my day, they shall be transmitted as an honourable certificate to posterity, that I have humbly imitated our illustrious WASHINGTON, in having exposed my health and life in the service of my country, without reaping any other reward than the glory of conquering in so arduous a contest.

CHARLOTTE

Well said heroics. Why, my dear Henry, you have such a lofty way of saying things, that I protest I almost tremble at the thought of introducing you to the polite circles in the city. The belles would think you were a player run mad, with your head filled with old scraps of tragedy; and as to the beaux, they might admire, because they would not understand you. But, however, I must, I believe, introduce you to two or three ladies of my acquaintance.

LETITIA

And that will make him acquainted with thirty or forty beaux.

CHARLOTTE

Oh! brother, you don't know what a fund of happiness you have in store.

MANLY

I fear, sister, I have not refinement sufficient to enjoy it.

CHARLOTTE

Oh! you cannot fail being pleased.

LETITIA

Our ladies are so delicate and dressy.

CHARLOTTE

And our beaux so dressy and delicate.

LETITIA

Our ladies chat and flirt so agreeably.

CHARLOTTE

And our beaux simper and bow so gracefully.

LETITIA

With their hair so trim and neat.

CHARLOTTE

And their faces so soft and sleek.

LETITIA

Their buckles so tonish and bright.

CHARLOTTE

And their hands so slender and white.

LETITIA

I vow, Charlotte, we are quite poetical.

CHARLOTTE

And then, brother, the faces of the beaux are of such a lily-white hue! None of that horrid robustness of constitution, that vulgar corn-fed glow of health, which can only serve to alarm an unmarried lady with apprehension, and prove a melancholy memento to a married one, that she can never hope for the happiness of being a widow. I will say this to the credit of our city beaux, that such is the delicacy of their complexion, dress, and address, that, even had I no reliance upon the honour of the dear Adonises, I would trust myself in any possible situation with them, without the least apprehensions of rudeness.

MANLY

Sister Charlotte!

CHARLOTTE

Now, now, now, brother [interrupting him], now don't go to spoil my mirth with a dash of your gravity; I am so glad to see you, I am in tiptop spirits. Oh! that you could be with us at a little snug party. There is Billy Simper, Jack Chaffe, and Colonel Van Titter, Miss Promonade, and the two Miss Tambours, sometimes make a party, with some other ladies, in a side-box at the play. Everything is conducted with such decorum. First we bow round to the company in general, then to each one in particular, then we have so many inquiries after each other's health, and we are so happy to meet each other, and it is so many ages since we last had that pleasure, and if a married lady is in company, we have such a sweet dissertation upon her son Bobby's chin-cough; then the curtain rises, then our sensibility is all awake, and then, by the mere force of apprehension, we torture some harmless expression into a double meaning, which the poor author never dreamt of, and then we have recourse to our fans, and then we blush, and then the gentlemen jog one another, peep under the fan, and make the prettiest remarks; and then we giggle and they simper, and they giggle and we simper, and then the curtain drops, and then for nuts and oranges, and then we bow, and it's pray, Ma'am, take it, and pray, Sir, keep it, and oh! not for the world, Sir; and then the curtain rises again, and then we blush and giggle and simper and bow all over again. Oh! the sentimental charms of a side-box conversation! [All laugh.]

MANLY

Well, sister, I join heartily with you in the laugh; for, in my opinion, it is as justifiable to laugh at folly as it is reprehensible to ridicule misfortune.

CHARLOTTE

Well, but, brother, positively I can't introduce you in these clothes: why, your coat looks as if it were calculated for the vulgar purpose of keeping yourself comfortable.

MANLY

This coat was my regimental coat in the late war. The public tumults of our state have induced me to buckle on the sword in support of that government which I once fought to establish. I can only say, sister, that there was a time when this coat was respectable, and some people even thought that those men who had endured so many winter campaigns in the service of their country, without bread, clothing, or pay, at least deserved that the poverty of their appearance should not be ridiculed.

CHARLOTTE

We agree in opinion entirely, brother, though it would not have done for me to have said it: it is the coat makes the man respectable. In the time of the war, when we were almost frightened to death, why, your coat was respectable, that is, fashionable; now another kind of coat is fashionable, that is, respectable. And pray direct the taylor to make yours the height of the fashion.

MANLY

Though it is of little consequence to me of what shape my coat is, yet, as to the height of the fashion, there you will please to excuse me, sister. You know my sentiments on that subject. I have often lamented the advantage which the French have over us in that particular. In Paris, the fashions have their dawnings, their routine, and declensions, and depend as much upon the caprice of the day as in other countries; but there every lady assumes a right to deviate from the general ton as far as will be of advantage to her own appearance. In America, the cry is, what is the fashion?

and we follow it indiscriminately, because it is so.

CHARLOTTE

Therefore it is, that when large hoops are in fashion, we often see many a plump girl lost in the immensity of a hoop-petticoat, whose want of height and en-bon-point would never have been remarked in any other dress. When the high head-dress is the mode, how then do we see a lofty cushion, with a profusion of gauze, feathers, and ribband, supported by a face no bigger than an apple! whilst a broad full-faced lady, who really would have appeared tolerably handsome in a large head-dress, looks with her smart chapeau as masculine as a soldier.

MANLY

But remember, my dear sister, and I wish all my fair country-women would recollect, that the only excuse a young lady can have for going extravagantly into a fashion is because it makes her look extravagantly handsome.—Ladies, I must wish you a good morning.

CHARLOTTE

But, brother, you are going to make home with us.

MANLY

Indeed I cannot. I have seen my uncle and explained that matter.

CHARLOTTE

Come and dine with us, then. We have a family dinner about half-past four o'clock.

MANLY

I am engaged to dine with the Spanish ambassador. I was introduced to him by an old brother officer; and instead of freezing me with a cold card of compliment to dine with him ten days hence, he, with the true old Castilian frankness, in a friendly manner, asked me to dine with him to-day—an honour I could not refuse. Sister, adieu—Madam, your most obedient—[Exit.

CHARLOTTE

I will wait upon you to the door, brother; I have something particular to say to you. [Exit.

LETITIA, alone

What a pair!—She the pink of flirtation, he the essence of everything that is outre and gloomy.—I think I have completely deceived Charlotte by my manner of speaking of Mr. Dimple; she's too much the friend of Maria to be confided in. He is certainly rendering himself disagreeable to Maria, in order to break with her and proffer his hand to me. This is what the delicate fellow hinted in our last conversation. [Exit.

SCENE II. THE MALL.
Enter JESSAMY.

Positively this Mall is a very pretty place. I hope the cits won't ruin it by repairs. To be sure, it won't do to speak of in the same day with Ranelagh or Vauxhall; however, it's a fine place for a young fellow to display his person to advantage. Indeed, nothing is lost here; the girls have taste, and I am very happy to find they have adopted the elegant London fashion of looking back, after a genteel fellow like me has passed them.—Ah! who comes here? This, by his awkwardness, must be the Yankee colonel's servant. I'll accost him.

Enter JONATHAN.

JESSAMY
Votre tres-humble serviteur, Monsieur. I understand Colonel Manly, the Yankee officer, has the honour of your services.

JONATHAN
Sir!—

JESSAMY
I say, Sir, I understand that Colonel Manly has the honour of having you for a servant.

JONATHAN
Servant! Sir, do you take me for a neger,—I am Colonel Manly's waiter.

JESSAMY
A true Yankee distinction, egad, without a difference. Why, Sir, do you not perform all the offices of a servant? do you not even blacken his boots?

JONATHAN
Yes; I do grease them a bit sometimes; but I am a true blue son of liberty, for all that. Father said I should come as Colonel Manly's waiter, to see the world, and all that; but no man shall master me. My father has as good a farm as the colonel.

JESSAMY
Well, Sir, we will not quarrel about terms upon the eve of an acquaintance from which I promise myself so much satisfaction;—therefore, sans ceremonie—

JONATHAN
What?—

JESSAMY

I say I am extremely happy to see Colonel Manly's waiter.

JONATHAN

Well, and I vow, too, I am pretty considerably glad to see you; but what the dogs need of all this outlandish lingo? Who may you be, Sir, if I may be so bold?

JESSAMY

I have the honour to be Mr. Dimple's servant, or, if you please, waiter. We lodge under the same roof, and should be glad of the honour of your acquaintance.

JONATHAN

You a waiter! by the living jingo, you look so topping, I took you for one of the agents to Congress.

JESSAMY

The brute has discernment, notwithstanding his appearance.—Give me leave to say I wonder then at your familiarity.

JONATHAN

Why, as to the matter of that, Mr.—; pray, what's your name?

JESSAMY

Jessamy, at your service.

JONATHAN

Why, I swear we don't make any great matter of distinction in our state between quality and other folks.

JESSAMY

This is, indeed, a levelling principle.—I hope, Mr. Jonathan, you have not taken part with the insurgents.

JONATHAN

Why, since General Shays has sneaked off and given us the bag to hold, I don't care to give my opinion; but you'll promise not to tell—put your ear this way—you won't tell?—I vow I did think the sturgeons were right.

JESSAMY

I thought, Mr. Jonathan, you Massachusetts men always argued with a gun in your hand. Why didn't you join them?

JONATHAN

Why, the colonel is one of those folks called the Shin—Shin—dang it all, I can't speak them lignum vitae words—you know who I mean—there is a company of them—they wear a china goose at their button-hole—a kind of gilt thing.—Now the colonel told father and brother,—you must know there are, let me see—there is Elnathan, Silas, and Barnabas, Tabitha—no, no, she's a she—tarnation, now I have it—there's Elnathan, Silas, Barnabas, Jonathan, that's I—seven of us, six went into the wars, and I staid at home to take care of mother. Colonel said that it was a burning shame for the true blue Bunker Hill sons of liberty, who had fought Governor Hutchinson, Lord North, and the Devil, to have any hand in kicking up a cursed dust against a government which we had, every mother's son of us, a hand in making.

JESSAMY

Bravo!—Well, have you been abroad in the city since your arrival?
What have you seen that is curious and entertaining?

JONATHAN

Oh! I have seen a power of fine sights. I went to see two marble-stone men and a leaden horse that stands out in doors in all weathers; and when I came where they was, one had got no head, and t'other wern't there. They said as how the leaden man was a damn'd tory, and that he took wit in his anger and rode off in the time of the troubles.

JESSAMY

But this was not the end of your excursion?

JONATHAN

Oh, no; I went to a place they call Holy Ground. Now I counted this was a place where folks go to meeting; so I put my hymn-book in my pocket, and walked softly and grave as a minister; and when I came there, the dogs a bit of a meeting-house could I see. At last I spied a young gentlewoman standing by one of the seats which they have here at the doors. I took her to be the deacon's daughter, and she looked so kind, and so obliging, that I thought I would go and ask her the way to lecture, and—would you think it?—she called me dear, and sweeting, and honey, just as if we were married: by the living jingo, I had a month's mind to buss her.

JESSAMY

Well, but how did it end?

JONATHAN

Why, as I was standing talking with her, a parcel of sailor men and boys got round me, the snarl-headed curs fell a-kicking and cursing of me at such a tarnal rate, that I vow I was glad to take to my heels and split home, right off, tail on end, like a stream of chalk.

JESSAMY

Why, my dear friend, you are not acquainted with the city; that girl you saw was a—[whispers.]

JONATHAN

Mercy on my soul! was that young woman a harlot!—Well! if this is New-York Holy Ground, what must the Holy-day Ground be!

JESSAMY

Well, you should not judge of the city too rashly. We have a number of elegant, fine girls here that make a man's leisure hours pass very agreeably. I would esteem it an honour to announce you to some of them.—Gad! that announce is a select word; I wonder where I picked it up.

JONATHAN

I don't want to know them.

JESSAMY

Come, come, my dear friend, I see that I must assume the honour of being the director of your amusements. Nature has given us passions, and youth and opportunity stimulate to gratify them. It is no shame, my dear Blueskin, for a man to amuse himself with a little gallantry.

JONATHAN

Girl huntry! I don't altogether understand. I never played at that game. I know how to play hunt the squirrel, but I can't play anything with the girls; I am as good as married.

JESSAMY

Vulgar, horrid brute! Married, and above a hundred miles from his wife, and thinks that an objection to his making love to every woman he meets! He never can have read, no, he never can have been in a room with a volume of the divine Chesterfield.—So you are married?

JONATHAN

No, I don't say so; I said I was as good as married, a kind of promise.

JESSAMY

As good as married!—

JONATHAN

Why, yes; there's Tabitha Wymen, the deacon's daughter, at home; she and I have been courting a great while, and folks say as how we are to be married; and so I broke a piece of money with her when we parted, and she promised not to spark it with Solomon Dyer while I am gone. You wouldn't have me false to my true-love, would you?

JESSAMY

May be you have another reason for constancy; possibly the young lady has a fortune? Ha! Mr. Jonathan, the solid charms: the chains of love are never so binding as when the links are made of gold.

JONATHAN

Why, as to fortune, I must needs say her father is pretty dumb rich; he went representative for our town last year. He will give her—let me see—four times seven is—seven times four—nought and carry one,— he will give her twenty acres of land—somewhat rocky though—a Bible, and a cow.

JESSAMY

Twenty acres of rock, a Bible, and a cow! Why, my dear Mr. Jonathan, we have servant-maids, or, as you would more elegantly express it, waitresses, in this city, who collect more in one year from their mistresses' cast clothes.

JONATHAN

You don't say so!—

JESSAMY

Yes, and I'll introduce to one of them. There is a little lump of flesh and delicacy that lives at next door, waitress to Miss Maria; we often see her on the stoop.

JONATHAN

But are you sure she would be courted by me?

JESSAMY

Never doubt it; remember a faint heart never—blisters on my tongue—I was going to be guilty of a vile proverb; flat against the authority of Chesterfield. I say there can be no doubt that the brilliancy of your merit will secure you a favourable reception.

JONATHAN

Well, but what must I say to her?

JESSAMY

Say to her! why, my dear friend, though I admire your profound knowledge on every other subject, yet, you will pardon my saying that your want of opportunity has made the female heart escape the poignancy of your penetration. Say to her! Why, when a man goes a-courting, and hopes for success, he must begin with doing, and not saying.

JONATHAN

Well, what must I do?

JESSAMY

Why, when you are introduced you must make five or six elegant bows.

JONATHAN

Six elegant bows! I understand that; six, you say? Well—

JESSAMY

Then you must press and kiss her hand; then press and kiss, and so on to her lips and cheeks; then talk as much as you can about hearts, darts, flames, nectar, and ambrosia—the more incoherent the better.

JONATHAN

Well, but suppose she should be angry with I?

JESSAMY

Why, if she should pretend—please to observe, Mr. Jonathan—if she should pretend to be offended, you must— But I'll tell you how my master acted in such a case: He was seated by a young lady of eighteen upon a sofa, plucking with a wanton hand the blooming sweets of youth and beauty. When the lady thought it necessary to check his ardour, she called up a frown upon her lovely face, so irresistibly alluring, that it would have warmed the frozen bosom of age; remember, said she, putting her delicate arm upon his, remember your character and my honour. My master instantly dropped upon his knees, with eyes swimming with love, cheeks glowing with desire, and in the gentlest modulation of voice he said: My dear Caroline, in a few months our hands will be indissolubly united at the altar; our hearts I feel are already so; the favours you now grant as evidence of your affection are favours indeed; yet, when the ceremony is once past, what will now be received with rapture will then be attributed to duty.

JONATHAN

Well, and what was the consequence?

JESSAMY

The consequence!—Ah! forgive me, my dear friend, but you New England gentlemen have such a laudable curiosity of seeing the bottom of everything;—

why, to be honest, I confess I saw the blooming cherub of a consequence smiling in its angelic mother's arms, about ten months afterwards.

JONATHAN

Well, if I follow all your plans, make them six bows, and all that, shall I have such little cherubim consequences?

JESSAMY

Undoubtedly.—What are you musing upon?

JONATHAN

You say you'll certainly make me acquainted?— Why, I was thinking then how I should contrive to pass this broken piece of silver—won't it buy a sugar-dram?

JESSAMY

What is that, the love-token from the deacon's daughter?—You come on bravely. But I must hasten to my master. Adieu, my dear friend.

JONATHAN

Stay, Mr. Jessamy—must I buss her when I am introduced to her?

JESSAMY

I told you, you must kiss her.

JONATHAN

Well, but must I buss her?

JESSAMY

Why, kiss and buss, and buss and kiss, is all one.

JONATHAN

Oh! my dear friend, though you have a profound knowledge of all, a pungency of tribulation, you don't know everything. [Exit.

JESSAMY, alone

Well, certainly I improve; my master could not have insinuated himself with more address into the heart of a man he despised. Now will this blundering dog sicken Jenny with his nauseous pawings, until she flies into my arms for very ease. How sweet will the contrast be between the blundering Jonathan and the courtly and accomplished Jessamy!

END OF THE SECOND ACT.

ACT III. SCENE I.
DIMPLE'S Room.

DIMPLE discovered at a Toilet, Reading

"Women have in general but one object, which is their beauty." Very true, my lord; positively very true. "Nature has hardly formed a woman ugly enough to be insensible to flattery upon her person." Extremely just, my lord; every day's delightful experience confirms this. "If her face is so shocking that she must, in some degree, be conscious of it, her figure and air, she thinks, make ample amends for it." The sallow Miss Wan is a proof of this. Upon my telling the distasteful wretch, the other day, that her countenance spoke the pensive language of sentiment, and that Lady Wortley Montague declared that if the ladies were arrayed in the garb of innocence, the face would be the last part which would be admired, as Monsieur Milton expresses it; she grinn'd horribly, a ghastly smile. "If her figure is deformed, she thinks her face counterbalances it."

Enter JESSAMY with letters.

DIMPLE

Where got you these, Jessamy?

JESSAMY

Sir, the English packet is arrived.

DIMPLE opens and reads a letter enclosing notes

"Sir,

"I have drawn bills on you in favour of Messrs. Van Cash and Co. as per margin. I have taken up your note to Col. Piquet, and discharged your debts to my Lord Lurcher and Sir Harry Rook. I herewith enclose you copies of the bills, which I have no doubt will be immediately honoured. On failure, I shall empower some lawyer in your country to recover the amounts.

"I am, Sir,
"Your most humble servant,
"JOHN HAZARD."

Now, did not my lord expressly say that it was unbecoming a well-bred man to be in a passion, I confess I should be ruffled. [Reads.] "There is no accident so unfortunate, which a wise man may not turn to his advantage; nor any accident so fortunate, which a fool will not turn to his disadvantage." True, my lord; but how advantage can be derived from this I can't see. Chesterfield himself, who made, however, the worst practice of the most excellent precepts, was never in so embarrassing a situation. I love the person of Charlotte, and it is necessary I should command the fortune of Letitia. As to Maria!—I doubt not by my sang-froid behaviour I shall compel her to decline the match; but the blame must not fall upon me. A prudent man, as my lord says, should take all the credit of a good action to himself, and throw the discredit of a bad one upon others. I must break with Maria, marry Letitia, and as for Charlotte—why, Charlotte must be a companion to my wife.—Here, Jessamy!

Enter JESSAMY.

DIMPLE folds and seals two letters.

DIMPLE

Here, Jessamy, take this letter to my love.

[Gives one.]

JESSAMY

To which of your honour's loves?—Oh! [reading] to Miss Letitia, your honour's rich love.

DIMPLE

And this [delivers another] to Miss Charlotte Manly. See that you deliver them privately.

JESSAMY

Yes, your honour. [Going.]

DIMPLE

Jessamy, who are these strange lodgers that came to the house last night?

JESSAMY

Why, the master is a Yankee colonel; I have not seen much of him; but the man is the most unpolished animal your honour ever disgraced your eyes by looking upon. I have had one of the most outre conversations with him!—He really has a most prodigious effect upon my risibility.

DIMPLE

I ought, according to every rule of Chesterfield, to wait on him and insinuate myself into his good graces.—Jessamy, wait on the colonel with my compliments, and if he is disengaged I will do myself the honour of paying him my respects.—Some ignorant, unpolished boor—

JESSAMY goes off and returns.

JESSAMY

Sir, the colonel is gone out, and Jonathan his servant says that he is gone to stretch his legs upon the Mall.—Stretch his legs! what an indelicacy of diction!

DIMPLE

Very well. Reach me my hat and sword. I'll accost him there, in my way to Letitia's, as by accident; pretend to be struck by his person and address, and endeavour to steal into his confidence. Jessamy, I have no business for you at present. [Exit.

JESSAMY [taking up the book]

My master and I obtain our knowledge from the same source;—though, gad! I think myself much the prettier fellow of the two. [Surveying himself in the glass.] That was a brilliant thought, to insinuate that I folded my master's letters for him; the folding is so neat, that it does honour to the operator. I once intended to have insinuated that I wrote his letters too; but that was before I saw them; it won't do now; no honour there, positively.—"Nothing looks more vulgar, [reading affectedly] ordinary, and illiberal than ugly, uneven, and ragged nails; the ends of which should be kept even and clean, not tipped with black, and cut in small segments of circles."—Segments of circles! surely my lord did not consider that he wrote for the beaux. Segments of circles; what a crabbed term! Now I dare answer that my master, with all his learning, does not know that this means, according to the present mode, let the nails grow long, and then cut them off even at top. [Laughing without.] Ha! that's Jenny's titter. I protest I despair of ever teaching that girl to laugh; she has something so execrably natural in her laugh, that I declare it absolutely discomposes my nerves. How came she into our house! [Calls.] Jenny!

Enter JENNY.

JESSAMY

Prythee, Jenny, don't spoil your fine face with laughing.

JENNY

Why, mustn't I laugh, Mr. Jessamy?

JESSAMY

You may smile, but, as my lord says, nothing can authorise a laugh.

JENNY

Well, but I can't help laughing.—Have you seen him, Mr. Jessamy? ha, ha, ha!

JESSAMY

Seen whom?

JENNY

Why, Jonathan, the New England colonel's servant. Do you know he was at the play last night, and the stupid creature don't know where he has been. He would not go to a play for the world; he thinks it was a show, as he calls it.

JESSAMY

As ignorant and unpolished as he is, do you know, Miss Jenny, that I propose to introduce him to the honour of your acquaintance?

JENNY

Introduce him to me! for what?

JESSAMY

Why, my lovely girl, that you may take him under your protection, as Madame Ramboulliet did young Stanhope; that you may, by your plastic hand, mould this uncouth cub into a gentleman. He is to make love to you.

JENNY

Make love to me!—

JESSAMY

Yes, Mistress Jenny, make love to you; and, I doubt not, when he shall become domesticated in your kitchen, that this boor, under your auspices, will soon become un amiable petit Jonathan.

JENNY

I must say, Mr. Jessamy, if he copies after me, he will be vastly, monstrously polite.

JESSAMY

Stay here one moment, and I will call him.—Jonathan!—Mr. Jonathan!—[Calls.]

JONATHAN [within]

Holla! there.—[Enters.] You promise to stand by me—six bows you say. [Bows.]

JESSAMY

Mrs. Jenny, I have the honour of presenting Mr. Jonathan, Colonel Manly's waiter, to you. I am extremely happy that I have it in my power to make two worthy people acquainted with each other's merits.

JENNY

So, Mr. Jonathan, I hear you were at the play last night.

JONATHAN

At the play! why, did you think I went to the devil's drawing-room?

JENNY

The devil's drawing-room!

JONATHAN

Yes; why an't cards and dice the devil's device, and the play-house the shop where the devil hangs out the vanities of the world upon the tenter-hooks of temptation? I believe you have not heard how they were acting the old boy one night, and the wicked one came among them sure enough, and went right off in a storm, and carried one quarter of the play-house with him. Oh! no, no, no! you won't catch me at a play-house, I warrant you.

JENNY

Well, Mr. Jonathan, though I don't scruple your veracity, I have some reasons for believing you were there: pray, where were you about six o'clock?

JONATHAN

Why, I went to see one Mr. Morrison, the hocus pocus man; they said as how he could eat a case knife.

JENNY

Well, and how did you find the place?

JONATHAN

As I was going about here and there, to and again, to find it, I saw a great crowd of folks going into a long entry that had lantherns over the door; so I asked a man whether that was not the place where they played hocus pocus? He was a very civil, kind man, though he did speak like the Hessians; he lifted up his eyes and said, "They play hocus pocus tricks enough there, Got knows, mine friend."

JENNY

Well—

JONATHAN

So I went right in, and they shewed me away, clean up to the garret, just like meeting-house gallery. And so I saw a bower of topping folks, all sitting round in little cabbins, "just like father's corn-cribs"; and then there was such a squeaking with the fiddles, and such a tarnal blaze with the lights, my head was near turned. At last the people that sat near me set up such a hissing—hiss—like so many mad cats; and then they went thump, thump, thump, just like our Peleg threshing wheat, and stampt away, just like the nation; and called out for one Mr. Langolee,—I suppose he helps act the tricks.

JENNY

Well, and what did you do all this time?

JONATHAN

Gor, I—I liked the fun, and so I thumpt away, and hiss'd as lustily as the best of 'em. One sailor-looking man that sat by me, seeing me stamp, and knowing I was a cute fellow, because I could make a roaring noise, clapt me on the shoulder and said, "You are a d—-d hearty cock, smite my timbers!" I told him so I was, but I thought he need not swear so, and make use of such naughty words.

JESSAMY

The savage!—Well, and did you see the man with his tricks?

JONATHAN

Why, I vow, as I was looking out for him, they lifted up a great green cloth and let us look right into the next neighbor's house. Have you a good many houses in New-York made so in that 'ere way?

JENNY

Not many; but did you see the family?

JONATHAN

Yes, swamp it; I see'd the family.

JENNY

Well, and how did you like them?

JONATHAN

Why, I vow they were pretty much like other families;—there was a poor, good-natured, curse of a husband, and a sad rantipole of a wife.

JENNY

But did you see no other folks?

JONATHAN

Yes. There was one youngster; they called him Mr. Joseph; he talked as sober and as pious as a minister; but, like some ministers that I know, he was a sly tike in his heart for all that. He was going to ask a young woman to spark it with him, and—the Lord have mercy on my soul!—she was another man's wife.

JESSAMY

The Wabash!

JENNY

And did you see any more folks?

JONATHAN

Why, they came on as thick as mustard. For my part, I thought the house was haunted. There was a soldier fellow, who talked about his row de dow, dow, and courted a young woman; but, of all the cute folk I saw, I liked one little fellow—

JENNY

Aye! who was he?

JONATHAN

Why, he had red hair, and a little round plump face like mine, only not altogether so handsome. His name was—Darby;—that was his baptizing name; his other name I forgot. Oh! it was Wig—Wag—Wag-all, Darby Wag-all,—pray, do you know him?—I should like to take a sling with him, or a drap of cyder with a pepper-pod in it, to make it warm and comfortable.

JENNY

I can't say I have that pleasure.

JONATHAN

I wish you did; he is a cute fellow. But there was one thing I didn't like in that Mr. Darby; and that was, he was afraid of some of them 'ere shooting irons, such as your troopers wear on training days. Now, I'm a true born Yankee American son of liberty, and I never was afraid of a gun yet in all my life.

JENNY

Well, Mr. Jonathan, you were certainly at the play-house.

JONATHAN

I at the play-house!—Why didn't I see the play then?

JENNY

Why, the people you saw were players.

JONATHAN

Mercy on my soul! did I see the wicked players?— Mayhap that 'ere Darby that I liked so was the old serpent himself, and had his cloven foot in his pocket. Why, I vow, now I come to think on't, the candles seemed to burn blue, and I am sure where I sat it smelt tarnally of brimstone.

JESSAMY

Well, Mr. Jonathan, from your account, which I confess is very accurate, you must have been at the play-house.

JONATHAN

Why, I vow, I began to smell a rat. When I came away, I went to the man for my money again; you want your money? says he; yes, says I; for what? says he; why, says I, no man shall jocky me out of my money; I paid my money to see sights, and the dogs a bit of a sight have I seen, unless you call listening to people's private business a sight. Why, says he, it is the School for Scandalization.—The School for Scandalization!—Oh! ho! no wonder you New-York folks are so cute at it, when you go to school to learn it; and so I jogged off.

JESSAMY

My dear Jenny, my master's business drags me from you; would to heaven I knew no other servitude than to your charms.

JONATHAN

Well, but don't go; you won't leave me so—

JESSAMY

Excuse me.—Remember the cash. [Aside to him, and—Exit.]

JENNY

Mr. Jonathan, won't you please to sit down? Mr. Jessamy tells me you wanted to have some conversation with me. [Having brought forward two chairs, they sit.]

JONATHAN

Ma'am!—

JENNY

Sir!—

JONATHAN

Ma'am!—

JENNY

Pray, how do you like the city, Sir?

JONATHAN

Ma'am!—

JENNY

I say, Sir, how do you like New-York?

JONATHAN

Ma'am!—

JENNY

The stupid creature! but I must pass some little time with him, if it is only to endeavour to learn whether it was his master that made such an abrupt entrance into our house, and my young mistress's heart, this morning. [Aside.] As you don't seem to like to talk, Mr. Jonathan—do you sing?

JONATHAN

Gor, I—I am glad she asked that, for I forgot what Mr. Jessamy bid me say, and I dare as well be hanged as act what he bid me do, I'm so ashamed. [Aside.] Yes, Ma'am, I can sing—I can sing Mear, Old Hundred, and Bangor.

JENNY

Oh! I don't mean psalm tunes. Have you no little song to please the ladies, such as Roslin Castle, or the Maid of the Mill?

JONATHAN

Why, all my tunes go to meeting tunes, save one, and I count you won't altogether like that 'ere.

JENNY

What is it called?

JONATHAN

I am sure you have heard folks talk about it; it is called Yankee Doodle.

JENNY

Oh! it is the tune I am fond of; and if I know anything of my mistress, she would be glad to dance to it. Pray, sing!

JONATHAN [Sings.]

Father and I went up to camp,
Along with Captain Goodwin;
And there we saw the men and boys,

As thick as hasty-pudding.
Yankee doodle do, etc.

And there we saw a swamping gun,
Big as log of maple,
On a little deuced cars,
A load for father's cattle.
Yankee doodle do, etc.
And every time they fired it off
It took a horn of powder,
It made a noise—like father's gun,
Only a nation louder.
Yankee doodle do, etc.
There was a man in our town,
His name was—

No, no, that won't do. Now, if I was with Tabitha Wymen and Jemima Cawley down at father Chase's, I shouldn't mind singing this all out before them—you would be affronted if I was to sing that, though that's a lucky thought; if you should be affronted, I have something dang'd cute, which Jessamy told me to say to you.

JENNY

Is that all! I assure you I like it of all things.

JONATHAN

No, no; I can sing more; some other time, when you and I are better acquainted, I'll sing the whole of it—no, no—that's a fib—I can't sing but a hundred and ninety verses; our Tabitha at home can sing it all.—[Sings.]

Marblehead's a rocky place,
And Cape-Cod is sandy;
Charlestown is burnt down,
Boston is the dandy.
Yankee doodle, doodle do, etc.

I vow, my own town song has put me into such topping spirits that I believe I'll begin to do a little, as Jessamy says we must when we go a-courting.—[Runs and kisses her.] Burning rivers! cooling flames! red-hot roses! pig-nuts! hasty-pudding and ambrosia!

JENNY

What means this freedom? you insulting wretch. [Strikes him.]

JONATHAN

Are you affronted?

JENNY

Affronted! with what looks shall I express my anger?

JONATHAN

Looks! why as to the matter of looks, you look as cross as a witch.

JENNY

Have you no feeling for the delicacy of my sex?

JONATHAN

Feeling! Gor, I—I feel the delicacy of your sex pretty smartly [rubbing his cheek], though, I vow, I thought when you city ladies courted and married, and all that, you put feeling out of the question. But I want to know whether you are really affronted, or only pretend to be so? 'Cause, if you are certainly right down affronted, I am at the end of my tether; Jessamy didn't tell me what to say to you.

JENNY

Pretend to be affronted!

JONATHAN

Aye, aye, if you only pretend, you shall hear how I'll go to work to make cherubim consequences. [Runs up to her.]

JENNY

Begone, you brute!

JONATHAN

That looks like mad; but I won't lose my speech. My dearest Jenny—your name is Jenny, I think?—My dearest Jenny, though I have the highest esteem for the sweet favours you have just now granted me—Gor, that's a fib, though; but Jessamy says it is not wicked to tell lies to the women. [Aside.] I say, though I have the highest esteem for the favours you have just now granted me, yet you will consider that, as soon as the dissolvable knot is tied, they will no longer be favours, but only matters of duty and matters of course.

JENNY

Marry you! you audacious monster! get out of my sight, or, rather, let me fly from you. [Exit hastily.]

JONATHAN

Gor! she's gone off in a swinging passion, before I had time to think of consequences. If this is the way with your city ladies, give me the twenty acres of rock, the Bible, the cow, and Tabitha, and a little peaceable bundling.

SCENE II. THE MALL.

Enter MANLY.

It must be so, Montague! and it is not all the tribe of Mandevilles that shall convince me that a nation, to become great, must first become dissipated. Luxury is surely the bane of a nation: Luxury! which enervates both soul and body, by opening a thousand new sources of enjoyment, opens, also, a thousand new sources of contention and want: Luxury! which renders a people weak at home, and accessible to bribery, corruption, and force from abroad. When the Grecian states knew no other tools than the axe and the saw, the Grecians were a great, a free, and a happy people. The kings of Greece devoted their lives to the service of their country, and her senators knew no other superiority over their fellow-citizens than a glorious pre-eminence in danger and virtue. They exhibited to the world a noble spectacle,—a number of independent states united by a similarity of language, sentiment, manners, common interest, and common consent, in one grand mutual league of protection. And, thus united, long might they have continued the cherishers of arts and sciences, the protectors of the oppressed, the scourge of tyrants, and the safe asylum of liberty. But when foreign gold, and still more pernicious foreign luxury, had crept among them, they sapped the vitals of their virtue. The virtues of their ancestors were only found in their writings. Envy and suspicion, the vices of little minds, possessed them. The various states engendered jealousies of each other; and, more unfortunately, growing jealous of their great federal council, the Amphictyons, they forgot that their common safety had existed, and would exist, in giving them an honourable extensive prerogative. The common good was lost in the pursuit of private interest; and that people who, by uniting, might have stood against the world in arms, by dividing, crumbled into ruin;—their name is now only known in the page of the historian, and what they once were is all we have left to admire. Oh! that America! Oh! that my country, would, in this her day, learn the things which belong to her peace!

Enter DIMPLE.

DIMPLE

You are Colonel Manly, I presume?

MANLY

At your service, Sir.

DIMPLE

My name is Dimple, Sir. I have the honour to be a lodger in the same house with you, and, hearing you were in the Mall, came hither to take the liberty of joining you.

MANLY

You are very obliging, Sir.

DIMPLE

As I understand you are a stranger here, Sir, I have taken the liberty to introduce myself to your acquaintance, as possibly I may have it in my power to point out some things in this city worthy your notice.

MANLY

An attention to strangers is worthy a liberal mind, and must ever be gratefully received. But to a soldier, who has no fixed abode, such attentions are particularly pleasing.

DIMPLE

Sir, there is no character so respectable as that of a soldier. And, indeed, when we reflect how much we owe to those brave men who have suffered so much in the service of their country, and secured to us those inestimable blessings that we now enjoy, our liberty and independence, they demand every attention which gratitude can pay. For my own part, I never meet an officer, but I embrace him as my friend, nor a private in distress, but I insensibly extend my charity to him.—I have hit the Bumkin off very tolerably.

[Aside.]

MANLY

Give me your hand, Sir! I do not proffer this hand to everybody; but you steal into my heart. I hope I am as insensible to flattery as most men; but I declare (it may be my weak side) that I never hear the name of soldier mentioned with respect, but I experience a thrill of pleasure which I never feel on any other occasion.

DIMPLE

Will you give me leave, my dear Colonel, to confer an obligation on myself, by shewing you some civilities during your stay here, and giving a similar opportunity to some of my friends?

MANLY

Sir, I thank you; but I believe my stay in this city will be very short.

DIMPLE

I can introduce you to some men of excellent sense, in whose company you will esteem yourself happy; and, by way of amusement, to some fine girls, who will listen to your soft things with pleasure.

MANLY

Sir, I should be proud of the honour of being acquainted with those gentlemen;—but, as for the ladies, I don't understand you.

DIMPLE

Why, Sir, I need not tell you, that when a young gentleman is alone with a young lady he must say some soft things to her fair cheek—indeed, the lady will expect it. To be sure, there is not much pleasure when a man of the world and a finished coquette meet, who perfectly know each other; but how delicious is it to excite the emotions of joy, hope, expectation, and delight in the bosom of a lovely girl who believes every tittle of what you say to be serious!

MANLY

Serious, Sir! In my opinion, the man who, under pretensions of marriage, can plant thorns in the bosom of an innocent, unsuspecting girl is more detestable than a common robber, in the same proportion as private violence is more despicable than open force, and money of less value than happiness.

DIMPLE

How he awes me by the superiority of his sentiments. [Aside.] As you say, Sir, a gentleman should be cautious how he mentions marriage.

MANLY

Cautious, Sir! No person more approves of an intercourse between the sexes than I do. Female conversation softens our manners, whilst our discourse, from the superiority of our literary advantages, improves their minds. But, in our young country, where there is no such thing as gallantry, when a gentleman speaks of love to a lady, whether he mentions marriage or not, she ought to conclude either that he meant to insult her or that his intentions are the most serious and honourable. How mean, how cruel, is it, by a thousand tender assiduities, to win the affections of an amiable girl, and, though you leave her virtue unspotted, to betray her into the appearance of so many tender partialities, that every man of delicacy would suppress his inclination towards her, by supposing her heart engaged! Can any man, for the trivial gratification of his leisure hours, affect the happiness of a whole life! His not having spoken of marriage may add to his perfidy, but can be no excuse for his conduct.

DIMPLE

Sir, I admire your sentiments;—they are mine. The light observations that fell from me were only a principle of the tongue; they came not from the heart; my practice has ever disapproved these principles.

MANLY

I believe you, Sir. I should with reluctance suppose that those pernicious sentiments could find admittance into the heart of a gentleman.

DIMPLE

I am now, Sir, going to visit a family, where, if you please, I will have the honour of introducing you. Mr. Manly's ward, Miss Letitia, is a young lady of immense fortune; and his niece, Miss Charlotte Manly, is a young lady of great sprightliness and beauty.

MANLY

That gentleman, Sir, is my uncle, and Miss Manly my sister.

DIMPLE

The devil she is! [Aside.] Miss Manly your sister, Sir? I rejoice to hear it, and feel a double pleasure in being known to you.—Plague on him! I wish he was at Boston again, with all my soul. [Aside.]

MANLY

Come, Sir, will you go?

DIMPLE

I will follow you in a moment, Sir. [Exit Manly.] Plague on it! this is unlucky. A fighting brother is a cursed appendage to a fine girl. Egad! I just stopped in time; had he not discovered himself, in two minutes more I should have told him how well I was with his sister. Indeed, I cannot see the satisfaction of an intrigue, if one can't have the pleasure of communicating it to our friends. [Exit.

END OF THE THIRD ACT.

ACT IV. SCENE I.

CHARLOTTE'S Apartment.

CHARLOTTE leading in MARIA.

CHARLOTTE

This is so kind, my sweet friend, to come to see me at this moment. I declare, if I were going to be married in a few days, as you are, I should scarce have found time to visit my friends.

MARIA

Do you think, then, that there is an impropriety in it?—How should you dispose of your time?

CHARLOTTE

Why, I should be shut up in my chamber; and my head would so run upon—upon—upon the solemn ceremony that I was to pass through!—I declare, it would take me above two hours merely to learn that little monosyllable—Yes. Ah! my dear, your sentimental imagination does not conceive what that little tiny word implies.

MARIA

Spare me your raillery, my sweet friend; I should love your agreeable vivacity at any other time.

CHARLOTTE

Why, this is the very time to amuse you. You grieve me to see you look so unhappy.

MARIA

Have I not reason to look so?

CHARLOTTE

What new grief distresses you?

MARIA

Oh! how sweet it is, when the heart is borne down with misfortune, to recline and repose on the bosom of friendship! Heaven knows that, although it is improper for a young lady to praise a gentleman, yet I have ever concealed Mr. Dimple's foibles, and spoke of him as of one whose reputation I expected would be linked with mine; but his late conduct towards me has turned my coolness into contempt. He behaves as if he meant to insult and disgust me; whilst my father, in the last conversation on the subject of our marriage, spoke of it as a matter which lay near his heart, and in which he would not bear contradiction.

CHARLOTTE

This works well; oh! the generous Dimple. I'll endeavour to excite her to discharge him. [Aside.] But, my dear friend, your happiness depends on yourself. Why don't you discard him? Though the match has been of long standing, I would not be forced to make myself miserable: no parent in the world should oblige me to marry the man I did not like.

MARIA

Oh! my dear, you never lived with your parents, and do not know what influence a father's frowns have upon a daughter's heart. Besides, what have I to alledge against Mr. Dimple, to justify myself to the world? He carries himself so smoothly, that every one would impute the blame to me, and call me capricious.

CHARLOTTE

And call her capricious! Did ever such an objection start into the heart of woman? For my part, I wish I had fifty lovers to discard, for no other reason than because I did not fancy them. My dear Maria, you will forgive me; I know your candour and confidence in me; but I have at times, I confess, been led to suppose that some other gentleman was the cause of your aversion to Mr. Dimple.

MARIA

No, my sweet friend, you may be assured, that though I have seen many gentlemen I could prefer to Mr. Dimple, yet I never saw one that I thought I could give my hand to, until this morning.

CHARLOTTE

This morning!

MARIA

Yes; one of the strangest accidents in the world. The odious Dimple, after disgusting me with his conversation, had just left me, when a gentleman, who, it seems, boards in the same house with him, saw him coming out of our door, and, the houses looking very much alike, he came into our house instead of his lodgings; nor did he discover his mistake until he got into the parlour, where I was; he then bowed so gracefully, made such a genteel apology, and looked so manly and noble!—

CHARLOTTE

I see some folks, though it is so great an impropriety, can praise a gentleman, when he happens to be the man of their fancy. [Aside.]

MARIA

I don't know how it was,—I hope he did not think me indelicate,—but I asked him, I believe, to sit down, or pointed to a chair. He sat down, and, instead of having recourse to observations upon the weather, or hackneyed criticisms upon the theatre, he entered readily into a conversation worthy a man of sense to speak, and a lady of delicacy and sentiment to hear. He was not strictly handsome, but he spoke the language of sentiment, and his eyes looked tenderness and honour.

CHARLOTTE

Oh! [eagerly] you sentimental, grave girls, when your hearts are once touched, beat us rattles a bar's length. And so you are quite in love with this he-angel?

MARIA

In love with him! How can you rattle so, Charlotte? am I not going to be miserable? [Sighs.] In love with a gentleman I never saw but one hour in my life, and don't know his name! No; I only wished that the man I shall marry may look, and talk, and act, just like him. Besides, my dear, he is a married man.

CHARLOTTE

Why, that was good-natured—he told you so, I suppose, in mere charity, to prevent you falling in love with him?

MARIA

He didn't tell me so; [peevishly] he looked as if he was married.

CHARLOTTE

How, my dear; did he look sheepish?

MARIA

I am sure he has a susceptible heart, and the ladies of his acquaintance must be very stupid not to—

CHARLOTTE

Hush! I hear some person coming.

Enter LETITIA.

LETITIA

My dear Maria, I am happy to see you. Lud! what a pity it is that you have purchased your wedding clothes.

MARIA

I think so. [Sighing.]

LETITIA

Why, my dear, there is the sweetest parcel of silks come over you ever saw! Nancy Brilliant has a full suit come; she sent over her measure, and it fits her to a hair; it is immensely dressy, and made for a court-hoop. I thought they said the large hoops were going out of fashion.

CHARLOTTE

Did you see the hat? Is it a fact that the deep laces round the border is still the fashion?

DIMPLE within

Upon my honour, Sir.

MARIA

Ha! Dimple's voice! My dear, I must take leave of you. There are some things necessary to be done at our house. Can't I go through the other room?

Enter DIMPLE and MANLY.

DIMPLE

Ladies, your most obedient.

CHARLOTTE

Miss Van Rough, shall I present my brother Henry to you? Colonel Manly, Maria,—Miss Van Rough, brother.

MARIA

Her brother! [turns and sees Manly.] Oh! my heart! the very gentleman I have been praising.

MANLY

The same amiable girl I saw this morning!

CHARLOTTE

Why, you look as if you were acquainted.

MANLY

I unintentionally intruded into this lady's presence this morning, for which she was so good as to promise me her forgiveness.

CHARLOTTE

Oh! ho! is that the case! Have these two penserosos been together? Were they Henry's eyes that looked so tenderly? [Aside.] And so you promised to pardon him? and could you be so good-natured? have you really forgiven him? I beg you would do it for my sake [whispering loud to Maria]. But, my dear, as you are in such haste, it would be cruel to detain you; I can show you the way through the other room.

MARIA

Spare me, my sprightly friend.

MANLY

The lady does not, I hope, intend to deprive us of the pleasure of her company so soon.

CHARLOTTE

She has only a mantua-maker who waits for her at home. But, as I am to give my opinion of the dress, I think she cannot go yet. We were talking of the fashions when you came in, but I suppose the subject must be changed to something of more importance now. Mr. Dimple, will you favour us with an account of the public entertainments?

DIMPLE

Why, really, Miss Manly, you could not have asked me a question more malapropos. For my part, I must confess that, to a man who has travelled, there is nothing that is worthy the name of amusement to be found in this city.

CHARLOTTE

Except visiting the ladies.

DIMPLE

Pardon me, Madam; that is the avocation of a man of taste. But for amusement, I positively know of nothing that can be called so, unless you dignify with that title the hopping once a fortnight to the sound of two or three squeaking fiddles, and the clattering of the old tavern windows, or sitting to see the miserable mummers, whom you call actors, murder comedy and make a farce of tragedy.

MANLY

Do you never attend the theatre, Sir?

DIMPLE

I was tortured there once.

CHARLOTTE

Pray, Mr. Dimple, was it a tragedy or a comedy?

DIMPLE

Faith, Madam, I cannot tell; for I sat with my back to the stage all the time, admiring a much better actress than any there—a lady who played the fine woman to perfection; though, by the laugh of the horrid creatures round me, I suppose it was comedy. Yet, on second thoughts, it might be some hero in a tragedy, dying so comically as to set the whole house in an uproar. Colonel, I presume you have been in Europe?

MANLY

Indeed, Sir, I was never ten leagues from the continent.

DIMPLE

Believe me, Colonel, you have an immense pleasure to come; and when you shall have seen the brilliant exhibitions of Europe, you will learn to despise the amusements of this country as much as I do.

MANLY

Therefore I do not wish to see them; for I can never esteem that knowledge valuable which tends to give me a distaste for my native country.

DIMPLE

Well, Colonel, though you have not travelled, you have read.

MANLY

I have, a little; and by it have discovered that there is a laudable partiality which ignorant, untravelled men entertain for everything that belongs to their native country. I call it laudable; it injures no one; adds to their own happiness; and, when extended, becomes the noble principle of patriotism. Travelled gentlemen rise superior, in their own opinion, to this; but if the contempt which they contract for their country is the most valuable acquisition of their travels, I am far from thinking that their time and money are well spent.

MARIA

What noble sentiments!

CHARLOTTE

Let my brother set out where he will in the fields of conversation, he is sure to end his tour in the temple of gravity.

MANLY

Forgive me, my sister. I love my country; it has its foibles undoubtedly;—some foreigners will with pleasure remark them—but such remarks fall very ungracefully from the lips of her citizens.

DIMPLE

You are perfectly in the right, Colonel—America has her faults.

MANLY

Yes, Sir; and we, her children, should blush for them in private, and endeavour, as individuals, to reform them. But, if our country has its errors in common with other countries, I am proud to say America—I mean the United States—has displayed virtues and achievements which modern nations may admire, but of which they have seldom set us the example.

CHARLOTTE

But, brother, we must introduce you to some of our gay folks, and let you see the city, such as it is. Mr. Dimple is known to almost every family in town; he will doubtless take a pleasure in introducing you.

DIMPLE

I shall esteem every service I can render your brother an honour.

MANLY

I fear the business I am upon will take up all my time, and my family will be anxious to hear from me.

MARIA

His family! but what is it to me that he is married! [Aside.] Pray, how did you leave your lady, Sir?

CHARLOTTE

My brother is not married [observing her anxiety]; it is only an odd way he has of expressing himself. Pray, brother, is this business, which you make your continual excuse, a secret?

MANLY

No, sister; I came hither to solicit the honourable Congress, that a number of my brave old soldiers may be put upon the pension-list, who were, at first, not judged to be so materially wounded as to need the public assistance. My sister says true [to Maria]: I call my late soldiers my family. Those who were not in the field in the late glorious contest, and those who were, have their respective merits; but, I confess, my old brother-soldiers are dearer to me than the former description. Friendships made in adversity are lasting; our countrymen may forget us, but that is no reason why we should forget one another. But I must leave you; my time of engagement approaches.

CHARLOTTE

Well, but, brother, if you will go, will you please to conduct my fair friend home? You live in the same street—I was to have gone with her myself— [Aside]. A lucky thought.

MARIA

I am obliged to your sister, Sir, and was just intending to go.
[Going.]

MANLY

I shall attend her with pleasure. [Exit with Maria, followed by Dimple and Charlotte.]

MARIA

Now, pray, don't betray me to your brother.

CHARLOTTE

[Just as she sees him make a motion to take his leave.] One word with you, brother, if you please. [Follows them out.]

Manent, DIMPLE and LETITIA.

DIMPLE

You received the billet I sent you, I presume?

LETITIA

Hush!—Yes.

DIMPLE

When shall I pay my respects to you?

LETITIA

At eight I shall be unengaged.

Re-enter CHARLOTTE.

DIMPLE

Did my lovely angel receive my billet? [to Charlotte.]

CHARLOTTE

Yes.

DIMPLE

At eight I shall be at home unengaged.

DIMPLE

Unfortunate! I have a horrid engagement of business at that hour.
Can't you finish your visit earlier and let six be the happy hour?

CHARLOTTE

You know your influence over me. [Exeunt severally.

SCENE II.
VAN ROUGH'S House.

VAN ROUGH, alone

It cannot possibly be true! The son of my old friend can't have acted so unadvisedly. Seventeen thousand pounds! in bills! Mr. Transfer must have been mistaken. He always appeared so prudent, and talked so well upon money matters, and even assured me that he intended to change his dress for a suit of clothes which would not cost so much, and look more substantial, as soon as he married. No, no, no! it can't be; it cannot be. But, however, I must look out sharp. I did not care what his principles or his actions were, so long as he minded the main chance. Seventeen thousand pounds! If he had lost it in trade, why the best men may have ill-luck; but to game it away, as Transfer says—why, at this rate, his whole estate may go in one night, and, what is ten times worse, mine into the bargain. No, no; Mary is right. Leave women to look out in these matters; for all they look as if they didn't know a journal from a ledger, when their interest is concerned they know what's what; they mind the main chance as well as the best of us. I wonder Mary did not tell me she knew of his spending his money so foolishly. Seventeen thousand pounds! Why, if my daughter was standing up to be married, I would forbid the banns, if I found it was to a man who did not mind the main chance.—Hush! I hear somebody coming. 'Tis Mary's voice; a man with her too! I shouldn't be surprised if this should be the other string to her bow. Aye, aye, let them alone; women understand the main chance.—Though, I' faith, I'll listen a little. [Retires into a closet.

MANLY leading in MARIA.

MANLY

I hope you will excuse my speaking upon so important a subject so abruptly; but, the moment I entered your room, you struck me as the lady whom I had long loved in imagination, and never hoped to see.

MARIA

Indeed, Sir, I have been led to hear more upon this subject than I ought.

MANLY

Do you, then, disapprove my suit, Madam, or the abruptness of my introducing it? If the latter, my peculiar situation, being obliged to leave the city in a few days, will, I hope, be my excuse; if the former, I will retire, for I am sure I would not give a moment's inquietude to her whom I could devote my life to please. I am not so indelicate as to seek your immediate approbation; permit me only to be near you, and by a thousand tender assiduities to endeavour to excite a grateful return.

MARIA

I have a father, whom I would die to make happy; he will disapprove—

MANLY

Do you think me so ungenerous as to seek a place in your esteem without his consent? You must—you ever ought to consider that man as unworthy of you who seeks an interest in your heart contrary to a father's approbation. A young lady should reflect that the loss of a lover may be supplied, but nothing can compensate for the loss of a parent's affection. Yet, why do you suppose your father would disapprove? In our country, the affections are not sacrificed to riches or family aggrandizement: should you approve, my family is decent, and my rank honourable.

MARIA

You distress me, Sir.

MANLY

Then I will sincerely beg your excuse for obtruding so disagreeable a subject, and retire. [Going.

MARIA

Stay, Sir! your generosity and good opinion of me deserve a return; but why must I declare what, for these few hours, I have scarce suffered myself to think?—I am—

MANLY

What?

MARIA

Engaged, Sir; and, in a few days, to be married to the gentleman you saw at your sister's.

MANLY

Engaged to be married! And have I been basely invading the rights of another? Why have you permitted this? Is this the return for the partiality I declared for you?

MARIA

You distress me, Sir. What would you have me say? You are too generous to wish the truth. Ought I to say that I dared not suffer myself to think of my engagement, and that I am going to give my hand without my heart? Would you have me confess a partiality for you? If so, your triumph is compleat, and can be only more so when days of misery with the man I cannot love will make me think of him whom I could prefer.

MANLY [after a pause]

We are both unhappy; but it is your duty to obey your parent—mine to obey my honour. Let us, therefore, both follow the path of rectitude; and of this we may be assured, that if we are not happy, we shall, at least, deserve to be so. Adieu! I dare not trust myself longer with you. [Exeunt severally.

END OF THE FOURTH ACT.

ACT V. SCENE I.

DIMPLE'S Lodgings.

JESSAMY meeting JONATHAN.

JESSAMY

WELL, Mr. Jonathan, what success with the fair?

JONATHAN

Why, such a tarnal cross tike you never saw! You would have counted she had lived upon crab-apples and vinegar for a fortnight. But what the rattle makes you look so tarnation glum?

JESSAMY

I was thinking, Mr. Jonathan, what could be the reason of her carrying herself so coolly to you.

JONATHAN

Coolly, do you call it? Why, I vow, she was fire-hot angry: may be it was because I buss'd her.

JESSAMY

No, no, Mr. Jonathan; there must be some other cause; I never yet knew a lady angry at being kissed.

JONATHAN

Well, if it is not the young woman's bashfulness, I vow I can't conceive why she shouldn't like me.

JESSAMY

May be it is because you have not the Graces, Mr. Jonathan.

JONATHAN

Grace! Why, does the young woman expect I must be converted before I court her?

JESSAMY

I mean graces of person: for instance, my lord tells us that we must cut off our nails even at top, in small segments of circles—though you won't understand that; in the next place, you must regulate your laugh.

JONATHAN

Maple-log seize it! don't I laugh natural?

JESSAMY

That's the very fault, Mr. Jonathan. Besides, you absolutely misplace it. I was told by a friend of mine that you laughed outright at the play the other night, when you ought only to have tittered.

JONATHAN

Gor! I—what does one go to see fun for if they can't laugh?

JESSAMY

You may laugh; but you must laugh by rule.

JONATHAN

Swamp it—laugh by rule! Well, I should like that tarnally.

JESSAMY

Why, you know, Mr. Jonathan, that to dance, a lady to play with her fan, or a gentleman with his cane, and all other natural motions, are regulated by art. My master has composed an immensely pretty gamut, by which any lady or gentleman, with a few years' close application, may learn to laugh as gracefully as if they were born and bred to it.

JONATHAN

Mercy on my soul! A gamut for laughing—just like fa, la, sol?

JEREMY

Yes. It comprises every possible display of jocularity, from an affettuoso smile to a piano titter, or full chorus fortissimo ha, ha, ha! My master employs his leisure hours in marking out the plays, like a cathedral chanting-book, that the ignorant may know where to laugh; and that pit, box, and gallery may keep time together, and not have a snigger in one part of the house, a broad grin in the other, and a d—-d grum look in the third. How delightful to see the audience all smile together, then look on their books, then twist their mouths into an agreeable simper, then altogether shake the house with a general ha, ha, ha! loud as a full chorus of Handel's at an Abbey commemoration.

JONATHAN

Ha, ha, ha! that's dang'd cute, I swear.

JESSAMY

The gentlemen, you see, will laugh the tenor; the ladies will play the counter-tenor; the beaux will squeak the treble; and our jolly friends in the gallery a thorough base, ho, ho, ho!

JONATHAN

Well, can't you let me see that gamut?

JESSAMY

Oh! yes, Mr. Jonathan; here it is. [Takes out a book.] Oh! no, this is only a titter with its variations. Ah, here it is. [Takes out another.] Now, you must know, Mr. Jonathan, this is a piece written by Ben Johnson, which I have set to my master's gamut. The places where you must smile, look grave, or laugh outright, are marked below the line. Now look over me. "There was a certain man"—now you must smile.

JONATHAN

Well, read it again; I warrant I'll mind my eye.

JESSAMY

"There was a certain man, who had a sad scolding wife,"—now you must laugh.

JONATHAN

Tarnation! That's no laughing matter though.

JESSAMY

"And she lay sick a-dying";—now you must titter.

JONATHAN

What, snigger when the good woman's a-dying! Gor, I—

JESSAMY

Yes, the notes say you must—"and she asked her husband leave to make a will,"—now you must begin to look grave;—"and her husband said"—

JONATHAN

Ay, what did her husband say? Something dang'd cute, I reckon.

JESSAMY

"And her husband said, you have had your will all your life-time, and would you have it after you are dead, too?"

JONATHAN

Ho, ho, ho! There the old man was even with her; he was up to the notch—ha, ha, ha!

JESSAMY

But, Mr. Jonathan, you must not laugh so. Why you ought to have tittered piano, and you have laughed fortissimo. Look here; you see these marks, A, B, C, and so on; these are the references to the other part of the book. Let us turn to it, and you will see the directions how to manage the muscles. This [turns over] was note D you blundered at.—You must purse the mouth into a smile, then titter, discovering the lower part of the three front upper teeth.

JONATHAN

How? read it again.

JESSAMY

"There was a certain man"—very well!—"who had a sad scolding wife,"—why don't you laugh?

JONATHAN

Now, that scolding wife sticks in my gizzard so pluckily that I can't laugh for the blood and nowns of me. Let me look grave here, and I'll laugh your belly full, where the old creature's a-dying.

JESSAMY

"And she asked her husband"—[Bell rings.] My master's bell! he's returned, I fear.—Here, Mr. Jonathan, take this gamut; and I make no doubt but with a few years' close application, you may be able to smile gracefully." [Exeunt severally.

SCENE II.
CHARLOTTE'S Apartment.

Enter MANLY.

MANLY

What, no one at home? How unfortunate to meet the only lady my heart was ever moved by, to find her engaged to another, and confessing her partiality for me! Yet engaged to a man who, by her intimation, and his libertine conversation with me, I fear, does not merit her. Aye! there's the sting; for, were I assured that Maria was happy, my heart is not so selfish but that it would dilate in knowing it, even though it were with another. But to know she is unhappy!—I must drive these thoughts from me. Charlotte has some books; and this is what I believe she calls her little library. [Enters a closet.

Enter DIMPLE leading LETITIA.

LETITIA

And will you pretend to say now, Mr. Dimple, that you propose to break with Maria? Are not the banns published? Are not the clothes purchased? Are not the friends invited? In short, is it not a done affair?

DIMPLE

Believe me, my dear Letitia, I would not marry her.

LETITIA

Why have you not broke with her before this, as you all along deluded me by saying you would?

DIMPLE

Because I was in hopes she would, ere this, have broke with me.

LETITIA

You could not expect it.

DIMPLE

Nay, but be calm a moment; 'twas from my regard to you that I did not discard her.

LETITIA

Regard to me!

DIMPLE

Yes; I have done everything in my power to break with her, but the foolish girl is so fond of me that nothing can accomplish it. Besides, how can I offer her my hand when my heart is indissolubly engaged to you?

LETITIA

There may be reason in this; but why so attentive to Miss Manly?

DIMPLE

Attentive to Miss Manly! For heaven's sake, if you have no better opinion of my constancy, pay not so ill a compliment to my taste.

LETITIA

Did I not see you whisper her to-day?

DIMPLE

Possibly I might—but something of so very trifling a nature that I have already forgot what it was.

LETITIA

I believe she has not forgot it.

DIMPLE

My dear creature, how can you for a moment suppose I should have any serious thoughts of that trifling, gay, flighty coquette, that disagreeable—

Enter CHARLOTTE.

DIMPLE

My dear Miss Manly, I rejoice to see you; there is a charm in your conversation that always marks your entrance into company as fortunate.

LETITIA

Where have you been, my dear?

CHARLOTTE

Why, I have been about to twenty shops, turning over pretty things, and so have left twenty visits unpaid. I wish you would step into the carriage and whisk round, make my apology, and leave my cards where our friends are not at home; that, you know, will serve as a visit. Come, do go.

LETITIA

So anxious to get me out! but I'll watch you. [Aside.] Oh! yes, I'll go; I want a little exercise. Positively [Dimple offering to accompany her], Mr. Dimple, you shall not go; why, half my visits are cake and caudle visits; it won't do, you know, for you to go. [Exit, but returns to the door in the back scene and listens.]

DIMPLE

This attachment of your brother to Maria is fortunate.

CHARLOTTE

How did you come to the knowledge of it?

DIMPLE

I read it in their eyes.

CHARLOTTE

And I had it from her mouth. It would have amused you to have seen her! She, that thought it so great an impropriety to praise a gentleman that she could not bring out one word in your favour, found a redundancy to praise him.

DIMPLE

I have done everything in my power to assist his passion there: your delicacy, my dearest girl, would be shocked at half the instances of neglect and misbehaviour.

CHARLOTTE

I don't know how I should bear neglect; but Mr. Dimple must misbehave himself indeed, to forfeit my good opinion.

DIMPLE

Your good opinion, my angel, is the pride and pleasure of my heart; and if the most respectful tenderness for you, and an utter indifference for all your sex besides, can make me worthy of your esteem, I shall richly merit it.

CHARLOTTE

All my sex besides, Mr. Dimple!—you forgot your tete-a-tete with Letitia.

DIMPLE

How can you, my lovely angel, cast a thought on that insipid, wry-mouthed, ugly creature!

CHARLOTTE

But her fortune may have charms?

DIMPLE

Not to a heart like mine. The man, who has been blessed with the good opinion of my Charlotte, must despise the allurements of fortune.

CHARLOTTE

I am satisfied.

DIMPLE

Let us think no more on the odious subject, but devote the present hour to happiness.

CHARLOTTE

Can I be happy when I see the man I prefer going to be married to another?

DIMPLE

Have I not already satisfied my charming angel, that I can never think of marrying the puling Maria? But, even if it were so, could that be any bar to our happiness? for, as the poet sings,

"Love, free as air, at sight of human ties,
Spreads his light wings, and in a moment flies."

Come, then, my charming angel! why delay our bliss? The present moment is ours; the next is in the hand of fate. [Kissing her.]

CHARLOTTE

Begone, Sir! By your delusions you had almost lulled my honour asleep.

DIMPLE

Let me lull the demon to sleep again with kisses. [He struggles with her; she screams.]

Enter MANLY.

MANLY

Turn, villain! and defend yourself.—[Draws.]

[VAN ROUGH enters and beats down their swords.]

VAN ROUGH

Is the devil in you? are you going to murder one another? [Holding Dimple.]

DIMPLE

Hold him, hold him,—I can command my passion.

Enter JONATHAN.

JONATHAN

What the rattle ails you? Is the old one in you? Let the colonel alone, can't you? I feel chock-full of fight,—do you want to kill the colonel?—

MANLY

Be still, Jonathan; the gentleman does not want to hurt me.

JONATHAN

Gor! I—I wish he did; I'd shew him Yankee boys play, pretty quick.—Don't you see you have frightened the young woman into the hystrikes?

VAN ROUGH

Pray, some of you explain this; what has been the occasion of all this racket?

MANLY

That gentleman can explain it to you; it will be a very diverting story for an intended father-in-law to hear.

VAN ROUGH

How was this matter, Mr. Van Dumpling?

DIMPLE

Sir,—upon my honour,—all I know is, that I was talking to this young lady, and this gentleman broke in on us in a very extraordinary manner.

VAN ROUGH

Why, all this is nothing to the purpose; can you explain it, Miss? [To Charlotte.]

Enter LETITIA through the back scene.

LETITIA

I can explain it to that gentleman's confusion. Though long betrothed to your daughter [to Van Rough], yet, allured by my fortune, it seems (with shame do I speak it) he has privately paid his addresses to me. I was drawn in to listen to him by his assuring me that the match was made by his father without his consent, and that he proposed to break with Maria, whether he married me or not. But, whatever were his intentions respecting your daughter, Sir, even to me he was false; for he has repeated the same story, with some cruel reflections upon my person, to Miss Manly.

JONATHAN

What a tarnal curse!

LETITIA

Nor is this all, Miss Manly. When he was with me this very morning, he made the same ungenerous reflections upon the weakness of your mind as he has so recently done upon the defects of my person.

JONATHAN

What a tarnal curse and damn, too!

DIMPLE

Ha! since I have lost Letitia, I believe I had as good make it up with Maria. Mr.

Van Rough, at present I cannot enter into particulars; but, I believe, I can explain everything to your satisfaction in private.

VAN ROUGH

There is another matter, Mr. Van Dumpling, which I would have you explain. Pray, Sir, have Messrs. Van Cash & Co. presented you those bills for acceptance?

DIMPLE

The deuce! Has he heard of those bills! Nay, then, all's up with Maria, too; but an affair of this sort can never prejudice me among the ladies; they will rather long to know what the dear creature possesses to make him so agreeable. [Aside.] Sir, you'll hear from me. [To Manly.]

MANLY

And you from me, Sir—

DIMPLE

Sir, you wear a sword—

MANLY

Yes, Sir. This sword was presented to me by that brave Gallic hero, the Marquis De la Fayette. I have drawn it in the service of my country, and in private life, on the only occasion where a man is justified in drawing his sword, in defence of a lady's honour. I have fought too many battles in the service of my country to dread the imputation of cowardice. Death from a man of honour would be a glory you do not merit; you shall live to bear the insult of man and the contempt of that sex whose general smiles afforded you all your happiness.

DIMPLE

You won't meet me, Sir? Then I'll post you for a coward.

MANLY

I'll venture that, Sir. The reputation of my life does not depend upon the breath of a Mr. Dimple. I would have you to know, however, Sir, that I have a cane to chastise the insolence of a scoundrel, and a sword and the good laws of my country to protect me from the attempts of an assassin—

DIMPLE

Mighty well! Very fine, indeed! Ladies and gentlemen, I take my leave; and you will please to observe in the case of my deportment the contrast between a gentleman who has read Chesterfield and received the polish of Europe and an unpolished, untravelled American. [Exit.

Enter MARIA.

MARIA

Is he indeed gone?—

LETITIA

I hope, never to return.

VAN ROUGH

I am glad I heard of those bills; though it's plaguy unlucky; I hoped to see Mary married before I died.

MANLY

Will you permit a gentleman, Sir, to offer himself as a suitor to your daughter? Though a stranger to you, he is not altogether so to her, or unknown in this city. You may find a son-in-law of more fortune, but you can never meet with one who is richer in love for her, or respect for you.

VAN ROUGH

Why, Mary, you have not let this gentleman make love to you without my leave?

MANLY

I did not say, Sir—

MARIA

Say, Sir!—I—the gentleman, to be sure, met me accidentally.

VAN ROUGH

Ha, ha, ha! Mark me, Mary; young folks think old folks to be fools; but old folks know young folks to be fools. Why, I knew all about this affair. This was only a cunning way I had to bring it about. Hark ye! I was in the closet when you and he were at our hours. [Turns to the company.] I heard that little baggage say she loved her old father, and would die to make him happy! Oh! how I loved the little baggage! And you talked very prudently, young man. I have inquired into your character, and find you to be a man of punctuality and mind the main chance. And so, as you love Mary and Mary loves you, you shall have my consent immediately to be married. I'll settle my fortune on you, and go and live with you the remainder of my life.

MANLY

Sir, I hope—

VAN ROUGH

Come, come, no fine speeches; mind the main chance, young man, and you and I shall always agree.

LETITIA

I sincerely wish you joy [advancing to Maria]; and hope your pardon for my conduct.

MARIA

I thank you for your congratulations, and hope we shall at once forget the wretch who has given us so much disquiet, and the trouble that he has occasioned.

CHARLOTTE

And I, my dear Maria,—how shall I look up to you for forgiveness? I, who, in the practice of the meanest arts, have violated the most sacred rights of friendship? I can never forgive myself, or hope charity from the world; but, I confess, I have much to hope from such a brother; and I am happy that I may soon say, such a sister.

MARIA

My dear, you distress me; you have all my love.

MANLY

And mine.

CHARLOTTE

If repentance can entitle me to forgiveness, I have already much merit; for I despise the littleness of my past conduct. I now find that the heart of any worthy man cannot be gained by invidious attacks upon the rights and characters of others;—by countenancing the addresses of a thousand;—or that the finest assemblage of features, the greatest taste in dress, the genteelest address, or the most brilliant wit, cannot eventually secure a coquette from contempt and ridicule.

MANLY

And I have learned that probity, virtue, honour, though they should not have received the polish of Europe, will secure to an honest American the good graces of his fair countrywomen, and, I hope, the applause of THE PUBLIC.

THE END.

3.15.2 Reading and Review Questions

1. What are American virtues, according to this play? How do you know?
2. What are European vices, according to this play? How do you know?
3. How does European culture "infect" American society, and to what effect?
4. What, if any, distinctions of class do you discern in this play? Which class, if any, is perceived in a positive light? Why?
5. How free are the characters in this play? What, if anything, constrains them? What liberates them?

3.16 HANNAH WEBSTER FOSTER

(1758–1840)

Image 3.24 | Hannah Webster Foster
Artist | Unknown
Source | Wikimedia Commons
License | Public Domain

Hannah Webster Foster was born in Salisbury, Massachusetts into a wealthy merchant family. She was educated for several years at a boarding school. In 1785, she married the Reverend John Foster (1735–1800), minister of the First Parish Church in Brighton, the only church in Brighton. She bore six children, three of whom were daughters, two of whom became writers as adults. As the wife of the only minister in Brighton, Foster was an important social leader of the town. After she published two novels, Foster focused her energies on her role as wife and mother. In 1827, a group within the First Parish Church broke away to establish the Brighton Evangelical Congregational Society. Soon afterwards, John Foster left the church. He died two years later. Foster moved to Montreal to live with her daughter Elizabeth, where she died in 1840.

Foster was wife, mother, and writer. Her writing considers women's lives as defined and constrained by their expected place in society as wives and mothers. Despite the hopes of such revolutionary minds as Abigail Adams, women were not freed from their dependence on the men who had legal authority over them after the American Revolution. Women were faced, at a remove, with the new nation's changes in economy, urbanization, and politics, and their only support, foundation, and stability amidst these changes was the institution of marriage, an institution that legally saw no change post-revolution.

Foster dramatizes these concerns in her epistolary novel *The Coquette* (1797), one of the first epistolary novels published in America. It is based on the life of Elizabeth Whitman (1752–1788), the daughter of the Reverend Elnathan Whitman (1708–1776) and a second cousin by marriage of Foster. Whitman's death gained great attention, for she died while using an assumed name as she waited at an inn for her presumed husband. She had no husband, and she died due to complications from giving birth to a stillborn child. Once she was identified as a relative of several well-known ministers, her story became a scandal about a woman's fall from grace. Foster's version of this story considers a woman's fall from grace, humiliation, repentance, and reassertion of rectitude, and in the process, gains sympathy for her. *The Coquette* displays women's limited options and limited choices within American society. Also concerned with women's choices, Foster's novel *The Boarding School; or, Lessons of a Preceptress to Her Pupils* (1798) considers women's education, what and how they should be taught, and how education should prepare women for their lives outside of school.

3.16.1 From *The Coquette: Or; the History of Eliza Wharton* (1797)

Letter I

TO MISS LUCY FREEMAN.
NEW HAVEN

An unusual sensation possesses my breast—a sensation which I once thought could never pervade it on any occasion whatever. It is pleasure, pleasure, my dear Lucy, on leaving my paternal roof. Could you have believed that the darling child of an indulgent and dearly-beloved mother would feel a gleam of joy at leaving her? But so it is. The melancholy, the gloom, the condolence which surrounded me for a month after the death of Mr. Haly had depressed my spirits, and palled every enjoyment of life. Mr. Haly was a man of worth—a man of real and substantial merit. He is, therefore, deeply and justly regretted by his friends. He was chosen to be a future guardian and companion for me, and was, therefore, beloved by mine. As their choice, as a good man, and a faithful friend, I esteemed him; but no one acquainted with the disparity of our tempers and dispositions, our views and designs, can suppose my heart much engaged in the alliance. Both nature and education had instilled into my mind an implicit obedience to the will and desires of my parents. To them, of course, I sacrificed my fancy in this affair, determined that my reason should concur with theirs, and on that to risk my future happiness. I was the more encouraged, as I saw, from our first acquaintance, his declining health, and expected that the event would prove as it has. Think not, however, that I rejoice in his death. No; far be it from me; for though I believe that I never felt the passion of love for Mr. Haly, yet a habit of conversing with him, of hearing daily the most virtuous, tender, and affectionate sentiments from his lips, inspired emotions of the sincerest friendship and esteem.

He is gone. His fate is unalterably, and I trust happily, fixed. He lived the life, and died the death, of the righteous. O that my last end may be like his! This event will, I hope, make a suitable and abiding impression upon my mind, teach me the fading nature of all sublunary enjoyments, and the little dependence which is to be placed on earthly felicity. Whose situation was more agreeable, whose prospects more flattering, than Mr. Haly's? Social, domestic, and connubial joys were fondly anticipated, and friends and fortune seemed ready to crown every wish; yet, animated by still brighter hopes, he cheerfully bade them all adieu. In conversation with me but a few days before his exit, "There is," said he, "but one link in the chain of life undissevered; that, my dear Eliza, is my attachment to you. But God is wise and good in all his ways; and in this, as in all other respects, I would cheerfully say, His will be done."

You, my friend, were witness to the concluding scene; and, therefore, I need not describe it.

I shall only add on the subject, that if I have wisdom and prudence to follow his advice and example, if his prayers for my temporal and eternal welfare be heard and answered, I shall be happy indeed.

The disposition of mind which I now feel I wish to cultivate. Calm, placid, and serene, thoughtful of my duty, and benevolent to all around me, I wish for no other connection than that of friendship.

This letter is all an egotism. I have even neglected to mention the respectable and happy friends with whom I reside, but will do it in my next. Write soon and often; and believe me sincerely yours,

ELIZA WHARTON.

Letter II

TO THE SAME.
NEW HAVEN.

Time, which effaces every occasional impression, I find gradually dispelling the pleasing pensiveness which the melancholy event, the subject of my last, had diffused over my mind. Naturally cheerful, volatile, and unreflecting, the opposite disposition I have found to contain sources of enjoyment which I was before unconscious of possessing.

My friends here are the picture of conjugal felicity. The situation is delightful—the visiting parties perfectly agreeable. Every thing tends to facilitate the return of my accustomed vivacity. I have written to my mother, and received an answer. She praises my fortitude, and admires the philosophy which I have exerted under what she calls my heavy bereavement. Poor woman! she little thinks that my heart was untouched; and when that is unaffected, other sentiments and passions make but a transient impression. I have been, for a month or two, excluded from the gay world, and, indeed, fancied myself soaring above it. It is now that I begin to descend, and find my natural propensity for mixing in the busy scenes and active pleasures of life returning. I have received your letter—your moral lecture rather;

and be assured, my dear, your monitorial lessons and advice shall be attended to. I believe I shall never again resume those airs which you term coquettish, but which I think deserve a softer appellation, as they proceed from an innocent heart, and are the effusions of a youthful and cheerful mind. We are all invited to spend the day to-morrow at Colonel Farington's, who has an elegant seat in this neighborhood. Both he and his lady are strangers to me; but the friends by whom I am introduced will procure me a welcome reception. Adieu.

ELIZA WHARTON.

Letter III

TO THE SAME.
NEW HAVEN.

Is it time for me to talk again of conquests? or must I only enjoy them in silence? I must write to you the impulses of my mind, or I must not write at all. You are not so morose as to wish me to become a nun, would our country and religion allow it. I ventured, yesterday, to throw aside the habiliments of mourning, and to array myself in those more adapted to my taste. We arrived at Colonel Farington's about one o'clock. The colonel handed me out of the carriage, and introduced me to a large company assembled in the hall.

My name was pronounced with an emphasis, and I was received with the most flattering tokens of respect. When we were summoned to dinner, a young gentleman in a clerical dress offered me his hand, and led me to a table furnished with an elegant and sumptuous repast, with more gallantry and address than commonly fall to the share of students. He sat opposite me at table; and whenever I raised my eye, it caught his. The ease and politeness of his manners, with his particular attention to me, raised my curiosity, and induced me to ask Mrs. Laiton who he was. She told me that his name was Boyer; that he was descended from a worthy family; had passed with honor and applause through the university where he was educated; had since studied divinity with success; and now had a call to settle as a minister in one of the first parishes in a neighboring state.

The gates of a spacious garden were thrown open at this instant, and I accepted with avidity an invitation to walk in it. Mirth and hilarity prevailed, and the moments fled on downy wings, while we traced the beauties of Art and Nature, so liberally displayed and so happily blended in this delightful retreat. An enthusiastic admirer of scenes like these, I had rambled some way from the company, when I was followed by Mrs. Laiton to offer her condolence on the supposed loss which I had sustained in the death of Mr. Haly. My heart rose against the woman, so ignorant of human nature as to think such conversation acceptable at such a time. I made her little reply, and waved the subject, though I could not immediately dispel the gloom which it excited.

The absurdity of a custom authorizing people at a first interview to revive the idea of griefs which time has lulled, perhaps obliterated, is intolerable. To have our enjoyments arrested by the empty compliments of unthinking persons for no other reason than a compliance with fashion, is to be treated in a manner which the laws of humanity forbid.

We were soon joined by the gentlemen, who each selected his partner, and the walk was prolonged.

Mr. Boyer offered me his arm, which I gladly accepted, happy to be relieved from the impertinence of my female companion. We returned to tea; after which the ladies sung, and played by turns on the piano forte; while some of the gentlemen accompanied with the flute, the clarinet, and the violin, forming in the whole a very decent concert. An elegant supper, and half an hour's conversation after it, closed the evening; when we returned home, delighted with our entertainment, and pleased with ourselves and each other. My imagination is so impressed with the festive scenes of the day that Morpheus waves his ebon wand in vain. The evening is fine beyond the power of description; all Nature is serene and harmonious, in perfect unison with my present disposition of mind. I have been taking a retrospect of my past life, and, a few juvenile follies excepted, which I trust the recording angel has blotted out with a tear of charity, find an approving conscience and a heart at ease. Fortune, indeed, has not been very liberal of her gifts to me; but I presume on a large stock in the bank of friendship, which, united with health and innocence, give me some pleasing anticipations of future felicity.

Whatever my fate may be, I shall always continue your

ELIZA WHARTON.

Letter IV

TO MR. SELBY.
NEW HAVEN.

You ask me, my friend, whether I am in pursuit of truth, or a lady. I answer, Both. I hope and trust they are united, and really expect to find Truth, and the Virtues and Graces besides, in a fair form. If you mean by the first part of your question whether I am searching into the sublimer doctrines of religion,—to these I would by no means be inattentive; but, to be honest, my studies of that kind have been very much interrupted of late. The respectable circle of acquaintances with which I am honored here has rendered my visits very frequent and numerous. In one of these I was introduced to Miss Eliza Wharton—a young lady whose elegant person, accomplished mind, and polished manners have been much celebrated. Her fame has often reached me; but, as the Queen of Sheba said to Solomon, the half was not told me. You will think that I talk in the style of a lover.

I confess it; nor am I ashamed to rank myself among the professed admirers of this lovely fair one. I am in no danger, however, of becoming an enthusiastic devotee. No; I mean I act upon just and rational principles. Expecting soon to settle in an eligible situation, if such a companion as I am persuaded she will make me may fall to my lot, I shall deem myself as happy as this state of imperfection will admit. She is now resident at General Richman's. The general and his lady are her particular friends; they are warm in her praises. They tell me, however, that she is naturally of a gay disposition. No matter for that; it is an agreeable quality, where there is discretion sufficient for its regulation. A cheerful friend, much more a cheerful wife, is peculiarly necessary to a person of a studious and sedentary life. They dispel the gloom of retirement, and exhilarate the spirits depressed by intense application. She was formerly addressed by the late Mr. Haly, of Boston. He was not, it seems, the man of her choice; but her parents were extremely partial to him, and wished the connection to take place. She, like a dutiful child, sacrificed her own inclination to their pleasure so far as to acquiesce in his visits. This she more easily accomplished, as his health, which declined from their first acquaintance, led her to suppose, as the event has proved, that he would not live to enter into any lasting engagements. Her father, who died some months before him, invited him to reside at his house for the benefit of a change of air, agreeably to the advice of his physicians. She attended him during his last illness with all the care and assiduity of a nurse and with all the sympathizing tenderness of a sister.

I have had several opportunities of conversing with her. She discovers an elevated mind, a ready apprehension, and an accurate knowledge of the various subjects which have been brought into view. I have not yet introduced the favorite subject of my heart. Indeed, she seems studiously to avoid noticing any expression which leads towards it; but she must hear it soon. I am sure of the favor and interest of the friends with whom she resides. They have promised to speak previously in my behalf. I am to call, as if accidentally, this afternoon just as they are to ride abroad. They are to refer me to Miss Wharton for entertainment till their return. What a delightful opportunity for my purpose! I am counting the hours—nay, the very moments. Adieu. You shall soon again hear from your most obedient,

J. BOYER.

Letter V

TO MISS LUCY FREEMAN.
NEW HAVEN.

These bewitching charms of mine have a tendency to keep my mind in a state of perturbation. I am so pestered with these admirers! Not that I am so very handsome neither; but, I don't know how it is, I am certainly very much the taste of the other sex. Followed, flattered, and caressed, I have cards and compliments in profusion. But I must try to be serious; for I have, alas! one serious lover. As I promised you to be particular in my writing, I suppose I must proceed methodically. Yesterday we had a party to dine. Mr. Boyer was of the number. His attention was immediately engrossed; and I soon perceived that every word, every action, and every look was studied to gain my approbation. As he sat next me at dinner, his assiduity and politeness were pleasing; and as we walked together afterwards, his conversation was improving. Mine was sentimental and sedate—perfectly adapted to the taste of my gallant. Nothing, however, was said particularly expressive of his apparent wishes. I studiously avoided every kind of discourse which might lead to this topic. I wish not for a declaration from any one, especially from one whom I could not repulse and do not intend to encourage at present. His conversation, so similar to what I had often heard from a similar character, brought a deceased friend to mind, and rendered me somewhat pensive. I retired directly after supper. Mr. Boyer had just taken leave.

Mrs. Richman came into my chamber as she was passing to her own. "Excuse my intrusion, Eliza," said she. "I thought I would just step in and ask you if you have passed a pleasant day."

"Perfectly so, madam; and I have now retired to protract the enjoyment by recollection." "What, my dear, is your opinion of our favorite, Mr. Boyer?" "Declaring him your favorite, madam, is sufficient to render me partial to him; but to be frank, independent of that, I think him an agreeable man." "Your heart, I presume, is now free." "Yes, and I hope it will long remain so." "Your friends, my dear, solicitous for your welfare, wish to see you suitably and agreeably connected." "I hope my friends will never again interpose in my concerns of that nature. You, madam, who have ever known my heart, are sensible that, had the Almighty spared life in a certain instance, I must have sacrificed my own happiness or incurred their censure. I am young, gay, volatile. A melancholy event has lately extricated me from those shackles which parental authority had imposed on my mind. Let me, then, enjoy that freedom which I so highly prize. Let me have opportunity, unbiased by opinion, to gratify my natural disposition in a participation of those pleasures which youth and innocence afford." "Of such pleasures, no one, my dear, would wish to deprive you; but beware, Eliza! Though strewed with flowers, when contemplated by your lively imagination, it is, after all, a slippery, thorny path. The round of fashionable dissipation is dangerous. A phantom is often pursued, which leaves its deluded votary the real form of wretchedness." She spoke with an emphasis, and, taking up her candle, wished me a good night. I had not power to return the compliment. Something seemingly prophetic in her looks and expressions cast a momentary gloom upon my mind; but I despise those contracted ideas which confine virtue to a cell. I have no notion of becoming a recluse. Mrs. Richman has ever been a beloved friend of mine; yet I always thought her rather prudish. Adieu.

ELIZA WHARTON.

Letter VI

TO THE SAME.
NEW HAVEN.

I had scarcely seated myself at the breakfast table this morning when a servant entered with a card of invitation from Major Sanford, requesting the happiness of my hand this evening at a ball given by Mr. Atkins, about three miles from this. I showed the billet to Mrs. Richman, saying, "I have not much acquaintance with this gentleman, madam; but I suppose his character sufficiently respectable to warrant an affirmative answer." "He is a gay man, my dear, to say no more; and such are the companions we wish when we join a party avowedly formed for pleasure." I then stepped into my apartment, wrote an answer, and despatched the servant. When I returned to the parlor, something disapprobating appeared in the countenances of both my friends. I endeavored, without seeming to observe, to dissipate it by chitchat; but they were better pleased with each other than with me, and, soon rising, walked into the garden, and left me to amuse myself alone. My eyes followed them through the window. "Happy pair!" said I. "Should it ever be my fate to wear the hymeneal chain, may I be thus united! The purest and most ardent affection, the greatest consonance of taste and disposition, and the most congenial virtue and wishes distinguish this lovely couple. Health and wealth, with every attendant blessing, preside over their favored dwelling, and shed their benign influence without alloy." The consciousness of exciting their displeasure gave me pain; but I consoled myself with the idea that it was ill founded.

"They should consider," said I, "that they have no satisfaction to look for beyond each other; there every enjoyment is centred; but I am a poor solitary being, who need some amusement beyond what I can supply myself. The mind, after being confined at home for a while, sends the imagination abroad in quest of new treasures; and the body may as well accompany it, for aught I can see."

General Richman and lady have ever appeared solicitous to promote my happiness since I have resided with them. They have urged my acceptance of invitations to join parties; though they have not been much themselves of late, as Mrs. Richman's present circumstances render her fond of retirement. What reason can be assigned for their apparent reluctance to this evening's entertainment is to me incomprehensible; but I shall apply the chemical powers of friendship, and extract the secret from Mrs. Richman to-morrow, if not before. Adieu. I am now summoned to dinner, and after that shall be engaged in preparation till the wished-for hour of hilarity and mirth engrosses every faculty of your

ELIZA WHARTON.

Letter VII

TO MR. SELBY.
NEW HAVEN.

Divines need not declaim, nor philosophers expatiate, on the disappointments of human life. Are they not legibly written on every page of our existence? Are they not predominantly prevalent over every period of our lives?

When I closed my last letter to you, my heart exulted in the pleasing anticipation of promised bliss; my wishes danced on the light breezes of hope; and my imagination dared to arrest the attention of, and even claim a return of affection from, the lovely Eliza Wharton. But imagination only it has proved, and that dashed with the bitter ranklings of jealousy and suspicion.

But to resume my narrative. I reached the mansion of my friend about four. I was disagreeably struck with the appearance of a carriage at the door, as it raised an idea of company which might frustrate my plan; but still more disagreeable were my sensations when, on entering the parlor, I found Major Sanford evidently in a waiting posture. I was very politely received; and when Eliza entered the room with a brilliance of appearance and gayety of manner which I had never before connected with her character, I rose, as did Major Sanford, who offered his hand and led her to a chair. I forgot to sit down again, but stood transfixed by the pangs of disappointment. Miss Wharton appeared somewhat confused, but, soon resuming her vivacity, desired me to be seated, inquired after my health, and made some commonplace remarks on the weather; then, apologizing for leaving me, gave her hand again to Major Sanford, who had previously risen, and reminded her that the time and their engagements made it necessary to leave the good company; which, indeed, they both appeared very willing to do. General Richman and lady took every method in their power to remove my chagrin and atone for the absence of my fair one; but ill did they succeed. They told me that Miss Wharton had not the most distant idea of my visiting there this afternoon, much less of the design of my visit; that for some months together she had been lately confined by the sickness of Mr. Haly, whom she attended during the whole of his last illness; which confinement had eventually increased her desire of indulging her natural disposition for gayety. She had, however, they said, an excellent heart and reflecting mind, a great share of sensibility, and a temper peculiarly formed for the enjoyments of social life. "But this gentleman, madam, who is her gallant this evening,—is his character unexceptionable? Will a lady of delicacy associate with an immoral, not to say profligate, man?" "The rank and fortune of Major Sanford," said Mrs. Richman, "procure him respect; his specious manners render him acceptable in public company; but I must own that he is not the person with whom I wish my cousin to be connected even for a moment. She never consulted me so little on any subject as that of his card this morning. Before I had time to object, she dismissed the servant; and I forbore to destroy her expected happiness by acquainting her with my disapprobation of her partner. Her omission was not design; it was juvenile indiscretion. We must, my dear sir," continued she, "look with a candid eye on such eccentricities. Faults, not foibles, require the severity of censure." "Far, madam, be it from me to censure any conduct which as yet I have observed in Miss Wharton; she has too great an interest in my heart to admit of that."

We now went into more general conversation. Tea was served; and I soon after took leave. General Richman, however, insisted on my dining with him on Thursday; which I promised. And here I am again over head and ears in the hypo—a disease, you will say, peculiar to students. I believe it peculiar to lovers; and with that class I must now rank myself, though I did not know, until this evening, that I was so much engaged as I find I really am. I knew, indeed, that I was extremely pleased with this amiable girl; that I was interested in her favor; that I was happier in her company than any where else; with innumerable other circumstances, which would have told me the truth had I examined them. But be that as it may, I hope and trust that I am, and ever shall be, a reasonable creature, and not suffer my judgment to be misled by the operations of a blind passion.

I shall now lay aside this subject; endeavor to divest even my imagination of the charmer; and return, until Thursday, to the contemplation of those truths and duties which have a happy tendency to calm the jarring elements which compose our mortal frame. Adieu.

J. BOYER.

Letter VIII

TO MR. CHARLES DEIGHTON.
NEW HAVEN.

We had an elegant ball, last night, Charles; and what is still more to the taste of your old friend, I had an elegant partner; one exactly calculated to please my fancy—gay, volatile, apparently thoughtless of every thing but present enjoyment. It was Miss Eliza Wharton—a young lady whose agreeable person, polished manners, and refined talents have rendered her the toast of the country around for these two years; though for half that time she has had a clerical lover imposed on her by her friends; for I am told it was not agreeable to her inclination. By this same clerical lover of hers she was for several months confined as a nurse. But his death has happily relieved her; and she now returns to the world with redoubled lustre. At present she is a visitor to Mrs. Richman, who is a relation. I first saw her on a party of pleasure at Mr. Frazier's, where we walked, talked, sang, and danced together. I thought her cousin watched her with a jealous eye; for she is, you must know, a prude; and immaculate—more so than you or I—must be the man who claims admission to her society. But I fancy this young lady is a coquette; and if so, I shall avenge my sex by retaliating the mischiefs she meditates against us. Not that I have any ill designs, but only to play off her own artillery by using a little unmeaning gallantry. And let her beware of the consequences. A young clergyman came in at General Richman's yesterday, while I was waiting for Eliza, who was much more cordially received by the general and his lady than was your humble servant; but I lay that up.

When she entered the room, an air of mutual embarrassment was evident. The lady recovered her assurance much more easily than the gentleman. I am just going to ride, and shall make it in my way to call and inquire after the health of my dulcinea. Therefore, adieu for the present.

PETER SANFORD.

Letter XI

TO MR. CHARLES DEIGHTON.
NEW HAVEN.

Well, Charles, I have been manoeuvring to-day a little revengefully. That, you will say, is out of character. So baleful a passion does not easily find admission among those softer ones which you well know I cherish. However, I am a mere Proteus, and can assume any shape that will best answer my purpose.

I called this afternoon, as I told you I intended, at General Richman's. I waited some time in the parlor alone before Eliza appeared; and when she did appear, the distant reserve of her manners and the pensiveness of her countenance convinced me that she had been vexed, and I doubted not but Peter Sanford was the occasion. Her wise cousin, I could have sworn, had been giving her a detail of the vices of her gallant, and warning her against the dangers of associating with him in future. Notwithstanding, I took no notice of any alteration in her behavior, but entered with the utmost facetiousness into a conversation which I thought most to her taste. By degrees she assumed her usual vivacity; cheerfulness and good humor again animated her countenance. I tarried as long as decency would admit. She having intimated that they were to dine at my friend Lawrence's, I caught at this information, and determined to follow them, and tease the jealous Mrs. Richman by playing off all the gallantry I was master of in her presence.

I went, and succeeded to the utmost of my wishes, as I read in the vexation visible in the one, and the ease and attention displayed by the other. I believe, too, that I have charmed the eye, at least, of the amiable Eliza. Indeed, Charles, she is a fine girl. I think it would hurt my conscience to wound her mind or reputation. Were I disposed to marry, I am persuaded she would make an excellent wife; but that, you know, is no part of my plan, so long as I can keep out of the noose. Whenever I do submit to be shackled, it must be from a necessity of mending my fortune. This girl would be far from doing that. However, I am pleased with her acquaintance, and mean not to abuse her credulity and good nature, if I can help it.

PETER SANFORD.

Letter XII

TO MISS LUCY FREEMAN.
NEW HAVEN.

The heart of your friend is again besieged. Whether it will surrender to the assailants or not I am unable at present to determine. Sometimes I think of becoming a predestinarian, and submitting implicitly to fate, without any exercise of free will; but, as mine seems to be a wayward one, I would counteract the operations of it, if possible.

Mrs. Richman told me this morning that she hoped I should be as agreeably entertained this afternoon as I had been the preceding; that she expected Mr. Boyer to dine and take tea, and doubted not but he would be as attentive and sincere to me, if not as gay and polite, as the gentleman who obtruded his civilities yesterday. I replied that I had no reason to doubt the sincerity of the one or the other, having never put them to the test, nor did I imagine I ever should. "Your friends, Eliza," said she, "would be very happy to see you united to a man of Mr. Boyer's worth, and so agreeably settled as he has a prospect of being." "I hope," said I, "that my friends are not so weary of my company as to wish to dispose of me. I am too happy in my present connections to quit them for new ones. Marriage is the tomb of friendship. It appears to me a very selfish state. Why do people in general, as soon as they are married, centre all their cares, their concerns, and pleasures in their own families? Former acquaintances are neglected or forgotten; the tenderest ties between friends are weakened or dissolved; and benevolence itself moves in a very limited sphere." "It is the glory of the marriage state," she rejoined, "to refine by circumscribing our enjoyments. Here we can repose in safety.

'The friendships of the world are oft
Confed'racies in vice, or leagues in pleasure:
Ours has the purest virtue for its basis;
And such a friendship ends not but with life.'

True, we cannot always pay that attention to former associates which we may wish; but the little community which we superintend is quite as important an object, and certainly renders us more beneficial to the public. True benevolence, though it may change its objects, is not limited by time or place. Its effects are the same, and, aided by a second self, are rendered more diffusive and salutary."

Some pleasantry passed, and we retired to dress. When summoned to dinner, I found Mr. Boyer below. If what is sometimes said be true, that love is diffident, reserved, and unassuming, this man must be tinctured with it. These symptoms were visible in his deportment when I entered the room. However, he soon recovered himself, and the conversation took a general turn. The festive board was crowned with sociability, and we found in reality "the feast of reason and the flow of soul." After we rose from table, a walk in the garden was proposed—an amusement we are all peculiarly fond of. Mr. Boyer offered me his arm. When at a sufficient distance from our company, he begged leave to congratulate himself on having an opportunity, which he had ardently desired for some time, of declaring to me his attachment, and of soliciting an interest in my favor; or, if he might be allowed the term, affection. I replied, "That, sir, is indeed laying claim to an important interest. I believe you must substitute some more indifferent epithet for the present." "Well, then," said he, "if it must be so, let it be esteem or friendship." "Indeed, sir," said I, "you are entitled to them both. Merit has always a share in that bank; and I know of none who has a larger claim on that score than Mr. Boyer." I suppose my manner was hardly serious enough for what he considered a weighty cause. He was a little disconcerted, but, soon regaining his presence of mind, entreated me, with an air of earnestness, to encourage his suit, to admit his addresses, and, if possible, to reward his love. I told him that this was rather a sudden affair to me, and that I could not answer him without consideration. "Well, then," said he, "take what time you think proper; only relieve my suspense as soon as may be. Shall I visit you again to-morrow?" "O, not so soon," said I; "next Monday, I believe, will be early enough. I will endeavor to be at home." He thanked me even for that favor, recommended himself once more to my kindness, and we walked towards the company, returned with them to the house, and he soon took leave. I immediately retired to write this letter, which I shall close without a single observation on the subject until I know your opinion.

ELIZA WHARTON.

Letter XIII

TO MISS ELIZA WHARTON.
HARTFORD.

And so you wish to have my opinion before you know the result of your own.

This is playing a little too much with my patience; but, however, I will gratify you this once, in hopes that my epistle may have a good effect. You will ask, perhaps, whether I would influence your judgment. I answer, No, provided you will exercise it yourself; but I am a little apprehensive that your fancy will mislead you. Methinks I can gather from your letters a predilection for this Major Sanford. But he is a rake, my dear friend; and can a lady of your delicacy and refinement think of forming a connection with a man of that character? I hope not; nay, I am confident you do not. You mean only to exhibit a few more girlish airs before you turn matron; but I am persuaded, if you wish to lead down the dance of life with regularity, you will not find a more excellent partner than Mr. Boyer. Whatever you can reasonably expect in a lover, husband, or friend, you may perceive to be united in this worthy man. His taste is undebauched, his manners not vitiated, his morals uncorrupted. His situation in life is, perhaps, as elevated as you have a right to claim. Forgive my plainness, Eliza. It is the task of friendship, sometimes, to tell disagreeable truths. I know your ambition is to make a distinguished figure in the first class of polished society, to shine in the gay circle of fashionable amusements, and to bear off the palm amidst the votaries of pleasure. But these are fading honors, unsatisfactory enjoyments, incapable of gratifying those immortal principles of reason and religion which have been implanted in your mind by Nature, assiduously cultivated by the best of parents, and exerted, I trust, by yourself. Let me advise you, then, in conducting this affair,—an affair big, perhaps, with your future fate,—to lay aside those coquettish airs which you sometimes put on; and remember that you are not dealing with a fop, who will take advantage of every concession, but with a man of sense and honor, who will properly estimate your condescension and frankness. Act, then, with that modest freedom, that dignified unreserve, which bespeak conscious rectitude and sincerity of heart.

I shall be extremely anxious to hear the process and progress of this business. Relieve my impatience as soon as possible; and believe me yours with undissembled affection.

LUCY FREEMAN.

Letter XIV

TO MISS LUCY FREEMAN.
NEW HAVEN.

I have received, and read again and again, your friendly epistle. My reason and judgment entirely coincide with your opinion; but my fancy claims some share in the decision; and I cannot yet tell which will preponderate. This was the day fixed for deciding Mr. Boyer's cause. My friends here gave me a long dissertation on his merits. Your letter, likewise, had its weight; and I was candidly summoning up the pros and cons in the garden, whither I had walked, (General Richman and lady having rode out,) when I was informed that he was waiting in the parlor. I went immediately in, (a good symptom, you will say,) and received him very graciously. After the first compliments were over, he seemed eager to improve the opportunity to enter directly on the subject of his present visit. It is needless for me to recite to you, who have long been acquainted with the whole process of courtship, the declarations, propositions, protestations, entreaties, looks, words, and actions of a lover. They are, I believe, much the same in the whole sex, allowing for their different dispositions, educations, and characters; but you are impatient, I know, for the conclusion.

You have hastily perused the preceding lines, and are straining your eye forward to my part of the farce; for such it may prove, after all. Well, then, not to play too long with the curiosity which I know to be excited and actuated by real friendship, I will relieve it. I think you would have been pleased to have seen my gravity on this important occasion. With all the candor and frankness which I was capable of assuming, I thus answered his long harangue, to which I had listened without interrupting him: "Self-knowledge, sir, that most important of all sciences, I have yet to learn. Such have been my situations in life, and the natural volatility of my temper, that I have looked but little into my own heart in regard to its future wishes and views. From a scene of constraint and confinement, ill suited to my years and inclination, I have just launched into society. My heart beats high in expectation of its fancied joys. My sanguine imagination paints, in alluring colors, the charms of youth and freedom, regulated by virtue and innocence. Of these I wish to partake. While I own myself under obligations for the esteem which you are pleased to profess for me, and, in return, acknowledge that neither your person nor manners are disagreeable to me, I recoil at the thought of immediately forming a connection which must confine me to the duties of domestic life, and make me dependent for happiness, perhaps, too, for subsistence, upon a class of people who will claim the right of scrutinizing every part of my conduct, and, by censuring those foibles which I am conscious of not having prudence to avoid, may render me completely miserable. While, therefore, I receive your visits, and cultivate towards you sentiments of friendship and esteem, I would not have you consider me as confined to your society, or obligated to a future connection. Our short acquaintance renders it impossible for me to decide what the operations of my mind may hereafter be. You must either quit the subject, or leave me to the exercise of my free will, which, perhaps, may coincide with your present wishes." "Madam," said he, "far is the wish from me to restrain your person or mind. In your breast I will repose my cause. It shall be my study to merit a return of affection; and I doubt not but generosity and honor will influence your conduct towards me. I expect soon to settle among a generous and enlightened people, where I flatter myself I shall be exempt from those difficulties and embarrassments to which too many of my brethren are subject. The local situation is agreeable, the society refined and polished; and if, in addition, I may obtain that felicity which you are formed to bestow in a family connection, I shall be happy indeed."

He spoke with emphasis. The tear of sensibility sparkled in his eye. I involuntarily gave him my hand, which he pressed with ardor to his lips; then, rising, he walked to the window to conceal his emotion. I rang the bell and ordered tea, during and after which we shared that social converse which is the true zest of life, and in which I am persuaded none but virtuous minds can participate. General Richman and lady returned with the shades of the evening. The penetrating eye of my cousin traced in our countenances the progress of the cause, and the smile of approbation animated hers. Mr. Boyer asked the favor of my company to ride to-morrow morning; which was granted. He tarried to supper, and took his leave. I retired immediately to my chamber, to which I was followed by Mrs. Richman. I related to her the conversation and the encouragement which I had given to Mr. Boyer. She was pleased, but insisted that I should own myself somewhat engaged to him. This, I told her, I should never do to any man before the indissoluble knot was tied. "That," said I, "will be time enough to resign my freedom." She replied, that I had wrong ideas of freedom and matrimony; but she hoped that Mr. Boyer would happily rectify them.

I have now, my dear friend, given you an account of my present situation, and leave you to judge for yourself concerning it. Write me your opinion, and believe me ever yours,

ELIZA WHARTON.

Letter XV

TO MISS ELIZA WHARTON.
HARTFORD.

I congratulate you, my dear Eliza, on the stability of your conduct towards Mr. Boyer. Pursue the system which you have adopted, and I dare say that happiness will crown your future days. You are indeed very tenacious of your freedom, as you call it; but that is a play about words. A man of Mr. Boyer's honor and good sense will never abridge any privileges which virtue can claim.

When do you return to embellish our society here? I am impatient to see you, and likewise this amiable man. I am much interested in his favor. By the way, I am told that Major Sanford has been to look at the seat of Captain Pribble, which is upon sale. It is reported that he will probably purchase it. Many of our gentry are pleased with the prospect of such a neighbor. "As an accomplished gentleman," say they, "he will be an agreeable addition to our social parties; and as a man of property and public spirit, he will be an advantage to the town." But from what I have heard of him, I am far from supposing him a desirable acquisition in either of these respects. A man of a vicious character cannot be a good member of society. In order to that, his principles and practice must be uncorrupted; in his morals, at least, he must be a man of probity and honor. Of these qualifications, if I mistake not, this gallant of yours cannot boast. But I shall not set up for a censor. I hope neither you nor I shall have much connection with him. My swain interests himself very much in your affairs. You will possibly think him impertinent; but I give his curiosity a softer name. Should I own to you that I place great confidence in his integrity and honor, you would, perhaps, laugh at my weakness; but, my dear, I have pride enough to keep me above coquetry or prudery, and discretion enough, I hope, to secure me from the errors of both. With him I am determined to walk the future round of life. What folly, then, would it be to affect reserve and distance relative to an affair in which I have so much interest! Not that I am going to betray your secrets; these I have no right to divulge; but I must be the judge what may, and what may not, be communicated. I am very much pressed for an early day of consummation; but I shall not listen to a request of that kind till your return. Such is my regard for you, that a union of love would be imperfect if friendship attended not the rites. Adieu.

LUCY FREEMAN.

Letter XVI

TO MISS LUCY FREEMAN.
NEW HAVEN.

We go on charmingly here, almost as soft and smooth as your ladyship. It seems to me that love must stagnate if it have not a light breeze of discord once in a while to keep it in motion. We have not tried any yet, however. We had a lovely tour this forenoon, were out three long hours, and returned to dinner in perfect harmony.

Mr. Boyer informed me that he should set out to-morrow morning for his future residence, and soon put on the sacred bands. He solicited an epistolary correspondence, at the same time, as an alleviation of the care which that weighty charge would bring on his mind. I consented, telling him that he must not expect any thing more than general subjects from me.

We were somewhat interrupted in our confidential intercourse, in the afternoon, by the arrival of Major Sanford. I cannot say that I was not agreeably relieved. So sweet a repast, for several hours together, was rather sickening to my taste. My inamorato looked a little mortified at the cheerful reception which I gave the intruder, and joined not so placidly in the social conversation as I could have wished.

When Mr. Boyer, after the major took leave, pressed me to give him some assurance of my constancy, I only reminded him of the terms of our engagement. Seeing me decided, he was silent on the subject, and soon bade me an affectionate adieu, not expecting, as he told me, the pleasure of a personal interview again for two or three months.

Thus far we have proceeded in this sober business. A good beginning, you will say. Perhaps it is. I do not, however, feel myself greatly interested in the progress of the negotiation. Time consolidate my affections, and enable me to fix them on some particular object. At present the most lively emotions of my heart are those of friendship, that friendship which I hope you will soon participate with your faithful

ELIZA WHARTON.

Letter XVII

TO MR. SELBY.
NEW HAVEN.

I have succeeded in my addresses to the lovely Eliza Wharton—as far, at least, as I had any reason to expect from our short acquaintance. I find the graces of her person and mind rise in my esteem, and have already enjoyed in her society some of the happiest hours of my life. She is kind, affable, and condescending; yet I must own that I have not been able to infuse into her bosom the ardor which I feel in my own. I know that the native modesty of the sex would restrain the discovery; but there is an animation of countenance, which betrays the sensations of the heart, that I find wanting in hers on this occasion.

I have just taken leave of my fair, and propose returning to-morrow morning to take upon me the solemn charge which lies with such weight upon my mind that I need every support, both human and divine. Eliza has promised to correspond with me. From this I anticipate a source of pleasure which alone can atone for her absence.

I am, &c.,

J. BOYER.

Letter XVIII

TO MR. CHARLES DEIGHTON.
NEW HAVEN.

Do you know, Charles, that I have commenced lover? I was always a general one, but now I am somewhat particular. I shall be the more interested, as I am likely to meet with difficulties; and it is the glory of a rake, as well as of a Christian, to combat obstacles. This same Eliza, of whom I have told you, has really made more impression on my heart than I was aware of, or than the sex, take them as they rise, are wont to do. But she is besieged by a priest—a likely lad though. I know not how it is, but they are commonly successful with the girls, even the gayest of them. This one, too, has the interest of all her friends, as I am told. I called yesterday at General Richman's, and found this pair together, apparently too happy in each other's society for my wishes. I must own that I felt a glow of jealousy, which I never experienced before, and vowed revenge for the pain it gave me, though but momentary. Yet Eliza's reception of me was visibly cordial; nay, I fancied my company as pleasing to her as that which she had before. I tarried not long, but left him to the enjoyment of that pleasure which I flatter myself will be but shortlived. O, I have another plan in my head—a plan of necessity, which, you know, is the mother of invention. It is this: I am very much courted and caressed by the family of Mr. Lawrence, a man of large property in this neighborhood. He has only one child—a daughter, with whom I imagine the old folks intend to shackle me in the bonds of matrimony. The girl looks very well; she has no soul, though, that I can discover; she is heiress, nevertheless, to a great fortune, and that is all the soul I wish for in a wife. In truth, Charles, I know of no other way to mend my circumstances. But lisp not a word of my embarrassments for your life. Show and equipage are my hobby horse; and if any female wishes to share them with me, and will furnish me with the means of supporting them, I have no objection. Could I conform to the sober rules of wedded life, and renounce those dear enjoyments of dissipation in which I have so long indulged, I know not the lady in the world with whom I would sooner form a connection of this sort than with Eliza Wharton. But it will never do. If my fortune or hers were better, I would risk a union; but as they are, no idea of the kind can be admitted. I shall endeavor, notwithstanding, to enjoy her company as long as possible. Though I cannot possess her wholly myself, I will not tamely see her the property of another.

I am now going to call at General Richman's, in hopes of an opportunity to profess my devotion to her. I know I am not a welcome visitor to the family; but I am independent of their censure or esteem, and mean to act accordingly.

PETER SANFORD.

Letter LXV

TO MR. CHARLES DEIGHTON.
HARTFORD.

Good news, Charles, good news! I have arrived to the utmost bounds of my wishes—the full possession of my adorable Eliza. I have heard a quotation from a certain book, but what book it was I have forgotten, if I ever knew. No matter for that; the quotation is, that "stolen waters are sweet, and bread eaten in secret is pleasant." If it has reference to the pleasures which I have enjoyed with Eliza, I like it hugely, as Tristram Shandy's father said of Yorick's sermon; and I think it fully verified.

I had a long and tedious siege. Every method which love could suggest, or art invent, was adopted. I was sometimes ready to despair, under an idea that her resolution was unconquerable, her virtue impregnable. Indeed, I should have given over the pursuit long ago, but for the hopes of success I entertained from her parleying with me, and, in reliance upon her own strength, endeavoring to combat and counteract my designs. Whenever this has been the case, Charles, I have never yet been defeated in my plan. If a lady will consent to enter the lists against the antagonist of her honor, she may be sure of losing the prize. Besides, were her delicacy genuine, she would banish the man at once who presumed to doubt, which he certainly does who attempts to vanquish it. But far be it from me to criticize the pretensions of the sex. If I gain the rich reward of my dissimulation and gallantry, that, you know, is all I want.

To return, then, to the point. An unlucky, but not a miraculous accident has taken place which must soon expose our amour. What can be done? At the first discovery, absolute distraction seized the soul of Eliza, which has since terminated in a fixed melancholy. Her health, too, is much impaired. She thinks herself rapidly declining, and I tremble when I see her emaciated form.

My wife has been reduced very low of late. She brought me a boy a few weeks past, a dead one though.

These circumstances give me neither pain nor pleasure. I am too much engrossed by my divinity to take an interest in any thing else. True, I have lately suffered myself to be somewhat engaged here and there by a few jovial lads who assist me in dispelling the anxious thoughts which my perplexed situation excites. I must, however, seek some means to relieve Eliza's distress. My finances are low; but the last fraction shall be expended in her service, if she need it.

Julia Granby is expected at Mrs. Wharton's every hour. I fear that her inquisitorial eye will soon detect our intrigue and obstruct its continuation. Now, there's a girl, Charles, I should never attempt to seduce; yet she is a most alluring object, I assure you. But the dignity of her manners forbids all assaults upon her virtue. Why, the very expression of her eye blasts in the bud every thought derogatory to her honor, and tells you plainly that the first insinuation of the kind would be punished with eternal banishment and displeasure. Of her there is no danger. But I can write no more, except that I am, &c.,

PETER SANFORD.

Letter LXVIII

TO MRS. M. WHARTON.
TUESDAY.

My honored and dear mamma: In what words, in what language shall I address you? What shall I say on a subject which deprives me of the power of expression? Would to God I had been totally deprived of that power before so fatal a subject required its exertion. Repentance comes too late, when it cannot prevent the evil lamented: for your kindness, your more than maternal affection towards me, from my infancy to the present moment, a long life of filial duty and unerring rectitude could hardly compensate. How greatly deficient in gratitude must I appear, then, while I confess that precept and example, counsel and advice, instruction and admonition, have been all lost upon me!

Your kind endeavors to promote my happiness have been repaid by the inexcusable folly of sacrificing it. The various emotions of shame and remorse, penitence and regret, which torture and distract my guilty breast, exceed description. Yes, madam, your Eliza has fallen, fallen indeed. She has become the victim of her own indiscretion, and of the intrigue and artifice of a designing libertine, who is the husband of another. She is polluted, and no more worthy of her parentage. She flies from you, not to conceal her guilt, (that she humbly and penitently owns,) but to avoid what she has never experienced, and feels herself unable to support—a mother's frown; to escape the heart-rending sight of a parent's grief, occasioned by the crimes of her guilty child.

I have become a reproach and disgrace to my friends. The consciousness of having forfeited their favor and incurred their disapprobation and resentment induces me to conceal from them the place of my retirement; but lest your benevolence should render you anxious for my comfort in my present situation, I take the liberty to assure you that I am amply provided for.

I have no claim even upon your pity; but from my long experience of your tenderness. I presume to hope it will be extended to me. O my mother, if you knew what the state of my mind is, and has been for months past, you would surely compassionate my case. Could tears efface the stain which I have brought upon my family, it would long since have been washed away; but, alas! tears are in vain; and vain is my bitter repentance; it cannot obliterate my crime, nor restore me to innocence and peace. In this life I have no ideas of happiness. These I have wholly resigned. The only hope which affords me any solace is that of your forgiveness. If the deepest contrition can make an atonement,—if the severest pains, both of body and mind, can restore me to your charity,—you will not be inexorable. O, let my sufferings be deemed a sufficient punishment, and add not the insupportable weight of a parent's wrath. At present I cannot see you. The effect of my crime is too obvious to be longer concealed, to elude the invidious eye of curiosity. This night, therefore, I leave your hospitable mansion. This night I become a wretched wanderer from my paternal roof. O that the grave were this night to be my lodging! Then should I lie down and be at rest. Trusting in the mercy of God, through the mediation of his Son, I think I could meet my heavenly Father with more composure and confidence than my earthly parent.

Let not the faults and misfortunes of your daughter oppress your mind. Rather let the conviction of having faithfully discharged your duty to your lost child support and console you in this trying scene.

Since I wrote the above, you have kindly granted me your forgiveness, though you knew not how great, how aggravated was my offence. You forgive me, you say. O, the harmonious, the transporting sound! It has revived my drooping spirits, and will enable me to encounter, with resolution, the trials before me.

Farewell, my dear mamma! Pity and pray for your ruined child; and be assured that affection and gratitude will be the last sentiments which expire in the breast of your repenting daughter,

ELIZA WHARTON.

Letter LXXI

TO MRS. LUCY SUMNER.
HARTFORD.

The drama is now closed! A tragical one it has proved!

How sincerely, my dear Mrs. Sumner, must the friends of our departed Eliza sympathize with each other, and with her afflicted, bereaved parent!

You have doubtless seen the account in the public papers which gave us the melancholy intelligence. But I will give you a detail of circumstances.

A few days after my last was written, we heard that Major Sanford's property was attached, and he a prisoner in his own house. He was the last man to whom we wished to apply for information respecting the forlorn wanderer; yet we had no other resource. And after waiting a fortnight in the most cruel suspense, we wrote a billet, entreating him, if possible, to give some intelligence concerning her. He replied that he was unhappily deprived of all means of knowing himself, but hoped soon to relieve his own and our anxiety about her.

In this situation we continued till a neighbor (purposely, we since concluded) sent us a Boston paper. Mrs. Wharton took it, and unconscious of its contents, observed that the perusal might divert her a few moments. She read for some time, when it suddenly dropped upon the floor. She clasped her hands together, and raising her streaming eyes to heaven, exclaimed, "It is the Lord; let him do what he will. Be still, O my soul, and know that he is God."

"What, madam," said I, "can be the matter?" She answered not, but, with inexpressible anguish depicted in her countenance, pointed to the paper. I took it up, and soon found the fatal paragraph. I shall not attempt to paint our heartfelt grief and lamentation upon this occasion; for we had no doubt of Eliza's being the person described, as a stranger, who died, at Danvers, last July. Her delivery of a child, her dejected state of mind, the marks upon her linen, indeed every circumstance in the advertisement, convinced us, beyond dispute, that it could be no other. Mrs. Wharton retired immediately to her chamber, where she continued overwhelmed with sorrow that night and the following day. Such in fact has been her habitual frame ever since; though the endeavors of her friends, who have sought to console her, have rendered her somewhat more conversable. My testimony of Eliza's penitence before her departure is a source of comfort to this disconsolate parent. She fondly cherished the idea that, having expiated her offence by sincere repentance and amendment, her deluded child finally made a happy exchange of worlds. But the desperate resolution, which she formed and executed, of becoming a fugitive, of deserting her mother's house and protection, and of wandering and dying among strangers, is a most distressing reflection to her friends; especially to her mother, in whose breast so many painful ideas arise, that she finds it extremely difficult to compose herself to that resignation which she evidently strives to exemplify.

Eliza's brother has been to visit her last retreat, and to learn the particulars of her melancholy exit. He relates that she was well accommodated, and had every attention and assistance which her situation required. The people where she resided appear to have a lively sense of her merit and misfortunes. They testify her modest deportment, her fortitude under the sufferings to which she was called, and the serenity and composure with which she bade a last adieu to the world. Mr. Wharton has brought back several scraps of her writing, containing miscellaneous reflections on her situation, the death of her babe, and the absence of her friends. Some of these were written before, some after, her confinement. These valuable testimonies of the affecting sense and calm expectation she entertained of her approaching dissolution are calculated to soothe and comfort the minds of mourning connections. They greatly alleviate the regret occasioned by her absence at this awful period. Her elopement can be equalled only by the infatuation which caused her ruin.

"But let no one reproach her memory.
Her life has paid the forfeit of her folly.
Let that suffice."

I am told that Major Sanford is quite frantic. Sure I am that he has reason to be. If the mischiefs he has brought upon others return upon his own head, dreadful indeed must be his portion. His wife has left him, and returned to her parents. His estate, which has been long mortgaged, is taken from him, and poverty and disgrace await him. Heaven seldom leaves injured innocence unavenged. Wretch that he is, he ought forever to be banished from human society! I shall continue with Mrs. Wharton till the lenient hand of time has assuaged her sorrows, and then make my promised visit to you. I will bring Eliza's posthumous papers with me when I come to Boston, as I have not time to copy them now.

I foresee, my dear Mrs. Sumner, that this disastrous affair will suspend your enjoyments, as it has mine. But what are our feelings, compared with the pangs which rend a parent's heart? This parent I here behold inhumanly stripped of the best solace of her declining years by the insnaring machinations of a profligate debauchee. Not only the life, but, what was still dearer, the reputation and virtue? of the unfortunate Eliza have fallen victims at the shrine of *libertinism*. Detested be the epithet. Let it henceforth bear its true signature, and candor itself shall call it *lust* and *brutality*. Execrable is the man, however arrayed in magnificence, crowned with wealth, or decorated with the external graces and accomplishments of fashionable life, who shall presume to display them at the expense of virtue and innocence. Sacred name attended with real blessings—blessings too useful and important to be trifled away. My resentment at the base arts which must have been employed to complete the seduction of Eliza I cannot suppress. I wish them to be exposed, and stamped with universal ignominy. Nor do I doubt but you will join with me in execrating the measures by which we have been robbed of so valuable a friend, and *society* of so ornamental a member. I am, &c.,

JULIA GRANBY.

Letter LXXII

TO MR. CHARLES DEIGHTON.
HARTFORD.

Confusion, horror, and despair are the portion of your wretched, unhappy friend. O Deighton, I am undone. Misery irremediable is my future lot. She is gone; yes, she is gone forever. The darling of my soul, the centre of all my wishes and enjoyments, is no more. Cruel fate has snatched her from me, and she is irretrievably lost. I rave, and then reflect; I reflect, and then rave. I have no patience to bear this calamity, nor power to remedy it. Where shall I fly from the upbraidings of my mind, which accuse me as the murderer of my Eliza? I would fly to death, and seek a refuge in the grave; but the forebodings of a retribution to come I cannot away with. O that I had seen her! that I had once more asked her forgiveness! But even that privilege, that consolation, was denied me! The day on which I meant to visit her, most of my property was attached, and, to secure the rest, I was obliged to shut my doors and become a prisoner in my own house. High living, and old debts incurred by extravagance, had reduced the fortune of my wife to very little, and I could not satisfy the clamorous demands of my creditors.

I would have given millions, had I possessed them, to have been at liberty to see, and to have had the power to preserve Eliza from death. But in vain was my anxiety; it could not relieve, it could not liberate me. When I first heard the dreadful tidings of her exit, I believe I acted like a madman; indeed, I am little else now. I have compounded with my creditors, and resigned the whole of my property. Thus that splendor and equipage, to secure which I have sacrificed a virtuous woman, is taken from me. That poverty, the dread of which prevented my forming an honorable connection with an amiable and accomplished girl,—the only one I ever loved,—has fallen with redoubled vengeance upon my guilty head, and I must become a vagabond on the earth.

I shall fly my country as soon as possible. I shall go from every object which reminds me of my departed Eliza; but never, never shall I eradicate from my bosom the idea of her excellence, nor the painful remembrance of the injuries I have done her. Her shade will perpetually haunt me; the image of her—as she appeared when mounting the carriage which conveyed her forever from my sight, waving her hand in token of a last adieu—will always be present to my imagination; the solemn counsel she gave me before we parted, never more to meet, will not cease to resound in my ears.

While my being is prolonged, I must feel the disgraceful and torturing effects of my guilt in seducing her. How madly have I deprived her of happiness, of reputation, of life! Her friends, could they know the pangs of contrition and the horrors of conscience which attend me, would be amply revenged.

It is said she quitted the world with composure and peace. Well she might. She had not that insupportable weight of iniquity which sinks me to despair. She found consolation in that religion which I have ridiculed as priestcraft and hypocrisy. But, whether it be true or false, would to Heaven I could now enjoy the comforts which its votaries evidently feel.

My wife has left me. As we lived together without love, we parted without regret.

Now, Charles, I am to bid you a long, perhaps a last farewell. Where I shall roam in future, I neither know nor care. I shall go where the name of Sanford is unknown, and his person and sorrows unnoticed.

In this happy clime I have nothing to induce my stay. I have not money to support me with my profligate companions, nor have I any relish, at present, for their society. By the virtuous part of the community I am shunned as the pest and bane of social enjoyment. In short, I am debarred from every kind of happiness. If I look back, I recoil with horror from the black catalogue of vices which have stained my past life, and reduced me to indigence and contempt. If I look forward, I shudder at the prospects which my foreboding mind presents to view both in this and a coming world. This is a deplorable, yet just, picture of myself. How totally the reverse of what I once appeared!

Let it warn you, my friend, to shun the dangerous paths which I have trodden, that you may never be involved in the hopeless ignominy and wretchedness of

PETER SANFORD.

Letter LXIII

TO MISS JULIA GRANBY.
BOSTON.

A melancholy tale have you unfolded, my dear Julia; and tragic indeed is the concluding scene.

Is she then gone? gone in this most distressing manner? Have I lost my once-loved friend? lost her in a way which I could never have conceived to be possible?

Our days of childhood were spent together in the same pursuits, in the same amusements. Our riper years increased our mutual affection, and maturer judgment most firmly cemented our friendship. Can I, then, calmly resign her to so severe a fate? Can I bear the idea of her being lost to honor, to fame, and to life? No; she shall still live in the heart of her faithful Lucy, whose experience of her numerous virtues and engaging qualities has imprinted her image too deeply on the memory to be obliterated. However she may have erred, her sincere repentance is sufficient to restore her to charity.

Your letter gave me the first information of this awful event. I had taken a short excursion into the country, where I had not seen the papers, or, if I had, paid little or no attention to them. By your directions I found the distressing narrative of her exit. The poignancy of my grief, and the unavailing lamentations which the intelligence excited, need no delineation. To scenes of this nature you have been habituated in the mansion of sorrow where you reside.

How sincerely I sympathize with the bereaved parent of the dear, deceased Eliza, I can feel, but have not power to express. Let it be her consolation that her child is at rest. The resolution which carried this deluded wanderer thus far from her friends, and supported her through her various trials, is astonishing. Happy would it have been had she exerted an equal degree of fortitude in repelling the first attacks upon her virtue. But she is no more, and Heaven forbid that I should accuse or reproach her.

Yet in what language shall I express my abhorrence of the monster whose detestable arts have blasted one of the fairest flowers in creation? I leave him to God and his own conscience. Already is he exposed in his true colors. Vengeance already begins to overtake him. His sordid mind must now suffer the deprivation of those sensual gratifications beyond which he is incapable of enjoyment.

Upon your reflecting and steady mind, my dear Julia, I need not inculcate the lessons which may be drawn from this woe-fraught tale; but for the sake of my sex in general, I wish it engraved upon every heart, that virtue alone, independent of the trappings of wealth, the parade of equipage, and the adulation of gallantry, can secure lasting felicity. From the melancholy story of Eliza Wharton let the American fair learn to reject with disdain every insinuation derogatory to their true dignity and honor. Let them despise and forever banish the man who can glory in the seduction of innocence and the ruin of reputation. To associate is to approve; to approve is to be betrayed.

I am, &c.,

LUCY SUMNER.

Letter LXXIV

TO MRS. M. WHARTON.
BOSTON.

Dear madam: We have paid the last tribute of respect to your beloved daughter. The day after my arrival, Mrs. Sumner proposed that we should visit the sad spot which contains the remains of our once amiable friend. "The grave of Eliza Wharton," said she, "shall not be unbedewed by the tears of friendship."

Yesterday we went accordingly, and were much pleased with the apparent sincerity of the people in their assurances that every thing in their power had been done to render her situation comfortable. The minutest circumstances were faithfully related; and, from the state of her mind in her last hours, I think much comfort may be derived to her afflicted friends.

We spent a mournful hour in the place where she is interred, and then returned to the inn, while Mrs. Sumner gave orders for a decent stone to be erected over her grave, with the following inscription:—

> THIS HUMBLE STONE, IN MEMORY OF ELIZA WHARTON, IS INSCRIBED BY HER WEEPING FRIENDS, TO WHOM SHE ENDEARED HERSELF BY UNCOMMON TENDERNESS AND AFFECTION. ENDOWED WITH SUPERIOR ACQUIREMENTS, SHE WAS STILL MORE DISTINGUISHED BY HUMILITY AND BENEVOLENCE. LET CANDOR THROW A VEIL OVER HER FRAILTIES, FOR GREAT WAS HER CHARITY TO OTHERS. SHE SUSTAINED THE LAST PAINFUL SCENE FAR FROM EVERY FRIEND, AND EXHIBITED AN EXAMPLE OF CALM RESIGNATION. HER DEPARTURE WAS ON THE 25TH DAY OF JULY, A.D.——, IN THE 37TH YEAR OF HER AGE; AND THE TEARS OF STRANGERS WATERED HER GRAVE.

I hope, madam, that you will derive satisfaction from these exertions of friendship, and that, united to the many other sources of consolation with which you are furnished, they may alleviate your grief, and, while they leave the pleasing remembrance of her virtues, add the supporting persuasion that your Eliza is happy.

I am, &c.,

JULIA GRANBY.

3.16.2 Reading and Review Questions

1. By whose perspective do we judge Eliza Wharton's character? Why? How does the epistolary genre contribute to this perspective?
2. What is Eliza's place in society, and why? Who supports her, and why? How do they communicate with, or for, her?
3. How liberated, or free, is Eliza Wharton? How do you know?
4. What are the forces, if any, that constrain Eliza, and why?
5. How, if at all, is Eliza's rebelliousness and desire for freedom confused with immorality? Why?

3.17 TECUMSEH

(1768–1813)

Tecumseh was born a Shawnee in what is now Ohio. His father was a Shawnee chief who fought white settlers and died in the Battle of Point Pleasant (1774). Tecumseh, too, would fight the ever-increasing westward expansion of white settlement. In 1811, William Henry Harrison (1773–1841) would describe Tecumseh to then secretary of war William Eustis (1753–1825) as an "uncommon genius" capable of founding an empire. Tecumseh's brother Tenskwatawa (c. 1775–1836), known as the Prophet, would also caution against Native American assimilation to white culture.

Image 3.25 | Tecumseh
Artist | Unknown
Source | Wikimedia Commons
License | Public Domain

In 1809, the Shawnees ceded huge tracts of their land to the United States. Tecumseh had already declared his view that such cession of land by one tribe was illegal without the consent of all other tribes. He responded to his tribe's cession of land by forming a multi-tribal alliance, a great confederation intended to stem the tide of white settlement. Tecumseh gave his *Speech to the Osage* as part of this unifying effort. With careful rhetoric, it persuades its audience of their commonality, of their all being children of the Great Spirit and enemies of the whites.

To add to the forces he already gathered, Tecumseh traveled in the south, leaving Tenskwatawa to act as leader. During Tecumseh's absence, Tenskwatawa's forces were attacked and defeated by Harrison at the Battle of Tippecanoe (1811). Harrison would later successfully use this victory over the Native Americans when running for president, with John Tyler as his vice-president, under the slogan "Tippecanoe and Tyler, too!"

After Tippecanoe, Tecumseh failed in subsequent attempts to unite tribes to defend their way of life against the whites. He fought with the British in the War of 1812 and was killed in the Battle of the Thames, near Thamesville, Ontario.

Tecumseh's *Speech to the Osages* was recorded in John Dunn Hunter's (1798–1827) *Memoirs of a Captivity among the Indians of North America* (1823). Dunn claimed to have heard this deeply-moving speech when he was ten years old. He lived as an Osage captive for fourteen years, publishing his memoir seven years after his release. Authentic or not, it is not unusual for a Native American's words or speech to be filtered (as this speech is) through whites.

3.17.1 Speech to the Osages

(1811, published 1823)

http://www.historyisaweapon.com/defcon1/tecumosages.html

3.17.2 Reading and Review Questions

1. Why does Tecumseh repeat the word "brothers," and to what effect?
2. By what means does Tecumseh create a sense of unity among the disparate tribes listening to his speech?
3. How does Tecumseh differentiate Native Americans from white people, and to what effect?
4. What temptations do the white people offer that Tecumseh exhorts Native Americans to resist?
5. On what grounds and by what means does Tecumseh foresee Native Americans' victory over white people?

3.18 CHEROKEE WOMEN

On September 8, 1787, Katteuha and three other Cherokee women sent a letter to Benjamin Franklin, then the Pennsylvania governor and delegate to the Constitutional Convention, asking him to encourage peace between their nations. In the matrilineal Cherokee social structure, women held considerable familial, economic, and political power. They had control over children and property, and they had key roles in councils and ceremonies. The highest position a Cherokee woman could attain was that of ghighua or Beloved Woman, and it is that position that entitles Ketteuha to act as Cherokee ambassador to the nascent United States. Women's power within the tribe was grounded in their connection to nature and childbirth; the latter is particularly emphasized in Katteuha's construction of her *ethos*. Unfortunately, Franklin essentially disregarded the communication, perhaps too fixed within his own culture's assumptions about female power.

Image 3.26 | Benjamin Franklin, 1767
Artist | David Martin
Source | Wikimedia Commons
License | Public Domain

Image 3.27 | Portrait of a Cherokee Woman
Artist | Edward Troye
Source | Wikimedia Commons
License | Public Domain

3.18.1 Cherokee Indian Women To Pres. Benjamin Franklin, September 8, 1787

Brother,

I am in hopes my Brothers & the Beloved men near the water side will heare from me. This day I filled the pipes that they smoaked in piece, and I am in hopes the smoake has Reached up to the skies above. I here send you a piece of the same Tobacco, and am in hope you & your Beloved men will smoake it in Friendship—and I am glad in my heart that I am the mother of men that will smoak it in piece.

Brother,

I am in hopes if you Rightly consider it that woman is the mother of All—and that woman Does not pull Children out of Trees or Stumps nor out od old Logs, but out of their Bodies, so that they ought to mind what a woman says, and look upon her as a mother—and I have Taken the privilege to Speak to you as my own Children, & the same as if you had sucked my Breast—and I am in hopes you have a beloved woman amongst you who will help to put her Children Right if they do wrong, as I shall do the same—the great men have all promised to Keep the path clear & straight, as my Children shall Keep the path clear & white so that the Messengers shall go & come in safety Between us—the old people is never done Talking to their Children—which makes me say so much as I do. The Talk you sent to me was to talk to my Children, which I have done this day, and they all liked my Talk well, which I am in hopes you will heare from me Every now & then that I keep my Children in piece—tho' I am a woman giving you this Talk, I am in hopes that you and all the Beloved men in Congress will pay particular Attention to it, as I am Delivering it to you from the Bottom of my heart, that they will Lay this on the white stool in Congress, wishing them all well & success in all their undertakings—I hold fast the good Talk I Received from you my Brother, & thanks you kindly for your good Talks, & your presents, & the kind usage you gave to my son.

From,
Katteuha
The Beloved woman of Chota

3.18.2 Reading and Review Questions

1. Why does this piece suggest women, let alone Cherokee women, should be listened to? How revolutionary or unconventional are its arguments?
2. What qualities characterize the authors of this letter, that is, Katteuha and the three other Cherokee women? How do you know?
3. What aspects of Cherokee culture can you discern from this letter?
4. Why is this letter sent by a group of women, rather than just one woman? To what effect?
5. What awareness of Benjamin Franklin's personality and/or culture does this letter reveal? How do you know?

3.19 CHARLES BROCKDEN BROWN

(1771–1810)

Charles Brockden Brown was born into a Quaker family in Philadelphia. He studied at the Friends Latin School in Philadelphia then learned law in a Philadelphia law office. However, he turned away from the practice of law due to moral repugnance and focused instead on making a living as a writer. He had literary ambitions from his youth onwards, including projecting poems on explorers of the New World.

Image 3.28 | Charles Brockden Brown
Artist | Unknown
Source | Wikimedia Commons
License | Public Domain

He found inspiration for writing through a circle of friends in New York City, where he lived from the 1790s onward. These friends included Timothy Dwight (1752–1817), a future president of Yale, and Noah Webster (1758–1843), the lexicographer. Brown was also influenced by the shift from the Age of Reason to early Romanticism occurring with contemporary British authors, particularly William Godwin (1756–1836), a radical political philosopher and Gothic novelist, and Mary Wollstonecraft (1759–1797), a women's rights advocate, novelist, and historian. The latter's influence appears in Brown's *Alcuin; a dialogue* (1798) which advocated women's equality and place in the public sphere, rather than only the domestic or private sphere. Godwin's influence may appear in the Gothic bent of Brown's work, which, though grounded in concrete reality, expands into Gothic extravagance and the irrational.

Starting in 1798, Brown published seven novels in four years, the most well-known of these being *Weiland*, a fictionalization of an actual Pennsylvania murder case. These works use American settings, stories, and events, including Native Americans, the American frontier, and a yellow fever epidemic in Philadelphia. They also include the uncanny, the mysterious, the psychotic, and the unconscious (or a mind not at one with itself). The titular character of *The Memoirs of Carwin the Biloquist*, for example, uses ventriloquism to suggest supernatural visitations of the dead. Brown thus serves as forerunner for Edgar Allen Poe, Nathaniel Hawthorne, and Herman Melville.

Brown relied for a living more pragmatically on journalistic writing, editing *The Monthly Magazine and American Review* (1799–1800), *The Literary Magazine and American Register* (1803–1807), and *The American Register and General Repository of History, Politics, and Science* (1807–1810).

3.19.1 *Memoirs of Carwin the Biloquist* (1805)

Chapter I

I was the second son of a farmer, whose place of residence was a western district of Pennsylvania. My eldest brother seemed fitted by nature for the employment to which he was destined. His wishes never led him astray from the hay-stack and the furrow. His ideas never ranged beyond the sphere of his vision, or suggested the possibility that to-morrow could differ from to-day. He could read and write, because he had no alternative between learning the lesson prescribed to him, and punishment. He was diligent, as long as fear urged him forward, but his exertions ceased with the cessation of this motive. The limits of his acquirements consisted in signing his name, and spelling out a chapter in the bible.

My character was the reverse of his. My thirst of knowledge was augmented in proportion as it was supplied with gratification. The more I heard or read, the more restless and unconquerable my curiosity became. My senses were perpetually alive to novelty, my fancy teemed with visions of the future, and my attention fastened upon every thing mysterious or unknown.

My father intended that my knowledge should keep pace with that of my brother, but conceived that all beyond the mere capacity to write and read was useless or pernicious. He took as much pains to keep me within these limits, as to make the acquisitions of my brother come up to them, but his efforts were not equally successful in both cases. The most vigilant and jealous scrutiny was exerted in vain: Reproaches and blows, painful privations and ignominious penances had no power to slacken my zeal and abate my perseverance. He might enjoin upon me the most laborious tasks, set the envy of my brother to watch me during the performance, make the most diligent search after my books, and destroy them without mercy, when they were found; but he could not outroot my darling propensity. I exerted all my powers to elude his watchfulness. Censures and stripes were sufficiently unpleasing to make me strive to avoid them. To effect this desirable end, I was incessantly employed in the invention of stratagems and the execution of expedients.

My passion was surely not deserving of blame, and I have frequently lamented the hardships to which it subjected me; yet, perhaps, the claims which were made upon my ingenuity and fortitude were not without beneficial effects upon my character.

This contention lasted from the sixth to the fourteenth year of my age. My father's opposition to my schemes was incited by a sincere though unenlightened desire for my happiness. That all his efforts were secretly eluded or obstinately repelled, was a source of the bitterest regret. He has often lamented, with tears, what he called my incorrigible depravity, and encouraged himself to perseverance by the notion of the ruin that would inevitably overtake me if I were allowed to persist in my present career. Perhaps the sufferings which arose to him from the disappointment, were equal to those which he inflicted on me.

In my fourteenth year, events happened which ascertained my future destiny. One evening I had been sent to bring cows from a meadow, some miles distant from my father's mansion. My time was limited, and I was menaced with severe chastisement if, according to my custom, I should stay beyond the period assigned.

For some time these menaces rung in my ears, and I went on my way with speed. I arrived at the meadow, but the cattle had broken the fence and escaped. It was my duty to carry home the earliest tidings of this accident, but the first suggestion was to examine the cause and manner of this escape. The field was bounded by cedar railing. Five of these rails were laid horizontally from post to post. The upper one had been broken in the middle, but the rest had merely been drawn out of the holes on one side, and rested with their ends on the ground. The means which had been used for this end, the reason why one only was broken, and that one the uppermost, how a pair of horns could be so managed as to effect that which the hands of man would have found difficult, supplied a theme of meditation.

Some accident recalled me from this reverie, and reminded me how much time had thus been consumed. I was terrified at the consequences of my delay, and sought with eagerness how they might be obviated. I asked myself if there were not a way back shorter than that by which I had come. The beaten road was rendered circuitous by a precipice that projected into a neighbouring stream, and closed up a passage by which the length of the way would have been diminished one half: at the foot of the cliff the water was of considerable depth, and agitated by an eddy. I could not estimate the danger which I should incur by plunging into it, but I was resolved to make the attempt. I have reason to think, that this experiment, if it had been tried, would have proved fatal, and my father, while he lamented my untimely fate, would have been wholly unconscious that his own unreasonable demands had occasioned it.

I turned my steps towards the spot. To reach the edge of the stream was by no means an easy undertaking, so many abrupt points and gloomy hollows were interposed. I had frequently skirted and penetrated this tract, but had never been so completely entangled in the maze as now: hence I had remained unacquainted with a narrow pass, which, at the distance of an hundred yards from the river, would conduct me, though not without danger and toil, to the opposite side of the ridge.

This glen was now discovered, and this discovery induced me to change my plan. If a passage could be here effected, it would be shorter and safer than that which led through the stream, and its practicability was to be known only by experiment. The path was narrow, steep, and overshadowed by rocks. The sun was nearly set, and the shadow of the cliff above, obscured the passage almost as much as midnight would have done: I was accustomed to despise danger when it presented itself in a sensible form, but, by a defect common in every one's education, goblins and spectres were to me the objects of the most violent apprehensions. These were unavoidably connected with solitude and darkness, and were present to my fears when I entered this gloomy recess.

These terrors are always lessened by calling the attention away to some indifferent object. I now made use of this expedient, and began to amuse myself by hallowing as loud as organs of unusual compass and vigour would enable me. I uttered the words which chanced to occur to me, and repeated in the shrill tones of a Mohock savage . . . "Cow! cow! come home! home!" . . . These notes were of course reverberated from the rocks which on either side towered aloft, but the echo was confused and indistinct.

I continued, for some time, thus to beguile the way, till I reached a space more than commonly abrupt, and which required all my attention. My rude ditty was suspended till I had surmounted this impediment. In a few minutes I was at leisure to renew it. After finishing the strain, I paused. In a few seconds a voice as I then imagined, uttered the same cry from the point of a rock some hundred feet behind me; the same words, with equal distinctness and deliberation, and in the same tone, appeared to be spoken. I was startled by this incident, and cast a fearful glance behind, to discover by whom it was uttered. The spot where I stood was buried in dusk, but the eminences were still invested with a luminous and vivid twilight. The speaker, however, was concealed from my view.

I had scarcely begun to wonder at this occurrence, when a new occasion for wonder, was afforded me. A few seconds, in like manner, elapsed, when my ditty was again rehearsed, with a no less perfect imitation, in a different quarter . . . . . To this quarter I eagerly turned my eyes, but no one was visible . . . . The station, indeed, which this new speaker seemed to occupy, was inaccessible to man or beast.

If I were surprized at this second repetition of my words, judge how much my surprise must have been augmented, when the same calls were a third time repeated, and coming still in a new direction. Five times was this ditty successively resounded, at intervals nearly equal, always from a new quarter, and with little abatement of its original distinctness and force.

A little reflection was sufficient to shew that this was no more than an echo of an extraordinary kind. My terrors were quickly supplanted by delight. The motives to dispatch were forgotten, and I amused myself for an hour, with talking to these cliffs: I placed myself in new positions, and exhausted my lungs and my invention in new clamours.

The pleasures of this new discovery were an ample compensation for the ill treatment which I expected on my return. By some caprice in my father I escaped merely with a few reproaches. I seized the first opportunity of again visiting this recess, and repeating my amusement; time, and incessant repetition, could scarcely lessen its charms or exhaust the variety produced by new tones and new positions.

The hours in which I was most free from interruption and restraint were those of moonlight. My brother and I occupied a small room above the kitchen, disconnected, in some degree, with the rest of the house. It was the rural custom to retire early to bed and to anticipate the rising of the sun. When the moonlight was strong enough to permit me to read, it was my custom to escape from bed, and hie with my book to some neighbouring eminence, where I would remain stretched on the mossy rock, till the sinking or beclouded moon, forbade me to continue my employment. I was indebted for books to a friendly person in the neighbourhood, whose compliance with my solicitations was prompted partly by benevolence and partly by enmity to my father, whom he could not more egregiously offend than by gratifying my perverse and pernicious curiosity.

In leaving my chamber I was obliged to use the utmost caution to avoid rousing my brother, whose temper disposed him to thwart me in the least of my gratifications. My purpose was surely laudable, and yet on leaving the house and returning to it, I was obliged to use the vigilance and circumspection of a thief.

One night I left my bed with this view. I posted first to my vocal glen, and thence scrambling up a neighbouring steep, which overlooked a wide extent of this romantic country, gave myself up to contemplation, and the perusal of Milton's Comus.

My reflections were naturally suggested by the singularity of this echo. To hear my own voice speak at a distance would have been formerly regarded as prodigious. To hear too, that voice, not uttered by another, by whom it might easily be mimicked, but by myself! I cannot now recollect the transition which led me to the notion of sounds, similar to these, but produced by other means than reverberation. Could I not so dispose my organs as to make my voice appear at a distance?

From speculation I proceeded to experiment. The idea of a distant voice, like my own, was intimately present to my fancy. I exerted myself with a most ardent desire, and with something like a persuasion that I should succeed. I started with surprise, for it seemed as if success had crowned my attempts. I repeated the effort, but failed. A certain position of the organs took place on the first attempt, altogether new, unexampled and as it were, by accident, for I could not attain it on the second experiment.

You will not wonder that I exerted myself with indefatigable zeal to regain what had once, though for so short a space, been in my power. Your own ears have witnessed the success of these efforts. By perpetual exertion I gained it a second time, and now was a diligent observer of the circumstances attending it. Gradually I subjected these finer and more subtle motions to the command of my will. What was at first difficult, by exercise and habit, was rendered easy. I learned to accommodate my voice to all the varieties of distance and direction.

It cannot be denied that this faculty is wonderful and rare, but when we consider the possible modifications of muscular motion, how few of these are usually exerted, how imperfectly they are subjected to the will, and yet that the will is capable of being rendered unlimited and absolute, will not our wonder cease?

We have seen men who could hide their tongues so perfectly that even an Anatomist, after the most accurate inspection that a living subject could admit, has affirmed the organ to be wanting, but this was effected by the exertion of muscles unknown and incredible to the greater part of mankind.

The concurrence of teeth, palate and tongue, in the formation of speech should seem to be indispensable, and yet men have spoken distinctly though wanting a tongue, and to whom, therefore, teeth and palate were superfluous. The tribe of motions requisite to this end, are wholly latent and unknown, to those who possess that organ.

I mean not to be more explicit. I have no reason to suppose a peculiar conformation or activity in my own organs, or that the power which I possess may not, with suitable directions and by steady efforts, be obtained by others, but I will do nothing to facilitate the acquisition. It is by far, too liable to perversion for a good man to desire to possess it, or to teach it to another.

There remained but one thing to render this instrument as powerful in my hands as it was capable of being. From my childhood, I was remarkably skilful at imitation. There were few voices whether of men or birds or beasts which I could not imitate with success. To add my ancient, to my newly acquired skill, to talk from a distance, and at the same time, in the accents of another, was the object of my endeavours, and this object, after a certain number of trials, I finally obtained.

In my present situation every thing that denoted intellectual exertion was a crime, and exposed me to invectives if not to stripes. This circumstance induced me to be silent to all others, on the subject of my discovery. But, added to this, was a confused belief, that it might be made, in some way instrumental to my relief from the hardships and restraints of my present condition. For some time I was not aware of the mode in which it might be rendered subservient to this end.

Chapter II

My father's sister was an ancient lady, resident in Philadelphia, the relict of a merchant, whose decease left her the enjoyment of a frugal competence. She was without children, and had often expressed her desire that her nephew Frank, whom she always considered as a sprightly and promising lad, should be put under her care. She offered to be at the expense of my education, and to bequeath to me at her death her slender patrimony.

This arrangement was obstinately rejected by my father, because it was merely fostering and giving scope to propensities, which he considered as hurtful, and because his avarice desired that this inheritance should fall to no one but himself. To me, it was a scheme of ravishing felicity, and to be debarred from it was a source of anguish known to few. I had too much experience of my father's pertinaciousness ever to hope for a change in his views; yet the bliss of living with my aunt, in a new and busy scene, and in the unbounded indulgence of my literary passion, continually occupied my thoughts: for a long time these thoughts were productive only of despondency and tears.

Time only enhanced the desirableness of this scheme; my new faculty would naturally connect itself with these wishes, and the question could not fail to occur whether it might not aid me in the execution of my favourite plan.

A thousand superstitious tales were current in the family. Apparitions had been seen, and voices had been heard on a multitude of occasions. My father was a confident believer in supernatural tokens. The voice of his wife, who had been many years dead, had been twice heard at midnight whispering at his pillow. I frequently asked myself whether a scheme favourable to my views might not be built upon these foundations. Suppose (thought I) my mother should be made to enjoin upon him compliance with my wishes?

This idea bred in me a temporary consternation. To imitate the voice of the dead, to counterfeit a commission from heaven, bore the aspect of presumption and impiety. It seemed an offence which could not fail to draw after it the vengeance of the deity. My wishes for a time yielded to my fears, but this scheme in proportion as I meditated on it, became more plausible; no other occurred to me so easy and so efficacious. I endeavoured to persuade myself that the end proposed, was, in the highest degree praiseworthy, and that the excellence of my purpose would justify the means employed to attain it.

My resolutions were, for a time, attended with fluctuations and misgivings. These gradually disappeared, and my purpose became firm; I was next to devise the means of effecting my views, this did not demand any tedious deliberation. It was easy to gain access to my father's chamber without notice or detection, cautious footsteps and the suppression of breath would place me, unsuspected and unthought of, by his bed side. The words I should use, and the mode of utterance were not easily settled, but having at length selected these, I made myself by much previous repetition, perfectly familiar with the use of them.

I selected a blustering and inclement night, in which the darkness was augmented by a veil of the blackest clouds. The building we inhabited was slight in its structure, and full of crevices through which the gale found easy way, and whistled in a thousand cadences. On this night the elemental music was remarkably sonorous, and was mingled not unfrequently with *thunder heard remote*.

I could not divest myself of secret dread. My heart faultered with a consciousness of wrong. Heaven seemed to be present and to disapprove my work; I listened to the thunder and the wind, as to the stern voice of this disapprobation. Big drops stood on my forehead, and my tremors almost incapacitated me from proceeding.

These impediments however I surmounted; I crept up stairs at midnight, and entered my father's chamber. The darkness was intense and I sought with outstretched hands for his bed. The darkness, added to the trepidation of my thoughts, disabled me from making a right estimate of distances: I was conscious of this, and when I advanced within the room, paused.

I endeavoured to compare the progress I had made with my knowledge of the room, and governed by the result of this comparison, proceeded cautiously and with hands still outstretched in search of the foot of the bed. At this moment lightning flashed into the room: the brightness of the gleam was dazzling, yet it afforded me an exact knowledge of my situation. I had mistaken my way, and discovered that my knees nearly touched the bedstead, and that my hands at the next step, would have touched my father's cheek. His closed eyes and every line in his countenance, were painted, as it were, for an instant on my sight.

The flash was accompanied with a burst of thunder, whose vehemence was stunning. I always entertained a dread of thunder, and now recoiled, overborne with terror. Never had I witnessed so luminous a gleam and so tremendous a shock, yet my father's slumber appeared not to be disturbed by it.

I stood irresolute and trembling; to prosecute my purpose in this state of mind was impossible. I resolved for the present to relinquish it, and turned with a view of exploring my way out of the chamber. Just then a light seen through the window, caught my eye. It was at first weak but speedily increased; no second thought was necessary to inform me that the barn, situated at a small distance from the house, and newly stored with hay, was in flames, in consequence of being struck by the lightning.

My terror at this spectacle made me careless of all consequences relative to myself. I rushed to the bed and throwing myself on my father, awakened him by loud cries. The family were speedily roused, and were compelled to remain impotent spectators of the devastation. Fortunately the wind blew in a contrary direction, so that our habitation was not injured.

The impression that was made upon me by the incidents of that night is indelible. The wind gradually rose into an hurricane; the largest branches were torn from the trees, and whirled aloft into the air; others were uprooted and laid prostrate on the ground. The barn was a spacious edifice, consisting wholly of wood, and filled with a plenteous harvest. Thus supplied with fuel, and fanned by the wind, the fire raged with incredible fury; meanwhile clouds rolled above, whose blackness was rendered more conspicuous by reflection from the flames; the vast volumes of smoke were dissipated in a moment by the storm, while glowing fragments and cinders were borne to an immense hight, and tossed everywhere in wild confusion. Ever and anon the sable canopy that hung around us was streaked with lightning, and the peals, by which it was accompanied, were deafning, and with scarcely any intermission.

It was, doubtless, absurd to imagine any connexion between this portentous scene and the purpose that I had meditated, yet a belief of this connexion, though wavering and obscure, lurked in my mind; something more than a coincidence merely casual, appeared to have subsisted between my situation, at my father's bed side, and the flash that darted through the window, and diverted me from my design. It palsied my courage, and strengthened my conviction, that my scheme was criminal.

After some time had elapsed, and tranquility was, in some degree, restored in the family, my father reverted to the circumstances in which I had been discovered on the first alarm of this event. The truth was impossible to be told. I felt the utmost reluctance to be guilty of a falsehood, but by falsehood only could I elude detection. That my guilt was the offspring of a fatal necessity, that the injustice of others gave it birth and made it unavoidable, afforded me slight consolation. Nothing can be more injurious than a lie, but its evil tendency chiefly respects our future conduct. Its direct consequences may be transient and few, but it facilitates a repetition, strengthens temptation, and grows into habit. I pretended some necessity had drawn me from my bed, and that discovering the condition of the barn, I hastened to inform my father.

Some time after this, my father summoned me to his presence. I had been previously guilty of disobedience to his commands, in a matter about which he was usually very scrupulous. My brother had been privy to my offence, and had threatened to be my accuser. On this occasion I expected nothing but arraignment and punishment. Weary of oppression, and hopeless of any change in my father's temper and views, I had formed the resolution of eloping from his house, and of trusting, young as I was, to the caprice of fortune. I was hesitating whether to abscond without the knowledge of the family, or to make my resolutions known to them, and while I avowed my resolution, to adhere to it in spite of opposition and remonstrances, when I received this summons.

I was employed at this time in the field; night was approaching, and I had made no preparation for departure; all the preparation in my power to make, was indeed small; a few clothes, made into a bundle, was the sum of my possessions. Time would have little influence in improving my prospects, and I resolved to execute my scheme immediately.

I left my work intending to seek my chamber, and taking what was my own, to disappear forever. I turned a stile that led out of the field into a bye path, when my father appeared before me, advancing in an opposite direction; to avoid him was impossible, and I summoned my fortitude to a conflict with his passion.

As soon as we met, instead of anger and upbraiding, he told me, that he had been reflecting on my aunt's proposal, to take me under her protection, and had concluded that the plan was proper; if I still retained my wishes on that head, he would readily comply with them, and that, if I chose, I might set off for the city next morning, as a neighbours waggon was preparing to go.

I shall not dwell on the rapture with which this proposal was listened to: it was with difficulty that I persuaded myself that he was in earnest in making it, nor could divine the reasons, for so sudden and unexpected a change in his maxims . . . . These I afterwards discovered. Some one had instilled into him fears, that my aunt exasperated at his opposition to her request, respecting the unfortunate Frank, would bequeath her property to strangers; to obviate this evil, which his avarice prompted him to regard as much greater than any mischief, that would accrue to me, from the change of my abode, he embraced her proposal.

I entered with exultation and triumph on this new scene; my hopes were by no means disappointed. Detested labour was exchanged for luxurious idleness. I was master of my time, and the chuser of my occupations. My kinswoman on discovering that I entertained no relish for the drudgery of colleges, and was contented with the means of intellectual gratification, which I could obtain under her roof, allowed me to pursue my own choice.

Three tranquil years passed away, during which, each day added to my happiness, by adding to my knowledge. My biloquial faculty was not neglected. I improved it by assiduous exercise; I deeply reflected on the use to which it might be applied. I was not destitute of pure intentions; I delighted not in evil; I was incapable of knowingly contributing to another's misery, but the sole or principal end of my endeavours was not the happiness of others.

I was actuated by ambition. I was delighted to possess superior power; I was prone to manifest that superiority, and was satisfied if this were done, without much solicitude concerning consequences. I sported frequently with the apprehensions of my associates, and threw out a bait for their wonder, and supplied them with occasions for the structure of theories. It may not be amiss to enumerate one or two adventures in which I was engaged.

Chapter III

I had taken much pains to improve the sagacity of a favourite Spaniel. It was my purpose, indeed, to ascertain to what degree of improvement the principles of reasoning and imitation could be carried in a dog. There is no doubt that the animal affixes distinct ideas to sounds. What are the possible limits of his vocabulary no one can tell. In conversing with my dog I did not use English words, but selected simple monosyllables. Habit likewise enabled him to comprehend my gestures. If I crossed my hands on my breast he understood the signal and laid down behind me. If I joined my hands and lifted them to my breast, he returned home. If I grasped one arm above the elbow he ran before me. If I lifted my hand to my forehead he trotted composedly behind. By one motion I could make him bark; by another I could reduce him to silence. He would howl in twenty different strains of mournfulness, at my bidding. He would fetch and carry with undeviating faithfulness.

His actions being thus chiefly regulated by gestures, that to a stranger would appear indifferent or casual, it was easy to produce a belief that the animal's knowledge was much greater than in truth, it was.

One day, in a mixed company, the discourse turned upon the unrivaled abilities of Damon. Damon had, indeed, acquired in all the circles which I frequented, an extraordinary reputation. Numerous instances of his sagacity were quoted and some of them exhibited on the spot. Much surprise was excited by the readiness with which he appeared to comprehend sentences of considerable abstraction and complexity, though, he in reality, attended to nothing but the movements of hand or fingers with which I accompanied my words. I enhanced the astonishment of some and excited the ridicule of others, by observing that my dog not only understood English when spoken by others, but actually spoke the language himself, with no small degree of precision.

This assertion could not be admitted without proof; proof, therefore, was readily produced. At a known signal, Damon began a low interrupted noise, in which the astonished hearers clearly distinguished English words. A dialogue began between the animal and his master, which was maintained, on the part of the former, with great vivacity and spirit. In this dialogue the dog asserted the dignity of his species and capacity of intellectual improvement. The company separated lost in wonder, but perfectly convinced by the evidence that had been produced.

On a subsequent occasion a select company was assembled at a garden, at a small distance from the city. Discourse glided through a variety of topics, till it lighted at length on the subject of invisible beings. From the speculations of philosophers we proceeded to the creations of the poet. Some maintained the justness of Shakspear's delineations of aerial beings, while others denied it. By no violent transition, Ariel and his songs were introduced, and a lady, celebrated for her musical skill, was solicited to accompany her pedal harp with the song of "Five fathom deep thy father lies" . . . She was known to have set, for her favourite instrument, all the songs of Shakspeare.

My youth made me little more than an auditor on this occasion. I sat apart from the rest of the company, and carefully noted every thing. The track which the conversation had taken, suggested a scheme which was not thoroughly digested when the lady began her enchanting strain.

She ended and the audience were mute with rapture. The pause continued, when a strain was wafted to our ears from another quarter. The spot where we sat was embowered by a vine. The verdant arch was lofty and the area beneath was spacious.

The sound proceeded from above. At first it was faint and scarcely audible; presently it reached a louder key, and every eye was cast up in expectation of beholding a face among the pendant clusters. The strain was easily recognized, for it was no other than that which Ariel is made to sing when finally absolved from the service of the wizard.

In the Cowslips bell I lie,
On the Bat's back I do fly . . .
After summer merrily, &c.

Their hearts palpitated as they listened: they gazed at each other for a solution of the mystery. At length the strain died away at distance, and an interval of silence was succeded by an earnest discussion of the cause of this prodigy. One supposition only could be adopted, which was, that the strain was uttered by human organs. That the songster was stationed on the roof of the arbour, and having finished his melody had risen into the viewless fields of air.

I had been invited to spend a week at this house: this period was nearly expired when I received information that my aunt was suddenly taken sick, and that her life was in imminent danger. I immediately set out on my return to the city, but before my arrival she was dead.

This lady was entitled to my gratitude and esteem; I had received the most essential benefits at her hand. I was not destitute of sensibility, and was deeply affected by this event: I will own, however, that my grief was lessened by reflecting on the consequences of her death, with regard to my own condition. I had been ever taught to consider myself as her heir, and her death, therefore, would free me from certain restraints.

My aunt had a female servant, who had lived with her for twenty years: she was married, but her husband, who was an artizan, lived apart from her: I had no reason to suspect the woman's sincerity and disinterestedness; but my aunt was no sooner consigned to the grave than a will was produced, in which Dorothy was named her sole and universal heir.

It was in vain to urge my expectations and my claims . . . . the instrument was legibly and legally drawn up . . . . Dorothy was exasperated by my opposition and surmises, and vigorously enforced her title. In a week after the decease of my kinswoman, I was obliged to seek a new dwelling. As all my property consisted in my cloths and my papers, this was easily done.

My condition was now calamitous and forlorn. Confiding in the acquisition of my aunt's patrimony, I had made no other provision for the future; I hated manual labour, or any task of which the object was gain. To be guided in my choice of occupations by any motive but the pleasure which the occupation was qualified to produce, was intolerable to my proud, indolent, and restive temper.

This resource was now cut off; the means of immediate subsistence were denied me: If I had determined to acquire the knowledge of some lucrative art, the acquisition would demand time, and, meanwhile, I was absolutely destitute of support. My father's house was, indeed, open to me, but I preferred to stifle myself with the filth of the kennel, rather than to return to it.

Some plan it was immediately necessary to adopt. The exigence of my affairs, and this reverse of fortune, continually occupied my thoughts; I estranged myself from society and from books, and devoted myself to lonely walks and mournful meditation.

One morning as I ranged along the bank of Schuylkill, I encountered a person, by name Ludloe, of whom I had some previous knowledge. He was from Ireland; was a man of some rank and apparently rich: I had met with him before, but in mixed companies, where little direct intercourse had taken place between us. Our last meeting was in the arbour where Ariel was so unexpectedly introduced.

Our acquaintance merely justified a transient salutation; but he did not content himself with noticing me as I passed, but joined me in my walk and entered into conversation. It was easy to advert to the occasion on which we had last met, and to the mysterious incident which then occurred. I was solicitous to dive into his thoughts upon this head and put some questions which tended to the point that I wished.

I was somewhat startled when he expressed his belief, that the performer of this mystic strain was one of the company then present, who exerted, for this end, a faculty not commonly possessed. Who this person was he did not venture to guess, and could not discover, by the tokens which he suffered to appear, that his suspicions glanced at me. He expatiated with great profoundness and fertility of ideas, on the uses to which a faculty like this might be employed. No more powerful engine, he said, could be conceived, by which the ignorant and credulous might be moulded to our purposes; managed by a man of ordinary talents, it would open for him the straightest and surest avenues to wealth and power.

His remarks excited in my mind a new strain of thoughts. I had not hitherto considered the subject in this light, though vague ideas of the importance of this art could not fail to be occasionally suggested: I ventured to inquire into his ideas of the mode, in which an art like this could be employed, so as to effect the purposes he mentioned.

He dealt chiefly in general representations. Men, he said, believed in the existence and energy of invisible powers, and in the duty of discovering and conforming to their will. This will was supposed to be sometimes made known to them through the medium of their senses. A voice coming from a quarter where no attendant form could be seen would, in most cases, be ascribed to supernal agency, and a command imposed on them, in this manner, would be obeyed with religious scrupulousness. Thus men might be imperiously directed in the disposal of their industry, their property, and even of their lives. Men, actuated by a mistaken sense of duty, might, under this influence, be led to the commission of the most flagitious, as well as the most heroic acts: If it were his desire to accumulate wealth, or institute a new sect, he should need no other instrument.

I listened to this kind of discourse with great avidity, and regretted when he thought proper to introduce new topics. He ended by requesting me to visit him, which I eagerly consented to do. When left alone, my imagination was filled with the images suggested by this conversation. The hopelessness of better fortune, which I had lately harboured, now gave place to cheering confidence. Those motives of rectitude which should deter me from this species of imposture, had never been vivid or stable, and were still more weakened by the artifices of which

I had already been guilty. The utility or harmlessness of the end, justified, in my eyes, the means.

No event had been more unexpected, by me, than the bequest of my aunt to her servant. The will, under which the latter claimed, was dated prior to my coming to the city. I was not surprised, therefore, that it had once been made, but merely that it had never been cancelled or superseded by a later instrument. My wishes inclined me to suspect the existence of a later will, but I had conceived that, to ascertain its existence, was beyond my power.

Now, however, a different opinion began to be entertained. This woman like those of her sex and class was unlettered and superstitious. Her faith in spells and apparitions, was of the most lively kind. Could not her conscience be awakened by a voice from the grave! Lonely and at midnight, my aunt might be introduced, upbraiding her for her injustice, and commanding her to attone for it by acknowledging the claim of the rightful proprietor.

True it was, that no subsequent will might exist, but this was the fruit of mistake, or of negligence. She probably intended to cancel the old one, but this act might, by her own weakness, or by the artifices of her servant, be delayed till death had put it out of her power. In either case a mandate from the dead could scarcely fail of being obeyed.

I considered this woman as the usurper of my property. Her husband as well as herself, were laborious and covetous; their good fortune had made no change in their mode of living, but they were as frugal and as eager to accumulate as ever. In their hands, money was inert and sterile, or it served to foster their vices. To take it from them would, therefore, be a benefit both to them and to myself; not even an imaginary injury would be inflicted. Restitution, if legally compelled to it, would be reluctant and painful, but if enjoined by Heaven would be voluntary, and the performance of a seeming duty would carry with it, its own reward.

These reasonings, aided by inclination, were sufficient to determine me. I have no doubt but their fallacy would have been detected in the sequel, and my scheme have been productive of nothing but confusion and remorse. From these consequences, however, my fate interposed, as in the former instance, to save me.

Having formed my resolution, many preliminaries to its execution were necessary to be settled. These demanded deliberation and delay; meanwhile I recollected my promise to Ludlow, and paid him a visit. I met a frank and affectionate reception. It would not be easy to paint the delight which I experienced in this man's society. I was at first oppressed with the sense of my own inferiority in age, knowledge and rank. Hence arose numberless reserves and incapacitating diffidences; but these were speedily dissipated by the fascinations of this man's address. His superiority was only rendered, by time, more conspicuous, but this superiority, by appearing never to be present to his own mind, ceased to be uneasy to me. My questions required to be frequently answered, and my mistakes to be rectified; but my keenest scrutiny, could detect in his manner, neither arrogance nor contempt. He seemed to talk merely from the overflow of his ideas, or a benevolent desire of imparting information.

Chapter IV

My visits gradually became more frequent. Meanwhile my wants increased, and the necessity of some change in my condition became daily more urgent. This incited my reflections on the scheme which I had formed. The time and place suitable to my design, were not selected without much anxious inquiry and frequent waverings of purpose. These being at length fixed, the interval to elapse, before the carrying of my design into effect, was not without perturbation and suspense. These could not be concealed from my new friend and at length prompted him to inquire into the cause.

It was not possible to communicate the whole truth; but the warmth of his manner inspired me with some degree of ingenuousness. I did not hide from him my former hopes and my present destitute condition. He listened to my tale with no expressions of sympathy, and when I had finished, abruptly inquired whether I had any objection to a voyage to Europe? I answered in the negative. He then said that he was preparing to depart in a fortnight and advised me to make up my mind to accompany him.

This unexpected proposal gave me pleasure and surprize, but the want of money occurred to me as an insuperable objection. On this being mentioned, Oho! said he, carelessly, that objection is easily removed, I will bear all expenses of your passage myself.

The extraordinary beneficence of this act as well as the air of uncautiousness attending it, made me doubt the sincerity of his offer, and when new declarations removed this doubt, I could not forbear expressing at once my sense of his generosity and of my own unworthiness.

He replied that generosity had been expunged from his catalogue as having no meaning or a vicious one. It was the scope of his exertions to be just. This was the sum of human duty, and he that fell short, ran beside, or outstripped justice was a criminal. What he gave me was my due or not my due. If it were my due, I might reasonably demand it from him and it was wicked to withhold it. Merit on one side or gratitude on the other, were contradictory and unintelligible.

If I were fully convinced that this benefit was not my due and yet received it, he should hold me in contempt. The rectitude of my principles and conduct would be the measure of his approbation, and no benefit should he ever bestow which the receiver was not entitled to claim, and which it would not be criminal in him to refuse.

These principles were not new from the mouth of Ludloe, but they had, hitherto, been regarded as the fruits of a venturous speculation in my mind. I had never traced them into their practical consequences, and if his conduct on this occasion had not squared with his maxims, I should not have imputed to him inconsistency. I did not ponder on these reasonings at this time: objects of immediate importance engrossed my thoughts.

One obstacle to this measure was removed. When my voyage was performed how should I subsist in my new abode? I concealed not my perplexity and he commented on it in his usual manner. How did I mean to subsist, he asked, in my own country? The means of living would be, at least, as much within my reach there as here. As to the pressure of immediate and absolute want, he believed I should be exposed to little hazard. With talents such as mine, I must be hunted by a destiny peculiarly malignant, if I could not provide myself with necessaries wherever my lot were cast.

He would make allowances, however, for my diffidence and self-distrust, and would obviate my fears by expressing his own intentions with regard to me. I must be apprized, however, of his true meaning. He laboured to shun all hurtful and vitious things, and therefore carefully abstained from making or confiding in promises. It was just to assist me in this voyage, and it would probably be equally just to continue to me similar assistance when it was finished. That indeed was a subject, in a great degree, within my own cognizance. His aid would be proportioned to my wants and to my merits, and I had only to take care that my claims were just, for them to be admitted.

This scheme could not but appear to me eligible. I thirsted after an acquaintance with new scenes; my present situation could not be changed for a worse; I trusted to the constancy of Ludloe's friendship; to this at least it was better to trust than to the success of my imposture on Dorothy, which was adopted merely as a desperate expedient: finally I determined to embark with him.

In the course of this voyage my mind was busily employed. There were no other passengers beside ourselves, so that my own condition and the character of Ludloe, continually presented themselves to my reflections. It will be supposed that I was not a vague or indifferent observer.

There were no vicissitudes in the deportment or lapses in the discourse of my friend. His feelings appeared to preserve an unchangeable tenor, and his thoughts and words always to flow with the same rapidity. His slumber was profound and his wakeful hours serene. He was regular and temperate in all his exercises and gratifications. Hence were derived his clear perceptions and exuberant health.

This treatment of me, like all his other mental and corporal operations, was modelled by one inflexible standard. Certain scruples and delicacies were incident to my situation. Of the existence of these he seemed to be unconscious, and yet nothing escaped him inconsistent with a state of absolute equality.

I was naturally inquisitive as to his fortune and the collateral circumstances of his condition. My notions of politeness hindered me from making direct inquiries. By indirect means I could gather nothing but that his state was opulent and independent, and that he had two sisters whose situation resembled his own.

Though, in conversation, he appeared to be governed by the utmost candour; no light was let in upon the former transactions of his life. The purpose of his visit to America I could merely guess to be the gratification of curiosity.

My future pursuits must be supposed chiefly to occupy my attention. On this head I was destitute of all stedfast views. Without profession or habits of industry or sources of permanent revenue, the world appeared to me an ocean on which my bark was set afloat, without compass or sail. The world into which I was about to enter, was untried and unknown, and though I could consent to profit by the guidance I was unwilling to rely on the support of others.

This topic being nearest my heart, I frequently introduced into conversation with my friend; but on this subject he always allowed himself to be led by me, while on all others, he was zealous to point the way. To every scheme that I proposed he was sure to cause objections. All the liberal professions were censured as perverting the understanding, by giving scope to the sordid motive of gain, or embuing the mind with erroneous principles. Skill was slowly obtained, and success, though integrity and independence must be given for it, dubious and instable. The mechanical trades were equally obnoxious; they were vitious by contributing to the spurious gratifications of the rich and multiplying the objects of luxury; they were destruction to the intellect and vigor of the artizan; they enervated his frame and brutalized his mind.

When I pointed out to him the necessity of some species of labour, he tacitly admitted that necessity, but refused to direct me in the choice of a pursuit, which though not free from defect should yet have the fewest inconveniences. He dwelt on the fewness of our actual wants, the temptations which attend the possession of wealth, the benefits of seclusion and privacy, and the duty of unfettering our minds from the prejudices which govern the world.

His discourse tended merely to unsettle my views and increase my perplexity. This effect was so uniform that I at length desisted from all allusions to this theme and endeavoured to divert my own reflections from it. When our voyage should be finished, and I should actually tread this new stage, I believed that I should be better qualified to judge of the measures to be taken by me.

At length we reached Belfast. From thence we immediately repaired to Dublin. I was admitted as a member of his family. When I expressed my uncertainty as to the place to which it would be proper for me to repair, he gave me a blunt but cordial invitation to his house. My circumstances allowed me no option and I readily complied. My attention was for a time engrossed by a diversified succession of new objects. Their novelty however disappearing, left me at liberty to turn my eyes upon myself and my companion, and here my reflections were supplied with abundant food.

His house was spacious and commodious, and furnished with profusion and elegance. A suit of apartments was assigned to me, in which I was permitted to reign uncontroled and access was permitted to a well furnished library. My food was furnished in my own room, prepared in the manner which I had previously directed. Occasionally Ludloe would request my company to breakfast, when an hour was usually consumed in earnest or sprightly conversation. At all other times he was invisible, and his apartments, being wholly separate from mine, I had no opportunity of discovering in what way his hours were employed.

He defended this mode of living as being most compatible with liberty. He delighted to expatiate on the evils of cohabitation. Men, subjected to the same regimen, compelled to eat and sleep and associate at certain hours, were strangers to all rational independence and liberty. Society would never be exempt from servitude and misery, till those artificial ties which held human beings together under the same roof were dissolved. He endeavoured to regulate his own conduct in pursuance of these principles, and to secure to himself as much freedom as the present regulations of society would permit. The same independence which he claimed for himself he likewise extended to me. The distribution of my own time, the selection of my own occupations and companions should belong to myself.

But these privileges, though while listening to his arguments I could not deny them to be valuable, I would have willingly dispensed with. The solitude in which I lived became daily more painful. I ate and drank, enjoyed clothing and shelter, without the exercise of forethought or industry; I walked and sat, went out and returned for as long and at what seasons I thought proper, yet my condition was a fertile source of discontent.

I felt myself removed to a comfortless and chilling distance from Ludloe. I wanted to share in his occupations and views. With all his ingenuousness of aspect and overflow of thoughts, when he allowed me his company, I felt myself painfully bewildered with regard to his genuine condition and sentiments.

He had it in his power to introduce me to society, and without an introduction, it was scarcely possible to gain access to any social circle or domestic fireside. Add to this, my own obscure prospects and dubious situation. Some regular intellectual pursuit would render my state less irksome, but I had hitherto adopted no scheme of this kind.

Chapter V

Time tended, in no degree, to alleviate my dissatisfaction. It increased till the determination became at length formed of opening my thoughts to Ludloe. At the next breakfast interview which took place, I introduced the subject, and expatiated without reserve, on the state of my feelings. I concluded with entreating him to point out some path in which my talents might be rendered useful to himself or to mankind.

After a pause of some minutes, he said, What would you do? You forget the immaturity of your age. If you are qualified to act a part in the theatre of life, step forth; but you are not qualified. You want knowledge, and with this you ought previously to endow yourself . . . . . Means, for this end, are within your reach. Why should you waste your time in idleness, and torment yourself with unprofitable wishes? Books are at hand . . . . books from which most sciences and languages can be learned. Read, analise, digest; collect facts, and investigate theories: ascertain the dictates of reason, and supply yourself with the inclination and the power to adhere to them. You will not, legally speaking, be a man in less than three years. Let this period be devoted to the acquisition of wisdom. Either stay here, or retire to an house I have on the banks of Killarney, where you will find all the conveniences of study.

I could not but reflect with wonder at this man's treatment of me. I could plead none of the rights of relationship; yet I enjoyed the privileges of a son. He had not imparted to me any scheme, by pursuit of which I might finally compensate him for the expense to which my maintenance and education would subject him. He gave me reason to hope for the continuance of his bounty. He talked and acted as if my fortune were totally disjoined from his; yet was I indebted to him for the morsel which sustained my life. Now it was proposed to withdraw myself to studious leisure, and romantic solitude. All my wants, personal and intellectual, were to be supplied gratuitously and copiously. No means were prescribed by which I might make compensation for all these benefits. In conferring them he seemed to be actuated by no view to his own ultimate advantage. He took no measures to secure my future services.

I suffered these thoughts to escape me, on this occasion, and observed that to make my application successful, or useful, it was necessary to pursue some end. I must look forward to some post which I might hereafter occupy beneficially to myself or others; and for which all the efforts of my mind should be bent to qualify myself.

These hints gave him visible pleasure; and now, for the first time, he deigned to advise me on this head. His scheme, however, was not suddenly produced. The way to it was circuitous and long. It was his business to make every new step appear to be suggested by my own reflections. His own ideas were the seeming result of the moment, and sprung out of the last idea that was uttered. Being hastily taken up, they were, of course, liable to objection. These objections, sometimes occurring to me and sometimes to him, were admitted or contested with the utmost candour. One scheme went through numerous modifications before it was proved to be ineligible, or before it yielded place to a better. It was easy to perceive, that books alone were insufficient to impart knowledge: that man must be examined with our own eyes to make us acquainted with their nature: that ideas collected from observation and reading, must correct and illustrate each other: that the value of all principles, and their truth, lie in their practical effects. Hence, gradually arose, the usefulness of travelling, of inspecting the habits and manners of a nation, and investigating, on the spot, the causes of their happiness and misery. Finally, it was determined that Spain was more suitable than any other, to the views of a judicious traveller.

My language, habits, and religion were mentioned as obstacles to close and extensive views; but these difficulties successively and slowly vanished. Converse with books, and natives of Spain, a steadfast purpose and unwearied diligence would efface all differences between me and a Castilian with respect to speech. Personal habits, were changeable, by the same means. The bars to unbounded intercourse, rising from the religion of Spain being irreconcilably opposite to mine, cost us no little trouble to surmount, and here the skill of Ludloe was eminently displayed.

I had been accustomed to regard as unquestionable, the fallacy of the Romish faith. This persuasion was habitual and the child of prejudice, and was easily shaken by the artifices of this logician. I was first led to bestow a kind of assent on the doctrines of the Roman church; but my convictions were easily subdued by a new species of argumentation, and, in a short time, I reverted to my ancient disbelief, so that, if an exterior conformity to the rights of Spain were requisite to the attainment of my purpose, that conformity must be dissembled.

My moral principles had hitherto been vague and unsettled. My circumstances had led me to the frequent practice of insincerity; but my transgressions as they were slight and transient, did not much excite my previous reflections, or subsequent remorse. My deviations, however, though rendered easy by habit, were by no means sanctioned by my principles. Now an imposture, more profound and deliberate, was projected; and I could not hope to perform well my part, unless steadfastly and thoroughly persuaded of its rectitude.

My friend was the eulogist of sincerity. He delighted to trace its influence on the happiness of mankind; and proved that nothing but the universal practice of this virtue was necessary to the perfection of human society. His doctrine was splendid and beautiful. To detect its imperfections was no easy task; to lay the foundations of virtue in utility, and to limit, by that scale, the operation of general principles; to see that the value of sincerity, like that of every other mode of action, consisted in its tendency to good, and that, therefore the obligation to speak truth was not paramount or intrinsical: that my duty is modelled on a knowledge and foresight of the conduct of others; and that, since men in their actual state, are infirm and deceitful, a just estimate of consequences may sometimes make dissimulation my duty were truths that did not speedily occur. The discovery, when made, appeared to be a joint work. I saw nothing in Ludlow but proofs of candour, and a judgment incapable of bias.

The means which this man employed to fit me for his purpose, perhaps owed their success to my youth and ignorance. I may have given you exaggerated ideas of his dexterity and address. Of that I am unable to judge. Certain it is, that no time or reflection has abated my astonishment at the profoundness of his schemes, and the perseverance with which they were pursued by him. To detail their progress would expose me to the risk of being tedious, yet none but minute details would sufficiently display his patience and subtlety.

It will suffice to relate, that after a sufficient period of preparation and arrangements being made for maintaining a copious intercourse with Ludlow, I embarked for Barcelona. A restless curiosity and vigorous application have distinguished my character in every scene. Here was spacious field for the exercise of all my energies. I sought out a preceptor in my new religion. I entered into the hearts of priests and confessors, the hidalgo and the peasant, the monk and the prelate, the austere and voluptuous devotee were scrutinized in all their forms.

Man was the chief subject of my study, and the social sphere that in which I principally moved; but I was not inattentive to inanimate nature, nor unmindful of the past. If the scope of virtue were to maintain the body in health, and to furnish its highest enjoyments to every sense, to increase the number, and accuracy, and order of our intellectual stores, no virtue was ever more unblemished than mine.

If to act upon our conceptions of right, and to acquit ourselves of all prejudice and selfishness in the formation of our principles, entitle us to the testimony of a good conscience, I might justly claim it.

I shall not pretend to ascertain my rank in the moral scale. Your notions of duty differ widely from mine. If a system of deceit, pursued merely from the love of truth; if voluptuousness, never gratified at the expense of health, may incur censure, I am censurable. This, indeed, was not the limit of my deviations. Deception was often unnecessarily practised, and my biloquial faculty did not lie unemployed. What has happened to yourselves may enable you, in some degree, to judge of the scenes in which my mystical exploits engaged me. In none of them, indeed, were the effects equally disastrous, and they were, for the most part, the result of well digested projects.

To recount these would be an endless task. They were designed as mere specimens of power, to illustrate the influence of superstition: to give sceptics the consolation of certainty: to annihilate the scruples of a tender female, or facilitate my access to the bosoms of courtiers and monks.

The first achievement of this kind took place in the convent of the Escurial. For some time the hospitality of this brotherhood allowed me a cell in that magnificent and gloomy fabric. I was drawn hither chiefly by the treasures of Arabian literature, which are preserved here in the keeping of a learned Maronite, from Lebanon. Standing one evening on the steps of the great altar, this devout friar expatiated on the miraculous evidences of his religion; and, in a moment of enthusiasm, appealed to San Lorenzo, whose martyrdom was displayed before us. No sooner was the appeal made than the saint, obsequious to the summons, whispered his responses from the shrine, and commanded the heretic to tremble and believe. This event was reported to the convent. With whatever reluctance, I could not refuse my testimony to its truth, and its influence on my faith was clearly shewn in my subsequent conduct.

A lady of rank, in Seville, who had been guilty of many unauthorized indulgences, was, at last, awakened to remorse, by a voice from Heaven, which she imagined had commanded her to expiate her sins by an abstinence from all food for thirty days. Her friends found it impossible to outroot this persuasion, or to overcome her resolution even by force. I chanced to be one in a numerous company where she was present. This fatal illusion was mentioned, and an opportunity afforded to the lady of defending her scheme. At a pause in the discourse, a voice was heard from the ceiling, which confirmed the truth of her tale; but, at the same time revoked the command, and, in consideration of her faith, pronounced her absolution. Satisfied with this proof, the auditors dismissed their unbelief, and the lady consented to eat.

In the course of a copious correspondence with Ludlow, the observations I had collected were given. A sentiment, which I can hardly describe, induced me to be silent on all adventures connected with my bivocal projects. On other topics, I wrote fully, and without restraint. I painted, in vivid hues, the scenes with which

I was daily conversant, and pursued, fearlessly, every speculation on religion and government that occurred. This spirit was encouraged by Ludloe, who failed not to comment on my narrative, and multiply deductions from my principles.

He taught me to ascribe the evils that infest society to the errors of opinion. The absurd and unequal distribution of power and property gave birth to poverty and riches, and these were the sources of luxury and crimes. These positions were readily admitted; but the remedy for these ills, the means of rectifying these errors were not easily discovered. We have been inclined to impute them to inherent defects in the moral constitution of men: that oppression and tyranny grow up by a sort of natural necessity, and that they will perish only when the human species is extinct. Ludloe laboured to prove that this was, by no means, the case: that man is the creature of circumstances: that he is capable of endless improvement: that his progress has been stopped by the artificial impediment of government: that by the removal of this, the fondest dreams of imagination will be realized.

From detailing and accounting for the evils which exist under our present institutions, he usually proceeded to delineate some scheme of Utopian felicity, where the empire of reason should supplant that of force: where justice should be universally understood and practised; where the interest of the whole and of the individual should be seen by all to be the same; where the public good should be the scope of all activity; where the tasks of all should be the same, and the means of subsistence equally distributed.

No one could contemplate his pictures without rapture. By their comprehensiveness and amplitude they filled the imagination. I was unwilling to believe that in no region of the world, or at no period could these ideas be realized. It was plain that the nations of Europe were tending to greater depravity, and would be the prey of perpetual vicissitude. All individual attempts at their reformation would be fruitless. He therefore who desired the diffusion of right principles, to make a just system be adopted by a whole community, must pursue some extraordinary method.

In this state of mind I recollected my native country, where a few colonists from Britain had sown the germe of populous and mighty empires. Attended, as they were, into their new abode, by all their prejudices, yet such had been the influence of new circumstances, of consulting for their own happiness, of adopting simple forms of government, and excluding nobles and kings from their system, that they enjoyed a degree of happiness far superior to their parent state.

To conquer the prejudices and change the habits of millions, are impossible. The human mind, exposed to social influences, inflexibly adheres to the direction that is given to it; but for the same reason why men, who begin in error will continue, those who commence in truth, may be expected to persist. Habit and example will operate with equal force in both instances.

Let a few, sufficiently enlightened and disinterested, take up their abode in some unvisited region. Let their social scheme be founded in equity, and how small soever their original number may be, their growth into a nation is inevitable.

Among other effects of national justice, was to be ranked the swift increase of numbers. Exempt from servile obligations and perverse habits, endowed with property, wisdom, and health. Hundreds will expand, with inconceivable rapidity into thousands and thousands, into millions; and a new race, tutored in truth, may, in a few centuries, overflow the habitable world.

Such were the visions of youth! I could not banish them from my mind. I knew them to be crude; but believed that deliberation would bestow upon them solidity and shape. Meanwhile I imparted them to Ludloe.

Chapter VI

In answer to the reveries and speculations which I sent to him respecting this subject, Ludloe informed me, that they had led his mind into a new sphere of meditation. He had long and deeply considered in what way he might essentially promote my happiness. He had entertained a faint hope that I would one day be qualified for a station like that to which he himself had been advanced. This post required an elevation and stability of views which human beings seldom reach, and which could be attained by me only by a long series of heroic labours. Hitherto every new stage in my intellectual progress had added vigour to his hopes, and he cherished a stronger belief than formerly that my career would terminate auspiciously. This, however, was necessarily distant. Many preliminaries must first be settled; many arduous accomplishments be first obtained; and my virtue be subjected to severe trials. At present it was not in his power to be more explicit; but if my reflections suggested no better plan, he advised me to settle my affairs in Spain, and return to him immediately. My knowledge of this country would be of the highest use, on the supposition of my ultimately arriving at the honours to which he had alluded; and some of these preparatory measures could be taken only with his assistance, and in his company.

This intimation was eagerly obeyed, and, in a short time, I arrived at Dublin. Meanwhile my mind had copious occupation in commenting on my friend's letter. This scheme, whatever it was, seemed to be suggested by my mention of a plan of colonization, and my preference of that mode of producing extensive and permanent effects on the condition of mankind. It was easy therefore to conjecture that this mode had been pursued under some mysterious modifications and conditions.

It had always excited my wonder that so obvious an expedient had been overlooked. The globe which we inhabit was very imperfectly known. The regions and nations unexplored, it was reasonable to believe, surpassed in extent, and perhaps in populousness, those with which we were familiar. The order of Jesuits had furnished an example of all the errors and excellencies of such a scheme. Their plan was founded on erroneous notions of religion and policy, and they had absurdly chosen a scene within reach of the injustice and ambition of an European tyrant.

It was wise and easy to profit by their example. Resting on the two props of fidelity and zeal, an association might exist for ages in the heart of Europe, whose influence might be felt, and might be boundless, in some region of the southern hemisphere; and by whom a moral and political structure might be raised, the growth of pure wisdom, and totally unlike those fragments of Roman and Gothic barbarism, which cover the face of what are called the civilized nations. The belief now rose in my mind that some such scheme had actually been prosecuted, and that Ludloe was a coadjutor. On this supposition, the caution with which he approached to his point, the arduous probation which a candidate for a part on this stage must undergo, and the rigours of that test by which his fortitude and virtue must be tried, were easily explained. I was too deeply imbued with veneration for the effects of such schemes, and too sanguine in my confidence in the rectitude of Ludloe, to refuse my concurrence in any scheme by which my qualifications might at length be raised to a due point.

Our interview was frank and affectionate. I found him situated just as formerly. His aspect, manners, and deportment were the same. I entered once more on my former mode of life, but our intercourse became more frequent. We constantly breakfasted together, and our conversation was usually prolonged through half the morning.

For a time our topics were general. I thought proper to leave to him the introduction of more interesting themes: this, however, he betrayed no inclination to do. His reserve excited some surprise, and I began to suspect that whatever design he had formed with regard to me, had been laid aside. To ascertain this question, I ventured, at length, to recall his attention to the subject of his last letter, and to enquire whether subsequent reflection had made any change in his views.

He said that his views were too momentous to be hastily taken up, or hastily dismissed; the station, my attainment of which depended wholly on myself, was high above vulgar heads, and was to be gained by years of solicitude and labour. This, at least, was true with regard to minds ordinarily constituted; I, perhaps, deserved to be regarded as an exception, and might be able to accomplish in a few months that for which others were obliged to toil during half their lives.

Man, continued he, is the slave of habit. Convince him to-day that his duty leads straight forward: he shall advance, but at every step his belief shall fade; habit will resume its empire, and tomorrow he shall turn back, or betake himself to oblique paths.

We know not our strength till it be tried. Virtue, till confirmed by habit, is a dream. You are a man imbued by errors, and vincible by slight temptations. Deep enquiries must bestow light on your opinions, and the habit of encountering and vanquishing temptation must inspire you with fortitude. Till this be done, you are unqualified for that post, in which you will be invested with divine attributes, and prescribe the condition of a large portion of mankind.

Confide not in the firmness of your principles, or the stedfastness of your integrity. Be always vigilant and fearful. Never think you have enough of knowledge, and let not your caution slumber for a moment, for you know not when danger is near.

I acknowledged the justice of his admonitions, and professed myself willing to undergo any ordeal which reason should prescribe. What, I asked, were the conditions, on the fulfilment of which depended my advancement to the station he alluded to? Was it necessary to conceal from me the nature and obligations of this rank?

These enquiries sunk him more profoundly into meditation than I had ever before witnessed. After a pause, in which some perplexity was visible, he answered:

I scarcely know what to say. As to promises, I claim them not from you. We are now arrived at a point, in which it is necessary to look around with caution, and that consequences should be fully known. A number of persons are leagued together for an end of some moment. To make yourself one of these is submitted to your choice. Among the conditions of their alliance are mutual fidelity and secrecy.

Their existence depends upon this: their existence is known only to themselves. This secrecy must be obtained by all the means which are possible. When I have said thus much, I have informed you, in some degree, of their existence, but you are still ignorant of the purpose contemplated by this association, and of all the members, except myself. So far no dangerous disclosure is yet made: but this degree of concealment is not sufficient. Thus much is made known to you, because it is unavoidable. The individuals which compose this fraternity are not immortal, and the vacancies occasioned by death must be supplied from among the living. The candidate must be instructed and prepared, and they are always at liberty to recede. Their reason must approve the obligations and duties of their station, or they are unfit for it. If they recede, one duty is still incumbent upon them: they must observe an inviolable silence. To this they are not held by any promise. They must weigh consequences, and freely decide; but they must not fail to number among these consequences their own death.

Their death will not be prompted by vengeance. The executioner will say, he that has once revealed the tale is likely to reveal it a second time; and, to prevent this, the betrayer must die. Nor is this the only consequence: to prevent the further revelation, he, to whom the secret was imparted, must likewise perish. He must not console himself with the belief that his trespass will be unknown. The knowledge cannot, by human means, be withheld from this fraternity. Rare, indeed, will it be that his purpose to disclose is not discovered before it can be effected, and the disclosure prevented by his death.

Be well aware of your condition. What I now, or may hereafter mention, mention not again. Admit not even a doubt as to the propriety of hiding it from all the world. There are eyes who will discern this doubt amidst the closest folds of your heart, and your life will instantly be sacrificed.

At present be the subject dismissed. Reflect deeply on the duty which you have already incurred. Think upon your strength of mind, and be careful not to lay yourself under impracticable obligations. It will always be in your power to recede. Even after you are solemnly enrolled a member, you may consult the dictates of your own understanding, and relinquish your post; but while you live, the obligation to be silent will perpetually attend you.

We seek not the misery or death of any one, but we are swayed by an immutable calculation. Death is to be abhorred, but the life of the betrayer is productive of more evil than his death: his death, therefore, we chuse, and our means are instantaneous and unerring.

I love you. The first impulse of my love is to dissuade you from seeking to know more. Your mind will be full of ideas; your hands will be perpetually busy to a purpose into which no human creature, beyond the verge of your brotherhood, must pry. Believe me, who have made the experiment, that compared with this task, the task of inviolable secrecy, all others are easy. To be dumb will not suffice; never to know any remission in your zeal or your watchfulness will not suffice. If the sagacity of others detect your occupations, however strenuously you may labour for concealment, your doom is ratified, as well as that of the wretch whose evil destiny led him to pursue you.

Yet if your fidelity fail not, great will be your recompence. For all your toils and self-devotion, ample will be the retribution. Hitherto you have been wrapt in darkness and storm; then will you be exalted to a pure and unruffled element. It is only for a time that temptation will environ you, and your path will be toilsome. In a few years you will be permitted to withdraw to a land of sages, and the remainder of your life will glide away in the enjoyments of beneficence and wisdom.

Think deeply on what I have said. Investigate your own motives and opinions, and prepare to submit them to the test of numerous hazards and experiments.

Here my friend passed to a new topic. I was desirous of reverting to this subject, and obtaining further information concerning it, but he assiduously repelled all my attempts, and insisted on my bestowing deep and impartial attention on what had already been disclosed. I was not slow to comply with his directions. My mind refused to admit any other theme of contemplation than this.

As yet I had no glimpse of the nature of this fraternity. I was permitted to form conjectures, and previous incidents bestowed but one form upon my thoughts. In reviewing the sentiments and deportment of Ludloe, my belief continually acquired new strength. I even recollected hints and ambiguous allusions in his discourse, which were easily solved, on the supposition of the existence of a new model of society, in some unsuspected corner of the world.

I did not fully perceive the necessity of secrecy; but this necessity perhaps would be rendered apparent, when I should come to know the connection that subsisted between Europe and this imaginary colony. But what was to be done? I was willing to abide by these conditions. My understanding might not approve of all the ends proposed by this fraternity, and I had liberty to withdraw from it, or to refuse to ally myself with them. That the obligation of secrecy should still remain, was unquestionably reasonable.

It appeared to be the plan of Ludloe rather to damp than to stimulate my zeal. He discouraged all attempts to renew the subject in conversation. He dwelt upon the arduousness of the office to which I aspired, the temptations to violate my duty with which I should be continually beset, the inevitable death with which the slightest breach of my engagements would be followed, and the long apprenticeship which it would be necessary for me to serve, before I should be fitted to enter into this conclave.

Sometimes my courage was depressed by these representations. . . . . . My zeal, however, was sure to revive; and at length Ludloe declared himself willing to assist me in the accomplishment of my wishes. For this end, it was necessary, he said, that I should be informed of a second obligation, which every candidate must assume. Before any one could be deemed qualified, he must be thoroughly known to his associates. For this end, he must determine to disclose every fact in his history, and every secret of his heart. I must begin with making these confessions with regard to my past life, to Ludloe, and must continue to communicate, at stated seasons, every new thought, and every new occurrence, to him. This confidence was to be absolutely limitless: no exceptions were to be admitted, and no reserves to be practised; and the same penalty attended the infraction of this rule as of the former. Means would be employed, by which the slightest deviation, in either case, would be detected, and the deathful consequence would follow with instant and inevitable expedition. If secrecy were difficult to practise, sincerity, in that degree in which it was here demanded, was a task infinitely more arduous, and a period of new deliberation was necessary before I should decide. I was at liberty to pause: nay, the longer was the period of deliberation which I took, the better; but, when I had once entered this path, it was not in my power to recede. After having solemnly avowed my resolution to be thus sincere in my confession, any particle of reserve or duplicity would cost me my life.

This indeed was a subject to be deeply thought upon. Hitherto I had been guilty of concealment with regard to my friend. I had entered into no formal compact, but had been conscious to a kind of tacit obligation to hide no important transaction of my life from him. This consciousness was the source of continual anxiety. I had exerted, on numerous occasions, my bivocal faculty, but, in my intercourse with Ludloe, had suffered not the slightest intimation to escape me with regard to it. This reserve was not easily explained. It was, in a great degree, the product of habit; but I likewise considered that the efficacy of this instrument depended upon its existence being unknown. To confide the secret to one, was to put an end to my privilege: how widely the knowledge would thenceforth be diffused, I had no power to foresee.

Each day multiplied the impediments to confidence. Shame hindered me from acknowledging my past reserves. Ludloe, from the nature of our intercourse, would certainly account my reserve, in this respect, unjustifiable, and to excite his indignation or contempt was an unpleasing undertaking. Now, if I should resolve to persist in my new path, this reserve must be dismissed: I must make him master of a secret which was precious to me beyond all others; by acquainting him with past concealments, I must risk incurring his suspicion and his anger. These reflections were productive of considerable embarrassment.

There was, indeed, an avenue by which to escape these difficulties, if it did not, at the same time, plunge me into greater. My confessions might, in other respects, be unbounded, but my reserves, in this particular, might be continued. Yet should I not expose myself to formidable perils? Would my secret be for ever unsuspected and undiscovered?

When I considered the nature of this faculty, the impossibility of going farther than suspicion, since the agent could be known only by his own confession, and even this confession would not be believed by the greater part of mankind, I was tempted to conceal it.

In most cases, if I had asserted the possession of this power, I should be treated as a liar; it would be considered as an absurd and audacious expedient to free myself from the suspicion of having entered into compact with a daemon, or of being myself an emissary of the grand foe. Here, however, there was no reason to dread a similar imputation, since Ludloe had denied the preternatural pretensions of these airy sounds.

My conduct on this occasion was nowise influenced by the belief of any inherent sanctity in truth. Ludloe had taught me to model myself in this respect entirely with a view to immediate consequences. If my genuine interest, on the whole, was promoted by veracity, it was proper to adhere to it; but, if the result of my investigation were opposite, truth was to be sacrificed without scruple.

Chapter VII

Meanwhile, in a point of so much moment, I was not hasty to determine. My delay seemed to be, by no means, unacceptable to Ludloe, who applauded my discretion, and warned me to be circumspect. My attention was chiefly absorbed by considerations connected with this subject, and little regard was paid to any foreign occupation or amusement.

One evening, after a day spent in my closet, I sought recreation by walking forth. My mind was chiefly occupied by the review of incidents which happened in Spain. I turned my face towards the fields, and recovered not from my reverie, till I had proceeded some miles on the road to Meath. The night had considerably advanced, and the darkness was rendered intense, by the setting of the moon. Being somewhat weary, as well as undetermined in what manner next to proceed, I seated myself on a grassy bank beside the road. The spot which I had chosen was aloof from passengers, and shrowded in the deepest obscurity.

Some time elapsed, when my attention was excited by the slow approach of an equipage. I presently discovered a coach and six horses, but unattended, except by coachman and postillion, and with no light to guide them on their way. Scarcely had they passed the spot where I rested, when some one leaped from beneath the hedge, and seized the head of the fore-horses. Another called upon the coachman to stop, and threatened him with instant death if he disobeyed. A third drew open the coach-door, and ordered those within to deliver their purses. A shriek of terror showed me that a lady was within, who eagerly consented to preserve her life by the loss of her money.

To walk unarmed in the neighbourhood of Dublin, especially at night, has always been accounted dangerous. I had about me the usual instruments of defence. I was desirous of rescuing this person from the danger which surrounded her, but was somewhat at a loss how to effect my purpose. My single strength was insufficient to contend with three ruffians. After a moment's debate, an expedient was suggested, which I hastened to execute.

Time had not been allowed for the ruffian who stood beside the carriage to receive the plunder, when several voices, loud, clamorous, and eager, were heard in the quarter whence the traveller had come. By trampling with quickness, it was easy to imitate the sound of many feet. The robbers were alarmed, and one called upon another to attend. The sounds increased, and, at the next moment, they betook themselves to flight, but not till a pistol was discharged. Whether it was aimed at the lady in the carriage, or at the coachman, I was not permitted to discover, for the report affrighted the horses, and they set off at full speed.

I could not hope to overtake them: I knew not whither the robbers had fled, and whether, by proceeding, I might not fall into their hands ..... These considerations induced me to resume my feet, and retire from the scene as expeditiously as possible. I regained my own habitation without injury.

I have said that I occupied separate apartments from those of Ludloe. To these there were means of access without disturbing the family. I hasted to my chamber, but was considerably surprized to find, on entering my apartment, Ludloe seated at a table, with a lamp before him.

My momentary confusion was greater than his. On discovering who it was, he assumed his accustomed looks, and explained appearances, by saying, that he wished to converse with me on a subject of importance, and had therefore sought me at this secret hour, in my own chamber. Contrary to his expectation, I was absent. Conceiving it possible that I might shortly return, he had waited till now. He took no further notice of my absence, nor manifested any desire to know the cause of it, but proceeded to mention the subject which had brought him hither. These were his words.

You have nothing which the laws permit you to call your own. Justice entitles you to the supply of your physical wants, from those who are able to supply them; but there are few who will acknowledge your claim, or spare an atom of their superfluity to appease your cravings. That which they will not spontaneously give, it is not right to wrest from them by violence. What then is to be done?

Property is necessary to your own subsistence. It is useful, by enabling you to supply the wants of others. To give food, and clothing, and shelter, is to give life, to annihilate temptation, to unshackle virtue, and propagate felicity. How shall property be gained?

You may set your understanding or your hands at work. You may weave stockings, or write poems, and exchange them for money; but these are tardy and meagre schemes. The means are disproportioned to the end, and I will not suffer you to pursue them. My justice will supply your wants.

But dependance on the justice of others is a precarious condition. To be the object is a less ennobling state than to be the bestower of benefit. Doubtless you desire to be vested with competence and riches, and to hold them by virtue of the law, and not at the will of a benefactor . . . . . . He paused as if waiting for my assent to his positions. I readily expressed my concurrence, and my desire to pursue any means compatible with honesty. He resumed.

There are various means, besides labour, violence, or fraud. It is right to select the easiest within your reach. It happens that the easiest is at hand. A revenue of some thousands a year, a stately mansion in the city, and another in Kildare, old and faithful domestics, and magnificent furniture, are good things. Will you have them?

A gift like that, replied I, will be attended by momentous conditions. I cannot decide upon its value, until I know these conditions.

The sole condition is your consent to receive them. Not even the airy obligation of gratitude will be created by acceptance. On the contrary, by accepting them, you will confer the highest benefit upon another.

I do not comprehend you. Something surely must be given in return.

Nothing. It may seem strange that, in accepting the absolute controul of so much property, you subject yourself to no conditions; that no claims of gratitude or service will accrue; but the wonder is greater still. The law equitably enough fetters the gift with no restraints, with respect to you that receive it; but not so with regard to the unhappy being who bestows it. That being must part, not only with property but liberty. In accepting the property, you must consent to enjoy the services of the present possessor. They cannot be disjoined.

Of the true nature and extent of the gift, you should be fully apprized. Be aware, therefore, that, together with this property, you will receive absolute power over the liberty and person of the being who now possesses it. That being must become your domestic slave; be governed, in every particular, by your caprice.

Happily for you, though fully invested with this power, the degree and mode in which it will be exercised will depend upon yourself . . . . . You may either totally forbear the exercise, or employ it only for the benefit of your slave. However injurious, therefore, this authority may be to the subject of it, it will, in some sense, only enhance the value of the gift to you.

The attachment and obedience of this being will be chiefly evident in one thing. Its duty will consist in conforming, in every instance, to your will. All the powers of this being are to be devoted to your happiness; but there is one relation between you, which enables you to confer, while exacting, pleasure . . . . . This relation is sexual. Your slave is a woman; and the bond, which transfers her property and person to you, is . . . . marriage.

My knowledge of Ludloe, his principles, and reasonings, ought to have precluded that surprise which I experienced at the conclusion of his discourse. I knew that he regarded the present institution of marriage as a contract of servitude, and the terms of it unequal and unjust. When my surprise had subsided, my thoughts turned upon the nature of his scheme. After a pause of reflection, I answered:

Both law and custom have connected obligations with marriage, which, though heaviest on the female, are not light upon the male. Their weight and extent are not immutable and uniform; they are modified by various incidents, and especially by the mental and personal qualities of the lady.

I am not sure that I should willingly accept the property and person of a woman decrepid with age, and enslaved by perverse habits and evil passions: whereas youth, beauty, and tenderness would be worth accepting, even for their own sake, and disconnected with fortune.

As to altar vows, I believe they will not make me swerve from equity. I shall exact neither service nor affection from my spouse. The value of these, and, indeed, not only the value, but the very existence, of the latter depends upon its spontaneity. A promise to love tends rather to loosen than strengthen the tie.

As to myself, the age of illusion is past. I shall not wed, till I find one whose moral and physical constitution will make personal fidelity easy. I shall judge without mistiness or passion, and habit will come in aid of an enlightened and deliberate choice.

I shall not be fastidious in my choice. I do not expect, and scarcely desire, much intellectual similitude between me and my wife. Our opinions and pursuits cannot be in common. While women are formed by their education, and their education continues in its present state, tender hearts and misguided understandings are all that we can hope to meet with.

What are the character, age, and person of the woman to whom you allude? and what prospect of success would attend my exertions to obtain her favour?

I have told you she is rich. She is a widow, and owes her riches to the liberality of her husband, who was a trader of great opulence, and who died while on a mercantile adventure to Spain. He was not unknown to you. Your letters from Spain often spoke of him. In short, she is the widow of Benington, whom you met at Barcelona. She is still in the prime of life; is not without many feminine attractions; has an ardent and credulent temper; and is particularly given to devotion. This temper it would be easy to regulate according to your pleasure and your interest, and I now submit to you the expediency of an alliance with her.

I am a kinsman, and regarded by her with uncommon deference; and my commendations, therefore, will be of great service to you, and shall be given.

I will deal ingenuously with you. It is proper you should be fully acquainted with the grounds of this proposal. The benefits of rank, and property, and independence, which I have already mentioned as likely to accrue to you from this marriage, are solid and valuable benefits; but these are not the sole advantages, and to benefit you, in these respects, is not my whole view.

No. My treatment of you henceforth will be regulated by one principle. I regard you only as one undergoing a probation or apprenticeship; as subjected to trials of your sincerity and fortitude. The marriage I now propose to you is desirable, because it will make you independent of me. Your poverty might create an unsuitable bias in favour of proposals, one of whose effects would be to set you beyond fortune's reach. That bias will cease, when you cease to be poor and dependent.

Love is the strongest of all human delusions. That fortitude, which is not subdued by the tenderness and blandishments of woman, may be trusted; but no fortitude, which has not undergone that test, will be trusted by us.

This woman is a charming enthusiast. She will never marry but him whom she passionately loves. Her power over the heart that loves her will scarcely have limits. The means of prying into your transactions, of suspecting and sifting your thoughts, which her constant society with you, while sleeping and waking, her zeal and watchfulness for your welfare, and her curiosity, adroitness, and penetration will afford her, are evident. Your danger, therefore, will be imminent. Your fortitude will be obliged to have recourse, not to flight, but to vigilance. Your eye must never close.

Alas! what human magnanimity can stand this test! How can I persuade myself that you will not fail? I waver between hope and fear. Many, it is true, have fallen, and dragged with them the author of their ruin, but some have soared above even these perils and temptations, with their fiery energies unimpaired, and great has been, as great ought to be, their recompence.

But you are doubtless aware of your danger. I need not repeat the consequences of betraying your trust, the rigour of those who will Judge your fault, the unerring and unbounded scrutiny to which your actions, the most secret and indifferent, will be subjected.

Your conduct, however, will be voluntary. At your own option be it, to see or not to see this woman. Circumspection, deliberation forethought, are your sacred duties and highest interest.

Chapter VIII

Ludloe's remarks on the seductive and bewitching powers of women, on the difficulty of keeping a secret which they wish to know, and to gain which they employ the soft artillery of tears and prayers, and blandishments and menaces, are familiar to all men, but they had little weight with me, because they were unsupported by my own experience. I had never had any intellectual or sentimental connection with the sex. My meditations and pursuits had all led a different way, and a bias had gradually been given to my feelings, very unfavourable to the refinements of love. I acknowledge, with shame and regret, that I was accustomed to regard the physical and sensual consequences of the sexual relation as realities, and every thing intellectual, disinterested, and heroic, which enthusiasts connect with it as idle dreams. Besides, said I, I am yet a stranger to the secret, on the preservation of which so much stress is laid, and it will be optional with me to receive it or not.

If, in the progress of my acquaintance with Mrs. Benington, I should perceive any extraordinary danger in the gift, cannot I refuse, or at least delay to comply with any new conditions from Ludloe? Will not his candour and his affection for me rather commend than disapprove my diffidence? In fine, I resolved to see this lady.

She was, it seems, the widow of Benington, whom I knew in Spain. This man was an English merchant settled at Barcelona, to whom I had been commended by Ludloe's letters, and through whom my pecuniary supplies were furnished . . . . Much intercourse and some degree of intimacy had taken place between us, and I had gained a pretty accurate knowledge of his character. I had been informed, through different channels, that his wife was much his superior in rank, that she possessed great wealth in her own right, and that some disagreement of temper or views occasioned their separation. She had married him for love, and still doated on him: the occasions for separation having arisen, it seems, not on her side but on his. As his habits of reflection were nowise friendly to religion, and as hers, according to Ludloe, were of the opposite kind, it is possible that some jarring had arisen between them from this source. Indeed, from some casual and broken hints of Benington, especially in the latter part of his life, I had long since gathered this conjecture . . . . Something, thought I, may be derived from my acquaintance with her husband favourable to my views.

I anxiously waited for an opportunity of acquainting Ludloe with my resolution. On the day of our last conversation, he had made a short excursion from town, intending to return the same evening, but had continued absent for several days. As soon as he came back, I hastened to acquaint him with my wishes.

Have you well considered this matter, said he. Be assured it is of no trivial import. The moment at which you enter the presence of this woman will decide your future destiny. Even putting out of view the subject of our late conversations, the light in which you shall appear to her will greatly influence your happiness, since, though you cannot fail to love her, it is quite uncertain what return she may think proper to make. Much, doubtless, will depend on your own perseverance and address, but you will have many, perhaps insuperable obstacles to encounter on several accounts, and especially in her attachment to the memory of her late husband. As to her devout temper, this is nearly allied to a warm imagination in some other respects, and will operate much more in favour of an ardent and artful lover, than against him.

I still expressed my willingness to try my fortune with her.

Well, said he, I anticipated your consent to my proposal, and the visit I have just made was to her. I thought it best to pave the way, by informing her that I had met with one for whom she had desired me to look out. You must know that her father was one of these singular men who set a value upon things exactly in proportion to the difficulty of obtaining or comprehending them. His passion was for antiques, and his favourite pursuit during a long life was monuments in brass, marble, and parchment, of the remotest antiquity. He was wholly indifferent to the character or conduct of our present sovereign and his ministers, but was extremely solicitous about the name and exploits of a king of Ireland that lived two or three centuries before the flood. He felt no curiosity to know who was the father of his wife's child, but would travel a thousand miles, and consume months, in investigating which son of Noah it was that first landed on the coast of Munster. He would give a hundred guineas from the mint for a piece of old decayed copper no bigger than his nail, provided it had aukward characters upon it, too much defaced to be read. The whole stock of a great bookseller was, in his eyes, a cheap exchange for a shred of parchment, containing half a homily written by St. Patrick. He would have gratefully given all his patrimonial domains to one who should inform him what pendragon or druid it was who set up the first stone on Salisbury plain.

This spirit, as you may readily suppose, being seconded by great wealth and long life, contributed to form a very large collection of venerable lumber, which, though beyond all price to the collector himself, is of no value to his heiress but so far as it is marketable. She designs to bring the whole to auction, but for this purpose a catalogue and description are necessary. Her father trusted to a faithful memory, and to vague and scarcely legible memorandums, and has left a very arduous task to any one who shall be named to the office. It occurred to me, that the best means of promoting your views was to recommend you to this office.

You are not entirely without the antiquarian frenzy yourself. The employment, therefore, will be somewhat agreeable to you for its own sake. It will entitle you to become an inmate of the same house, and thus establish an incessant intercourse between you, and the nature of the business is such, that you may perform it in what time, and with what degree of diligence and accuracy you please.

I ventured to insinuate that, to a woman of rank and family, the character of a hireling was by no means a favourable recommendation.

He answered, that he proposed, by the account he should give of me, to obviate every scruple of that nature. Though my father was no better than a farmer, it is not absolutely certain but that my remoter ancestors had princely blood in their veins: but as long as proofs of my low extraction did not impertinently intrude themselves, my silence, or, at most, equivocal surmises, seasonably made use of, might secure me from all inconveniences on the score of birth. He should represent me, and I was such, as his friend, favourite, and equal, and my passion for antiquities should be my principal inducement to undertake this office, though my poverty would make no objection to a reasonable pecuniary recompense.

Having expressed my acquiescence in his measures, he thus proceeded: My visit was made to my kinswoman, for the purpose, as I just now told you, of paving your way into her family; but, on my arrival at her house, I found nothing but disorder and alarm. Mrs. Benington, it seems, on returning from a longer ride than customary, last Thursday evening, was attacked by robbers. Her attendants related an imperfect tale of somebody advancing at the critical moment to her rescue. It seems, however, they did more harm than good; for the horses took to flight and overturned the carriage, in consequence of which Mrs. Benington was severely bruised. She has kept her bed ever since, and a fever was likely to ensue, which has only left her out of danger to-day.

As the adventure before related, in which I had so much concern, occurred at the time mentioned by Ludloe, and as all other circumstances were alike, I could not doubt that the person whom the exertion of my mysterious powers had relieved was Mrs. Benington: but what an ill-omened interference was mine! The robbers would probably have been satisfied with the few guineas in her purse, and, on receiving these, would have left her to prosecute her journey in peace and security, but, by absurdly offering a succour, which could only operate upon the fears of her assailants, I endangered her life, first by the desperate discharge of a pistol, and next by the fright of the horses . . . . My anxiety, which would have been less if I had not been, in some degree, myself the author of the evil, was nearly removed by Ludloe's proceeding to assure me that all danger was at an end, and that he left the lady in the road to perfect health. He had seized the earliest opportunity of acquainting her with the purpose of his visit, and had brought back with him her cheerful acceptance of my services. The next week was appointed for my introduction.

With such an object in view, I had little leisure to attend to any indifferent object. My thoughts were continually bent upon the expected introduction, and my impatience and curiosity drew strength, not merely from the character of Mrs. Benington, but from the nature of my new employment. Ludloe had truly observed, that I was infected with somewhat of this antiquarian mania myself, and I now remembered that Benington had frequently alluded to this collection in possession of his wife. My curiosity had then been more than once excited by his representations, and I had formed a vague resolution of making myself acquainted with this lady and her learned treasure, should I ever return to Ireland . . . . . Other incidents had driven this matter from my mind.

Meanwhile, affairs between Ludloe and myself remained stationary. Our conferences, which were regular and daily, related to general topics, and though his instructions were adapted to promote my improvement in the most useful branches of knowledge, they never afforded a glimpse towards that quarter where my curiosity was most active.

The next week now arrived, but Ludloe informed me that the state of Mrs. Benington's health required a short excursion into the country, and that he himself proposed to bear her company. The journey was to last about a fortnight, after which I might prepare myself for an introduction to her.

This was a very unexpected and disagreeable trial to my patience. The interval of solitude that now succeeded would have passed rapidly and pleasantly enough, if an event of so much moment were not in suspense. Books, of which I was passionately fond, would have afforded me delightful and incessant occupation, and Ludloe, by way of reconciling me to unavoidable delays, had given me access to a little closet, in which his rarer and more valuable books were kept.

All my amusements, both by inclination and necessity, were centered in myself and at home. Ludloe appeared to have no visitants, and though frequently abroad, or at least secluded from me, had never proposed my introduction to any of his friends, except Mrs. Benington. My obligations to him were already too great to allow me to lay claim to new favours and indulgences, nor, indeed, was my disposition such as to make society needful to my happiness. My character had been, in some degree, modelled by the faculty which I possessed. This deriving all its supposed value from impenetrable secrecy, and Ludloe's admonitions tending powerfully to impress me with the necessity of wariness and circumspection in my general intercourse with mankind, I had gradually fallen into sedate, reserved, mysterious, and unsociable habits. My heart wanted not a friend.

In this temper of mind, I set myself to examine the novelties which Ludloe's private book-cases contained. 'Twill be strange, thought I, if his favourite volume do not show some marks of my friend's character. To know a man's favourite or most constant studies cannot fail of letting in some little light upon his secret thoughts, and though he would not have given me the reading of these books, if he had thought them capable of unveiling more of his concerns than he wished, yet possibly my ingenuity may go one step farther than he dreams of. You shall judge whether I was right in my conjectures.

Chapter IX

The books which composed this little library were chiefly the voyages and travels of the missionaries of the sixteenth and seventeenth centuries. Added to these were some works upon political economy and legislation. Those writers who have amused themselves with reducing their ideas to practice, and drawing imaginary pictures of nations or republics, whose manners or government came up to their standard of excellence, were, all of whom I had ever heard, and some I had never heard of before, to be found in this collection. A translation of Aristotle's republic, the political romances of sir Thomas Moore, Harrington, and Hume, appeared to have been much read, and Ludlow had not been sparing of his marginal comments. In these writers he appeared to find nothing but error and absurdity; and his notes were introduced for no other end than to point out groundless principles and false conclusions . . . . . The style of these remarks was already familiar to me. I saw nothing new in them, or different from the strain of those speculations with which Ludlow was accustomed to indulge himself in conversation with me.

After having turned over the leaves of the printed volumes, I at length lighted on a small book of maps, from which, of course, I could reasonably expect no information, on that point about which I was most curious. It was an atlas, in which the maps had been drawn by the pen. None of them contained any thing remarkable, so far as I, who was indeed a smatterer in geography, was able to perceive, till I came to the end, when I noticed a map, whose prototype I was wholly unacquainted with. It was drawn on a pretty large scale, representing two islands, which bore some faint resemblance, in their relative proportions, at least, to Great

Britain and Ireland. In shape they were widely different, but as to size there was no scale by which to measure them. From the great number of subdivisions, and from signs, which apparently represented towns and cities, I was allowed to infer, that the country was at least as extensive as the British isles. This map was apparently unfinished, for it had no names inscribed upon it.

I have just said, my geographical knowledge was imperfect. Though I had not enough to draw the outlines of any country by memory, I had still sufficient to recognize what I had before seen, and to discover that none of the larger islands in our globe resembled the one before me. Having such and so strong motives to curiosity, you may easily imagine my sensations on surveying this map. Suspecting, as I did, that many of Ludlow's intimations alluded to a country well known to him, though unknown to others, I was, of course, inclined to suppose that this country was now before me.

In search of some clue to this mystery, I carefully inspected the other maps in this collection. In a map of the eastern hemisphere I soon observed the outlines of islands, which, though on a scale greatly diminished, were plainly similar to that of the land above described.

It is well known that the people of Europe are strangers to very nearly one half of the surface of the globe. [*] From the south pole up to the equator, it is only the small space occupied by southern Africa and by South America with which we are acquainted. There is a vast extent, sufficient to receive a continent as large as North America, which our ignorance has filled only with water. In Ludlow's maps nothing was still to be seen, in these regions, but water, except in that spot where the transverse parallels of the southern tropic and the 150th degree east longitude intersect each other. On this spot were Ludlow's islands placed, though without any name or inscription whatever.

I needed not to be told that this spot had never been explored by any European voyager, who had published his adventures. What authority had Ludlow for fixing a habitable land in this spot? and why did he give us nothing but the courses of shores and rivers, and the scite of towns and villages, without a name?

As soon as Ludlow had set out upon his proposed journey of a fortnight, I unlocked his closet, and continued rummaging among these books and maps till night. By that time I had turned over every book and almost every leaf in this small collection, and did not open the closet again till near the end of that period. Meanwhile I had many reflections upon this remarkable circumstance. Could Ludlow have intended that I should see this atlas? It was the only book that could be styled a manuscript on these shelves, and it was placed beneath several others, in a situation far from being obvious and forward to the eye or the hand. Was it an oversight in him to leave it in my way, or could he have intended to lead my curiosity and knowledge a little farther onward by this accidental disclosure? In either case how was I to regulate my future deportment toward him? Was I to speak and act as if this atlas had escaped my attention or not? I had already, after my first examination of it, placed the volume exactly where I found it. On every supposition I thought this was the safest way, and unlocked the closet a second time, to see that all was precisely in the original order . . . . . How was I dismayed and confounded on inspecting the shelves to perceive that the atlas was gone. This was a theft, which, from the closet being under lock and key, and the key always in my own pocket, and which, from the very nature of the thing stolen, could not be imputed to any of the domestics. After a few moments a suspicion occurred, which was soon changed into certainty by applying to the housekeeper, who told me that Ludlow had returned, apparently in much haste, the evening of the day on which he had set out upon his journey, and just after I had left the house, that he had gone into the room where this closet of books was, and, after a few minutes' stay, came out again and went away. She told me also, that he had made general enquiries after me, to which she had answered, that she had not seen me during the day, and supposed that I had spent the whole of it abroad. From this account it was plain, that Ludlow had returned for no other purpose but to remove this book out of my reach. But if he had a double key to this door, what should hinder his having access, by the same means, to every other locked up place in the house?

This suggestion made me start with terror. Of so obvious a means for possessing a knowledge of every thing under his roof, I had never been till this moment aware. Such is the infatuation which lays our most secret thoughts open to the world's scrutiny. We are frequently in most danger when we deem ourselves most safe, and our fortress is taken sometimes through a point, whose weakness nothing, it should seem, but the blindest stupidity could overlook.

My terrors, indeed, quickly subsided when I came to recollect that there was nothing in any closet or cabinet of mine which could possibly throw light upon subjects which I desired to keep in the dark. The more carefully I inspected my own drawers, and the more I reflected on the character of Ludlow, as I had known it, the less reason did there appear in my suspicions; but I drew a lesson of caution from this circumstance, which contributed to my future safety.

From this incident I could not but infer Ludlow's unwillingness to let me so far into his geographical secret, as well as the certainty of that suspicion, which had very early been suggested to my thoughts, that Ludlow's plans of civilization had been carried into practice in some unvisited corner of the world. It was strange, however, that he should betray himself by such an inadvertency. One who talked so confidently of his own powers, to unveil any secret of mine, and, at the same time, to conceal his own transactions, had surely committed an unpardonable error in leaving this important document in my way. My reverence, indeed, for Ludlow was such, that I sometimes entertained the notion that this seeming oversight was, in truth, a regular contrivance to supply me with a knowledge, of which, when I came maturely to reflect, it was impossible for me to make any ill use. There is no use in relating what would not be believed; and should I publish to the world the existence of islands in the space allotted by Ludlow's maps to these incognitae, what would the world answer? That whether the space described was sea or land was of no importance. That the moral and political condition of its inhabitants was the only topic worthy of rational curiosity. Since I had gained no information upon this point; since I had nothing to disclose but vain and fantastic surmises; I might as well be ignorant of every thing. Thus, from secretly condemning Ludlow's imprudence, I gradually passed to admiration of his policy. This discovery had no other effect than to stimulate my curiosity; to keep up my zeal to prosecute the journey I had commenced under his auspices.

I had hitherto formed a resolution to stop where I was in Ludlow's confidence: to wait till the success should be ascertained of my projects with respect to Mrs. Benington, before I made any new advance in the perilous and mysterious road into which he had led my steps. But, before this tedious fortnight had elapsed, I was grown extremely impatient for an interview, and had nearly resolved to undertake whatever obligation he should lay upon me.

This obligation was indeed a heavy one, since it included the confession of my vocal powers. In itself the confession was little. To possess this faculty was neither laudable nor culpable, nor had it been exercised in a way which I should be very much ashamed to acknowledge. It had led me into many insincerities and artifices, which, though not justifiable by any creed, was entitled to some excuse, on the score of youthful ardour and temerity. The true difficulty in the way of these confessions was the not having made them already. Ludlow had long been entitled to this confidence, and, though the existence of this power was venial or wholly innocent, the obstinate concealment of it was a different matter, and would certainly expose me to suspicion and rebuke. But what was the alternative? To conceal it. To incur those dreadful punishments awarded against treason in this particular. Ludlow's menaces still rung in my ears, and appalled my heart. How should I be able to shun them? By concealing from every one what I concealed from him? How was my concealment of such a faculty to be suspected or proved? Unless I betrayed myself, who could betray me?

In this state of mind, I resolved to confess myself to Ludlow in the way that he required, reserving only the secret of this faculty. Awful, indeed, said I, is the crisis of my fate. If Ludlow's declarations are true, a horrid catastrophe awaits me: but as fast as my resolutions were shaken, they were confirmed anew by the recollection—Who can betray me but myself? If I deny, who is there can prove? Suspicion can never light upon the truth. If it does, it can never be converted into certainty. Even my own lips cannot confirm it, since who will believe my testimony?

By such illusions was I fortified in my desperate resolution. Ludlow returned at the time appointed. He informed me that Mrs. Benington expected me next morning. She was ready to depart for her country residence, where she proposed to spend the ensuing summer, and would carry me along with her. In consequence of this arrangement, he said, many months would elapse before he should see me again. You will indeed, continued he, be pretty much shut up from all society. Your books and your new friend will be your chief, if not only companions. Her life is not a social one, because she has formed extravagant notions of the importance of lonely worship and devout solitude. Much of her time will be spent in meditation upon pious books in her closet. Some of it in long solitary rides in her coach, for the sake of exercise. Little will remain for eating and sleeping, so that unless you can prevail upon her to violate her ordinary rules for your sake, you will be left pretty much to yourself. You will have the more time to reflect upon what has hitherto been the theme of our conversations. You can come to town when you want to see me. I shall generally be found in these apartments.

In the present state of my mind, though impatient to see Mrs. Benington, I was still more impatient to remove the veil between Ludlow and myself. After some pause, I ventured to enquire if there was any impediment to my advancement in the road he had already pointed out to my curiosity and ambition.

He replied, with great solemnity, that I was already acquainted with the next step to be taken in this road. If I was prepared to make him my confessor, as to the past, the present, and the future, without exception or condition, but what arose from defect of memory, he was willing to receive my confession.

I declared myself ready to do so.

I need not, he returned, remind you of the consequences of concealment or deceit. I have already dwelt upon these consequences. As to the past, you have already told me, perhaps, all that is of any moment to know. It is in relation to the future that caution will be chiefly necessary. Hitherto your actions have been nearly indifferent to the ends of your future existence. Confessions of the past are required, because they are an earnest of the future character and conduct. Have you then—but this is too abrupt. Take an hour to reflect and deliberate. Go by yourself; take yourself to severe task, and make up your mind with a full, entire, and unfailing resolution; for the moment in which you assume this new obligation will make you a new being. Perdition or felicity will hang upon that moment.

This conversation was late in the evening. After I had consented to postpone this subject, we parted, he telling me that he would leave his chamber door open, and as soon as my mind was made up I might come to him.

Chapter X

I retired accordingly to my apartment, and spent the prescribed hour in anxious and irresolute reflections. They were no other than had hitherto occurred, but they occurred with more force than ever. Some fatal obstinacy, however, got possession of me, and I persisted in the resolution of concealing one thing. We become fondly attached to objects and pursuits, frequently for no conceivable reason but the pain and trouble they cost us. In proportion to the danger in which they involve us do we cherish them. Our darling potion is the poison that scorches our vitals.

After some time, I went to Ludloe's apartment. I found him solemn, and yet benign, at my entrance. After intimating my compliance with the terms prescribed, which I did, in spite of all my labour for composure, with accents half faultering, he proceeded to put various questions to me, relative to my early history.

I knew there was no other mode of accomplishing the end in view, but by putting all that was related in the form of answers to questions; and when meditating on the character of Ludloe, I experienced excessive uneasiness as to the consummate art and penetration which his questions would manifest. Conscious of a purpose to conceal, my fancy invested my friend with the robe of a judicial inquisitor, all whose questions should aim at extracting the truth, and entrapping the liar.

In this respect, however, I was wholly disappointed. All his inquiries were general and obvious.—They betokened curiosity, but not suspicion; yet there were moments when I saw, or fancied I saw, some dissatisfaction betrayed in his features; and when I arrived at that period of my story which terminated with my departure, as his companion, for Europe, his pauses were, I thought, a little longer and more museful than I liked. At this period, our first conference ended. After a talk, which had commenced at a late hour, and had continued many hours, it was time to sleep, and it was agreed that next morning the conference should be renewed.

On retiring to my pillow, and reviewing all the circumstances of this interview, my mind was filled with apprehension and disquiet. I seemed to recollect a thousand things, which showed that Ludloe was not fully satisfied with my part in this interview. A strange and nameless mixture of wrath and of pity appeared, on recollection, in the glances which, from time to time, he cast upon me. Some emotion played upon his features, in which, as my fears conceived, there was a tincture of resentment and ferocity. In vain I called my usual sophistries to my aid. In vain I pondered on the inscrutable nature of my peculiar faculty. In vain I endeavoured to persuade myself, that, by telling the truth, instead of entitling myself to Ludloe's approbation, I should only excite his anger, by what he could not but deem an attempt to impose upon his belief an incredible tale of impossible events. I had never heard or read of any instance of this faculty. I supposed the case to be absolutely singular, and I should be no more entitled to credit in proclaiming it, than if I should maintain that a certain billet of wood possessed the faculty of articulate speech. It was now, however, too late to retract. I had been guilty of a solemn and deliberate concealment. I was now in the path in which there was no turning back, and I must go forward.

The return of day's encouraging beams in some degree quieted my nocturnal terrors, and I went, at the appointed hour, to Ludloe's presence. I found him with a much more cheerful aspect than I expected, and began to chide myself, in secret, for the folly of my late apprehensions.

After a little pause, he reminded me, that he was only one among many, engaged in a great and arduous design. As each of us, continued he, is mortal, each of us must, in time, yield his post to another.—Each of us is ambitious to provide himself a successor, to have his place filled by one selected and instructed by himself. All our personal feelings and affections are by no means intended to be swallowed up by a passion for the general interest; when they can be kept alive and be brought into play, in subordination and subservience to the great end, they are cherished as useful, and revered as laudable; and whatever austerity and rigour you may impute to my character, there are few more susceptible of personal regards than I am.

You cannot know, till you are what I am, what deep, what all-absorbing interest I have in the success of my tutorship on this occasion. Most joyfully would I embrace a thousand deaths, rather than that you should prove a recreant. The consequences of any failure in your integrity will, it is true, be fatal to yourself: but there are some minds, of a generous texture, who are more impatient under ills they have inflicted upon others, than of those they have brought upon themselves; who had rather perish, themselves, in infamy, than bring infamy or death upon a benefactor.

Perhaps of such noble materials is your mind composed. If I had not thought so, you would never have been an object of my regard, and therefore, in the motives that shall impel you to fidelity, sincerity, and perseverance, some regard to my happiness and welfare will, no doubt, have place.

And yet I exact nothing from you on this score. If your own safety be insufficient to controul you, you are not fit for us. There is, indeed, abundant need of all possible inducements to make you faithful. The task of concealing nothing from me must be easy. That of concealing every thing from others must be the only arduous one. The first you can hardly fail of performing, when the exigence requires it, for what motive can you possibly have to practice evasion or disguise with me? You have surely committed no crime; you have neither robbed, nor murdered, nor betrayed. If you have, there is no room for the fear of punishment or the terror of disgrace to step in, and make you hide your guilt from me. You cannot dread any further disclosure, because I can have no interest in your ruin or your shame: and what evil could ensue the confession of the foulest murder, even before a bench of magistrates, more dreadful than that which will inevitably follow the practice of the least concealment to me, or the least undue disclosure to others?

You cannot easily conceive the emphatical solemnity with which this was spoken. Had he fixed piercing eyes on me while he spoke; had I perceived him watching my looks, and labouring to penetrate my secret thoughts, I should doubtless have been ruined: but he fixed his eyes upon the floor, and no gesture or look indicated the smallest suspicion of my conduct. After some pause, he continued, in a more pathetic tone, while his whole frame seemed to partake of his mental agitation.

I am greatly at a loss by what means to impress you with a full conviction of the truth of what I have just said. Endless are the sophistries by which we seduce ourselves into perilous and doubtful paths. What we do not see, we disbelieve, or we heed not. The sword may descend upon our infatuated head from above, but we who are, meanwhile, busily inspecting the ground at our feet, or gazing at the scene around us, are not aware or apprehensive of its irresistible coming. In this case, it must not be seen before it is felt, or before that time comes when the danger of incurring it is over. I cannot withdraw the veil, and disclose to your view the exterminating angel. All must be vacant and blank, and the danger that stands armed with death at your elbow must continue to be totally invisible, till that moment when its vengeance is provoked or unprovokable. I will do my part to encourage you in good, or intimidate you from evil. I am anxious to set before you all the motives which are fitted to influence your conduct; but how shall I work on your convictions?

Here another pause ensued, which I had not courage enough to interrupt. He presently resumed.

Perhaps you recollect a visit which you paid, on Christmas day, in the year ——, to the cathedral church at Toledo. Do you remember?

A moment's reflection recalled to my mind all the incidents of that day. I had good reason to remember them. I felt no small trepidation when Ludloe referred me to that day, for, at the moment, I was doubtful whether there had not been some bivocal agency exerted On that occasion. Luckily, however, it was almost the only similar occasion in which it had been wholly silent.

I answered in the affirmative. I remember them perfectly.

And yet, said Ludloe, with a smile that seemed intended to disarm this declaration of some of its terrors, I suspect your recollection is not as exact as mine, nor, indeed, your knowledge as extensive. You met there, for the first time, a female, whose nominal uncle, but real father, a dean of that ancient church, resided in a blue stone house, the third from the west angle of the square of St. Jago.

All this was exactly true.

This female, continued he, fell in love with you. Her passion made her deaf to all the dictates of modesty and duty, and she gave you sufficient intimations, in subsequent interviews at the same place, of this passion; which, she being fair and enticing, you were not slow in comprehending and returning. As not only the safety of your intercourse, but even of both your lives, depended on being shielded even from suspicion, the utmost wariness and caution was observed in all your proceedings. Tell me whether you succeeded in your efforts to this end.

I replied, that, at the time, I had no doubt but I had.

And yet, said he, drawing something from his pocket, and putting it into my hand, there is the slip of paper, with the preconcerted emblem inscribed upon it, which the infatuated girl dropped in your sight, one evening, in the left aisle of that church. That paper you imagined you afterwards burnt in your chamber lamp. In pursuance of this token, you deferred your intended visit, and next day the lady was accidentally drowned, in passing a river. Here ended your connexion with her, and with her was buried, as you thought, all memory of this transaction.

I leave you to draw your own inference from this disclosure. Meditate upon it when alone. Recal all the incidents of that drama, and labour to conceive the means by which my sagacity has been able to reach events that took place so far off, and under so deep a covering. If you cannot penetrate these means, learn to reverence my assertions, that I cannot be deceived; and let sincerity be henceforth the rule of your conduct towards me, not merely because it is right, but because concealment is impossible.

We will stop here. There is no haste required of us. Yesterday's discourse will suffice for to-day, and for many days to come. Let what has already taken place be the subject of profound and mature reflection. Review, once more, the incidents of your early life, previous to your introduction to me, and, at our next conference, prepare to supply all those deficiencies occasioned by negligence, forgetfulness, or design on our first. There must be some. There must be many. The whole truth can only be disclosed after numerous and repeated conversations. These must take place at considerable intervals, and when all is told, then shall you be ready to encounter the final ordeal, and load yourself with heavy and terrific sanctions.

I shall be the proper judge of the completeness of your confession.—Knowing previously, and by unerring means, your whole history, I shall be able to detect all that is deficient, as well as all that is redundant. Your confessions have hitherto adhered to the truth, but deficient they are, and they must be, for who, at a single trial, can detail the secrets of his life? whose recollection can fully serve him at an instant's notice? who can free himself, by a single effort, from the dominion of fear and shame? We expect no miracles of fortitude and purity from our disciples. It is our discipline, our wariness, our laborious preparation that creates the excellence we have among us. We find it not ready made.

I counsel you to join Mrs. Benington without delay. You may see me when and as often as you please. When it is proper to renew the present topic, it shall be renewed. Till then we will be silent.—Here Ludloe left me alone, but not to indifference or vacuity. Indeed I was overwhelmed with the reflections that arose from this conversation. So, said I, I am still saved, if I have wisdom enough to use the opportunity, from the consequences of past concealments. By a distinction which I had wholly overlooked, but which could not be missed by the sagacity and equity of Ludloe, I have praise for telling the truth, and an excuse for withholding some of the truth. It was, indeed, a praise to which I was entitled, for I have made no additions to the tale of my early adventures. I had no motive to exaggerate or dress out in false colours. What I sought to conceal, I was careful to exclude entirely, that a lame or defective narrative might awaken no suspicions.

The allusion to incidents at Toledo confounded and bewildered all my thoughts. I still held the paper he had given me. So far as memory could be trusted, it was the same which, an hour after I had received it, I burnt, as I conceived, with my own hands. How Ludloe came into possession of this paper; how he was apprised of incidents, to which only the female mentioned and myself were privy; which she had too good reason to hide from all the world, and which I had taken infinite pains to bury in oblivion, I vainly endeavoured to conjecture.

3.19.2 Reading and Review Questions

1. What is the effect of this work being unfinished, and why?
2. How reliable a narrator is Carwin? How do you know?
3. How, if at all, are Carwin's ambitions uniquely American?
4. How does Carwin's ability to imitate the voices of other people affect his individuality, or character?
5. How does Carwin's ventriloquism connect with nature, particularly with nature in America?

www.ingramcontent.com/pod-product-compliance
Lightning Source LLC
Chambersburg PA
CBHW070704100726
47907CB00001B/47

* 9 7 8 1 9 4 0 7 7 1 6 3 2 *